W9-AJO-023

FRANCHISE OPPORTUNITIES

• 21ST •
EDITION

 Sterling Publishing Co., Inc.   New York

TABLE OF CONTENTS

Published in 1989 by Sterling Publishing Co., Inc.
Two Park Avenue New York, New York 10016
Reprint of the 21st edition of "Franchise Opportunities Handbook"
issued in 1988 by the U.S. Government Printing Office
Sterling ISBN 0-8069-6970-9

INDEX OF FRANCHISING PARTICIPANTS

By Category

CONSTRUCTION/REMODELING-MATERIALS/SERVICES

COSMETICS/TOILETRIES

DENTAL CENTERS

DRUG STORES

EDUCATIONAL PRODUCTS/SERVICES

INDEX OF FRANCHISING PARTICIPANTS—BY CATEGORY

**FOODS-RESTAURANTS/DRIVE-INS/
CARRY-OUTS**

INDEX OF FRANCHISING PARTICIPANTS—BY CATEGORY

RETAILING—FLORIST

RETAILING—NOT ELSEWHERE CLASSIFIED

SECURITY SYSTEMS

INDEX OF FRANCHISING PARTICIPANTS

Alphabetical

INDEX OF FRANCHISING PARTICIPANTS—ALPHABETICAL

INTRODUCTION

Franchising is both an old and new concept. The term from the French originally meant to be free from servitude. Its meaning in the context of present-day promotions is the opportunity for an individual to own his or her own business, even if they are inexperienced and lacking adequate capital. During recent years, franchising, as a type of business operation, has been expanding rapidly and entering into new areas of application. Statistical evidence of such expansion is contained in the study entitled *Franchising in the Economy*, published annually by the International Trade Administration. The latest study, covering the period 1986-88 reveals that franchised businesses accounted for $591 billion in annual sales in 1987. Retail franchising, amounting to $515 billion, is equal to 33 percent of total U.S retail sales.

What Is Franchising?

Franchising is a form of licensing by which the owner (the franchisor) or a product, service or method obtains distribution through affiliated dealers (the franchisees). The holder of the right is often given exclusive access to a defined geographical area.

The product, method or service being marketed is identified by a brand name, and the franchisor maintains control over the marketing methods employed.

In many cases the operation resembles that of a large chain with trademarks, uniform symbols, equipment, storefronts, and standardized services or products, and maintains uniform practices as outlined in the franchise agreement.

The International Franchise Association, the major trade association in the field, defines franchising as ''a continuing relationship in which the franchisor provides a licensed privilege to do business, plus assistance in organizing, training, merchandising, and management in return for a consideration from the franchise.''

A former president of the International Franchise Association described franchising as ''a convenient and economic means for the filling of a drive or desire (for independence) with a minimum of risk and investment and maximum opportunities for success through the utilization of a proven product or service and marketing method.'' However, the owner of a franchised business must give up some options and freedom of action in business decisions that would be open to the owner of a non-franchised business.

In a way, the franchisee is not his own boss, because in order to maintain the distinctiveness and uniformity of the service and to insure that the operations of each outlet will reflect favorably on the organization as a whole to protect and build its good will, the franchisor usually exercises some degree of continuing control over the operations of franchisees, and requires them to meet stipulated standards of quality. The extent of such control varies. In some cases, franchisees are required to conduct every step of their operation in strict conformity with a manual furnished by the franchisor—and this may be desirable.

In return, the individual franchisee can share in the good will built up by all other outlets which bear the same name.

A company which depends upon the successful operation of franchise outlets needs individuals who are willing to learn the business and have the energy for a considerable amount of effort. It can supply the other essentials for successful operation of the outlet. Among the services franchisors may provide to the franchise operators are as follows: (1) location analysis and counsel; (2) store development aid, including lease negotiation; (3) store design and equipment purchasing; 4) initial employee and management training, and continuing management counseling; (5) advertising and merchandising counsel and assistance; (6) standardized procedures and operations; (7) centralized purchasing with consequent savings; and (8) financial assistance in the establishment of the business.

Investing in a Franchise

Be Aware of Risks

Everyone knows that there is some risk in investing money in the stock market. Investing in a franchise is not much different. In some ways, the risks are even greater than the risks of buying stock. After all, if you buy a franchise you usually expect to invest not only your time, but a good part of your working life.

Some franchises carry a greater degree of risk than others. There are ''blue chip'' franchises which, like ''blue chip'' stocks, are offered by companies with a track record of successful operation. There are also high risk franchises that are offered, like speculative stocks, by new companies without a proven track record, or by some fly-by-night operators.

The risk of buying a franchise is usually greater than the risk of buying a stock for another reason. When you buy stock, you are relying only on the business skills of the company that issued the stock. When you buy a franchise, you are relying not only on the business skills of the franchisor, but also on your own business aptitude and experience. If you give up a good job to purchase and operate a franchise, you will obviously have a lot more to lose than your financial investment if the franchise does not work out.

Protect Yourself By Self-Evaluation

How can you protect youself against making a mistake in buying a franchise? No answer to that question is 100 percent reliable. But, there are some important steps you can take before you make a commitment to buy a franchise that may help to reduce the risk.

The first step, and often the most difficult, is to take a hard look at yourself. Ask yourself whether you are really willing to make the personal sacrifices—long hours at the franchise, hard work, financial uncertainty that are often necessary for a successful business. Do you enjoy working with others? Are you a good supervisor? Are you an organized person? Or are you simply attracted by the potential profits?

Some franchisors will help you to take this careful look at yourself. A reputable franchisor, after all, is investing in you because the franchisor will profit from your continued success. Others may only check to be sure that you have the necessary money or credit to invest. In that case, you will have to do your best to ask these questions yourself. Your family and friends can make an important contribution to your self-evaluation, and their answers will probably be more objective than the answers of a franchise salesman.

Protect Yourself By Investigating The Franchise

The second step is to investigate the franchisor and the franchise business as thoroughly as you can. The best way to proceed is to do what most people do when they buy a new car or a new home. Do some comparison shopping, look at more than one franchise, just as you would look at more than one car or house before deciding to buy.

If you have only talked with one franchisor about its franchise, the most important step you can take to protect yourself is to look at other similar franchises in the same line of business. This Franchise Opportunities Handbook will help you get started, since the first part of the index categorizes franchisors by the type of franchise they offer.

Look at the brief descriptions in this handbook of the franchises offered of the type you are considering. However, don't stop your investigation there. Call or write to at least a few of the franchisors listed in the same category for more detailed information. You may discover that some of them offer benefits not available with the franchise you have been considering.

Protect Yourself By Studying Disclosure Statements

If the initial information you receive from a franchisor does not include a disclosure statement (sometimes called an "offering circular" or "prospectus"), be sure to ask for one. It will be a great help in comparing one franchise with another, understanding the risks involved, and learning what to expect and what not to expect from the franchise in which you finally decide to invest. You

should study the disclosure statement carefully before making an investment decision.

A trade regulation rule issued by the Federal Trade Commission requires the nationwide use of disclosure statements. Franchisors are also required by state law in 15 states to provide disclosure statements to prospective franchisees.

The disclosure statement will contain detailed information on some 20 different subjects that may influence your decision to invest or not to invest:

1. Information identifying the franchisor and its affiliates, and describing their business experience.

2. Information identifying and describing the business experience of each of the franchisor's officers, directors and management personnel responsible for franchise services, training and other aspects of the franchise program.

3. A description of the lawsuits in which the franchisor and its officers, directors and management personnel have been involved.

4. Information about any previous bankruptcies in which the franchisor and its officers, directors and management personnel have been involved.

5. Information about the initial franchise fee and other initial payments that are required to obtain the franchise.

6. A description of the continuing payments franchisees are required to make after the franchise opens.

7. Information about any restrictions on the quality of goods and services used in the franchise and where they may be purchased, including restrictions requiring purchases from the franchisor or its affiliates.

8. A description of any assistance available from the franchisor or its affiliates in financing the purchase of the franchise.

9. A description of restrictions on the goods or services franchisees are permitted to sell.

10. A description of any restrictions on the customers with whom franchisees may deal.

11. A description of any territorial protection that will be granted to the franchisee.

12. A description of the conditions under which the franchise may be repurchased or refused renewal by the franchisor, transferred to a third party by the franchisee, and terminated or modified by either party.

13. A description of the training programs provided to franchisees.

14. A description of the involvement of any celebrities or public figures in the franchise.

15. A description of any assistance in selecting a site for the franchise that will be provided by the franchisor.

16. Statistical information about the present number of franchises, the number of franchises projected for the future, and the number of franchises terminated, the number the franchisor has decided not to renew, and the number repurchased in the past.

17. The financial statements of the franchisors.

18. A description of the extent to which franchisees must personally participate in the operation of the franchise.

19. A complete statement of the basis for any earnings claims made to the franchisee, including the per-

centage of existing franchises that have actually achieved the results that are claimed.

20. A list of the names and addresses of other franchisees.

Protect Yourself By Checking Out The Disclosures

After you have read the disclosure statement carefully, and have compared it to other disclosure statements you should check the accuracy of the information disclosed. A good way to start is to contact several of the franchisees listed in the disclosure statement, and ask them about their experience in the business. They can tell you whether the information provided, and any other claims that are made by the franchisor, accurately reflect their experience in the business.

Be sure to talk to more than one franchisee. No single franchisee can ever be a very adequate representative of a franchise program. He is likely to be either better than the average franchisee or below average. If the franchise is worth considering at all, it should be worth your time to talk to three or more franchisees. While you may wish to talk to franchisees recommended by the franchisor, you should also make a point of talking to franchisees who have not been recommended.

Look for franchisees who have been in the business for at least a year. If none has been in business that long because the franchise is a new one, the risks you will run by investing in the franchise will obviously be higher than those you would face if you invested, instead, in a well-established franchise with an established track record in your area.

You should also talk to franchisees who have been in business for only a few years. They are the ones who will be able to give you the best advice about what to expect during your first year of operation. That is important because the first year of operation is often the period during which the success or failure of a new franchise is determined.

Protect Yourself By Questioning Earnings Claims

If the franchisor or its representative makes any claims about the sales, income, or profits you can expect from the franchise, you should examine these earnings claims carefully, and demand written substantiation for them. Remember: earnings claims are only estimates and there is absolutely no assurance that you will do as well.

Franchisors are now required by law in 15 states to provide detailed substantiation to prospective franchisees of any earnings claims they make. A trade regulation rule issued by the Federal Trade Commision extends that protection to prospective franchisees in every state.

This documentation of earnings claims, which will either appear in the disclosure statement or in a separate document, is required whenever an earnings claims is made—whether it is presented orally, in writing or in advertising or other promotional materials. It is required regardless of whether the earnings claim is based on actual or projected results, or an average figures for all

franchisees as opposed to arbitrary figures met by a small number of franchisees.

You should examine the documentation carefully and be certain that you understand the basis for the earnings claim and the assumptions that were made in preparing it. Ask yourself what would happen if an assumption proved to be wrong. For example, what if the wages you must pay employees turn out to be higher than predicted or if you must pay a higher than usual rate of interest for any financing you need in order to obtain the franchise?

If you do nothing else, be sure to note what percentage of the franchisor's present franchisees have actually had sales, profits or income that equalled or exceeded the amount claimed. Then find out how many franchisees did that well during their first year of operation, when their operating results may not have been as good. Your own first year operating results are more likely to be like those of other first-year franchisees than those of franchisees who have been in business for several years.

Protect Yourself By Obtaining Professional Advice

You would be well advised to obtain independent professional assistance in reviewing and evaluating any franchise you are considering. Such assistance is particularly important in reviewing the financial statements of the franchise and the franchise agreement to be signed.

The reason state and federal law requires franchisors to include their financial statements in the disclosure statement is to permit you to determine whether the franchisor has adequate financial resources to fulfill its commitments to you. The financial statements will reveal to a professional accountant, banker or other experienced business advisor whether a franchisor's financial condition is sound, or whether there is a risk that it will not be able to meet its financial and other obligations.

Unless you have had considerable business experience, you may need professional assistance in reviewing the franchisor's financial statements to determine whether special precautions should be taken to insure that you receive the services and assistance that have been promised in return for your investment. The cost of securing this advice before you invest will be a small price to pay if it saves you from getting involved with a franchisor that cannot meet its obligations.

The advice of a lawyer is unquestionably the most important professional assistance to obtain before investing in a franchise. Do not make the mistake of assuming that the disclosure statement tells all that you need to know about the consequences of signing a franchise agreement and related contracts. The disclosure statement is not designed to serve that purpose.

A lawyer can advise fully about your legal rights if you enter a franchise agreement, and the obligations which will be legally binding on you as a result. In addition, a lawyer may be able to suggest important changes in the contracts you are asked to sign so that they will provided better protection for your interests.

A lawyer will be able to advise you about any requirements of state and local law that will affect the franchised business, and to assist with the taxation and personal liablity questions which must be considered in establishing any new business.

The cost of obtaining legal advice will be relatively small in comparison to the total initial investment for a franchise. Moreover, the cost of legal advice at the outset is invariably less than the cost of later representation to solve legal problems that could have been avoided in the first place.

At the very least, you should be certain that every promise you consider important made by the franchisor and its representative is stated clearly in writing in the franchise agreement. If such promises do not clearly appear in the contracts you sign, you may be legally obligated to comply with your own continuing obligations under the franchise agreement.

Protect Yourself By Knowing Your Legal Rights

The trade regulation rule issued by the Federal Trade Commission will give you and other prospective franchisees a number of important legal rights under federal law:

1. The right to receive a disclosure statement at your first personal meeting with a representative of the franchisor to discuss the purchase of a franchise; but in no event less than 10 business days before you sign a franchise or related agreement, or pay any money in connection with purchase of a franchise.

2. The right to receive documentation stating the basis and assumptions for any earnings claims that are made at the time the claims are made; but in no event less than 10 business days before you sign a franchise or related agreement, or pay any money in connection with the purchase of a franchise. If an earnings claim is made in advertising, you have the right to receive the required documentation at your first personal meeting with a representative of the franchisor.

3. The right to receive sample copies of the franchisor's standard franchise and related agreements at the same time as you receive the disclosure statement and the right to receive the final agreements you are to sign at least 5 business days before you sign them.

4. The right to receive any refunds promised by the franchisor, subject to any conditions or limitations on that right which have been disclosed by the franchisor.

5. The right not to be misled by oral or written representations made by the franchisor or its representatives that are inconsistent with the disclosures made in the disclosure statement.

No federal agency will have reviewed the disclosure statements and other documents you receive from franchisors before you obtain them. If you think they are inaccurate, or that you have been denied any of your other rights under federal law, you should send a letter describing the violation to John M. Tifford, Program Advisor, Franchise and Business Oportunities Program, Federal Trade Commission, Washington, D.C. 20580.

If a violation of federal law has occurred, the Federal Trade Commission is authorized to obtain civil penalties against the franchisor of up to $10,000 for each violation. If you and other prospective franchisees have been injured by a violation, the Commission may also be able to obtain a court order that will remedy the injury you suffered. Such remedies may include compensation for any money you lost, and relief from your future contractual obligations, where appropriate.

You should be aware that the Federal Trade Commission may not be able to act on your behalf in every case. In that event, you will need to consult a lawyer about your other legal rights, which may include the right to obtain relief in a private lawsuit for the violation of any of your rights under federal law.

You may have additional rights under state law if you are a resident of a state with a franchise disclosure law, of if the franchise you are considering is to be located in such a state. The 14 states which now have such laws are California, Hawaii, Illinois, Indiana, Maryland, Minnesota, North Dakota, Oregon, Rhode Island, South Dakota, Virginia, Washington, Wisconsin and New York. You should contact the state agency, usually the state securities commission, which administers the applicable state law to obtain information about your rights and to report any violations.

The best protection, in the long run, is to know your legal rights, candidly evaluate your own abilities, and thoroughly investigate a franchise before you make a commitment to invest. To do this will take some time and effort at the outset, but you may save yourself a great deal of time and money later on—the time and money you could lose if the franchise does not work out.

One final word of caution is important. Do not make the mistake of thinking that an investment in a franchise is risk-free, or virtually risk-free, just because federal or state law may provide you with some protection. That protection is subject to a limitation, and may not be able to remedy every case.

As a result, investing in a franchise will always involve a certain degree of risk, which you can ignore only at your peril. It is always better to do everything you can to protect yourself than to be forced to rely on your legal rights and potential remedies.

In addition, you should investigate the territory you are considering and the market potential for the product or service you will handle.

For each of these factors there are questions to be asked, and many facts to be secured. A list of 25 questions was devised which should be helpful in evaluating a franchise opportunity. These questions are incorporated in this booklet under the heading "Evaluating a Franchise."

To assist you in acquiring the necessary background, we have included with this publication an annotated bibliography of current franchise reading material which should be reviewed prior to investing. In addition, the prospective franchisee should consult the *Readers Guide to Perodical Literature* at the local library. The local librarians can be of assistance to those unfamiliar with library procedures.

There also are many local special business career counseling services which can help and individual determine his own qualifications by organizing the facts about himself and by surveying franchise opportunities in depth.

Such counseling usually increases a franchisee's chances for success.

The obligations of a franchisor to the franchisee are in the Code of Ethics adopted by the International Franchise Association. A study of this code will help the franchisee evaluate the franchisor under consideration before making his final commitment.

Code of Ethics

(International Franchise Association)

Each member company pledges:

1. In the advertisement and grant of franchises or dealerships, a member shall comply with all applicable laws and regulations and the member's offering circulars shall be complete, accurate, and not misleading with respect to the franchisee's or dealer's investment, the obligations of the member, and the franchise or dealer under the franchise or dealership and all material facts relating to the franchise or dealership.

2. All matters material to the member's franchise or dealership shall be contained in one or more written agreements, which shall clearly set forth the terms of the relationship and the respective rights and obligations of the parties.

3. A member shall select and accept only those franchisees or dealers who, upon reasonalbe investigation, appear to possess the basic skills, education, experience, personal characteristics and financial resources requisite to conduct the franchised business or dealership and meet the obligations of the franchise or dealer under the franchise and other agreements. There shall be no discrimination in the granting of franchises based solely on race, color, religion, national origin or sex. However, this in no way prohibits a franchisor from granting franchises to prospective franchisees as part of a program to make franchises available to persons lacking the capital, training, business experience, or other qualifications ordinarily required of franchisees or any other affirmative action program adopted by the franchisor.

4. A member shall provided reasonable guidance to its franchisees or dealers in a manner consistent with its franchise agreement.

5. Fairness shall characterize all dealings between a member and its franchisees or dealers. A member shall make every good faith effort to resolve complaints by and disputes with its franchisees or dealers through direct communication and negotiation. To the extent reasonably appropriate in the circumstances, a member shall give its franchisee or dealer notice of, and a reasonable opportunity to cure, a breach of their contractual relationship.

6. No member shall engage in the pyramid system of distribution. A pyramid is a system wherein a buyer's future compensation is expected to be based primarily upon recruitment of new participants, rather than upon the sale of products or services.

FRANCHISE COMPANY DATA

*Denotes Member International Franchise Association

AUTOMOTIVE PRODUCTS/SERVICES

*AAMCO TRANSMISSIONS, INC.
Presidential Boulevard
Bala Cynwd, Pennsylvania 19004
Don Limbert, Director of Franchising

Description of Operation: AAMCO centers service transmissions for all vehicles. Services include unique "Lifetime Warranty" for as long as customer owns car (honored throughout U.S. and Canada).

Number of Franchisees: Nearly 900 in U.S. and Canada

In Business Since: 1964

Equity Capital Needed: $42,500

Financial Assistance Available: None.

Training Provided: A comprehensive 5 week training course is provided at the company headquarters.

Managerial Assistance Available: Consulting and operations departments continually work with each center to insure proper operation. Technical seminars are held in the field on a regular basis.

Information Submitted: May 1987

ABT SERVICE CENTERS
Division of ABT SERVICE CORPORATION
2339 South 2700 West
Salt Lake City, Utah 84119

Description of Operation: Alignment—Brakes—Tune-up repair centers which specialize in the one day, high profit automobile and truck service needs. Guaranteed, fast, economical service performed in a "new" 8 bay facility, with the "right" equipment and the "right" training, is the backbone of this franchise. A strong managerial background is essential—training will provide the rest.

Number of Franchisees: 5 in 2 States

In Business Since: 1977

Equity Capital Needed: $51,000 (includes $10,000 operating capital).

Financial Assistance Available: Franchise includes 8 bay facility, signs, equipment, training with no need for additional equipment. Should a franchiseee want additional equipment, financing through leasing companies, banks and ABT is available to qualified applicants. Franchisee must be financiallly qualified to guarantee construction.

Training Provided: 2 weeks will be spent in an ABT Service Center and at the company headquarters in Salt Lake City, Utah. This schedule will be increased if necessary. ABT operational people will then shift to franchisee's center for the training of his manpower. A grand opening will be prepared and held during this period.

Managerial Assistance Available: On a regular basis ABT personnel visit the franchisee to provide consultation in day to day operations and to analyze monthly progress. ABT provides operation manuals, traning manuals, bookkeeping systems, insurance programs, advertising assistance and other management tools.

Information Submitted: June 1987

ACC-U-TUNE & BRAKE
2510 Old Middle Field Way
Mountain View, California 94043
Stan Shore, President

Description of Operation: ACC-U-Tune & Brake centers specialize in automotive tune-ups, brakes, oil changes, air conditioning, state inspections and other minor repair and auto maintenance services. Typical tune-up and complete lube, oil and filter change is less than $68, is done in about 1 hour, while customer waits and guaranteed in writing for 12,000 miles. Prices include both parts and labor

Number of Franchisees: 9 in California and 9 company-owned centers.

In Business Since: 1975

Equity Capital Needed: $45,000 and excellent credit

Financial Assistance Available: Total investment of $85,000, financial assistance available.

Training Provided: Extensive pre-opening training, classroom training (about 2 weeks) and 4 weeks on-the-job training. Training includes technical aspects of repair work, bookkeeping, marketing, customer relations, shop maintenance, sales.

Managerial Assistance Available: Complete technical manuals, advertising manuals, and operations manuals covering all day-to-day aspects of managing a profitable tune-up center.

Information Submitted: June 1987

*ACTION AUTO, INC.
2128 South Dort Highway
Flint, Michigan 48507
Richard A. Sabo, President

Description of Operation: Retail auto parts, service and gasoline store.

Number of Franchisees: 50 company stores in Michigan plus 1 franchise.

In Business Since: 1976

Equity Capital Needed: Minimum investment of $125,000, excluding real estate.

Financial Assistance Available: None

Training Provided: Retail sales and automotive repair—30days (combination of classroom and store/service center).

Managerial Assistance Available: 7 week management program—time being spent in corporate office in the accounting, data processing, and personnel departments; distribution center; and store location.

Information Submitted: May 1987

AID AUTO STORES, INC.
475 Doughty Boulevard
P. O. Box 1100
Inwood, New York 11696
Philip L. Stephen, President

Description of Operation: Retail sales of automotive parts, tools and accessories.

Number of Franchisees: 80 in New York and New Jersey

In Business Since: 1954

Equity Capital Needed: $140,000

Financial Assistance Available: 140,000 financial assistance available to qualified applicants.

Training Provided: Continual assistance after initial training.

Managerial Assistance Available: All necessary to properly train franchisee to maintain a stable business.

Information Submitted: May 1987

AL & ED'S AUTOSOUND
516 Monterey Pass Road
Monterey Park, California 91754
Margaret Sins, Franchise Director

Description of Operation: Al & Ed's Autosound sell, install and service mobile electronics products such as cellular telephones, auto security devices and car sterios. Turnkey retail stores.

Number of Franchisees: 5 in California

In Business Since: 1954

Equity Capital Needed: $45,000, complete franchise $93,000 to $165,000.

Financial Assistance Available: Yes.

Training Provided: 4 week training program in sales, administration and technical procedures. 2 weeks at corporate location and 2 weeks in-store location.

Managerial Assistance Available: Training and installations manuals provided. Franchisor locates sites, offers continuing field consultation in problem solving and keeps franchisee abreast of innovations and changes in industry. Franchisor assists in marketing strategy and trends.

Information Submitted: May 1987

AMERICAN TRANSMISSIONS
17177 N. Laurel Park Drive
Suite 256
Livonia, Michigan 48152
John F. Folino, President

Description of Operation: American Transmissions centers service all types of transmissions, foreign or domestic. Specially trained mechanics are on-site.

Number of Franchisees: 17 in Michigan and Ohio

In Business Since: 1979

Equity Capital Needed: Approximately $83,000 depending upon location.

Financial Assistance Available: Personnel from American Transmissions can arrange for financial assistance, or franchisee has the option to acquire for his own outside financing.

Training Provided: A 2 week training program is offered which directs the new franchisee in management, advertising techniques, warranty and adjustment procedures, etc. This program consists of classroom and on-site training. Additional training programs and refresher courses will be made available on a regular basis.

Managerial Assistance Available: The home office continually works with the franchisee and his operation. Complete manuals are provided which cover operation, marketing, inventory, etc.

Information Submitted: May 1987

AMMARK CORPORATION
10 West Main Street
Carmel, Indiana 46032
Curtis J. Butcher, President

Description of Operation: Service, installation and repair of automobile transmissions. Only area franchises available with the right to sub-franchise in your area.

Number of Franchisees: 29 franchise locations in operation in Indiana, Ohio, Kentucky, and Florida.

In Business Since: 1974

Equity Capital Needed: Operating capital of $2,000 per bay and the ability to obtain loan to pay for franchise, parts, equipment and inventory.

Financial Assistance Available: AmMark Corporation, works closely with franchisee in attempting to locate outside financing sources.

Training Provided: Initial training of from 2 to 4 weeks is provided for each new franchisee.

Managerial Assistance Available: The company will provide up to 12 hours of consultation and technical services per year without charge to the franchisee and that additional consulting services will be provided when a suitable fee has been agreed upon. The company will sponsor at least one seminar each year for franchise managers.

Information Submitted: May 1987

APPEARANCE RECONDITIONING CO., INC.
12833 Industrial Park Boulevard
Plymouth, Minnesota 55441
Daniel Almen, President

Description of Operation: Appearance Reconditioning Co. Inc., offers a complete service to the ever expanding used car market that reconditions the auto interior or wherever vinyls, plastics, cloth and leather is found. The priority of the Appearance Reconditioning Co. Inc., provides its franchisees with continued support

Number of Franchisees: 6 in 6 states.

In Business Since: 1977

Equity Capital Needed: $13,500 minimum

Financial Assistance Available: A total investment of $25,000 is necessary for a Appearance Reconditioning Co. Inc., franchise. The minimum of $7,500 is needed with an financing available to qualified franchisees. (A approved vehicle must be obtained which is not included in the franchise package.) The balance, if financed, is payable over three years. Franchise has option to arrange own outside financing.

Training Provided: A 1 week training course must be completed before each franchise is in operation. Within 30 days of completion, a representative from the home office provides the franchisee with continued training. The home office provides constant support with each of its franchisees.

Managerial Assistance Available: Appearance Reconditioning Co. Inc., provides a continual management support in areas of market awareness, inventory control, bookkeeping, advertising and technical guidelines. A manual of operations and training is provided and each franchisee is expected to know them throughly. Problem solving is offered at any time for each franchisee.

Information Submitted: May 1987

APPLE POLISHING SYSTEMS, INC.
6005 Benjamin Road, Suite 100
Tampa, Florida 33634
Jimmy Morrison, National Sales Manager

Description of Operation: Apple Systems Inc., is a very unique paint sealant for use on automotive, mairne and aviation. We have a full line of products to be applied on both commercial and individual vehicles, with up to a system warranty.

Number of Franchisees: 300 in Florida.

In Business Since: 1981

Equity Capital Needed: $10,000.

Financial Assistance Available: None.

Training Provided: Intensive 3-day mandatory training class is scheduled for all new franchisees and personnel.

Managerial Assistance Available: Apple Systems provides continual management assistance and provide training sessions to review and update sales and marketing techniques and to disseminate other information and training to assist franchisees.

Information Submitted: July 1987.

ATLAS AUTOMATIC TRANSMISSION, INC.
10615 Perrin Beitel Rd.
Suite 401
San Antonio, Texas 78217
Harold L. Rinn, President

Description of Operation: Service and repair of automotive and standard transmissions, clutch, flywheel, and U-joints.

Number of Franchisees: 33 in 7 states.

In Business Since: 1964

Equity Capital Needed: $55,000 to $65,000.

Financial Assistance Available: No financial assistance.

Training Provided: 4 weeks of on job and classroom training.

Managerial Assistance Available: All 4 weeks of training, consist of business management twenty-four-hour wats line for help with transmission problems or business related problems.

Information Submitted: May 1987.

AUTO CARE EXPRESS, INC. (ACE)
1699 Wall Street, #425
Mt. Prospect, Illinois 60056
George R. Haines, Vice President

Description of Operation: Auto Care Express services consist of oil change, replacement of oil filter and lubrication of chassis at a cost of under $20. The basic services are performed in ten minutes. Other automotive products and services are offered at additional costs.

Number of Franchisees: 7 in Illinois

In Business Since: 1985

Equity Capital Needed: Minimum $50,000 for start up costs and operating capital

Financial Assistance Available: None

Training Provided: Franchisee and managers must attend mandatory 2 week training program in an operating Auto Care Express Center.

Managerial Assistance Available: Auto Care Express will provide follow up training in all phases of the operation including service cycle, bookkeeping, inventory management, safety instruction, equipment maintenance and public relations and will supply operations manual and advertising suggestions.

Information Submitted: May 1987

AUTO ONE ACCESSORIES AND GLASS, INC.
580 Ajax Drive
Madison Heights, Michigan 48071
Michael Daniels, President

Description of Operation: Auto One Appearance and Protection Centers specialize in the service and installation of auto and truck replacement glass, burglar alarms, running boards, sunroof tops, rustproofing, paint sealant, fabric protection and a complete line of automotive accessories. Glass suppliers, tooling, sealant compounds, technical data, marketing are provided by Auto One.

Number of Franchisees: 28 in 2 states, Michigan and Florida.

In Business Since: 1963

Equity Capital Needed: $40,000 to $70,000.

Financial Assistance Available: None.

Training Provided: 1 week at corporation, 1 week at operational shop, 1 week on their site with follow-up assistance as needed.

Managerial Assistance Available: Auto One provides continuing management assistance in sales, marketing and technical operations. Field service managers are on staff to support franchisees. Technical manuals and operations manuals are continually updated. Advertising assistance is always available.

Information Submitted: May 1987

*AUTOSPA CORP.
70-65 Queens Boulevard
Woodside, New York 11377
Joel Tenzer, Vice President, Franchising

Description of Operation: Autospa facilities provide a 10 minute oil change and lubrication service. Special bays eliminate the need for lifts and new technology dispenses oil without cans. Building is approximately 2,000 square feet. The operation is similar to a car wash since it is an assemblyline operation and a drive-thru.

Number of Franchisees: 110 in 12 states

In Business Since: 1981

Equity Capital Needed: $50,000 minimum

Financial Assistance Available: If franchisee has a good credit rating, company will arrange to have the equipment package consisting of tools, tanks, computerized cash register, T.V. cameras and monitors, equipment,and signs put on a monthly lease. This comes to $35,000 for the total equipment package. Franchisee will own equipment after 5 years.

Training Provided: 1 week training program at franchisor's headquarters for franchisee and his personnel.

Managerial Assistance Available: Autospa provides a continual management service during the term of the franchise agreement in such areas as bookkeeping, inventory control and advertising. Operations manuals are provided. Field representatives are provided to assist franchisees and visit locations. Autospa continually conduct marketing and research to maintain high consumer acceptance.

Information Submitted: June 1987

AUTO VALET, INC.
7110 Blondo Street
Omaha, Nebraska 68104
Marty Brown, President

Description of Operation: Auto Valet offers full-time or part-time opportunities for an individual. We offer to the public a guaranteed paint protection for the vehicle, guaranteed interior protection, dry cleaning for the interior, under-coating, rust proofing, and other detail services. The dealer can be mobile or have a store location.

Number of Franchisees: 11 in 5 states

In Business Since: 1978, starting franchising in 1982

Equity Capital Needed: From $3,000 to $25,000

Financial Assistance Available: None

Training Provided: On the job training, in house as well as on location.

Managerial Assistance Available: Management, advertisement and marketing assistance.

Information Submitted: June 1987

*AVIS SERVICE, INC.
900 Old Country Road
Garden City, NY 11530
Laurence Bader, Director, Franchise Development

Description of Operation: Avis Service Inc., D/B/A Avis Lube Fast Oil Change Centers will provide basic preventive maintenance for automobiles and light trucks. Service will include oil change, oil filter change, lubrication of chassis, checking brake, differential, battery and windshield washer fluid. A transmission system fluid and filter change and a coolant system flush will also be available.

Number of Franchisees: 2 in New York and Virginia.

In Business Since: 1986

Equity Capital Needed: A net worth of $250,000 ($100,000 in liquid assets)) is required.

Financial Assistance Available: No financing is available. However, a total turn-key opportunity is available to qualifying candidates. A candidates total cash investment is between $100,000 and $160,000.

Training Provided: Avis Service Inc., shall provide a 2-week training course for franchise owners and managers, and on the job training of franchisees/initial technicians. Training will include instruction and product knowledge, identity, hiring/interviewing techniques, scheduling, benefits, incentive programs, how to train technicinas, hands on experience, computer operation, customer con tact and selling skills, operating procedures, advertising/marketing programs.

Managerial Assistance Available: Avis Service Inc. will furnish management assistance to franchisees on a continuing basis during the term or the franchise agreement. Assistance will include manuals on the operation of the business, system identity, real estate, advertising and accounting. Area managers will be available to work closely with the franchisee. He/she will periodically visit the lube center to discuss operations, advertising, new producers and merchandising, quality standards, and assist in hiring and training new employees.

Information Submitted: August 1987.

BRAKO SYSTEMS, INC.
BARGAIN BRAKES & MUFFLERS
740 Valley Forge Plaza
King of Prussia, PA 19406
Milt Entner, Franchise Director

Description of Operation: BRAKO SYSTEMS Franchises BARGAIN BRAKES & MUFFLERS Centers. Having In-House Staffs of Finance, Real Estate, Training, Back-up support & Marketing personnel. BARGAIN BRAKES & MUFFLERS Centers offers complete turnkey discount Brake and Muffler Centers.

Number of Franchisees: 33 in New Jersey, Pennsylvania and Delaware.

In Business Since: 1985

Equity Capital Needed: Approximately $20,000. Total turn-key investment $69,000.

Financial Assistance Available: Franchisor has financial personnel to arrange and/or assist in financing. Franchisee has option of arranging own financing.

Training Provided: Franchisee receives 2 weeks of Formal Classroom Training, then 3 weeks of "Hands-On" Training in their Centers.

Managerial Assistance Available: Full help and back-up support plus training "up-date" for the duration of the Agreement.

Information Submitted: May 1987

JALCO, INC.
dba THE BATTERY BANK
2011 Johns Drive
Glenview, Illinois 60025
Alan Schulman, President

Description of Operation: The Battery Bank is designed to be an additional profit center for an existing business. As specialists in the battery business each store sells and installs a complete line of automotive, truck, marine, motorcycle and other batteries for all applications. Existing businesses should have a good traffic location, an area to install car batteries and a small showroom area. National brands as well as private label are stocked. Wholesale business also is obtainable due to the "Factory Direct" pricing that is available.

Number of Franchisees: 12 in Illinois

In Business Since: 1983

Equity Capital Needed: $15,000

Financial Assistance Available: None

Training Provided: 3 days of product and operations training.

Managerial Assistance Available: Complete technical product information and applications provided. Training manual provides complete managerial and customer relations guidance.

Information Submitted: July 1987

* BIG O TIRE DEALERS, INC.
6021 South Syracuse Way
P. O. Box 3206
Englewood, Colorado 80155
Kevin Kormondy, Executive Director, Regional Support Division

Description of Operation: Retail tire store selling tires, wheels, shocks and other automotive products and services.

Number of Franchisees: 261 in 14 States

In Business Since: 1962

Equity Capital Needed: $100,000 plus

Financial Assistance Available: None

Training Provided: Mandatory training of at least the designated store manager at one 5-day sales school and one 5-day management school in Denver, Colorado. Additional regional training is also mandatory.

Managerial Assistance Available: See offering circular

Information Submitted: July 1987

BRAKE WORLD AUTO CENTERS
700 North State Road 7
Plantation, Florida 33317
Gerald D. Hopkins, President

Description of Operation: Brakes, alignment, front end repairs, mufflers, and other light repairs.

Number of Franchisees: 9 in Florida

In Business Since: 1970

Equity Capital Needed: $25,000

Financial Assistance Available: Will hold mortgage on balance.

Training Provided: On-the-job training in all phases of operation.

Managerial Assistance Available: Managerial assistance provided in any way possible.

Information Submitted: April 1987

CAP-A RADIATOR SHOPS OF AMERICA, INC.
dba CAP-A RADIATOR SHOPS
2879 Long Beach Road
Oceanside, New York
Joseph Fels, President

Description of Operation: Cap-A Radiator Shops are clean, attractive shops located in high trafficked areas designed to appeal to the retail customers for service of auto radiators, heaters and air conditioners.

Number of Franchisees: 7 in New York

In Business Since: 1971, franchise business established 1980

Equity Capital Needed: $24,000

Financial Assistance Available: Franchisor is willing to render assistance to franchisee in locating outside financing.

Training Provided: Franchisor offers a complete 2 week training program at company headquarters, which includes training in technical and managerial aspects of operating a Cap-A Radiator Shop. Franchisee will also receive 1 week of training and assistance at his location.

Managerial Assistance Available: Franchisor offers many managerial and technical aids including complete operating manual (describing proper operation of a Cap-A Radiator Shop), text books on technical aspects of the business, advertising and merchandising programs, and a sustained program of cooperation for the duration of the franchise.

Information Submitted: June 1987

CAR CARE INTERNATIONAL
2608 S.E. Gladstone
Portland, Oregon 97202
R. L. Abraham

Description of Operation: Complete automatic car wash business with options to do waxing, polishing, lube and oil, tune-up as a complete car care center.

Number of Franchisees: 50 in 13 States

In Business Since: 1974

Equity Capital Needed: Minimum cash $50,000. Total investment $200,000 to $2,000,000.

Financial Assistance Available: None

Training Provided: On site for time required. Training in factory locations as required by customer. Market study, site selection, financial engineering, layout, building design, services, equipment, installation, drawings, construction supervision, training, operations management.

Managerial Assistance Available: Complete management training in all phases

Information Submitted: May 1987

CAR-MATIC SYSTEMS, INC.
P. O. Box 12466
Norfolk, Virginia 23502
W. W. Vail, President

Description of Operation: Car-Matic System operates a 2 level merchandising program. A distributor covers an entire marketing area. Retail profit centers handle the direct to consumer sales. A Car-Matic distributor supplies the retail profit centers in his marketing area with rebuilt transmissions, engines, and other parts. He also operates a retail transmission and engine exchange center at the same location.

Number of Franchisees: 12 in 4 States

In Business Since: 1919

Equity Capital Needed: Approximately—Distributor—$150,000, Retail Outlets—$26,000

Financial Assistance Available: $37,500 assistance is available to qualified people for distributor franchise.

Training Provided: Complete overall training available.

Managerial Assistance Available: Initial training of 4 weeks, and continual consultation services available when needed.

Information Submitted: May 1987

CAR-X MUFFLER SHOPS
444 North Michigan Avenue, Suite 800
Chicago, Illinois 60611
Joseph Marley, Director of Franchise Sales

Description of Operation: Retail automotive repair chain that specializes in exhaust, suspension, front end and brake repairs. Franchising since 1973, Car-X is a component of Tenneco Automotive's Retail Division that also includes the Speedy Muffler King and Pit Stop chains.

Number of Franchisees: Presently operating over 115 Car-X locations in the mid-west United States. Tenneco Automotive retail has currently over 600 locations worldwide, both company-owned and franchised.

In Business Since: 1971

Equity Capital Needed: $135,000-$155,000. Franchise fee $12,500

Financial Assistance Available: Provide assistance to franchisee to help secure their own financing. Equipment financing packages from outside sources are also available.

Training Provided: Franchisor provides complete initial training program at company headquarters that includes training in operations, accounting, marketing and new store start-up. Also a comprehensive on-the-job training program is provided in a regional training center. Training is supported by a series of manuals, clinics and seminars.

Managerial Assistance Available: Franchisor assists new franchisees in site selection, financing, shop operations, local marketing, sales and financial statement analysis. Field supervisors are also available for inventory, sales updates and training.

Information Submitted: May 1987

CHAMPION AUTO STORES, INC.
5520 County Road 18 North
New Hope, Minnesota 55428
Mark S. Wold, Market Developer

Description of Operation: Retail sale of automotive parts, accessories and tires.

Number of Franchisees: 118 in 9 States

In Business Since: 1956

Equity Capital Needed: $55,000 to $90,000

Financial Assistance Available: None

Training Provided: Sales and management training with minimum required by franchisor of 20 days. Training program could last up to 90 days.

Managerial Assistance Available: Franchisor gives assistance in advertising, inventory control, purchasing, sales, merchandising, expense control and employee management through out the affiliation.

Information Submitted: May 1987

CLEANCO INC.
8018 Sunnyside Road
Minneapolis, Minnesota 55432
James a. Trapp, President

Description of Operation: Truck washing—mobile units and drive thru. A complete chemical wash.

Number of Franchisees: 16 in Minnesota, Wisconsin, Illinois, Georgia and Florida

In Business Since: 1963

Equity Capital Needed: $20,000

Financial Assistance Available: None

Training Provided: 1 week full training in Minneapolis, Minnesota.

Managerial Assistance Available: Ongoing in all areas of the franchise.

Information Submitted: May 1987

CONTINENTAL TRANSMISSION INTERNATIONAL
2328 Fort Street
Lincoln Park, Michigan 48146
Aaron Conley, Jr.

Description of Operation: Auto and truck transmission service.

Number of Franchisees: 6 plus 4 company-owned in Michigan.

In Business Since: 1978.

Equity Capital Needed: Minimum $25,000.

Financial Assistance Available: None.

Training Provided: 2 weeks classroom, 2 weeks shop.

Managerial Assistance Available: Continental provides ongoing assistance such as bookkeeping, advertising, inventory control, will provide operating manual. Visit center on an ongoing basis.

Information Submitted: May 1987

*COTTMAN TRANSMISSION SYSTEM, INC.
240 New York Drive
Fort Washington, Pennsylvania 19034
John Bulluck, Director of Franchise
Development

Description of Operation: Cottman Transmission Centers repair, service and remanufacture automatic transmissions for wholesale and retail trade. Operator does not need previous automotive experience.

Number of Franchisees: 147 throughout the United States and Canada

In Business Since: 1962

Equity Capital Needed: $35,000 (total cost: $87,500)

Financial Assistance Available: A financial package designed to aid franchisee in loan negotiations with lending institutions.

Training Provided: 3 weeks training at the home office and 1 week training at operator's location. We also assist in the training of proven procedures.

Managerial Assistance Available: The home office continually works with each operator on all phases of operation, advertising, sales, management, employee relations, remanufacturing techniques, etc.

Information Submitted: June 1987

DETAIL PLUS CAR APPEARANCE CENTERS
P. O. Box 14276
Portland, Oregon 97214
R. L. Abraham

Description of Operation: A complete-one-stop car appearance center with unique semi-automatic equipment and proven procedures to provide these car care services: waxing, polishing, shampooing, engine cleaning, pin stripping, body molding.

Number of Franchisees: 15 in 11 States, Saudi Arabia and Japan

In Business Since: 1981

Equity Capital Needed: $75,000 total investment, not including building.

Financial Assistance Available: None

Training Provided: Ongoing training after initial training in training center.

Managerial Assistance Available: Ongoing

Information Submitted: June 1987

NICK'S SYSTEMS INC.
dba DR. NICK'S TRANSMISSIONS INC.
150 Broad Hollow Road
Melville, New York 11747
Richard G. Brown, Franchise Director

Description of Operation: Transmission Service Centers providing quality repairs to all types of auto and light duty commercial vehicles in both the retail and wholesale trade.

Number of Franchisees: 24 Centers

In Business Since: 1972—Franchising since 1977

Equity Capital Needed: Up to $75,000. $21,500 franchise fee, $10,000 working capital required—remainder depending on inventory, lease equipment available, leasehold improvements necessary and personal credit rating.

Financial Assistance Available: Financial advice and counseling is available when necessary and upon request. The prospective franchisee is responsible for an investment to cover initial licensing fees and operating capital.

Training Provided: A comprehensive home office training program into all phases necessary to successfully operate your transmissions center. Also continuous field support and counseling.

Managerial Assistance Available: Prospective franchisee need not have any automotive technical experience. We provide ongoing training and assistance in all phases of center operations, including but not restricted to Center Management— Personnel selection and financial management. A professional Co-Op Advertising Program. Site selection assistance. Regular monthly meetings.

Information Submitted: May 1987

DR. VINYL & ASSOCIATES, LTD.
3001 Cherry Street
Kansas City, Missouri 64108
Tom Rafter, Franchise Development Director

Description of Operation: Dr. Vinyl franchisees provide a mobile wholesale service to the auto dealership community in their franchise territory. The service includes vinyl, leather and dashboard repair to car interiors and tops as well as complete recoloring of vinyl and leather, either to match or change colors; also installation of pin stripes, side moldings, real window deicers, and other cosmetic add-ons, plus exterior paint touch up where needed.

Number of Franchisees: 65 in Missouri and surrounding States.

In Business Since: 1972

Equity Capital Needed: Minimum franchise is $14,900 which includes all materials and training but does not include necessary vehicle.

Financial Assistance Available: Qualified applicants may receive financing assistance up to 40 percent of the required investment.

Training Provided: 2 weeks of training is required by the franchisor at the Kansas City headquarters. Franchisee is only responsible for room and board during training interval.

Managerial Assistance Available: All managerial and technical assistance is provided during the two week training period in Kansas City, Missouri. Technical, sales, accounting and business practices are included.

Information Submitted: May 1987

EAGLESPEED OIL AND LUBE
20 Brace Road
Cherry Hill, New Jersey 08034
Donald Zimmer, Franchise Director

Description of Operation: Eaglespeed Oil and Lube centers feature a 16 pt. 19.90 oil change and lube. Eaglespeed provides a complete turnkey franchise package including location, signs, equipment, inventory, personnel, and training. The Eaglespeed management team has over 20 years experience in the auto motive aftermarket.

Number of Franchisees: 73 in New Jersey, Pennsylvania, Massachusetts, Connecticut, Florida, Utah, locations are currently available in most States.

In Business Since: 1985

Equity Capital Needed: $49,500 minimum.

Financial Assistance Available: The total investment is $49,500. $17,500 is the franchise fee, the balance of $32,000 is for equipment, inventory, signs, location training. Eaglespeed will assist the franchise in financing based upon the collateral of the franchise.

Training Provided: A 2 week training program includes classroom and on-site in an operating center. Training covers operations, sales, purchasing, quality con trol, technical, personnel relations, accounting, etc.

Managerial Assistance Available: Eaglespeed provides continual guidance and support for the life of the agreement (10 years) and options. Guidance covers operations and technical areas and includes, seminars, income analysis, sales performance, newsletters, etc.

Information Submitted: July 1987

ECONO LUBE N'TUNE, INC.
4911 Birch Street
Newport Beach, California 92660
Mr. Savage

Description of Operation: "Turn-key" franchise offering full-service menu specializing in 10 minute lube, oil and filter change, 30 minute tune-up, smog inspection and certification, brakes, air conditioning service, transmission service, valve adjustments, belts, hoses and shock absorbers. Company builds 5 or 6 bay free-standing buildings.

Number of Franchisees: 100 in California, Nevada and Arizona.

In Business Since: 1973

Equity Capital Needed: Approximately $160,000

Financial Assistance Available: $80,000 O.A.C.

Training Provided: Mandatory 3 weeks in all phases of operation.

Managerial Assistance Available: Day to day managerial and technical assistance is provided through the life of the franchise.

Information Submitted: April 1987

END-A-FLAT
1725 Washington Road
Suite 205
Pittsburgh, Pennsylvania 15241
Gary B. Griser, Vice President

Description of Operation: A revolutionary product that eliminates flat tires. Distributorship available in all major cities. End-A-Flat offers each distributor a protected territory.

Number of Franchisees: 10 locations

In Business Since: 1982

Equity Capital Needed: $10,000 inventory plus working capital.

Financial Assistance Available: None

Training Provided: Company training in all phases of operations.

Managerial Assistance Available: Ongoing assistance.

Information Submitted: May 1987

ENDRUST INDUSTRIES
1725 Washington Road
Suite 205
Pittsburgh, Pennsylvania 15241
Gary B. Griser, Vice President

Description of Operation: Engaged in establishing dealerships for Endrust Car Care Centers. Services include Endrust professional rustproofing, sound deadening, undercoating, exterior paint sealant, fabric protection and car detailing. Excellent supplement to a present automotive business or can be established as a separate center.

Number of Franchisees: 80 in 9 States

In Business Since: 1969

Equity Capital Needed: $30,000

Financial Assistance Available: None

Training Provided: Company training in all phases of operation.

Managerial Assistance Available: All that is required by dealer.

Information Submitted: May 1987

E.P.I. INC.
P. O. Box 543
Longboat Key, Florida 34235
W. C. Koppel, President

Description of Operation: Manufacturers of world famous "Sparky Washmobile" car wash equipment. **Sparky,** portable self-service coin-operated "50 cents and $1.00" car wash and wax systems. Also washes trucks, vans, campers, boats, etc. Washes with cold water. **Washmobile** "countdown" has a functional stainless steel housing, completely automatic, and consists of motors, gear boxes, air cylinders, industrial brushes, electric controls to run machine automatically, all copper piping, with automatic detergent system and detergent and wax tanks and gauges. Optional: window brushes, 20 H.P. high volocity dryer, wheel washer, spray wax system, truck and guide, hose and trolly assembly, power pump, hot water heater, coin meter, vacuum cleaner, signs, towel dispenser and waste receptacles.

Number of Franchisees: 180 in 21 States and throughout the world.

In Business Since: 1948

Equity Capital Needed: $44,900

Financial Assistance Available: Depending upon personal statements of applicants.

Training Provided: Company training in all phases of operation including merchandising and marketing programs and direction.

Managerial Assistance Available: As above plus marketing sales manager and factory engineers available for sales and technical experience as requested. This is available for as long as owner or franchisee has equipment and is without default technical experience as requested.

Information Submitted: May 1987

* FAIR MUFFLER SHOPS
Division of FAIR AUTOMOTIVE REPAIR, INC.
531 East Roosevelt Road
Wheaton, Illinois 60187

Description of Operation: Fair offers franchises under the tradename Fair Muffler Shops. Fair Muffler Shops specialize in the business of installing and repairing automotive exhaust systems and related services such as shock absorbers, coil springs, leaf springs, McPherson struts and brakes.

Number of Franchisees: 40 including company shops, located in Illinois and Indiana, Missouri and Wisconsin.

In Business Since: 1980

Equity Capital Needed: Approximately $20,000

Financial Assistance Available: Personnel counsel and assist franchisees to obtain necessary assistance through third party sources, depending on personal financial status of applicants.

Training Provided: As a Fair Muffler Shop owner, you are trained to manage. No previous mechanic or automotive experience is necessary. Training period is dependent upon individual proficiency and may range from 2 to 6 weeks.

Managerial Assistance Available: Ongoing, consisting of seminars, conferences, and field counselling.

Information Submitted: June 1987

FANTASY COACHWORKS LTD
6034 S. Lindbergh
St. Louis, Missouri 63123
James Smoot, Jr., President

Description of Operation: A new concept in automotive retailing, the "Auto Boutique" featuring practical and functional motoring accessories for all cars, vans, imports and pickups, plus designer wearables for the driving enthusiast. Packaged in "high fashion" themes.

Number of Franchisees: 35 in 8 States

In Business Since: 1975

Equity Capital Needed: $20,000 per single unit.

Financial Assistance Available: Finance package preparation assistance.

Training Provided: 2 weeks intensive training at an existing boutique, operations manual, bi-monthly newsletter, site selection and grand opening planning and assistance.

Managerial Assistance Available: Managerial assistance provided in advertising, public relations, promotions, accounting/bookkeeping, co-op buying, product testing, sales, personnel, periodic visits from company field consultants.

Information Submitted: June 1987

THE FIRESTONE TIRE & RUBBER COMPANY
1200 Firestone Parkway
Akron, Ohio 44317
W. F. Tierney, Dealer Sales Manager

Description of Operation: Complete business franchise includes all phases of selling tires, auto supplies, and automotive services, backed up with national and local television, radio and newspaper advertising, periodic retail sales plans, display materials, and many other sales and merchandising plans for increased sales and profits. Master-care service program available to qualified operators. Complete identification program includes illumination signs available where practable.

Number of Franchisees: Over 10,000 direct including many associate dealers oerating throughout the USA and Canada.

In Business Since: 1900

Equity Capital Needed: $85,000 or more; varies as to locations, business, equipment and inventory.

Financial Assistance Available: Sales and credit personnel counsel and assist franchisee to obtain necessary assistance through local source or through company's assistance programs.

Training Provided: Home office and field personnel are available at all times to train the dealer and his employees in all phases of sales and business management. This continuous program helps to insure an efficient and successful operation. Firms, self-training programs, on-the-job training programs, etc., are constantly being revised and up-dated to keep dealer informed on all aspects of his business.

Managerial Assistance Available: Home office and local sales personnel are available to give assistance on any matter requested, including all phases of retail selling.

Information Submitted: May 1987

* GIBRALTAR TRANSMISSIONS
One Hollow Lane
Lake Success, New York 11042
Dennis Ballen, President

Description of Operation: Gibraltar Transmissions Centers, specialize in quality repair, rebuilding and servicing of automotive transmissions.

Number of Franchisees: 71 in 11 States

In Business Since: 1974—franchising since 1977

Equity Capital Needed: Approximately $120,000

Financial Assistance Available: Sales and Administrative personnel assist franchisee to obtain necessary assistance through financial institutions.

Training Provided: We have a 6 week training program: 3 weeks of classroom and 3 weeks on-the-job.

Managerial Assistance Available: Continuous management and technical assistance.

Information Submitted: June 1987

B. F. GOODRICH COMPANY
Tire Group
500 South Main Street
Akron, Ohio 44318 D/0636
Walter S. Stashklw, Director—Dealer Sales Marketing Operations

Description of Operation: Establishes a total franchise to sell and service B. F. Goodrich tires and related automotive service merchandise. Franchise is supported by effective national advertising coupled with all necessary marketing support.

Number of Franchisees: Thousands of direct dealers and associate dealers throughout the United States.

In Business Since: 1870

Equity Capital Needed: Varies as to market, style of business, projected volume, etc.

Financial Assistance Available: Assistance is provided to help franchisee obtain required financing through local sources and/or franchisor's assistance programs. Required financing is dependent upon market potential, requirements and projected profitability.

Training Provided: Training on a continuous basis is provided by the company on salesmanship, product knowledge, servicing techniques and business manage ment.

Managerial Assistance Available: Sale as "Training" above.

Information Submitted: May 1987

THE GOODYEAR TIRE & RUBBER COMPANY
1144 East Market Street
Akron, Ohio 44316
H. M. Harding, Manager, Tire Centers Division

Description of Operation: Retail and wholesale sale of tires, tire and automotive service and other car and home related merchandise. These are marketed through a long-established independent dealer organization and a more recently developed chain of franchised tire centers.

Number of Franchisees: Approximately 4,500 independent Goodyear dealers including 650 tire center franchisees in most States.

In Business Since: 1898. Tire center franchise program has operated since 1968.

Equity Capital Needed: Varies for regular Goodyear dealership. $50,000 minimum required for Tire Center.

Financial Assistance Available: Lease real estate; equipment and fixtures, long-term note line as needed and justified; and open account credit as needed and justified.

Training Provided: Formal 10 weeks training plus continued on-the-job training.

Managerial Assistance Available: Business counsel and data processing provided on a continuing and permanent basis. Program also includes local, cooperative advertising to tie-in with national advertising, display and point-of-sale advertising, identification and fixture assistance, monthly and quarterly marketing and merchandising program; complete sales training program.

Information Submitted: May 1987

* GREASE 'N GO, INC.
305 East Main
Suite 400
Mesa, Arizona 85202

Description of Operation: Grease 'n Go 3-bay quick-lube centers provide 10-minute lube and oil service and other fluid-maintenance services for all vehicles, using nationally advertised brand-name products.

Number of Franchisees: 15 open and 176 sold in 15 States.

In Business Since: 1984

Equity Capital Needed: $98,900 including franchise fee and operating capital.

Financial Assistance Available: Grease 'n Go assists as needed in preparing bank packets and in arranging financing, but does not offer financial assistance directly.

Training Provided: Grease 'n Go provides classroom and hands-on training to franchisee or designated manager and initial staff as well as ongoing training to new employees.

Managerial Assistance Available: On call franchise supervisor provides support in all operational areas at no additional charge.

Information Submitted: June 1987

* GREASE MONKEY INTERNATIONAL, INC.
Subsidiary of: GREASE MONKEY HOLDING CORP.
1660 Wynkoop Street Suite 1160
Denver, Colorado 80202
Arthur P. Sensenig, President

Description of Operation: Franchisor is in the business of providing convenient quick-service lubrication and oil changes for automobiles and trucks and of licensing franchisees to use the mark Grease Monkey, The 10 Minute Lube and Oil Pros, and other trademarks, service marks, copyrights and concepts regarding the establishment of operation of automotive lubrication centers.

Number of Franchisees: 409 open or under development contracts in 37 States.

In Business Since: 1978

Equity Capital Needed: $50-80,000 excluding land and building. Building may be leased or purchased.

Financial Assistance Available: Providing the franchisee establishes credit worthiness, financing through franchisor may be available up to $25,000. In addition, equipment leasing programs are normally available for certain items and construction funds for building available from company.

Training Provided: The franchisor will provide training and instruction to franchisee and its employees in the operation and management of each center.

Managerial Assistance Available: Franchisor provides a recommended system of accounting and internal accounting control, grand opening and promotional advertising package, technical advice and assistance re. installation of equipment, construction of building, technical service, marketing and accounting manuals are provided, national and regional advertising programs, provide a system of quality control over all franchisees to maintain uniform quality of the products, services and inventory control. Franchisor also protects its trade and service marks.

Information Submitted: May 1987

GREAT BEAR AUTO CENTERS, INC.
31 Frost Lane
Lawrence, New York 11559
Ken Loderhose, Director of Franchising

Description of Operation: Great Bear Auto Centers, specializing in automotive aftermarket sales and installation of parts for front end, brakes, shocks, alignment, mufflers, springs and tune-ups. All work performed by specially trained mechanics. Franchisees do not require an automotive background but should have some managerial experience.

Number of Franchisees: 55 in New York, Connecticut, New Jersey and Florida

In Business Since: 1934

Equity Capital Needed: $75,000

Financial Assistance Available: A minimum investment of $125,000 is necessary to open a Great Bear Auto Center in a major marketing area. Company will assist in obtaining financing for franchisees with good credit references.

Training Provided: Basic training at company headquarters followed by field training at the franchisee's own location to guarantee a well planned operation and an organized opening.

Managerial Assistance Available: Continued managerial, technical and advertising assistance at all times during the time of the franchise.

Information Submitted: May 1987

GUARANTEED TUNE UP
59 Main Street
Suite 202
West Orange, New Jersey 07052
William Okita, President

Description of Operation: Automotive tune up and automobile repair service business.

Number of Franchisees: 11 in New Jersey and Pennsylvania and Virginia.

In Business Since: 1983

Equity Capital Needed: Turnkey operation approximately $86,400; $15,000 cash, $21,000 equipment lease and balance financed.

Financial Assistance Available: Will assist in securing outside financing.

Training Provided: An intensive training program is provided for shop managers, mechanics and owners.

Managerial Assistance Available: Continuous managerial assistance is provided in all phases of operation to insure proper operation of the business.

Information Submitted: May 1987

HOLLYWOOD AUTO DECOR LTD.
420 Sunrise Highway
Lynbrook, New York 11563
Martin Baland, President

Description of Operation: Automotive accessories, seat covers, etc. Boutique type operation.

Number of Franchisees: 5 in New York.

In Business Since: 1984

Equity Capital Needed: $40,000

Financial Assistance Available: Finance available through banking program set-up.

Training Provided: 10 days in all phases of operation.

Managerial Assistance Available: Managerial assistance in administration, buying and supply of all products sold, merchandising, advertising and promotions. Complete turnkey set-up.

Information Submitted: March 1987

HOUSE OF MUFFLERS ENTERPRISES
8504 L Street
Omaha, Nebraska 68127
Ronald H. Bettger, President

Description of Operation: House of Mufflers is an auto exhaust repair shop with a large inventory of pipes and mufflers plus custom bending.

Number of Franchisees: 15 in Iowa, Nebraska and Colorado, including com pany owned.

In Business Since: 1972

Equity Capital Needed: $50,000

Financial Assistance Available: None

Training Provided: 30 days of shop procedures and management.

Managerial Assistance Available: Provide bookkeeping assistance and advertising assistance. Some advertising provided.

Information Submitted: June 1987

INTERNATIONAL COOLING EXPERTS SYSTEMS LTD. (I.C.E.)
402 Pierce Street
Suite 300
Houston, Texas 77002
Joe Baccus, President

Description of Operation: International Cooling Experts Systems Ltd. (I.C.E.) is a professionally operated retail service center specializing in the repair, sale and servicing of automobile radiators and related cooling system components such as heaters and air conditioners.

Number of Franchisees: 60 in 11 States.

In Business Since: 1984

Equity Capital Needed: $30,000 to $75,000

Financial Assistance Available: None

Training Provided: I.C.E. will provide 2 to 3 weeks of instruction at an I.C.E. training school in shop management as well as the diagnosis and repair of automotive cooling and heating systems components; information regarding pricing procedures, accounting, general business and sales techniques; a detailed operations manual; advanced and ongoig training.

Managerial Assistance Available: I.C.E. will provide an advertising package containing ad slicks of the logo and newspaper layouts, sample television and radio commercials, an initial supply of work order forms, stationery, envelopes and business cards; assorted signage; newsletters and up-date bulletins; seminars and conventions.

Information Submitted: May 1987

INTERSTATE AUTOMATIC TRANSMISSION CO., INC.
29200 Vassar Avenue
Suite 501
Livonia, Michigan 48152
Aaron A. Reavis, Vice President

Description of Operation: Interstate Transmission Centers service, repair and replace all types of standard and automatic transmissions for automobiles, small truck and RV's. They are usually in a building large enough to service 5 or 6 vehicles with outside parking for up to 20 cars. Each center is completely equipped with new and unique labor saving and parts reconditioning equipment.

Number of Franchisees: 98 in 13 States

In Business Since: 1973

Equity Capital Needed: Subject to franchisees' financial status.

Financial Assistance Available: A total investment of $85,500 excluding working capital, is required. Because of the amount of equipment involved in an Interstate Transmission Center, and depending upon the individual licensee's credit standing, financing can usually be arranged.

Training Provided: 2 weeks of intensive management training is provided at the home office and then additional on-site training is given during the opening period.

Managerial Assistance Available: Interstate Transmissions provides operational support in both management and technical services. Field operation managers visit each center on a periodic basis and each week each licensee submits a report on his individual Interstate Transmissions Centers' operation which is reviewed by the home office.

Information Submitted: May 1987

JIFFIWASH, INC.
P. O. Box 2489
San Francisco, California 94126
Merle Akers, President

Description of Operation: Service institutional clients at their locations, washing, brushing and cleaning their fleet of vehicles from a Jiffiwash mobile unit equipped with patented pressure washing equipment. Work is done mostly in the evenings and on weekends when rolling stock is parked in their respective yards.

Number of Franchisees: 31 now—exclusive franchises in 10 States

In Business Since: 1959

Equity Capital Needed: $5,000-$25,000

Financial Assistance Available: Franchisee is to arrange own financing for the purchase price. $5,000-$20,000 is needed to purchase a Jiffiwash franchise. The additional $5,000 is necessary to defray initial operating expenses for the first six months the franchisee is in business, or until such time sufficient revenue is generated for the franchisee to be self-sufficient with positive cash flow.

Training Provided: 1 week of on-site training with established Jiffiwash Dealer washing vehicles and making sales calls. Optional: a visit to the home office in San Francisco for additional sales training and a training period at the Jiffiwash machine shop to acquaint franchisee with Jiffiwash patented equipment. Franchisee to pay all expenses incurred during training period.

Managerial Assistance Available: Jiffiwash will do all accounting functions on behalf of franchisee until the franchise is terminated. Jiffiwash will conduct periodic sales campaign in and around the area serviced by franchisee. Franchisee is to follow up leads thus generated, calling on interested parties selling the Jiffiwash Mobile Washing Service in and around his service area. Jiffiwash machine shop is available for technical assistance during normal shop hours. All equipment received by the franchisee is covered by a 90-day warranty. After the warranty period, replacements will be shipped, at cost, to franchisee to keep the equipment working on-the-job.

Information Submitted: June 1987

* **JIFFY LUBE INTERNATIONAL, INC.**
7008 Security Boulevard
Suite 300
Baltimore, Maryland 21207
Judy Bungori, Manager, Franchise Sales

Description of Operation: Jiffy Lube International, Inc., offers a unique quick lubrication system for all motor vehicles, including recreational vehicles. Each service center is approximately 2,000 square feet and open 10 hours daily 6 days a week. Jiffy Lube products, as well as selected brand name merchandise, is maintained.

Number of Franchisees: 532

In Business Since: 1979

Equity Capital Needed: $35,000

Financial Assistance Available: Jiffy Lube International, Inc., may assist franchisees in locating sources of financing.

Training Provided: Jiffy Lube International, Inc., provides an intensive mandatory course to franchisee or approved manager for a minimum of 2 weeks at Jiffy Lube headquarters. Training is also provided at franchisee's initial location of all other initial employees and is given by a representative of franchisor.

Managerial Assistance Available: Jiffy Lube International, Inc., provides continual management service for the life of the franchise in such areas as accounting, advertising, policies and procedures and operations. Complete manuals are provided. Regional managers are available to work closely with franchisees and visit service centers regularly to assist in solving problems. Jiffy Lube International, Inc., sponsors an annual meeting with seminars for franchisees.

Information Submitted: June 1987

JOHNNY RUTHERFORD TUNE/LUBE CORP.
2418 Jackson Keller
San Antonio, TX 78230
Terry Nelsen, Director, Franchise Sales

Description of Operation: Simultaneous automotive tune-up and oil change service; including diagnostics, carburetor service, fuel injection service, a/c recharge service and transmission fluid and filter service.

Number of Franchisees: 107 commitments in Texas, New Jersey and Michigan

In Business Since: Incorporated in 1984, franchising 1986

Equity Capital Needed: $30,000 initial investment/total $90,000-$110,000.

Financial Assistance Available:

Training Provided: 2 weeks training which includes everything from the every day paperwork to operating sophisticated diagnostic systems. Forty hours on daily operations—40 hours on computer diagnostic systems; which includes P.C. operations, cash procedures, opening and closing the center, customer relations,, employee evaluations, scheduling and more along with:

Managerial Assistance Available: Site selection, advertising/marketing, ac counting and field support.

Information Submitted: May 1987.

KENNEDY TRANSMISSION
5740 Humboldt Avenue South
Bloomington, Minnesota 55431
Dennis A. Bain, Vice President

Description of Operation: Kennedy Transmission offers a unique, single purpose service. Each store is approximately 6,000 square feet with ample parking and is open 5 days per week.

Number of Franchisees: 10 in Minnesota

In Business Since: 1962

Equity Capital Needed: Approximately $50,000, total investment is approximately $150,000.

Financial Assistance Available: Franchisee to arrange own financing.

Training Provided: Franchisor will assist franchisee in setting up the operation, ordering equipment and supplies and will assist on-site during first 10 days of operation.

Managerial Assistance Available: Field managers are available on an "as-needed" basis to assist franchisees. In addition periodic visits and training sessions are conducted by franchisor.

Information Submitted: June 1987

*KING BEAR ENTERPRISES, INC.
1390 Jerusalem Avenue
North Merrick, New York 11566

Description of Operation: Automotive repairs, brake, front-end, shock, mufflers, and under car repairs. All parts are sold to franchisees at jobber prices, or less.

Number of Franchisees: 61 in New York, New Jersey and California.

In Business Since: 1973

Equity Capital Needed: $60,000

Financial Assistance Available: Limited financing available, to qualified individuals.

Training Provided: In shop training for 2 weeks, plus full management training in our home office. Additional training provided in franchisee's shop on a continuing basis and assistance at all times thereafter.

Managerial Assistance Available: A divisional field consultant works with each franchise dealer to promote success with updated marketing formulas, technical information, and sales training.

Information Submitted: May 1987

*LEE MYLES ASSOCIATES CORP.
25 East Spring Valley Avenue
Maywood, New Jersey 07607
Edward R. Possumato, Chief Executive Officer

Description of Operation: Lee Myles Franchised Transmission Centers offer complete one-stop transmission service. These centers perform complete quality automatic transmission service, from minor adjustments through and including major repairs and reconditioning. It is not necessary for franchisees to have a technical background: Lee Myles provides a comprehensive training course and shop set-up assistance by a training staff equipped with experience, knowledge and developments of 30 years in the automotive field.

Number of Franchisees: 122 in 9 States and Puerto Rico

In Business Since: 1948

Equity Capital Needed: $40,000

Financial Assistance Available: Assistance in obtaining partial financing to qualified individuals. Franchisor provides financing to qualified franchisees based on the evaluation of credit records, history and factors derived from the application and other sources.

Training Provided: 2 week training course, parent company classroom. Staff of experienced field consultants provides continuing guidance and assistance at all times thereafter.

Managerial Assistance Available: A unit manager works with each franchise dealer to promote success with updated marketing formulas, technical information, and sales training.

Information Submitted: May 1987

LUBEPRO'S INTERNATIONAL, INC.
1900 N. Roselle Rd.
Suite #403
Schaumburg, Illinois 60195
David Beebe, Franchise Director

Description of Operation: Automotive—Quick Lubrication and Oil Change Franchise.

Number of Franchisees: 29 in 7 states.

In Business Since: 1978

Equity Capital Needed: $200,000 minimum.

Financial Assistance Available: Direction to 3rd party lenders and build to suit developers.

Training Provided: 17 days of training including on location

Managerial Assistance Available: Field service provided periodically and on site evaluation.

Information Submitted: June 1987

THE LUBE SHOP
3507 North Central Avenue
Suite 312 Phoenix, Arizona 85012
Roger Goins

Description of Operation: Automotive lubrication.

Number of Franchisees: 6

In Business Since: 1978

Equity Capital Needed: $60,000

Financial Assistance Available: None

Training Provided: Yes, in both home office location as well as franchisee location.

Managerial Assistance Available: Yes, through S.O.P. a home office support.

Information Submitted: June 1987

*MAACO ENTERPRISES, INC.
381 Brooks Road
King of Prussia, Pennsylvania 19404
Linda Kemp, Franchising Sales Administrator

Description of Operation: MAACO Auto Painting and Body Centers are complete production auto paint centers that also perform bodywork. Knowledge of the auto paint business is not necessary as MAACO provides a thorough training course and shop opening assistance by a staff fully experienced in the field.

Number of Franchisees: 450 open and 96 others sold.

In Business Since: 1972

Equity Capital Needed: $45,000—cost of complete franchise $134,920.

Financial Assistance Available: MAACO will consider applicants with $45,000 investment capital and will assist franchisee in applying for balance required. MAACO, however, does not in any way guarantee financing.

Training Provided: Complete 4 week training program in company's home office as well as initial training in franchisee's own shop.

Managerial Assistance Available: Continuous as long as the franchise in in operation.

Information Submitted: May 1987

*MAD HATTER MUFFLER INTERNATIONAL, INC.
3493 Tyrone Boulevard North
St. Petersburg, Florida 33710
Joseph Kotow, President

Description of Operation: Complete undercar specialists offering fast, professional automotive services such as exhaust repair, brakes, struts and shock absorbers, front and alignment, and lubrication. Computerized inventory control and billing procedures, in an updated, clean, sales inducing atmosphere.

Number of Franchisees: 47 in 10 States

In Business Since: 1986

Equity Capital Needed: $98,500 to $113,500 is total investment for inventory, equipment, signs, lease deposits, utility deposits, start-up expenses and working capital.

Financial Assistance Available: Minimum of $25,000 cash required. Franchisee will receive assistance in obtaining necessary financing through various financial institutions including banks, business finance companies and SBA.

Training Provided: Training for franchisee and one employee. 4 week training classes conducted by industry professional in Chicago and Florida National Training Center. Training will cover all aspects for successful shop operation. Weekly shop analysis, monthly territorial meetings, continuous and follow-up training provided by franchisor.

Managerial Assistance Available: A complete operations manual is provided along with computer training and accounting procedures. Technical bulletins issued on periodic basis. Toll free incoming WATTS line for immediate access.

Information Submitted: June 1987

---

*MAGIC FRANCHISE SYSTEMS, INC.
14300 Cornerstone Village Drive
Suite 517
Houston, Texas 77014
Joe A. Lambert

Description of Operation: Magic Franchise System, Inc., offers a system of automotive glass replacement retail service centers serving the insurance i:•dustry, leasing equipment companies, car rental agencies, etc. The system in cludes a volume discount purchasing program, national accounts marketing pro gram of services and other benefits associated with a network of experienced owners.

Number of Franchisees: 41 in 9 States

In Business Since: 1982

Equity Capital Needed: Franchise fee—$7,500 plus equipment, tools, inventory, working capital—total estimated to be $65,000—including the franchise fee.

Financial Assistance Available: No financial assistance available through com pany sources. Franchisor will assist Franchisee in securing outside financing.

Training Provided: Limited training assistance provided because franchisor pro gram directed primarily toward conversion of independent auto glass re placement centers.

Managerial Assistance Available: Franchisor provides support through manuals, technical publications, meetings and seminars, and personal counseling by ex perienced glass shop operators.

Information Submitted: May 1987

MALCO PRODUCTS, INC.
361 Fairview Avenue
P. O. Box 892
Barberton, Ohio 44203
J. Ginley

Description of Operation: Distributorship to sell complete line of automotive chemical specialities including cleaners, oil aaditives, brake fluid, etc., to service stations, garages, new and used car dealers, and industrial outlets. He is assigned a territory that can support him. The distributor and his men travel the area using step vans, selling to the above accounts.

Number of Franchisees: 430 throughout the United States

In Business Since: 1953

Equity Capital Needed: $6,000 for inventory investment only.

Financial Assistance Available: None

Training Provided: Thorough field and product training in the distributor's area by regional sales manager. Periodically during the year the regional sales manager spends time with the distributor and salesmen for training both in product knowledge and field training.

Managerial Assistance Available: Distributor sales meetings are held twice a year for further training. Complete managerial assistance provided through company personnel and field representatives.

Information Submitted: June 1987

MARK I AUTO SERVICE CENTERS, INC.
10825 Old Halls Ferry
St. Louis, Missouri 63136

Description of Operation: Mark I Auto Service Centers, Inc., offers computerized automotive diagnostic and repair services on all vehicles. The company employs nationally-certified mechanics, offers appointments and service while-you-wait, extensive guarantees, all at reasonable prices. Center is a complete "turnkey" operation, including all equipment, tools, furniture, fixtures, signs, inventory, forms, and procedures. No prior automotive experience is required.

Number of Franchisees: 2 plus 5 company-owned in Missouri

In Business Since: 1971

Equity Capital Needed: Total investment is approximately $85,000, with about $45,000 required in cash.

Financial Assistance Available: Mark I will indirectly assist franchisee in possibly acquiring financing through equipment manufacturers and other suppliers. Mark I will offer substantial savings on equipment, tools and auto parts through its own automotive warehouse.

Training Provided: Franchisee is required to attend an extensive 2 week classroom and on-the-job training session at an operational center. In addition, a company representative will spend the first week at the franchisee's center for the grand opening. Continual training and advice is provided as needed.

Managerial Assistance Available: Mark I Auto Service Centers, Inc., provides a complete operations manual. Mark I also provides regular on-site visits from company representatives to assist franchisee. Updated technical and business bulletins are sent regularly. Regular meetings are held with franchisees and company personnel. Mark I offers, as an option, computerized accounting and statistical analysis to its franchisees.

Information Submitted: May 1987

---

*MCQUIK'S OILUBE INC.
P. O. Box 32
Muncie, Indiana 47305
Sam Julian, Director of Franchising

Description of Operation: The McQuik's Oilube system provides for convenient and expert preventive auto care maintenance. The service include changing oil and oil filter, complete chassis lubrication and automatic transmission service. This service is performed in ten minutes in a clean and attractive McQuick's Oilube center at a reasonable price.

Number of Franchisees: 37 plus 25 company-owned stores in 8 States.

In Business Since: 1978

Equity Capital Needed: $75,000, exclusive of land and building.

Financial Assistance Available: None

Training Provided: 5 weeks—2 weeks in company store, 1 week at corporate office and 2 weeks at the franchise location.

Managerial Assistance Available: McQuick's Oilube will make available the privilege of consultation with its staff at our Executive Offices so that you will have available the experience of McQuick's Oilube and of all its franchisees.

Information Submitted: May 1987

---

*MEINEKE DISCOUNT MUFFLER SHOPS, INC.
First Citizens Bank Plaza
128 South Tryon Street, Suite 900
Charlotte, North Carolina 28284
Ron Smythe, President

Description of Operation: Meineke Discount Muffler Shops, Inc., offer fast, courteous service in the merchandising of automotive exhaust systems, shock absorbers, struts and brakes. Unique inventory control and group purchasing power enable Meineke Dealers to adhere to a "Discount Concept" and delivering quality service. No mechanical skills required.

Number of Franchisees: 840 in 46 States and Canada

In Business Since: 1972

Equity Capital Needed: $48,500. Total of $89,900 investment for inventory, equipment, signs, furniture, fixtures, estimated lease, utility deposits, start-up costs and working capital.

Financial Assistance Available: Up to $25,000 to qualified applicants.

Training Provided: 3-1/2 weeks schooling and on-the-job training at Charlotte headquarters. In addition, Meineke provides continuous field supervision and group operational meetings.

Managerial Assistance Available: Meineke Discount Muffler operations manual provides clear and concise reference for every phase of the business. Home office staff analysis of weekly reports is provided on a continuous basis.

Information Submitted: May 1987

MERLIN MUFFLER SHOPS, INC.
1250 Grove Avenue
Barrington, Illinois 60010
Thomas Barret, Coordinator of Franchise Development

Description of Operation: Merlin is an upscale automotive specialty shop providing full underbody automotive services such as exhaust repair, brake replacement and suspension services.

Number of Franchisees: 20 in Illinois, Wisconsin, Michigan, 12 company-owned in Illinois and Wisconsin.

In Business Since: 1975

Equity Capital Needed: $154,000 is necessary to open a Merlin's Muffler and Brake franchise. This includes inventory, equipment, sign fees, working capital and start-up expenses.

Financial Assistance Available: Minimum $45,000 cash required. Subject to individual qualification, franchise is readily financable through third parties such as banks, business finance companies, etc.

Training Provided: Franchisees and their designated managers must attend and successfully complete a 5 week training program conducted at Merlin's headquarters in Barrington, Illinois. Training will cover sales techniques, shop management, product installation, communication and personnel policies and procedures.

Managerial Assistance Available: Technical and managerial support provided on a continuing basis.

Information Submitted: June 1987

MERMAID MARKETING INC.
526 Grand Canyon Drive
Madison, Wisconsin 53711
Peter H. Aspinwall, President
John M. Aspinwall, Vice President

Description of Operation: Mermaid Car Wash is a service business franchise devoted to the total service washing, cleaning, waxing and detailing of cars, vans and pick-up trucks.

Number of Franchisees: 2 in Wisconsin and Minnesota

In Business Since: 1984

Equity Capital Needed: $200,000 to $400,000

Financial Assistance Available: Mermaid Marketing, Inc., indirectly offers financing to the franchise on the initial franchise fee. The franchisor will not guarantee any note, lease or other payments and has no agreement with any lender to offer financing.

Training Provided: Provide training for franchisee, managers, assistant managers, salespersons, off line persons, and cashiers at Madison, Wisconsin for a period up to 60 days after opening at no additional charge.

Managerial Assistance Available: Mermaid Marketing, Inc., provides complete training, assistance and consultation for the life of the franchise. This service provides the franchisee with technical and operational help at all times for the duration of the franchise.

Information Submitted: May 1987

* MIDAS INTERNATIONAL CORPORATION
225 North Michigan Avenue
Chicago, Illinois 60601

Description of Operation: Automotive exhaust system, brake, shock absorbers, and front end alignment. Shops offer fast service "while you wait" in clean, pleasant, modern surroundings.

Number of Franchisees: 1,596 in 50 States

In Business Since: 1956

Equity Capital Needed: $170,000 investment for inventory, equipment, sign, furniture, fixtures, fees and working capital.

Financial Assistance Available: Franchisee will receive assistance in obtaining necessary financing from appropriate lending agencies with which Midas has working arrangements.

Training Provided: Both a dealer orientation program and on-the-job training programs are initially provided, followed by continuous in-the-shop field counseling and periodic dealer seminar-type meetings on all aspects of shop operations. Provide formal training program at National Training Center, Palatine, Illinois.

Managerial Assistance Available: A shop operator's manual is provided along with record keeping and accounting manual. Training received from regional directors covers all aspects of management, marketing, and sales.

Information Submitted: May 1987

* MIGHTY DISTRIBUTION SYSTEM OF AMERICA, INC.
50 Technology Park
Norcross, Georgia 30092
Roger Buddington

Description of Operation: The Mighty franchise sells a complete automotive parts and services system to independent repair shops, service stations, fleet operators, and new car and truck dealers. Inventory control for the customer, a unique double guarantee and diagnostic assistance capabilities are important parts of the system.

Number of Franchisee: 216 in 47 States

In Business Since: 1963; franchising since 1970

Equity Capital Needed: $50,000 to $200,000

Financial Assistance Available: Franchisor will assist in preparation of loan application and in locating sources of financing. Full range of business and personal insurances available at reduced rates through group plans.

Training Provided: Franchisees are provided with a 2 week business management and sales technique course at the Corporate Office. Periodic visits are scheduled to assist franchisees in the overall conduct of their businesses. 9-1/2 days of seminars a year are scheduled for franchisees for product, marketing, sales, business and productivity management training.

Managerial Assistance Available: Hotlines to corporate office expertise are maintained. Computer services are available as well as business management assistance and monthly individual profit and loss statements for participating franchisees.

Information Submitted: May 1987

MILEX OF AMERICA, INC.
4914 North Lincoln Avenue
Chicago, Illinois 60625

Description of Operation: Milex service centers provide written warranties on all work performed. Although tune-ups and brake services are the mainstay of the operation, other car care services may be offered subject to Milex approval. Milex shops are equiipped with the latest computerized diagnostic equipment and utilize such to give an exclusive Milex diagnosis. Milex franchisees come from many different walks of life; some have a mechanical background--others do not.

Number of Franchisees: 27 in Illinois and New York

In Business Since: 1972

Equity Capital Needed: $15,000 minimum

Financial Assistance Available: The total investment ranges from $40,000 to $69,940 depending upon the equipment needed in the location. Milex Finance Department will assist the franchisees by recommending procedures by which such loans previously have been obtained and will counsel in preparing any applications or presentations necessary to submit to the lending institutions or government agencies.

Training Provided: Prior to the opening of a center for business, a new franchisee must attend Milex's comprehensive training program which takkes place in a classroom and/or service center for a period of 24 working days.

Managerial Assistance Available: Since 1972, most principals of Milex have been successfully owning and operating auto care service centers specializing in tune-ups and brakes. Continuous managerial and sales counseling is provided throughout the life of the franchise. The Operations Division will put special emphasis on counseling the franchisees during their first year in business. Ongoing counseling in such areas as advertising, accounting, complete operating procedure manuals, and forms and directions are provided.

Information Submitted: June 1987

MING OF AMERICA, INC.
7526 Metcalf
Overland Park, Kansas 66204
Joseph L. Stokely, Franchise Director

Description of Operation: Automotive beautification and protection services, including Ming Mirror Finish, complete appearance reconditioning, Ming custom rust protection.

Number of Franchisees: 32 in the United States and Canada; also in Australia and Japan plus 3 corporate owned stores.

In Business Since: 1968

Equity Capital Needed: $75,000-$115,000

Financial Assistance Available: Ming of America, Inc., will assist in preparation of loan application and in locating sources of financing.

Training Provided: 3 week mandatory training program for manager and 1 employee at the corporate training center. 1 week training provided on-site at time of store opening.

Managerial Assistance Available: Technical and managerial support is provided on a continuing basis including operations manuals, on-site inspections and updated technical information.

Information Submitted: May 1987

MIRACLE AUTO PAINTING
Division of MULTIPLE ALLIED SERVICES, INC.
Century Plaza One Building
1065 East Hillsdale Boulevard
Suite 110
Foster City, California 94404

Description of Operation: Miracle Auto Painting offers quality body repair work and baked enamel auto painting with a written guarantee at a volume-producing low price. Miracle provides high quality, rapid service and lowest cost through the production line process. Assistance is provided to the franchisee in site selection, equipment installation, and sales promotion. Supplies and materials are available through Miracle's volume purchasing.

Number of Franchisees: 48 in California, Oregon, Washington, Nevada and Texas

In Business Since: 1953

Equity Capital Needed: $35,000 minimum

Financial Assistance Available: The franchisee usually needs a minimum of $79,000 cash to establish the business on a profitable basis. Financing assistance is available.

Training Provided: A 4 week training course is scheduled for new franchisees. Two weeks of the training is at a "Miracle" location and 2 weeks at the franchisee's location. Training covers systems and procedures for production painting and bodywork as well as sales and business procedures. Miracle operates training centers in San Mateo and Burlingame, California.

Managerial Assistance Available: Miracle provides continuing consultation not only for production techniques and procedures but also for sales and business management, accounting and record keeping and employee recruiting and training.

Information Submitted: June 1987

MOBILE AUTO TRIM, INC.
P. O. Box 38108
11460 Garland Road
Dallas, Texas 75238C. E. "Butch" Davis, Jr., President

Description of Operation: Mobile Auto Trim, Inc., provides the franchisee the opportunity to offer their prospective market area with one of the most complete mobile reconditioning and trim concepts in the country. Services include body side molding, pin striping, custom dye for carpet, vinyl, and leather surfaces, vinyl repair, trunk reconditioning, auto paint chip repair, windshield repair, etc. No prior experience required; methods and techniques highly effective towards success.

Number of Franchisees: 15 in Texas, Oklahoma, Louisiana, Arkansas, Indiana, and Michigan.

In Business Since: 1981

Equity Capital Needed: $10,000 minimun

Financial Assistance Available: Total investment for a Mobile Auto Trim franchise operation is approximately $25,000. Investment includes $15,000 franchise fee, and $10,000 equipment and supplies.

Training Provided: Complete 3 day administrative orientation required at home office in Dallas, Texas followed by a 4 week field training program. Training program includes establishment of customer base, familiarization with product line, and how to professionally and proficiently perform the range of services offered through Mobile Auto Trim.

Managerial Assistance Available: In addition to initial training program outlined above, Mobile Auto Trim provides continual management services for the life of the franchise (i.e., bookkeeping, advertising, inventory control). Complete manuals of operations, solving any problems of the franchise operation. Dissemination of new methods and products as they are tested and become available.

Information Submitted: May 1987

MORALL BRAKE CENTERS
160 Larrabee Road
Westbrook, Maine 04092
Gary T. Tryon, Vice President

Description of Operation: Morall Brake Centers provide fast efficient low cost automotive brake service. Morall Brake Centers carry complete brake part inventories as well as all equipment to perform required services. All work is backed by Morall's unique Lifetime Guarantee. Using Morall techniques most vehicles can be serviced in one hour or less. All makes and models of vehicles are serviced up to one ton trucks.

Number of Franchisees: 4 in Maine and Massachusetts, New Hampshire and Rhode Island, plus 3 corporate owned stores.

In Business Since: 1978, franchising since 1984

Equity Capital Needed: Total investment required $59,000 includes $10,000 franchise fee, and 10,000 working capital. Approximately 80 percent of tools and inventory can be financed.

Financial Assistance Available: None currently.

Training Provided: 2 weeks mandatory training at franchisors home office. Includes technical development, management seminar, inventory control, sales, employee relations and on-the-job training at a company-owned center. Follow-up training at franchisee's location conducted by a Morall representative.

Managerial Assistance Available: Morall provides continuous managerial development through periodic training meetings of franchisees. Besides a comprehensive operations manual, Morall also provides a complete system of forms, work orders, and guarantees, as well as a brake service technical bulletin file. A regional manager is available to assist in training, management, sales and inventory control.

Information Submitted: May 1987

*MOTRA CORP.
4912 North Lincoln
Chicago, Illinois 60625
Werner E. Ament, Chairman of the Board

Description of Operation: MOTRA Transmission Service Centers provide transmission rebuilding and repair services with warranties from 6 months to lifetime. MOTRA Centers provide free 23-point diagnostic Motran checks. MOTRA will make recommendations as to the equipment requirements for each center. Franchisee does not need a mechanical background.

Number of Franchisees: 33 in Illinois, Arizona and Florida

In Business Since: 1980

Equity Capital Needed: $15,000

Financial Assistance Available: The total investment ranges from $40,000 to $70,000 depending upon the equipment needed in the location. MOTRA will assist the franchisee by recommending procedures by which such loans previously have been obtained and will counsel in preparing any applications or presentations necessary to submit to the lending institutions or government agencies.

Training Provided: Prior to opening center for business, franchisee must attend MOTRA's comprehensive training program.

Managerial Assistance Available: The principals of MOTRA have over 30 years of successful experience in owning and operating transmission shops, and continue to own and operate MOTRA Centers. Continuous managerial, technical, and sales counseling is provided throughout the life of the franchise. The Operations Division will put special emphasis on operators during the first year in business. Ongoing counseling in such areas as advertising and accounting is provided. Complete operating procedure manuals and forms and directions are provided. Operations director and other representatives are available to counsel franchisees through MOTRA's Operations Division.

Information Submitted: June 1987

*MR. TRANSMISSION DIVISION
AUTOMOTIVE FRANCHISE CORPORATION
P. O. Box 111060
Nashville, Tennessee 37222-0568
Walter W. Smith, President

Description of Operation: Transmission repair centers.

Number of Franchisees: 176 in 21 States

In Business Since: Incorporated in 1968

Equity Capital Needed: Approximately $105,000 ($82,500 franchise fee, $2,500 inventory, capital and start-up cost.

Financial Assistance Available: Will assist the franchisee in obtaining financing.

Training Provided: A 4 to 6 weeks in-office/on the job training school is required of franchisee.

Managerial Assistance Available: A review of the franchisee's business is made monthly by the home office; a seminar of the office staff periodically visits the franchisee to offer assistance; the franchise shop is periodically audited; and if the franchisee needs assistance, it is provided and if franchisee needs assistance, he can contact the Nashville office.

Information Submitted: May 1987

MUFFLER CRAFTERS, INC.
4911 Birch Street
Newport Beach, California 92660
Mr. Savage

Description of Operation: A complete 'turnkey' muffler, brakes and front end alignment.

Number of Franchisees: 7 in California

In Business Since: Parent company 1973

Equity Capital Needed: Approximately $80,000

Financial Assistance Available: None

Training Provided: 6 weeks training in all phases of operation. We hire and train all employees.

Managerial Assistance Available: Day-to-day managerial and technical assistance is provided.

Information Submitted: April 1987

*NATIONAL CAR CARE CENTERS, INC.
2470 Windy Hill Road
Marietta, Georgia 30067
D. J. Zachman, President

Description of Operation: National provides specialty automotive services with emphasis on brake and exhaust systems, shock absorbers and MacPherson struts, trailer hitches and towing systems, quik lube and filter and ACD service quick oil/filter change. Each Center offers fast service and popular prices in well equipped, clean facilities. Franchisee does not need a mechanical back ground.

Number of Franchisees: 12 in Georgia, Florida and Louisiana.

In Business Since: 1977

Equity Capital Needed: Total investment between $75,000 and $90,000 with financing available. Initial cash requirement approximately $40,000, including $20,000 franchisee fee.

Financial Assistance Available: Financial packages and leasing are available to qualified franchisee's through various approved sources. Assistance is avail able in preparing and presenting financial packages to lending institutions or government agencies. Joint ventures can be coordinated and other finan cial assistance extended based on the personal financial statement of the ap plicant.

Training Provided: National provides a unique 3 phase technical and man agement training for programs for franchisee and manager. Hands-on training is provided at National headquarters. Assistance is also provided prior to and during grand opening. Ongoing support, assistance and training is rigidly structured and includes field counseling, periodic meetings on all aspects of Center management and technical updates.

Managerial Assistance Available: An extensive operations manual is pro vided and complete managerial assistance is provided on a continuing basis through company personnel and field supervisors.

Information Submitted: May 1987

NOVUS WINDSHIELD REPAIR AND
SCRATCH REMOVAL
10425 Hampshire Avenue South
Minneapolis, Minnesota 55438
Gerald E. Keinath, President

Description of Operation: Company has developed a process to repair, rather than replace stone-damaged windshields. In addition, the company now has introduced a process for removing scratches from windshields.

Number of Franchisees: 600

In Business Since: 1972

Equity Capital Needed: Approximately $10,000

Financial Assistance Available: None

Training Provided: 5 day formal factory training.

Managerial Assistance Available: Regional sales manager and research and development laboratory support.

Information Submitted: May 1987

*OIL CAN HENRY'S
P. O. Box 19295
Portland, Oregon 97212
Holli Ringgenberg, Director of Franchising

Description of Operation: Oil Can Henry's are the quick lube/fast oil change professionals offering a twenty point courtesy check as well as additional preventative maintenance services on the auto's filters and fluids.

Number of Franchisees: 4 in Oregon, Florida, Washington and Arizona. Twenty four service centers including company-owned.

In Business Since: Franchising since 1987, business since 1978.

Equity Capital Needed: $75,000 liquidity with net worth of $150,000

Financial Assistance Available: Franchisor estimates a total investment of $60,000 to $75,000 which includes franchise fee of $20,000; pre-paid expenses such as security deposits, first and last month's rent; opening inventory, and working capital. Leasebacks for land and building are possible, equipment financing available through suppliers. Franchisee has option to arrange own outside financing. Oil Can Henry's will match up to $3,000 for the franchisee's grand opening advertising program.

Training Provided: No tuition charged. 6 weeks intensive training required for operator and available for managerial personnel; conducted in classroom facility and company service center. Additional training assistance at franchisee's service center prior to opening. Opening team of four supervises and assists in training of franchisee's crew. Ongoing training provided for new procedures, new equipment, managerial techniques, etc., during life of the franchise.

Managerial Assistance Available: Oil Can Henry's provides coaching and counseling for the full term of the franchise through the franchise consultant. The consultant is a technical expert as well as a business generalist able to offer assistance in administrative controls, marketing and advertising; he visits each center on a regular basis. Complete manuals on operations are provided along with manuals for grand opening and local center marketing, as well as manuals for in-center crew training. Oil Can Henry's conducts ongoing marketing and product research to maintain high customer acceptance.

Information Submitted: June 1987

OIL EXPRESS NATIONAL, INC.
22 Orchard Place
Hinsdale, Illinois 60521
Daniel R. Barnas, Executive Vice President

Description of Operation: 10 minute oil, filter and lubrication service for cars and trucks.

Number of Franchisees: 20 in Illinois, Indiana and Tennessee.

In Business Since: 1979

Equity Capital Needed: $75,000 minimum.

Financial Assistance Available: None

Training Provided: Complete operations for at least 10 days.

Managerial Assistance Available: Above training, plus store development and advertising and site location assistance.

Information Submitted: May 1987

PARTS PLUS
Sponsored by ASSOCIATION OF AUTOMOTIVE
AFTER MARKET DISTRIBUTORS
P. O. Box 40672
Memphis, Tennessee 38174
Joe Matlock, Executive Vice President

Description of Operation: Affiliation is a jobber (auto parts store) operation wholesaling and/or retailing automotive parts, supplies, equipment and accessories. Inventory selection is from over 200 brand names and nationally adver tised product lines.

Number of Franchisees: 2,200 in 43 States

In Business Since: Affiliating since 1958

Equity Capital Needed: Varies on basis of inventory investment.

Financial Assistance Available: Arranged if franchisee has outside collateral.

Training Provided: General management, to include bookkkeeping and accounting system, operations manual, advertising and merchandising programs, market surveys, product and technical clinics, companies retains field representatives as well as specialty sales representatives.

Managerial Assistance Available: Maintain daily contact through field representatives and/or through WATS telephone calls to assist jobber in any phase of his business and to supplement written operating manuals, bookkeeping and accounting system manuals, cost books, catalog services. Financial ratios, expense control and inventory control are designed to improve the jobber's sales, profits and return on investment. Owners have the option of utilizing in-store computer terminal which accomplishes the following: inventory management, accounts receivable, sales analysis, profit analysis and general ledger.

Information Submitted: May 1987

THE PIT PROS
9657 Distribution Avenue
San Diego, California 92121
Timonthy W. Whyte, President

Description of Operation: The Pit Pros specialize in 9 minute oil changes. We operate with a limited menu and focus on quick professional service. No appointments are needed and the customer waits in our clean pleasant surroundings. The operator does not need previous automotive experience. The Pit Pros concept includes low start up cost, low overhead, low inventory, and high margins.

Number of Franchisees: 57 in 9 States

In Business Since: 1981

Equity Capital Needed: $20,000

Financial Assistance Available: Franchisee receives complete assistance in obtaining necessary financing from appropriate lending agencies with which the Pit Pros has a working arrangement.

Training Provided: The Pit Pros provides an intensive course to franchisee or approved manager for a minimun of 10 days at an operating Pit Pros location. Training includes actual operation of a center by the franchisee.

Managerial Assistance Available: Pit Pros provides continual management service for the life of the franchise in areas such as accounting, advertising, policy and procedures, and operations. Complete manuals are provided. Regional managers are available to work with franchise and visit service centers regularly.

Information Submitted: June 1987

PLUG BUGGY, INC.
7864 Gloria Avenue
Van Nuys, California 91406
Edward R. Hier, President

Description of Operation: Mobile auto parts distribution (auto parts store on wheels). Selling auto parts, wholesale to repair garages, service stations dealers both foreign and American from an attractive well organized van in a protected area.

Number of Franchisees: 10 in California and Hawaii

In Business Since: 1970, franchised since 1979

Equity Capital Needed: $27,500

Financial Assistance Available: Franchisor will assist in obtaining franchisee his own financing.

Training Provided: Product knowledge, product identification, sales, accounting, buying and selling.

Managerial Assistance Available: Ongoing field assistance, technical assistance from franchisor and manufacturers representatives.

Information Submitted: June 1987

•**PRECISION TUNE INC.**
1319 Shepard Drive
P.O. Box 379
Sterling, Virginia 22170
Donald E. Ervin, Chairman and Chief Executive Officer

Description of Operation: Precision Tune, Inc., is America's largest automotive tune-up specialty franchise. No automotive or mechanical experience is needed. Precision Tune Centers are usually 3-6 bays and are open 6 days a week. Franchisees may offer oil change and lubrication services. Franchisees may either convert an existing building into a Precision Tune Center or construct the center. Precision Tune centers specialize in both tune-ups and engine performance repair and maintenance for newer computer-assisted vehicles. Precision Tune centers provide a cost effective alternative to higher priced repair facilities with no sacrifice in quality.

Number of Franchisees: 360 centers in operation in 31 States—80 additional centers sold and not yet open.

In Business Since: 1975

Equity Capital Needed: Approximately $101,000-$120,000 total capital required—this includes franchise fee, advertising, working capital, equipment, inventory, etc. ($30,000 cash plus the ability to finance balance.)

Financial Assistance Available: Not available

Training Provided: 5 weeks basic training at corporate headquarters. No mechanical or technical experience necessary.

Managerial Assistance Available: Management assistance is provided through Precision Tune Corporate Headquarters' Operations Department, video training tapes, in-field seminars, correspondence courses, and corporate produced training manuals.

Information Submitted: May 1987

QUICK-O
c/o QUICK-O ENTERPRISES INC.
1490 Interstate Drive
Cookeville, Tennessee 38501
Ken Standlifer, General Manager

Description of Operation: QUICK-O is a retail muffler and brake repair business offering customers quality products and services, including limited guarantees, at reasonable prices. IPC exhaust systems, Bendix brake parts and Monroe shock absorbers are distributed to franchises by franchisor.

Number of Franchisees: 14 in Tennessee

In Business Since: 1977

Equity Capital Needed: $25,000-$30,000

Financial Assistance Available: Franchisor will arrange equipment leases for franchisee for equipment purchased for operations to $25,000-$30,000 making total investment by franchisee $50,000.

Training Provided: The normal training period is 2 weeks, however it can be extended until such time as the dealer feels confident that he can manage his own QUICK-O Muffler Center. Training is available not only to the dealer, but also to any of his employees at any time. Training is carried out in both the QUICK-O Training Center in Cookeville, Tennessee and the dealer's QUICK-O shop.

Managerial Assistance Available: Training covers how to run a profitable muffler business, exhaust system and shock inspection, job estimating, exhaust system and shock removal and installation, customer relations, billing, advertising, tube bending and welding, bender and hoist operation and maintenance, and inventory control, bookkeeping and financial statements.

Information Submitted: June 1987

SERVICE CENTER
HIGH PERFORMANCE AUTO PARTS
1530 West El Segundo Boulevard
Gardena, California 90249
Sheldon Konblatt

Description of Operation: A complete "turnkey" retail store specializing in high performance auto parts, accessories, marine and off road, etc.

Number of Franchisees: 32 in Washington, California, Nevada, Texas and Arizona including 12 company-owned stores.

In Business Since: 1963

Equity Capital Needed: Approximately $50,000

Financial Assistance Available: None

Training Provided: Complete 2 weeks of training period which will take place at our warehouse, offices and retail stores.

Managerial Assistance Available: We assist our franchise stores in inventory control and offer substantial discount prices on all merchandise. Assistance is offered in merchandising and how to profitably run a small business.

Information Submitted: May 1987

60 MINUTE TUNE
11811 N.E. 1st Street, Suite 208
Bellevue, Washington 98005
Colin Wallace, Franchise Director

Description of Operation: 60 Minute Tune is two businesses integrated into one service center. 60 Minute Tune provides a complete computerized diagnostic tune-up service with a warranty of 6,000 miles or 6 months, and a complete drive thru 10 minute lube oil filter change. In addition, 60 Minute Tune provides preventative service and replacement of belts, hoses, air conditioning, computer modules, starters, generators and batteries.

Number of Franchisees: 50 in Washington, Florida, Oregon Texas and Alaska

In Business Since: 1979

Equity Capital Needed: Single Unit—$45,000 cash requirement, $100,000 total investment; 3 Unit Package—$75,000 cash requirement, $245,000 total investment; 5 Unit Package—$120,000 cash requirement, $395,000 total investment.

Financial Assistance Available: No direct financing available, equipment financing available from suppliers, SBA and bank financial assistance available.

Training Provided: Mandatory 40 hours classroom and on-site training at franchisor's training centers for 40 hours of opening training at franchisee site for both franchisee and technician.

Managerial Assistance Available: Franchisor provides real estate, equipment, inventory, signs, operations manuals, accounting system, advertising, quality control systems. Franchisor has monthly mandatory technical training classes for mechanics.

Information Submitted: May 1987

* **SPARKS TUNE-UP, INC.**
381 Brooks Road
King of Prussia, Pennsylvania 19405
Edward L. Campbell, Director, Franchise Sales

Description of Operation: Sparks Tune-Up provides a complete tune-up service including parts and labor at one low price, with a warranty good for 6,000 miles or 6 months, whichever comes first, and an oil change and lubrication service within 15 minutes. Sparks diagnoses the automobiles on highly sophisticated computerized equipment before the work begins. The centers are open 6 days a week, Monday thru Friday—8 am to 6 pm and Saturday—8 am to 2 pm.

Number of Franchisees: 155

In Business Since: 1981

Equity Capital Needed: $32,000

Financial Assistance Available: The franchisee is responsible for the total investment of $127,834. Sparks' finance department will assist the franchisee by recommending procedures by which such loans have been previously obtained, and will assist in preparing any applications or presentations necessary to be submitted to lending institutions or government agencies.

Training Provided: An intensive 2 week training program is scheduled at the Corporate Headquarters, and another 8 days of training at the franchisee's Sparks center by a full-time Sparks Tune-Up, Inc. employee.

Managerial Assistance Available: Sparks Tune-Up, Inc., provides continual management services for the life of the franchise in such areas as advertising, inventory control and accounting. Complete operating procedures manuals, technical manuals, forms and directions are provided. An operations director and field representative are available to work closely with the franchisee both telephonically and by visiting the centers regularly to assist whenever needed. Sparks operations department will hold regional meetings and conventions for the franchisees, and conduct marketing and product research to assure the best service available to our customers.

Information Submitted: June 1987

* **SPECIALTY LUBRICATION CORP.**
4770 Cromwell Road
Memphis, Tennessee 38118
Allen Castleman, Vice President, Franchising

Description of Operation: Operating the franchise operation provides three ongoing profit centers under one roof: (1) quick lube and oil change, (2) Mobile lube servicing small fleet operators, and (3) wholesale sales of 21 specialty lubricants to auto parts stores, gas stations, and chain stores.

Number of Franchisees: 103 in 12 states.

In Business Since: 1981

Equity Capital Needed: $100,000

Financial Assistance Available: Assistance with equipment, furniture and fixtures. Joint ventures available for land and building.

Training Provided: 1 week in Memphis, Tennessee, 1 week at franchisee's location and grand opening team assistance for 3 days. Training covers: lube center mobile lube operations; marketing; accounting, duration product application; site selection and construction build out.

Managerial Assistance Available: Franchisor visits franchisee 4 times per year to help with overall operations to include: lube center, mobile lube and wholesale sales. Toll free number to handle daily problems.

Information Submitted: May 1987

* **SPEEDEE OIL CHANGE & TUNE-UP**
6660 Riverside Drive
Suite 101
Metairie, Louisiana 70003
Kevin Bennett, Vice President/Director of Franchising

Description of Operation: Specializing in 9 minute oil changes and 30 minute tune-ups. Also perform transmission services, radiator flushes, and related fluid maintenance.

Number of Franchisees: 30 in Louisiana, Mississippi, Florida, and Texas.

In Business Since: 1980

Equity Capital Needed: $75,000

Financial Assistance Available: Supplier financing on equipment.

Training Provided: 2 week training class, covering the operation of the shop.

Managerial Assistance Available: Site selection, construction, advertising, accounting, public relations and ongoing support and training.

Information Submitted: June 1987

* **SPEEDY MUFFLER KING**
444 N. Michigan Avenue
Suite 800
Chicago, Ill. 60611
James Lentz, Franchise Director

Description of Operation: Retail automotive repair chain that specializes in exhaust, suspension, front end and brake repairs. Speedy is currently celebrating its 31st anniversary in the muffler replacement business. Speedy Muffler King is the main component of Tenneco Automotive's Retail Division that also includes the U.S. Car-X chain as well as the Pit Stop chain in Belgium and Germany. Speedy announced its franchise program in 1985 and is granting franchises in the eastern U.S. during 1987 with outward expansion to follow.

Number of Franchisees: Presently operating 600 company-owned units in the United States, Canada and Europe, including 60 franchised Car-X locations.

In Business Since: 1956

Equity Capital Needed: $135,000-$150,000. Franchise fee $12,500.

Financial Assistance Available: Provide assistance to franchisee to help secure their own financing. Equipment financing packages from outside sources are also available.

Training Provided: Franchisor provides a complete initial training program at company headquarters and includes training in operations, accounting and marketing and new store start-up. Also a comprehensive on-the-job training program is provided in a regional training center. The training is supported by a series of manuals, seminars and clinics provided to the franchisee. 5 week in total training program.

Managerial Assistance Available: Franchisor assists new franchisee in site selection, financing, shop operations, local marketing and sales, financial statement analysis. Field supervisors are available for inventory and sales updates and training.

Information Submitted: May 1987

SPEEDY TRANSMISSION CENTERS
1239 E. Newport Center Drive, #115
Deerfield Beach, FL 33442
D.Arcy J. Williams, President

Description of Operation: Speedy Transmission Centers repair, rebuild, and recondition automatic and standard transmissions for automobiles and trucks. Franchisees do not require a mechanical background. Trained mechanics are used for the technical aspect of the operation.

Number of Franchisees: 19 in Florida, New York and California

In Business Since: 1973

Equity Capital Needed: Total investment $60,000

Financial Assistance Available: Financial packages are available to qualified franchisees through various suppliers of the franchisor. Both financing and leasing is available in most areas. Franchisor will assist applicant in preparing and the presenting of a financial plan to secure financing.

Traning Provided: Prior to opening the franchisor provides a 3 week course covering sales, management systems, advertising, accounting and operations management and on-the-job training.

Managerial Assistance Available: The franchisor assists in securing a location, building design and layout, initial equipment and stock ordering, pre-opening and post opening operations and management supervision by the operations department. Continued periodic operations support, advertising and technical support is supplied on an "ongoing basis."

Information Submitted: May 1987

SPOT-NOT CAR WASHES
(A Division of RACO CAR WASH SYSTEMS, INC.)
2011 West Fourth Street
Joplin, Missouri 64801
Stanley J. Osweiler, Director of Marketing

Description of Operation: The Spot-Not Car Wash franchise system is a division of RACO Car Wash Systems, Inc., an acknowledged leader in the car wash industry for nearly twenty years. Spot-Not's technological superiority is recognized in the industry and the company continues to be a pioneer in the development of brushless, frictionless car washing and exclusive No-Spot Rinse systems.

Number of Franchisees: 12 in 5 states.

In Business Since: As RACO Car Wash Systems, Inc. since 1968; franchising since 1985.

Equity Capital Needed: 15-25 percent of total investment.

Financial Assistance Available: Assistance in preparation of presentation to lending institutions.

Training Provided: 6 days of comprehensive factory-based, technical and management training; additional 5 to 7 days training at franchisee site, following startup. Full complement of Operations Manuals. Franchisees do not need a technical background, but should be strongly motivated to achieve success through owning their own business.

Managerial Assistance Available: The Spot-Not management team assists franchisees in site selection, start-up and ongoing training, marketing and advertising planning and implementation, and operational management.

Information Submitted: May 1987

STAR TECHNOLOGY WINDSHIELD REPAIR, INC.
4593 North Broadway
Boulder, Colorado 80302
Henry E. Skelton, Franchise Director
David A. Casey, General Manager

Description of Operation: The franchisor develops, owns and operates, and authorizes franchisees' to operate and own mobile and fixed windshield repair business utilizing franchisors registered trademarks and exclusive ADP windshield repair system. Many franchises are operated as mobile service units in conjunction with an answering service and Post Office box for mailing and collection of receipts. The primary business of the franchise is the mobile repair of rock damaged windshields, guaranteeing the windshield against further breakage for the life of the windhield. Complete customer satisfaction is guaranteed. The income base is primarily provided by service to commercial fleets, car sales lots, auto rental, insurance independent motorists.

Number of Franchisees: 87 in 30 States, 3 under construction.

In Business Since: 1983

Equity Capital Needed: $14,000 to $35,000, includes franchise fee, all equipment and materials, training and city set-up and three months personal expenses.

Financial Assistance Available: 70 percent down payment required. Franchisor will finance remainder to persons with approved credit at 10 percent A.P.R.

Training Provided: An intensive 2 week training course is mandatory. 1 week at the national training center in Boulder, Colorado, and 1 week in the franchisees' territory setting up working accounts with a certified corporate senior technician. Training manuals, operation manuals, account cross reference catalogues, a complete bookkeeping system, all equipment and accessories, complete uniform package, all printed materials, continuous newsletters and follow-up marketing support are all included in the franchise package.

Managerial Assistance Available: A full-time corporate staff is available to provide technical assistance, counsel and marketing guidance as needed. A full-time national account marketing department is in effect. Seminars and advanced training are available full-time. An annual convention is held.

Information Submitted: May 1987

STEREO WORKSHOP, INC.
2396 Gulf To Bay Blvd.
Clearwater, Florida 34625

Description of Operation: Stereo Workshop Centers specialize in the sale, service, and installation of car stereo products and related items such as car alarms, CB radios, radar detectors, car telephones, and othr car accessories.

Number of Franchisees: 2 including company-owned in Florida

In Business since: 1974, franchising 1987

Equity Capital Needed: $75,000 average. Varies with size, site location, leasehold, improvements and construction costs. Includes franchise fee.

Financial Assistance Available: None

Training Provided: Comprehensive 2 week training program. 1 week in corporate office, 1 week in franchisees' center. The training covers all phases of operation and is accordingly comprehenisve and detailed. franchisee is provided with operations and training manual.

Managerial Assistance Available: Franchisor provides ongoing assistance to aid franchisee in operating a successful business.

Information Submitted: June 1987

• **STEVE'S DETAILING**
1545 Newport Boulevard
Costa Mesa, California 92627
Jeff Parks, Vice President, Marketing

Description of Operation: A full service automotive detailing and hand car wash business geared toward the "Upscale" automobile owners. Acessories are sold through a nationally known distributor. Complete car service is performed.

Number of Franchisees: 38 throughtout the United States.

In Business Since: 1972

Equity Capital Needed: $130,000

Financial Assistance Available: None at this time.

Training Provided: Extensive training pertaining to operations, management, detailing, and marketing in Costa Mesa, California (2 weeks). Continual ongoing assistance; Field Support, Custom Software.

Managerial Assistance Available: In addition to field visits, systems analysis is provided.

Information Submitted: June 1987

SUNSHINE POLISHING SYSTEMS, INC.
4560 Alvarado Road
Suite 2-A
San Diego, California 92120
Dennis Soto, Vice President/Marketing

Description of Operation: Sunshine Polishing Systems offers both a mobile and a fixed base franchise providing car care service offering exclusive teflon paint sealants, fabric protection, rustproofing, undercoating, window tinting, pinstriping, and a complete line of automotive accessories. Site selection, training, advertising, and continued support are provided with both franchise opportunities.

Number of Franchisees: 298 in 39 States

In Business Since: 1982

Equity Capital Needed: $3,000 mobile franchise, $50,000-$70,000 auto appearance center franchise.

Financial Assistance Available: None

Training Provided: MOBILE FRANCHISE: The training and support offered to mobile franchise owners includes a business portfolio and operations manual containing technical training and reference material. Training is further enhanced by a 22-minute training video. Sales and marketing guidelines including ad slicks for the print media and a 60 second TV commercial, for establishing and maintaining a franchisee's operation. Franchisor offers continuing support through Toll Free (800) hotline number, Contract negotiation assistance, Newsletters and technical updates. **FIXED BASE FRANCHISE:** The franchisor provides ongoing training and support in all areas for the Auto Appearance Center including a 200 + pages operations manual, 10 days training @ Corporate Center/5 days on-site taining, initial site selection, complete interior/exterior building design, shop facility design, interior/exterior building decor, signage, complete research and development, equipment selection, accessories showroom displays, marketing and advertising assistance, newsletters and periodic updates. Toll free 800 numbers and technical troubleshooting.

Managerial Assistance Available: Full business and technical manual including sales manual provided to all new franchise owners. Quarterly newsletter for technical updates to all franchise owners. Toll free 800 numbers and tech nical troubleshooting.

Information Submitted: May 1987

SUPERFORMANCE FRANCHISING, INC.
2950 Airway Avenue A5
Costa Mesa, California 92626
Geoff Hirson, President

Description of Operation: Independent repairs and service to Mercedes Benz, BMW and Porsche. Fully computerized, unique customer service, and full support from franchisor, including training, hiring, and inventory purchasing.

Number of Franchisees: 4 plus 3 company-owned in California.

In Business Since: 1980

Equity Capital Needed: $140,000

Financial Assistance Available: Introduction to financial institutions.

Training Provided: Minimum 20 days—up to 90 days.

Managerial Assistance Available: Complete managerial assistance, including bookkeeping, estimating, invoicing, technical updates, price increases. District manager to work closely with franchisee in all areas of the business, including customer relations, advertising, and technical problems.

Information Submitted: May 1987

THREE STAR MUFFLER, INC.
Franchise Development Center
Suite 300-B
3373 Poplar Avenue
Memphis, Tennessee 38111
Ray Zedlitz, President

Description of Operation: Three Star Muffler Inc., sells franchises to owner-operator individuals who desire to operate a car body repair specialty center with a choice of doing exhausts systems, brakes, shocks, struts, ANSC.U. joints, or any choice of the above including transmissions and front ends. We are underbody professionals that work on all vehicles, foreign and American made.

Number of Franchisees: 10 in Tennessee and Missouri

In Business Since: 1978

Equity Capital Needed: $49,000

Financial Assistance Available: Total investment of $69,000 is necessary to open a Three Star Muffler franchise—$24,000 of equipment can be lease purchased from manufacture. Three Star Muffler does not finance but will help arrange financing with 25 percent down payment. Can place whole package if franchisee desires to buy real estate.

Training Provided: Intensive 2 week training prior to opening center, assist week of grand opening, and providing any other training Three Star Muffler feels that franchisee needs. Also continuous assistance during term of contract.

Managerial Assistance Available: Continues assistance in shop management, advertising, bookkeeping, inventory control, and technical assistance is provided by field representatives and home office staff that work closely with franchisee. Operations manual is provided for assistance. All new research is maintained and passed on to franchisee.

Information Submitted: May 1987

* TIDY CAR INC.
1515 North Federal Highway
Suite 411
Boca Raton, Florida 33432
Gary Goranson, President

Description of Operation: Two types of franchises are available. One is mobile polishing and interior detailing. The other is a one-stop center for automotive appearance and protection service including full detailing; exterior polishing, paint sealants, deoxidation, interior drycleaning, stainproofing, rust protection, sunroof installation, bedliners, running boards, window tinting, pinstriping.

Number of Franchisees: The original franchise offering consisted of a mobile polishing and interior detailing service. Today there are approximately 300 Tidy Car's throughout the United States and Canada, of which 150 are located in permanent locations, with additional franchisees in several foreign countries.

In Business Since: 1976

Equity Capital Needed: Initial investment, including working capital ranges from $28,000-$60,000 depending on type of franchise.

Financial Assistance Available: None

Training Provided: Extensive training is provided through a 4 week program and is supplemented with a variety of technical video training films. Supplemented by field visits as well as annual seminars and conventions.

Managerial Assistance Available: Site selection, lease negotiations, architectural design, store setup and assistance with inventory requirements. Monthly newsletter and technical "info-Grams." Advertising programs are administered by Tidy Car Inc., for both opening launch and ongoing campaigns. A professionally produced custom sales training cassette program is provided to all new franchise owners. Ongoing assistance provided by Regional Managers and head office personnel. Supplemented by Operations Manuals.

Information Submitted: June 1987

TOTAL SYSTEMS TECHNOLOGY, INC.
65 Terence Drive
Pittsburgh, Pennsylvania 15236
Leonard S. Felman, Vice President

Description of Operation: Aircraft, auto, marine and RV protective coatings and application for the effects of acid rain, industrial fallout and environmental effects. TST manufactures 88 very unique products for new vehicle dealers, utilities, and the public. Products include—acid resistant waxes, Teflon paint and fabric protection, corrosion preservatives, and paint restoration.

Number of Franchisees: Distributors and agents—36 serving 2,300 auto and truck dealers in the United States and Australia.

In Business Since: 1978

Equity Capital Needed: $100,000 minimum

Financial Assistance Available: (As in #4 on franchise offer.)

Training Provided: 2 weeks at factory, TST area manager on-site at least 1 week after opening—regular visits thereafter. The industries largest source of information and data supplied with in excess of nine hours of VHS tapes on operations and sales procedures.

Managerial Assistance Available: Complete operations manuals computer tie in and technical backup, in house laboratory and competitive analysis. Regular bulletins, data sheets and the industries most comprehensive catalog to back up franchise. Monthly factory training classes for employees and staff available for technical presentation to professional groups.

Information Submitted: May 1987

* TUFF-KOTE DINOL, INC.
15045 Hamilton Avenue
Highland Park, Michigan 48203
Deane Presar, Vice President, Marketing

Description of Operation: Western Hemisphere office for world's largest rust-proofing organization. TKD shops offer automotive aftermarket services to the public on a retail basis, and to automotive dealers on a wholesale basis. Services include rust protection for new and used vehicles, paint glaze, fabric protection, trim and moldings, sunroofs, sound deadener, security systems, truck/van running boards, windows, and bedliners, plus older vehicle renewal.

Number of Franchisees: 152 in U.S. and Canada

In Business Since: 1967

Equity Capital Needed: $36,000-$60,000 initial investment including franchise fee of $4,000-$11,000.

Financial Assistance Available: Yes

Training Provided: Complete technical training, both theory and hands-on, plus comprehensive business management, advertising, and sales training is provided at company expense. Franchisee is responsible for transportation, food, lodging for 2 week training course.

Managerial Assistance Available: Beyond classroom training, technical and management manuals are issued at graduation. Continually updated. Supported by field service and quality control personnel regularly helping franchisee in his own territory. Advertising representatives also aid dealers.

Information Submitted: May 1987

* **TUFFY ASSOCIATES CORP.**
dba TUFFY SERVICE CENTERS, INC.
1414 Baronial Plaza
Toledo, Ohio 43619
John Healey, Vice President

Description of Operation: Tuffy Service Centers, Inc., offers a franchise to sell and install at retail mufflers, exhaust pipes, tail pipes, exhaust installation hardware, shock absorbers and brake parts. The franchise will also perform exhaust system services, brake adjustment, front end and spring service.

Number of Franchisees: 80 in 7 States

In Business Since: 1970

Equity Capital Needed: Between $70,000 and $90,000 is necessary to open a Tuffy Service Center franchise. This includes inventory, equipment, sign, fees, working capital and start-up costs and the franchise fee of $18,500.

Financial Assistance Available: The franchisee receives complete assistance in obtaining equipment financing from lending agencies with which Tuffy has working arrangements. All cost and working capital are included in the equity requirements.

Training Provided: 3 weeks of training are provided at Toledo Tuffy Service Center for franchisees/managers. An additional 5 days of training is provided at the franchise location when the shop opens.

Managerial Assistance Available: Tuffy Service Centers, Inc., provides the management and technical assistance of a field manager as requested and manages the advertising function.

Information Submitted: June 1987

tuneOmize TUNE-UP CENTERS
AUTOMOTIVE FRANCHISE CORP.
402A Harding Industrial Drive
Nashville, Tennessee 37222
Walter Smith, President

Description of Operation: Engine analysis is done by computer checking engine's performance against manufacturer's specifications. Customer is given a print out of analysis with quotation before necessary repairs are done. Average job ticket and customer satisfaction are higher than with fixed price tune-up. Also perform oil and lubrication services; brake and A.C. repairs, we fill the void created by the service stations going out of business.

Number of Franchisees: 8 plus 3 company-owned in Kentucky, Arkansas, Georiga, Ohio, Florida, Tennessee and Virginia.

In Business Since: 1980

Equity Capital Needed: Total capital investment is approximately $110,000. Franchisee should have approximately 1/3 to 1/2 total cash and the ability to finance the balance.

Financial Assistance Available: Co-ordinate financing with financial institutions. Joint ventures can also be co-ordinated.

Training Provided: We provide a 30 day intensive training program for franchisees and their managers to assure proper operation of the computer testing equipment, proper servicing techniques, proper customer relations and sales training. In addition, we provide 1 week on-site assistance when the store opens and continuing assistance as needed.

Managerial Assistance Available: 1 week each in basic training, and training on-the-job in a company store and on-site assistance at franchisees center.

Information Submitted: June 1987

* **TUNEX INTERNATIONAL, INC.**
556 East 2100 South
Salt Lake City, Utah 84106
Rudy Zitzmann, Vice President, Franchise Development

Description of Operation: Attractive six- and eight-bay Tunex Centers offer a complete one-stop tune-up service. From low-priced maintenance tune-up to full analysis and repair of ignition, fuel, cooling and emission control systems, a full service of the automotive air conditioning system, and the (newly added) Tunex Lube and Oil Service, using the latest equipment and skilled technicians. Franchisee does not need special automotive skills. Strong business management abilities are essential.

Number of Franchisees: 50 operating in 9 Western States plus 2 company-owned.

In Business Since: 1972

Equity Capital Needed: $65,000 plus adequate credit to lease $30,000 worth of equipment. Capital includes $15,000 working capital and $19,000 franchise fee.

Financial Assistance Available: Direct financial assistance is not available, however, guidance in preparing application for SBA guaranteed or commercial loans can be provided.

Training Provided: 3 weeks training is provided for franchisee/manager and his technical staff at company headquarters and the service centers, which includes opening week training in the franchisee's center.

Managerial Assistance Available: Technical and managerial support provided on a continuing basis. Technical bulletins and toll-free hot line.

Information Submitted: May1987

ULTRA WASH, INC.
8100 Cambridge Street
Suite 121Houston, Texas 77054
Brian Peskin, President

Description of Operation: A state-of-the-art mobile pressure washing franchise specializing in truck fleet washing at the customer's location. All equipment, training, and initial supplies are included. An optional on-site salesman will come to franchisee's area to secure sales. This has proved very successful!

Number of Franchisees: 14 in Utah, California, and Texas.

In Business Since: 1981, franchising since 1984.

Equity Capital Needed: $30,000 cash. Can usually finance the remainder. Total franchise is approximately $55,000-$80,000.

Financial Assistance Available: Sources provided

Training Provided: Mandatory unlimited training at corporate headquarters in Houston, Texas, plus 1 week on location. Optional sales specialist will go to franchisee's area to assist in securing sales. Ongoing support is continual in the form of monthly newsletters, videotapes, etc.

Managerial Assistance Available: Over 15 years fleet washing experience. Mr. Peskin has been a manager with a Fortune 500 company. Our sale's expertise numbers over 12 in selling this service to truck fleet managers. We have over 5 man-years in equipment design and the washing equipment can bring in more sales per system than any other competitor due to its vastly reliable design.

Information Submitted: May 1987

USA AUTO APPEARANCE CENTERS, INC.
274 Union Boulevard
Suite 480
Lakewood, Colorado 80228
Robert Palmer, Jr., President

Description of Operation: Offering centers specializing in auto detailing, window tinting, auto glass replacement, and other appearance and protection services.

Number of Franchisees: 6 in Colorado

In Business Since: 1987

Equity Capital Needed: $50,000

Financial Assistance Available: Financing available to qualified applicants.

Training Provided: Training provided to owners and employees in all operations and management as well as ongoing training to new employees.

Managerial Assistance Available: Training staff available for all assistance in opening and ongoing activities.

Information Submitted: August 1987

USA FAST LUBE SYSTEMS
274 Union Boulevard
Suite 480
Lakewood, Colorado 80228
Robert Palmer, Jr., President

Description of Operation: Provides 10 minute oil change and automotive service centers.

Number of Franchisees: 58 in 5 States

In Business Since: 1984

Equity Capital Needed: $103,000 full investment, including land and building.

Financial Assistance Available: Financing can be obtained up to $30,000 to qualified applicants. Equipment leasing programs are also available.

Training Provided: Training provided to owners and employees in all operations and management as well as ongoing training to new employees.

Managerial Assistance Available: Training staff available for all assistance in opening and ongoing activities.

Information Submitted: August 1987

VICTORY LANE QUICK OIL CHANGE
2608 West Liberty
Ann Arbor, Michigan 48103
John Stegeman, Director of Franchising

Description of Operation: Quick oil change centers in which vehicles are given oil and filter change, chasis lubed and all fluids filled in addition to window cleaned, tires checked and inflated to current pressure and a general vehicle inspection. That is done in 10 minutes on a drive-thru basis.

Number of Franchisees: 4 plus 5 company-owned in Michigan and Ohio

In Business Since: 1980

Equity Capital Needed: $65,000

Financial Assistance Available: Franchisee to arrange own financing.

Training Provided: 1 week training course in Ann Arbor, Michigan covering site and personnel selection, pre-opening requirements, marketing, advertising, P&L statements accounting and control procedures. In addition, 25 hours are designated to on-site training.

Managerial Assistance Available: Victory Lane will provide continual assistance in "overseeing" the complete operation of the franchise. Manuals, technical bulletins, slide presentations and continual training are provided. In addition, an area supervisor will assist in franchisee's initial opening in an "on-site" capacity and continue to oversee the operation on an ongoing basis.

Information Submitted: May 1987

WASH-O-TEL, INC.
1501 Arkansas Avenue
Monroe, Louisiana 71201
Wayne Williamson, President

Description of Operation: We are in the vehicle maintenance service and we provide top quality cleaning and waxing service with our own hand applied technique while consuming no more than 1 gallon of water. A patented detergent combined with hand work makes the system successful.

Number of Franchisees: 15 plus 11 company-owned in Louisiana, Oklahoma, Texas, Tennessee, Arkansas and Florida

In Business Since: 1982

Equity Capital Needed: $15,000 franchise fee

Financial Assistance Available: Possible source of financing provided.

Training Provided: 3 days corporate training and 3 days in field training.

Managerial Assistance Available: Ongoing assistance of both types, as needed by franchisee.

Information Submitted: May 1987

*WESTERN AUTO
2107 Grand Avenue
Kansas City, Missouri 64108
James R. Randolph, Director, Store Development

Description of Operation: Retailing of hard lines and other home items—principal lines are automotive, lawn and garden and wheel goods, appliances, and electronics.

Number of Franchisees: Over 1,700 stores in all States except North Dakota. Dealer stores in Bahama Islands, British west Indies.

In Business Since: 1909: Began dealership in 1935

Equity Capital Needed: $75,000 minimum

Financial Assistance Available: Financing available on store fixtures. Floor planning of major items and deferred terms on some seasonal merchandise offered. Other financial assistance extended depending on personal financial statements of prospects.

Training Provided: 4 week training course, 4 weeks hands-on training in a company operated store. Company personnel continue to offer training, counseling and sales assistance after formalized training school is completed.

Managerial Assistance Available: Dealer contacted regularly in store by company personnel, offering counseling on sales, credit and store operation.

Information Submitted: May 1987

*ZIEBART CORPORATION
1290 East Maple Road
Troy, Michigan 48099
Richard Johnson, Director of Licensing

Description of Operation: Automotive appearance and protection services specializing in: rustproofing auto and truck bodies via special tooling and sealant, exterior paint protection, fabric protection, installation of quality sunroofs and running boards. Ziebart (newly added) automotive radiator, heat and air conditioning repair and service.

Number of Franchisees: 750 plus in 35 States and 35 Countries.

In Business Since: 1963

Equity Capital Available: Total project including operating capital averages $60,000-$80,000 of which $15,000 is the franchise fee.

Financial Assistance Available: None

Training Provided: Ziebart provides 18 days of marketing and technical training at the home office in Troy, Michigan followed by 5 days of intensive on-the-job training in a company-owned center. Formal training is followed by expert technical assistance in setting up the dealership and marketing assistance in implementing comprehensive programs to serve all channels of trade including retail, fleet and associate car dealers. Follow-up training continues with frequent visits by a district sales manager who is experienced in all technical areas and marketing techniques.

Managerial Assistance Available: A district sales manager continues to call on the dealer to assist in making sales calls, as well as reviewing new procedures for marketing Ziebart Services. Annual national seminar and special training and technical help are available to dealers at all times. Dealers participate in new product promotions and up-to-date advertising programs.

Information Submitted: May 1987

AUTO/TRAILER RENTALS

AFFORDABLE USED CAR RENTAL SYSTEM, INC.
P. O. Box 33
Keyport, New Jersey 07735-0033

Description of Operation: Affordable License is available to new car **dealers only.** It provides training, forms, follow-up and insurance for new car dealers desiring to enter the used car rental business. Price of license includes all forms necessary. District representatives call on dealer members regularly in person.

Number of Franchisees: 227 in 36 States

In Business Since: 1981

Equity Capital Needed: $3,500 to $13,000 depending on population. Monthly management fee depending on cars in service. Average $3,500 per unit put into service (Dealer's inventory).

Financial Assistance Available: None currently.

Training Provided: 3 days at training center in Hazlet, New Jersey. Training program mandatory.

Managerial Assistance Available: Affordable has trained executives to personally counsel dealers on regular basis. Forms are provided at no cost. Advertising techniques are exchanged. Low cost insurance is available but not compulsory. All former new car dealers, auto manufacturers former employees and rental professionals.

Information Submitted: May 1987

A.I.N LEASING SYSTEMS
80 Cuttermill Road
Great Neck, New York 11021
Garry Rothbaum

Description of Operation: An automobile and equipment leasing franchise. A.I.N. provides training, marketing plan, and all necessary lease financing.

Number of Franchisees: 265 nationwide

In Business Since: 1980

Equity Capital Needed: $15,000

Financial Assistance Available: Will assist in obtaining financing.

Training Provided: 4 days of training covers, marketing and merchandising.

Managerial Assistance Available: Ongoing support and assistance.

Information Submitted: June 1987

AIRWAYS RENT A CAR CO.
4025 North Mannheim
Schiller Park, Illinois 60176
Michael H. Zaransky, President

Description of Operation: Car rental firm in business 20 years. Offers national reservations system including 800 number and airline automated system listing.

Number of Franchisees: 2 in Illinois and New Jersey

In Business Since: 1967

Equity Capital Needed: $100,000

Financial Assistance Available: Arrange for auto purchase financing.

Training Provided: Comprehensive at franchisor's premises for up to 2 weeks.

Managerial Assistance Available: Throughout franchise term.

Information Submitted: May 1987

AMERICAN INTERNATIONAL RENT A CAR
4801 Spring Valley Road,
Dallas, Texas 75244
Marge Wavernek, Vice President Franchise Development

Description of Operation: American International is a world-wide network of car rental operations servicing customers at airport, suburban, and downtown locations. All outlets are franchised-owned, there are no corporate locations.

Number of Franchisees: The American International network consists of over 1,300 locations in more than 25 countries throughout the North America, Europe, the Middle East, South America, and the Caribbean.

In Business Since: 1968

Equity Capital Needed: Varies with size and location of the territory. Average initial franchise investment: $50,000.

Financial Assistance Available: Arrangements are discussed on a individual basis.

Training Provided: Initial training available at the corporate headquarters location. Complete operations manuals are provided and updated by the Systems Office. Ongoing consultation and assistance will be provided as needed.

Managerial Assistance Available: The management team at American International assists new franchisees in selecting sites, financing and managing their fleets, analyzing financial statements, obtaining corporate accounts, government contracts and local marketing and advertising. American International has standardized everything their franchisees need, including signs, rental agreements, uniforms and promotional materials.

Information Submitted: May 1987

AMTRALEASE
1415 Rt. 70 East
Suite 505A
Cherry Hill, New Jersey 08034
Douglas Clark, Executive Director

Description of Operation: AMTRALEASE is a franchise system of independent truck leasing companies dedicated to reciprocal service and exchange of information among its members.

Number of Franchisees: 57 presently operating in 38 States with expansion to the remaining States being planned.

In Business Since: 1979

Equity Capital Needed: Not applicable

Financial Assistance Available: Not applicable

Training Provided: Not applicable

Managerial Assistance Available: AMTRALEASE provides 1 and 2 day seminars throughout the year. These seminars and conventions are voluntary for the members.

Information Submitted: June 1987

ATLANTIC RENT-A-CAR, INC.
P. O. Box 3744
West Palm Beach, Florida 33402
David E. Russell, President
David E. Christy, Vice President

Description of Operation: Atlantic Rent-A-Car, Inc., offers two revenue sources to all franchisee's: (1) daily, weekly and seasonal rentals, and (2) credit lines for long-term leasing, one of the fastest growing businesses today. Extensive knowledge in rental insurance and where to get it. Finally, the most creative financing plans for rental inventory available.

Number of Franchisees: 3 in Florida

In Business Since: 1985

Equity Capital Needed: $60,000 is necessary to begin. This includes franchisee fee, all deposits (phone, electric insurance and care) also office furniture, computers and supply is to begin your progress.

Financial Assistance Available: When possible Atlantic can help arrange financing for qualified applicants.

Training Provided: 2 weeks training at the location and assistance on an ongoing basis. How to advertise, counterpractices and best methods of how to succeed.

Managerial Assistance Available: Atlantic provides continual management assistance to all franchisee's for the life of the program. Operation manuals are provided and updated periodically. Management is constantly looking for better insurance programs, more practical car programs and marketing outlets are always being sought after.

Information Submitted: May 1987

AVIS RENT A CAR SYSTEM, INC.
Licensee Relations Department
900 Old Country Road
Garden City, New York 11530

Description of Operation: Avis is in the business of renting passenger cars to members of the general public directly and through franchisees who purchase Avis car rental franchises from Avis. Avis offers franchises within the United States for car rental (including the sale of used cars) and truck rental and leasing.

Number of Franchisees: Over 700 locations throughout the United States

In Business Since: 1946

Equity Capital Needed: Varies according to the size of franchised area.

Financial Assistance Available: None

Training Provided: An Avis field director will spend approximately 1 week prior to or during the opening of the franchised business to assist the franchisee, to acquaint the franchisee with the Avis car rental system and to assist in training rental sales agents.

Managerial Assistance Available: Avis personnel are available for consultation on advertising, promoting, operating and developing the franchisee's car rental business. Periodic business conventions will be held.

Information Submitted: June 1987

*BUDGET RENT A CAR CORPORATION
200 North Michigan Avenue
Chicago, Illinois 60601
Rick J. Santella, Director of Franchise

Description of Operation: Automobile and truck rental.

Number of Franchisees: 3,230 locations worldwide

In Business Since: 1960

Equity Capital Needed: Varies with size of operation.

Financial Assistance Available: Occasionally, depending on circumstances.

Training Provided: Management and operational training at the Budget training center, at selected locations and on-site.

Managerial Assistance Available: During the term of the franchise, Budget has a complete management team available to assist licencees in areas of: franchising, operations, promotions, local marketing, advertising, trucks, training and insurance. Site selection assistance is provided prior to the opening of each location.

Information Submitted: May 1987

DOLLAR RENT A CAR SYSTEMS, INC.
6141 West Century Boulevard
Los Angeles, California 90045
E. Woody Francis

Description of Operation: Automobile and truck rental. Heavy concentration in airport operations.

Number of Franchisees: Over 1,800 worldwide. Locations throughout Europe, Middle East and Africa will be under Inter-Rent-Dollar.

In Business Since: 1966

Equity Capital Needed: Approximately $100,000

Financial Assistance Available: Occasionally assist in financing.

Training Provided: Standardized accounting system set up. Operational training by franchisor's representative at site.

Managerial Assistance Available: Assistance in-site selection. Standardized free-standing building. Consultant on-site during construction. Guidance in selection and balance of fleet. Continuing guidance in accounting and operations. Nationwide advertising campaign, co-op program available, and nationwide reservations service.

Information Submitted: June 1987

FANCY FLIVVERS NATIONAL FRANCHISE
311 North Henry Street
Alexandria, Virginia 22314
Kevin Ghezzi

Description of Operation: Full service automobile rental franchise featuring new, mid-year and used automobiles.

Number of Franchisees: 4 in Virginia

In Business Since: 1978

Equity Capital Needed: $55,000

Financial Assistance Available: None

Training rovided: Each franchise owner will receive training in all areas of the business operation. Training will be conducted in our new facility located in Alexandria, Virginia.

Managerial Assistance Available: Exclusive territory, state of the art computer system, complete insurance package assistance, operations manual, advertising, promotions and mass purchasing power are all provided through Fancy Flivvres National Franchise.

Information Submitted: May 1987

FREEDOM RENT-A-CAR SYSTEM
1320 West Frank Phillips Boulevard
Bartlesville, Oklahoma 74005
Neil Wilderom, President

Description of Operation: Freedom Rent-A-Car offers daily car and truck rentals throughout the United States. Operators offer new and used rental cars to both airport and local markets at inexpensive rates.

Number of Franchisees: 165 locations in 35 States

In Business Since: 1982

Equity Capital Needed: Varies in size of franchise territory.

Financial Assistance Available: Franchisor will assist licensee in obtaining vehicle financing from lending institutions. Franchisor will extend financing for a portion of franchise purchase to select licensees.

Training Provided: Each licensee receives a comprehensive 3-day classroom training course in Bartlesville, Oklahoma. On-site training within first 2 weeks of operation. The training program is open to any new staff members on continuing basis.

Managerial Assistance Available: Periodic reviews conducted by regional managers. Qualified in all aspects of the car rental industry. Operating manuals and a toll-free number maintained for licensee assistance.

Information Submitted: June 1987

HERTZ CORPORATION
660 Madison Avenue
New York, New York 10021

Description of Operation: Hertz System, Inc., offers franchises for the conduct of car and truck rental and leasing businesses in the United States under the "Hertz" name.

Number of Franchisees: Over 1,100 car and truck rental locations in all states except Florida and Hawaii.

In Business Since: 1918

Equity Capital Needed: Varies according to franchise-operating capital as required by location.

Financial Assistance Available: None

Training Provided: Zone System Manager trains new franchisee before operation opens with Hertz Starter Kit (kit includes all forms needed to run a location). Visits by System Manager on a periodic basis. Manager rental representative training classes. Manuals and guides for running a location issued. Corporate training class available to franchisees. Annual business meeting.

Managerial Assistance Available: Accounting and operational guides are provided to run the location. Visits by Corporate Zone System Manager to act as a liaison between the corporate and licensee locations. All forms and training classes provided business (e.g., insurance, advertising, accounting, etc.).

Information Submitted: June 1987

PAYLESS CAR RENTAL
dba HOLIDAY PAYLESS RENT-A-CAR SYSTEM
5510 Gulfport Boulevard
St. Petersburg, Florida 33707
Les Netherstrom, President

Description of Operation: Automobile renting of current model cars.

Number of Franchisees: 160 in 37 States and 5 in foreign countries.

In Business Since: 1971

Equity Capital Needed: Varies—franchise fee $10,000-$50,000 plus $11.750 to $39,100 working capital plus net worth is guarantee rental fleet financing.

Financial Assistance Available: Assistance in establishing necessary lines of credit with which to acquire vehicles. Assistance in procuring fleet insurance.

Training Provided: Theory complete with procedure manual, 1 day. On-the-job training, 5 days. Opening assistance and review, 5 days. Follow-up visit and review, 2-3 days.

Managerial Assistance Available: Training as necessary in vehicle procurement, insurance procurement, office and counter procedures, customer qualifications, hiring and training personnel, business development, advertising, accounting, vehicle disposal and fleet maintenance procedures. Periodic visits, regional and international meetings.

Information Submitted: May 1987

MR. RENT A CAR, MR. LEASE A CAR, INC.
45 Haverhill Street
Andover, Massachusetts 01810
Carl Harrington, Franchise Director

Description of Operation: Mr. Rent A Car, Mr. Lease A Car offers a system unique in the auto industry. Operating from an office approximately 600 to 1,200 square feet with parking facilities for 8 to 10 vehicles, franchisee's can rent, lease and sell new cars. Makes and models of the vehicles are selected by the franchisee and financed by Mr. Rent A Car, Mr. Lease A Car, Inc.

Number of Franchisees: 22 in New England States only.

In Business Since: 1977

Equity Capital Needed: $50,000

Financial Assistance Available: Mr. Rent A Car provides all financing for rental vehicles. This is the only financing assistance available.

Training Provided: Intensive 1 month mandatory training program, consisting of 2, 6 day weeks prior to opening at a company training outlet. This is followed by a minimum of 2, 6 day, weeks in the franchisee's office under the supervision of a Mr. Rent A Car, Mr. Lease A Car field supervisor.

Managerial Assistance Available: Mr. Rent A Car, Mr. Lease A Car provides continuous training and management services for the duration of the franchise agreement in such areas as sales, leasing, accounting, fleet size, vehicle acquisition and disposal. Operations manual, forms and advertising assistance are provided. Field supervisors are available for business consultation and problem solving at the franchisee's request. Frequent visits are scheduled by field personnel to assist the franchisee. Mr. Rent A Car, Mr. Lease A Car sponsors bi-monthly meetings and annual conventions.

Information Submitted: June 1987

*PRACTICAL USED CAR RENTAL
9th Floor, P. O. Box 111
1177 Hornby Street
Vancouver, B.C. V6Z 2E9
Mr. James M. Hodge, President

Description of Operation: Rental and leasing of clean, late model used cars at lower prices than new car companies. Leasing is offered on primarily a 1 year basis.

Number of Franchisees: 197 in United States, Canada and England

In Business Since: 1976

Equity Capital Needed: $10,000-$50,000 franchise fee. $30,000-$250,000 total investment.

Financial Assistance Available: Complete preparation of bank proposals, budgets, proformas, 3 month supply of all operational needs with the exception of cars and leaseholds.

Training Provided: Intensive 1 week mandatory training course at free standing training center. Two days opening assistance. Ongoing assistance and seminars.

Managerial Assistance Available: Opening and ongoing assistance. Visits from operations supervisors as required along with regular telephone contact. Regional meetings, bi-annual zone meetings. Workshop on various aspects of the business e.g., car sales, leasing promotion etc. Assistance in preparation of monthly statements if required.

Information Submitted: May 1987

RENT-A-DENT CAR RENTAL SYSTEMS, INC.
19415 Pacific Highway South
Suite 413
Seattle, Washington 98188

Description of Operation: Used automobile rental franchise.

Number of Franchisees: 95 in 13 States

In Business Since: 1977

Equity Capital Needed: Minimum $5,000-$10,000 franchise fee. $25,000-$250,000 total investment. Franchise fee and total investment would be more for a master franchise.

Financial Assistance Available: Financial assistance available to prospective franchisees with good credit.

Training Provided: 1 week intensive training in Seattle, plus 1 week opening assistance at location.

Managerial Assistance Available: Ongoing, including National "800" reservation System. Visits from marketing supervisors, regular telephone contact, national advertising, national convention, and any and all assistance provided as needed.

Information Submitted: June 1987

RENT-A-WRECK OF AMERICA, INC.
1100 Glendon Avenue
Suite 1250
Los Angeles, California 90024
Donald B. Marks, Chief Operating Officer

Description of Operation: Automobile rental and leasing.

Number of Franchisees: 305 in 44 States and Australia

In Business Since: 1977

Equity Capital Needed: Capitalization $73,000 to $200,000. Each new affiliate pays an initial license fee which ranges from $3,000 to $50,000 depending on the size and location of his market.

Financial Assistance Available: See automobile financing available.

Training Provided: Each new licensee receives a mandatory 4-day intensive training course in Los Angeles which covers all aspects of the operation of a Rent-A-Wreck facility in compliance with the standards set by the company. Ongoing training is provided through regional meetings, regional representatives, national conventions and refresher courses.

Managerial Assistance Available: During the four-day training period management and technical training are the foremost areas addressed to prepare new licensees in running a Rent-A-Wreck operation; licensees are free to send new management personnel to Rent-A-Wreck school as needed. A complete operations manual, as well as rental business forms with directions for their use, and a marketing planner, containing advertising and promotional materials, are provided. Trained Bundy personnel are available by telephone for ongoing consultation and assistance.

Information Submitted: June 1987

THRIFTY RENT-A-CAR SYSTEM, INC.
P. O. Box 35250
4608 Exchange Center
Tulsa, Oklahoma 74153
Brett M. Thomas, Director-Franchise Development

Description of Operation: Franchisor of automobile renting and leasing business throughout the world.

Number of Franchisees: Over 650 locations in North America, South America, the Carribbean, Europe, the Middle East, and the Asia-Pacific areas, and Great Britian.

In Business Since: 1962

Equity Capital Needed: Varies in proportion to the size and potential of the franchise area.

Financial Assistance Available: Franchisor will assist licensee in obtaining vehicle financing from lending institutions. Additional financial assistance is provided via credit card programs, national and local advertising programs, and national insurance programs.

Training Provided: Company maintains and operates an ongoing car rental operation which is used exclusively for the training of licensees, testing of marketing theories and programs. In addition, field assistance is provided by trained personnel at the time of opening, and periodically thereafter.

Managerial Assistance Available: Thrifty furnishes continuing management assistance to its licensees by way of a headquarters staff trained in all areas of the car rental operation, including: financial, legal, operational, sales and marketing, insurance, and vehicle purchases and disposal. Trained regional directors call on the licensee on a regular basis offering assistance designed to insure the success of the licensee.

Information Submitted: May 1987

UGLY DUCKLING RENT-A-SYSTEM, INC.
7750 East Broadway
Suite 100
Tucson, Arizona 85710

Description of Operation: Each franchise is individually owned and operated. Rental of preowned vehicles aimed at local market with few customers at or from airports. Licensee provides capital and vehicles except as noted below. Current licensees include new and used car dealerships and automotive related businesses, such as, body shops, tune-up centers, transmission repair shops, etc.

Number of Franchisees: 500 plus in 41 States and Canada

In Business Since: 1977

Equity capital Needed: $10,000 to $50,000

Financial Assistance Available: None

Training Provided: Fully comprehensive 4 day training program at our Tucson national office. Company provides round trip air fare up to $750.

Managerial Assistance Available: Eight hundred number available for all problems relative to the business. Zone managers and service rep available for technical assistance. Monthly information and bulletins keeps franchisees abreast of market development.

Information Submitted: June 1987

U-SAVE AUTO RENTAL OF AMERICA, INC.
P. O. Box 1651
Salisbury, North Carolina 28144
Trauisa Tefft, Home Office Contact

Description of Operation: Designed for small as well as large populated areas. Most locations are independent car dealers renting preconditioned cars, servicing insurance customers as well as off the street rentals and the business community.

Number of Franchisees: 460 in 42 States

In Business Since: 1979

Equity Capital Needed: $15,000-$20,000

Financial Assistance Available: None

Training Provided: On premise training by State or regional manager as required, normally for 1 day. Visits by State manager. Manuals and guides for operating a location issued.

Managerial Assistance Available: Periodic visits by State and regional managers, toll free number to home office for official assistance. Assistance available in all phases of rental and reservation system (i.e., accounting, legal, insurance, etc.).

Information Submitted: May 1987

BEAUTY SALONS/SUPPLIES

AMERICUTS
501 West Clenoaks Boulevard
Suite 201
Glendale, California 91202
Victor Seprakian

Description of Operation: mericuts offers a full service franchise concept providing both men and women a complete hair care package—dedicating its energies and resources to cutting hair better and in a better environment. The marketing emphasis on the franchise salons is the precision that its hair stylists employ and the precise planning that went into building exceptional stores with a bustling trade based upon repeat and new customers. As well as the availability of new franchise outlets, franchises may be available for fully improved, operational, company-owned shops.

Number of Franchisees: 3 plus 4 company-owned in California

In Business Since: 1982

Equity Capital Needed: Total investment, including initial franchise fee, ranges from $65,000 to $92,000 depending upon the size and leasehold improvements of franchise outlets.

Financial Assistance Available: None

Training Provided: The franchise, 1 person employed in a managerial capacity and 3 licensed operators are required to be trained prior to the opening of the franchise. Training is generally 1 week and includes shop management and business operations and procedures. The training program includes both classroom and practical instruction.

Managerial Assistance Available: The franchisor provides members of its operations staff and shop personnel to assist franchisee in the operation of the shop, in establishing shop procedures and training shop personnel. The franchisor also provides a staff and shop personnel at its expense for up to 4 weeks following the opening of the franchise outlet. Periodically, franchisor may make available advertising plans and advice and in-shop promotional materials for franchisees' use and may assist in designing special advertising and promotional programs. Additional training courses or programs may become available to franchisee at the discretion of the franchisor to include sales techniques, training of personnel, performance standards and advertising programs.

Information Submitted: June 1987

THE MANE EVENT FRANCHISING CO., INC.
dba AUTUMN ROSE HAIR DESIGNERS
700 Franklin Avenue
Franklin Square, New York 11010
Lee Meyer, President

Description of Operation: The franchise offered is for the establishment and operation of a hair care salon featuring traditional "beauty parlor" services, such as full sets, in addition to basic haircutting, styling and hair care services, at a designated location under the name "Autumn Rose Hair Designers." The marketing emphasis on the franchise salons is a haircutting and styling for women as the primary market target, although services are available to men. Personalized attention in a relaxing atmosphere is stressed. Private brand hair care products packaged under the name "Autumn Rose" are also featured at franchise salons for retail sales to customers.

Number of Franchisees: 4 in New York

In Business Since: 1979

Equity Capital Needed: Initial estimated total cost, including initial franchise fee, ranges between $24,945 to $56,250.

Financial Assistance Available: Initial franchise fee of $9,500 may be paid in installments. Most installment payment plans require the franchisee to pay at least $3,500 upon signing the franchise agreement, at least $1,500 upon signing the sublease for the franchise premises and the balance of the initial franchise fee by no later than 3 months after the franchise salon opens for business. However, in individual cases different payment plans may be available.

Training Provided: Initial training is in 2 parts: hands-on training at a company-owned location and on-site assistance at the franchise location following the opening of the franchise business to the public. The length of the initial training program varies in individual cases opening of the franchise business to the public. The length of the initial training program varies in individual cases depending upon the franchisee's prior business and trade experience. Training covers all aspects of autumn Rose franchise system. There is no training fee (fee is included in initial franchise fee), except the franchisee is responsible for all personal expenses incurred in attending the training program. An unlimited number of employees and managers of the franchisee may attend the initial training program.

Managerial Assistance Available: The franchisor will periodically inspect the franchise premises to provide on-site operations assistance. Franchisees will be provided with the names of recommended suppliers for equipment, signs, fixtures, nonproprietary supplies and materials. The franchisor may periodically make available advertising plans and advice and in-shop merchandising materials for franchisees' local use and may assist in designing special advertising and promotional programs for individual market regions. The franchisor will periodically offer free optional and mandatory workshops for franchisees and their employees in haircutting and hair styling and may hold franchisee conferences to discuss sales techniques, training of personnel, performance standards, advertising programs and merchandising procedures.

Information Submitted: June 1987

* **THE BARBERS, HAIRSTYLING FOR MEN AND WOMEN, INC.**
300 Industrial Boulevard
Minneapolis, Minnesota 55413
Vaughn Berg, Director of Franchise Sales

Description of Operation: A completely systemized men's and women's hairstyling shop with inventory controls, accounting systems, advertising, public relations, business management programs, and turnkey built locations.

Number of Franchisees: 82 in 9 States plus 16 company-owned

In Business Since: 1963

Equity Capital Needed: $25,000 to $40,000

Financial Assistance Available: Investor partners welcomed.

Training Provided: Management and technical, 1 week, then quarterly seminars.

Managerial Assistance Available: Business management, including advertising, public relations, accounting and recordkeeping, training in hairstyling and all related services.

Information Submitted: May 1987

* **COMMAND PERFORMANCE**
355 Middlesex Avenue
Wilmington, Massachusetts 01887
Carl Youngman, C.E.O.

Description of Operation: Precision haircutting and styling salons for men and women. Company encourages owner-operators.

Number of Franchisees: 140 franchisees own 450 franchises in 40 States

In Business Since: 1976

Equity Capital Needed: Total cost to purchase, construct and open salon:$41,500 to $124,500

Financial Assistance Available: None

Training Provided: In addition to recruiting and training the salon's manager and staff, the franchisor conducts a comprehensive 30 hour initial training courses for its franchisees in all phases of operations, advertising, promotion, legal and financial considerations.

Managerial Assistance Available: In addition to initial site selection, lease negotiations, hiring and training of staff, construction counsel, the franchisor furnishes continuing management, marketing, operational and technical assistance to franchisee and his employees.

Information Submitted: May 1987

• COST CUTTERS FAMILY HAIR CARE SHOPS
A Division of THE BARBERS, HAIRSTYLING FOR MEN & WOMEN, INC.
300 Industrial Boulevard NE
Minneapolis, Minnesota 55413
Vaughn Berg, Director of Franchise Sales

Description of Operation: No-frills hair care services and related retail products for men, women and children.

Number of Franchisees: 205 in 16 States and 4 in Canada plus 36 company-owned.

In Business Since: 1982

Equity Capital Needed: $15,000-$40,000

Financial Assistance Available: None

Training Provided: Mandatory 2-1/2 day program for the franchisee and manager to include operating and management skills, customer relations, handling of personnel, inventory control, advertising and promotional techniques.

Managerial Assistance Available: Additional training for stylists available upon request at charges based on the type, location and duration of training provided. Such training may be custom designed to fit the franchisees needs.

Information Submitted: May 1987

EASH HAIR FRANCHISE, INC.
2625 Sandy Plains Road
Suite 206
Marietta, Georgia 30066
Cliff Hicks

Description of Operation: Value priced hair care salon. Computerized operations with full-time manager. Stores approximately 1,500 square feet.

Number of Franchisees: 3 in Georgia

In Business Since: 1986

Equity Capital Needed: $20,000 franchise fee.

Financial Assistance Available: We will assist in obtaining satisfactory financing.

Training Provided: 2 weeks prior to opening, 1 week on operations and 1 week on actual daily business.

Managerial Assistance Available: Pre-opening training for all parties involved. Each store is also assigned a business consultant who calls on them weekly.

Information Submitted: May 1987

ELAN HAIR DESIGN FRANCHISING LTD.
3 River Run
East Greenwich, Rhode Island 02818
Elaine Shapiro, President

Description of Operation: Hair, skin care and nail salon. Full service—unisex. Full line of products—total retail centre.

Number of Franchisees: 4 including company-owned in Rhode Island

In Business Since: 1977

Equity Capital Needed: $44,500

Financial Assistance Available: None

Training Provided: Initially, 1-2 weeks training in record keeping, managerial operations and inventory control. If necessary more time will be given.

Managerial Assistance Available: 1 week intense training in record keeping, managerial operations and inventory control. If necessary more time will be given.

Information Submitted: June 1987

FANTASTIC SAM'S, THE ORIGINAL FAMILY HAIRCUTTERS
3180 Old Getwell Road
P. O. Box 18845
Memphis, Tennessee 38181-0845
Sam M. Ross, Chairman of the Board
George H. Carnall, II, President

Description of Operation: The company sells licenses for Fantastic Sam's, the Original Family Haircutters, a unique retail haircare establishment oriented to the demands, pocketbooks and convenience of all American families.

Number of Franchisees: 1,100 licenses are open and located in 43 States and Canada.

In Business Since: 1974

Equity Capital Needed: (1) one Fantastic Sam's store—$44,000-$62,000 which includes the license fee and all amounts to open that store. (2) Regional license to sell and provide service to Fantastic Sam's licensees within that region—$25,000-$300,000.

Financial Assistance Available: The company provides payment terms on initial product inventory and will finance shop equipment to qualified licensees.

Training Provided: The company provides training classes for all licensees, their shop managers, hairstylists and staff members in the training facilities of the company. Further, experienced trainers assist all of the licensees in their store openings, provide seminars around the country and Canada, conduct in-store consultation and training, and provide a complete technical training program.

Managerial Assistance Available: In-store seminars and regional seminars are provided to all licensees and their store managers. Additionally, week long management classes and daily training classes for all licensees and their store managers are scheduled regularly at the training facilities of the company.

Information Submitted: June 1987

FIRST CHOICE HAIRCUTTERS, LTD.
6535 Millcreek Drive
Unit 64
Mississauga, Ontario L5N 2M2
George Kostopoulos, Director of Franchise Development

Description of Operation: First Choice Haircutters is in the business of providing high volume, low cost retail haircutting and hair care services for the entire family. Our a la carte price structure allows customers to purchase only services required: cut, shampoo, style dry, perms, hennas etc. Licensed stylists, all services fully guaranteed. Convenience-emphasized—no appointments, one-stop shopping for entire family; free parking. Also private label shampoo and conditioners for retail trade.

Number of Franchisees: 27 franchisees with 115 franchised stores, plus a strong corporate base of 90 stores; strategically located in the United States and Canada.

In Business Since: 1980

Equity Capital Needed: $35,000 to $40,000 for a single store franchise includes franchise fees, furniture and equipment, leaseholds, grand opening, advertising and working capital. $65,000 to $70,000 for an area franchise includes exclusive territory for multiple shop franchises and 2 initial stores complete, as indicated.

Financial Assistance Available: Preparation of proformas and assistance in obtaining bank financing, or internal financing of franchise fees for qualified individuals.

Training Provided: 2 week complete franchisee training program includes operations, site selection and lease negotiations, advertising, staff hiring and motivation. Plus 10-13 days on-site store opening assistance and continued support. Plus 2 store visits per year by one of the training officers/operations manager for updates, reviews and progress reports. Plus operations and training manuals, video training tapes, television commercials and radio ads. All included in the franchise fee.

Managerial Assistance Available: All haircutters are trained in the First Choice Haircutters method of cutting and customer service techniques. On-site opening assistance, frequent shop visits, ongoing support and consultation, franchisee seminars, advertising advisory council and refresher course.

Information Submitted: June 1987

FIRST PLACE, INC.
2190-H Parkway Lake Drive
Birmingham, Alabama 35244
Michael Darnell, President

Description of Operation: Family hair care center servicing the entire family. The stores are characterized by a distinctive interior design, color scheme, layout and specially-designed decor.

Number of Franchisees: 13 stores including company-owned.

In Business Since: 1977

Equity Capital Needed: $64,225 to $92,200

Financial Assistance Available: None

Training Provided: Training consists of an initial 2 week session on procedures and techniques for hair care, methods of implementing operating cash and financial controls, and manuals including advertising and marketing programs.

Managerial Assistance Available: During the first week of franchisee's opening, franchisor provides an employee at franchisee's location for opening assistance. Franchisor offers continuing services relating to the conduct of franchisee's business.

Information Submitted: May 1987

GREAT CLIPS, INC.
3601 West 77th Street #145
Minneapolis, Minnesota 55435
Raymond L. Barton, Chief Executive Officer

Description of Operation: A Great Clips shop is a high quality, high volume haircutting shop for the entire family. The Great Clips franchise is designed for the business person—investor.

Number of Franchisees: 150 in 10 States

In Business Since: 1982

Equity Capital Needed: $50,000 to $60,000

Financial Assistance Available: Assistance in preparing bank presentations to secure up to 100 percent financing through various outside financial institutions.

Training Provided: Complete franchisee training and assistance including: site selection, lease negotiations, manager selection, equipping and suppling a Great Clips shop, and professional advertising and promotion programs.

Managerial Assistance Available: Professional technical training and assistance for all shop managers and stylists. Regularly scheduled visits fro Great Clips training and management consulting staffs. District manager employed by Great Clips training and management consulting staffs. District manager employed by Great Clips in every major market. Continuing advertising and promotion support and assistance.

Information Submitted: May 1987

*GREAT EXPECTATIONS PRECISION HAIRCUTTERS
125 South Service Road
P. O. Box 265
Jericho, New York 11753
Don vonLiebermann, Exeuctive Vice President

Description of Operation: Great Expectations is a distinctive haircutting establishment primarily servicing men and women aged 18-34, appealing to the contemporary hair care customer. The franchise package offers: a thoroughly modern, attractively designed shop, streamlined equipment, operational support, training, site selection and personnel recruitment.

Number of Franchisees: 288 in 40 States, 9 in Japan

In Business Since: 1955

Equity Capital Needed: Total initial investment $81,000 to $169,000

Financial Assistance Available: Financial assistance available up to $50,000 to qualified applicants.

Training Provided: In salon training about 10 days. Pre-opening training in franchisee's salon and complete supply of manuals.

Managerial Assistance Available: Home office, technical seminars, new techniques, and management training. Advertising materials and promotions.

Information Submitted: June 1987

*HAIRCRAFTERS
125 South Service Road
P. O. Box 265
Jericho, New York 11753
Don vonLiebermann, Executive Vice President

Description of Operation: Full service hair care salons servicing men and women, combines popular unisex styling services with the traditional selection to meet the needs of all ages. The franchise package offers: a thoroughly modern, attractively designed shop, streamlined equipment, operational support, training, site selection and personnel recruitment.

Number of Franchisees: 356 in 28 States, Canada and Japan

In Business Since: 1955

Equity Capital Needed: $71,000 to $124,500

Financial Assistance Available: Financial assistance available up to $50,000 to qualified applicants.

Training Provided: In-salon training about 10 days. Pre-opening training in franchisee's salon and complete supply of manuals.

Managerial Assistance Available: Home office, technical seminars, new techniques, and management training. Advertising materials and promotions.

Information Submitted: June 1987

HAIRCUTS COMPANY
20900 Swenson Drive
Suite 100
Waukesha, Wisconsin 53186
Ken Smith/Bernard J. Conway

Description of Operation: Haircuts operates a chain of family affordable hair care shops. Locations are in strip mall centers and are approximately 1,500 square feet. Haircuts provides site location, remodeling plans and a complete operations manual to each franchisee. Television commercials and print promotions are a part of the extensive marketing plan available to franchisees.

Number of Franchise: 3 plus 23 company-owned in Ohio, and Wisconsin.

In Business Since: 1983, franchising since 1985.

Equity Capital Needed: $85,000-$95,000 total investment.

Financial Assistance Available: While Haircuts does not provide any direct financing to franchisees, assistance is provided in obtaining outside financing.

Training Provided: Separate training programs are conducted for franchisees and their personnel. Haircuts provides franchisees with on-site assistance during shop opening process.

Managerial Assistance Available: Haircuts provides ongoing quality control assurance through field operations management. Marketing and advertisingprograms are implemented in conjunction with the franchisees.

Information Submitted: June 1987

*HAIR PERFORMERS
c/o JOHN F. AMICO & CO., INC.
7327 West 90th Street
Bridgeview, Illinois 60455
William H. Patton, Director of Sales

Description of Operation: Family hair care center which provides styling and hair cutting for the entire family. Most franchisees operate store on limited hours (8 to 10) all business and management aids provided. Regional offices and training facilities throughout the U.S. Two basic schools in Chicago.

Number of Franchisees: 217 franchised units in 17 States, plus 9 company-owned.

In Business Since: 1962

Equity Capital Needed: $25,000 to $50,000

Financial Assistance Available: Assistance provided by company.

Training Provided: Staffing, recruiting, management selection and training provided for franchisees. Training conducted at home office, regional offices, company-owned college and in-store programs.

Managerial Assistance Available: Complete site selection, lease negotiations, salon design, full staffing and continual management assistance and full training at Hair Performers college.

Information Submitted: June 1987

JOAN M. CABLE'S LA FEMMINA BEAUTY SALONS, INC.
3301 Hempstead Turnpike
Levittown, New York 11756
John L. Wagner, Vice President

Description of Operation: Joan M. Cable's La Femmina Beauty Salons, Inc., offers to qualified applicants, franchises to operate retail ladies beauty parlors under the name **Joan Cable's La Femmina Beauty Salons.** La Femmina offers total service to women with complete haircare and grooming services including manicures, pedicures, facials, using only the highest quality name brand products—all at affordable prices and convenient hours for today's active women.

Number of Franchisees: 14 in New York/Long Island areas

In Business Since: 1974

Equity Capital Needed: Total investment ranges from $27,265.21 to 33,265.21

Financial Assistance Available: Franchisor will possibly assist franchisee in obtaining appropriate financing or franchisor may offer a portion of such financing for the purpose of all necessary machinery and equipment.

Training Provided: The training program shall last no less than 5 days and provides the franchisee with the certain knowledge to assist the franchisee in the operation of the La Femmina Beauty Parlor. Throughout the training program, which will be held on a one to one bases such topics as payroll, advertising, insurance, products, and scheduling will be discussed in conjunction with the direct use of the operations manual.

Managerial Assistance Available: Joan M. Cable's La Femmina Beauty Salons, Inc., provides continual and ongoing training and management service for the term of the franchise in areas of bookkeeping, advertising, workshops, seminars and promotional programs, all on an as needed basis.

Information Submitted: May 1987

JOAN M. CABLE'S LA FEMMINA BEAUTY SALONS, INC.
dba THE LEMON TREE
3301 Hempstead Turnpike
Levittown, New York 11756
John L. Wagner, Vice President

Description of Operation: Joan M. Cable's La Femmina Beauty Salons, Inc., offers franchises to qualified applicants. Franchises to operate Unisex Haircutting Establishments under the name of **The Lemon Tree, a "Unisex Haircutting Establishment."** Lemon Tree offers complete haircare and grooming service to men, women and children using only the highest quality name brand products all at affordable prices and convenient hours for today's active people.

Number of Franchisees: 48 in Long Island/Staten Island/Brooklyn Westchester and New Jersey.

In Business Since: 1976

Equity Capital Needed: Total investment ranges from $26,600.00 to $33,100.00.

Financial Assistance: Franchisor will possibly assist franchisee in obtaining appropriate financing or franchisor may offer a portion of such financing for the purchase of all necessary machinery and equipment.

Training Provided: The training program shall last no less than 5 days and provides the franchisee with the certain knowledge to assist the franchisee in the operation of the Lemon Tree, a "Unisex Haircutting Establishment." Throughout the training program, which will be held on a one to one bases such topics as payroll, advertising, insurance, products, and scheduling will be discussed in conjunction with the direct use of the operations manual.

Managerial Assistance Available: Joan M. Cable's La Femmina Beauty Salons, Inc., provides continual and ongoing training and management service for the term of the franchise in areas of bookkeeping, advertising, workshops, seminars and promotional programs, all on an as needed basis.

Information Submitted: May 1987

LORD'S & LADY'S HAIR SALONS
450 Belgrade Avenue
Boston, Massachusetts 02132
Michael M. Barsamian, President
Harry G. Mitchell, Executive Vice President and Treasurer

Description of Operation: Professional haircutting for men and women is the main service of a full service operaion requiring a minimum of 15 hours per week from the franchisee. The salons have a wide range of professional hair care products including a private label "Lord's & Lady's" line.

Number of Franchisees: 8 franchises plus 18 company-owned units in 7 States.

In Business Since: Lord's & Lady's began operations in 1971 and has been franchising since 1978.

Equity Capital Needed: "Turnkey" operation ranges from $80,000 to $140,000. This includes a $25,000 franchise fee.

Financial Assistance Available: Reduced royalties during initial year of operations; reduced franchise fee for multi-salon commitments and exclusive territory agreements.

Training Provided: Comprehensive management and business training programs for franchisee and manager. Further the Director of Education and members of the Lord's & Lady's Styling Team provide in-salon technical and motivation training workshops on a periodic basis.

Managerial Assistance Available: Four operations supervisors provide regular salon managerial assistance. The corporate office has several certified public accounts to assist franchisees with such matters as corporate structure, accounting, bookkeeping systems, cash bugeting, tax planning and inventory purchasing and control. The company also provides support and guidance in advertising, marketing and merchandising programs.

Information Submitted: June 1987

MAGICUTS, INC.
2105 Midland Avenue
Scarborough, Ontario
Canada M1P 3E3
Alan Shawn, President

Description of Operation: Magicuts "a great haircut for everyone," offers what people demand today—style, value and convenience. With well over 100 stores operating in prime shopping centres in the United states and across Canada. The Magicuts system is a complete and comprehensive franchise opportunity. The system is proven, successful and growing.

Number of Franchisees: 13 in California and Georgia, 101 in Canada

In Business Since: 1981

Equity Capital Needed: Investment of approximately $90,000. Start-up cash required.

Financial Assistance Available: Financial assistance is not available for Magicuts.

Training Provided: Magicuts operations department will hire and train all initial staff. They will spend the first week in the store familiarizing the staff with the Magicuts system.

Managerial Assistance Available: Magicuts provides a complete operations manual, forms and instructions for completion. The operations department personnel are available to help solve any problems which may arise and make regular store visits.

Information Submitted: May 1987

THE MANE EVENT FRANCHISING CO., INC.
dba THE MANE EVENT UNISEX HAIR DESIGNERS
700 Franklin Avenue
Franklin Square, New York 11010
Les Meyers, President

Description of Operation: The franchise offered is for the establishment and operation of a precision "unisex" haircutting, styling and hair care salon at a designated location under the name "The Mane Event Unisex Hair Designers." The marketing emphasis of the franchise salons is on servicing all members of the family as well as the working population. Franchise salons are required to be open for extended hours, seven days a week, with limited holiday closings to accommodate this diverse potential market. Private brank hair care products packaged under the name "The Mane Event" are also featured at franchise salons for retail sale to customers.

Number of Franchisees: 12 plus 3 company-owned in New York

In Business Since: 1979

Equity Capital Needed: Initial estimated total cost, including initial franchise fee, ranges between $24,945 to $56,250.

Financial Assistance Available: Initial franchise fee of $9,500 may be paid in installments. Most installment payment plans require the franchisee to pay at least $3,500 upon signing the franchise agreement, at least $1,500 upon signing the sublease for the franchise premises and the balance of the initial franchise fee by no later than 3 months after the franchise salon opens for business. However, in individual cases different payment plans may be available.

Training Provided: Initial training is in 2 parts: hands-on training at a company-owned location and on-site assistance at the franchise location following the opening of the franchise business to the public. The length of the initial training program varies in individual cases depending upon the franchisee's prior business and trade experience. Training covers all aspects of The Mane Event franchise system. There is no training fee (fee is included in initial franchise fee), except the franchisee is responsible for all personal expenses incurred in attending the training program. An unlimited number of employees and managers of the franchisee may attend the initial training program.

Managerial Assistance Available: The franchisor will periodically inspect the franchise premises to provide on-site operations assistance. Franchisees will be provided with the names of recommended suppliers for equipment, signs, fixtures, non-proprietary supplies and materials. The franchisor may periodically make available advertising plans and advice and in-shop merchandising materials for franchisees' local use and may assist in designing special advertising and promotional programs for individual market regions. The franchisor will periodically offer free optional and mandatory workshops for franchisees and their employees in haircutting and hair styling and may hold franchisee conferences to discuss sales techniques, training of personnel, performance standards, advertising programs and merchandising procedures.

Information Submitted: June 1987

MANTRAP PROFESSIONAL HAIR SALONS
780 94th Avenue North
Suite 108
Joseph V. Sansonetti, Marketing Director

Description of Operation: Mantrap franchise offers professional hair salon for men and women, and retail centers.

Number of Franchisees: 18 in Florida and 3 under construction

In Business Since: 1967

Equity Capital Needed: $25,000

Financial Assistance Available: Yes

Training Provided: Complete training program is provided and consists of two parts: one part is designed for the training of the franchisee and/or the franchisee's manager. The second part of the training program is designed for the franchisee's hair styling/cutting employees.

Managerial Assistance Available: Mantrap continual management service for the life of the franchise in such areas as bookkeeping, advertising, and inventory control. Complete manuals of operations, forms, field managers are available in all regions to work closely with franchises and visit stores regularly to assist solving problems. Mantrap sponsors franchise meetings and product and styling training.

Information Submitted: June 1987

POPPERS FAMILY HAIR CARE CENTER, INC.
5 Canty Lane
Fairview Heights, Illinois 62206
Thomas M. Kendall, President

Description of Operation: Family hair care center catering to the whole family with value prices, a highly trained staff of stylists in a contemporary designed salon to meet the needs of all clients. Open 7 days a week.

Number of Franchisees: 2 in Illinois and Missouri plus 1 company owned

In Business Since: 1984

Equity Capital Needed: $60,000-$85,000

Financial Assistance Available: None

Training Provided: Initial 2 weeks training in salon for entire staff and additional regional seminars for salon. We will initially train a salon trainer (styles director) who will direct stylist technical hair stills every week for 8 weeks and then twice a month thereafter.

Managerial Assistance Available: We assist in the hiring of a manager, if this position is not filled by the owner. We provide 2 weeks in salon management training and 1 week salon operations training. Complete supply of manuals: 13

weeks pre-opening manual, 2 operations manuals, and employee handbook. Blanket advertising assistance in site selection, lease negotiations, hiring and staff training, marketing and company support.

Information Submitted: June 1987

PRO-CUTS, INC.
3716 Rufe Snow Drive
Fort Worth, Texas 76180
Don Stone, Director of Franchise Sales

Description of Operation: Pro-cuts offers guaranteed quality haircuts, shampoos and blowdrys for men, women, and children. Stores normally employ 6-8 haircutters and are open 6 days a week. Pro-cuts represents a special niche in the haircutting industry, which, along with family orientation, accounts for our rapid and successful growth pattern.

Number of Franchisees: 39 in Texas, Oklahoma, New Mexico, and Louisiana

In Business Since: 1982

Equity Capital Needed: $65,000 to $85,000

Financial Assistance Available: None

Training Provided: Extensive training for as long as the franchisee feels necessary or about 4 days, with ongoing assistance for a long-term relationship.

Managerial Assistance Available: In-shop assistance in the form of field supervisors, executive level assistancwe where needed. Extensive management training for shop managers.

Information Submitted: May 1987

RAINY DAY PEOPLE, INC.
1215 Golf Road
Schaumburg, Illinois 60195

Description of Operation: Family haircare salons— complete hairdesign service for women, men and children.

Number of Franchisees: 3 including company-owned in Illinois.

In Business Since: 1974

Equity Capital Needed: $80,000

Financial Assistance Available: Possible

Training Provided: 2 weeks management training.

Managerial Assistance Available: Same as above plus site selection, staff selection, organizational and business techniques etc. All round assistance in every facet. Blanket advertising, continued education in hairdesign.

Information Submitted: June 1987

SUPERCUTS
555 Northgate Drive
San Rafael, California 94903
Teresa A. Guerin, Franchise Administration
Coordinator

Description of Operation: The companny offers franchises for SUPERCUTS shops which provide guaranteed quality haircuts to men, women and children at an affordable price and delivered in a bright, open and efficient environment. Shampoo and blow dry services are also available along with SUPERCUTS own line of high quality haircare products.

Number of Franchisees: 150 with 502 open shops in 40 States and Canada.

In Business Since: 1975

Equity Capital Needed: $77,000 to $128,000 is the estimated cost to open a shop and includes the franchise fee.

Financial Assistance Available: None

Training Provided: Training begins with a course onsite selection and lease negotiations. Franchisee training is an intensive one week training which includes shop build-out, operations, accounting, personnel and marketing. A one week advanced operations training is also available on an ongoing basis without additional charge. All haircutters are trained in the SUPERCUTS technique and shop managers also attend specialized training.

Managerial Assistance Available: Extensive field staff provide quality control and operations assistance, as well as providing refresher courses for haircutters. Four regional offices along with corporate headquarters provide ongoing assistance in all phases of the business.

*THIRD DIMENSION CUTS, INC.
8015 Broadway
Everett, Washington 98203
Rob Jurries, New Development Director

Description of Operation: Third Dimension Cuts offers a unique design and no appointment style hair salon for men and women with a concept that appeals to the largest segment of the population. (You need not be a hair stylist to own or operate.)

Number of Franchisees: 13 plus 31 company-owned in Alaska, Idaho, Washington, Oregon and Utah.

In Business Since: 1979

Equity Capital Needed: Approximately $25,000

Financial Assistance Available: Investment is between $65,000 to $120,000 of which approximately $25,000 is start up capital for franchise fee, down payments, grand opening advertising, and start up capital depending on financial arrangements.

Training Provided: Training is done at the nearest location or 3D headquarters of 25 to 120 hours training in all aspects of the operation plus all manuals and operation formulas are provided.

Managerial Assistance Available: Third Dimension Cuts offers handbooks, manager manuals, continued hair styling training from company representatives, plus national company training from products companies throughout the life of the franchise.

Information Submitted: May 1987

BUSINESS AIDS AND SERVICES

A NIGHT WITH THE STARS FRANCHISE CORPORATION
8484 Wilshire Boulevard
Suite 550
Beverly Hills, California 90211
Burt Ward, President

Description of Operation: Motion picture distribution for fund raising.

Number of Franchisees: 11 in 6 States and Canada

In Business Since: 1984

Equity Capital Needed: $29,500 minimum

Financial Assistance Available: Case by case credit extended on original purchase price only. Franchisee has option to arrange outside financing.

Training Provided: Intensive 3 days in Beverly Hills office, follow-up trip by franchisor to franchisee's territory for grand opening (2-3 days).

Managerial Assistance Available: 800 toll free number for assistance during week days and during regular business hours.

Information Submitted: May 1987

A-SCRIPT, INC.
130 Pleasant Street
Mablehead, Massachusetts 01945

Description of Operation: A-Script is a custom-crafted resume and career development consultation company. Franchisees provide resumes developed using A-Script's proven method of information focusing. The company also provides career development consultation, cover-letter writing, computer storage, and resume typesetting and printing services.

Number of Franchisees: 2

In Business Since: 1981

Equity Capital Needed: $21,400 to $29,000

Financial Assistance Available: None

Training Provided: Franchisees participate in an intensive 10 day training program which includes resume and cover-letter creation, video-taped role-playing, business practices, advertising, and promotions. The training takes place at both the Home Office and the franchisee's location.

Managerial Assistance Available: Ongoing managerial support in all phases of the A-Script business is provided on-site, at the Home Office, and by telephone. A corporate newsletter will continually keep franchisees informed about changes in the industry. Franchisees may participate in company sponsored seminars and conferences.

Information Submitted: August 1987

ADAM GROUP, INC.
140 South Dearborn Street
Suite 1615
Chicago, Illinois 60603
John S. Meers

Description of Operation: Financial firm specializing in aid to small business in locating funding, government loan packaging, real estate mortgage banking and consulting to troubled companies.

Number of Franchisees: 29 in 17 States

In Business Since: 1965

Equity Capital Needed: $10,000

Financial Assistance Available: None

Training Provided: Original—3 days to 1 week and then continuous

Managerial Assistance Available: Daily and weekly releases, phone and personal calls.

Information Submitted: May 1987

ADVANTAGE PAYROLL SERVICES
800 Center Street
P. O. Box 1330
Auburn, Maine 04210
David Friedrich, Vice President, Marketing

Description of Operation: Payroll service bureau providing payroll and payroll taxes to small businesses.

Number of Franchisees: 10 in 5 States, 1 company-owned.

In Business Since: 1967

Equity Capital Needed: $13,000-$17,500 including equipment, franchise fee and training.

Financial Assistance Available: $5,000 at 10 percent approximately for 3 years. No payments for 1 year.

Training Provided: Up to 2 weeks at company headquarters with additional 10 days in field. Ongoing service and support.

Managerial Assistance Available: Ongoing

Information Submitted: May 1987

AGVISE
Box 510
Northwood, North Dakota 58267
Edward H. Lloyd

Description of Operation: AGVISE is a privately owned agricultural consulting firm. We provide farmer with technical skills and information used to make farm management decisions. AGVISE neither sells nor promotes any products. AGVISE has it's own testing facilities and research farms. The franchisee will operate his or her own field consulting business with support systems such as: testing, research, educational training, ongoing field training, resource people, business management, etc., all coming from AGVISE the franchisor.

Number of Franchisees: 2 in Minnesota and North Dakota

In Business Since: AGVISE has been in business since 1976

Equity Capital Needed: Range of $10,000 to $20,000

Financial Assistance Available: AGVISE will finance 50 percent of franchise fee up to three years at 12 percent. AGVISE also provides a bookkeeping and tax service for the franchisee.

Training Provided: Training is provided through a series of workshops scheduled at various times during the year. Training is a continuous process during the life time of franchisee's business. On-the-job or field training is the most valuable part of and most in-depth experience of franchisee's training.

Managerial Assistance Available: AGVISE's managerial and technical assistance to franchisee is in business.

AIR BROOK LIMOUSINE
115 West Passaic Street
Rochelle Park, New Jersey 07662
Mark Milmar, Director of Franchising

Description of Operation: Provide transportation service to the general public, including corporations, travel agencies, group and individuals with a fleet of late model sedans, station wagons, vans and stretch limousines. Areas of operation include the metropolitan New York area as well as Rockland, Orange County, New York and New Jersey, including the Atlantic City area. Complete service is also provided to and from the major metropolitan airports.

Number of Franchisees: 110 in New Jersey

In Business Since: 1969

Equity Capital Needed: $7,000—New Sedan $12,000—New Van or Stretch Limousine

Financial Assistance Available: Air Brook will finance up to $3,000 on a $7,000 investment and up to $5,000 on a $12,000 investment at no interest charge.

Training Provided: 5 day program consisting of 3 days classroom training and 2 days on-the-road training. This program is available for owners and their employed drivers.

Managerial Assistance Available: Air Brook actively markets its services through a team of sales professionals and maintains a fully-staffed reservations and dispatch departments seven days to coordinate work. Air Brook also provides all accounting and bookkeeping services at no cost; in addition, Air Brook provides all necessary vehicle liability insurance.

Information Submitted: May 1987

ALLAN & PARTNERS
603 Lawyers Building
428 Forbes Avenue
Pittsburgh, Pennsylvania 15219
Allan L. Hyman, General Partner

Description of Operation: Executive marketing, outplacement, resume services to corporate and private sector clients.

Number of Franchisees: 2

In Business Since: 1972—franchise operations since 1984

Equity Capital Needed: $25,000

Financial Assistance Available: None

Training Provided: Initial year's start up training approximately 30 days and approximately 10 days training each succeeding year. All selected franchises are appointed senior consultants and receive, with no additional cost: a complete set of training, operations, and client information manuals which outline company policy and operations methods; computerized resume reference files; 2 weeks of initial training plus 1 week of advanced training in Pittsburgh, Pennsylvania; periodic field training in the franchisees office as needed: training and individual assistance continues through experienced home office personnel and senior partners to be assigned in the future.

Managerial Assistance Available: Each franchisee is trained in the use of PAAR Plan-A job search program for professional, executive, technical and other white collar workers that is based on effective and proven marketing and communications procedures. Full assistance is provided continuously to franchisees and their clients by home office personnel. In addition, the company provides professional writing, research and computer support services to franchisees and their clients.

Information Submitted: July 1987

*AMERICAN ADVERTISING DISTRIBUTORS, INC.
234 South Extension Road
Mesa, Arizona 85202
John D. Alig, Vice President—Marketing/Sales

Description of Operation: American Advertising Distributors, Inc., has trademarked techniques, methods, experience and knowhow in establishing a professional direct mail business. Franchisee shall have the exclusive marketing license for a particular territory. The company has complete 80,000 square feet facilities for the printing and production of coupons and other mailing pieces, for nationwide delivery.

Number of Franchisees: 108 in 35 States

In Business Since: 1976

Equity Capital Needed: $25,000 to $50,000 depending on population of the territory.

Financial Assistance Available: Partial, in some States

Training Provided: 2 weeks of formal training school at the company's home office, 2 weeks of training at either a similar operation, or in the licensee's territory by a company representative. Complete training manual and start-up materials.

Managerial Assistance Available: Provided for in training school. Further training at regional sessions 2-3 times per year. Also national convention once a year.

Information Submitted: May 1987

*AMERICAN BUSINESS ASSOCIATES FRANCHISE CORP.
475 Park Avenue
New York, New York 10016
Jerome P. Feltenstein, President

Description of Operation: ABA offers a unique system for executive networking councils. Each franchise operates 5 councils in a specific geographic area. A business category can be represented by only one company so there is no competition.

Number of Franchisees: 5 in Connecticut

In Business Since: 1983

Equity Capital Needed: $25,000-$50,000

Financial Assistance Available: 60 percent financeable

Training Provided: 1 week intensive training, working with existing ABA councils and ABA representatives.

Managerial Assistance Available: ABA offers continual advisory services, as well as financial administration, and national and public relations.

Information Submitted: May 1987

AMERICAN HERITAGE AGENCY, INC.
Heritage Building
104 Park Road
West Hartford, Connecticut 06119
Rita Ann Gellinas, Director

Description of Operation: 1 Wedding consulting business furnishes services tailored to the needs of the brides-to-be.

Number of Franchisees: 6 in Connecticut, Massachusetts and New York

In Business Since: 1925

Equity Capital Needed: $500-$10,000

Financial Assistance Available: Financing of up to 50 percent of the franchise fee provided credit standards can be met.

Training Provided: 12 days of formal classroom training and on-the-job training at established office; up to 30 days training at franchsee's own office; periodic briefings and meetings.

Managerial Assistance Available: Liaison officer available to help in solving problems, expanding operations and suggesting improvements.

Information Submitted: July 1987

AMERISTAR, INC.
Number One Financial Centre
Suite 100
Little Rock Arkansas 72211
Roy Huddle, National Marketing Coordinator

Description of Operation: AmeriStar, Inc. is a national company of independently owned franchised businesses which professionally market manufactured and modular homes through AmeriStar Home Display Centers. AmeriStar, Inc. is presently the only national business format franchise within the manufactured housing industry. Franchise services include nationally trademarked signs and logos, site and office appearance standards, local consumer market research, national advertising, local advertising support, complete operational training, exclusive home financing sources, business insurance services, increased purchasing control of goods and service, and a national referral network. New entry assistance includes state and local licensing requirements, site analysis, and home manufacturer selection.

Number of Franchisees: 32 in 8 States

In Business Since: AmeriStar was incorporated in 1986, and began offering franchises in 1987.

Equity Capital Needed: Conversion: $15,000 to 425,000. New Entry: $50,000 minimum.

Financial Assistance Available: AmeriStar, Inc. will assist in arranging third-party financing for conversion and new entry franchise fee and start-up costs.

Training Provided: AmeriStar, Inc. requires the following mandatory training: New Franchise Orientation (2 day training seminar prior to opening), Management Academy (3 days of training held quarterly), Professional Management Development (mandatory 3 day course held annually). The following training seminars are periodically offered as voluntary courses: Financial Service Course, Star-Traiing (sales training), Professional Services.

Managerial Assistance Available: AmeriStar, Inc. provides continual service to franchisees for the life of the franchise agreement. Each franchise is assigned to a franchise services representative who, in turn, is a primary contact between appropriate AmeriStar corporate personnal and franchisees.

Information Submitted: June 1987

ANA
c/o ANACO PARTNERS, L.P.
3711 Long Beach Boulevard, Suite 824
Long Beach, California 90807
Steven A. Kriegsman, Chairman of the Board
Dean I. Ader, President

Description of Operation: Unique system for providing administrative-oriented and marketing support services to independently owned and operated certified public accounting offices. To qualify, franchisees must be certified public accounts.

Number of Franchisees: 6 in California

In Business Since: 1985

Equity Capital Needed: Range $11,300 to $23,300 (includes initial license fee of $7,500).

Financial Assistance Available: Franchisor does not presently offer financing to franchisees. Franchisor may, in the future, offer deferred payment and/or financing arrangements.

Training Provided: Initial training period required is 80 hours. Initial training will consist of lectures and on-the-job training designed to instruct franchisees in every aspect of ANA system.

Managerial Assistance Available: Franchisor will provide a series of confidential operations and technical manuals. At the request of franchisee, franchisor will provide a comprehensive system requirements analysis regarding computerization. In addition, franchisor provides name brand image and ongoing marketing systems, along with systems to improve the management of franchisee's CPA practice.

Information Submitted: July 1987

AN INTERNATIONAL WORLD OF WEDDINGS, INC.
Box 66318, Department 2CD
Portland, Oregon 97266
Francine M. Hansen, President

Description of Operation: The companys principal business is as a franchisor of business opportunities to own and operate bridal consulting and wedding design firms, catering not only to the planning and creation of traditional Christian ceremonies, but also creating custom ethnic and religous ceremonies for the Hindu, Buddist, Jewish and Moslem brides and co-ordinating a variety of formal occasions, such as proms, balls, cotillions and anniversary parties. The rental of bridesmaid gowns, and wedding gowns, and other formal women's attire also included in the franchise.

Number of Franchisees: 5 in Oregon

In Business Since: 1973

Equity Capital Needed: $17,500-$31,500

Financial Assistance Available: None at this present time.

Training Provided: A 1 week training program includes comprehensive training for 2, covering all aspects of wedding, consultation, planning, and design. The traning is conducted by 7 qualified instructors in Portland, Oregon, teaching not only traditional American wedding planning, but the planning of many authentic ethnic or religious groups, including, but not limited to the Hindu, Buddist, Jewish and Moslem weddings.

Managerial Assistance Available: Complete support system including confidential operations manuals, training manuals, full color photo presentation manual, initial supply of brochures, flyers, coupons, newspaper slick ads, business cards and VHS tape to assist franchisee in selling the service. Regional representatives to assist in ongoing advice and counseling, and a newsletter with the most up to date information in the wedding industry. Regional and/or national advertising through a co-operative effort in combining our advertising dollars.

Information Submitted: July 1987

ASI SIGN SYSTEMS
4082 Glencoe Aveue
Marina del Rey, California 90292
Vic Stalley, Vice President

Description of Operation: ASI Sign Systems, Inc., offers franchises which gives franchisees the license and right to opreate a sign business using the ASI Sign System. The ASI Sign System consists of various components. Together, they offer to franchisees the techniques, know-how, information, equipment, materials, supplies and business and marketing formats which enable the franchisee: to manufacture subsurface imaged signs, to obtain from qualified sources other kinds of finished signs and other products, materials and consumable supplies; and, to officially conduct a sign business.

Number of Franchisees: 34 in 26 States

In Business Since: 1977

Equity Capital Needed: $40,000

Financial Assistance Available: A total investment of approximately $140,000 is needed to cover additional equipment, supplies, rental space and operating capital. The franchisor offers financial assistance.

Training Provided: An intensive 5 day training course is held for all new franchisees at the home office. An additional 3 days of training and opening assistance is held at the franchisee's location.

Managerial Assistance Available: ASI Sign Systems provides ongoing assistance in sales, marketing, manufacturing and administration. Comprehensive operations manuals are provided. ASI has field personnel who regularly visit and work with the franchisees in all phases of the business.

Information Submitted: May 1987

*ASSOCIATED AIR FREIGHT, INC.
3333 New Hyde Park Road
New Hyde Park, New York 11042
Walter G. Mahland, Director-Development

Description of Operation: Associated Air Freight currently ranks in the top 15 air freight forwarders. Franchisees must have either transportation sales experience or an extensive background in business-to-business sales. Each location is staffed with customer service and operations personnel in addition to sales personnel. Associated offers an extensive product line including domestic same day, overnight, second day and international priority service, 3-5 Day deferred, and courier express service. Inventory requirements are minimal, and inventory items are provided free of charge during the first year of operation.

Number of Franchisees: Associated has 13 company-owned locations, 5 franchises, 21 joint-venture operations in the U.S., and 10 international joint-venture operations as well as 300 U.S. and 100 international agents.

In Business Since: 1958

Equity Capital Needed: $20,000-$50,000, depending upon market area (this includes franchise fees of $5,000-$15,000).

Financial Assistance Available: Associated offers in direct financing. Also, franchisees have immediate credit with all suppliers; and Associated assists in marketing for first year of operation at no cost to franchisee. Franchisees are not required to purchase trucks or aircraft. Approximately 40 percent of working capital is spent of facility and the remaining on staffing.

Training Provided: Training consists of 5 days training at world headquarters to include sales, marketing and advertising presentations and demonstrations of accounting and billing procedures, routing guidelines, reporting and claims. An additional 5 days training is held at an Associated field location to include joint sales calls and hands-on operational training.

Managerial Assistance Available: Associated provides ongoing assistance in the management of the franchise operation. Associated handles the majority of accounting functions, including accounts receivable and accounts payable to suppliers. On a monthly basis, Associated does an analysis of each franchise location and provides directional support. Franchisees benefit from national account purchasing arrangements with major airlines. Special attention is paid to the support of each newly opened office.

Information Submitted: April 1987

•BANACOM INSTANT SIGNS
16715 Von Karman Avenue
Irvine, California 92714
Mike Farley, President

Description of Operation: Banners and signs produced instantly retailed through Banacom Instant Sign Centers using unique system manufactured and developed by Bana com to proved full sign service.

Number of Franchisees: 34 in 17 States and Puerto Rico.

In Business Since: 1985

Equity Capital Needed: $95,000

Training Provided: 1 week of technical and marketing training in Irvine, California. Regional infield training.

Managerial Assistance Available: Ongoing support in marketing, customer service, direct mail, in field and back up of 47 service staff at head office. Regional, national and international conventions.

Information Submitted: May 1987

BARTER EXCHANGE, INC.
Twin Towers
1106 Clayton Lane
Suite 480 West
Austin, Texas 78723
Robert Sander, Executive Vice President

Description of Operation: Barter Exchange, Inc., operates as a third party record keeper for businesses (clients) throughout the U.S. and abroad. Clients are able to buy and sell goods and services for trade dollars instead of cash. The national headquarters in Austin is responsible for billing, receiving, monthly statements, credit lines, and long-term loans. Each franchise officeregisters new clients and brokers each client's product/service. Client's financial position is enhanced by the new sales generated and the ability to offset cash expenses with the trade dollars received for their goods and services. BEI provides each client with a client directory, client cards (similar to credit cards), and a subscription to BEI's bi-monthly newspaper, Tradewinds. BEI provides each franchise with a computer hardware and software package which includes BarterLine, a central computer access system.

Number of Franchisees: 22 in 20 States

In Business Since: 1983

Equity Capital Needed: $30,000

Financial Assistance Available: BEI provides ongoing materials and accounting services to franchises and their clients.

Training Provided: 1 day orientation for prospective buyers, 2 day training in the overall operation which is followed by 3 days of training for sales people and 3 days training for trade brokers.

Managerial Assistance Available: BEI processes all new clients, generates client cards, sets up client accounts in the data base, and provides ongoing accounting services with monthly statements. BEI also provides toll-free watts lines for authorizations on transactions. Along with this administrative support, BEI provides all printed brochures, directories, newspapers, and logos for creation of letterhead, envelopes, etc. BEI provides operations and sales manuals which directs and instructs the franchisee in virtually every aspect of the business.

Information Submitted: May 1987

BEST RESUME SERVICE
Suite 1870
Three Gateway Center
Pittsburgh, Pennsylvania 15222
Richard D. Hindman, President

Description of Operation: Best Resume Service provides a broad range of professional business communication services for the educational, commercial and individual client markets. These services include professional resume preparation, job consulting executive marketing services, corporate outplacement services, marketing proposal resumes, automatic typing and word processing.

Number of Franchisees: 37 throughout the United States

In Business Since: 1962

Equity Capital Needed: None. Requires $5,0000 working capital.

Financial Assistance Available: Financing available to qualified persons.

Training Provided: Franchisor conducts a formal, intensive training program for all new franchisees in the corporate office. Complete operational manuals of systems and procedures are provided. Update training seminars are conducted periodically.

Managerial Assistance Available: Best Resume Service provides a continuous program of assistance to all franchisees in all phases of their business operations and management, finances and recordkeeping, marketing and personnel. Visits to the franchisee's office are made by home office staff and all franchisee's participate in periodic refresher training seminars. Market research and testing of new products and services is done continuously by the franchisor's home office.

Information Submitted: June 1987

BINEX-AUTOMATED BUSINESS SYSTEMS, INC.
441 Auburn Blvd., Suite E
Sacramento, California 95481
Walter G. Heidig, President

Description of Operation: Binex licenses offer a broad range of computerized services to small and medium sized businesses. Services include financial reports, general ledgers, accounts receivable, accounts payable, job cost, payroll and specialized computer services are also available, and you can develop your own. You may operate your business in various ways from a bookkeeping office to a full computer service. The computer programs are licensed to you for use on your computer or a central Binex computer. Complete small business computer systems may be installed in your clients office.

Number of Franchisees: 60 in 21 States, Canada, and New Zealand

In Business Since: 1965

Equity Capital Needed: $11,500. The fee covers training, manuals, and startup supplies. No expensive equipment is required.

Financial Assistance Available: A computer can be purchased for $4,500. Lease arrangements available if a computer is purchased.

Training Provided: Home study course and 1 week home office. Individuals may return for further training as needed.

Managerial Assistance Available: Support is provided on a continuous basis. Frequent newsletters are sent out covering a variety of subjects including business operation, marketing, technical, taxes, etc. New programs and services are developed, documented, and made available regularly to all licensees. Periodic regional meetings provide upgrading and review.

Information Submitted: May 1987

•H & R BLOCK INC.
4410 Main Street
Kansas City, Missouri 64111
Christoper Meck, Director, Franchise Operations

Description of Operation: The function of an H & R Block franchisee is to prepare individual income tax returns. The franchisee is operated as a sole proprietorship or partnership. The only warranty made by the franchisee is to respect and uphold a specific code of ethics and to abide by the policy and procedures of the company.

Number of Franchisees: Over 8,800 offices throughout the United States, Canada and 17 foreign countries. Over 4,000 offices are franchised with the balance operated by the parent company.

In Business Since: 1946

Equity Capital Needed: $2,000-$3,000

Financial Assistance Available:

Training Provided: Each year a training program is held for all new owners. Prior to tax season each year, a training program for all employees is conducted in major centers. Each fall a meeting is held for all owners for 2-3 days to discuss all phases of the operation and new developments and ideas.

Managerial Assistance Available: We work very closely with our franchisees through a network of Satellite franchise directors and provide any and all assistance required or needed.

Information Submitted: May 1987

THE BREAD BOX
1010 South Taylor
Little Rock, Arkansas 72204
John Reynolds, President

Description of Operation: The Bread Box is a co-op direct mail advertising company. Our licensees provide the local business owners in their territories a media that target his advertising into a specific geographical area. All printing and production is handled by The Bread Box from their corporate headquarters in Little Rock, Arkansas. No inventory required and low overhead operation for our licensees.

Number of Franchisees: 5 in Arkansas, Texas and Oklahoma.

In Business Since: 1976

Equity Capital Needed: $8,000-$15,000

Training Provided: 1 week classroom training program is mandatory for all new franchisees. Field training is available. Complete operations manual, sales presentation manual and coupon library are provided.

Managerial Assistance Available: Regional and annual meetings, work shops, home office support on a continuous basis, periodic newsletters, awards and incentive programs.

Information Submitted: May 1987

BROKER ONE
230 East Wheeling Street
Lancaster, Ohio 45130
Raymond A. Strohl, President

Description of Operation: Stockbroker offering stocks, bonds, options, mutual funds, penny stocks, tax shelters, retirement plans, diamonds, and precious metals.

Number of Franchisees: 7 in Ohio, New York, Florida, California, and Pennsylvania.

In Business Since: 1983

Equity Capital Needed: None

Financial Assistance Available: Varies, but usually is small.

Training Provided: Varies, depending on the background and experience of the franchisee.

Managerial Assistance Available: Perpetual assistance as needed.

Information Submitted: July 1987

*THE BUILDING INSPECTOR OF AMERICA
684 Main Street
Wakefield, Massachusetts 01880
Larry Finklestone, Director of Marketing

Description of Operation: The Building Inspector of America is a national organization of home and building inspection consultants. The service is used primarily by buyers of homes, condominiums and property investors. It is designed to alert buyers to potential problem areas as well as show buyers how to maintain their property and possibly save money by conserving on energy.

Number of Franchisees: 31 in 11 states and Washington, D.C.

In Business Since: 1985

Equity Capital Needed: $15,000 to $50,000 depending on size of territory.
Financial Assistance Available: None

Training Provided: Intense 2 week in-field and in-franchisee. Audio and video tapes provided. Workbook on sales promotion and advertising is included.

Managerial Assistance Available: Extensive ongoing market research for franchisee benefit. Report writing clinics and sales training and promotion workshops run several times a year at corporate headquarters. Regular newsletters, slide show programs, national referral slstem in place.

Information Submitted: May 1987

*BUSINESS AMERICA ASSOCIATES, INC.
5815 Library Road
Bethel Park, Pennsylvania 15102
Thomas D. Atkins, Executive Vice President

Description of Operation: Listing and sales of businesses. Listings of businesses for sale are shared by all offices on a confidential basis. Buyers are prequalified by interview in franchise office locations. Franchises are offered for sale as well as established businesses.

Number of Franchisees: 4 in Pennsylvania

In Business Since: 1984

Equity Capital Needed: $45,000

Financial Assistance Available: Terms may be considered.

Training Provided: 1 week at corporate offices and 1 week at franchisee's location. Training by video with training manual. All forms and systems provided.

Managerial Assistance Available: Ongoing support with regular meetings for franchise owners.

Information Submitted: May 1987

BUSINESS CONSULTANTS OF AMERICA
Affiliate of: HORIZONS OF AMERICA
P. O. BOX 4098
Waterbury, Connecticut 06714
Gregg Nolan, Franchise Director

Description of Operation: Franchisor offers time tested practice, dealing with advisory services for small and medium sized business operations. Training in services to include: management, market, tax advisory and financial advisory services. Additional training to include programs for mergers/acquisition, business brokerage and franchise coverage. Franchisor provides a client lead service through a computer hookup to franchisee's office.

Number of Franchisees: 26 in 11 States.

In Business Since: 1973

Equity Capital Needed: $20,000 plus $5,000-$10,000 working capital. Computer equipment optional.

Financial Assistance Available: Assistance with bank/government financing/franchisor financing.

Training Provided: 3 weeks intensive training at franchise headquarters, 1 week at franchisee's office, followed by 2 months cassette courses packaged by franchisor and other professional organizations. Continuing franchisor advisory newsletters and tapes. Fully computerized national listing and consulting service.

Managerial Assistance Available: Technical and advisory services at discretion of franchisee. Continued services on an as needed basis from franchisor. Additional memberships arranged in professional associations.

Information Submitted: May 1987

BUSINESS DIGEST, INC.
25 Circus Time Road
South Portland, Maine 04106
Leo Girr or Patti Crabtree

Description of Operation: Business Digest is the first franchised monthly business publication that pays special attention to local small- and medium-size businesses of all sizes.

Number of Franchisees: 16 in 8 States

In Business Since: 1976

Equity Capital Needed: $100,000 (approximately) depending on the market and size of trade area. (Includes $20,000 franchise fee.)

Financial Assistance Available: Franchisor will assist in obtaining working capital and equipment loans.

Training Provided: Minimum 3 day initial training at franchisors headquarters.

Managerial Assistance Available: Because of the nature of the publishing business the franchisor will assist the franchisee in selecting copywriters, layout and design staff, coordinate the relationship with printers and train the franchisees sales staff on the techniques of selling advertising. Further, as the franchisee gains experience, the franchisor will assist in incorporating other income sources at the franchisees level, such as business opportunity shows and ways to derive income from the equipment involved in running a magazine.

Information Submitted: May 1987

BUYING AND DINING GUIDE
80 Eighth Avenue
Suite 315
New York, New York 10011
Allan Horwitz, President

Description of Operation: Buying and Dining Guide is a unique money-making for the publishers and the advertisers. A fre publication offering total market coverage of the active "buyers", and "diners" throughout the area. It's a direct route to prime spenders—those who enjoy spending money even more than they like saving it. Publishing and distribution costs are minimal, and the advertiser receives 14 days of effective advertising—and at the price of just a single ad.

Number of Franchisees: 3 in New York

In Business Since: 1980, franchising since 1987

Equity Capital Needed: $19,900 with a money-back guarantee.

Financial Assistance Available: Company sponsored financing available with a down payment of $14,400.

Training Provided: 9 days of classroom, infield and on-site training for franchisees and their employees. Covers how to sell advertising, acquire co-op from manufacturers, profit from barter, service accounts, ad design, layout, distribution, and bookkeeping. Includes extensive confidential operations manual, audio and video cassettes, training films and video-taped role playing sessions.

Managerial Assistance Available: Continuous assistance provided by the home office. Includes our unique "head start" program to get you off to a flying start, with $1,500 free printing, a direct mailing to your prospects by the company, and our special charter advertiser program to produce immediate income for both the franchisee and his advertisers. In addition, the company contributes $1,000 for each new franchise plus 12 percent of all royalty fees for direct mailing, sweepstakes, and other promotions funded entirely by the company to make the franchisees more successful.

Information Submitted: July 1987

BUY LOW ENTERPRISES, INC.
801 North Cass Avenue
Suite 104
Westmont, Illinois 60559
Irv Silver, President
Russell B. Chevalier, Vice President

Description of Operation: To provide merchandising displays, sales promotions and advertising under the trade name of "Buy Low" to franchisees engaged in the sale of alcoholic beverages at retail for consumption off premises.

Number of Franchisees: 83 in Illinois

In Business Since: The form of business of the franchisor is corporated by Low Enterprises, Inc., was incorporated under the law of Illinois on October 1960.

Equity Capital Needed: Franchisee and initial investment is estimated at a low-high range of $500-$1,000.

Financial Assistance Available: Neither the franchisor nor any agents, directly or indirectly offers any financial management to franchisees.

Training Provided: There are training programs supplied by the franchisor.

Managerial Assistance Available: The licensor is obligated to (1) permit the licensee to represent himself as a "Buy Low" store, (2) permit licensee to use its service marks, trademarks, trade names and logotypes, in accordance with licensor's policy, (3) provide assistance to the licensee in establishing a retail promotional plan for the location, including merchandise displays and general sales promotion and advertising, and (4) place advertisements in newspapers and other media chosen solely by licensor which is published and circulated in the greater metropolitan Chicago land area at lease once each week. Other various assistance may be provided by the franchisor on a voluntary basis to franchisees in addition to the above.

Information Submitted: May 1987

CAM-TEL PRODUCTIONS, INC.
Box 280 Harding Highway
Richland, New Jersey 08350
Jack Campbell, President

Description of Operation: A nationally-trademarked company, Cam-Tel Productions, Inc., specializes in the creation and production of customized video, film and other audio/visual presentations that currently range from training seminar, plant safety programs and recruitment, to sales and marketing, presentations, new product demonstrations, trade shows and corporate overviews.

Number of Franchisees: 2 in Pennsylvania

In Business Since: 1981

Equity Capital Needed:

Financial Assistance Available: None

Training Provided: Classroom training held a corporate headquarters, 1 week and 1 week on location training.

Managerial Assistance Available: Cam-Tel provides franchisee with ongoing support group. Consisting of creative and technical personnel at corporate headquarters as well as key field representatives to work with franchisee at their location.

Information Submitted: May 1987

CARING LIVE—IN'S, INC.
214 East 72nd Terrace
Kansas City, Missouri 04114
George Fetekamp, President

Description of Operation: Consultation and referral service for elderly.

Number of Franchisees: 10 in Missouri, Texas, Kansas, Ohio and Florida

In Business Since: 1982

Equity Capital Needed: $10,000 to $15,000

Financial Assistance Available: None

Training Provided: 4 days of training in all phases of operation.

Managerial Assistance Available: Ongoing consultation.

Information Submitted: July 1987

CERTIFIED CAPITAL CORRESPONDENT, INC.
4220 South Maryland Parkway
Suite 201
Las Vegas, Nevada 89119
R. J. Robinson, President

Description of Operation: The offer and sale to franchisees of a financial correspondent loan application processing and packaging business under the name "Certified Capital Correspondent, Inc.," together with the furtherance of such other general business purpose and objects as allowed by law.

Number of Franchisees: 3 in Nevada and Arizona

In Business Since: CCC Inc.—1982.

Equity Capital Needed: $38,500

Financial Assistance Available: None

Training Provided: Intensive 5 day mandatory training at home office, 3 days field training and continuous updating thereafter, both within and without the franchisees office under supervision of a regional coordinator.

Managerial Assistance Available: CCC Inc., provides continual management service for the life of the franchise, in such areas as bookkeeping, advertising, merchandising, and market updating. Complete policy and procedures manual, forms and directions are provided. Regional coordinators are available in all regions to work closely with franchises and visit offices regularly to assist solving problems.

Information Submitted: May 1987

CONVENIENCE MONEY CENTERS, INC.
dba CHECK MART
1055 Wazee
Suite 100
Denver, Colorado 80204
Terry Paige, Franchise Sales Manager

Description of Operation: Variety of financial services— cash checks, sell money orders, postage, postal services offer notary service, Western Union, Utility payments, and other related services.

Number of Franchisees: 5 in Colorado, Oregon, Louisiana and Arizona.

In Business Since: 1982

Equity Capital Needed: $125,000

Financial Assistance Available: Finance plan available.

Training Provided: All facets of check cashing operations (5 years duration).

Managerial Assistance Available: We offer complete training in all phases of check cashing business (5 years duration).

Information Submitted: May 1987

CHECK-X-CHANGE CORPORATION
111 S.W. Columbia
Suite 1080
Portland, Oregon 97201
John Collins, National Development Director

Description of Operation: Check cashing for a fee, money order sales, and photo I.D.'s.

Number of Franchisees: 56 in 11 States

In Business Since: 1982

Equity Capital Needed: $60,000-$80,000

Financial Assistance Available: None

Training Provided: 2 weeks at corporate headquarters

Managerial Assistance Available: On-site training after opening, continuing on-site consulting on as needed basis.

Information Submitted: May 1987

*CHROMA COPY FRANCHISING OF AMERICA, INC.
423 West 55th Street
New York, New York 10019
David J. Manning

Description of Operation: Photographic service for business.

Number of Franchisees: 15 in 10 States

In Business Since: 1982

Equity Capital Needed: $300,000

Financial Assistance Available: None

Training Provided: Management, printmaking, sales 2 weeks.

Managerial Assistance Available: Organizing assistance relating to all areas of the operation is provided as needed by each franchise.

Information Submitted: July 1987

CHROMA INTERNATIONAL
342 West 200 South
Suite 20, Fine Arts Bldg.
Salt Lake City, Utah 84101
Marlene R. Jones, President
Roger G. Jones, Senior Vice President

Description of Operation: Chroma International offers a unique and extensive personal appearance and image consultation service. The franchisees are trained to do individual group and business analyses and seminar presentations. The Chroma franchise system offers some special types of clothing, accessories, jewelry and cosmetics.

Number of Franchisees: 68 in 22 States, Canada, Hong Kong, Australia, New Zealand, Great Britain and Singapore.

In Business Since: 1983

Equity Capital Needed: $12,000 minimum

Financial Assistance Available: The total investment of $12,000 plus airfare is necessary to open a Chroma franchise. The down payment of $7,500 secures a place in the franchise school and is used for equipment, inventory, licenses, training and hotel accommodations. No special financing is offered by Chroma.

Training Provided: Intensive 14-day training is held at the corporate headquarters and training facilities. Classes are limited to 10 participants and 1 instructor per each 2 trainees. Trainees will have "hands-on" experience with up to 80 subjects while in class. Marketing, demonstrations, and business time and management skills are presented.

Managerial Assistance Available: Chroma offers ongoing assistance through newsletters, update seminars and personal consultations. Complete manuals of franchise operation, forms, bookkeeping and technical information for Chromatype identification, style, texture and personal appearance. Chroma principals attend national and international fashion and clothing shows in order to keep the franchisees current with the latest trends.

Information Submitted: May 1987

CLOSETTEC FRANCHISE CORPORATION
123 East Street
Dedham, Massachusetts 02026
Dan Peek, Director of Marketing

Description of Operation: The Closettec franchise opportunity combines elements of management, sales, and light manufacturing to provide a benchmark approach to the custom closet and storage systems industry. Closettec Custom Systems utilize 100 percent of existing storage space. The Closettec franchise system is designed to maximize franchisee success in this emerging industry.

Number of Franchisees: 11 in 7 States

In Business Since: 1985

Equity Capital Needed: $65,000

Financial Assistance Available: None

Training Provided: Formal initial training is 2 weeks for owners and manager. Additional training is available to all franchisees and their personnel at any time. Initial training is supplemented through periodic seminars.

Managerial Assistance Available: Closettec offers complete managerial and technical assistance to all franchisees through training and operations manuals, periodic seminars and visits from the franchisors operations staff. An authorized supplies program and assistance programs ranging from advertising to accounting assure the Closettec franchise complete support.

Information Submitted: May 1987

CLOSET-TIER, INC.
5800 Forward Avenue
Pittsburgh, Pennsylvania 15217
Arlene Mogerman, Franchise Coordinator

Description of Operation: Closet and storage area organization system made up of component parts for versatile use.

Number of Franchisees: 3 in Pennsylvania

In Business Since: 1976

Equity Capital Needed: $50,000

Financial Assistance Available:

Training Provided: 8 days of intensive training in the corporate office and shop, 1 week in franchisee operation before opening and 1 week after opening. Ongoing support by phone and field representatives.

Managerial Assistance Available: The franchisor is available for assistance by phone or field representatives an time for franchisee assistance.

Information Submitted: May 1987

COLBRIN AIRCRAFT EXCHANGE
c/o COLBRIN FRANCHISE SYSTEMS, INC.
Centerpark I
Suite 710
4041 Powder Mill Rd.
Calverton, MD 20705
Colter C. Brinkley, President

Description of Operation: Colbrin Aircraft Exchange is the world's first full service aircraft brokerage franchise network. As a Colbrin Aircraft Exchange franchise owner, you will put Colbrin principles into practice, providing aircraft buyers and sellers with a comprehensive package of services (unique and needed) to the aircraft brokerage industry. You will oversee all activities involved in the transfer of an aircraft from one party to another. Franchises are being made available to licensed pilots or to entrepreneurs capable of employing the required staff. Colbrin Aircraft Exchange is establishing a network of aircraft brokerages across the United States and Canada.

Number of Franchisees: 29, 50 percent sold in the United States.

In Business Since: Founder started in 1981, Incorporated as Colbrin franchise Systems, Inc. in 1985.

Equity Capital Needed: Based on territory size. Contact company for full information.

Financial Assistance Available: None

Training Provided: An intensive and structured 3-week certification course will be conducted at Colbrin headquarters in Baltimore, Maryland. Training covers all aspects of the business-operational procedures, management, personnel, marketing and sales, brokerage procedures, computer and network operations, and accounting and finance. During the first week of operation in the franchisee's business, an operations consultant will be present to provide additional training and to assist in the opening of the franchise.

Managerial Assistance Available: At Colbrin Aircraft Exchange, we are dedicated to making every franchise a success. A company operations consultant will visit a franchisee's unit periodically for inspection and assistance. Home office personnel are always available for whatever assistance is needed. Franchisee's are issued a confidential operations manual to spell-out everything needed to operate the franchise efficiently. Professional advertising and marketing support will help you promote your business and cultivate a growing recognition of Colbrin aircraft Exchange as the industry leader.

Information Submitted: May 1987

● **COMMUNICATIONS WORLD INTERNATIONAL, INC.**
14828 West 6th Avenue
Suite 13B
Golden, Colorado 80401
Aletha Oster, Franchise Director

Description of Operation: Sale and service of Business Telephone Systems to companies with 2 to 100 employees.

Number of Franchisees: 42 in 12 States

In Business Since: 1979

Equity Capital Needed: $40,000, $10,000 cash and $30,000 line of credit, for Sales Franchise. $100,000, $40,000 cash and $60,000 line of credit for Master Franchise.

Financial Assistance Available: None

Training Provided: Initial 5 days at company headquarters, involving administrative and product knowledge.

Managerial Assistance Available: Continuous technical help via 800 number for telephone technicians. Managerial support in researching acceptable product lines and providing sales advice. Business telephone centers are established in each city to provide administrative, service and demonstration back-up.

Information Submitted: May 1987

● **COMPREHENSIVE ACCOUNTING CORPORATION**
2111 Comprehensive Drive
Aurora, Illinois 60505
Edward D. Muse, President

Description of Operation: Comprehensive franchise independent accountants to provide a monthly computerized accounting, bookkeeping, tax and business consultation service to small- and medium-sized businesses of all types. Services include complete computerized preparation of monthly balance sheets, operating statements, general ledger and payroll ledgers, accounts receivable, and job cost statements. Comprehensive trains its franchisees to use the Comprehensive Client Acquisition System. The franchisee can build his practice as fast as he is able to grow and maintain quality service.

Number of Franchisees: Approximately 400 in 40 States and Puerto Rico

In Business Since: 1949; licensing since 1967

Equity Capital Needed: $20,000 initial franchise fee; $35,000 marketing service fee for interns; $50,000 marketing fee for affiliates.

Financial Assistance Available: The franchise fee is paid in cash. The marketing training and assistance fee, or the marketing service fee, may be financed

Training Provided: The franchisee is required to complete a 5-week course at the corporate headquarters after sufficient home study preparation in Comprehensive's production methods. Training at corporate headquarters is divided equally between production and marketing. In addition, a post-graduate course lasting 1 week is given in the corporate headquarters.

Managerial Assistance Available: Comprehensive provides on an ongoing basis a production consultant, a marketing consultant and a data processing consultant. Each consultant is available by phone or in person for each franchisee. Also provided are detailed production procedures and methods, client reporting forms, plus sales aids for use in obtaining accounts, one professional film portraying Comprehensive's service to prospective clients, desk top visual for client presentation, sample computer financial statements and various sales brochures. Comprehensive gives the franchisee the benefit of Comprehensive's experience gained through current licensees who are providing services for over 20,000 monthly accounting, bookkeeping, tax and business consultation service clients. A manage-

ment information system provides statistics monthly and annually of continuing education and interchange of ideas. Other seminars are conducted for franchisees' staff and clients.

Information Submitted: May 1987

COMPUFUND NATIONAL MORTGAGE NETWORK
4900 Hopyard Road
Suite 100
Pleasonton, California 94566

Description of Operation: CompuFund's National Mortgage Network's computerized mortgage service organization linking the consumer with the lender through independent license network. Our franchisees are offered the opportunity to utilize the company's state-of-the-art proprietary software designed to provide the full spectrum of mortgage and financial services from lender and loan information to the realtor and/or homebuyer to complete processing/underwriting and in some cases funding of the loan transaction.

Number of Franchisees: 55 in California and Texas

In Business Since: 1983

Equity Capital Needed: $20,000-$50,000

Financial Assistance Available: None

Training Provided: 1 day management overview; 3 days loan processor training program, and 2 days sales training program plus ongoing training.

Managerial Assistance Available: Loan products from over 50 lenders, cooperative advertising, lead referral program, use of the company's proprietary application software, sales and management training programs, ongoing business consultation, and marketing programs.

Information Submitted: June 1987

CONCEPT III INTERNATIONAL
2120 Newburg Road
Louisville, Kentucky 40205
Debbie Tross, Marketing Coordinator

Description of Operation: The company licenses a management consulting business operation specializing in organization, management and leadership development. Each franchisee is granted an exclusive territory and offers consulting assistance to all types of companies and organizations and offers regularly scheduled public seminars and workshops. Concept III International makes available a total program which includes all staff personnel and a total impact marketing system which allows the franchisee to begin operations immediately. Management, marketing or training and development background helpful but not essential.

Number of Franchisees: 9 plus 7 company owned

In Business Since: 1968, franchising since 1982

Equity Capital Needed: $3,500 to $4,500

Financial Assistance Available: None

Training Provided: Concept III International offers complete training in marketing and consulting skills. There are 2 one week training schools in the first 3 months of operation. Ongoing training includes quarterly training and development conferences throughout the year. Consulting and performance certification training programs are offered on a regularly scheduled basis which enables qualified franchisees to join the company's professional staff.

Managerial Assistance Available: The company maintains a continuous supportive effort through correspondence, telephone and field visitations. The company also provides a computerized and totally automated mailing program, record keeping, clerical and secretarial assistance, furnishes promotional and advertising materials and assistance.

Information Submitted: July 1987

CORPORATE FINANCE ASSOCIATES
600 Seventeenth Street
Suite 710N
Denver, Colorado 80202
James Sorensen-Michael Rothberg

Description of Operation: Financial consultants on loans, mergers—acquisition brokers. For executives only.

Number of Franchisees: 65 in 18 States plus 2 international offices.

In Business Since: 1956

Equity Capital Needed: $35,000 for operating capital

Financial Assistance Available: No financial assistance except for sources for loan and venture funds.

Training Provided: For executives—one on one. Operating manuals are provided. Semi-annual seminars and periodic regional meetings. Total of 8 training days annually.

Managerial Assistance Available: Ongoing—case by case training.

Information Submitted: May 1987

CORPORATE INVESTMENT BUSINESS BROKERS, INC.
1515 East Missouri Avenue
Phoenix, Arizona 85014
Russel Branch, Chairman of the Board

Description of Operation: A international network of franchised business brokerage companies.

Number of Franchisees: 130 operating throughout the U.S. and Canada

In Business Since: 1977

Equity Capital Needed: Varies between $32,500-$70,000

Financial Assistance Available: A portion of the investment can be financed to qualified applicants.

Training Provided: Complete ongoing training is provided through the 10 year franchise agreement.

Managerial Assistance Available: Continuous in all phases of operation as needed.

Information Submitted: May 1987

CORRECT CREDIT CO. OF HOWELL, INC.
228 Highway 9
Howell, New Jersey 07731
Pat Fasano, President

Description of Operation: Credit restoration service, each office is approximately 500 square feet with 2-12 salespeople, who see clients in their homes 6 days a week.

Number of Franchisees: 8 in Pennsylvania, Massachusetts, Florida and Georgia.

In Business Since: 1983

Equity Capital Needed: $6,500 total fee $19,500.

Financial Assistance Available: Approximately $3,000-$5,000 operating capital needed for office and advertising for first 6 weeks. A portion of the investment finances to qualified applicants $11,000.

Training Provided: In-out office training for 1 week and follow up at franchisee's office whenever needed.

Managerial Assistance Available: Always available to assist franchisees whenever needed.

Information Submitted: May 1987

CREDIT CLINIC, INC.
P. O. Box 10323
Marina Del Rey, California 90291
Irv Sylvern, President

Description of Operation: Credit improvement services—(consumer) and business, establishing and reestablishing excellent credit ratings.

Number of Franchisees: 162 throughout the USA.

In Business Since: 1979

Equity Capital Needed: Minimum $100

Financial Assistance Available: Complete cost $100

Training Provided: Complete training manual, continuous home office upgrading and training.

Managerial Assistance Available: Continuous phone and mail contact to effectuate better service to credit clinic clients. Utilizing: (1) newest court and Federal Trade Commission rulings effecting consumer credit, and (2) newest and most liberal credit grantors.

Information Submitted: May 1987

CYCLE SERVICE MESSENGERS
47 Wooster Street
New York, New York 10013
Thomas Martinez, Franchise Director

Description of Operation: Pick-up and delivery within city limits via bicycle on normal 2-hour and rush 1-hour service. Pick-up and delivery within 50 miles of location via motorcycle, cars, and trucks. No company vehicles; all owner operated.

Number of Franchisees: 2 including company-owned in New York and Pennsylvania.

In Business Since: 1977

Equity Capital Needed: $27,000—start up, $40,000-$60,000 working capital recommended.

Financial Assistance Available: None

Training Provided: 4 day course in New York City followed by 4 days to 1 week on-site.

Managerial Assistance Available: Initial training in New York City 4 days, additional training on-site 4 days to 1 week, periodic assistance as necessary and operations manual supplied.

Information Submitted: July 1987

DATA DESTRUCTION SERVICES, INC.
dba DDS FRANCHISE CORPORATION
140 Brookline Avenue
Boston, Massachusetts 02215
Richard Hannon, President

Description of Operation: DDS Franchise Corporation offers a unique new business—a mobile shredding service providing on-site shredding of confidential documents or materials. Franchisor provides a completely equipped vehicle. Customers are high tech, governmental, banks, insurance companies and medical facilities.

Number of Franchisees: 1 company-owned unit in New England

In Business Since: 1982, franchising 1985

Equity Capital Needed: $75,000-$200,000

Financial Assistance Available: None

Training Provided: A 2 week training program is provided by the franchisor.

Managerial Assistance Available: Continual operating support is provided in all aspects of business operation.

Information Submitted: July 1987

DEBIT ONE, INC.
3433-S South Campbell
Springfield, Missouri 65807
Jack D. Dunn, President

Description of Operation: Debit One offers a unique concept in bookkeeping services. Our mobile vans are a custom designed office with computer and software used to travel to the client's place of business where their bookkeeping is done "at the door of their store."

Number of Franchisees: 65 in 26 States

In Business Since: 1983

Equity Capital Needed: $44,025 minimum plus $5,000 operating capital.

Financial Assistance Available: Franchisee provides no financial assistance but the $26,025 for the vehicle and equipment can be financed through local banks or leasing company.

Training Provided: Intensive 80 hours, mandatory training course is scheduled for all new franchisees and/or their personnel. 56 hours of training is conducted at the home office and 24 hours is held in franchisee's territory.

Managerial Assistance Available: Debit One provides continued management service. Complete manuals of operations, (computer and sales) and directions are provided. A director of franchisees is available to work closely with franchisee and to assist in solving problems. Debit One provides a bi-monthly newsletter in order to keep the franchisees up to date on any software changes; changes in tax laws; etc.

Information Submitted: July 1987

DELIVEREX, INC.
2054 Zanker Road
Suite F
San Jose, California 95131
Steven H. Rowen, President

Description of Operation: Off-site storage, management and delivery of medical industry records, business records and computer tapes.

Number of Franchisees: 20 nationwide

In Business Since: 1973

Equity Capital Needed: Approximately $100,000

Financial Assistance Available: None

Training Provided: 2 weeks home office training and assistance as needed at franchise location.

Managerial Assistance Available: Ongoing as needed.

Information Submitted: May 1987

DEVELOPMENT SERVICES, INC.
A Subsidiary of HOME SAVINGS & LOAN
2 South Carroll Street
Madison, Wisconsin 53703
Roderick A. Ritcherson, Vice President/Marketing

Description of Operation: Development Services, Inc., franchises a junior saver's program called Homer's club to savings and loans and credit unions. The program is designed to teach children the importance of saving money. We sell promotional items to accompany the Homer's Club program such as T-shirts, buttons, ballons, safari hats, yo-yo's, frisbees, coin banks, stuffed annimals, etc.

Number of Franchisees: 8 in 5 States

In Business Since: 1977

Equity Capital Needed: Does not apply

Financial Assistance Available: Does not apply

Training Provided: 1 day training session involving operational and promotional training. Continuous supervision and aid afterwards.

Managerial Assistance Available: Included in the same 1 day training session.

Information Submitted: May 1987

＊DIAL ONE INTERNATIONAL, INC.
4100 Long Beach Boulevard
Long Beach, California 90807
James F. Hand, President

Description of Operation: Must be a qualified property service or selected retail company operator, with good recommendations from customers, suppliers and financial institutions. Franchisees may be in one or more of over forty-five trades and services.

Number of Franchisees: 865 nationally and 125 internationally.

In Business Since: 1982

Equity Capital Needed: Master district approximately $100,000—$175,000 and working capital

Financial Assistance Available: Local financing where applicable.

Training Provided: Monthly management training for owners and managers, periodic (quarterly) for employees.

Managerial Assistance Available: Management Workshops, Support groups and technical counsel where applicable.

Information Submitted: May 1987

DIXON COMMERCIAL INVESTIGATORS, INC.
728 Center Street
Lewiston, New York 14092
E. L. Dixon, President

Description of Operation: Complete range of credit and collection services. Territories available by city or state/province (U.S. and Canada locations available).

Number of Franchisees: 6 in New York, Pennsylvania, Ohio, California and Canada

In Business Since: 1956

Equity Capital Needed: $5,000

Financial Assistance Available: None

Training Provided: 1 or 2 weeks head office training. Continuous supervision and aid afterwards.

Managerial Assistance Available: Franchisee is trained in all areas of credit collection. Franchisee is in continuous contact with head office.

Information Submitted: May 1987

DYNAMIC AIR FREIGHT, INC.
1732 Old Minters Chapel Road
Suite 100
Grapevine, Texas 76051
Daniel J. Herron, Jr., Executive Vice President

Description of Operation: Dynamic Air Freight is an air freight forwarder, transporting a customer's cargo from pick-up at the point or origin to delivery at destination. The company's purpose is to provide effective and efficient air freight forwarding services to businesses, industry, institutions and governmental entities.

Number of Franchisees: 23 in 10 States and Canada

In Business Since: 1978

Equity Capital Needed: $7,500 minimum

Financial Assistance Available: For qualified individuals, the company offers to finance up to three quarters of the franchisee's initial license fee. The company does not offer financing for any other purpose relating to either the establishment or operation of the franchise business.

Training Provided: 2 week mandatory training program is provided all new franchisee's and their management personnel. Training program is conducted at both the company's headquarters and the franchisee's outlet.

Managerial Assistance Available: Dynamic provides continual administrative and managerial assistance for the life of the franchise business. Complete manuals of operations are provided each franchisee.

Information Submitted: June 1987

EASTERN ONION, INC.
333 North Rancho Drive
Suite 444
Las Vegas, Nevada 89106
James Flatt, President

Description of Operation: Singing telegram, gift-giving, entertainment service. OVer 30 trademarked performances and 120 original copyrighted songs. Low overhead, high profit, fun business dealing with general public and celebrities.

Number of Franchisees: 30 nationwide

In Business Since: 1976

Equity Capital Needed: $25,000-$40,000

Financial Assistance Available: None

Training Provided: Manuals, training tapes, updated material for the growth of Eastern Onion. Continuous newsletters.

Managerial Assistance Available: Material is sent on an ongoing process as business progresses. Advertising, songs, costumes, gifts, proposals for quality control, efficiency programs, profit making programs.

Information Submitted: July 1987

ECONOTAX
365 West Northside Drive
Jackson, Mississippi 39206
James T. Marsh, E.A.

Description of Operation: EconoTax provides the public with a professional, full-service tax office. In addition to income tax preparation, EconoTax offers audit representation, tax planning, and tax-oriented services. EconoTax began and continues to operate in the spirit of a cooperative of tax professionals with low franchise fees and a maximum of local independent decision-making.

Number of Franchisees: 51 nationwide

In Business Since: 1965

Equity Capital Needed: $9,500 minimum (includes start-up working capital) with no franchise fee.

Financial Assistance Available: None

Training Provided: EconoTax provides a comprehensive technical training program for franchisees and their employees. Technical backup normally provides a response within 30 minutes during tax season.

Managerial Assistance Available: Managerial assistance is provided as needed. EconoTax offers a full service tax operation with support in site selection; recruiting; hiring; and training; work scheduling; internal controls and procedures; financial controls and complete advertising packages.

Information Submitted: July 1987

EKW SYSTEMS (EDWIN K. WILLIAMS & CO.)
5324 Ekwill Street
Santa Barbara, California 93111
Duane B. Walsh, Executive Vice President

Description of Operation: EKW Systems is a producer of accounting systems and a franchisor of accounting and business management counseling services for small business. For many years, the leading supplier of these products and services to the retail petroleum industry, EKW Systems now also includes most other small businesses in the scope of activities. Turnkey computer packages are available to franchisees.

Number of Franchisees: 260 licensed offices in the United States

In Business Since: 1935 and franchising since 1947

Equity Capital Needed: Will vary by individual and by territory, depending upon the practice (if any) to be purchased, training required and other considerations. Initial cash requirements will be $15,000 or more.

Financial Assistance Available: Limited to a portion of the franchise fee by franchisor. Terms for business generally available from seller.

Training Provided: Initial training available includes hands-on training in existing licensee offices plus continuing guidance by the company's regional managers after installation. Training is also available in internal procedures, business management counseling, computer operation, tax preparation, sales, marketing of services and more from both company and affiliated outside sources.

Managerial Assistance Available: Field staff provides follow-up counseling and guidance in licensee operations. Technical support and other assistance is available through EKW Systems' headquarters staff. Periodic meetings and promotional programs are made available throughout the year.

Information Submitted: July 1987

EXTENDED SERVICE OF AMERICA, INC.
P. O. Box 9568
Wichita, Kansas 67277-0568

Description of Operation: Offering "extended warranties" on televisions, appliances, VCR's, microwaves, satellite TV systems, home computers and central heating and air conditioning. Warranties offered through retailers.

Number of Franchisees: 85 in 26 States

In Business Since: 1981

Financial Assistance Available: Will finance up to half the investment. Reserve and all claims handled by franchisor.

Training Provided: 1 to 2 weeks initial training in franchisee's area, establishing several retail outlets on warranty program. Continuous training every 90 days thereafter.

Managerial Assistance Available: Same as above. Franchisee provides continual updating on market trends, competition and new marketing techniques.

Information Submitted: July 1987

FINANCIAL TRANSACTION CORPORATION
7 Mt. Lassen Drive C-251
San Rafael, California 94903
Douglas R. Brim, Executive Vice President

Description of Operation: Real estate loan brokerage. Franchisee should be a licensed real estate person with experience in real estate finance.

Number of Franchisees: 11 in California

In Business Since: 1982

Equity Capital Needed: Approximately $10,000-$20,000

Financial Assistance Available: Per agreement.

Training Provided: Training manual; ongoing updates, seminars on underwriting and other important functions of real estate finance.

Managerial Assistance Available: Operations manuals and setting up assistance. Management seminars, advertising and recruiting assistance.

Information Submitted: May 1987

FOCUS ON BINGO MAGAZINE
GUIDES PUBLISHING, INC.
One Anderson Avenue, Dept. FOB
P. O. Box 133
Fairview, New Jersey 07022
Louis C. Fernandez, President

Description of Operation: Focus On Bingo is a free bingo guide magazine whose main advertisers are bingo sponsors who otherwise are unable to advertise in most newspapers because of postal regulations. No experience necessary. We produce the complete magazine for you. Complete training and protected territory.

Number of Franchisees: 5 in 4 States

In Business Since: 1980

Equity Capital Needed: $1,800 license fee.

Financial Assistance Available: None

Training Provided: Complete training and continuous support.

Managerial Assistance Available: Continuous assistance via telephone "hot line" and periodic bulletins.

Information Submitted: May 1987

FOCUS ON HOMES MAGAZINE
GUIDES PUBLISHING, INC.
One Anderson Avenue, Dept. FOH
P. O. Box 133
Fairview, New Jersey 07022
Louis C. Fernandez, President

Description of Operation: Focus On Homes is a free pictorial "houses-for-sale" magazine whose main advertisers are the real estate agencies in your territory. No previsou experience necessary. We produce the complete magazine for you. Complete training and protected territory.

Number of Franchisees: 10 in 5 States

In Business Since: 1980

Equity Capital Needed: $1,800 license fee.

Financial Assistance Available: None

Training Provided: Complete training and continuous support.

Managerial Assistance Available: Continuous assistance via telephone "hot line" and periodic bulletins.

Information Submitted: July 1987

THE FRANCHISE ARCHITECTS—CONSULTANTS FOR FRANCHISING, INC.
240 East Ontario
Suite 203
Chicago, Illinois 60611
Craig S. Slavin, President

Description of Operation: The Franchise Architects franchises franchise development, consulting, marketing and sales services through offices known as "The Franchise Architects."

Number of Franchisees: 4 currently in the United States and Australia

In Business Since: 1980

Equity Capital Needed: Varies according to markets $35,000-$85,000

Financial Assistance Available: Partial financing for computer systems through traditional sources.

Training Provided: Minimum 2 weeks initially covering various aspects of franchising, the proprietary development process and the brokering of client franchises.

Managerial Assistance Available: See above. Additionally, the corporate staff is available to conduct seminars on the various aspects of franchising for franchisees in their markets, advertising layouts and guidance, investment assistance, and continued education throughout the system.

Information Submitted: July 1987

*FRANCHISE NETWORK USA, INC.
3025 South Parker Road
Suite 400
Aurora, Colorado 80014
Carol Green, President

Description of Operation: National network of independent franchise marketing specialists selling selected franchises to qualified buyers via specialized seminars, franchise shows and indepth personal interviews.

Number of Franchisees: 13 in 13 States plus 1 company owned.

In Business Since: 1984

Equity Capital Needed: $29,000-$50,000 dependent on population of area served.

Financial Assistance Available: None.

Training Provided: Minimum 1 week covering franchise sales, advertising, office set up, conducting seminars plus an overview of current franchise law.

Managerial Assistance Available: Constant communication to field offices assisting in up to date sales and marketing techniques, client franchisor information, advertising/promotion formats, seminar and franchise show assistance. Due dilligence for client franchisors monitored by home office. Investment assistance and continued education systemwide.

Information Submitted: May 1987

THE FRANCHISE STORE
5100 Poplar, Suite 1219
Memphis, Tennessee 38137

Description of Operation: The franchise is a business utilize certain methods of service and sales to the public for the marketing and sales of franchises of others from a center location throughout the United States through promotional efforts.

Number of Franchisees: 9 regions with 57 sub licensees.

In Business Since: 1976

Equity Capital Needed: $25,000-$50,000. Dependent on population of area served.

Financial Assistance Available: None

Training Provided: The training is available in Memphis, Tennessee, and extensiveness is dependent upon experience.

Managerial Assistance Available: See above

Information Submitted: May 1987

FRANKLIN TRAFFIC SERVICE, INC.
5251 Shawnee Road
Ransomville, New York 14131
John M. Maxon, Manager Sales/Franchising

Description of Operation: Franklin Traffic Service, Inc., is a prominent company providing its nationwide clientele with audit and payment of freight bills; management reporting; management services; and complete industrial traffic services.

Number of Franchisees: 6 in New York, Pennsylvania and Georgia.

In Business Since: 1969

Equity Capital Needed: $19,000-$25,000

Financial Assistance Available: $11,000-$14,000 required in advance. Financing on balance to qualified applicants.

Training Provided: Intensive 3 week, mandatory training program for all new franchisees. Training consists of in-house programs and time in the field with an existing franchisee.

Managerial Assistance Available: Franklin Traffic Service maintains a bonafide interest in all franchises. Manuals of operations, forms, and directions are provided. In-the-field assistance is provided on a regular basis. Franchisees benefit from all new marketing concepts which are developed. Franklin sponsors regular franchise meetings, and continually upgrades and maintains the highest level of quality possible.

Information Submitted: May 1987

FUTURE SEARCH MANAGEMENT CORP.
50 East Palisade Avenue
Suite 322
Englewood, New Jersey 07631
Mary Ann Liscio, President

Description of Operation: Future Search provides college and career planning services to high school students, transfer students, graduate students, students with disabilities and even to adults re-entering the college or job market. Services include: college planning, occupational interest analysis, aptitude testing, private secondary school planning, financial aid planning, athletic scholarship availability.

Number of Franchisees: 10 in New Jersey, Connecticut and New York.

In Business Since: 1985

Equity Capital Needed: $15,000-$19,000

Financial Assistance Available: The franchisor will assist the franchisee in applying to local banks for financing.

Training Provided: 3-day classroom instruction at company site; franchisor provides continual ongoing training and advise.

Managerial Assistance Available: Assistance and direction given by direct phone, seminars and in-office visits. Complete operations manuals provided in counseling techniques and procedures as well as marketing and promotional activities.

Information Submitted: May 1987

GASCARD CLUB, INC.
11025 North Torrey Pines Road
P. O. Box 389700
La Jolla, California 92038
Danny Brown

Description of Operation: Computerized automated fuel management system.

Number of Franchisees: 628 open and operating in 38 States

In Business Since: 1981

Equity Capital Needed: $50,000

Financial Assistance Available: Gascard Club will supply a list of contacts for franchisees who wish to lease equipment in place of purchasing equipment needed.

Training Provided: Minimum 5 days training at national headquarters in La Jolla, California is required of new franchisees. Gascard's total program and C.R.T. hands-on are only 2 of the many subjects covered. Detailed training manuals are issued and updated for a continuing reference tool. Gascard advertising guidelines and new sales development ideas are passed on to franchisees. Sales training seminars are available to franchisees.

Managerial Assistance Available: Gascard Club provides member services, which is a franchisee's direct contact to any department in the event of questions or problems. A toll free customer service line is also available 24 hours a day, 7 days a week to meet franchisees needs. Technicians are based at Gascard region offices across the nation for service as needed. Management and sales seminars and program enhancements are offered on a regular continuing basis.

Information Submitted: July 1987

*GENERAL BUSINESS SERVICES, INC.
20271 Goldenrod Lane
Germantown, Maryland 20874-4090
Robert Pirtle, President

Description of Operation: General Business Services franchised business counselors provide financial management, business counseling, tax planning, and computer services to small businesses and professionals. Supported by the GBS national office, franchisees provide clients the proper recordkeeping system, guaranteed correct tax return preparation, computer services, and financial planning services. GBS provides its business counselors and their clients with continuous training and support. The franchisee can be operated as either a sole proprietorship or corporation.

Number of Franchisees: Hundreds nationwide

In Business Since: 1962

Equity Capital Needed: Franchise fee is $21,500 plus $3,500 for inventory. Should also have sufficient operating capital for living expenses and for business "start-up" period—will vary by individual.

Financial Assistance Available:

Training Provided: Initial and continuous training is provided. Approximately 30 days training provided during the first year and approximately 10 days training each year thereafter. GBS business counselors are trained in all aspects of counseling, client acquisition and operating an independent business based on GBS' 20-plus years experience. All new franchisees received without additional expense: (1) a 4-volume operations manual containing all operating instructions, company policies, and procedures; (2) 1-1/2 week basic training institute and 1 week advanced training institute at GBS' national training center; (3) 1 week individual training in the franchisee's own marketing area by an experienced business counselor; (4) necessary sales aids, client servicing and practice management forms; and (5) ongoing training and individual guidance through assigned regional director.

Managerial Assistance Available: In addition to local assistance provided by an experienced regional director, a staff of over 200 in the national office is available for managerial assistance and technical support as required; 20 continuing support services are provided franchisees: e.g., annual series of seminars for professional development and continuing education; business management self-study services; lending library of books, tapes and pamphlets; sales brochures, client advertising and ongoing public relations program; toll-free numbers for order placement, computer assistance and tax advisory services; ongoing communications through bi-weekly and monthly newsletters and field-represented President's Advisory Council.

Information Submitted: May 1987

* GO-VIDEO
4141 North Scottsdale Road
Suite 204
Scottsdale, Arizona 85251-3940
Timothy L. Kuhn, Manager, Franchise Development

Description of Operation: The Go-Video concept revolves around a complete mobile video production studio housed inside an economically designed, attractive mini-van. This van is retrofitted with video editing equipment along with video camera and lighting packages. Go-Video has developed a professional, 1/2" production system that enables the owner/operator to provide quick, convenient production and on long edition services at almost any location the client chooses and has the capability to provide the client with the finished product choices and has the capability to provide the client with the finished product on-site.

Number of Franchisees: 2 in Arizona

In Business Since: 1984

Equity Capital Needed: Approximately $60,000 with use of leasing program.

Financial Assistance Available: A leasing program has been developed by Go-Video to assist in lowering the effective initial start-up costs. Under this program a qualified franchisee could lease the equipment from Go-Video, thus lowering the total initial investment to the $60,000 range.

Training Provided: Initial training is 12 day course provided at Go-Video's learning center in Scottsdale, Arizona. The curriculum includes hands-on training in video production operations, management, marketing, computer familiarization, and accounting. The company will provide previously trained and experienced Go-Video system managers/operators with refresher and/or advanced training course, particularly when there have been significant improvements in the "state of the art."

Managerial Assistance Available: Throughout the term of the franchise, franchisee is provided not only ongoing training but support from regular visits of our field service executives. Training manuals are furnished in manual and video formats. Franchisee is assisted by a national and regional advertising program and is given supplemental material and recommendations for local ads. Technical bulletins as well as 800 number are in place for continued assistance.

Information Submitted: May 1987

THE HEADQUARTERS COMPANIES
900 Larkspur Landing Circle
Suite 270
Larkspur, California 94939
T. J. Tison

Description of Operation: Lease executive offices with complete support services. Offices and support services available to both full-time users and occasional users. Each client receives, in addition to use of office, a receptionist, telephone answering, secretarial, word processing, office supplies and an array of other support services such as radio paging, facsimile transmission, electronic document distribution, telex, conference rooms, furniture rental, printing, direct mail and more. The various services are made available to the business community in general, not only those using the office space. The office center functions as a business support service bureau for the entire city in which it is located. Company officials stress that the array of support services will continue to change as the new office technology unfolds in the future. The overall concept envisions licensed locations in both major and minor business cities across the country linked together in a communications network of office centers providing support services to the business community.

Number of Franchisees: 42 with 60 locations in 30 States.

In Business Since: 1967, franchising since October 1978

Equity Capital Needed: An initial investment of approximately $250,000.

Financial Assistance Available: Assistance is available only in arranging financing.

Training Provided: License trademark only, no training.

Managerial Assistance Available: Marketing, advertising, sales and administration assistance.

Information Submitted: July 1987

HEIMER INSPECTIONS
1923 New York Avenue
Huntington, New York 11746
Irwin Heimer, Vice President, Marketing

Description of Operation: The Heimer Home Inspection Report gives the prospective home buyer a 40-50 page narrative report that informs the client of the total condition of the house; the good points, deficiencies and potential problem areas. The report is bound in a booklet and promptly submitted to the client.

Number of Franchisees: 3 in New York, Massachusetts, and New Jersey

In Business Since: 1985

Equity Capital Needed: Approximately $60,000

Financial Assistance Available: Co-Signature on equipment available.

Training Provided: 2 weeks, 60 hour course given in the home office.

Managerial Assistance Available: Continuous

Information Submitted: May 1987

* HOMECALL, INC.
30 East Patrick Street
Frederick, Maryland 21701
Marty Kinkiad, Coordinator of Franchise Services

Description of Operation: HomeCall, Inc., provides comprehensive home care services. These services range from non-medical services such as: homemaker, chore, transportation, to nursing, therapy and home health aids. Most of our franchises participate in the Medicare program.

Number of Franchisees: 6 in Oklahoma, Oregon, Washington, Maryland and Virginia

In Business Since: 1974

Equity Capital Needed: $50,000-$70,000

Financial Assistance Available: None

Training Provided: Minimum 1 week classroom training at home office. Additional training on-the-job, in one of branches. On-site assistance for start-up.

Managerial Assistance Available: Complete manuals of operations are provided. Training and management development, seminars and conferences, management, finance and medical review advisory assistance, professional health services consultation.

Information Submitted: July 1987

HOMES & LAND PUBLISHING CORPORATION
dba HOMES & LAND MAGAZINE
2365 Centerville Road
Tallahassee, Florida 32308
Ken Ledford, Vice President, Sales

Description of Operation: Nation's largest publisher of community real estate magazines. Magazines are black/white or color and contain property listings of real estate companies. Franchisees sell advertising space to real estate brokers and distribute the magazines in the community. Separate franchises offered for quality magazines and for economy magazines.

Number of Franchisees: 300 under contract in 35 States

In Business Since: 1973

Equity Capital Needed: $6,000 for quality magazine; $1,500 for economy magazine.

Financial Assistance Available: None

Training Provided: 1 week orientation at company offices, including instruction in production, sales and financial management, field assistance provided for initial sales.

Managerial Assistance Available: Operating manuals and sales aids provided. Regional meetings and annual sales convention provide opportunities for further training and interaction. Home office technical assistance is provided by telephone; sales assistance is available from district sales managers.

Information Submitted: June 1987

HOMEWATCH CORPORATION
2865 South Colorado Boulevard
Denver, Colorado 80222
Paul A. Sauer, President

Description of Operation: A checking and sitting service which provides attentive care for peoples homes, pets and elderly people. Homesitting 24 hours or overnight, companion sitting, and in-home personal services (errands), odd jobs and handyman services.

Number of Franchisees: 19 in 8 states

In Business Since: 1973

Equity Capital Needed: Initial fee is $6,000 to $12,000. The total investment not to exceed $12,000-$25,000. Area development available.

Financial Assistance Available: Financial assistance available for multiple sales or large franchises.

Training Provided: 4-day (mandatory) training program at corporate office or on-site. Manuals, bookkeeping and advertising/marketing manuals. Continuous support and consultation, bi-monthly newsletters, and voice and video cassettes telephone helpline.

Managerial Assistance Available: Continuous assistance available whenever needed. Newsletters, regional seminars, and national convention.

Information Submitted: May 1987

*HOUSEMASTER OF AMERICA, INC.
421 West Union Avenue
Bound Brook, New Jersey 08805
Robert J. Hardy, President

Description of Operation: HouseMaster of America is an organization of home inspection professionals. Qualified technical people conduct the inspections, while marketing-oriented people run the business end. Home buyers who want to know the condition of perhaps the largest investment of their lifetime are the primary users. There are no inventory requirements and no need for fancy office space.

Number of Franchisees: 86 in 31 States

In Business Since: 1979

Equity Capital Needed: $17,000-$35,000, depending upon the number of owner-occupied homes in area.

Financial Assistance Available: It is advised that an additional $10,000 to $15,000 is needed to get started. Sources of financial assistance are provided by the franchisor.

Training Provided: 3-day orientation training; this is for the person who will run the business. 5-day technical training course; this is for the designated technical director. Also provided are: (1) sales and promotion manual, (2) operations manual, (3) technical training manual.

Managerial Assistance Available: Ongoing counseling in all aspects of the business. Administration of referral system (WATS Line), advertising, publicity and promotion programs, regular newsletters, both technical and sales, as well as bulletins, trade digests. Periodic seminars. Both technical and marketing research and development. A warranty program.

Information Submitted: May 1987

INCOTAX SYSTEMS, INC.
1401 South J Street
Lake Worth, Florida 33460
Richard B. Vondrak, President

Description of Operation: Incotax Systems is a volume, multi unit tax service system. It has developed an outstanding method of providing high quality, accurate tax returns to the public at a minimum cost.

Number of Franchisees: 15 in Florida and 1 in Maryland and 3 in Arizona

In Business Since: 1967

Equity Capital Needed: $15,000

Financial Assistance Available: $10,000 of equity capital is prorated thru first year of operation.

Training Provided: Complete management and tax preparation training for 2 persons is conducted by the home office. Complete cost of training, including air fare, hotel, etc., is included in equity capital.

Managerial Assistance Available: Continuous home office inspection and management training is conducted. Home office consultation and management suggestions are made to all franchisees, complete procedural manuals and forms are furnished franchisees as well as monthly news bulletins.

Information Submitted: July 1987

INFORMERIFIC CORPORATION
P. O. Box 2833
Charleston, West Virginia 25330
Charles L. Counts, President

Description of Operation: Franchised business forms retailing.

Number of Franchisees: 11 in 6 states.

In Business Since: 1984

Equity Capital Needed: $29,000.

Financial Assistance Available: Assist in financing franchise fee

Training Provided: Varies with experience of franchisee.

Managerial Assistance Available: Ongoing training for all franchisees at training center as well as at each franchisees location.

Information Submitted: July 1987

INTERNATIONAL MERGERS AND ACQUISITIONS
8100 East Indian School Road
Suite 7 West
Scottsdale, Arizona 85251
Neil D. Lewis, President

Description of Operation: International Mergers and Acquisitions is a national affiliation of members engaged in the profession of servicing merger and acquisition minded companies on a confidential basis. Our program embraces all aspects essential to a successful merger or acquisition.

Number of Franchisees: 35 in 13 States

In Business Since: 1970

Equity Capital Needed: $10,000 minimum

Financial Assistance Available: A total investment of $10,000 is necessary. We request a down payment of $5,000 and will finance the balance if franchisee has good credit references.

Training Provided: Quarterly regional creative work sessions, plus orientation sessions for each new member as needed.

Managerial Assistance Available: International Mergers and Acquisitions provides complete procedures and operations manual, forms and provide product research to all members.

Information Submitted: May 1987

K & O PUBLISHING
7522 20th N.E.
Seattle, Washington 98115
Warren E. Kraft, Jr., President

Description of Operation: K & O Publishing franchises a special interest newspaper called the Bingo Bugle. The franchisee has the opportunity to become the editor and publisher of his/her own newspaper even with no previous publishing experience. This publication is extremely popular with bingo players. The Bingo bugle is America's largest group of bingo newspapers.

Number of Franchisees: 37 in 16 States and District of Columbia.

In Business Since: 1982

Equity Capital Needed: $2,000-$10,000

Financial Assistance Available: None

Training Provided: Franchisor provides a 2 day seminar.

Managerial Assistance Available: An operation manual and ongoing assistance are provided by franchisor.

Information Submitted: May 1987

K & W COMPUTERIZED TAX SERVICE, INC.
1607 Minnesota Avenue
Kansas City, Kansas 66102
Herb Buchanan, Franchise Director

Description of Operation: Computerized tax and accounting services.

Number of Franchisees: 75 in 8 States

In Business Since: 1979

Equity Capital Needed: $500

Financial Assistance Available: No

Training Provided: Continuous training and update of current tax laws and accounting procedures. Franchisees are trained on a unique interview technique developed by K & W for tax and accounting preparation. Training mandatory

Managerial Assistance Available: Continuous

Information Submitted: May 1987

KELLY'S LIQUIDATORS, INC.
1310 N.W. 21st Street
Fort Lauderdale, Florida 33311
Edward Kelly, President

Description of Operation: Kelly's Liquidators is a unique clearing house service agency for bringing buyers and sellers of used, second-hand (or "pre-owned") personal property together. (i.e., household goods, antiques, etc.) We sell piece-meal (by appointment), package-deal, or at one-day public sale (especially estates) NOT auctions! We charge 20 or 25 percent commission of gross sales on a contractual basis. We sell other people's goods on their premises.

Number of Franchisees: 3 in Florida (

franchises available in Florida only).

In Business Since: 1954

Equity Capital Needed: $2,500 minimum

Financial Assistance Available: $2,000 is the cost of a franchise. $1,000 must be paid before training begins. The $1,000 balance may be paid in installments. An additional $500 is needed for start-up and 3 months operations. Franchisee must arrange his own financing if necessary.

Training Provided: Intensive 5-day mandatory training course is given only to franchisee at Ft. Lauderdale. Training based on confidential manual of operations and supplemented wherever possible by on-the-job supervision by a Kelly's officer or experienced franchisee.

Managerial Assistance Available: KLI provides continuing managerial, technical and operational assistance for 6 months in such areas as obtaining contracts, listing, advertising, and selling, as they relate to the various methods of selling (i.e., appointment, package deal, or public sales—especially estates) and record control. A complete manual of operations is provided.

Information Submitted: May 1987

THE LETTER WRITER, INC.
9357 Haggerty Road
Plymouth, Michigan 48170
Ginny Eades, President

Description of Operation: Franchisor is offering for sale the right to use the trademarks and logos of The Letter Writer in connection with the operation of a resume writing, creative writing, letter writing, full secretarial services, answering service and technical writing/advertising service. Franchisor has developed training, policies and procedures, marketing and advertising procedures, accounting systems, printing and reproducing systems, supplier contacts, equipment contracts, methods of client development, methods of preparing client services and working with clients in operating a Letter Writer franchise.

Number of Franchisees: 2 including company-owned in Michigan.

In Business Since: 1981/franchising since 1985.

Equity Capital Needed: Franchise fee: $7,500. Equipment costs: $2,850.

Financial Assistance Available: Franchisor will advise and assist franchisee in obtaining necessary financing, including methods of purchasing or leasing equipment. Franchisor will require $5,000, as a down-payment and allow franchisee to pay the $2,500 balance in monthly payments of $425 for six months.

Training Provided: Franchisee or franchisee's designated manager will receive a combination of lecture, self-study and on-the-job training. Policies, procedures and methods of operation will be reviewed. Training will be given in both management

and in delivery of services to the public, including training in typing skills, resume writing, bookkeeping, advertising, hiring practices, use of equipment, purchasing and telephone methods—a minimum of 80 hours.

Financial Assistance Available: None

Training Provided: 2 weeks with ongoing support.

Managerial Assistance Available: Continuous in all phases of operation.

Information Submitted: May 1987

THE MANAGEMENT CENTER, INC.
TMC BUSINESS BROKERS
7122 Forest Hill Avenue
Richmond, Virginia 23225
C. Scott Pugh, President

Description of Operation: Business brokerage franchise. Complete system of business brokerage to assist buyers and sellers of small businesses. Comprehensive training, networking of listings, ongoing consultation.

Number of Franchisees: 6 in 3 states.

In Business Since: 1984

Equity Capital Needed: $45,000

Financial Assistance Available: Negotiable

Training Provided: Depending on prior experience of applicant for 3 days to 2 weeks.

Managerial Assistance Available: Start-up training and guidance and ongoing consultation.

Information Submitted: July 1987

MANAGEMENT REPORTS & SERVICES, INC.
Westin Building, Suite 2501
2001 Sixth Avenue
Seattle, Washington 98121

Description of Operation: Management Reports & Services provides business and non-profit owner/operators with custom-designed management reports that focus on key performance indicators. The reports often include analysis of cash flow, accounts receivable, inventory, sales analysis and productivity of people and assets.

Number of Franchisees: 2 in Washington and Arizona

In Business Since: 1986

Equity Capital Needed: $28,000 to $140,500

Financial Assistance Available: None

Training Provided: MR&S provides a comprehensive 3 week training program at headquarters, and spends 1 week with new franchisees in the field reinforcing the training, following the franchisees return to the field. In addition, focused field training is provided to solve a franchise owner's need for re-education, as required.

Managerial Assistance Available: MR&S provides regular field visits by managerial staff and technical field support, as required for smooth operation by the franchise owner.

Information Submitted: May 1987.

* **MAIL BOXES ETC. USA**
5555 Oberlin Drive
San Diego, California 92121
Tony DeSio, President

Description of Operation: Postal and business service centers. Provide services to consumer and small businessmen in the following areas: P. O. Box rentals, mail receipt and forwarding, electronic mail and wire services, parcel packaging and shipping, copy service and printing, secretarial services, word processing.

Number of Franchisees: 500 in 38 States and Washington, D.C.

In Business Since: 1980

Equity Capital Needed: Individual franchise - $55,000 (includes $10,000 in heasehold improvements and $10,000 working capital).

Financial Assistance Available: Yes.

Training Provided: Combination of classroom and on-the-job training. Individual franchise—1 week at franchisor headquarters (optional) and 1 week at franchisees location. Area franchise—2 weeks at franchise headquarters and 2 weeks at franchise location.

Managerial Assistance Available: Initial assistance provided in setting up turnkey operation—including site selection, lease negotiation, facility design, construction management (optional), purchase of equipment and supplies (optional), set up of facility, grand opening promotional assistance. Continuing assistance provided in promotions and new profit center development.

Information Submitted: May 1987

MAIL SORT, INC.
4781 Commercial Plaza
Winston-Salem, North Carolina 27102
William G. Norris, Jr., Chairman

Description of Operation: Manual mail processing centers designed primarily for the presorting of 1st and 3rd class mail volume for mailers. Mail volume is manually sorted by zip code to qualify for the presort postage discount offered by the United States Postal Service.

Number of Franchisees: 12 in 8 States

In Business Since: 1978

Equity Capital Needed: $100,000 to $500,000

Financial Assistance Available: None

Training Provided: Franchisee will receive at least 2 months of on-site training at a Mail Sort, Inc., mail processing center. Additional training in operational procedures and marketing techniques will be given at Mail Sort, Inc., headquarters. This training must be completed before the franchisee can actually begin actively pursuing customers for the proposed Mail Sort franchise or begin active mail processing operations.

Managerial Assistance Available: For the first 14 days after mail processing begins in the operation of the franchisee, the Mail Sort representative on-site will directly assist and instruct the franchisee and/or his representative in the areas of marketing, operations, management, postal regulations and all other areas pertaining to the efficient and profitable operation of a Mail Sort franchise.

Information Submitted: July 1987

*MARCOIN, INC.
1924 Cliff Valley Way, N.E.
Atlanta, Georgia 30329
J. T. Rhodes

Description of Operation: Marcoin, Inc., is a business management service specializing in the "how to" of maximizing small business profits through a nationwide network of company-owned and franchised offices. This network of local offices provides the most up-to-date accounting, tax and business counseling services plus a wide range of computer services to independently owned businesses. Marcoin has developed and markets financial recordkeeping systems for small businesses, and these systems and the allied services Marcoin offers have received the endorsement of numerous organizations which represent potential management service clients.

Number of Franchisees: 134 offices of which 16 are company-operated in 37 States.

In Business Since: 1952

Equity Capital Needed: Initial franchise fee is $20,000. Additional expenditures are required for travel and lodging for training. Optional computer hardware and software are available. To cover these expenses, office equipment, working capital, a total investment of $35,000 to $45,000 is needed. Some financing is available.

Financial Assistance Available: A portion of the initial fee for qualified candidates.

Training Provided: A 3 week basic orientation course is conducted to instruct licensees in the day-to-day business operations and techniques. In addition, a week long seminar in advanced business applications is attended within a year. Field training sessions are conducted throughout the year.

Managerial Assistance Available: After the initial basic orientation course, a Marcoin employee spends up to one week of on-the-job training in the first couple of months of business operation. Licensees are provided in in-depth and complete operations manuals, and Marcoin conducts field training sessions throughout the year. Computer systems software for processing client work is available and supported from the General Office. An in-house staff of data processing professionals provides computer training, support, and maintenance.

Information Submitted: May 1987

MCTAGGART MORTGAGE ASSISTANCE CENTERS, INC.
450 Seminola Boulevard
Casselberry, Florida 32707
Edward J. McTaggart

Description of Operation: Offering assistance to families who are behind with their house payments...we have several options available to solve 80 percent of the cases.

Number of Franchisees: 2 in Florida and Ohio

In Business Since: 1983

Equity Capital Needed: $35,000 down payment

Financial Assistance Available: Yes

Training Provided: An extensive 2 week training period at the home office in Orlando, FLorida, will show new office owners a working office atmosphere' where they can have "hands-on training." Followed by 1 week training in their office location.

Managerial Assistance Available: Each new office will receive assistance in regards to office location, necessary forms and office management. In addition to this, each office will receive training in Orlando, Florida prior to opening date....a manual of instructions is available covering all aspects of operation. Special group benefits are offered and available.

Information Submitted: May 1987

MEDICAL INSURA FORM SERVICE
609 14th Street
Sioux City, Iowa 51105
Mary P. Phillips

Description of Operation: A business that coordinates and processes all medicare and medical insurance claims. Medical reimbursement consultants, particularly of interest to people with medical background.

Number of Franchisees: 2 in Iowa

In Business Since: 1980

Equity Capital Needed: $35,000 to $40,000

Financial Assistance Available: None

Training Provided: 10 days to 3 weeks training in home office in all operations of the business.

Managerial Assistance Available: Monthly visits for the first 6 months of operations in addition to training.

Information Submitted: July 1987

*MEL JACKSON, INC.
6513 College Park Square
Virginia Beach, Virginia 23464
Carolyn Buzek, Vice President, Franchise Operations

Description of Operation: A Mel Jackson Income Tax franchise will offer computerized income tax preparation, bookkeeping, and other related services. Franchisees are licensed to use the Mel Jackson System which includes proprietary software, accounting methods, merchandising, equipment selection, advertising, sales and promotional techniques, personnel training, and other related matters.

Number of Franchisees: 17 in Virginia, 2 in New York

In Business Since: 1985

Equity Capital Needed: $12,500-$13,000 (estimated) including initial franchise fee.

Financial Assistance Available: Mel Jackson Inc., will not offering financing to any franchisee, either directly or indirectly.

Training Provided: Prior to franchisee's commencement of business Mel Jackson Inc., will provide a minimum of 5 days of training in all aspects of the operation and management of a Mel Jackson Income Tax Franchise, including the use of the computerized tax programs. In addition, annual refresher training is provided.

Managerial Assistance Available: Mel Jackson Inc., will provide assistance in advertising and marketing, recommendations and advice concerning site selection, ongoing advice and guidance as requested by franchisees concerning operations and tax problems as well as concerning new and improved techniques and operating methods, business procedures, management and promotional materials, and updated software programs.

Information Submitted: May 1987

* MIFAX SERVICE AND SYSTEMS, INC.
3070 West Airline Highway
Box 5800
Waterloo, Iowa 50704
Tom Mullen, Vice President/General Manager

Description of Operation: Franchised dealers selling Control-o-fax 800/553-2003 office systems, and computer services to the healing arts professions throughout the U.S.

Number of Franchisees: 70 in all but 6 States

In Business Since: 1969

Equity Capital Needed: $21,340—$11,800 down, 2 year note for balance.

Financial Assistance Available: All but $7,500 (disclosure and administrative costs) will cover 3 direct mailings; demonstration and advertising supplies; and three basic classes, 2 telemarketing classes and 1 management class.

Training Provided: Ongoing formal sales and management training at home office, ongoing field help by Control-o-fax on products. Each class has a duration of 5-1/2 days, with 6 months field follow-up by company representatives.

Managerial Assistance Available: Business and financial planning, assistance in recruiting of salespeople and service people by Mifax field representatives on an ongoing basis. An operations manual covering all facets of the business is made available. A yearly regional meeting is also conducted.

Information Submitted: May 1987

MILLION AIR INTERLINK
4300 Westgrove
Dallas, Texas 75248
Ed Blair, President

Description of Operation: Aviation franchise or general aviation operators. Fixed Base Operations (FBO). operations provide fuel, maintenance charters, aircraft sales, etc., to the general aviation community.

Number of Franchisees: 26 in 11 States

In Business Since: 1985

Equity Capital Needed: Aviation Facility

Financial Assistance Available: Finances franchise fee and leases refueling equipment.

Training Provided: Initial 2 day session in Dallas. Training done periodically at franchise location.

Managerial Assistance Available: Operational training on-site, manuals, monthly operational and marketing ideas, annual sessions, and semi-annual owners meetings.

Information Submitted: May 1987

* MONEY CONCEPTS INTERNATIONAL, INC.
Golden Bear Plaza
11760 U.S. Highway One
North Palm Beach, Florida 33408
John P. Walsh, President
Jerry Darnell, Vice President

Description of Operation: Money Concepts International, Inc., is a financial services franchisor. Money Concepts provides its franchisees with a complete "turnkey" marketing system for a financial planning center.

Number of Franchisees: Over 300 in the United States, Caribbean, United Kingdom, Australia, canada and Northern Ireland.

In Business Since: 1979. Franchising since 1982.

Equity Capital Needed: Franchisee needs to rent office space, office help approximately $1,100 monthly; conducts seminars, $2,200; needs working capital $5,000; and possible purchase of furniture and equipment, approximately $5,000. Franchisee contributes 2 percent of gross receipts for advertising.

Financial Assistance Available: Money Concepts may accept a note for 50 percent or less of the franchise fee as a cash substitute for the full payment of the franchise fee upon execution of the agreement. There is no interest on the note, which shall be paid in no more than 10 installments, and within one year.

Training Provided: Franchise includes basic and advanced management seminars. Other training is available such as: product and marketing seminar, financial planning school, office administration seminar, equity products seminar, hard assets seminar. These schools and seminars each last 2 to 5 days.

Managerial Assistance Available: Council of Presidents meeting for all franchise presidents held each quarter, (2 or 3 days). Back up support in all areas of franchise operations (both sales and administration) on an ongoing basis.

Information Submitted: May 1987

* MONEY MAILER, INC.
15472 Chemical Lane
Huntington Beach, California 92649
Kris O. Friedrich, President

Description of Operation: Money Mailer sell regional subfranchises through which its independent regions individually sell and service local franchises. Each of these independent local franchises provides an inexpensive but highly effective form of advertising to merchants, service businesses, and professionals in their local areas. Each region provides a wealth of sales aids and continuing marketing support to their local franchisees as well as complete production support from Money Mailer, including artwork, printing and mailing through the U.S. Post Office.

Number of Franchisees: 96 in 29 States

In Business Since: 1979

Equity Capital Needed: Regional owner: $37,700-$58,000, local franchisee: $8,600-$15,000.

Financial Assistance Available: Yes O.A.C.

Training Provided: An intensive 1 week classroom training is provided for regional owners. Local franchisees receive a mandatory 2 week training course, this training includes 1 week classroom training and 1 week field training in their local area.

Managerial Assistance Available: Money Mailer produces complete training manuals, forms and sales aids. The region owner is obligated to provide these materials as well as continuous consultation to the local franchisees for all aspects of the business. The region and local franchisee receive constant updates on the results of our product and market research. In addition, Money Mailer sponsors an annual convention and aids communication between regions, local franchisees and the corporate office with regional conferences and a bi-monthly newsletter.

Information Submitted: June 1987

* MORTGAGE SERVICE ASSOCIATES
21 Brock Street
North Haven, Connecticut 06473
Joseph D. Raffone, President

Description of Operation: Franchisor currently has over 100 clients nationwide, including banks, S&L's, insurance companies and others who hold mortgages on properties throughout the United States, Canada and other countries. Franchisee's operate through franchisor's computer system and conduct property inspections, delinquency interviews, insurance inspections, property maintenance, securing and sales make ready work. Franchisor provides daily work orders to franchisee's who in turn assign work and supervise local representatives.

Number of Franchisees: 2 in Texas, 2 in Florida and 1 company-owned in Connecticut.

In Business Since: 1978

Equity Capital Needed: Minimum equity capital $35,000 (franchise fee $25,000 and working capital $10,000)

Financial Assistance Available: Franchisor will finance up to $10,000 for qualified applicants.

Training Provided: Mortgage Service Associates provides 40 hours of training at headquarters covering: industry overview; the business of property inspections and maintenance; marketing; formulating a business plan; finance; use of our computer program; additional 30 hours at franchisee's location; continual toll free telephone support through a 20 person support staff; 600 representatives nationwide help the franchisee get started and stay on track.

Managerial Assistance Available: 3 kinds of continual managerial support and technical training are provided: 1) marketing to prospective clients through national advertising; trade shows, exhibits, seminars and convention; direct mail; direct client contact by national marketing staff. 2) day-to-day support by team of 20. Each support person has an area of expertise, including: mortgage servicing, finance, human resources; marketing and advertising; construction, renovation, cost estimating and special writing. 3) direct local support from representatives in place. Representatives have been hired and trained by the franchisor and are available to support and work for/with franchisees.

Information Submitted: May 1987

MOTIVATIONAL SYSTEMS
395 Pleasant Valley Way
West Orange, New Jersey 07052
Candace Deasy, Vice President, Franchise Sales

Description of Operation: Motivational Systems conducts training programs on communications skills, interpersonal and motivational skills, and persuasion and influence skills for corporations, government agencies and associations.

Number of Franchisees: 2 including company-owned in New Jersey

In Business Since: 1970

Equity Capital Needed: $20,000-$50,000, depending on location of franchise.

Financial Assistance Available: Franchisee arranges own financing.

Training Provided: Mandatory 2-week training college provides training to new franchisees in selling and conducting training programs, marketing, bookkeeping, and other necessary business skills. Additional training colleges are scheduled every 6 months to improve/increase skills.

Managerial Assistance Available: Continual telephone and problem-solving support ongoing. Updating training on technical areas and new programs. Our quality assurance rep will visit franchisee periodically, and will be available via telephone.

Information Submitted: May 1987

MR. SIGN FRANCHISING CORP.
159 Keyland Court
Bohemia, New York 11716
Harold L. Kesterbaum, President

Description of Operation: Sign business.

Number of Franchisees: 20 in New York and New Jersey.

In Business Since: 1985

Equity Capital Needed: $49,948

Financial Assistance Available: $9,000

Training Provided: 3 weeks of training.

Managerial Assistance Available: Complete ongoing support through term of contract.

Information Submitted: June 1987

MUZAK
915 Yale Avenue North, 3rd Floor
Seattle, WA 98109
Tom Evans, Sr., Vice President, Sales & Marketing

Description of Operation: Lease of special work and public area music programs to businesses of all kinds. Sound systems and related communication systems included as lease or sale to customers. Available franchises limited to U.S.; wide opportunities overseas.

Number of Franchisees: Approximately 170 in all 50 States plus 10 owned operations, 26 franchisees in 14 countries.

In Business Since: 1934

Equity Capital Needed: Varies—information from Muzak

Financial Assistance Available: None

Training Provided: Continuing sales and technical training sessions help at various sites.

Managerial Assistance Available: Field visits by Muzak corporate staff providing evaluations, assistance, progress reports on continuous basis. National advertising, sales brochures, equipment specification sheets, etc., provided at all times.

Information Submitted: May 1987

NAMCO SYSTEMS, INC.
7 Strathmore Road
Natick, Massachusetts 01760
Elizabeth Oksanen

Description of Operation: Professional advertising program for businesses sold by appointment.

Number of Franchisees: 50 in 19 States

In Business Since: 1952

Equity Capital Needed: $21,000-$35,000, depending on size of territories.

Financial Assistance Available: None

Training Provided: Classroom training consists of 4 days at franchisor's headquarters in Natick, Massachusetts. two weeks of field training in the franchisees' territory, subsequent regional meetings and advance training seminars, on-going support and advice.

Managerial Assistance Available: All administrative functions such as contract processing, artwork and initial client billing is done by franchisor. Franchisor produces and delivers the product. Franchisor provides a weekly newsletter and contests to motivate its franchisees.

Information Submitted: May 1987

NATIONAL HOUSING INSPECTIONS
1817 North Hills Boulevard NE
Knoxville, Tennessee 37917
Rex Raney, Rentals Supervisor

Description of Operation: National Housing Inspections is a service-oriented business performing individual inspections of residential and commercial properties for purchasers and/or sellers. Generally, inspections are 90 percent for "used" or existing housing and 10 percent for new homes. NHI makes NO appraisals, merely acts as "house detectives" enabling would-be purchasers to make better decisions, while oftentimes helping them receive better prices, terms.

Number of Franchisees: 301 in 47 States; 1 in Canada.

In Business Since: 1970

Equity Capital Needed: National Housing Inspections is rented for 60 day trial—"Try it before you buy it"—"test before you invest." Rental fee applies to down payment Rent is $29 for 60 days.

Financial Assistance Available: Full purchase price after down payment of $1,250 financed by parent company for up to 48 months, with 2 percent simple interest.

Training Provided: NHI's initial training is augmented by "trail-run" grading sessions and personal follow-up, if needed. Parent firm maintains computerized service of 125,000 housing items, problems, causes, el al, available to dealer through out life-time of franchise.

Managerial Assistance Available: Continuing without cost during life of franchise and/or financing term, whichever is greater, including proven ad information, telephone dialogues, copyrighted inspection sheets and specialized inspectional forms.

Information Submitted: May 1987

NATIONAL TENANT NETWORK, INC.
P. O. Box 1664
Lake Grove, Oregon 97035
Edward F. Byczynski, President

Description of Operation: Unique computerized tenant tracking and screening systrem for residential and commercial tenants. Extremely high cash flow potential.

Number of Franchisees: 3 in Florida, Pennsylvania and Washington

In Business Since: 1981

Equity Capital Needed: $15,000

Financial Assistance Available: Start-up financing

Training Provided: Computer and marketing for 3 month period, when needed.

Managerial Assistance Available: Marketing assistance, bookkeeping, advertising and data control. Hardware and software supplies.

Information Submitted: May 1987

NATIONWIDE INCOME TAX SERVICE COMPANY
14507 West Warren
Dearborn, Michigan 48126
Carl Gilbert, President

Description of Operation: Preparation of State and Federal income tax returns for individuals.

Number of Franchisees: 32 franchised plus 8 company offices

In Business Since: 1965

Equity Capital Needed: Dependent upon number of offices to be opened.

Financial Assistance Available: None

Training Provided: 2 day training period in home office in various phases of income tax preparation and in the systems and procedures developed by Nationwide Tax Service.

Managerial Assistance Available: The company (franchisor) will: assist franchisee in selecting sites most suitable for business; provide guidance for personnel recruitment, selection and training of employees; office layout and design counselling; franchisor designs advertising and promotional materials, recommends media and ad schedules; will maintain continuous liaison with franchisees through mail, telephone.

Information Submitted: May 1987

NEEDLE IN A HAYSTACK AUDIO VIDEO SERVICE CENTER
Gateway Building
Suite 216
Dulles International Airport
Washington, D.C. 20041
James Bowser, Director of Franchise Sales

Description of Operation: Needle in a Haystack Audio Video Service Center delivers what consumres want and need: fast, expert repair of their audio and video components and performance accessories and maintenance products to enhance their audio and video systems. Through service express and our national service center, franchisees can provide this service without the substantial investment a service operation normally demands.

Number of Franchisees: 6 in Ohio, Massachusetts and Virginia

In Business Since: 1974

Equity Capital Needed: A total investment of $115,200-$142,700 is needed (which includes the franchise fee).

Financial Assistance Available: Franchisor does not offer a financing program, but can recommend sources of financing to the franchisee.

Training Provided: An intensive 1 week store manager's training is held at the corporate office and flagship store on all facets of the day-to-day business. A 2 day training is held for the store owner on-site selection, store construction, pre-opening and store operations. On-site training as well as continuous communication with the franchisee is provided.

Managerial Assistance Available: Advertising materials, training seminars, newsletters and on-site support are provided, along with continuous communication regarding sales and service techniques.

Information Submitted: May 1987

OFFICE ALTERNATIVE, INC.
One SeaGate
Suite 1001
Toledo, Ohio 43604
Steven B. Hanson

Description of Operation: By joining the Office Alternative team, you'll offer telephone answering, mail receiving and the use of a time share mini-office. Because of Office Alternative's exclusive telephone answering equipment, you'll be able to offer telephone answering by company name at a cost to you of only $3 per line per month! Imagine being able to offer your services for less than half of what your competition does! Your clients will also be able to receive their mail and have the use of a desk and an office to return calls, open mail, etc. A real Office Alternative!

This business is ideal for adding to an existing business or can be opened in almost any location in just a matter of weeks! Because you'll cater to business clients, your business can be operated successfully during normal business hours. For more information about owning your own Office Alternative franchise or territory, please write to the address above.

Number of Franchisees: 22 in 5 States

In Business Since: 1983

Equity Capital Needed: $10,000 total package.

Financial Assistance Available: Telephone system

Training Provided: Training to be conducted at corporate headquarters in Toledo with all expenses including travel and lodging paid for. Franchisee get "hands-on" training, all necessary manuals and extensive marketing and advertising assistance.

Managerial Assistance Available: Continuous in all phases of operation.

Information Submitted: May 1987

THE OFFICE, LTD.
1111 South Alpine Road
Suite 201
P. O. Box 6391
Rockford, Illinois 61125
Basant Patel

Description of Operation: Custom secretarial service/word processing service.

Number of Franchisees: 2 in Illinois

In Business Since: 1974

Equity Capital Needed: $25,000

Financial Assistance Available: None

Training Provided: 2 weeks in home office, 1 week sales in the franchisee location, and continuing support through the years of the agreement.

Managerial Assistance Available: A book of operations is provided plus monthly newsletter. Personnel available to visit franchise location. A minimum of 2 yearly visits available on call for any problems. Hot line is open for calls from 8:00 a.m. to 5:00 p.m., Monday through Friday. An accounting, marketing and advertising package is provided.

Information Submitted: July 1987

PACKAGING KNOW-HOW AND GIFT SHIPPING INCORPORATED
5400 Cornell Road
Cincinnati, Ohio 45242
Thomas R. Sizer, President

Description of Operation: P.Kg.'s is a unique service business, providing wrapping, packaging, and shipping services for customers wanting to send anything, anywhere in the world. This fresh new concept provides a "hassle-free" retail store environment as well as pick-up services for retail, commercial and industrial customers. System includes exclusive, professional packaging techniques and materials and an array of gift sending merchandise.

Number of Franchisees: 45 in 10 states.

In Business Since: 1983

Equity Capital Needed: Approximately $33,900

Financial Assistance Available: None

Training Provided: Provide an initial training program for franchisee, manager and employees consisting primarily of instruction and discussion concerning franchisor's objectives and policies, operations and use of equipment in franchise business, packaging, shipping, marketing and customer service, as well as business procedures.

Managerial Assistance Available: Provide consultation and assistance on a continuing basis including site selection, store development, marketing and advertising programming and planning, operations planning and routine field visits.

Information Submitted: May 1987

*THE PACKAGING STORE, INC.
8480 East Orchard Road
Englewood, Colorado 80111
Richard T. Godwin, President

Description of Operation: Custom packaging and shipping service. Wholesale and retail sales of packaging supplies.

Number of Franchisees: 130 in 27 States

In Business Since: 1980

Equity Capital Needed: $25,000 to $35,000

Financial Assistance Available: None

Training Provided: Intensive, 1 week mandatory training session for all new franchisees and their employees in an authorized training store and opening assistance at franchise store.

Managerial Assistance Available: The Packaging Store provides continual management service for the life of the franchise in the areas of advertising and marketing, operations and management reviews. Complete manuals of operations, forms and directions are provided. Field managers are available in all regions to work closely with franchisees and visit stores regularly to assist solving problems. The Packaging Store sponsors meetings of franchisees and conducts marketing and product research to maintain high Packaging store consumer acceptance.

Information Submitted: May 1987

PADGETT BUSINESS SERVICES
PBS Building
263 West Clayton Street
Athens, Georgia 30601
Hub Brightwell, Jr., Franchise Division

Description of Operation: PBS grants licenses to individuals who desire to operate their own accounting, income tax and business counseling practice, utilizing the unique forms and successful systems of operations developed by the franchisor. The PBS franchisee remains, at all times, in control of his practice subject only to quality control and performance prescribed by the franchisor. The franchisee markets small to medium-size businesses located in an area which franchisee is able to service from his assigned territory.

Number of Franchisees: 70 in 21 States

In Business Since: 1965, franchising since 1975

Equity Capital Needed: The PBS franchise fee is $12,000 with an additional training fee. First year operating capital is also necessary.

Financial Assistance Available: Yes—through a local financial institution.

Training Provided: The franchisor offers an initial 3 week training program. The first week of this program consists of training in the PBS systems and client services with emphasis on establishing and working a large number of monthly clients; the second week consists of training in the PBS marketing techniques and the third week is held in an established franchise working with the office owner, employees, clients and prospective clients. A fourth week will be in field training conducted by a home office representative.

Managerial Assistance Available: PBS offers 2 seminars annually. One is a thorough 3 day income tax seminar, the other is a 2 day update on PBS procedures and new marketing techniques. There are no charges for these seminars. A year around income tax answering service is also included. Special visits to each franchise office are made to examine additional needs of franchisee and to update PBS forms, tax procedures and marketing advice. Re-training and new employee training are also available at no cost to the franchisee.

Information Submitted: July 1987

PENNYSAVER
80 Eighth Avenue
Suite 315
New York, New York 10011
Allan Horwitz, President

Description of Operation: A free publication offering advertisers total market coverage of the households and businesses throughout the community. Usually delivered by mail, the Pennysaver is recognized as the number 1 local shopping guide throughout the U.S. because the Pennysaver has no wasted or duplicated circulation and little editorial, the advertiser receives more circulation, and at a lower cost than with any daily or weekly newspaper. Many Pennysavers have started out in garges and basements, and have grown into multi-million dollar publishing empires.

Number of Franchisees: Over 200 throughout the United States.

In Business Since: 1973

Equity Capital Needed: $19,000 with a money back gauarantee

Financial Assistance Available: Company sponsored financing available with a down payment of $14,400.

Training Provided: 9 days of classroom, in-field and on-site training for franchisees and their employees. Teaches how to sell Pennysaver advertising, acquire co-op ads from manufacturers, profit from barter, service accounts, design ads, layout the publication, distribution, and bookkeeping. Includes confidential operations manual, audio and video tapes, training films and video-taped role playing sessions.

Managerial Assistance Available: Continuous assistance provided by the home office. Includes our unique "head start" program to get you off to a flying start with $1,500 free printing, a direct mailing to your prospects by the company, and our special charter advertising program to produce immediate income for the franchisee and his advertisers. In addition, the company contributes $1,000 per each new franchise plus 12 percent of all royalty fees for direct mailings, sweepstakes, and other promotions funded 100 percent by the company to produce greater profits for all franchisees.

Information Submitted: July 1987

PENSION ASSISTANCE THROUGH HICKS, INC.
2416 West Shaw Avenue
Fresno, California 93711
Michael L. Temer, Franchise Director

Description of Operation: Qualified Pension and Profit Sharing Plan Administration including plan design, installation, annual administration and actuarial services for the small plan market (employers with fewer than 100 employees).

Number of Franchisees: 23 in 13 States. No additional franchises will be offered until after January 1, 1988.

In Business Since: 1977

Equity Capital Needed: $50,000-$75,000

Financial Assistance Available: None

Training Provided: Initial 2 weeks plus ongoing training classes including regional seminars. Continual phone assistance and support and video tapes.

Managerial Assistance Available: Complete support for plan administration including availability of specialized software. Additional assistance provided in marketing training, and business management techniques including budgeting and goal setting.

Information Submitted: May 1987

PETRO BROKERAGE & SERVICE, LTD.
P. O. Box 568
1645 Falmouth Road
Centerville, Massachusetts 02632
Attn: John Wargin

Description of Operation: National group exclusively servicing petroleum marketers in the following essential areas: company and site appraisals, sales and divestiture service, merger and acquisition specialists, and consultant and valuation opinions.

Number of Franchisees: 11 covering 22 States

In Business Since: 1982

Equity Capital Needed: $9,500-$25,000 plus working capital.

Financial Assistance Available: Notes can be extended for 10 months at 10.5 percent.

Training Provided: 4 days in-house, and approximately 4 days in territory. Additional on-site and call-in reinforcement.

Managerial Assistance Available: Sales, financial, and operational furnished; with constant support and update monthly.

Information Submitted: July 1987

PEYRON ASSOCIATES, INC.
P. O. Box 175
Sellersburg, Indiana 47172
Dan Peyron, President

Description of Operation: Company provides a series of warranty services to Tax Services firms, public accountants and others already engaged in the tax return preparation business. Company also provides other services (see below) thru individual licensing agreements which give the franchisee the right to sub franchise, become a franchisor or a national distributor of the companies two monthly newsletters, one for tax practitioners and one for the general public.

Number of Franchisees: 200 in 20 States

In Business Since: 1960

Equity Capital Needed: Minimum $500

Financial Assistance Available: Numerous installment plans for large multi office operations.

Training Provided: None, franchise available only to tax service owners, public accountants and others with tax return preparation experience.

Managerial Assistance Available: Monthly newsletters for managers and owners plus separate newsletters for clients. Company provides tax audit warranty services to clients and compensation to franchisee for audit work, reimbursement for mistakes and other warranties plus technical assistance on tax matters the year round.

Information Submitted: May 1987

PILOT AIR FREIGHT CORPORATION
Route 352
P. O. Box 97
Lima, Pennsylvania 19037
John J. Edwards, President

Description of Operation: Pilot provides the service of handling air freight shipping requirements of their customers both domestically and internationally.

Number of Franchisees: 62 in 29 States, Canada and Puerto Rico.

In Business Since: 1970

Equity Capital Needed: $10,000-$30,000 determined by market.

Financial Assistance Available: None

Training Provided: 2 weeks classroom, pilot headquarters, with emphasis on operation, customer service, sales and accounting procedures.

Managerial Assistance Available: Ongoing communications with corporate headquarters and visitation by Pilot regional managers.

Information Submitted: July 1987

PINNACLE 1 INTERNATIONAL, INC.
3350 Lenape Street
North Charleston, South Carolina 29405
Bob Roe

Description of Operation: Pinnacle 1 International, Inc., is a tax/accounting franchisee serving the public and small business.

Number of Franchisees: 30 in South Carolina, North Carolina, Georgia and Florida.

In Busniess Since: 1981

Equity Capital Needed: $25,000

Financial Assistance Available: None

Training Provided: Back up assistance for the duration of the franchise.

Managerial Assistance Available: Computer systems and technical back up.

Information Submitted: May 1987

PNS, INC.
P. O. Box 428
Racine, Wisconsin 53401
Rexford M. Rossi, President

Description of Operation: PNS, Inc., (Pack'N Ship and Packy the Shipper) is a franchisor of local packing and shipping locations specializing in parcel post packages for the general public and small business. Generally this is an addedum to a retail or wholesale operation which adds this service to build additional in-store traffic and create extra cash sales.

Number of Franchisees: 1,125 in 48 States

In Business Since: 1981

Equity Capital Needed: $995-$1,295

Financial Assistance Available: Investment includes materials, equipment and to introduce the program, no other funds are necessary except to replace supplies as needed.

Training Provided: Training on franchise's premises by trained representative including audio-visual cassettes and operations manual.

Managerial Assistance Available: Periodic calls by representative—WATS line available for information on operations—strong support from home office for record maintenance and claim activity. A continuous co-op program instituted.

Information Submitted: May 1987

PONY MAILBOX AND BUSINESS CENTER, INC.
13110 Northeast 177th Place
Woodinville, Washington 98072
Robert E. Howell, President

Description of Operation: Commercial mail receiving center, providing private mailboxes, Western Union, FAX (electronic mail), U.P.S. and Emery Shipping and Receiving, word processing, cartons and mailing supplies, answering service, business cards, wedding announcements, stationery, parcel packing, rubber stamps and copying machine work. Serving the small business and private sector of a community with emphasis on "service!"

Number of Franchisees: 5 in Washington, Oregon, Illinois, Texas and California

In Business Since: 1986

Equity Capital Needed: $37,000-$42,000 is necessary to open a Pony Mailbox and Business Center.

Financial Assistance Available: Franchisor does not provide financing. The equity capital purchases all the necessary equipment and supplies to begin operations. Estimated costs for leadhold improvements are included in the equity capital needed by the franchisee. Franchisee must arrange his or her own financing, if needed.

Training Provided: Intensive, but personalized 3-4 day mandatory training course for all new franchisees. Course provided at home office and conducted by corporate officers who operate their own Pony Mailbox and Business Center. Refresher course given at no cost upon request of franchisee.

Managerial Assistance Available: Pony Mailbox and Business Center provides continual advisory assistance for the life of the franchise on the services offered by a franchisee and the marketing of the services. Franchisor furnishes manuals on operations, forms and directions are provided. Franchisor offers advisory assistance for new services introduced by franchisor and approved services desired by the franchisee to meet local market conditions. Franchisor assists with location advice, layout and design of the franchise business.

Information Submitted: May 1987

THE PRIME-PM CORPORATION
1117 Perimeter Center West
5th Floor East
Atlanta, Georgia 30338
Paul D. Lapides, President

Description of Operation: Real estate management franchise for existing experienced real estate management firms with good reputation and proven ability.

Number of Franchisees: 48 in 25 States

In Business Since: 1980

Equity Capital Needed: $10,000

Financial Assistance Available: None

Training Provided: Intensive 3 day mandatory training course is scheduled for all new franchisees. On-site training and assistance also provided.

Managerial Assistance Available: Prime-PM provides management and marketing assistance for the life of the franchise. Complete series of operation manuals are provided. Insurance review programs, tax assistance, mass purchasing programs also provided.

Information Submitted: July 1987

PRINCETON ENERGY PARTNERS, INC.
2221 Stackhouse Drive
Yardley, Pennsylvania 19067
David M. Brown, President

Description of Operation: Market comfort improvement and energy savings to the home owner and new construction markets and deliver and instrumented energy analysis and retrofit service based on technology originally developed at Princeton University under a U.S. Department of Energy grant.

Number of Franchisees: 8 in Pennsylvania, New York and Minnesota.

In Business Since: 1981

Equity Capital Needed: $45,000 to $77,000

Financial Assistance Available: None

Training Provided: 1 week intensive training of Princeton, New Jersey, followed by a week of on-the-job training with other franchisees. Followed by a 3 day training at franchisee's location, followed a month later by a 2 day training at franchisee's location. Training covers all technical and marketing aspects of delivering instrumented energy analysis and retrofitting services in residential building markets.

Managerial Assistance Available: P.E.P. provides ongoing technical, marketing, and managerial assistance for the life of the franchise through its home office and field representatives. P.E.P. sponsors franchisee meetings and sponsors market development on behalf of franchisees. P.E.P. technical staff is closely connected to the residential energy research community.

Information Submitted: July 1987

PRIORITY MANAGEMENT SYSTEMS, INC.
2401 Gateway Drive
Suite 115
Irving, Texas 75063-2728
Jonathan Harshaw, Manager, Franchise Marketing

Description of Operation: Priority Management is the 1 management training franchise in North America. Franchisees work with busy professionals and instruct them in the development of personal effectiveness skills.

Number of Franchisees: 60 in 17 States plus 60 in Canada.

In Business Since: 1984

Equity Capital Needed: $35,000 including franchise fee.

Financial Assistance Available: None

TrainingProvided: 2 weeks intensive training in the "Priority Management" program. 6 days in-house plus 1 week in-field. Minimum 3 follow-up training sessions each year.

Managerial Assistance Available: Teach franchisee the "Priority Management" program. Sales techniques, presentation skills, marketing methods, bookkeeping, general business management skills. Work with franchisee on sales calls, conduct (at franchisee's request) first 2 workshops.

Information Submitted: May 1987

*PROFORMA, INC.
4705 Van Epps Road
Cleveland, Ohio 44131
John Campbell, Director of Franchise Development

Description of Operation: Business products. Distributors of business forms, commercial printing, office supplies, computer supplies, and computers. This is not a quick print shop or retail operation.

Number of Franchisees: 33 in 17 States

In Business Since: 1978, franchising started 1985

Equity Capital Needed: $15,000-$25,000

Financial Assistance Available: Available for qualified and needy individuals.

Training Provided: Up to 2 weeks intensive training program covering industry/product knowledge and selling skills.

Managerial Assistance Available: Franchise owner does not need to hire any administrative employees because most administrative functions are performed by franchisor. Franchisor answers franchisee's telephone (toll free number), generates billings, does computer input, logs cash receipts, and generates monthly business reports. Continuous managerial advice is available from an experienced team of professionals in selling, product knowledge, manufacturer sourcing, and administration.

Information Submitted: May 1987

PROPERTY DAMAGE APPRAISERS, INC.
P. O. Box 9230
Fort Worth, Texas 76107
David T. Clayton, President

Description of Operation: Property Damage Appraisers, Inc., grants franchises to highly qualified automobile damage appraisers in cities with sufficient business potential to provide a good income for the franchisee.

Number of Franchisees: 148 in all States except Hawaii and Montana

In Business Since: 1963

Equity Capital Needed: $3,000-$10,000

Financial Assistance Available: None, Property Damage Appraisers does not sell franchises, we provide all forms, procedure manual, advertising materials and marketing service—equity capital required is needed to purchase office equipment, automobile, insurance and etc., necessary to start a business.

Training Provided: No formal training program is provided as only experienced appraisers are considered.

Managerial Assistance Available: Through a staff of regional managers we provide at least 2 weeks of intensive marketing support when an office opens. A bookkeeping system is provided at no cost to franchisee and is installed by a company accounting representative. Periodic visits are made by regional managers to market services of all franchisees.

Information Submitted: July 1987

PROPERTY INSPECTION SERVICE
1741 Saratoga Avenue
Suite 106
San Jose, California 95129
Ben Vitcov, President

Description of Operation: Property Inspection Service Provides residential building inspections for the purpose of giving the prospective buyer a full disclosure of the structural and mechanical condition of the property. The inspection includes a roof to foundation inspection and the electrical, plumbing and heating systems.

Number of Franchisees: 4 in California

In Business Since: 1980

Equity Capital Needed: $50,000

Financial Assistance Available: None

Training Provided: Full training for field inspector and one office person. Training is performed at our San Jose location and includes 30 days of actual operational experience.

Managerial Assistance Available: Property Inspection Service provides all computer software including updates. All operational manuals and forms. A dynamic statewide marketing program and continuing education program is also provided to all franchises.

Information Submitted: May 1987

PROTOCOL MESSAGE MANAGEMENT CENTERS, INC.
12200 Sunrise Valley Drive
Reston, Virginia 22091
F. R. Jacques, President

Description of Operation: The grant of conversion and strat-up franchises to the telephone answering service industry.

Number of Franchisees: 20 in 8 States

In Business Since: 1985

Equity Capital Needed: Conversion—$30,000 to $51,000. Start-up—$189,500 to $362,000.

Financial Assistance Available: The franchisor provides financing on the initial franchise fee of up to $15,000 through the execution of a promissory note.

Training Provided: A professional management module which provides for the initial training to new franchisees. This indoctrination course lasts 6 days. Additionally, other ongoing training in areas of telereceptionists training, supervisors training and sales and marketing training which run for an average of 3 days.

Managerial Assistance Available: Protocol offers their franchisees managerial assistance through an extensive training program outlined above plus additional managerial assistance from field consultants employed by Protocol who regularly travel to the franchisee's location to provide ongoing feedback on the management and operation of the bureaus. Also, Protocol offers its franchisees an 800 action line that franchisees can call for assistance. In the area of technical assistance, Protocol has an engineering staff that offers support to the franchisees when there is a major equipment problem, when the decision has been made to convert their equipment to an automated system, and when dealing with the telephone company.

Information Submitted: May 1987

PROVENTURE, INC.
79 Parkingway
Quincy, Massachusetts 02169
Leo F. Meady, Chairman

Description of Operation: Professional business brokers—specializing in the listing and sale of medium priced going businesses. Also represent franchise companies in the sale and location of their franchised units.

Number of Franchisees: 10 plus 1 company-owned in Massachusetts, Pennsylvania and New Jersey. Seeking franchisees for all areas of the U.S.

In Business Since: 1979

Equity Capital Needed: $15,000 franchise fee plus about $30,000 for working capital.

Financial Assistance Available: None

Training Provided: Intensive classroom training program for 1 week in Quincy, followed by on-the-job training in franchisee's own office. Assistance offered in recruiting and training commissioned sales staff. proVENTURE prefers that franchisees (of their associates) have real estate licenses, or they obtain one as soon as possible.

Managerial Assistance Available: Continued training and management assistance for all franchised units. Parent company co-ordinates the distribution of "VENTURElist" to all offices. "VENTURElist" contains all the listings of all local offices plus selected listings nationally. Participating franchisees share proportionately in the sale of business listed by one office and sold by another.

Information Submitted: May 1987

REALTY COUNSEL BROKERAGE MANAGEMENT CORPORATION
199 East Linda Mesa, Suite 12
Danville, California 94526
D. LeMoine Bond, President

Description of Operation: Realty Counsel franchisees are independently practicing general real estate brokers who are interfacing single agency, flat fee consultive brokerage techniques as an alternative to the consumer over the traditional commission methods. Regional "Broker Consultant" licensing is selectively available to experienced brokers. Both non-contingent fee and contingent fee methods are utilized within the realty counsel sales methods.

Number of Franchisees: 8 in California

In Business Since: 1979

Equity Capital Needed: $8,500 minimum broker consultant license, $1,000 minimum initial fee for franchisee. No other projections are made 5 percent royalty—$5,000 maximum per year.

Financial Assistance Available: Franchise financing available.

Training Provided: Broker reorientation; plus unlimited management consultation and support. No rookie recruiting or freshman training for salesmen. Only broker and franchisee training for the client related consultive broker. Periodic technical sessions and support media and personal telephone consultation. Video franchise and client sales presentation. Operations manuals and contracts.

Managerial Assistance Available: Continuous brokerage management assistance for the duration of the franchise. Advertising media packages, referrals, because of the nature and degree of sophistication that is required of a Realty Counsel, the firm recommends university, and college post graduate training plus certain approved certification and continuing education of the bar and realty professions.

Information Submitted: May 1987

*RECOGNITION EXPRESS INTERNATIONAL, LTD.
(formerly BADGEMAN)
31726 Rancho Viejo Road
Suite 115 (Dept. DC)
San Juan Capistrano, California 92675
Richard L. Ferguson, President

Description of Operation: Recognition Express franchise owners manufacture and sell Corporate Recognition and Specialty Advertising products—personalized badges, nameplates, plaques, awards, office signage, buttons, lapel pins, to name a few. Recognition Express is the oldest and largest chain of full service recognition shops. Our owners have been providing service to medium and large corporations. Our customers include Hilton Hotels, Century 21 Real Estate, Baskin Robbins, Rotary, Mary Kay Cosmetics, etc. Recognition Express dealers operate from a commercial location. Our shops feature state of the art showrooms and do light manufacturing with the latest technology including computer engraving, automatic hot stamping, and automatic pinning machines. In addition other items are offered which are purchased from approved trade suppliers.

Number of Franchisees: 100 throughout the U.S. and 50 units throughout Canada, U.K., Sweden, Australia, and Belgium

In Business Since: Founder began manufacturing name badges in 1972. BadgeMan franchises were first awarded in 1974 to part time, homebased owners who manufactured name badges only. Recognition express units tested since 1981, franchised since 1983.

Equity Capital Needed: $27,000

Financial Assistance Available: A total investment of $60,000 to $90,000 is needed to cover opening inventory, equipment, franchise fee, training costs, start up promotion and advertising, as well as working capital. Financing can be arranged fro $60,000.

Training Provided: An intensive training course is conducted for the new owner at the home office. A field development person will help you in your new shop during opening. He will insure that you are capable of developing your business properly.

Managerial Assistance Available: Complete ongoing support and managerial assistance in all phases of the business.

Information Submitted: May 1987

RELIABLE BUSINESS SYSTEMS, INC.
19 Ransom Road
Newton, Massachusetts 02159
M. Michael Licker, President

Description of Operation: Firm publishes the Reliable Business and Tax Service System, a service designed to meet the needs of all business, offering them a bookkeeping system that complies with all Federal and State tax laws, together with an advisory service.

Number of Franchisees: 3 in Vermont and Massachusetts

In Business Since: 1955

Equity Capital Needed: $1,950

Financial Assistance Available: None

Training Provided: 1 week in the field training by another experienced distributor and further training at the home office if needed, continuous upgrading of distributor's knowledge.

Managerial Assistance Available: Continuous flow of new material, home office consultation available on an unlimited and continuous basis. Close contact with distributor maintained. Additional help regarding tax matters for client when called upon through homeoffice accounting tax staff.

Information Submitted: July 1987

ROOM-MATE REFERRAL SERVICE CENTERS, INC.
P. O. Box 94305
Oklahoma City, Oklahoma 73143
Florence S. Cook, President

Description of Operation: Room-Mate Referral Service Center is a service company that handles the placement of persons as roommates, for economic and a variety of other needs.

Number of Franchisees: 8 in Texas, Oklahoma, Pennsylvania and California

In Business Since: 1979

Equity Capital Needed: $3,500 to $30,000

Financial Assistance Available: Our franchise fee is determined by the population of the franchise area. The franchise can be from $7,500 to $45,000. We would carry one-third of the franchise fee on a promisory note.

Training Provided: We have a 3-1/2 day training session at the home office. We also help the franchisee find the right location, help with grand opening, also give ongoing assistance.

Managerial Assistance Available: We give continuous assistance for the life of the franchise. We assist with new advertising ideas and training on new services that we are adding. We are always available to solve any problems that may come up.

Information Submitted: May 1987

SANDY HOOK SCIENTIFIC, INC.
P. O. Box 539
Columbia, North Carolina 27925
D. N. Sneed, CDP

Description of Operation: An opportunity exists to aid owner-operated small business to plan, develop and control qualified goals for improvement of service to its market and consequently to increase profits. Using proven techniques and (in most cases) a small computer, the results can be most dramatic and far-reaching.

Number of Franchisees: 7 in Connecticut, New York, Massachusetts, and North Carolina

In Business Since: 1976

Equity Capital Needed: $5,000 plus ability to live on reduced income for first few months of operation.

Financial Assistance Available: None

Training Provided: 5 day training course at the home office school with visits to local clients. Assistance is given to franchisee at his location to find clients, install initial phases of system and to follow-up programs. On a continuing basis there is constant monitoring of progress and results.

Managerial Assistance Available: New business leads to supplement franchisees efforts. Project and program products constantly being developed/refined. Assistance with monitoring and controlling projects. Additional training as required. Manuals and other training aids for clients.

Information Submitted: July 1987

*SARA CARE FRANCHISE CORPORATION
1200 Golden Key Circle
Suite 368
El Paso, Texas 79925
Sara Addis, President

Description of Operation: Sales of Sara Care Service franchise—specializing in temporary companion aaand home support personnel. Provides companion care, sleepovers, baby/child sitters, house sitters, hospital sitters, pet sitters, plant/garden sitters, drop-ins (companion, teens, pets, house) and sub-contracting services to all home health agencies and hospitals. We pride ourselves in being the largest franchisor of specialized services in the United States and the first company specifically organized to concentrate in the field of home support personnel.

Number of Franchisees: 46 in 18 States

In Business Since: 1978, franchising since 1983.

Equity Capital Needed: Initial fee ranges from $12,500-$25,500. Total investment ranges from $35,975 to $48,475.

Financial Assistance Available: We will negotiate with persons interested in purchasing more than one franchise.

Training Provided: A 5-business day intensive management training program at corporate headquarters. Training will continue even after the opening of your office to sharpen your skills and to make certain that your new business is operating as efficiently as possible. You even have the option of 1 week of on-site training at your location.

Managerial Assistance Available: You will have an effective support system behind you at corporate headquarters every step of the way. You will receive instructions and constant updates in the use of all Sara Care manuals and forms in addition to training in recruiting, interviewing, and applicant processing techniques as well as detailed training and handling customer requirements.

Information Submitted: May 1987

SAV-PAC—THE MONEY SAVER
6115 Wirhc Road
Cincinnati, Ohio 45237
P. Thomas Ellinor, Ph.D.,President

Description of Operation: Cooperative direct mail. Printing

Number of Franchisees: 6

In Business Since: 1978

Equity Capital Needed: $12,000-$35,000

Financial Assistance Available: Partial

Training Provided: Yes, through S.O.P. and home office support.

Managerial Assistance Available: S.O.P. and managerial assistance.

Information Submitted: May 1987

SELECTRA-DATE CORPORATION
2175 Lemoine Avenue
Ft. Lee, New Jersey 07024
Robert Friedman, President

Description of Operation: Computer-dating has been around since Art Linkletter started playing matching games with a Univac Computer in the late fifties. But that was just for laughs. Today its for love and money, with a score of computer-dating firms throughout the country reporting brisk business. Selectra-Date, one of the pioneers, now offers a complete turnkey package that makes it possible for any reputable individual with a sound business or professional background to enter this facinating work. Since all computer processing is handled entirely by the company, no technical knowledge is required.

Number of Franchisees: 9 in 10 States

In Business Since: 1967, oldest existing franchise operational since 1969

Equity Capital Needed: $6,000 to $10,000

Financial Assistance Available: The total required investment for promotional material, initial advertising, franchise fee, and for forms and stationery is $9,000, of which Selectra-Date will finance $3,500 for qualified franchisees. In addition the franchisee should have sufficient capital to adequately equip his office and to see him through the first 30 days of operation.

Training Provided: A full-time Selectra-Date executive thoroughly trains each franchisee in all phases of the business during the first week he is in operation.

Managerial Assistance Available: Selectra-Date furnishes continuing individual guidance and support in all phases of the franchisee's operation.

Information Submitted: May 1987

THE SIGNERY CORPORATION
614 West 5th Avenue
Naperville, Illinois 60540
Richard Gretz, President

Description of Operation: The Signery Quick Service Sign Shops offer a new and different approach to sign making service. Automated with computer driven equipment franchises serve almost exclusively other businesses. Store sizes range from 800 to 1,200 square feet. No artistic or sign making experience is needed. Ideal for husband and wife teams or multiple store ownership.

Number of Franchisees: 8 in Illinois and Ohio

In Business Since: 1986

Equity Capital Needed: Varies according to size and leasing - $30,000-$60,000.

Financial Assistance Available: Will assist in obtaining financing and equipment leasing.

Training Provided: Complete and extensive classroom and in-store training at corporate headquarters in Naperville, Illinois, lasting 2 weeks. Ongoing support and continued training from field personnel for life of agreement.

Managerial Assistance Available: The Signery parent company is dedicated to providing ongoing support in creative design, profitable and effective business management, and advertising/marketing.

Information Submitted: May 1987

*SIGN EXPRESS
6 Clarke Circle
P. O. Box 309
Bethel, Connecticut 06801
Gary A. Gass, National Sales Manager

Description of Operation: Company offers complete sign store that offers 24 hour service. Signs are made by a computer with complete design functions. Signs include indoor and outdoor signs, vehicle lettering magnetic signs, banners, business signs.

Number of Franchisees: 8 in 6 states

In Business Since: 1985

Equity Capital Needed: $12,000 to $25,000

Financial Assistance Available: A total investment of $25,000 to $40,000 is necessary to open a Sign Express store. Up to $18,000 can be financed by qualified buyers.

Training Provided: 1 week in sign layout, design and sign shop operations at company operated sign shop.

Managerial Assistance Available: Sign Express offers technical assistance, newsletters, telephone consultation and workshops.

Information Submitted: May 1987

*SIGN STOP, INC.
191 Post Road West
Westport, Connecticut 06880
John Oudheusden, President

Description of Operation: Strong customer demand and new technology creates the opportunity to market high quality custom signs to small businesses. Operating from a store location and using computer-generated vinyl lettering, Sign Stop fabricates custom signs, trade exhibits, banners, graphs and charts, backlit awnings, and lettering for vans, trucks, and boats.

Number of Franchisees: 2 in Connecticut and Massachusetts

In Business Since: 1985

Equity Capital Needed: $58,000

Financial Assistance Available: Independent company offers equipment lease.

Training Provided: No experience is necessary. Company provides minimum of 1 week traiing, operations manual, plus on-site assistance.

Managerial Assistance Available: Sign Stop offers ongoing marketing and advertising assistance, on-site visits, seminars and newsletters.

Information Submitted: May 1987

*SMI INTERNATIONAL, INC.
(SUCCESS MOTIVATION INSTITUTE, INC.)
1600 Lake Air Drive
Waco, Texas 76710
Charles G. Williams

Description of Operation: The Company's international distributorship organization markets specialized management, sales, and personal development programs to individuals, companies, governments, and other organizations. Materials are printed and recorded, using modern learning methods, personal goal setting, and management by objective techniques.

Number of Franchisees: Approximately 3,000 in 50 States and 26 foreign countries.

In Business Since: 1960

Equity Capital Needed: $20,000

Financial Assistance Available: Financial assistance provided.

Training Provided: Complete distributorship training program in printed and recorded form furnished with initial investment; continuous home office sales training and sales management seminars available monthly. Field sales training also available in many areas.

Managerial Assistance Available: Continuous sales consultant assistance provided by home office to distributors through use of monthly mailings, telephone and prompt response to mail communications.

Information Submitted: May 1987

SNC TELECOM PROBLEM SOLVERS
101 West Waukau Avenue
Oshkosh, Wisconsin 54901
Wally Petersen

Description of Operation: Providing sales, installation and consultation services to businesses with telecommunication problems. Customers include telephone and electric power utilities, interconnects and businesses with their own computer, telephone and data equipment. Proven product line with 15 year sales history. Only source for many items. Exclusive territories. Individual and master franchises available.

Number of Franchisees: 2 in Texas

In Business Since: 1986

Equity Capital Needed: $18,500-$47,400

Financial Assistance Available: None

Training Provided: Training and support provided by franchisor: intensive 8 day managerial, sales and technical training at corporate headquarters plus 5 days in-market start-up assistance. Comprehensive operations manual.

Managerial Assistance Available: Continuing technical support and seminars.

Information Submitted: May 1987

SOUND TRACKS RECORDING STUDIO, INC.
424 Parkway
Sevierville, Tennessee 37862
J. Andre Veal, Franchise Director

Description of Operation: Sound Tracks allows the general public to record their voice on over 300 pre-recorded tapes. They can do audio or video productions in many of our studios across the U.S.

Number of Franchisees: 27 in 14 States

In Business Since: 1984

Equity Capital Needed: Approximately $60,000. $40,000 minimum.

Financial Assistance Available: Finance of hard cost, such as equipment.

Training Provided: At the franchisee's location—1 week.

Managerial Assistance Available: At he franchisee's location—1 week.

Information Submitted: June 1987

SOUTHWEST PROMOTIONAL CORPORATION
P. O. Box 81023
San Diego, California 92138
Jerry Nesler, President

Description of Operation: SouthWest Promotional Corporation offers a proofs-of-purchase, advertising and marketing plan for franchisees to sell to radio, television and cable TV stations or to operate themselves. A franchisee's territory may include an area, one state, or more. The franchisee, besides receiving cash income from each station's advertising sales through the marketing plan, in addition, receives a number of broadcast commercial spot announcements, as additional payment, with each station signed. The "network" of spot announcements may be sold to advertisers, by the franchisee, for additional franchisee income or barter. Potential franchisees may be multi-station representatives, advertising agencies, sales marketing companies, experienced men and women broadcast advertising sales representatives or other experienced media sales persons. Telephone: 619/588-0664.

Number of Franchisees: 15 in the West

In Business Since: 1970—franchising since 1975

Equity Capital Needed: $10,000 area. Equity capital required for a territory is separately negotiated according to size and potential.

Financial Assistance Available: Yes

Training Provided: 2 weeks training in franchisee's own area or territory. Training by an experienced existing franchisee or by the franchisor. Also, additional assistance with any franchisee advertising sales through franchisor's existing account lict and from account lists of other existing franchisees.

Managerial Assistance Available: Continual assistance for the life of the franchise.

Information Submitted: May 1987

STORK NEWS OF AMERICA
6537 Raeford Road
Fayetteville, North Carolina 28304
John Nelson, Franchise Director

Description of Operation: Newborn announcement service. Announce new arrivals by large stork in front yard, office or any location desired by parents, grandparents, friends, etc. Also retail other pre birth products, stork wireing in F.T.D. fashion.

Number of Franchisees: 78 in 28 States and Canada

In Business Since: 1984

Equity Capital Needed: $5,000

Financial Assistance Available: None

Training Provided: Book, telephone and visit the headquarters, newsletter..

Managerial Assistance Available: Assistance ongoing to help them and develop business

Information Submitted: May 1987

STUFFIT COMPANY, INC.
12450 Automobile Boulevard
Clearwater, Florida 33520
Regina Anderson

Description of Operation: Co-operative direct mail advertising program.

Number of Franchisees: 17 in Florida, Louisiana, Alabama and New Jersey

In Business Since: 1978

Equity Capital Needed: $25,000

Financial Assistance Available: None

Training Provided: 1 week of training in plant for systems, product knowledge, and sales techniques. One week of training in the field to set up office procedures and make sales calls.

Managerial Assistance Available: Ongoing assistance to franchisees' to help them with training and development of their geographical area.

Information Submitted: July 1987

SUPER COUPS
180 Bodwell Street
Avon, Massachusetts 02322
Scott Berry, President

Description of Operation: Super Coups franchises service local retailers and contractors by mailing money savings coupons to local residents. Corporate headquarters handles all manufacturing. Franchises responsibilities include sales and service of local and regional advertisers and management of accounts and collection of payments due. Each protected territory totals 60,000 homes.

Number of Franchisees: 40 in 8 States

In Business Since: 1982

Financial Assistance Available: In addition to training, start-up manuals, samples, etc., the first 40,000 homes are mailed at 50 percent off regular charge. This provides the new owner with positive cash flow from the beginning.

Training Provided: Intensive 1 week training at Corporate headquarters and field training of 1 week preceed our ongoing education which addresses the specific details an owner needs to know on a day-to-day basis to be successful in the field of co-operative direct mail advertising.

Managerial Assistance Available: Super Coups provides a wide range of managerial and technical assistance via 800 phone lines, meetings, franchise conferences, newsletter and bulletins. Coverage includes sales,marketing, book-keeping, accounting, operations, recruitment, training, finance, advertising layouts and design, as well as specific problem identification and solution forums.

Information Submitted: May 1987

TAX MAN, INC.
674 Massachusetts Avenue
Cambridge, Massachusetts 02139
Robert G. Murray, President

Description of Operation: Preparation of individual income tax returns. Interested in franchisees in

New England Only.

Number of Franchisees: 6 in Massachusetts plus 20 company-owned units.

In Business Since: 1967

Equity Capital Needed: $4,500 minimum plus means of support for first 2 years.

Financial Assistance Available: Advertising support. Bookkeeping income opportunity for rest of year.

Training Provided: Tax preparation training (8 weeks). Tax office management training (3 days).

Managerial Assistance Available: Complete tax advice, management assistance, site selection, advertising and marketing.

Information Submitted: May 1987

TAX OFFICES OF AMERICA
Box 4098
Waterville, Connecticut 06714
Gregg Nolan, Franchise Director

Description of Operation: Income tax preparation for individuals and small businesses. Thorough training program, exclusive territories. Estate planning and business consulting services.

Number of Franchisees: 15

In Business Since: 1966

Equity Capital Needed: Approximately $12,000 plus $7,500 working capital.

Financial Assistance Available: Financing arranged through Horizons of America, Inc., parent company.

Training Provided: About 2 weeks training provided at Waterbury headquarters, 2 weeks at franchisee's location plus a mail order course. If available in franchisee's area the company pays all expenses to a special training course set up by a nationally known organization.

Managerial Assistance Available: Company always available for counseling, plus on-site office organization.

Information Submitted: May 1987

54

TBC BUSINESS BROKERS, INC.
1171 Main Avenue
Warwick, Rhode Island 02886
Stephen A. Brassard, President

Description of Operation: A New England network of business brokerage offices specializing in the marketing of businesses and franchises. We have a developed method of evaluating and marketing of companies ranging from the mom and pop operations to the large corporations. Cooperation thru our network enables brokers to reach a large market.

Number of Franchisees: 3 in Massachusetts and Rhode Island

In Business Since: 1978

Equity Capital Needed: Approximately $30,000-$40,000 including $14,000 franchise fee.

Financial Assistance Available: None

Training Provided: 1 week training at corporate office by the owner, followed by 1 week training in the field, followed by training at franchisee's office. Support will be provided to you on a continuous basis and will take the form of assisting you with obtaining listings, evaluation and sales techniques.

Managerial Assistance Available: Supervision will be provided to assist franchisees from the corporate office on an ongoing basis. Assistance will be provided in recruiting, training, advertising, marketing, sales, closings, office management, etc. Management support will be available by telephone, and regular office visits.

Information Submitted: May 1987

∗TENDER SENDER VENTURE
7370 S.W. Durham Road
Portland, Oregon 97224-7307

Description of Operation: Tender Sender is a unique opportunity to provide a vital service to consumers in the retail community. It provides the chance to be a part of a new and exciting concept which offers professional gift wrapping, packaging, and shipping in stores located in major malls.

Number of Franchisees: 35 throughout the United States

In Business Since: 1982

Equity Capital Needed: Approximately $45,000-$85,000

Financial Assistance Available: None

Training Provided: Comprehensive 5-day classroom and in-store training program prior to store opening. Ongoing training and support provided as necessary.

Managerial Assistance Available: Tender Sender will continue to be a vital source of supplies, information, and direction to the franchise owner.

Information Submitted: May 1987

TOTE-A-SHOWER, INC.
R. 1, Box 172
Toledo, Illinois 62468
Kathy Black, President

Description of Operation: Tote-A-Shower offers an unique at home franchise business. Our franchisees may work out of their homes to provide baby showers, bridal showers, and birthday party services. Each franchisee is guaranteed an exclusive territory. Tote-A-Shower also offers the unique opportunity to share in the profits of a new franchisee by the recruiting franchisee.

Number of Franchisees: 9 in Illinois, 3 in Indiana

In Business Since: 1985

Equity Capital Needed: $1,150

Financial Assistance Available: None

Training Provided: 1 day program plus VCR tape and training manual

Managerial Assistance Available: Each new franchisee is given written instructions as well as the on-the-spot assistance from an experienced franchisee owner at the first showing and during the first party.

Information Submitted: May 1987

TRANSFORMATIONAL TECHNOLOGIES
207-D Second Street
Sausalito, California 94965
Gordon Starr, Vice President

Description of Operation: Management consulting, management training and related organizational services.

Number of Franchisees: 50 in the United States, Canada and Europe

In Business Since: 1984

Equity Capital Needed: $20,000 iniial fee plus 3 months operating capital (variable).

Financial Assistance Available: None

Training Provided: 2 day orientation, 5 day program/technology training, 3 day advanced training program, 2 day business skills workshop, 3 days sales training, 240 hours video tape training.

Managerial Assistance Available: On-call coaching, site reveiw, and 1 meeting annually for purpose of technical development.

Information Submitted: May 1987

* TRIMARK
184 Quigley Boulevard
P.O. Box 10530
New Castle, Delaware 19720
Wilmington, DE 19720
Contact: David H. Clayton, Senior V.P. Sales & Marketing

Description of Operation: Co-op direct mail marketing company. Franchisor is a printing and publishing company in the business of co-op direct mail advertising which consists of mailing advertisements, usually in the form of redeemable coupons and special discount notices, to homes throughout the United States. TriMark has refined the co-op concept, which brings together non-competitive business into a single "coupon" package. TriMark can assist the businessman in targeting his market area in as few as 10,000 homes or in excess of 20 million homes on an annual basis.

Number of Franchisees: 10 in 29 States

In Business Since: 1969. Franchising sicne 1977

Equity Capital Needed: $24,900-$33,900 (varies with size of exclusive territory granted).

Financial Assistance Available: TriMark provides, to the new franchisee, a "Cash Flow Assistance Program" which, at no charge by TriMark, will produce the franchisee's first mailing to 20 thousand homes. Franchisee's obligation is for postage only.

Training Provided: 1 week of intensive in-house classroom training. Franchisor has developed and provides to franchisee a system of operation,uniform standards, quality and uniformity of products and services offered. The training consists of procedures for layout design, artwork, printing, labeling and inserting. Heavy emphasis on marketing, sales, administration, procedures for bookkeeping, accounting. In-field training provided. Operation and sales manual provided.

Managerial Assistance Available: Continual regional meetings, field support, marketing, and technical assistance.

Information Submitted: May 1987

* TRIPLE CHECK INCOME TAX SERVICE
727 South Main Street
Burbank, California 91506
David W. Lieberman, President

Description of Operation: Triple Check Income Tax Service offers a unique method of operating a tax preparation business utilizing a proprietary interview worksheet system integrated with an all-encompassing training program and year-round technical assistance. Group promotional programs and a sophisticated, low cost computer service are also an integral feature of a Triple Check Franchise. Through a sister company, Triple Check Financial Services, Inc., a fully registered (NASD-SIPC) broker/dealer, franchisees also have the opportunity to qualify to provide financial and investment services to clients.

Number of Franchisees: 223 offices in 29 States

In Business Since: 1968

Equity Capital Needed: Ownership of a pre-existing business offering tax preparation services or approximately $5,000

Financial Assistance Available: Triple Check offers indirect financing in that the company may act as a guarantor with respect to loans made by an outside commercial bank in payment of the company's annual fees and for those participating in certain advertising programs. These loans are short-term (less than 1 year) made by an outside commercial bank.

Training Provided: Triple Check offers a comprehensive 72 hour training in the first year designed to familiarize franchisees and his employees with the "Triple Check" system, to improve their existing expertise as tax return preparers and to expand their knowledge of the tax laws. In addition, the company offers an annual training program consisting of 24-hours designed to maintain the expertise of its franchisees in tax theory. This training is given both live via seminars in selected areas and made available to others through cassettes and workbooks.

Managerial Assistance Available: Triple Check provides ongoing technical assistance by providing year round "hot line" research, technical memoranda as to changes in the applicable laws and administrative practices as it relates to the typical client expected to be served by franchisee. In addition, Triple Check provides various supplies and other items common to the operation of a tax preparation business on a substantial cost saving basis. Advertising and promotional programs are also an integral part of the ongoing service provided by the franchisor.

Information Submitted: May 1987

TV FACTS
1638 New Highway
Farmingdale, New York 11735

Description of Operation: TV Facts offers readers a localized weekly television guide with 7 days of national and local TV programming, cable TV, local news and advertising. Individually owned publications are operated by local associate publishers.

Number of Franchisees: Almost 300 in 36 States and Canada

In Business Since: 1971

Equity Capital Needed: $16,500

Financial Assistance Available: None

Training Provided: 1 week home office training in sales, advertising and circulation.

Managerial Assistance Available: Continuous assistance is provided by home office and area supervisors.

Information Submitted: July 1987

TV FOCUS
Guides Publishing, Inc.
One Anderson Avenue
Fairview, New Jersey 07022
Lou Fernandez, President

Description of Operation: TV Focus weekly magazine is a free and localized TV, cable and shopping guide. It contains crossword puzzles, horoscope, and TV, movie and sports articles. It is designed to help local advertisers focus their advertising efforts effectively and economically on their immediate trading areas. No previous experience is necessary. No equipment, no inventory and no writing is required. Individually-owned publication by associate publisher.

Number of Franchisees: More than 200 in 35 States

In Business Since: 1980

Equity Capital Needed: Distributorship fee of $1,800; $4,000 working capital suggested.

Financial Assistance Available: None

Training Provided: TV Focus provides the associate publisher with a comprehensive franchise operations manual. Continuous assistance is provided via telephone "hot line" and periodic memoranda.

Managerial Assistance Available: Continuous assistance is provided via a telephone "hot line."

Information Submitted: July 1987

TV NEWS
COMMUNITY PUBLICATIONS OF AMERICA, INC.
80 Eighth Avenue
New York, New York 10011
Allan Horwitz, President

Description of Operation: TV News is an award-winning free community publication combining the 7-day readership of a TV Guide with the community saturation of a shopper, and teh efficiencies of scale of a major national publication. TV News is an exciting editorial product that attracts readers, while the low advertising rates and concentrated circulation attract the advertisers. The publisher of TV News was formerly the sales strategy planner for the Wall Street Journal. As a leader in the publishing field he has been interviewed by Barbara Walters on "20/20" and appeared as a panelist on the "Phil Donahue Show."

Number of Franchisees: 8 in New York, Florida and South Carolina with no solicitation and no advertising.

In Business Since: 1973—TV News is a successful, respected and highly profitable publication, company-owned in New York. We have been franchising since 1979.

Equity Capital Needed: $19,900 with a Money Back Guarantee.

Financial Assistance Available: Yes

Training Provided: 9 days of classroom, in-field and on-site training for the franchisees and their employees. Covers how to sell TV News, how to get co-op advertising, financial leverage thru barter, servicing of accounts, distribution ad design, layout, and accounting. Includes extensive training manual, audio and video cassettes, numerous films, and video taped role-playing sessions.

Financial Assistance Available: Continuous assistance provided by the home office. Includes our unique start-up program to get you off to a flying start, with $1,500 of free printing, a direct mailing to your prospects by the company, and our special charter advertising program to produce immediate income for the franchisee and his advertisers. Also the company contributes $1,000 for each new franchise purchased plus 12 percent of all royalty fees for direct mailings, sweepstakes and special promotions to make the franchisees more successful.

Information Submitted: May 1987

TV SCENE, INC.
11641 Marshwood Lane S.W.
Fort Myers, Florida 33908
William W. Anderson, President

Description of Operation: TV Scene is an international network of local television magazines. TV Scene, Inc., has adopted the successful concept of TV Guide nationally and localized a weekly television magazine for specific markets. TV Scene is operated on a local level by independent franchisees who publish the weekly magazine with the approved and prescribed format developed and successfully tested for 58years. The finished product (TV Scene) is distributed through high traffic retail areas. TV Scene, Inc., is responsible for the actual production of the finished product (composition and printing) and securing the television/cable listings for a specific market. The responsibility of the franchisee/publisher is to sell and service advertising to the local business and distribute the well accepted magazine to the consumer. No particular publishing or advertising experience are necessary but management and/or marketing skills are adviseable.

Number of Franchisees: 72 in the United States.

In Business Since: 1982

Equity Capital Needed: $21,500

Financial Assistance Available: N/A

Training Provided: TV Scene, Inc., provides a "Publishers College and Sales Training Seminar" which is available to all franchisees and their employees. The program consists of 5 intensive days of publishing/advertising fundamentals, sales, accounting, distribution, marketing/promotions and video recording of sales presentations. The TV Scene, Inc., infield training director then returns to the franchisees market for 3 additional days of onsight training.

Managerial Assistance Available: TV Scene's department heads stand prepared to serve the franchisees needs in their particular areas of responsibility. A marketing/promotion director creates monthly sales contest, promotions and marketing programs. An annual convention is also hosted by TV Scene, Inc., to improve, refine and suggest the skills of sales, advertising, publishing and administration.

Information Submitted: May 1987

TV TEMPO, INC.
3131 Atlanta Highway
Athens, Georgia 30606
Paul M. King, President

Description of Operation: TV Tempo, Inc., offers a unique system of "free" weekly television and cable TV scheduling, and home entertainment guides. Each associate publisher (franchisee) owns and operates his/her local edition of TV Tempo magazine which is distributed "free" in high traffic retail areas. Individual associate publishers place advertising around Saturday through Friday television scheduling listings and readership features such as crossword puzzle, horoscope and movie descriptions. No need for expensive equipment, fixtures or offices. Excellent cash flow and low operational costs. Excellent localized guides.

Number of Franchisees: 101 in 19 States

In Business Since: 1975

Equity Capital Needed: $22,500.00 up depending on the population of associate publisher area.

Financial Assistance Available: None, interium financing only.

Training Provided: 5 days in intensive classroom learning fundamentals of business operation. Follow-up field training at the actual site assisting the associate publisher to put into operation the techniques of a successful operation. Classroom training available to associate publisher on repeated basis for associate publisher, if needed. Periodic seminars conducted by home office.

Managerial Assistance Available: TV Tempo, Inc., offers guidance and assistance to franchisee on a continuing basis to enhance franchisee's ability and skills. Basic managerial control is always within the control of the associate publisher's business operations. Advertising rates are in the control of the associate publisher.

Information Submitted: May 1987

TWP ENTERPRISES, INC.
11128 John Galt Boulevard
Suite 512
Omaha, Nebraska 68137
Kenneth Nanfito, Vice President, Marketing

Description of Operation: The Wedding Pages (TWP) is a wedding planner (250 page book) that contains a 168 page wedding planner and an advertising section for local area advertisers. The local advertisers receive a monthly listing of brides-to-be names, addresses, phone numbers and wedding dates, making this the most targeted direct marketing tool available in the wedding market today. Franchisee sells the local advertising.

Number of Franchisees: 17 in 15 States and Washington, DC

In Business Since: 1982

Equity Capital Needed: $15,000 minimum

Financial Assistance Available: None

Training Provided: 2 day in-house training at home office in Omaha, Nebraska. 1 week in market with franchisee or franchisee's sales force for field training.

Managerial Assistance Available: Franchisor provides support for all questions regarding sales and servicing of the markets. Updating and creation of products is constantly done to maintain a quality product. Franchisor publishes the advertising section and the books.

Information Submitted: July 1987

UBI BUSINESS BROKERS, INC.
11965 Venice Boulevard
Suite 204
Los Angeles, California 90066
David Scribner, President

Description of Operation: Opportunity to enter highly profitable field of business brokerage. Thorough training, ongoing marketing and technical support from the industry's oldest, most successful firm. Internal multiple listing service provides listings of thousands of businesses for sale. Exclusive computerized appraisal system, protected territories. UBI Financial Network, Inc., merger, acquisition division.

Number of Franchisees: 45 in 10 States

In Business Since: 1970

Equity Capital Needed: $27,500 franchise fee plus $30,000.

Financial Assistance Available: Franchisor option.

Training Provided: 2 weeks at corporate headquarters— indefinite ongoing training.

Managerial Assistance Available: Comprehensive and ongoing.

Information Submitted: May 1987

VOICE ENTERPRISES, INC.
70 West Streetsboro Street
Hudson, Ohio 44236
Charles Feuer, Executive Vice President

Description of Operation: Voice messaging service bureaus, providing the transmission, storage and retrieval of verbal messages through a combination of computer and telephone. Opportunities for single or master franchises available.

Number of Franchisees: 6 in Ohio, Virginia, and North Carolina

In Business Since: 1986

Equity Capital Needed: Single franchise—$30,000. Minimum master franchise—$45,000 minimum.

Financial Assistance Available: Total investment: Single franchise is $120,000. Total investment master franchise, $175,000. Investment includes franchise fees, equipment and working capital. Third-party leasing available for equipment packages.

Training Provided: All master franchisees and master franchisees must attend an initial 10 day intensive training program at home office school. Master franchisees are required to attend an additional 5 day training program after at least 30 days of operations as a franchisee.

Managerial Assistance Available: Voice Enterprises provides continual managerial and field support during the life of the franchise in such areas as sales and marketing techniques, public relations services, equipment operations, accounting and information systems, business controls and personnel management. Operational manuals and training guides are provided as reference tools. Frequent seminars, training meetings and conventions are bringing our people the newest ideas in voice messaging. Master franchisees in each region will provide ongoing field support for equipment and sales marketing.

Information Submitted: May 1987

* VR BUSINESS BROKERS, INC.
230 Western Avenue
Boston, Massachusetts 02134
George Naddaff, C.E.O

Description of Operation: A national network of business brokerage offices, specializing in the marketing of businesses and franchises. Proven and consistent operational techniques are used in all offices to ensure satisfaction of both buyer and seller. Regional and national advertising, plus an instant inventory of available businesses listed through an exclusive national multi-listing system leads to cooperative success of all offices. Offices typically open six days a week and are staffed by 10 professionally trained account executives.

Number of Franchisees: 300 in the U.S. and Canada

In Business Since: 1979

Equity Capital Needed: Approximately $60,000-$65,000 including $35,000 franchise fee.

Financial Assistance Available: Yes

Training Provided: 2-week classroom at regional centers, plus 1 week (specialized) franchise sales training and 1 week (specialized) preferred investment training. Supplemented by continuing assistance of regional operations supervisors, bi-weekly regional seminars, and in-office training of sales associates.

Managerial Assistance Available: Regional operations supervision from experienced business brokers who assist franchisees in all aspects of their business: recruiting, training, advertising, marketing, sales, closings, office management, etc. In addition, full management support available by telephone, newsletter, bulletins, and a regular program of office visits by regional operations staff.

Information Submitted: July 1987

WESTERN APPRAISERS
Division of WEST/APP INC.
P. O. Box 5211
El Dorado Hills, California 95630
Bert K. McMillian, Executive Vice President

Description of Operation: Western Appraisers provides material damage appraisals, total loss evaluation and mechanical failure inspections to major insurance companies, lending institutions and fleet operators.

Number of Franchisees: 33 in 7 States

In Business Since: 1960

Equity Capital Needed: $7,500 to $15,000 depending upon population count of area desired.

Financial Assistance Available: None; exceptions may be made under certain circumstances.

Training Provided: Intensive 4 week training period at one of our California training offices prior to franchisee opening business.

Managerial Assistance Available: West/App Inc., provides continued management service for the life of the franchise in such areas as work product quality control, customer development and profit structure. Many services such as medical insurance, manuals and printing can be purchased from West/App Inc., at a considerable discount. Semi-annual training seminars are also provided.

Information Submitted: May 1987

CAMPGROUNDS

KAMP DAKOTA, INC.
103 West 20th Street South
Brookings, South Dakota 57006
M. L. Thorne, President

Description of Operation: Franchising of campgrounds to be used by camping and trailering vacationers.

Number of Franchisees: 36 nationwide

In Business Since: 1964

Equity Capital Needed: $50,000 and up

Financial Assistance Available: Other than assistance in preparation and presentation of loan requests to potential financiers, Kamp Dakota, Inc., offers no financial assistance.

Training Provided: Training is provided at each campground as required and as may be necessary.

Managerial Assistance Available: Managerial assistance offered franchisees on a continuous basis. Kamp Dakota, Inc., also provides franchisee with complete engineering and construction planning for their particular campground.

Information Submitted: March 1987

* KAMPGROUNDS OF AMERICA, INC.
P. O. Box 30558
Billings, Montana 59114
Dave Johnson

Description of Operation: Kampgrounds of America, Inc., (KOA) is America's largest system of campgrounds for recreational vehicles. The average campground contains 100 sites equipped with water and electrical hookups; many sites have sewer hookups. Each campground features clean restrooms with hot showers, a convenience store, laundry equipment and playground equipment. Most have swimming pools.

Number of Franchisees: Over 650 in the United States and Canada

In Business Since: 1964

Equity Capital Needed: $80,000 minimum

Financial Assistance Available: KOA does not provide direct financing to franchisees for campground construction. However, it does provide assistance in obtaining financing such as, assisting the franchisee is preparing his prospectus, developing operating projections, and meeting with potential lenders.

Training Provided: KOA provides formal classroom training in campground development and campground operations for franchisees and their personnel. Each school (development and operations) last 2 days and several sessions are conducted throughout the year.

Managerial Assistance Available: KOA provides formal classroom training and continual engagement services for the life of the franchise in such areas as development, general operations, advertising and merchandising. In addition, complete manuals of development, operations and supply catalogs are provided. Regional consultants are available in all regions to work closely with franchisees. Each campground is visited regularly to insure conformance with standards and to assist franchisees in solving problems. KOA publishes a Kampground Directory annually and sponsors an annual meeting of franchisees.

Information Submitted: May 1987

* YOGI BEAR'S JELLYSTONE PARK
CAMP-RESORTS
LEISURE SYSTEMS, INC.
Rt. 209
Bushkill, PA 18324
J A. Lovejoy, Chief Operating Officer

Description of Operation: Has designed a standardized method of marketing and operation under a nationwide system known as Jellystone Park Camp-Resorts. Jellystone has granted and desires to grant franchises for exclusive territories in which to operate a Jellystone Park Camp-Resort. Jellystone will also accept certain existing unaffiliated campgrounds for conversion to their system.

Number of Franchisees: 73 in 22 States and Canada

In Business Since: 1969

Equity Capital Needed: $12,500 to $100,000 plus. Depends on location, size and other considerations.

Financial Assistance Available: Up to 60% of Franchise Fee.

Training Provided: 1 week manager training school, opening assistance, and a manual.

Managerial Assistance Available: Consultation regarding acceptable site criteria and selection. Construction assistance by way of campground layout and building plans. Consulting engineering also available. Ongoing consultation on all facets of campground operation and promotion. Inspection visits to insure chainwide adherence to quality standards. Field consulting. A national 800 toll free reservation service is provided by the national office as well as a national directory and national advertising.

Information Submitted: May 1987

CHILDRENS STORES/FURNITURE/PRODUCTS

BABY'S ROOM USA, INC.
752 North Larch Avenue
Elmhurst, Illinois 60126
Richard G. Levine

Description of Operation: Retail infants and juvenile furniture and accessories.

Number of Franchisees: 9 in 8 States

In Business Since: 1985

Equity Capital Needed: $88,000 to $199,000

Financial Assistance Available: No direct financial assistance, however our in-house CPA is available for advice and counsel. In most cases we are able to negotiate 60 to 90 day terms on initial stock orders.

Training Provided: Complete 2 week training program for franchisee and up to 2 additional employees at our headquarters in Elmhurst, Illinois.

Managerial Assistance Available: An operations specialist will spend 1 week during the first month of operation. Regular visits by our field representatives thereafter. A complete operations manual covering all facets of the business as well as periodic newsletters. Two meetings per year which all franchisees attend.

Information Submitted: May 1987

* **BELLINI JUVENILE DESIGNER FURNITURE CORPORATION**
1305 Second Avenue
New York, New York 10021
Ronald Sommers, Franchise Sales Agent

Description of Operation: Bellini offers exclusive juvenile designer furniture.

Number of Franchisees: 26 in 11 States, plus 7 company-owned

In Business Since: 1982

Equity Capital Needed: $110,000-$140,000

Financial Assistance Available: The franchiser will assist the franchisee in applying to local banks for financing.

Training Provided: Training provided in New York or California locations for 2 weeks includes extensive training in furniture sales and merchandising.

Managerial Assistance Available: Additional assistance and direction given by direct phone, correspondence and store visits. Complete operations manual provided covering all aspects of the retail operation.

Information Submitted: July 1987

LEWIS OF LONDON INC.
25 Power Drive
Hauppauge, New York 11788
Joel Rallo, President of Franchise Operations

Description of Operation: Retail juvenile furniture and accessories imported exclusively for Lewis of London stores.

Number of Franchisees: 21 in 10 States including 5 company-owned.

In Business Since: 1950

Equity Capital Needed: Determined by the area.

Financial Assistance Available: None

Training Provided: As much as needed for the franchisee to feel confortable with the opening of their store. Full training is provided in all aspects of the business such as complete knowledge of sales, inventory help to start-up books, in tracking inventory, full understanding of all fees and the billing procedures.

Managerial Assistance Available: Same as above

Information Submitted: June 1987

PEPPERMINT FUDGE FRANCHISE, INC.
P.O. Box 77243
Oklahoma City, Oklahoma 73177
Bob Giggs, Franchise Director

Description of Operation: Children's designer clothing, infant to pre-teen (maternity optional) including accessories, furniture and toys. Small and distinctive collections by highest quality designers of children's fashions. Presented in an atmosphere to attract discriminating clientele. Our concept combines superiod retail merchandising with personal services and amenities creating loyal, repeat sales. Ongoing support and analysis of total store activities allow the franchisee to access and forecast inventory needs as well as business strategy adjustments.

Number of Franchises: 10 in 7 States

In Business Since: 1980 (franchising since 1985)

Equity Capital Needed: $115,000 to $220,000, includes franchise fee and all start-up costs.

Financial Assistance Available: Assistance provided to position franchisee for third-party financing.

Training Provided: Training manual, class attendance in Oklahoma City and in your area minimum 1 week. Personnel provided for grand opening in your city. Continued education 4 days per year requrired.

Managerial Assistance Available: Assistance in site location and lease negotiation. In-house buyer. Operations director for ongoing support and guidance. Computerized analysis of toal store activities. Industry reports and trends in bi-monthly newsletters. Advertising-promotional master copies, accounting, marketing and management system provided in "operations manual." Store design and architecture specifications provided and approved vendor list.

Information Submitted: May 1987

PREGNANT INC. 4 BABYS ONLY
8938 East Valley Boulevard
Rosemead, California 91770
Bernard Zwick, President

Description of Operation: The "4 Babys Only" and "4 Kids Only" retail baby and teen furniture stores are approximately 8,000 square feet. With off site warehousing of 2,000 square feet. These specialty stores display import and American name brand merchandise in addition to exclusive merchandise to "4 Babys Only." The unique geometric display distinguish our supermarket effect.

Number of Franchisees: 10 in California, Arizona and Nevada.

In Business Since: 1970

Equity Capital Needed: $160,000-$200,000

Financial Assistance Available: Total investment ranges from $160,000-$200,000. $10,000 of which is the franchise fee. $60,000 for leasehold improvements, deposits, fixtures, delivery truck, cash registers, computer equipment, etc. $90,000-$140,000 for inventory depending on product mix and size of store.

Training Provided: A 116 page store operation manual and 5 days of in-store training and two days in our training center.

Managerial Assistance Available: 4 Babys only provides management advice and consultation in inventory control, operations, advertising, accounting and personnel. We provide purchasing information on a continual basis and pass on additional cash and volume discounts negotiated by 4 Babys Only management team.

Information Submitted: April 1987

CLOTHING/SHOES

*ALLISON'S PLACE, INC.
3161 East Washington Boulevard
Los Angeles, California 90023
Maria deBoer, Franchise Director
Leonora Hafen, Franchise Director

Description of Operation: Allison's Place is the leader of the one price concept in womens apparel and accessories. Allison's Place offers first quality merchandise, (no seconds or irregulars) for fashion merchandise that would normally retail for $14, to $49 and higher in major department stores and specialty shops. With over 50 years of combined experience in the apparel industry, and our huge buying power, Allison's Place can consistently buy in volume manufacturer cancellations, close-outs and over-runs, allowing us to provide our customers with current fashions and recognizable labels, at prices that are all $7 or less. A typical store is 1,500 to 2,000 square feet, and is located in strip centers, malls and shopping centers.

Number of Franchisees: 83 in 23 States plus the Virgin Islands and Guam

In Business Since:

1980

Equity Capital Needed: $99,500 total turn-key investment

Financial Assistance Available: Franchisor will finance 20 percent of initial investment if franchisee is collateralized and qualified.

Training Provided: Allison's Place will provide airfare and hotel accommodations (one trainee) for 3 days in Los Angeles, as arranged by franchisor, plus 7 days on-site supervision at franchisee's location. Franchisee is trained in merchandising the store, displays, daily reports and inventory control. Allison's Place also provides the confidential operations manual.

Managerial Assistance Available: Our toll free numbers provide our franchisees convenient access to our inventory and merchandise control department, to facilitate franchisee's needs. A franchisee can expect periodic visits from our trained supersisors to assist them in the latest merchandising and selling techniques, utilizing employee's services for maximum efficiency. Allison's Place will ship merchandise to the franchisees' on a regular basis 1 to 2 times a week depending on the demographics and sales of each individual franchisee.

Information Submitted: June 1987

*ATHLETE'S FOOT MARKETING ASSOCIATES, INC.
3735 Atlanta Industrial Parkway
Atlanta, Georgia 30331
Paul Modzelewski, Director of Sales/Marketing

Description of Operation: Company franchises its name and services, on a national basis, to individually owned stores that specialize in athletic shoes offering top quality retail priced lines of shoes and related clothing. Company also offers a private label program that enhances the bottom line profitability of its franchised stores.

Number of Franchisees: 473 in the United States, Japan, Australia and France.

In Business Since: 1971

Equity Capital Needed: $10,000 for franchise fee plus approximately $100,000 to $150,000 investment including opening inventory.

Financial Assistance Available: No financing provided by headquarters company. They do provide a package to present to bankers, and will assist in helping to negotiate loan package.

Training Provided: 2 weeks intensive training program provided by headquarters prepares franchisee for complete operation of store. Written manuals also provided.

Managerial Assistance Available: Assistance in lease negotiations and site selection. Complete competitively priced package for store design and construction. Continuous ongoing help in the form of store visitations by franchise coordinators.

Information Submitted: May 1987

ATHLETIC ATTIC MARKETING, INC.
P. O. Box 14503
Gainesville, Florida 32604
C. J. Collins, Director of Franchise Sales

Description of Operation: A retail sporting goods operation specializing in the sale of active-wear apparel, athletic footwear and related sporting goods (racquetball, tennis, soccer, etc.).

Number of Franchisees: 160 in 40 States, District of Columbia, Puerto Rico, New Zealand and Japan.

In Business Since: 1974

Equity Capital Needed: $7,500 for franchise fee. $125,000 to $175,000 total investment. Minimum $45,000 cash required.

Financial Assistance Available: No financial assistance is provided by the franchisor, however, all necessary information for loan applications is available.

Training Provided: Training program includes 1 week of classroom instruction in all aspects of store operations and 1 week of in-store instruction at franchisor's training store.

Managerial Assistance Available: Assistance includes, but not limited to the following: site selection, lease negotiations, store design, basic construction drawings, product mix assistance, opening suppliers accounts, accounting systems, inventory systems, on-site opening assistance, complete operations manual, advertising manual, local advertising materials, national advertising and publicity support, monthly management and newsletters, annual sales meetings.

Information Submitted: May 1987

ATHLETIC ATTIC MARKETING, INC.
dba ATHLETIC LADY
P. O. Box 14503
Gainesville, Florida 32604
C. J. Collins, Director of Franchise Sales

Description of Operation: A retail sporting goods operation specializing in the sale of women's fashion active wear and footwear (aerobic, tennis, running, swimming, etc.).

Number of Franchisees: 5 in Georgia, Florida, and North Carolina

In Business Since: Athletic Attic—1974—started franchising Athletic Lady in 1983

Equity Capital Needed: $7,500 for initial fee. $125,000 to $175,000 total investment. Minimum $45,000 cash required.

Financial Assistance Available: No financial assistance is provided by franchisor. However, all necessary information for loan application is available.

Training Provided: Training program includes 1 week of classroom instruction in all aspects of store operation and 1 week of in-store instruction at franchisor's training store.

Managerial Assistance Available: Assistance includes, but not limited to the following: site selection, lease negotiations, store design, basic construction drawings, product mix assistance, opening suppliers accounts, accounting systems, inventory systems, on-site opening assistance, complete operations manual, advertising manual, local advertising materials, national advertising and publicity support, monthly management and newsletters, annual sales meetings.

Information Submitted: May 1987

BAGS & SHOES, INC.
P. O. Box 51273
Jacksonville Beach, Florida 32240
W. H. Bonneau, President

Description of Operation: Step into leather with over 100 designer and brand name bags and shoes. A warehouse outlet for $20,000 to $40,000. A designer and brand name Bag & Shoes store for $75,000 to $150,000. We taylor your business to meet your individual needs and resources offering our turnkey operations which are geared for high traffic strip centers and malls for a flat fee or on a plus basis with no hidden charges.

Number of Franchisees: 37

In Business Since: 1985

Equity Capital Needed: $50,000 to $150,000

Financial Assistance Available: None

Training Provided: We will hire and train sufficient personnel at your Bags & Shoes Boutique. Our program is ideal for absentee ownership.

Managerial Assistance Available: Bags & Shoes will continually provide you with the latest in fashion footwear and handbags. We will make available to you our expertise in buying pricing, merchandising and advertising on a cost plus basis.

Information Submitted: June 1987

BENCONE OUTLET CENTER
121 Carver Avenue
Westwood, New Jersey 07675
Ronald Sommers, Franchise Sales

Description of Operation: "Off-price" retail outlet center featuring uniforms, lingerie and maternity.

Number of Franchisees: 2 including company-owned in New Jersey and Illinois.

In Business Since: Retailing/mail order service since 1973, franchising since 1985.

Equity Capital Needed: $70,000-$90,000

Financial Assistance Available: Bencone does not directly provide financing but will assist franchisee in obtaining financing through a financial institution of franchisee's choice.

Training Provided: All franchisee owners must attend an extensive training program in Bencone's training store in Westwood, New Jersey. The company provides at no charge, the personnel, materials, and equipment, franchisee is responsible for all other expenses including transportation, lodgings and meals.

Managerial Assistance Availble: Franchisee receives a Bencone operations manual covering all facets of the operation. This manual is updated from time to time to adjust to new products and procedures. Periodic visits are made to the store by management. They will consult on all aspects of the store operation. Additional continuing assistance includes site selection, lease negotiations, store layout, design, merchandise buying and guidance, and the monitoring of cash flow and budgets.

Information Submitted: July 1987

CANTERBURY OF NEW ZEALAND
101 Lincoln Center Drive
Suite 125
Foster City, California 94404
Graham C. Wong, President

Description of Operation: Specialty sports active and leisurewear retailers selling Canterbury of New Zealand branded products and associated accessories.

Number of Franchisees: 11 in California, Louisiana, Texas and Maryland

In Business Since: Company franchising in New Zealand and Australia since 1982

Equity Capital Needed: $100,000

Financial Assistance Available: None

Training Provided: 2 weeks in-house in San Francisco, California

Managerial Assistance Available: Ongoing support by corporate retail and field personnel.

Information Submitted: July 1987

CHEROKEE FRANCHISING CORP.
12544 Saticoy Street
North Hollywood, California 91603
Dan Zuckerman, Executive Vice President

Description of Operation: Retail stores featuring exclusively Cherokee brand women's apparel, shoes and accessories, supported by a multi-million dollar national advertising program. Cherokee merchandise is moderately priced and casual in design, and enjoys nationwide consumer acceptance and recognition.

Number of Franchisees: 13 including company-owned in California.

In Business Since: Parent company since 1973; franchising since 1986.

Equity Capital Needed: Maximum equity investment of $15,000.

Financial Assistance Available: None

Training Provided: Prior to opening of the store, a training program of up to 2 weeks long is provided in Southern California on all aspects of operations. After opening of the store, continuing advice and guidance is provided. Each franchisee also receives a comprehensive operations manual.

Managerial Assistance Available: Ongoing managerial and technical assistance in all areas including the following: merchandise display and merchandising, advertising and marketing, store appearance, sales techniques, operations and use of bookkeeping and reporting forms.

Information Submitted: July 1987

FLEET FEET
2410 J Street
Sacramento, California 96816
Sally Edwards

Description of Operation: Retail active footwear/sports/wear/triathlons with an emphasis on a sporting lifestyle. Brand names only—owners must be involved in physical fitness.

Number of Franchisees: 26 in California, Nevada, Washington, DC and Florida

In Business Since: Retail business 1975, franchise since 1978.

Equity Capital Needed: $10,000

Financial Assistance Available: Financial advice and preparation of papers for financial institutions. The total capitalization costs range from $50,000-$100,000 including inventory. Fixtures, fees, working capital. Bank financing is available but the franchisees responsibility. We will help with the preparation of forms.

Training Provided: Strenuous training program and franchise manual which involves all aspects of business operations and management. Course is 2 weeks long, mandatory attendance in Sacramento, California. Following course, franchisor-Fleet Feet—spends 1 week with the new store owner during the first week in business.

Managerial Assistance Available: Ongoing weekly bulletin "Fleet Feet Weekly Memo" to announce inventory and management news. Weekly phone calls to each franchise to offer assistance. Warehouse facilities which offer franchises inventory goods. Three times annually franchisee/franchisor meetings to improve managerial, technical, and other business skills. Discount buying programs.

Information Submitted: May 1987

FORMAL WEAR SERVICE
639 V.F.W. Parkway
Chestnut Hill, Massachusetts 03267
Jay Kuritsky

Description of Operation: Formal specialists in the sale and rental of men's formal clothes. Dealers receive stock plus photo album of every fashion and color we stock plus rental and sales catalog.

Number of Franchisees: 34 in Massachusetts, New Hampshire, New York and Connecticut.

In Business Since: 1940

Equity Capital Needed: $65,000 minimum for stock and fixtures.

Financial Assistance Available: Formal Wear Service will finance if franchisee has good credit rating.

Training Provided: 2 weeks at store. Complete training course in all aspects of formal rental business to all franchisees plus a 60 page book "Can A Nice Guy Succeed in Formals."

Managerial Assistance Available: The home office provides bookkeeping, inventory control and national and local cooperative advertising.

Information Submitted: May 1987

* GINGISS INTERNATIONAL, INC.
180 North LaSalle Street
Chicago, Illinois 60601
John Heiser, Vice President

Description of Operation: Specialists in the sale and rental of men's formal wear.

Number of Franchisees: 215 in 37 States

In Business Since: 1936 franchising since 1968

Equity Capital Needed: $40,000-$95,000

Financial Assistance Available: Through external sources franchisor arranges and guarantees $60,000 financing for inventory and equipment.

Training Provided: 2 week comprehensive training at Gingiss International Training Center in Chicago approximately 1 month before center's opening. One week on-site training during initial opening week. Regular visits by training directors and various department heads on a continuing basis.

Managerial Assistance Available: Franchisor provides regular visits by field training advisors, a comprehensive instructional manual, periodic bulletins and constant telephone assistance as required.

Information Submitted: May 1987

*HATS IN THE BELFRY FRANCHISE CORPORATION
Suite 33, 1410 Forest Drive
Annapolis, Maryland 21403
Courtney Gorton President

Description of Operation: Dynamic hat boutique featuring fashion, functional, and fun headwear for women and men. More than 500 styles from classic to casual to costume, traditional to theatrical.

Number of Franchisees: 14 in 13 States and Washington, DC

In Business Since: 1978

Equity Capital Needed: $80,000-$150,000

Financial Assistance Available: None

Training Provided: 10 day training program at home office, company owned shop on location. Intensive training in all areas of the business. A wide range of training materials utilized. Comprehensive operations manuals and information packets also provided.

Managerial Assistance Available: Ongoing assistance in areas such as merchandise control, advertising and daily operations. Continuous communication through weekly phone contact, informative shop-keepers's newsletter, regularly scheduled store visits, and buying sessions and owners' meetings held for franchisees two times per year at home office.

Information Submitted: May 1987

JILENE, INC.
1560 Holding Hill
Goleta, California 93117
Jim Klobucher, President

Description of Operation: Jilene offers two different opportunities to the retail clothing business. One store is called "Kimo's Polynesian Shop," which specializes in colorful clothing for women and men. The other store, is called "Shandar," which specializes in quality women's fashions. Jilene provides expert site selection, complete retail training program, professional buying service, merchandise control system, and advertising and sales promotion assistance.

Number of Franchisees: 10 in California and Florida

In Business Since: 1969

Equity Capital Needed: $35,000 and up depending on size of store.

Financial Assistance Available: None

Training Provided: 2 weeks training provided in franchisee's store. Training covers all general aspects of a retail clothing store operation. A complete operations manual is provided to each store owner.

Managerial Assistance Available: After initial 2 week training period Jilene is always available for assistance for the duration of the franchise contract. Jilene also functions as a buying service for the franchisee.

Information Submitted: July 1987

JUST PANTS
1034 Bonaventure Drive
Elk Grove Village, Illinois 60007
Robert Tischler

Description of Operation: Just Pants stores average 2,000 square feet with expansion geared to new mall developments, existing malls and other potential retail locations available now and in the future. Just Pants stores sell quality branded casual tops, bottoms and junior wear to young men and young women.

Number of Franchisees: 14 (94 units) in 21 States. Areas available in all States.

In Business Since: 1969

Equity Capital Needed: Regional mall $108,000 to $202,500. No initial franchise fee. Investment covers: site selection and development, inventory, fixtures and working capital.

Financial Assistance Available: None

Training Provided: Just Pants will furnish a training program consisting of "on-the-job-training" plus much additional instruction to the manager with respect to other aspects of the business. The licensee will be responsible for the travel and living expenses and the compensation of the manager while enrolled in the training program.

Managerial Assistance Available: Operating assistance will include advice and guidance with respect to (1) buying pants, tops and other merchandise; (2) additional products authorized for sale by Just Pants stores; (3) hiring and training

of employees; (4) formulating and implementing advertising and promotional programs; (5) pricing and special sales; (6) the establishment and maintenance of administrative, bookkeeping, accounting, inventory control and general operating procedures. Further, Just Pants will advise the licensee from time to time of operating problems of the store disclosed by financial statements submitted to or inspections made by Just Pants. Just Pants will make no separate change to the licensee for such operating assistance.

Information Submitted: May 1987

THE KIDDIE KOBBLER LTD.
68 Robertson Road
Suite 106
Nepean, Ontario
K2H 8P5 Canada
Fred Norman, President

Description of Operation: Largest franchisor of children's full line shoe stores in North America. Stores carry complete lines of America's leading children's branded footwear for all seasons as well as athletic, orthopedic and dancewear needs.

Number of Franchisees: 70 in Massachusetts, Connecticut and Canada

In Business Since: 1951

Equity Capital Needed: 50 percent of investment. Total investment $110,000 to $130,000.

Financial Assistance Available: Assistance in preparation of loan application and possible S.B.A. financing.

Training Provided: Minimum 3 months in-store training with an established franchisee, covering all phases of customer service and recordkeeping, marketing, ordering, store maintenance, on-site assistance before and after grand opening.

Managerial Assistance Available: Regular visits by field consultants, operations manual, buying assistance, regular information memos, head office personnel on-call for advice, franchise meetings semi annually, advertising assistance, new products advisory, leasing and store design services.

Information Submitted: May 1987

LADY MADONNA MANAGEMENT CORP.
A DIV. OF D.F. COREY ENT. INC.
561 Richmond Street West
Toronto, Ontario M5V 1Y6
Canada

Description of Operation: Manufacture, wholesale and retail women's maternity apparel and related accessories.

Number of Franchisees: 76 in 30 States

Equity Capital Needed: $70,000-$90,000

Financial Assistance Available: No financing available; however, company provides a business package to present to bankers to qualified applicants. Licensee arranges own outside financing.

Training Provided: Intensified training program provided.

Managerial Assistance Available: Continuous merchandising guidance, buying service, all advertising material, forms and systems and continuous field supervision of retail operations.

Information Submitted: May 1987

LANZ FRANCHISING, INC.
8680 Hayden Place
Culver City, California 90232
James Howard, Marketing and Operations

Description of Operation: Classic yet contemporary women's wear specialty stores. Featuring full-line of Lanz quality merchandise in the upper-moderate pricelines and other well known brands. Each fashion store is uniquely tailored to reflect the tasts of the women and the flavor of the community in which they do business.

Number of Franchisees: 29 stores including company-owned in California and Utah.

In Business Since: 1983

Equity Capital Needed: $125,320 to $308,030

Financial Assistance Available: 100 percent financing available for Lanz merchandise. Company provides assistance in developing proposals for obtaining financing.

Training Provided: 10 day extensive management training program, conducted at the corporate headquarters in Los Angeles, and in the California apparel mart with our staff of buyers. The program consists of seminars covering all areas essential to the operation of a Lanz Fashion Store.

Managerial Assistance Available: Prior to the grand opening, a Lanz area supervisor will help train local staff. The areas covered in these training sessions include product knowledge, multiple-sales technique, customer service, development of a personal trade file and more. As part of the ongoing training and support system, the area supervisor will visit the fashion store periodicallly to make recommendations and provide basic training for sales staff and ascertain that all stores are adhering to Lanz standards.

Information Submitted: May 1987

THE MARK-IT STORES, INC.
316 Yale
P. O. Box 187
St. Joseph, Missouri 64504
Tim Burtner, President

Description of Operation: The Mark-It Stores franchise system consists of retail stores in regional malls. We specialize in imprinted sportswear and accessory items. Average store size of 700 square feet. We operate a complete screenprinting plant.

Number of Franchisees: 33 in 17 States

In Business Since: 1975

Equity Capital Needed: $20,000 to $80,000

Financial Assistance Available: None

Training Provided: 2 days in store, 2 days in office. Available for assistance when needed.

Managerial Assistance Available: Monthly newsletters, product location service, advertising assistance, store display.

Information Submitted: May 1987

MODE O'DAY COMPANY
2130 North Hollywood Way
Burbank, California 91505
Ronald G. Diharce, Vice President, Operations

Description of Operation: Mode O'Day presently operates and licenses women's apparel specialty shops under the trade names Mode O'Day and Fashion Crossroads. These stores specialize in popular and moderately priced merchandise in size ranges which may include junior, misses, and large sizes. Licensees do not purchase inventory from Mode O'Day; all Mode O'Day inventory is placed in licensee's store on consignment.

Number of Franchisees: Approximately 453 in 26 States.

In Business Since: 1933

Equity Capital Needed: Variable—estimated range: $23,850 to $68,000 to cover initial license fee, lease deposit, leasehold improvements, equipment and fixtures, working capital, insurance and security deposit.

Financial Assistance Available: No merchandise investment, all merchandise supplied on consignment. Licensee pays Mode O'Day for merchandise after it has been sold to the ultimate consumer. Mode O'Day requires a security deposit from all licensees. Under certain circumstances, portions of a security deposit may be withdrawn by licensee for the purpose of financing the purchase of fixtures and or improvements for the licensee's store. In the event of withdrawal, licensee is required to make additional monthly payments to Mode O'Day until the entire amount has been repaid. No other financing arrangement is customarily offered directly or indirectly by Mode O'Day.

Training Provided: Mandatory training is conducted at a site designated by Mode O'Day. Mode O'Day customarily provides a 2-week training period for each new licensee in a comparable store by a qualified Mode O'Day licensee with 1-10 years experience. Trainee is responsible for travel and living expenses during training period. Otherwise, there is no charge to licensee for training program. Additional licensee training is provided in the form of Mode O'Day's continuous in-store training program which is based upon periodic visits by the licensee's supervisor, a Mode O'Day employee, and various training materials prepared by Mode O'Day. Typically, the licensee's supervisor will visit the licensee's store at regular intervals in order to provide the licensee with guidance concerning operation and management of store.

Managerial Assistance Available: Mode O'Day agrees from time to time to provide and make available to licensee retail operations assistance and supplies. The assistance provided by Mode O'Day shall include, but not be limited

to: Training of licensee; supervision and assistance in store leasing, store operation, personnel management, inventory control, advertising, sales promotion, and window display; providing without additional charge store improvement plans, lay-out plans, advertising productions, seasonal window backgrounds, window signs, interior signs and merchandise bags; and making available insurance, store fixtures, gift boxes, sales checks, bookkeeping supplies and other miscellaneous items. Licensee is not required to make use of any or all of these services in order to obtain merchandise on consignment.

Information Submitted: May 1987

NEW YORK CITY SHOES
Marple Springfield Center
Route 1 and 320
Springfield, Pennsylvania 19064
Barry S. Borsky, Director of Franchising

Description of Operation: One price women's discount shoes store, selling shoes, boots, handbags, and related items at one low price.

Number of Franchisees: 69 franchised and 45 company-owned stores in Pennsylvania, New Jersey, Maryland and Florida

In Business Since: 1982

Equity Capital Needed: $75,000 to $95,000

Financial Assistance Available: None presently

Training Provided: 1 week intensive training in company-owned store, 1 week in franchises store and continuing supervision at franchisee's store.

Managerial Assistance Available: New York City shoes provides assistance in finding the right location. Will provide fixtures and most signage at franchisee's cost which is included above. Expert advise for the duration of the business relative to the purchasing of shoes from our vast selections. Periodic visits to the franchisee's location for the purpose of finding ways to increase sales.

Information Submitted: May 1987

PRESIDENT TUXEDO, INC.
29212 Hoover Road
Warren, Michigan 48093
Michael A. Sbrocca, Vice President

Description of Operation: President Tuxedo stores rent and sell the finest in mens formalwear and accessories. Each store is approximately 1,000-1,500 square feet and usually located in regional malls or high traffic, easily accessible street locations. President Tuxedo specializes in servicing proms, weddings, fraternal groups, and black tie occasions.

Number of Franchisees: 12 plus 22 company-owned stores in Michigan, Ohio, Colorado and California.

In Business Since: 1970, the concept of franchising began in 1985

Equity Capital Needed: Between $60,000-$100,000 plus good credit.

Financial Assistance Available: President Tuxedo will help in arranging credit with all suppliers and manufacturers. President Tuxedo will also locate, negotiate, and secure leases for stores.

Training Provided: A complete 2 week training course is given for every franchisee at President Tuxedo's training facilities in Warren, Michigan. After the in-house training, a President Tuxedo field supervisor will be on hand for the official opening plus the following 2 weeks, or longer.

Managerial Assistance Available: President Tuxedo will have a field supervisor available to the franchisee on an ongoing basis, including help with local promotions, buying, store operations, merchandising, and any accounting support needed. President Tuxedo is dedicated to continuing the high quality standards our customers have come to expect. Therefore, we feel obligated to give our franchisees any and all support necessary to have an efficient and profitable business.

Information Submitted: May 1987

SALLY WALLACE BRIDES SHOP, INC.
2210 Pine Terrace
Scotch Plains, New Jersey 07076
John Van Drill, President

Description of Operation: Sally Wallace Brides Shops offer a complete bride shop and bridal service. Wedding gowns, bridsmaids, mothers, party, cocktail, dance and formals plus all accessories. Inventory consists of all the leading designers and manufacturers. Advertised in brides and Modern Bride Magazine.

Number of Franchisees: 12 in 5 States

In Business Since: 1955

Equity Capital Needed: $50,000

Financial Assistance Available: A total investment of approximately $50,000 is needed for a complete turnkey operation including inventory and $5,000 operating fund back-up. We will finance 30 percent if franchisee has good credit reference.

Training Provided: 3 week mandatory training course in one of our shops. Trainer spend 1 week with franchisee to open new shop. Six months follow thru by trainer with close supervision via written reports and telephone.

Managerial Assistance Available: Continuous. Consultant buyer and merchandise manager supervision on a weekly basis, checking sales, money, inventory and cost controls. Field personnel available as needed, to visit shops and assist in solving problems. Buying service supplies as part of franchise agreement.

Information Submitted: May 1987

> **SECOND SOLE, INC.**
> **9605 Scranton Road #840**
> **San Diego, California 92111**
> **Richard Hertz, President**

Description of Operation: Athletic shoe retail stores combined with athletic shoe resoling operations.

Number of Franchisees: 54 in 6 States

In Business Since: 1976

Equity Capital Needed: $70,000 to $100,000 ($10,000 franchise fee plus inventory, leasehold improvements, machinery etc.).

Financial Assistance Available: None

Training Provided: a comprehensive training program is conducted in San Diego and includes all aspects of athletic shoe sales and resoling as well as buying systems, inventory systems, advertising and promotional activities. Training course lasts a minimum of 7 days and a maxium of 14 days.

Managerial Assistance Available: Second Sole provides management assistance and consultation for the life of the franchise. Complete manual of operations, forms and systems are provided at well as complete seasonal advertising assistance on a quarterly basis. Second Sole management is continually available to assist in problem solving.

Information Submitted: May 1987

> **SOX APPEAL**
> **Designers Guild Building**
> **401 North Third Street**
> **Suite 4900**
> **Minneapolis, Minnesota 55401**
> **Barbara McCormick, Franchise Coordinator**

Description of Operation: Sox Appeal businesses are retail establishments that sell specialty and quality socks, hosiery and a limited number of approved items such as Sox Appeal t-shirts and sweatshirts, footsie roll mailing tubs, slipper socks, washing bags and washing soap. Sox Appeal imports from 5 different countries and is currently completing a private lable program. Each store is approximately 500-900 square feet.

Number of Franchisees: 3 in Colorado and Minnesota.

In Business Since: Sox Appeal originally started in 1984 and the franchise program started in 1986.

Equity Capital Needed: Low $69,800—High $128,600. Sox Appeal currently does not provide financial assistance.

Training Provided: The training program will include classroom and on-the-job instruction on basic operations, product knowledge, merchandising, employee relations, customer relations and other topics selected by Sox Appeal. The training program will be for no less than 4 days.

Managerial Assistance Available: Sox Appeal provides continual management services for the life of the franchise in such areas as bookkeeping, advertising, inventory control and the day-to-day operations. Complete and updated training manuals of the operations, forms and directions are provided. A franchise coordinator is available to work closely with the franchisees and visit the stores when necessary. A Sock Market Report is mailed after each buying market to keep the franchisee informed on what is approved merchandise to buy.

Information Submitted: May 1987

> **SPORTIQUE, INC.**
> **1405 Old Square Road**
> **Jackson, Mississippi 39211**
> **Carol V. Dunn, President**

Description of Operation: Retail clothing—actionwear for individual sports.

Number of Franchisees: 4 in Mississippi and Louisiana

In Business Since: 1975

Equity Capital Needed: $75,000

Financial Assistance Available: None

Training Provided: 1 week in store—continual help through life of franchise.

Managerial Assistance Available: All needed during life of franchise.

Information Submitted: July 1987

> **SPORTS FANTASY MARKETING, INC.**
> **P. O. Box 1847**
> **Columbus, GA 31902**
> **Eddie Hofstetter, Director of Sales & Marketing**

Description of Operation: A Sports Fantasy Store specializes in "The Clothes of the Pros." The Stores are typically 1,000 square feet and carry professional and collegiate licensed sporting apparel and novelty items.

Number of Franchisees: 5 including company-owned in Kentucky, Georgia, Florida, and South Carolina.

In Business Since: 1986

Equity Capital Needed: $60,000-$90,000

Financial Assistance Available: None available—Sports fantasy assists franchisee in developing a business plan for third party financing.

Training Provided: Sports Fantasy marketing provides intensive 1 week training at the company headquarters and store in Columbus, Georgia in all phases of operations, merchandising, inventory control, bookkeeping, and purchasing.

Managerial Assistance Available: Ongoing managerial and busineess operations assistance to maximize store performance via phone contact, company newsletter, promotional and point of sales programs.

Information Submitted: May 1987

> **T-SHIRTS PLUS**
> **P. O. Box 20608**
> **3630 I-35 South**
> **Waco, Texas 76702-0608**
> **Larry Meyer, President**

Description of Operation: Family oriented specialty stores selling T-shirts and associated garments, individualized according to the wishes of each buyers; personalization done while buyer waits. Also make up special orders for businesses, teams, clubs, and similar groups with whatever design they desire.

Number of Franchisees: 250 in 42 States

In Business Since: 1975

Equity Capital Needed: $50,000-$100,000

Financial Assistance Available: None

Training Provided: Attendance of 1 week at T-shirts college before store opens, followed by second week after store opens. Company personnel assist in setting up and opening stores; then make periodic visits to assist as needed. Company provides WATS service to enable store operators to obtain answers to specific questions. Monthly publications to all stores includes merchandising plans, helpful ideas·and other information.

Managerial Assistance Available: Company provides field representatives who visit stores. Company provided WATS service makes home office personnel constantly available to store operators and managers to assist as needed as well as for fast handling of shirt orders. Company's publications and regional meetings and annual meetings also keep all franchisees abreast of developments. Regularly updated operators manuals are furnished all operators for continuing use. Advertising and merchandising materials supplied monthly.

Information Submitted: May 1987

> **TYLER'S COUNTRY CLOTHES**
> **8136 Ritchie Highway**
> **Pasadena, Maryland 21122**
> **Marvin Jacobs**

Description of Operation: Retail family apparel stores. Features apparel and footwear for men, women, and children in medium pricelines and well known brands. Emphasis is on customer service and community involvement to develop repeat business and long-term success.

Number of Franchisees: 4 in Maryland, Virginia and Pennsylvania

In Business Since: 1975

Equity Capital Needed: $75,000-$100,000

Financial Assistance Available: Company provides assistance in developing proposals for obtaining bank financing.

Training Provided: Intensive in-store training in existing franchises, prior to opening. Continuous on-site training after store opening.

Managerial Assistance Available: Continuous merchandising guidance, operating and financial guidance and supervision, advertising materials; systems, forms, and supplies offered. Franchisor conducts meetings and seminars on an ongoing basis. Retail specialist in each area of operations visit franchises regularly.

Information Submitted: May 1987

WILD TOPS
NATIONAL DEVELOPMENT GROUP, INC.
400 Cochituate Road
Framingham, MA 01701
Richard Gold, President

Description of Operation: Wild Tops T-Shirt Stores are contemporary in design and are located in major regional malls. Average location size is 400 to 1,000 square feet. Wild Tops features an extensive selection of imprinted sportswear highlighted by T-Shirts, sweatshirts, custom flock lettering, numbers, transfers, trendy fashion tops, sweaters, infantwear and related items.

Number of Franchisees: 37 franchised and 3 company-owned.

In Business Since: Predecessor: 1980; current company 1985

Equity Capital Needed: $40,000 and leasehold improvements.

Financial Assistance Available: The total investment of $40,000 and construction, (if any) includes all equipment and fixtures as: heat press, cash register, press table, cash and wrap table counter, glass shelving, decal display book, promotional advertising, lease negotiation, home office training and inventory.

Training Provided: Intensive on-the-job training at Wild Tops training center will last 1 week and cover the following topics: store opening and closing, transfer application, purchasing, store set-up, advertising, hiring procedures, customer relations, etc.

Managerial Assistance Available: Wild Top's representatives will be present for all franchisee's grand openings and home office personnel are available on a daily basis to assist franchisees on a consultancy basis. A manual is also provided that outlines all policies, forms and procedures.

Information Submitted: July 1987

CONSTRUCTION/REMODELING MATERIALS/SERVICES

ABC SEAMLESS, INC.
2004 1st Avenue South
Fargo, North Dakota 58103
Jerry Beyers, President

Description of Operation: ABC franchise sales for seamless steel sliding, seamless gutters. All products manufactured on location. ABC seamless steel siding replaces the obsolesant method of applying siding in 12' lengths. Factory direct suppliers.

Number of Franchisees: 220 in 14 States and Canada

In Business Since: 1973

Equity Capital Needed: $30-$50,000

Financial Assistance Available: Leasing available for equipment to qualified buyers.

Training Provided: Training in sales, product information and application.

Managerial Assistance Available: Accounting services—product service—equipment service.

Information Submitted: May 1987

*ACRYSYL INTERNATIONAL CORPORATION (AIC)
11 South 11th Street
P. O. Box 7858
Reading, Pennsylvania 19603
Dr. Donald G. Snyder, President

Description of Operation: AIC is engaged in franchising nationwide a unique patent-pending 3-stage elastomeric roofing and siding coating system called AcrySyl.

Number of Franchisees: 11 in Pennsylvania, New Jersey, North Carolina, and South Carolina

In Business Since: 1982

Equity Capital Needed: License fee minimum $15,000 plus $20,000 initial operating capital.

Financial Assistance Available: None

Training Provided: Technical aspects of the AcrySyl line of products; estimates; evaluations; application procedures; customer service and relations; marketing, management, and administrative procedures. Individual training in the field. On-going assistance on unusual roofing/siding service-related matters. Group meetings or training sessions to exchange marketing, administrative, and technical know-how among franchisees and for the transfer of specialized and advanced technical information and procedures from AIC to franchisee personnel.

Managerial Assistance Available: See above.

Information Submitted: May 1987

ADD-VENTURES OF AMERICA, INC.
38 Park Street Station
Medfield, Massachusetts 02052
Thomas D. Sullivan, President

Description of Operation: Add-Ventures of America, Inc., specializes in remodeling construction for both residential and commercial tradesman. Developed business system and documentation for assisting carpenters/general contractors in administrating their operations. Region franchise owners have exclusive rights to sell local franchises in defined territories.

Number of Franchisees: Regional franchise owners—2, local franchise owners—12.

In Business Since: 1977

Equity Capital Needed: Regional franchise ($45,000), local franchise ($2,500).

Financial Assistance Available: Will assist in arranging financing.

Training Provided: Initial 10 day training, spread-over 2-3 different sessions at regional franchise owners location.

Managerial Assistance Available: Assistance in preparation of business plan and ongoing management training.

Information Submitted: August 1987

AMERICAN LEAK DETECTION
1750 East Arenas
Suite 1
Palm Springs, California 92262
Dick Rennick, Chief Executive Officer

Description of Operation: Electronically located leaks in concealed walls and gas pipes. Job includes finding leaks in pools, spas, fountains, under concrete slabs of homes and commercial buildings. Locate hidden and concealed sewer lines, septic tanks, etc. Building energy loss, roof moisture analysis by the use of infra-red thermography.

Number of Franchisees: 60 in 6 States

In Business Since: 1975

Equity Capital Needed: $20,000

Financial Assistance Available: Franchises start at $40,000—50 percent can be financed in-house by franchisor with good credit rating.

Training Provided: 4 to 6 week training—50 hours plus per week—very intensive course. Ongoing quarterly training.

Managerial Assistance Available: Ongoing public relations and marketing support given periodically or upon special request. Yearly training conventions and sales meetings, continual equipment and technique updates.

Information Submitted: May 1987

ARCHADECK WOODEN PATIO DECKS
P. O. Box 5185
Richmond, Virginia 23220
Richard Provost, Vice President

Description of Operation: Archadeck (R-KA-DEK) markets, sells, and builds custom-designed, stick-built wooden patio decks for residential, builder, and commercial clients.

Number of Franchisees: 4 plus 8 company-owned in Virginia, Georgia, Pennsylvania, New York, and New Jersey.

In Business Since: 1980, franchising since 1984

Equity Capital Needed: $12,500 franchise fee; additional capital requirements from $10,000.

Financial Assistance Available: None

Training Provided: Minimum 10 days intensive training covering the areas of:office management; marketing and advertising; sales; construction documentation and management; and design and estimating.

Managerial Assistance Available: Unlimited managerial support via telephone and mails. Regular on-site services include support in all facets of business with special emphasis on sales support and business management. We provide working drawings for each project with specs, details, and material takeoffs. We also have an architectural rendering service and an in-house advertising agency.

Information Submitted: April 1987

* BATHCREST INC.
2425 South Progress Drive
Salt Lake City, Utah 84119
Scott Peterson, President

Description of Operation: Specializing in porcelain resurfacing on bathtubs, sinks, ceramic wall tile, kitchen appliances, chip repair on new tubs, fiber glass and acrylic spa repair. Bathcrest Inc., services motels, hotels, apartment houses, home owners, contractors, and repairs for manufacturers of new porcelain bathroom fixtures.

Number of Franchisees: 70 in 27 States

In Business Since: 1979

Equity Capital Needed: $19,500

Financial Assistance Available: None

Training Provided: 5 days of (on-the-job) training by trained technicians. Complete equipment, printed materials, supplies, advertising, and enough Glazecote to return investment. Yearly dealers meetings and newsletters. Protected territory.

Managerial Assistance Available: Continual support.

Information Submitted: May 1987

BATH GENIE, INC.
109 East Main Street
Marlborough, Massachusetts 01752
John J. Foley, President

Description of Operation: The franchisor through a uniquely developed and refined process, offers the service of restoring and resurfacing bathroom fixtures. This service includes the restoration, recolor and recoating of standard bathroom fixtures which include bathtubs, sinks, and wall tiles.

Number of Franchisees: 50 in 12 States and Canada

In Business Since: 1978

Equity Capital Needed: $19,500

Financial Assistance Available: The franchisor does not offer any specific kind or amount of financial assistance to prospective franchisees. Assistance is rendered to prospective franchisees with regard to mode and method of financing where the same is needed.

Training Provided: Prior to the start of the franchise business, the franchisor has the obligation to provide full training for a period of approximately 4 to 5 days in all phases of the business to include on-the-job training, revelation of all technical aspects and procedures of the business; instruction with regard to marketing, public relations and accounting procedures. Training is mandatory.

Managerial Assistance Available: Beyond the training period, the franchisor keeps a continual liaison with the franchisee with regard to all details pertaining to training of personnel; public relations; marketing; and with regard to advertising. In addition the franchisor provides the franchisee with periodical newsletters and newsworthy items pertaining to doings in the industry and also with regard to

pertinent changes in the law and other factors that effect the conduct of the franchisee's problems of any kind or nature directly with the home office of the franchisor. All such communications are attended to by the franchisor's office immediately upon notification from the franchisee.

Information Submitted: July 1987

* B-DRY SYSTEM, INC.
1341 Copley Road
Akron, Ohio 44320
Joseph Garfinkel, Vice President

Description of Operation: Franchisor has developed and formulated unique procedures and techniques for the operation of a basement waterproofing business. Franchisor provides to franchisee a uniform system of procedures for the operation of a B-Dry franchise including the right to use the B-Dry patented process and the use of B-Dry logos and trademarks.

Number of Franchisees: 80 franchises in 25 States and Canada

In Business Since: 1958

Equity capital Needed: $39,500-$94,500

Financial Assistance Available: Up to 50 percent of the initial franchisee fee may be extended up to 24 months at no interest.

Training Provided: Franchisor provides the complete initial training on all aspects of technical, marketing, and administrative phases of the operation. Initial training approximately 10 days. Regular follow-up training provided at no charge.

Managerial Assistance Available: During operation of franchise, regular managerial and technical assistance is provided on an ongoing basis.

Information Submitted: May 1987

* CALIFORNIA CLOSET CO.
6409 Independence Avenue
Woodland Hills, California 91367
Neil Balter

Description of Operation: Custom closet installation—complete interior renovation and designed individually. Space savers. Double handing space. A place for all articles in a closet.

Number of Franchisees: 79 in 23 States, Canada/Australia

In Business Since: 1979

Equity Capital Needed: $51,000

Financial Assistance Available: None

Training Provided: Initial 5-10 days ongoing sales, installation and bookkeeping.

Managerial Assistance Available: Ongoing—advertising, sales and carpentry.

Information Submitted: July 1987

CAPTAIN GLIDES INC.
20832 Roscoe Boulevard
Canoga Park, California 91306
John Benach

Description of Operation: Specializing in sliding door and window repair. Screens, tub and shower enclosures, wardrobe doors, security for home. "If your door don't slide call Captain Glides."

Number of Franchisees: 7 in California, Florida and Georgia

In Business Since: 1981

Equity Capital Needed: $25,000

Financial Assistance Available: Bulk rate purchasing, contractors license, advertising, complete training on installed services.

Training Provided: 2 weeks minimum, in field and complete office procedure. Additional 4 weeks in franchisee's territory.

Managerial Assistance Available: Through the term of the contract constant supervision, constant upgrade of services.

Information Submitted: July 1987

CHIMNEY RELINING INTERNATIONAL, INC.
105 West Merrimack Street
P. O. Box 4035
Manchester, New Hampshire 03108
Clifford R. Martel, President

Description of Operation: Using the PermaFlu Chimney Lining System the PermaFlu franchisee can reline cracked, crooked or deteriorated chimney flues and restore them to safe, efficient use with any heating fuel, including wood, oil, gas and coal. complete contractor package includes a mortar mixer mounted on a hopper which flows into a pump. Special PermaFlu Mix pumped into chimney around inflated rubber flue-former. When mix hardens, former is deflated and removed. New round flue. All cracks sealed.

Number of Franchisees: 35 in 21 States and Canada. Affiliate in United Kingdom.

In Business Since: 1981

Equity Capital Needed: $14,700, $11,700 or $6,900

Financial Assistance Available: Will provide model business plan.

Training Provided: 1 week intensive training in actual on-the-job chimney relining work; also classroom work reviewing operations guidelines, marketing, estimating, profit and cost analysis; warehouse instructions on maintenance of PermaFlu Chimney Lining System.

Managerial Assistance Available: Guidance in advertising and publicity, office operations, use of programmed estimating computer (provided by CRI); letters of introduction on franchisees behalf sent with complete testing and descriptive package to franchisee's local (1) building inspectors, (2) insurance adjusters, (3) fire marshalls, (4) real estate brokers and (5) local newspapers. Advertising and publicity sales lead program on monthly basis—Permaflu information sent to franchisee's customer, with copy to franchisee. Full package of franchisee identity materials provided—business cards, letterheads, invoices, envelopes and brochures, all custom printed with the franchisee name, address, etc.

Information Submitted: May 1987

CLOSETTEC FRANCHISE CORPORATION
123 East Street
Dedham, Massachusetts 02026
Dan Peek

Description of Operation: Custom designed closets and storage systems for both the consumer and commercial markets. Using furniture grade wood products and European steel hardware to create custom designed and installed fully adjustable storage systems.

Number of Franchisees: 24 in 13 States

In Business Since: 1985

Equity Capital Needed: $65,000

Financial Assistance Available: Equipment leasing package.

Training Provided: 2 weeks initial training for owners and managers at corporate office. Additional 1 week courses for other personnel. Ongoing regional seminars and on-site training and support.

Managerial Assistance Available: Ongoing in all phases of the business.

Information Submitted: August 1987

COLLEGE PRO PAINTERS (U.S.), LTD.
108 Water Street
Watertown, Massachusetts 02172
Seth W. Hamot, President

Description of Operation: Student contractors are recruited on college campuses each fall. Successful contractors are chosen to operate house painting franchises, usually in their home town. During the winter the student painting contractors are given a 600 page manager's manual which describes in detail how to run a house painting business. During the winter they also receive 5 days of management training and in the spring they and their painters receive extensive on-the-job training. In may the student painting contractors open up for business, ready to paint 100 plus homes during the summer before they return to school in September.

Number of Franchisees: 125 in 10 States

In Business Since: 1971

Equity Capital Needed: Nil

Financial Assistance Available: $2,000 is prepaid expenses and advertising.

Training Provided: 5 days of extensive management training on how to run your own house painting business, and 5 days of on-the-job training.

Managerial Assistance Available: Ongoing advice and assistance is available from experienced people at any time to the franchisee.

Information Submitted: July 1987

THE DRAIN DOCTOR
P. O. Box 3071
Reading, Pennsylvania 19604

Description of Operation: The Drain doctor, Inc., is a 24 hour emergency sewer service for the purpose of cleaning and opening drains, sewer pipes, etc.

Number of Franchisees: 4 in Florida and Pennsylvania

In Business Since: 1981; franchisor offered franchises since 1984.

Equity Capital Needed: $18,000

Financial Assistance Available: Any financing of the above is the sole responsibility of the franchisee. The franchisor will make good faith efforts to find the franchisee a creditor, if possible, but can not guarantee any rates or terms of such arrangements.

Training Provided: 7 to 10 days of intensive training in the operation and conduct of his business including a complete course of home office training and field office training with respect to the following; marketing techniques, bookkeeping, equipment operation and maintenance; the science of drain pipe cleaning.

Managerial Assistance Available: Periodic visits to franchisee's location by an executive of the company and unlimited consultation, advice and information concerning the growth and operation of franchisee's business. Organization and sponsorship of district, regional, and national meetings of franchisees for the dissemination and exchange of ideas, experiences, techniques, and developments. Assistance as may be deemed necessary by the company within the provisions of the agreement.

Information Submitted: July 1987

EASI-SET INDUSTRIES
RT 28
Midland, Virginia 22728
Ashley Smith, Director

Description of Operation: ESI provides a service to concrete products producers who are seeking diversification and to persons interested in establishing a precast concrete business. the approach is to supply them fulll developed standards products which have been proven successful and profitable and to provide them an ongoing comprehensive program of service.

Number of Franchisees: 38 in 13 States, Canada and Belgium

In Business Since: 1978

Equity Capital Needed: Varies with product selected and franchisee's manufacturing capabilities range $35,000-$215,000

Financial Assistance Available: None

Training Provided: Production training—1-2 weeks, sales training—1-2 weeks

Managerial Assistance Available: Marketing consultation, production consultation, provide co-op regional advertising, and periodic field visits—quarterly.

Information Submitted: May 1987

ELDORADO STONE CORPORATION
P. O. Box 27 Z
Carnation, Washington 98014
John E. Bennett, President

Description of Operation: Franchisee will manufacture and sell Eldorado Stone, simulated stone and brick building products. No technical background is necessary.

Number of Franchisees: 23 in 16 States and international

In Business Since: 1969

Equity Capital Needed: $46,000 minimum

Financial Assistance Available: None

Training Provided: Company provides 1 week of training in an established manufacturing plant, 1 week in franchisee's plant, and continuous supervision thereafter.

Managerial Assistance Available: Company provides continuous managerial assistance and sponsors annual meetings of franchisees.

Information Submitted: May 1987

EUREKA LOG HOMES INC.
Industrial Park
Berryville, Arkansas 72616
Allen McNelis

Description of Operation: Wholesaling through an international network of distributors and dealers.

Number of Franchisees: 300 in 38 States, Japan and Switzerland

In Business Since: 1976

Equity Capital Needed: $19,700 for 2,000 square foot log home display model.

Financial Assistance Available: None

Training Provided: Excellent training manual and constant assistance from International Marketing and Production Division.

Managerial Assistance Available: Same as above

Information Submitted: July 1987

FACELIFTERS
800 Snediker Avenue
Brooklyn, New York 11207

Description of Operation: Kitchen cabinet refacing and kitchen remodeling.

Number of Franchisees: 4

In Business Since: Parent since 1978, franchising 1984

Equity Capital Needed: $20,000-$25,000

Financial Assistance Available: Yes

Training Provided: 3 weeks of training is provided

Managerial Assistance Available: Sales, marketing, installation and production, and administration. Also financial management assistance ongoing for life of agreement.

Information Submitted: July 1987

FIREDEX, INC.
611 County Line Road
Huntingdon Valley, Pennsylvania 19006
James A. Lees, Vice President, Marketing

Description of Operation: Property damage restoration due to fire, smoke, water, wind or other insured perils.

Number of Franchisees: 17 in Georgia, New Jersey, New York, Pennsylvania and South Carolina

In Business Since: 1980

Equity Capital Needed: $38,500

Financial Assistance Available: None

Training Provided: 2 weeks in national insurance training school for property damage estimating and 1 week of field training in franchisor's headquarters.

Managerial Assistance Available: 2 weeks on location prior to opening of franchisee's office available upon request thereafter.

Information Submitted: July 1987

FLEX-SHIELD INTERNATIONAL, INC.
P. O. Box 1790
636 West Commerce
Gilbert, Arizona 85234
Charles Carroll

Description of Operation: Total maintenance products for the floor to the roof. Cold applied elastomeric roof system—the toughest rubber nonbrake roof system manufactured—the quickest to install, the best warranty. Also features commercial floor care products and service.

Number of Franchisees: 12 including company-owned

In Business Since: 1976

Equity Capital Needed: $25,000 franchise fee. Initial investment of $50,000 to $150,000.

Financial Assistance Available: Yes, some on both franchise fee and equipment.

Training Provided: Complete 5 day training in Gilbert, Arizona with classroom and on-the-job training. Continued training on-site for several installation and follow up training on an ongoing basis.

Managerial Assistance Available: Complete corporate resource staff and new product development staff for ongoing assistance.

Information Submitted: May 1987

*FOUR SEASONS GREENHOUSES, DESIGN
  AND REMODELING CENTER
5005 Veterans Memorial Highway
Holbrook, New York 11741
Chris Esposito, President

Description of Operation: Four Seasons Greenhouse, Design and Remodeling centers franchise presents a unique opportunity in the remodeling and construction industry through its unique and very popular Four Seasons greenhouse—solarium—room addition product line. Each center will be approximately 1,500-3,000 square feet and have "showroom" type displays of products, builders, remodelers, restaurant owners as well as residential home owners and condo owners are only a few of the many different types of potential customers.

Number of Franchisees: 200 throughout the United States and 10 in Canada

In Business Since: 1975

Equity Capital Needed: Approximately $50,000-$100,000

Financial Assistance Available: No financing available

Training Provided: Intensive 2 weeks mandatory training program is scheduled for all new franchisees at the FOur Seasons training center in Farmingdale, New York or Hayward, California, plus an additional 1 week of on-site assistance at the franchised location.

Managerial Assistance Available: Four Seasons will provide ongoing administrative, sales, installation and service training and guidance during the life of the franchise. Complete manuals, forms and directions are provided. Regional sales and service representatives are available to work closely with the franchisees.

Information Submitted: May 1987

GNU SERVICES CORPORATION
1010 University Park Drive
Waco, Texas 76707

Description of Operation: Porcelain and fiberglass repair and refinishing.

Number of Franchisees: 27 in 14 States

In Business Since: 1971

Equity Capital Needed: $10,000 plus service truck

Financial Assistance Available: $8,000 purchases license agreement for area, all necessary equipment, 2 weeks training and materials inventory. Does not include transportation to and from school, motel and meals. $2,000 will be needed for start-up funds, plus initial advertising.

Training Provided: Intensive 2 week training for dealer and one mechanic. Training is in school and on-the-job.

Managerial Assistance Available: GNU Services provides upon request, management services in areas of bookkeeping, advertising, inventory control. Complete operations and service manuals are furnished to all dealers. District dealer meetings are conducted at home office or in designated area. GNU is constantly developing new product and technical information to be distributed to all GNU Tub dealers.

Information Submitted: May 1987

HERITAGE LOG HOMES, INC.
Box 610
Gatlinburg, Tennessee 37738

Description of Operation: Manufacture pre-cut log home(s) kits in verious attractive design plans for year-round living. Meets all national building codes, H.U.D. approval and material grades for quality. Sell through dealership and provide training and development of sales force.

Number of Franchisees: 45 in 19 States

In Business Since: 1974

Equity Capital Needed: $50,000 to $100,000 model home construction on commercial lot.

Financial Assistance Available: Co-op advertising after open house/grand opening.

Training Provided: 2 days sales, policies and technical training at national headquarters in Gatlinburg, Tennessee. Annual follow-up

Managerial Assistance Available: Technical assistance construction training provided upon delivery of model home.

Information Submitted: May 1987

HYDROFLO SYSTEM BASEMENT WATERPROOFING
3729 Linden, Southwest
Wyoming, Michigan 49508
Wayne L. Nichols, Jr., President

Description of Operation: Franchisor has developed unique procedures for waterproofing an entire basement within one day without the use of any chemicals. All work carries a life-of-structure guarantee against leakage - regardless of ownership. Franchises are geared for high volume through refined marketing techniques.

Number of Franchisees: 3 in Michigan and Indiana

In Business Since: 1972

Equity Capital Needed: $50,000

Financial Assistance Available: Franchisor will assist in securing financial assistance through leasing companies.

Training Provided: 4 to 6 weeks intensive classroom and on-the-job training at the home office and at the franchisees location.

Managerial Assistance Available: Monthly personal assistance by both marketing representatives and installation supervisors.

Information Submitted: May 1987

K-KRETE, INC.
7711 Computer Avenue
Edina, Minnesota 55435
Dick Dahlstrom

Description of Operation: K-Krete, controlled density fill, is a patented formulation of cement, fillers and pozzolanic materials used in place of compacted earth. It is delivered and placed by standard ready mix concrete trucks.

Number of Franchisees: 20 in 9 States

In Business Since: 1972

Equity Capital Needed: $3,000 minimum plus plant capability of mixing and delivering concrete.

Financial Assistance Available: None

Training Provided: Training course covering manufacturing qualityl control, and marketing of K-Krete products—1 day duration.

Managerial Assistance Available: Technical manuals, brochures and marketing aids are made available to franchisees. Engineering personnel are available to assist in technical response.

Information Submitted: May 1987

KITCHEN SAVERS, INC.
715 Rose Street
La Crosse, Wisconsin 54603
Gerald A. Baldner, President

Description of Operation: Kitchen Savers remodels kitchen cabinets by first removing the existing doors and drawer fronts. Then we reface the existing framework with 1/8", 3-ply oak paneling. The old doors and drawer fronts are then replaced with new, 3/4" solid oak doors and drawer fronts.

Number of Franchisees: 6 in Wisconsin

In Business Since:b08 1982

Equity Capital Needed: $10,000 broken down: $7,500 for franchise fee and $2,500 for initial start-up cost, advertising.

Financial Assistance Available: None

Training Provided: 2 days of extensive training at home office and 2 days at franchisee's location.

Managerial Assistance Available: Ongoing training and consultation will be provided upon request.

Information Submitted: May 1987

LAVASTONE INTERNATIONAL, INC.
P. O. Box 26699
Dallas, Texas 75226
Jack G. Busby, President

Description of Operation: Manufacturing and sales of a complete system and product line; Lavastone, Lite Stone, Fireplace Surrounds, Lava Crete, Lavastone Grout, and Lavastone Sealer.

Number of Franchisees: 8

In Business Since: 1969

Equity Capital Needed: Determined by size of operation and franchise territory.

Finanancial Assistance Available: None

Training Provided: Company provides 2 weeks of comprehensive training in franchisee's plant, plus 2 weeks training in sales. Company personnel are available upon request at all times.

Managerial Assistance Available: Company provides continuous managerial assistance and sponsors semi-annual meetings for franchisees each year. A manual is provided for all policies and procedures.

Information Submitted: May 1987

THE LINC CORPORATION
4 North Shore Center
Pittsburgh, Pennsylvania 15212
Preston D. Bond, President

Description of Operation: Franchising leading existing independent heating and air conditioning contractors to offer commercial and industrial building owners and operators a full service heating, ventilating and air conditioning maintenance program (LINC Service). This program also includes energy management, system installation, replacement, repair and modernization and 24-hour emergency service. As part of the LINC System franchise arrangement, the contractor is provided with computerized programs for customer invoicing, accounting and management information reporting. The computerized programs are part of the LINC System which links a computer terminal in each franchisee's office to a main computer at The LINC Corporation headquarters in Pittsburgh. This total franchise program, which is unique in the industry, offers independent contractors a comprehensive and cost-effective maintenance and service program for today's professional HVAC contractors.

Number of Franchisees: 87 in 37 States

In Business Since: 1980

Equity Capital Needed: Not applicable; only franchising existing businesses. (Approximately $35,000 initial cost.)

Financial Assistance Available: $20,000 of initial fee with interest

Training Provided: Business format, management, marketing, sales and operations.

Managerial Assistance Available: Consultation is available without charge ongoing. Initial start-up training is up to 15 instructor days.

Information Submitted: May 1987

LINDAL CEDAR HOMES, INC.
P. O. Box 24426
Seattle, Washington 98124
Sir Walter Lindal, Chairman

Description of Operation: Manufacture and sale of Cedar Homes including precut Cedar Homes and Cedar Log Homes.

Number of Franchisees: 250 in all 50 States

In Business Since: 1945

Equity Capital Needed: $3,000 minimum, none to Lindal (no franchise fee).

Financial Assistance Available: Long-term mortgage financing for homes sold.

Training Provided: 4 days training seminar initially. 1 day seminars 3 times a year.

Managerial Assistance Available: Area representative continually assists.

Information Submitted: May 1987

MAGNUM PIERING INC.
720 A. West Fourth Street
Eureka, Montana 63025
Tom Zagel, Vice President

Description of Operation: Mechanical correction of settled building foundations and flatwork done by hydraulically driving steel piers to bedrock and locking same to the corrected portion.

Number of Franchisees: 6 in Kansas, Missouri, Texas and Colorado.

In Business Since: 1987

Equity Capital Needed: $85,000 includes: franchise fee, supplies, equipment, material and training.

Financial Assistance Available: Partial financing of the franchise fee with no interest charged.

Training Provided: Complete training in office procedure, advertising, estimating presentation of contracts, closing and all facets of Piering, including "hands-on" field work.

Managerial Assistance Available: Franchisor features through training in both managerial and technical aspects and offers ongoing support without reservation.

Information Submitted: May 1987

MASTER REMODELERS NATIONAL, INC.
11747 Firestone Boulevard
Norwalk, California 90650
Leslie D. Wilson, President

Description of Operation: Franchising of home remodeling contractors.

Number of Franchisees: 6 in California

In Business Since: 1981

Equity Capital Needed: $7,500 plus business office—$20,000 working capital.

Financial Assistance Available: $3,500 deposit on franchise purchase price with monthly payments of $200 until paid in full.

Training Provided: Sales and managment training provided before start-up of operation. Ongoing sales training for sales personnel plus help as needed regarding management.

Managerial Assistance Available: Additional training in management or sales and marketing assistance as company deems necessary.

Information Submitted: July 1987

MIRACLE METHOD, INC.
BATHROOM RESTORATION
950 Detroit Avenue
Suite 1-B
Concord, California 94518
Robert D. Gray, President

Description of Operation: Miracle Method Bathroom Restoration franchisees provide durable high quality repair and refinishing of bathroom and kitchen fixtures and tile, either porcelain or fiberglass. Our franchises use a unique system, proven for its outstanding durability. Miracle Method Inc., also offers program to back up our franchise's, with a 5 year warranty.

Number of Franchisees: 65 in 12 States

In Business Since: 1977

Equity Capital Needed: $20,000-$25,000

Financial Assistance Available: Third party lease of equipment.

Training Provided: 14 days in-house and in-field training at franchisee's location in U.S. Continued technical and managerial assistance. Advertising program.

Managerial Assistance Available: As above and assistance provided as needed and required for as long as franchise exists.

Information Submitted: May 1987

MISTER RENOVATOR
Suite 201
105 North Washington Street
Alexandria, Virginia 22320
R. J. Kaufman, President

Description of Operation: Is involved with the franchising of independent general contractors.

Number of Franchisees: 45 in Washington, Virginia, Maryland, Canada and Australia

In Business Since: 1976

Equity Capital Needed: $7,500

Financial Assistance Available: None

Training Provided: Franchisor provides an initial 3 day orientation program followed up with 1/2 day per week and a formal (all in attendance) 1/2 day per month.

Managerial Assistance Available: The franchisor has been involved in the business for many years. Through the ongoing training programs which cover all aspects of the weekly and monthly programs all management areas of the business are covered thoroughly.

Information Submitted: July 1987

MR. BUILD INTERNATIONAL
One Univac Lane
Suite 402
Windsor, Connecticut 06095
Thomas M. Tyska, President/CEO

Description of Operation: National franchisor of residential and commercial remodeling, maintenance, service and repair tradespeople.

Number of Franchisees: Over 500 throughout the United States, Canada and Japan

In Business Since: 1981

Equity Capital Needed: $3,900-$6,900 franchise fee, depending upon classification, plus net worth requirements.

Financial Assistance Available: Various financing programs available through independent lending institutions if franchisee qualifies.

Training Provided: Marketing management on a continuous basis.

Managerial Assistance Available: Various industry-related computer program sales and management courses available on a continuous basis.

Information Submitted: May 1987

NATURAL LOG HOMES, INC.
RT 2 Box 164, South Kings Highway
Noel, Missouri 64854
Ernest Bramlett, President

Description of Operation: International log home manufacturer.

Number of Franchisees: 137 in 23 States

Equity Capital Needed: $40,000-$50,000 (log model home)

Financial Assistance Available: 50 percent is provided to qualified applicants.

Training Provided: Expense free at our national office excluding travel.

Managerial Assistance Available: Technical manual, blueprints and etc.

Information Submitted: May 1987

* NEW ENGLAND LOG HOMES, INC.
2301 State Street
P. O. Box 5427
Hamden, Connecticut 06518

Description of Operation: New England Log Homes, Inc. (NELHI), manufactures precut, hand-peeled log homes from pine timber. Over 40 models are available encompassing a wide variety of home sizes and styles. NELHI can also design and manufacture custom homes. Franchise dealers are established from Maine to Florida and as far West as California. The dealer is required to erect a model home which serves as his office. This is provided at dealers cost.

Number of Franchisees: 70 nationwide.

In Business Since: 1969

Equity Capital Needed: $100,000-$150,000 (this includes the log home cost, land, furnishings, etc., which are then the franchisees personal property).

Financial Assistance Available: Yes

Training Provided: 5 days classroom in Hamden, Connecticut, 5 days construction when model home erected. A yearly sales meetings is designed is designed to upgrade the dealers in the latest changes in the log homes, sales methods, etc.

Managerial Assistance Available: Yes, depending on the individuals needs, assistance is provided by regional managers in franchisee's area as well as by corporate staff.

Information Submitted: May 1987

NORTHERN PRODUCTS LOG HOMES, INC.
P. O. Box 616, Bomarc Road
Bangor, Maine 04401-0616
Judi Perkins, Director of Marketing

Description of Operation: Northern Products Log Homes, Inc., manufacturers pre-cut log home packages for both residential and commercial use. The company offers 23 standard models and a free custom design service. Franchised dealers are required to purchase and erect a display building which may also be used as the franchisee's residence.

Number of Franchisees: 24 in 19 States

In Business Since: 1968

Equity Capital Needed: $66,600-$199,980 (includes cost of log home, equipment, furnishings, signage and sales and promotional material).

Financial Assistance Available: None

Training Provided: Mandatory initial training and orientation at main office in Bangor, Maine. Further training at the franchisee's location. Annual national sales training and business meeting held.

Managerial Assistance Available: Managerial and technical assistance provided as required or requested throughout the term of the franchise.

Information Submitted: May 1987

NOVUS PLATE GLASS REPAIR, INC.
10425 Hampshire Avenue, South
Minneapolis, Minnesota 55438
Gerald E. Keinath, President

Description of Operation: Company has developed a process to repair, rather than replace, BB and stone-damaged plate glass windows. This is a company affiliated with Novus Windshield Repair which has over 1,200 dealers worldwide.

Number of Franchisees: 6

In Business Since: 1972 (franchising since 1982).

Equity Capital Needed: Approximately $12,000 (depending on size of exclusive area)

Financial Assistance Available: None

Training Provided: 3 day formal factor training

Managerial Assistance Available: Regional sales manager and research and development laboratory support.

Information Submitted: May 1987

PAUL W. DAVIS SYSTEMS, INC.
1100 Cresery Boulevard
Suite 20
Jacksonville, Florida 32211
Paul W. Davis, President

Description of Operation: Paul W. Davis Systems, Inc., is a totally computerized insurance restoration contracting company with approximately 80 percent of its business obtained from insurance adjusters for the repair of fire, water and windstorm damage; the other 20 percent comes from home and commercial improvements. A unique system of computer estimates and cost controls enable our franchises to experience early success with no previous experience in this field. A good personality and a willingness to work is required.

Number of Franchisees: 90 in 25 States

In Business Since: 1966

Equity Capital Needed: The franchise fee is $35,000. The franchise needs $25,000 operating capital. $42,500 minimum cash required to start.

Financial Assistance Availble: Franchisor finances part of franchise fee with payment tied to sales income.

Training Provided: Franchisee trains in home office school for 3 weeks. Franchisor works with franchisee on location. Franchisor can assist in all recruiting, hiring and training.

Managerial Assistance Available: Managerial and technical assistance continues throughout the life of the franchise including computer software and other management programs.

Information Submitted: May 1987

PERMA CERAM ENTERPRISES, INC.
65 Smithtown Boulevard
Smithtown, New York 11787
Joseph Tumolo, President

Description of Operation: Resurfacing and repair of porcelain and fiberglass bathroom fixtures such as tubs, sinks and wall tile with Perma Ceram's Porcelaincote. Process used in private homes, apartments, hotels/motels, institutions, etc. Available in white and all colors. Established national accounts.

Number of Franchisees: Approximately 175 in 39 States, Bermuda, Bahamas, Canada and Puerto Rico

In Business Since: 1975

Equity Capital Needed: $19,500 total investment. Includes all equipment, materials, supplies and training.

Financial Assistance Available: 100 percent financing available through independent lending institutions.

Training Provided: 5 days training at established location. All expenses included in cost of dealership. Technical, training, sales training, management, marketing, etc. Operation manual provided.

Managerial Assistance Available: Advertising, sales and promotional materials; ongoing managerial and technical assistance provided. Continual updating of information provided through bulletins, newsletters, personal contact. Return visits to training facilityl available if necessary.

Information Submitted: May 1987

PERMA-GLAZE, INC.
132 South Sherwood Village Drive
Tucson, Arizona 85710
Dale R. Young, President

Description of Operation: Perma-Glaze specializes in the restoration and refinishing of bathroom and kitchen fixtures such as bathtubs, sinks and ceramic wall tiles. Materials to be refinished consist of porcelain, fiberglass, acrylic, cultured marble, formica, kitchen appliances, whirlpool tubs, shower enclosures and most building materials. Service includes chip repair, fiberglass and acrylic spa repairs, restoration and recoating of fixtures. Available in 30 colors including white. ALl work under complete warranty. Perma-Glaze services home owners, apartments, hotels/motels, institutions, hospitals, contractors, property managers, plumbing contractors and many more.

Number of Franchisees: 40 in the United States

In Business Since: 1978

Equity Capital Needed: $16,500 to $19,500 includes all training, equipment and supplies with enough product to earn back your initial investment.

Financial Assistance Available: Franchisor does not offer any specific kind or amount of financial assistance to prospective franchises. Assistance is rendered to prospective franchises with regard to mode and method of financing and payment where a small amount of assistance is needed.

Training Provided: 5 day (hands-on) training session by trained technician at established location. "Lodging and air fare included in cost of franchise." Technical training provided with operations manual, "hotline" service and newsletter.

Managerial Assistance Available: Info provided for support in advertising, sales, promotional sales, mailing lists, business contacts. Advertising format for yellow pages, newspapers and manazines plus availability of material for TV commercial. Continual exposure from national advertising in popular well known magazines as well as many trade publications. Continual updating of information provided thru bulletins, newsletters and personal contact.

Information Submitted: May 1987

PERMA-JACK CO.
9066 Watson Road
St. Louis, Missouri 63126
Joan L. Robinson, President

Description of Operation: A fast inexpensive building foundation stabilizing system. Hydraulically driven steel pipe colums support the building foundation on rock.

Number of Franchisees: 13 in Missouri, Texas, California, Oklahoma, Mississippi and Colorado

In Business Since: 1974, incorporated 1975

Equity Capital Needed: Inventory and working capital $60,000. Franchise fee, according to population $7,500 to $20,000.

Financial Assistance Available: None

Training Provided: Field training and complete instructions are given at the St. Louis, Missouri home office. Further training at the franchisee's location and job sites. Continuing informational assistance and training is given. Art work, layouts, and outlines for advertising and suggested business forms and brochures are included.

Managerial Assistance Available: Managerial and technical assistance provided throughout length of franchise. Top management makes field visits as deemed necessary.

Information Submitted: May 1987

PORCELAIN PATCH & GLAZE COMPANY OF AMERICA
140 Watertown Street
Watertown, Massachusetts 02172
Philip J. Gleason

Description of Operation: Refinishing, spraying, glazing, spot-blending and patching of porcelain and enamel finishes of all kinds, spray painting of lacquer and lacquer blending work of all kinds. Performed for appliance stores, home owners, movers, apratment house owners, plumbers, distributors of major appliances, dentists. A shop is not necessary.

Number of Franchisees: 15 in 15 States

In Business Since: 1938

Equity Capital Needed: $3,500

Financial Assistance Available: 50 percent down to good credit risks.

Training Provided: 10 days at main office

Managerial Assistance Available: Periodic visits, direct mail advertising.

Information Submitted: July 1987

PORCELITE INTERNATIONAL, INC.
15745 Crabbs Branchway
Rockville, Maryland 28855
M. D. Berardi, President

Description of Operation: The Porcelite franchise offers a process for the repair and refinishing of porcelain plumbing fixtures such as bathtubs and sinks for both commercial and residential use. Chips are repaired and complete fixtures refinished and restored. Used in homes, motels, apartment houses, etc. In white or choice of any color.

Number of Franchisees: 72 in 26 States

In Business Since: 1963

Equity Capital Needed: $17,500 minimum

Financial Assistance Available: None

Training Provided: 5 day training session from 9 am to 5 pm covering all aspects of procelain repair, refinishing, and restoration.

Managerial Assistance Available: Advertising and sales promotional materials, continuing guidance and assistance is required. Operations manual provided.

Information Submitted: May 1987

REDI—STRIP CO., INC.
P. O. Box 2745
Santa Fe Springs, California 90670
J. Paul Derlinger, President

Description of Operation: The Redi—Strip system offers a unique nondestructive paint and coating removal by a simple immersion system. The electrolytic deruster immersion "floats" the rust off of steel parts with no metal loss. Redi—Strip provides the tanks, chemical and some other equpment to start your business.

Number of Franchisees: 23 in 16 States and Canada

In Business Since: 1951

Equity Capital Needed: $40,000 to $89,000. No franchise fee or royalties are involved.

Financial Assistance Available: This would be answered by J. Paul Deringer

Training Provided: Intensive 1 week mandatory work and training program at one of our plants. One week at the franchise location.

Managerial Assistance Available: Redi—Strip is available at all times to answer any and all questions.

Inforamtion Submitted: July 1987

RYAN HOMES, INC.
100 Ryan Court
Pittsburgh, Pennsylvania 15205
Ronald T. Blair, Vice President, Ryan Building Systems

Description of Operation: Ryan Homes, Inc., is a residential single family homebuilder. Ryan is presently one of the largest builders in the country. They offer to an individual complete systems and products to allow them to build and sell houses in preselected markets.

Number of Franchisees: 7 in 7 States

In Business Since: 1948

Equity Capital Needed: $150,000-$250,000

Financial Assistance Available: Franchisor will provide no assistance in financing operation. Franchisor provides construction financing for model homes and sold houses and assistance in securing permanent mortgages for customers.

Training Provided: Initial training includes Ryan manager spending approximately 4 months on-site with franchisee to set up systems and start up operation. Ryan has ongoing field training and franchisee can attend Ryan training center for any of 16 courses.

Managerial Assistance Available: Field support is administered by a staff and is involved in marketing, merchandising, sales, construction, administration and management. Field staff works closely with franchisee in all phases of operation.

Information Submitted: July 1987

THE SCREENMOBILE INC.
538 East Dalton Avenue
Glendora, California 91740
Monty M. Walker, President

Description of Operation: Mobile window and door screening and rescreening service.

Number of Franchisees: 18 in California, Arizona, Idaho and Nevada.

In Business Since: 1982

Equity Capital Needed: $32,000

Financial Assistance Available: None

Training Provided: Field training, shop training, classroom training, approximately 2 weeks.

Managerial Assistance Available: Ongoing 24 hour telephone and field assistance.

Information Submitted: July 1987

SERVICE AMERICA
4415 Metro Parkway
Suite 202
Fort Myers, FLorida 33901
Al Roach, President

Description of Operation: Service America offers a unique service/replacement marketing program for existing heating and air conditioning dealers.

Number of Franchisees: 37 in 10 states

In Business Since: 1984

Equity Capital Needed: $9,900 minimum

Financial Assistance Available: None

Training Provided: 10 days of initial training is provided at the home office school. Ongoing training and support is provided at franchisee's location every month.

Managerial Assistance Available: Service America provides continual ongoing management service for the life of the franchise.

Information Submitted: May 1987

SMOKEY MOUNTAIN LOG HOMES
P. O. Box 549
Maggie Valley, North Carolina 28751

Description of Operation: Manufacturer of pre-fabricated log homes.

Number of Franchisees: 16 in Virginia, North Carolina, South Carolina, Georgia and Florida.

In Business Since: 1974

Equity Capital Needed: No franchise fee or liability. However, dealer must be capable of erecting a model home.

Financial Assistance Available: Financing must be obtained through various establishing loaning institutions.

Training Provided: Franchisee is required to familiarize himself/herself with Smokey Mountain Log Home production methods by visiting the production facility in Maggie Valley, North Carolina. Knowledge of construction related procedures is a prerequisite. A paid 2 day training seminar is offered.

Managerial Assistance Available: Technical assistance in the field on a personal basis is provided along with a dealer support kit that has been compiled to aid advertising and marketing of SMokey Mountain Log Home kits.

Information Submitted: July 1987

SPEED FAB-CRETE CORPORATION INTERNATIONAL
1150 East Mansfield Highway
P. O. Box 15580
Fort Worth, Texas 76119
David Bloxom, Jr., President

Description of Operation: Speed Fab-Crete is a patented precast concrete building system utilizing lightweight loadbearing concrete wall panels as its core component. Each franchise acts as a manufacturer, general contractor, and sub-contractor. The franchisor provides complete training program and technical back-up support services.

Number of Franchisees: 2 in 2 States

In Business Since: 1968

Equity Capital Needed: $30,000-$50,000

Financial Assistance Available: None

Training Provided: Minimum 1 week traning provided by franchisor at national headquarters for franchisee and key personnel. Periodic 1 and 2 day training seminars held at national headquarters

Managerial Assistance Available: On-site managerial assistance periodically provided at expense of franchisor. On-site technical assistance on request of franchisee. Complete manuals of operations, forms, and directions as provided.

Information Submitted: May 1987

SPR INTERNATIONAL BATHTUB REFINISHING, INC.
3800 Wendell Drive
Suite 302
Atlanta, Georgia 30336
Larry Stevens, Franchise Director

Description of Operation: SPR franchise system offers; confidential technical knowhow, and an exclusive chemical system to repair, refinish or change color on porcelain, fiberglass, cultured marble—bathtubs, sinks, appliance surfaces, counter tops, etc. SPR also offer a system for ceramic tile restoration which includes: leakproofing ceramic walls and floors, stain and mildew removal, regrouting sealing or complete color change without removal. SPR franchise system includes use of all trademark and service marks including the service trucks, etc., for the use of all dealers.

Number of Franchisees: 16 in 9 States and 1 in Canada

In Business Since: 1971

Equity Capital Needed: $5,000-$10,000

Financial Assistance Available: Yes

Training Provided: 2 weeks training for franchisee and personnel at home office and on-the-job training. SPR also provides periodic training year round to assist franchisee and employees in any aspect of their business—at no charge or VHS video training tapes.

Managerial Assistance Available: SPR provides continual management aid for the life of the franchise. Including: advertisment formats for newspapers, magazines, TV commercials, etc. Co-op advertisement is also available. Complete manual of operations and directions are provided. SPR personnel offers telephone consultation daily on problem solving.

Information Submitted: May 1987

SURFACE SPECIALISTS, INC.
Route 3, Box 272
Isanti, Minnesota 55040
Wayne McClosky, President

Description of Operation: Repair, refinishing, recoloring of acrylic spas, formica countertops, cultured marble vanities and whirlpool tubs, fiberglass tubs and showers, porcelain tubs and sinks. P.V.C. tubs and showers and kitchen appliances. Factory authorized warranty service for 26 plumbingware manufacturers. Service work for apartments, hospitals and major hotel/motel chains. Supplier of repair materials to acrylic spa and P.V.C. tub manufacturers.

Number of Franchisees: 5 in Illinois, Minnesota, Nebraska and Kansas.

In Business Since: 1980

Equity Capital Needed: $20,500 includes franchise fee.

Financial Assistance Available: Finance $4,000 of the $14,500 franchise fee. Payable over 3 years at 10 percent interest. Fee includes equipment and material to complete $10,000 to $15,000 in service work.

Training Provided: 2 weeks at the Minnesota location. After training we spend 4 days at the franchisee's city contacting apartments, hotels/motels, distributors, etc. Periodic re-training, newsletters, operations manual.

Managerial Assistance Available: Continual management service for the duration of the franchise in all phases including: bidding, technical problems, new services and materials, and problem solving.

Information Submitted: May 1987

TIMBERMILL STORAGE BARNS, INC.
1 Wolf Run
Glen Ellen, California 95442
A. G. Phillips, III, President

Description of Operation: Timbermill Storage Barns, Inc., prefabricates, sells and constructs on-site storage barns and greenhouses. Gazebos are manufactured centrally and sold by the franchisees in kit form. The barns and greenhouses are constructed of top quality materials purchased locally by the franchisee. Some prefabrication is required before construction takes place at the job site.

Number of Franchisees: 19 nationwide

In Business Since: 1985

Equity Capital Needed: $18,000

Financial Assistance Available: None

Training Provided: Extensive 5 day training program at franchisee's location designed to educate him in all aspects of the Timbermill business plan. The loan of the Timbermill operations manual that includes such topics as material inventory, purchasing and construction procedures, marketing, bookkeeping, and much more.

Managerial Assistance Available: Total training and ongoing assistance with advertising, technical bulletins and managerial support. Conducts market research to aid franchisees in promoting their products. Timbermill Storage Barns, Inc., provides all assistance necessary to achieve and maintain the high quality that is becoming a trademark with our Barns.

Information Submitted: May 1987

WALL FILL WORLDWIDE, INC.
649 Childs Street
Wheaton, Illinois 60187
Edmund G. Lowrie, President

Description of Operation: Business format franchise. Trains the franchisee in the areas of sales, management, and basic installation procedures. The business operation consists of the sale and installation of siding, gutters, windows and doors.

Number of Franchisees: 2 in Illinois including company-owned

In Business Since: 1986—Parent in business since 1928.

Equity Capital Needed: $31,250

Financial Assistance Available: None

Training Provided: 10 days in sales, basic installation, crew management, and office management.

Managerial Assistance Available: Ongoing—intensive in first 5 days of operation.

Information Submitted: June 1987

THE WINDOWS OF OPPORTUNITIES, INC.
711 Rigsbee Avenue
Durham, North Carolina 27701
Jack Huisman

Description of Operation: The Windows of Opportunities offers franchises in "The Window Man," for exclusive solid vinyl replacement windows and new construction vinyl windows, sun and garden room enclosures and state of the art wireless security systems.

Number of Franchisees: 36 in North Carolina, South Carolina, Georgia

In Business Since: 1983

Equity Capital Needed: Varies from $15,000 to $35,000.

Financial Assistance Available: Financing assistance to qualified applicants.

Training Provided: Extensive 1 week training at corporate training center in Durham, North Carolina. On-site start-up support and continual ongoing training and operational support.

Managerial Assistance Available: Assistance in management, sales and marketing, business operations, advertising, lead operations, etc.

Information Submitted: July 1987

COSMETICS/TOILETRIES

ALOETTE
345 Lancaster Avenue
Malvern, Pennsylvania 19355
John E. Defibaugh

Description of Operation: Distribution of high quality cosmetics through sales representatives conducting shows in customers' homes.

Number of Franchisees: 75 in 33 States, and 51 in Canada, United Kingdom, Australia, New Zealand, Bahamas and Hong Kong.

In Business Since: 1978

Equity Capital Needed: $60,000; $10,000 cash downpayment, balance financed.

Financial Assistance Available: Franchisor has provided financing of franchise note.

Training Provided: Extensive training provided in areas of sales, recruiting, operations, and financial accounting.

Managerial Assistance Available: Sales training manuals and videotapes available. Accounting manual and journals. District set-up allows for technical assistance and support. Regional and national meetings held throughout the year.

Information Submitted: March 19877

CASWELL-MASSEY
111 Eighth Avenue
New York, New York 10011
Herbert Leeds, Business Counselor

Description of Operation: Caswell-Massey, the oldest chemists and perfumers in America was founded in 1752. It is the source for high quality toiletry and personal care items. From its historical register are still made the colognes loved by George Washington and Dolly Madison. With all its products, Caswell-Massey pays attention to product packaging, creating beautiful variegated designs that are representations of its image.

Number of Franchisees: 20 in 12 States including company-owned.

In Business Since: 1976

Equity Capital Needed: $150,000

Financial Assistance Available: None at this time.

Training Provided: 1 week intensive training, refresher training during the initial set-up and on-site training.

Managerial Assistance Available: Complete retail management staff which consists of the director, associate director and the administrative assistant are available to assist and direct franchisees in all aspects of operating a retail store.

Information Submitted: July 1987

* **"i" NATURAL COSMETICS NUTRIENT COSMETIC, LTC.**
355 Middlesex Avenue
Wilmington, Massachusetts 01887
Robert Greenberg

Description of Operation: A unique cosmetic boutique, primarily located in regional malls, offering a complete skin care and cosmetic line with more than 350 products, plus services like: make-up stylings, facials, waxing, nail sculpturing and manicuring. Products are based on natural ingredients and are exclusively distributed through "i" Natural Cosmetics shops.

Number of Franchisees: 70 shops in 20 States plus 25 company-owned in 18 States.

In Business Since: 1970

Equity Capital Needed: Total capital required, $50,000 to $100,000 depending upon location.

Financial Assistance Available: "i" Natural may assist a franchisee with arrangements for financing new locations and may offer financing from franchisees purchasing company-owned or managed shops.

Training Provided: "i" Natural provides a 1 week business seminar at corporate headquarters. Topics include, but are not limited to management, marketing, merchandising and accounting. A 9 day training program covering merchandising, product knowledge and sales training is provided at the shop for the franchisee and shop staff. Additional on-site visits are provided periodically.

Managerial Assistance Available: Includes, but not limited to real estate, architectural, construction, equipment, initial and ongoing training, opening assistance, marketing research, advertising and promotions, insurance and operational manuals.

Information Submitted: July 1987

JUDITH SANS INTERNATIONALE, INC.
3853 Oakcliff Industrial Court
Atlanta, Georgia 30340
Judith Sans, President

Description of Operation: A total "Judith Sans Total Image" makeover center with skin care, body care, hair care, private label manufacturer (cosmetics) and complete skin care cosmetic line for the ethnic market, traded under the name "Women of Color Inc." Complete start-up packages available.

Number of Franchisees: 34 in 9 States plus distributors which approximate 500 plus over 1,000 private label accounts throughout the country in various beauty salons, department stores, boutiques, etc., and in several foreign countries. "Women of Color," retail line for the ethnic market is mall marketed throughout the United States.

In Business Since: 1969, franchising, distributoring, private label 1978.

Equity Capital Needed: $40,000 to $70,000 for distributors. No minimum order for private label.

Financial Assistance Available: None

Training Provided: 14 days intensive training provided by franchiser, distributor at company's training school in Atlanta, Georgia comprehensive, technical, administrative manuals, and recordkeeping, advertising assistance, and quarterly fresh-up training, site location and layout help provided. Field personnel start-up, on-site help, and periodic evaluation.

Managerial Assistance Available: Continuous

Information Submitted: May 1987

**KEY WEST FRAGRANCE & COSMETIC FACTORY, INC.,/
KEY WEST ALOE INC.**
524 Front Street
Key West, Florida 33040
Kathleen Stauss, Director of Marketing

Description of Operation: Manufacture and distribution of over 300 unique and high quality Aloe based cosmetics: hair care, suntan, bath, men's products and skin care products, as well as an unusual and extensive fragrance line. Seven company-owned stores are in operation, over 40 full-line stores and over 1,000 wholesale accounts. Mailing list numbers over 100,000. Our mail order department promises next day shipment.

Number of Franchisees: 1 in Hawaii plus 5 company-owned

In Business Since: 1971

Equity Capital Needed: Franchise fees begin at $25,000.

Financial Assistance Available: None

Training Provided: Concentrated training at corporate headquarters before franchisor opens for business; ongoing training during preparations for opening at site. Staff available at all times for refresher training as needed.

Managerial Assistance Available: Technical assistance is available at all times. Managerial assistance is also available at all times. Training in both areas is provided at corporate headquarters and on-site before franchisee opens for business.

Information Submitted: July 1987

SUZANNE MOREL COSMETICS & SKIN CARE
c/o MOREL MARKETING MANAGEMENT COMPANY
3115 Northwest 10th Terrace
Suite 110
Ft. Lauderdale, Florida 33309
Pierre Morel, President and Chief Executive Officer

Description of Operation: A unique, exclusive concept in retail sales of high quality cosmetics and skin care products in an approximate 200 square foot kiosk located in the middle of upscale malls with high density traffic.

Number of Franchisees: 5 in Florida

In Business Since: 1977

Equity Capital Needed: $100,000 for a complete turnkey operation.

Financial Assistance Available: Opening inventory of $20,000 may be financed by the distributors depending on the merit of franchisee.

Training Provided: An extensive 4 week training program between the corporate headquarters, existing mall locations and on-site prior to the grand opening.

Managerial Assistance Available: Assistance in all phases of operation is ongoing at all times, including training, bookkeeping, advertising, site selection, lease negotiations and cost control. District managers are available for on-site consultations.

Information Submitted: May 1987

SYD SIMONS COSMETICS, INC.
2 East Oak Street
Chicago, Illinois 60611
Jerome Weitzel, President

Description of Operation: Syd Simons Cosmetics offers a unique completely equipped makeup and skin care studio for the sale of a complete line of cosmetic products and accessories as well as related services. The package includes all furniture, fixtures, studio supplies, opening inventory, decorating, brochures and advertising and promotional materials.

Number of Franchisees: 5 in Illinois and Kansas

In Business Since: Retailing 1940. Franchising 1972.

Equity Capital Needed: Approximately $60,000

Financial Assistance Available: Franchisor will assist franchisee in obtaining business loan from appropriate lending institution.

Training Provided: Syd Simons Cosmetics provides basic 60 day training period in makeup and skin care as well as studio operations and business procedures at the franchisors home office. Additional on-site training conducted periodically.

Managerial Assistance Available: Syd Simons provides continual managerial, legal, financial and promotional guidance in accordance with the needs of the franchisee, as well as assistance in sales areas.

Information Submitted: April 1987

DENTAL CENTERS

AMERICAN DENTAL COUNCIL, INC.
16250 Ventura Boulevard
Suite 335
Encino, California 91436
Martin M. Cooper, President

Description of Operation: Dental referral service providing free referral to private-practice general dentist or orthodontist in local area. Panel consists of at least 25 private dental practices, composed of dentists who wish to gain more patients by bonding together, pooling advertising (TV, newspaper) funds, and creating a total marketing program.

Number of Franchisees: 2 in California and 1 in Michigan

In Business Since: 1980

Equity Capital Needed: $75,000

Financial Assistance Available: None

Training Provided: Ongoing

Managerial Assistance Available: Assistance with creation of dental panel by putting on group meetings and involvement with personal sales followup. Providing of complete operational handbook ·and hands-on assistance with such details as staffing, office procedures, patient relations, dental law and ethics. Furnishing of turnkey advertising program, including actual commercials, ongoing media buying and placement, marketing strategy, publicity, etc.

Information Submitted: July 1987

DENTAL HEALTH SERVICES
6302 Benjamin Road
Suite 414
Tampa, Florida 33614
George Linsey, Chief Executive Officer

Description of Operation: Traditional dental offices in high traffic locations. DHS is popularly priced and advertises. We provide complete management services, bookkeeping, laboratory advertising etc.

Number of Franchisees: 15

In Business Since: 1981

Equity Capital Needed: $50,000 (working capital and franchise fee)

Financial Assistance Available: We arrange financing

Training Provided: Extensive and ongoing—we train all individuals in our business systems.

Managerial Assistance Available: DHS provides ongoing assistance to its franchisees. We are responsible for new advertising campaigns, implementation of new profit centers, aid in professional hiring, purchasing, etc.

Information Submitted: June 1987

DENTAL POWER INTERNATIONAL
5530 Wisconsin Avenue
Suite 735
Chevy Chase, Maryland 20815
Merle Baboyian, President

Description of Operation: Dental Power is a profitable, nationally recognized personnel placement and consulting network serving the dental community exclusively. Each office uses professional, proven methods of operations, sophisticated and innovative advertising and marketing techniques and is staffed by former members of the dental office team. Services include temporary and permanent staffing, seminars and workshops, in-office consulting and placement of associates and "locum tenens."

Number of Franchisees: 30 in the U.S. and Canada.

In Business Since: 1984 (Prototype, Dental Power of Washington, in business since 1974).

Equity Capital Needed: Approximately $30,000 including franchise fee.

Financial Assistance Available: Yes

Training Provided: Consultation and assistance available by telephone or personal visit. Updates on advertising and video-taped updates on recruitment, seminars, and new services ongoing. Review and analysis of financial statements quarterly.

Managerial Assistance Available: Consultation and assistance available by telephone or personal visit. Updates on advertising, recruitment, seminars, and new services ongoing. review and analysis of financial statements quarterly.

Information Submitted: May 1987

DWIGHT SYSTEMS, INC.
Suite 204
Ronald F. Saverin, CEO

Description of Operation: Quality, full-service dental care facility in retail shopping centers.

Number of Franchisees: 12 in Pennsylvania and Florida, operating 20 units

In Business Since: 1982

Equity Capital Needed: Initial franchise fee: $20,000, turnkey package:$95,000-$185,000, working capital: $20,000.

Financial Assistance Available: None

Training Provided: 5-days intensive program for franchisees and their office managers.

Managerial Assistance Available: Periodic review of business, operating and clinical procedures. Peer review program and operating manuals provided.

Information Submitted: May 1987

JONATHAN DENTAL INC.
7114 Shady Oak Road
Eden Prairie, Minnesota 55344
Brad Matushak, Director of Franchise Sales

Description of Operation: Jonathan Dental is a franchisor of independently owned, traditional fee-for-service dental practices located in high traffic retail settings. Jonathan provides franchisees a full realm of services including site selection, construction materials, staffing assistance, training, practice management consulting, quality assurance, marketing and advertising, and a comprehensive computerized business system.

Number of Franchisees: 15 in Minnesota, 2 in Illinois

In Business Since: 1980

Equity Capital Needed: $14,500

Financial Assistance Available:

Training Provided: 3-5 days initial training for franchisee, managing dentists, and business manager encompassing personnel and dental business systems.

Managerial Assistance Available: Heavy on-site assistance in practice management during the first operating year, tapering to 4-6 days per year thereafter.

Information Submitted: June 1987

NU-DIMENSIONS DENTAL SERVICES
1386 Palisade Avenue
Fort Lee, New Jersey 07024
Charles Hedbavny, Chief Operating Officer

Description of Operation: Nu-Dimensions Dental Centers are comprehensive, consumer-oriented, group dental practices, operating 7 days and 5 evenings a week, and utilizing sophisticated business systems appropriate for high-volume dental practices. Fee structure is less than prevailing community averages, but practices are not discount-oriented.

Number of Franchisees: 9 in New Jersey and New York (excludes company-owned units)

In Business Since: 1978

Equity Capital Needed: $250,000

Financial Assistance Available: Franchisor is able to introduce qualified prospective franchisees to major regional banks with which successful banking relationships have long been established.

Training Provided: Formal training program is one month prior to opening, plus 75 days after opening; ongoing technical assistance is also provided throughout franchise relationship.

Managerial Assistance Available: Nu-Dimensions provides a complete managerial and business systems format for its franchisees and provides technical assistance as an ongoing component of its management services throughout the duration of the franchise. This includes, but is not limited to, marketing and advertising services, financial controls and managerial systems support, operational guidance, group purchasing arrangements, organizational collaboration on systems improvement, and general updating of all business procedures as improvements become indicated.

Information Submitted: May 1987

DRUG STORES

DRUG CASTLE FRANCHISES, INC.
810 East High Street
Springfield, Ohio 45505
Dale A. Obracay, Director of Franchising

Description of Operation: High volume, low margin, deep discount drug stores.

Number of Franchisees: 5 in Ohio and 2 in Indiana, and 1 in Florida

In Business Since: 1984

Equity Capital Needed: $600,000

Financial Assistance Available: Counsel and introduction to banking sources and governmet programs

Training Provided: Initially—30 days, balance of franchise agreement—on demand.

Managerial Assistance Available: Initially—30 days, balance of franchise agreement—on demand.

Information Submitted: May 1987

DRUG EMPORIUM, INC.
7760 Olentangy River Road
Suite 207
Worthington, Ohio 43085
Pat Hiller, Vice President-Franchising

Description of Operation: Drug Emporium is a high-volume, low-margin retail drug store that carries a broad line of health and beauty aids, cosmetics, greeting cards, and a full service pharmacy.

Number of Franchisees: 66 in 20 States plus 54 company-owned

In Business Since: 1977

Equity Capital Needed: $600,000

Financial Assistance Available: Guidance only

Training Provided: 200 hours training in Columbus, manuals are furnished with documentation of start-up and operations including forms needed for operation function.

Managerial Assistance Available: Assistance is constant and predicated on the fact that our income starts after the franchisee is successful.

Information Submitted: July 1987

*HEALTH MART, INC.
1220 Senlac Road
Carrollton, Texas 75006
Gary W. Swords, President

Description of Operation: Health Mart will provide franchises with substantial assistance in the operational and merchandising aspects of operating a full line drug store which includes private label products.

Number of Franchisees: 395 stores in 23 States

In Business Since: 1982

Equity Capital Needed: $5,750 to $55,750—existing operation—$145,000 to $192,000—new operation

Financial Assistance Available: Fixturing, signage and decor is available on a lease basis.

Training Provided: The H/M training department provides intensive 3 day managerial training seminars, 1 day intense clerk seminars, a monthly training newsletter, various video training programs, and a complete retail operations manual. The H/M district manager provides in-store training at the time of store set up and ongoing training during the monthly store visits.

Managerial Assistance Available: Assistance is provided during the initial store set up phase and ongoing throughout the franchise. Assistance is provided in the areas of trade area analysis, site selection, lease negotiation, finance negotiations, fixturing, design, decor, signage, store layout, merchandising product selection, planograming, pricing, in-store promotion, advertising, personnel selection and training, inventory control and basic store operations.

Information Submitted: July 1987

LE$-ON RETAIL SYSTEMS, INC.
dba LE$-ON DRUGS
4722 West Touhy Avenue
Lincolnwood, Illinois 60646
Leslie B. Masover, President

Description of Operation: Retail drug stores.

Number of Franchisees: 8 in Illinois

In Business Since: 1968

Equity Capital Needed: $10,000 to $50,000 depending on size of store and type

Financial Assistance Available: Counsel and introduction to banking sources

Training Provided: Minimum 2 weeks of training

Managerial Assistance Available: Managerial assistance provided for duration of license agreement.

Information Submitted: July 1986

*MEDICAP PHARMACIES, INC.
10202 Douglas Avenue
Des Moines, Iowa 50322
Calvin Jones, Vice President-Franchise Development

Description of Operation: Medicap Pharmacies are convenient and low cost professional pharmacies. they typically operate in a 700 square feet location with 80 to 90 percent of the business being the filling of prescriptions. Providing over the counter medically oriented products is 10 to 20 percent of the business.

Number of Franchisees: 67 in 7 states

In Business Since: 1971

Equity Capital Needed: $30,000

Financial Assistance Available: On behalf of the franchisee our assistance includes: preparation of growth projections and capital needs as well as the actual presentation of the program to the lending institution.

Training Provided: A minimum of 3 days in the Des Moines area provides 3 day of classroom situation and 1 day in several Medicap Pharmacies with on-the-job experience. Training covers all aspects of operation from bookkeeping and cash register procedures to proper handling of patients and employees. A complete procedures manual is fully discussed.

Managerial Assistance Available: A full management training course is provided by Medicap Pharmacies, Inc. In addition to the initial 3 days in the Des Moines area, continuing training and guidance is provided through periodic store visits by home office personnel. Periodic seminars, workshops and equipment exhibits are held. Much of the annual 3 day convention is devoted to technical and managerial assistance.

Information Submitted: May 1987

*MEDICINE SHOPPE INTERNATIONAL, INC.
10121 Paget Drive
St. Louis, Missouri 63132
Jerome F. Sheldon, President

Description of Operation: Retail prescription and health care centers, emphasizing prescriptions, OTC items and professional health care programs. The format includes major emphasis on the pharmacist/manager being an integral part of the health care delivery team in the store's market area. Approximately 90 percent of the sales volume is generated by prescriptions, with the remainder being over-the-counter drugs, Medicine Shoppe brand label products, and health care related items.

Number of Franchisees: 708 in 48 States

In Business Since: 1970

Equity Capital Needed: $70,000-$80,000 which includes fee, fixtures, supplies, inventory and opening promotion.

Financial Assistance Available: Franchisor provides financial assistance up to 75 percent of the cost of the franchise, or guidance in dealing with commercial and SBA lenders, leasing packages, etc.

Training Provided: Intensive 1 week training seminar at corporate headquarters with direct instruction by all department heads. Two days or longer at store location during store opening. Franchisor also conducts district, regional and national meetings for the continued training of franchisee.

Managerial Assistance Available: Substantial assistance is given in all of the following key areas: site selection, lease negotiations, store layout, fixturing, personnel selection and training, opening procedures, purchasing guidelines and sales and expense, and an operations report. Stores have individual operations representatives who work closely with the manager/owner in the monthly analysis of sales, gross profit, expenses and other sallient areas. Heavy emphasis is given to public relations efforts, advertising and marketing programs at all times.

Information Submitted: May 1987

SNYDER DRUG STORES, INC.
14525 Highway #7
Minnetonka, Minnesota 55345
Philip D. Perkins, Jr., Vice President/Wholesale Operations

Description of Operation: Full line wholesaler of health and beauty aids, drugs, and general merchandise from its 363,000 square feet company-owned warehouse. It wholesales to approximately 200 independent retail drug store operators and operates 57 company-owned stores. There is no franchise fee.

Number of Franchisees: 200 in Iowa, Michigan, Minnesota, South Dakota, Illinois and Wisconsin plus 56 company-owned stores.

In Business Since: 1928

Equity Capital Needed: Equity plus loan availability to $300,000

Financial Assistance Available: Company assists operator in developing bank and SBA credit.

Training Provided: While most of Snyder Independent Retail Operators are pharmacists or individuals with retail experience, training in a company-owned store can be provided.

Managerial Assistance Available: Complete new store assistance from market survey, site selection, store fixturing and merchandise layout. Continuous management counciling by experienced store operations personnel, year round advertising and promotional program.

Information Submitted: May 1987

EDUCATIONAL PRODUCTS/SERVICES

*BARBIZON INTERNATIONAL, INC.
3 East 54th Street
New York, New York 10022
B. Wolff, President

Description of Operation: Barbizon operates modeling and personal development schools for teenage girls, homemakers, and career girls. the schools also offer a male modeling program, fashion merchandising course, acting course, make-up artistry, and sell Barbizon cosmetics. We are the largest organization in this field.

Number of Franchisees: 91 in 40 States

In Business Since: 1939

Equity Capital Needed: $25,000-$50,000

Financial Assistance Available: Franchisee can finance 50 percent of franchise fee with franchisor. Total franchise fee is $19,500 to $35,000.

Training Provided: Intensive 1 week training program for franchisee and his director at corporate office. Extensive on-site field visits at franchisee's location by home office staff during first 6 months. Periodic staff visits and conferences at home office thereafter on a continuing basis.

Managerial Assistance Available: In addition to initial training indicated above, Barbizon makes available continuing staff programs, sales aids, new programs, brochures, direct mail pieces, etc.

Information Submitted: May 1987

BETTER BIRTH FOUNDATION, INC.
733 Main Street
Stone Mountain, Georgia 30083
Brenda Seagraves, President

Description of Operation: Better Birth Foundation offers unique courses in family centered child birth preparation for expectant couples, and post partum classes for new mothers and infants. Better Birth Foundation is presently designing additional classes for expectant couples, families and children.

Number of Franchisees: 4 in Georgia and 1 in Colorado.

In Business Since: 1981

Equity Capital Needed: $19,000

Financial Assistance Available: $15,000 franchise fee. The balances for working capital, there is no financing available through the Better Birth Foundation.

Training Provided: Intensive 15 module educational home study program. An additional 1 week intensive training program at Better Birth's home office, which would include team teaching, practice teaching with supervision, and training for the general business operation of the franchise.

Managerial Assistance Available: Better Birth provides continual management with manuals of operation, forms, etc. better birth Foundation works closely with franchisees to assist in ongoing training, to maintain a high degree of service and professionalism.

Information Submitted: May 1987

THE CAROLE RIGGS STUDIOS
Corporate Headquarters
416-420 Main Street
Lynchburg, Virginia 24504
Carole Harris, President

Description of Operation: Instructional system, largely aimed at children and young adults which offers to the public, including but not limited to the teaching of dance, motor development skills, modeling, karate, and musical programs.

Number of Franchisees: 3 company-owned in Virginia

In Business Since: 1966

Equity Capital Needed: $19,900

Financial Assistance Available: No financial assistance provided. Fee paid in two installments.

Training Provided: Franchisee must stay 1 week at corporate headquarters to be trained in operations and procedures. Franchisee may bring 1 additional person. Advisory service with corporate headquarters.

Managerial Assistance Available: Continual service for length of franchise. Complete operational manual also records, cassettes and videos on operations and syllabus.

Information Submitted: May 1987

CHILD ENRICHMENT CENTERS
6 Passaic Street
Hackensack, New Jersey 07601
Russell J. Rupon, General Manager

Description of Operation: A prestige pre school, kindergarten, and summer camp. 4,000 square foot building together with outdoor playground. Can be operated by owner or as absentee management. You don't have to be an educator. ALphabetland assist franchisee in obtaining land and building.

Number of Franchisees: 15 in New York, New Jersey, and Florida

In Business Since: 1975

Equity Capital Needed: $20,000 plus operating capital

Financial Assistance Available: A total of $70,000 is required to own a Alphabetland franchise. A down payment of $20,000 is made on contract, balance can be financed both short-term and over 5 years, if qualified. An additional $15,000-$20,000 is needed for operating capital.

Training Provided: 10 days pre-training is offered to franchisee at home office. Minimum of 21 days post-training at franchisee's school.

Managerial Assistance Available: Advertising, bookkeeping, operations and curriculum manuals. Seminars to maintain consumer acceptance of our curriculum and methodology.

Information Submitted: July 1987

COLLEGE CENTERS OF SOUTHERN CALIFORNIA, INC.
10801 National Boulevard
Suite 600
Los Angeles, California 90064
W. Cartwright Sheppard, President

Description of Operation: College Centers provides college planning services to high school, vocational and college students. Specializing in career guidance, college selection, SAT score improvement and financial aid planning. All services are computer assisted.

Number of Franchisees: 1 in California, plus 2 company-owned

In Business Since: 1984

Equity Capital Needed: $75,000 including working capital.

Financial Assistance Available: None

Training Provided: 1 week of training at franchisor's facilities plus additional time at franchisee's place of business.

Managerial Assistance Available: In addition to continually updating all manuals, franchisor will communicate constantly with franchisee, periodically visit and always be available by telephone. New training will be provided when significant additions or modifications are made.

Information Submitted: July 1987

CREATIVE TRAINING AND MOTIVATIONAL SERVICES, INC.
Heritage Executive Plaza
1873 Rt. 70
Suite 205-23
Cherry Hill, New Jersey 08003
P. John Judice, President

Description of Operation: Automotive and sales training with subliminal motivational tapes.

Number of Franchisees: 2 in New Jersey

In Business Since: 1987

Equity Capital Needed: Minimum $250,000 backed by inventory.

Financial Assistance Available: None

Training Provided: 2 weeks at commencement; 1 week every 90 days for 12 months.

Managerial Assistance Available: Franchisee receives full management and technical information for duration of contract.

Information Submitted: June 1987

ECHOLS INTERNATIONAL TRAVEL AND HOTEL SCHOOLS, INC.
303 East Ohio Street
Time Life Building
Chicago, Illinois 60611

Description of Operation: Echols International Travel and Hotel Schools, established in 1962. The purpose of the schools is to train students for positions in travel agencies, with airlines, steamship companies and major hotel chains. The teaching staff of Echols schools is comprised of executives, department heads and training personnel from major hotels, airlines and travel agencies.

Number of Franchisees: 2 in California and 1 in Washington, DC.

In Business Since: 1982

Equity Capital Needed: $150,000. This capital is required for operating costs, including advertising, rent, furniture, etc., for first year of operations. Cost of an INTTCO franchise is $50,000. Franchisees also pay INTTCO 10 percent of the gross for the first 5 years and 7-1/2 percent of the gross thereafter. Contract renewable at option of either party every 5 years.

Training Provides: Intensive mandatory training is scheduled for all new franchisees at headquarters in Chicago. During this time franchisee is trained in sales and marketing and also audits classes in session. New personnel are also offered the opportunity for this type training.

Managerial Assistance Available: Echols International Travel and Hotel Schools, provides continual management service for the life of the franchise in the areas of marketing, advertising, and sales. All training materials are purchased through International Travel Training Courses at a very low cost. Executive personnel from International Travel Training Courses spend a minimum of 3 weeks in their area prior to, and 1 week after, the opening of the first class. They then visit each franchise 12 days per year to assist in interviewing, selling and marketing. There is 1 meeting each year in the Chicago office for reorientation for the franchisee.

Information Submitted: July 1987

ELS INTERNATIONAL, INC.
5761 Buckingham Parkway
Culver City, California 90230
Jerry D. Loudenback, President

Description of Operation: ELS International, Inc., is offering franchises to operate ELS International Language Schools for the teaching of English as a Second Language in foreign countries. ELS International is related to ELS Language Centers which owns and operates 20 language centers.

Number of Franchisees: 10 in Japan, Korea, Thailand, Peru, Taiwan and Indonesia, plus 20 company-owned in 16 states.

In Business Since: 1961

Equity Capital Needed: $150,000-$300,000

Financial Assistance Available: No financing is available from franchisor or its affiliates.

Training Provided: Prior to franchisee's opening, franchisor will conduct a minimum 8 day training session at franchisor's headquarters. A "start-up" kit is provided which includes curriculum guides, tests, courses syllabi and outlines.

Franchisor will also conduct a 5 day training session at franchisee's premises prior to opening. Franchisor will conduct an additional 5 day on-the-job training session at franchisee's premises approximately 6 months after the franchisee commences.

Managerial Assistance Available: ELS International provides continued support throughout the term of the franchise by conducting professional seminars for franchisee's teachers, providing updated curriculum guides and manuals for professional English courses and a communication system with each franchisee. Franchisor will also provide each franchisee with its operations manual which sets forth franchisor's unique program of English language instruction. Franchisor's designated representatives will visit each language school at least 2 times per year to inspect the operations and assist the franchisee.

Information Submitted: July 1987

*GYMBOREE CORPORATION
577 Airpost Blvd., #400
Burlingame, California 94010
Bob Campbell, Director of Training Sales

Description of Operation: Gymboree, a quality developmental play program, offers weekly classes to parents and their children, age 3 months to 4 years, on custom-designed equipment for infants, toddlers and preschoolers. The program is based on sensory integration theory, positive parenting, child development principles, and the importance of play.

Number of Franchisees: Over 245 Gymboree centers in operation (including 5 company-owned). Franchises have been granted to over 125 franchisees covering market plans for the development of over 125 centers in 31 States and Canada, Australia and France.

In Business Since: 1976

Equity Capital Needed: $7,000-$14,000 fee per site depending on number of sites. Approximately $7,500-$9,000 per site for equipment and supplies; $4,000-$6,000 working capital.

Financial Assistance Available: None

Training Provided: All franchisees attend a 9 day training seminar with a follow-up visit to their location(s) after opening and once a year thereafter. Regional training programs are held on an ongoing basis.

Managerial Assistance Available: There is an annual seminar for ongoing training. All franchisees are visited annually. Phone contact regularly.

Information Submitted: May 1987

HUNTINGTON LEARNING CENTERS, INC.
660 Kinderkamack Road
Oradell, New Jersey 07649
Michael Ward, Franchise Director

Description of Operation: Individualized instruction is provided for school-aged children and adults in remedial and speed reading, study skills, spelling, phonics, math, and SAT preparation. Prior to admission, each student receives an educational evaluation. During a parent conference, recommendations are made regarding the type and degree of help needed. The system of diagnosis and conferencing incorporates an educationally sound assessment of skills with a professional presentation. This presentation is designed to "sell" the parents on the importance of the center in their child's academic life.

Number of Franchisees: 14 company-owned centers in New York, New Jersey and Pennsylvania and over 45 franchised centers in 22 States.

In Business Since: 1977

Equity Capital Needed: From $45,000 to $150,000

Financial Assistance Available: No financing arrangements are offered by the franchisor.

Training Provided: Intensive 2 week initial training program covering educational and testing materials; phone call training to get parents to bring the child for testing; initial conference procedures to help parents help the child and to keep the student enrolled; management systems for the center's efficient operation; quality control procedures. Follow-up on-site training is also conducted.

Managerial Assistance Available: Franchisor provides franchisee with the management and administrative systems to minimize time spent on non-productive miscellaneous administrative matters. To aide in the center's efficient operation seasoned professionals are available to provide additional advice and assistance over the phone or in person. In addition, periodic visits to each center are planned in advance. Franchisor provides statistical tools to compare franchisee's performance to an over-all average. This statistical information permits franchisor to review each center for possible weaknesses, and to schedule additional problem-solving visits.

Information Submitted: May 1987

INSTITUTE OF READING DEVELOMENT FRANCHISING CORP.
1360 9th Avenue
Suite D
San Francisco, California 94122
Paul Cooperman, President

Description of Operation: The Institute of Reading Development (IRD) offers several programs of speed reading and comprehension training for college students, professional persons, and junior high and senior high school students. The programs are marketed solely to institutions, such as corporations, universities, and public and private schools, municipal governments and professional associations. They are endorsed by a number of major California universities, and were developed by IRD's founder and president, Paul Cooperman, who is the author of the widely acclaimed book on the decline of academic achievement of American students. The Literacy Hoax (Fall 1978, William Morrow and Company).

Number of Franchisees: 3 in California

In Business Since: 1971

Equity Capital Needed: $55,000

Financial Assistance Available: None

Training Provided: IRD will supply extensive and continuous training in 3 areas; marketing, management, and reading instruction. The initial training consists of a 5 week session for franchisee at IRD's home office.

Managerial Assistance Available: IRD will supply franchisee with all marketing and instructional materials (including training manuals for all jobs), bookkeeping forms, and a cost accounting/sales analysis system. IRD will also supply continuous training and supervision in all phases of marketing and reading instruction, including training in new marketing and instructional programs as they are developed. This is an extraordinary opportunity for someone with a strong marketing/sales background who wants to work in private education.

Information Submitted: July 1987

JOHN ROBERT POWERS FINISHING, MODELING
& CAREER SCHOOL WORLD HEADQUARTERS
9 Newbury Street
Boston, Massachusetts 02116
Barbara J. Tyler, Executive Vice President

Description of Operation: John Robert Powers School offers finishing, self-improvement, drama, modeling, executive grooming, fashion merchandising, interior design, make-up arts, TV acting/drama, flight attendants , pre-teen and communications in today's world to women and men of all ages. Classes are held year 'round—day and evening.

Number of Franchisees: 70 in 26 States and Singapore; Manila, Philippines; Jakarta, Indonesia; Bangkok, Thailand; Sidney and Adelaide, Australia and Japan.

In Business Since: 1923

Equity Capital Needed: $25,000

Financial Assistance Available: None

Training Provided: 3 weeks of teaching and administrative training plus semi-annual seminars.

Managerial Assistance Available: We provide managerial and technical assistance during the life of the franchise by visiting field personnel. Accounting assistance is provided by home office personnel. Conferences are held during the year.

Information Submitted: July 1987

KINDERDANCE INTERNATIONAL, INC.
P. O. Box 881
Melbourne Beach, Florida 32951
Bernard Friedman, Vice President

Description of Operation: Kinderdance offers a unique educational dance and motor development program designed specifically for preschool children and to be taught primarily in various types of child care centers. The program is presently being taught in hundreds of locations in several States and is highly recommended by most of the major child care organizations.

Number of Franchisees: 4 in Arizona, Texas and Florida.

In Business Since: 1979

Equity Capital Needed: Depends on size of territory purchased—$5,000 to $25,000 total investment.

Financial Assistance Available: Financial assistance is not provided.

Training Provided: An intensive 10 days training program is provided at company headquarters in Orlando, Florida area. This is followed up with a 2 to 3 day visit to the franchisee's area by company personnel.

Managerial Assistance Available: Kinderance offers continual advanced training and management services for the life of the franchise. Complete operators manuals, instructional cassette audio and visual tapes, operational forms and directions are provided.

Information Submitted: May 1987

MAC TAY AQUATICS, INC.
P. O. Box 753
Champaign, Illinois 61820
Karen N. Taylor, President

Description of Operation: Mac Tay Acquatic Schools are known as a unique, self-motivating approach to swimming instruction. Based upon positive reinforcement, praise, and reward our program offers semiprivate lessons and the classes facilitate flexability in techniques and approaches. Mac Tay Aquatics, Inc., will help with site selection, lease negotiation and will provide extensive training.

Number of Franchisees: 3 locations in Illinois, Arizona and Indiana.

In Business Since: 1974, franchising began in 1985.

Equity Capital Needed: In order to obtain and/or commence the franchise operation the franchisee must pay $10,000. The total initial investment in the franchise is $15,950-$19,300.

Financial Assistance Available: Franchisee must arrange all financing.

Training Provided: 1-2 weeks intensive training course which includes classroom work, observation, discussion and "hands-on" training course is held at home location in Illinois. A manual is provided which serves as a reference for procedures, techniques and business details.

Managerial Assistance Available: Mac Tay Aquatics, Inc., will be involved in initial media coverage, grand opening procedures, and follow-up consultation. Ongoing assistance in advertising, business aspects and regularly scheduled seminars are also part of the Mac Tay Aquatics franchise.

Information Submitted: July 1987

MODEL MERCHANDISING INTERNATIONAL, LTD.
111 East 22nd Street
New York, New York 10010
Fernando Casablancas, President

Description of Operation: MMI franchises the John Casablancas Modeling, and Career Centers. MMI, a subsidiary of Elite Model Management, offers a complete franchise package that includes course programs, operations manuals, advertising and promotion material and audio visuals, ongoing guidance, and a promotional/placement link with Elite, the world's leading model agency group.

Number of Franchisees: 93 throughout the world

In Business Since: 1980

Equity Capital Needed: $22,000-$88,000 (depending on type of franchise and location)

Financial Assistance Available: The franchise fee is $6,000 to $27,000 (depending on population and type), with terms offered. A conversion franchise with existing premises and cash flow may require only promotional outlay to establish itself as a John Casablancas Center. A Center starting from scratch will require working capital through breakeven. details on request.

Training Provided: Offered at other Centers, in New York and at the new franchise's place of business (1 week minimum) with regular visits by MMI and Elite personnel.

Managerial Assistance Available: Service and management guidance, market information, merchandising material, model recruitment, advertising and promotional material and events, plus new programs and audio visual updates are provided by MMI on an ongoing basis.

Information Submitted: May 1987

PERKINS FIT BY FIVE, INC.
1606 Penfield Road
Rochester, New York 14625
Betty Perkins-Carpenter, President

Description of Operation: Athletically oriented pre-school program for children 2-1/2 to 5 years. The fundamental approach to instruction is through development of physical skills as the key to the acquisition of self-confidence, social interaction, tolerance, self-discipline, and verbal-conceptual understandings. The means by which the above purpose is accomplished is through a revolutionary new idea in pre-school education, utilizing unique teaching techniques, special equipment, and unusual activities. Exercises, music, and basic motor skills are but some of the tools of instruction which is success oriented, heavily flavored with kindness, consideration, respect, and love.

Number of Franchisees: 2 in Maryland and 1 in New York not including company-owned

In Business Since: 1969, $21,000 to $35,000

Equity Capital Needed: $18,000-$20,000 fee per site depending on number of sites, approximately $6,000 per site for equipment and supplies.

Financial Assistance Available: Financial assistance is not provided

Training Provided: All franchisees attend a 3 week training program. Follow-up visits to their location(s). Also additional training in Rochester, New York as needed on ongoing basis.

Managerial Assistance Available: All franchisees are visited twice annually. Phone contact as needed. written communications monthly.

Informatoin Submitted: May 1987

PERSONAL COMPUTER LEARNING CENTERS OF AMERICA, INC.
230 Park Avenue
New York, New York 10169
Jack Fox, Chief Executive Officer

Description of Operation: PCLC trains executives, businessmen, managers, professionals, and their staffs to use the most popular software application programs designed for micro and personal computers.

Number of Franchisees: 3 in New York City, White Plains, New York and Washington, D.C. including company-owned.

In Business Since: 1981

Equity Capital Needed: $75,000 to $100,000

Financial Assistance Available: None

Training Provided: 2 weeks intensive training covering various popular business software, as well as operation of business. At the completion of the training, the franchisee will be qualified to teach classes in the use of these software programs.

Managerial Assistance Available: The company provides periodic training to upgrade teaching skills and for new classes which are developed as new business software products are introduced.

Information Submitted: May 1987

PLAYFUL PARENTING FRANCHISE CORP.
3026 Penn Avenue
West Lawn, Pennsylvania 19609
Gary R. Seibert, President

Description of Operation: Child/Parent Play Development center that caters to children 6 weeks to 6 years old. Classes are taught by professionally trained teachers that provide a fun filled, educational environment for children and their parents.

Number of Franchisees: Over 80 sold in the United States, Australia and Canada.

In Business Since: Program developed in 1972, franchising started in January 1984.

Equity Capital Needed: $30,000

Financial Assistance Available: Assistance in negotiating bank financing.

Training Provided: 5 day teacher training provided at our national headquarters. Use of lecture demonstration, video tapes, hands-on experience in our lab schook, along with a detailed training manual provides a well rounded learning environment.

Managerial Assistance Available: 3 day business management course for the owner/director is mandatory prior to sending anyone to the teacher training. A detailed operations and procedures manual is used as the course outline. We also re-certify teachers each year, provide a national convention, monthly newsletters, workshops, advertising, marketing, public relations, as well as have a full-time franchise services department to handle the day-to-day managerial assistance.

Information Submitted: July 1987

PLAYORENA, INC.
125 Mineola Avenue
Roslyn Heights, New York 11577
Fred Jaroslow, Executive Vice President

Description of Operation: Playorena is a recreational and exercise program for children 3 months to 4 years old who attend weekly sessions with a parent. Activities and equipment are custom designed and time tested for the rapidly shiftly stages of motor development. Program is based on learning through natural play.

Number of Franchisees: 45 in 6 States

In Business Since: 1981

Equity Capital Needed: $14,000 fee per site depending on number of sites. Approximately $8,000 per site for equipment. Additional working capital required.

Financial Assistance Available: Up to 50 percent of franchise fee may be financed.

Training Provided: 8 day training program encompassing the business as well as program aspects of Playorena. Upgrading and refresher training on a continuing basis.

Managerial Assistance Available: Complete manuals provided. On-site visits by management. Seminars and franchisee meetings. Ongoing bulletin service. Public relations assistance. Marketing direction and advise.

Information Submitted: May 1987

PRIMARY PREP PRE-SCHOOLS
5690 Roosevelt Blvd.
Clearwater, Florida 33520
James P. Nault, C.E.O.

Description of Operation: Primary Prep offers quality pre-school franchisees to qualified franchisees at a reasonable cost. $55,000 initial investment covers all equipment, training and includes working capital. Primary Prep arranges for $250-$300,000 pre-school facility to be built and leased to the franchisee, who then has the option to purchase the facility once his/her business is established.

Number of Franchisees: 9 in Florida

In Business Since: 1984

Equity Capital Needed: $55,000 total (no debt), includes $12,000 working capital.

Financial Assistance Available: Lease/option available on new custom-built pre-school facilities.

Training Provided: Initial training lasts 1 month and is conducted both at the franchisor's home office and at the franchisee's new school. Intensive monitoring and additional training lasts an additional 6 months. Monitoring, management and educational consulting continue for the life of the franchise, which is perpetual.

Managerial Assistance Available: Monitoring, management and educational consulting last for the life of the franchise (which is perpetual) on both a regular and a as-needed basis.

Information Submitted: May 1987

SANDLER SYSTEMS, INC.
P. O. Box 183
2005 Greenspring Valley Road
Stevenson, Maryland 21153
David Sandler, President

Description of Operation: The franchise being offered consists of the right to operate a business devoted to a distinctive style of training persons in the fields of management consulting, leadership development and sales techniques; and also the methods of teaching such subjects through seminars and workshops including programs known as the Sandler Selling System and Systematic Sales Management and other programs to be offered in the future.

Number of Franchisees: 47 in USA

In Business Since: 1983

Equity Capital Needed: $20,000 minimum

Financial Assistance Available: The total investment of $20,000, pays for inventory, training, administrative expenses, and opening costs. Franchisor does not offer any financing arrangements to franchisee.

Training Provided: Franchisor provides regular, periodic training every 90 days, held during business hours at franchisor's principal office in Baltimore. The training program consists of 2 full days, and includes such techniques, expertise, and trade secrets as developed by the franchisor. The training program is mandatory. Periodic newsletters, bulletins, phone consultations will be made available to franchisee.

Managerial Assistance Available: Sandler Systems provides continual assistance for the life of the franchise, and a sales support manager is assigned to each franchisee to work directly with him to answer any technical questions. Sandler Systems sponsors meetings of franchisees to discuss marketing ideas, present new material, etc., in order to maintain high standards of motivation.

Information Submitted: May 1987

SEXTON EDUCATIONAL CENTERS
443 East 3rd Avenue
Roselle, New Jersey 07203
Frank Berlen, President

Description of Operation: We offer courses preparing college grads for the "LSAT," "GMAT," "GRE," "MAT." For the high school student we offer help with the "SAT," and for the foreign student we offer the "TDEFL."

Number of Franchisees: 12 in New York, New Jersey, Massachusetts, Ohio, Maine and Georgia and Canada.

In Business Since: 1978

Equity Capital Needed: $5,000 to $50,000 depending on location.

Financial Assistance Available: Franchisor will accept 1/3 of license fee as down payment and give liberal terms for balance.

Training Provided: Franchisor will recruit and train first cadre of teachers. Training lasts for 2-1/2 days.

Managerial Assistance Available: Administrative manual is provided and managerial assistance is provided during teacher training.

Information Submitted: May 1987

SPORTASTIKS INC.
510 South Staley Road
Champaign, Illinois 61821
James M. Wilkins, Vice President

Decription of Operation: A childrens fitness and gymnastics training center. For children from 18 months to 18 years. Pre-school motor development program, recreational class program, accelerated program that leads into competition. Each program is designed so each child feels success, builds confidence and cordination.

Number of Franchisees: 9 in Illinois, Missouri, Indiana, Washington, South Carolina and Virginia

In Business Since: 1979

Equity Capital Needed: Minimum investment $100,000. Maximum investment will depend on demographic requirements and individual needs.

Financial Assistance Available: Equipment leasing available depending on analysis of financial statement.

Training Provided: 24 months of ongoing training, includes: 6 week correspondence course, complete with videos, 10 day training at national headquarters in Champaign and 22 month ongoing training by phone and visitation.

Managerial Assistance Available: Sportastiks will train each franchisee in daily operations of their business. We will also train a master coach for each facility to assist in daily operations and to provide the gymnastics knowledge necessary to operate a sportasticks franchise. The owner-operator need no previous gymnastics experience.

Information Submitted: June 1987

*SYLVAN LEARNING CORPORATION
2400 Presidents Drive
Montgomery, Alabama 36103-5605

Description of Operation: Diagnostic testing and prescriptive programs in reading, math and other curriculum for children and adults. Individualized instruction by certified teachers using proven learning materials and Sylvan innovative educational techniques.

Number of Franchisees: 300 in 42 States, and 4 Canadian Provinces

In Business Since: 1979

Equity Capital Needed: $75,000. Total investment $90,000-$115,000.

Financial Assistance Available: Equipment financing.

Training Provided: 2 weeks initial training in methods of instruction and business plan.

Managerial Assistance Available: Continual franchisee operational and service support.

Information Submitted: May 1987

TEGELER TIME DAY CARE SYSTEM
10 Forbes Road
Braintree, Massachusetts 02184
Dean E. Tegeler, President

Description of Operation: Operation is providing day care services for children through a network of screened and qualified franchised home day care providers. Training, enrollment, billing, curriculum, supervision and support are provided by the company.

Number of Franchisees: 2 in Massachusetts

In Business Since: 1986

Equity Capital Needed: $2,000

Financial Assistance Available: None at this time.

Training Provided: Mandatory training is offered, utilizing a professionally prepared curriculum. An early childhood specialist supervises, monitors and supports the providers on an ongoing basis.

Managerial Assistance Available: An early childhood specialist supervises, monitors, and supports the providers on an ongoing basis.

Information Submitted: July 1987

*TELLER TRAINING DISTRIBUTORS, INC.
400 Ual Building
2033 Sixth Avenue
Seattle, Washington 98121
David Lonay, President

Description of Operation: Teller Training Distributors, Inc., owns and franchises post-secondary proprietary schools (Teller Training Institutes) specializing in the training of persons for entry-level positions in the banking industry. The student completes 80 hours of instruction which includes training on all standard banking machines, computer training, and all methods and procedures necessary to begin work with minimal orientation. The course is approved and accredited for five credits by the American Institute of Banking. Graduates are given ongoing placement assistance until employed. Placement rates are very high. Exclusive franchise territories are available to persons who will be personally involved in the operation of the franchise.

Number of Franchisees: 33 in 20 States

In Business Since: 1971

Equity Capital Needed: Up to $25,000 in addition to franchise fee which varies by territory.

Financial Assistance Available: Franchisor will assist franchise owner in obtaining financing.

Training Provided: No prior experience required. Up to 1 month at corporation headquarters for franchise owners in administration, marketing, financing, hiring, recruiting, and placement. Up to 1 month at corporation headquarters for head instructor in instruction methodology and curriculum. Periodical meetings of all franchise-owners provides exchange of current and new methodology in all phases of the business.

Managerial Assistance Available: Franchisor will provide the franchisee with continual support and assistance. Included in franchisor services are: (1) aid in selection of school location; (2) aid in negotiating a favorable lease; (3) provide information and research requirements for city, county, and state licenses; (4) selection of office furniture, school equipment, and supplies; (5) establishment of an advertising program and schedule including prepared print advertisements and television commercials; (6) establishment of an operations budget; (7) assistance

in employing and training employees; and (8) accounting and recordkeeping through the corporation's computer. In addition to the continual communication between the franchise-owner and the franchisor by telephone, and the continued furnishing of information through the mail, visits, a detailed operations manual as well as other reference manuals and guides. There is always available to the franchise-owner someone at corporation headquarters to assist in any area that is required.

Information Submitted: May 1987

THE TRAVEL TRADE SCHOOL, INC.
609 West Littleton Boulevard
Suite 201
Littleton, Colorado 80120
Adonna L. Hipple, President

Description of Operation: Educational institutions which are individually owned and operated that prepare students for a career in the travel industry. Franchisor provides complete start-up assistance, including site selection, marketing, state approval, for operating a school, guidelines for advertising, equipment and furniture needs and training for directors, and instructors.

Number of Franchisees: 5 in Colorado and 1 in New Mexico

In Business Since: 1975

Equity Capital Needed: $17,000 in addition to franchise fee which varies by territory.

Financial Assistance Available: Franchisee must be able to handle their own financing.

Training Provided: Start-up assistance and continuing assistance throughout duration: assistance in obtaining state licenses, certification and approval assistance in setting up office system, record keeping, recruitment, enrollment and continuing education program. Training of director and guidelines for hiring instructors (testing), complete curriculum and guide—all teaching materials.

Managerial Assistance Available: Technical assistance throughout duration of relationship with franchisor: advertising co-operation, revision of teaching materials, printing of catalogue and materials, workshops to up-date skills and implement changes, training of new personnel (director and instructors), and maintain quality control and train in methods of monitor success.

Information Submitted: May 1987

USA TRAVEL SCHOOLS, INC.
260 Sunny Isles Boulevard
North Miami Beach, Florida 33160
Reto Lingenhag, President

Description of Operation: Complete training in the travel business. Courses may be taken days or evenings. 130 hours class work, 130 hours home work. Continuous updating for teachers.

Number of Franchisees: 2 in Florida

In Business Since: 1967

Equity CapitalNeeded: $20,000

Financial Assistance Available: Financing available.

Training Provided: Initial training and ongoing consultation.

Managerial Assistance Available: Consultation as needed.

Information Submitted: July 1987

WEIST-BARRON, INC.
35 West 45th Street
New York, New York 10036
Bob Barron

Description of Operation: Teaching the performance of commercials to adults and children, both TV and radio. Also teaching soap opera technique to actors. Classes in newscasting; auditioning techniques for musical comedy, classes in sit com technique, classes in performing musical and comedy and remedial acting classes.

Number of Franchisees: 6 in Georgia, Pennsylvania, California and Massachusetts.

In Business Since: 1958

Equity Capital Needed: $20,000

Financial Assistance Available: None

81

Training Provided: Training sessions on the premises conducted by the franchisor for all classes to be in curriculum. Expenses paid by franchisee. Once a year visits to hold seminars and re-training sessions. Paid for by franchisee. Money made by seminars held by franchisee.

Managerial Assistance Available: All the consultation in our New York studios required by franchisee.

Information Submitted: May 1987

EMPLOYMENT SERVICES

AAA EMPLOYMENT FRANCHISE, INC.
5533 Central Avenue
St. Petersburg, Florida 33710
Carolyn Weathinston, Vice President

Description of Operation: AAA Employment Franchise, Inc., offers a highly ethical and professional service to both applicants and employers. AAA offices do not limit themselves to specialized areas of employment—full service is available— executive to domestic placement—both temporary and permanent employment. The low-discount placement fee of only 2-1/2 weeks salary has proven to be in great demand for the past 30 years. Coast to coast, border to border territories available on a first to qualify basis.

Number of Franchisees: 43 in 13 States plus 88 company-owned offices in 4 States

In Business Since: AAA Employment, Inc.—1957; AAA Employment Franchise, Inc.—1977

Equity Capital Needed: Down payment depends on size of territory selected (minimum $4,000—maximum $15,000) and approximately $4,000 (includes office space, furnishings, office supplies, and licensing).

Financial Assistance Available: Once down payment is made, the balance of the fee is paid $50 per week until paid off.

Training Provided: The franchisor's staff will provide the franchisee with an intensive 2 week training program at the corporate headquarters in St. Petersburg, Florida. Additional on-the-job training will be conducted in the field for the franchisee and employees. A representative from the home office will spend the first week of operation in the franchisees office to offer assistance. Seminars are held semi-annually to keep franchisees updated on new ideas and techniques.

Managerial Assistance Available: The staff of the franchisor will provide the franchisee with continual support and assistance. Some of the services provided by the franchisor are: 1) aid in selecting a prime location, 2) aid in negotiating a lease, 3) providing information and research requirements for city, county and State licenses, 4) selection of office furniture and supplies, 5) establishing an advertising schedule, 6) establishing a budget schedule, 7) hiring and training employees, and 8) record keeping. In addition to the continual communication between the franchisee and franchisor by phone, and the continued furnishings of information through the mail, visits will be made periodically into the field by a representative of the corporation. The franchisee will also be provided with a detailed operations manual as well as other reference guides. Every effort will be made by AAA Employment Franchise, Inc.

Information Submitted: May 1987

*ADIA PERSONNEL SERVICES
64 Willow Place
Menlo Park, California 94025
Richard E. Benson, Vice President Franchise Operations

Description of Operation: ADIA Personnel Services, Inc., is principally engaged in providing a full-service temporary help franchise to independently owned franchisees, who furnish office, clerical, word processing, sales, marketing and industrial personnel to clients on a temporary, as needed, basis. The franchise is offered to qualified "start-up" and existing business owners. ADIA has both company-owned and franchised operations in major markets throughout the United States and is part of an international organization based in Lausane, Switzerland, with over 800 offices worldwide. The franchise offered includes permanent place, in addition to temporary services. The ADIA System provides the franchisee with research, marketing programs, advertising techniques, materials, publicity methods, awards programs, accounts receivable financing and billing systems, temporary employee benefits programs, management reports and management and staff training. For further information call (800) 343-ADIA, or in California, (415) 324-0696 collect.

Number of Franchisees: 86 franchisees plus 140 company operated offices in 33 States and the District of Columbia

In Business Since: 1957

Equity Capital Needed: $70,000 plus, inclusive of $17,500 initial franchise fee. Initial capital required also depends on whether the franchise is for an established or "start-up" operation.

Financial Assistance Available: ADIA finances 100 percent of the temporary employees' payroll and accounts receivable financing for 90 days. In addition, ADIA participates in the franchise's local advertising through a co-operative advertising plan which funds up to 50 percent of local costs for pre-approved programs. In addition, ADIA may assist applicants in locating other sources of financing for capitalization. ADIA does not finance directly any portion of the initial franchise fee or other costs.

Training Provided: ADIA provides initial training to the franchisee in 3 phases, coinciding with the opening of the franchisee's office. Initial orientation in operations is provided through manuals, branch observation, and video programs. The second phase, sales and management, is conducted at the U.S. headquarters in the San Francisco area. The training program involves 5 days of intensive instruction in ADIA sales and office management techniques. The third phase of initial training involves on-site support and implementation of programs and systems during the first 2 weeks that the franchisee opens for business, and includes instruction and guidance for both the franchisee and his or her staff. Ongoing training is provided through field support, national meetings, written publications, and field consultation throughout the franchise relationship.

Managerial Assistance Available: Ongoing consulting services and managerial guidance are provided on a regular basis. In addition to initial training, ADIA maintains headquarters and field staff proficient in the entire industry spectrum. These resources are available to each franchisee, offering advice and assistance in such areas as management, marketing, sales, operations, administration, computer information, training, office lay-out and design, legal affairs, insurance, government regulations, finance, purchasing, word processing, employee benefits, public relations, and advertising. Regularly scheduled visits are conducted to assist the franchisee in establishing objectives and to review progress, as well as to ascertain additional services to be provided by ADIA to focus support on areas of specific need.

Information Submitted: June 1987

ATLANTIC PERSONNEL SERVICE SYSTEMS, INC.
4806 Shelly Drive
Wilmington, North Carolina 28405
Lorraine G. Owens, Vice President, Marketing

Description of Operation: Premanent job placement, targeting entry level to middle management positions.

Number of Franchisees: 24 in North Carolina and South Carolina. Soliciting new franchisees in other southeastern states.

In Business Since: 1985

Equity Capital Needed: $14,500-$24,500

Financial Assistance Available: Training Provided: 1 week training (classroom - corporate headquarters) and 1 week additional training (on-site).

Managerial Assistance Available: Automatic periodic visitation by corporate operations consultants and specific visitation on request. Financial and bookkeeping forms, business cards, letterhead and envelopes. Periodic franchise meetings and seminars.

Information Submitted: May 1987

*AUNTIE FAY, INC.
9404 Genesee Avenue
Suite 262
La Jolla, California 92037
Fay McGrath

Description of Operation: Employment agencies that specializes in professional domestic placement. We recruit, train and place mature Americans and legal immigrants to care for homes and families. We fill the fragmented family void created by today's fast pace changes.

Number of Franchisees: 2 in California

In Business Since: 1982

Equity Capital Needed: Under $20,000

Financial Assistance Available: None

Training Provided: 4 days of intensive training at headquarters in La Jolla, California. Assistance at location during opening week. Continuing assistance for duration of the contract (5 years).

Managerial Assistance Available: Training on how to operate an employment agency, location, policies, procedures, bookkeeping, advertising, public relations, recruiting of clients and applicants, the usage of resources, networks and linkages. Training on how to facilitate a training video which is included. Regularly scheduled conferences and follow-up assistance. Training manual of 125 pages. For the duration of the contract (5 years).

Information Submitted: May 1987

BAILEY EMPLOYMENT SYSTEM, INC.
51 Shelton Road
Monroe, Connecticut 06468
Sheldon Leighton, President

Description of Operation: Profitable, nationally scoped, placementship techniques augmented with a centralized, electronically computerized, data retrieval system. Centrally filed applicants and centrally filed job specifications, registered by individual Bailey Employment System offices, allows all franchisees a constant pool of qualified applicants and employers with which to work with at all times. Bailey offers extensive training in the use of the intelligent computer Bailey provides to each franchisee. This computer permits instant retrieval of valuable candidate and/or company data in order for Bailey offices to hold a competitive advantage.

Number of Franchisees: 18 in 3 States

In Business Since: 1960

Equity Capital Needed: $40,000

Financial Assistance Available: If desired, purchase price may be financed at going bank rates.

Training Provided: Complete training in the profitable operation of a Bailey Employment Service office is given to each franchise operator before a new office is opened for business. Our training courses may be attended again and again by the franchise operator and his or her staff at their convenience. Additional traiing in advanced techniques of professional placementship is offered 52 weeks a year. All such additional training is free of charge to all franchise operators and personnel. Conventions are offered at least four times a year to insure continued interoffice cooperation, camaraderie and profits.

Managerial Assistance Available: Every conceivable service to insure the owner a profitable return on his or her investment is offered.

Information Submitted: May 1987

BAKER & BAKER EMPLOYMENT SERVICE, INC.
P. O. Box 364
3 Jackson
Athens, Tennessee 37303
Kathleen Baker, President

Description of Operation: Franchising of employment service agencies for small towns of 20,000 population and city metropolitan area.

Number of Franchisees: 8 in 3 States

In Business Since: 1967

Equity Capital Needed: $10,000 to $20,000 dependent on location, plus $2,500 working capital.

Financial Assistance Available: Yes

Training Provided: Comprehensive training course before opening and additional periodical on-the-job training at the franchise location.

Managerial Assistance Available: Selection of suitable location, a nationally aimed public-relations program and instructions and materials for obtaining maximum publicity in local advertising media, all forms required for the first 12 months of operation, an established accounting system, national placement Tele-System operating between offices, assistance in interpreting State laws and complying with license regulations. Trained assistance on call at all hours on any agency problem.

Information Submitted: June 1987

*BRYANT BUREAU
A Division of SNELLING AND SNELLING, INC.
Executive Offices
4000 South Tamiami Trail
Sarasota, Florida 33581

Description of Operation: Employment services primarily offering executive placement and recruitment services to client companies and candidates alike. High demand disciplines such as data processing, finance, marketing, oil and gas, etc.

Number of Franchisees: 35 in U.S.

In Business Since: 1976 (parent company since 1951)

Equity Capital Needed: $53,000 to $73,000

Financial Assistance Available: Yes

Training Provided: 2 weeks training at home office in Sarasota, Florida plus additional initial training in the field for franchisees and their employees. Training includes the use of copyrighted training manuals—one each—for the director, staffing specialist, and registrar. The franchisor is available for counselling and at the present time national marketing consultants travel throughout the U.S. offering additional management advice, assistance, and training.

Managerial Assistance Available: Pre-opening aid selection, lease negotiation, phone systems, furniture selection, etc., provided by staff at home office and initial supply package and video player are supplied at no extra charge.

Information Submitted: June 1987

BUSINESS & PROFESSIONAL CONSULTANTS, INC.
3255 Wilshire Boulevard
Suite 1732
Los Angeles, California 90010
W. J. LaPerch, President

Description of Operation: Operations in the executive search, recruitment and placement of managerial and executive talent at the professional level. Covers engineering, banking, insurance, accounting, finance, data processing, sales, marketing, and an employment agency but as executive recruiters. The ideal franchise owner will come from industry at the middle to senior management level, will be degreed or equivalent (an advanced degree is desirable), will be people-proented, will work well as part of a national team, and yet be capable of individual accomplishment and leadership. An additional facet of this franchise is the inclusion of a professional level temporary service to serve the same customer base and thus be able to satisfy all of the customer's needs. The company finances and handles all details of payroll and billing for the franchisee, so no large amount of payroll capital is required.

Number of Franchisees: 5 in California

In Business Since: 1961

Equity Capital Needed: $10,000 franchise fee

Financial Assistance Available: Will finance portion of franchise fee at no interest.

Training Provided: An initial 2 week program at the home office to cover the basics of executive search, hiring and training of staff personnel, operational and accounting procedures and market penetration. This is followed by an on-site training program of 1 full week at the franchisee's location, and by further field visits by home office training personnel.

Managerial Assistance Available: Continuous on an as needed basis and may consist of seminars, field visits, refresher training at franchisor's home office, and constant communication.

Information Submitted: May 1987

*CAREER EMPLOYMENT SERVICES, INC.
1600 Stewart Avenue
Westbury, New York
Howard Fader, Vice President, Marketing

Description of Operation: Career Employment Services, Inc., offers a unique franchise opportunity for entrance into the temporary help industry using its nationally registered name Temp Force in all States other than Georgia, Texas and Minnesota where it operates at Temp Staff supported by a comprehensive program of providing training, payroll funding, promotion and all bookkeeping functions.

Number of Franchisees: 70 Temp Force and 2 Temp staff in 22 States

In Business Since: 1962

Equity Capital Needed: $2,500-$15,000

Financial Assistance Available: The franchisor accepts $7,500 down and the balance in monthly payments at 12 percent per annum commencing nine months after start-up.

Training Provided: The franchisor offers an optional 1 week training program at its training center in New York at no cost to the franchisee other than transportation, room and board for those attending, followed by a mandatory 1 week training session conducted at the franchisee's office at no cost to the franchisee.

Managerial Assistance Available: Ongoing support and training by way of periodic visits by a field service representative and fully computerized statistical management reports for ongoing analysis and consultation by home office with owner.

Information Submitted: July 1987

COSMOPOLITAN CARE CORPORATION
330 Seventh Avenue
New York, New York 10001
Elmer H. Maack, Director of Licensing

Description of Operation: Temporary help service providing a highly professional service to general business. Banking, insurance, financial, accounting, advertising, manufacturing, distribution, merchandising, etc., communities. Categories of temporary help employees available include general clerical, secretarial, word processing, personal computer operators, law services, records management, food services, skilled/semi-skilled trades, light industrial, factory and general labor.

Number of Franchisees: 36 company-owned offices, offering franchises in all States.

In Business Since: 1971

Equity Capital Needed: $50,000

Financial Assistance Available: For qualified candidates will finance part of the franchise fee. Once in operation will finance the payroll cash flow of the business and accounts receivable.

Training Provided: 1 full week at home office in all aspects of the business plus pre-opening guidance and 1 full week on-site opening training. Another 2 days of follow-up on-site training after 6 months of opening. Continued follow-up training after open. Also provide training of new full-time manager at the home office whenever turnover occurs.

Managerial Assistance Available: Pre-opening assistance and guidance re site selection, insurance coverage, staff recruiting, office layout, accounting systems, operational forms, etc. Continued post-opening assistance for duration of franchise. Operational guidance and analysis, continual availability, phone guidance, sales promotions, co-op advertising, operational guidance field visits, training assistance of staff, computerized terminals for payroll, billing, testing, retrieval, sales tracking, etc. Complete set of operations manuals.

Information Submitted: May 1987

DENNIS & DENNIS PERSONNEL SERVICE
1600 North Broadway #110
Santa Ana, California 92706
Lita L. Watson, President

Description of Operation: Dennis & Dennis Personnel Service offers franchises for the operation of employment agency and personnel services business and has been successfully operating in the franchise business since 1969. Franchising currently in State of California.

Number of Franchisees: 3 in California

In Business Since: 1969

Equity Capital Needed: $10,000 initial fee and an additional $50,000 to $100,000 for first year.

Financial Assistance Available: None with the exception of initial fee covers all supplies (initial) and initial training and assistance in start-up.

Training Provided: 2 weeks intense beginning training, weekly training thereafter and as required at the option of franchisor.

Managerial Assistance Available: Continual training as necessary on all aspects of business.

Information Submitted: May 1987

DIVISION 10 PERSONNEL SERVICE
499 Thornhall Street
Edison, New York 08837
David Roth, President

Description of Operation: Placement of office service personnel.

Number of Franchisees: 8 in 7 States

In Business Since: 1979

Equity Capital Needed: Approximately $42,000.

Financial Assistance Available: Negotiable

Training Provided: Initial training of 2 weeks at home office, 1 week at licensee's office. Further training as determined by licensor.

Managerial Assistance Available: Office visits, seminars, conventions, bulletins, manuals, etc., all at licensor's discretion.

Information Submitted: May 1987

*DUNHILL OFFICE PERSONNEL
DUNHILL PERSONNEL SYSTEM, INC.
One Old Country Road
Carle Place, New York 11514

Description of Operation: Dunhill Office Personnel specializes in the placement of high demand executive and legal secretaries, word processing operators, bookkeepers, receptionists and other office personnel job classifications.

Number of Franchisees: 2

In Business Since: 1982

Equity Capital Needed: $22,000 minimum initial investment. This includes a portion of the franchise fee, start-up and working capital.

Financial Assistance Available: Two-thirds of the franchise fee is financed over a 3 year period at 8 percent interest, commencing 10 months after the opening of business.

Training Provided: 2 weeks training program includes managing, marketing, market research, financial planning, applicant interviewing and testing, selling, recruiting, advertising and publicity. Initial inventory of forms and promotion material provided.

Managerial Assistance Available: Continuous follow-up and support provided through field service and telephone contact by field representatives specializing in the office personnel market. All new systems and promotional materials developed by franchisor is made available to franchisee.

Information Submitted: July 1987

*DUNHILL PERSONNEL SYSTEM, INC.
One Old Country Road
Carle Place, New York 11514

Description of Operation: Dunhill Personnel System is an international company offering three different franchises in peronnnel services. The Full Service franchise is recruitment and search for management and professional personnel on a national level, the Office Personnel franchise specializes in the high demand area of executive and legal secretaries, word processing operators and other office personnel job classifications and the Temporary Service franchise, which is the business that contracts out office and light industrial staff for both short- and long-term assignments.

Number of Franchisees: 298

In Business Since: 1952

Equity Capital Needed: The Full Service franchise requires minimum capital of $30,000, exclusive of personal needs. The Office Personnel franchise requires capital of $17,500. Capital needed for the Temporary Service franchise, depending on the size or scope of the operation ranges between $53,000 to $116,000. These amounts include the down payment of the franchise fee.

Financial Assistance Available: Dunhill System will finance up to 60 percent of the franchise fee over a 4 year period, commencing 10 months after opening at 8 percent interest.

Training Provided: Dunhill Personnel System provides intensive, continuous and updated training. The initial training provides 2 weeks of hands-on training in New York covering the search and placement cycle and the managerial aspects of the business. Extensive follow-up training is continuously provided on a regional and national basis. Motivational training and special industry training in the form of workshops and seminars are provided for franchisees and their consultants.

Managerial Assistance Available: Follow-up support is provided through our qualified field representatives both in the franchisee's office and through constant telephone contact. Audio visual programs and resource material for in-house training are also available.

Information Submitted: July 1987

EMPLOYERS OVERLOAD
Employers Overload Building
8040 Cedar Avenue South
Minneapolis, Minnesota 55420
Cynthia Wuori, Franchise Director

Description of Operation: One of the nation's largest temporary help services with 75 offices Coast-to-Coast and Canada. EO provides guaranteed, quality temporary help in all job classifications to business and industry.

Number of Franchisees: 64 franchises and 11 branch offices.

In Business Since: 1947

Equity Capital Needed: $25,000 to $100,000 depending on choice of plan.

Financial Assistance Available: Option of financing temporary payrolls and billings or funding by franchises.

Training Provided: Comprehensive training at corporate headquarters and additional training at office location.

Managerial Assistance Available: Complete support and assistance through corporate support staff on continual basis.

Information Submitted: May 1987

*EXPRESS SERVICES, INC.
6300 NW Expressway
Oklahoma City, Oklahoma 73132
Tom Gunderson, Franchise Director

Description of Operation: Express is a national corporation with more than 73 offices in 19 States. With three distinct divisions, the franchised offices provide clients with temporary help, permanent placements, and executive recruitment. Express Temporary Service supplies office, clerical, word processing, marketing, technical, and light industrial temporaries for short-term needs or long-term growth. Express Personnel Service provides qualified permanent employees for entry level through management positions. Robert William James & Associates, the management recruiting division, offers a professional approach to executive search. Together, the three divisions of Express give **total,** guaranteed personnel service. Acquired franchise service corporation in 1986 (15 offices).

Number of Franchisees: 73 in 19 States

In Business Since: 1983

Equity Capital Needed: $12,000 franchise fee per office, plus start-up capital (approximately $40,000). Initial investment depends upon whether operation is established or a start-up.

Financial Assistance Available: Temporary payroll is 100 percent financed by Express and accounts receivable are financed for 60 days. Express also participates in a local franchise advertising plan which is funded according to the franchisee's sales.

Training Provided: An intensive week-long training class is provided initially, followed by on-site visits by a traveling training director. Regional seminars, an annual company-wide meeting, and an ongoing supply of publications and training materials complete the program. A tape library is also available to franchise owners for in-service programs and individual use.

Managerial Assistance Available: Express supplies complete operations manuals, all forms, marketing brochures and promotional programs, advertising campaigns, and general PR help. Computer payrolling, client billing, and management consulting are included in the system. Field personnel are available for on-site help in planning and implementation of the Express program after initial training is completed.

Information Submitted: May 1987

FIVE STAR TEMPORARIES, INC.
1415 Elbridge Payne
Chesterfield, Missouri 63017
A. H. Harter, Jr., President

Description of Operation: We provide temporary personnel to businesses, factories, municipalities. Personnel provided includes secretaries, typists, clerical workers; also engineers as well as general laborers.

Number of Franchisees: 3 in Missouri, 1 in Indiana

In Business Since: 1981

Equity Capital Needed: Maximum of $40,000.

Financial Assistance Available: There is no franchise fee.

Training Provided: 2 months concentrated training at franchisee and franchisor location. Manuals are provided plus follow-up training and assistance for 2 years.

Managerial Assistance Available: Complete assistance in every aspect of the operations including sales, accounting, legal office management and general management. There is also a buy-back agreement at the option of the franchiser.

Information Submitted: May 1987

F-O-R-T-U-N-E FRANCHISE CORPORATION
655 Third Avenue
Suite 1805
New York, New York 10017
Michael Meyerson, Director of Sales

Description of Operation: F-O-R-T-U-N-E Personnel Consultants offers a quality middle management/executive recruiting service, utilizing unique, proven methods of operation to achieve its present status of industry leadership. F-O-R-T-U-N-E's 27 year reputation is highlighted by its prefessional service, innovative marketing concepts and sophisticated system of exchange of applicants and job orders, together with an excellent program of support for its franchise offices.

Number of Franchisees: 45 in 21 States

In Business Since: Founding company, F-O-R-T-U-N-E Personnel started in business, 1959, 1967 as F-O-R-T-U-N-E Personnel System and 1973 as F-O-R-T-U-N-E Franchise Corporation.

Equity Capital Needed: $35,000 plus

Financial Assistance Available: $25,000 is the minimum franchise fee, additional funds are required to meet pre-opening expenses and working capital, which in aggregate should be between $20,000 and $35,000. This amount will vary by the size of the office and number of personnel employed.

Training Provided: Intensive 20 day training program is required. 10 days are conducted for the owner at F-O-R-T-U-N-E home office on business fundamentals and management controls; 10 days are spent on location by F-O-R-T-U-N-E executives training franchise owner and staff. Additional training is also available at the home office and on field visits.

Managerial Assistance Available: F-O-R-T-U-N-E provides ongoing management assistance in the areas of franchise controls, exchange programs for applicants and companies and daily operational support. Communication is maintained by regular telephone contact, workshops, bulletins, newsletters, national conventions and on-site visits. Innovative techniques to improve quality and profitability of the F-O-R-T-U-N-E offices are continual. Special attention is paid and as much time as required given to the support of each newly opened office until they are well-established.

Information Submitted: June 1987

GEROTOGA ENTERPRISES, INC.
211 Park Avenue
Scotch Plains, New Jersey 07076
Audrey Hull

Description of Operation: A permanent professional, technical and clerical employment service under the names "Gerotoga" and "Plusmates," as well as temporary help service, under the name of "Apoxiforce" specializing in clerical and industrial temporaries.

Number of Franchisees: 10 in New Jersey

In Business Since: 1960

Equity Capital Needed: $16,000 (includes franchise fee and office set-up), plus approximately $10,000 operating capital for first 3 months.

Financial Assistance Available: None

Training Provided: Prior to opening of business, company will provide 3 weeks training at corporate headquarters, training and assistance is also provided the licensee and his personnel at the licensee's office. Operations and training manuals and training aids provided.

Managerial Assistance Available: Company provides printing and operating forms sufficient to do business for 90 days, continuous follow-up and support and field trips to licensee's office. Company will assist and/or advise the complete set-up of office, advertising, accounts, hiring and training of initial personnel. Meetings and seminars are conducted to improve expertise and efficiency.

Information Submitted: May 1987

GILBERT LANE PERSONNEL SERVICE
221 Main Street
Hartford, Connecticut 06106
Howard Specter, President

Description of Operation: Gilbert Lane Personnel Service offers a broad based employment recruiting system which specializes in middle-management and professional level placement with quotas ans concentration on engineering and high technology recruitment.

Number of Franchisees: 7 in 5 States, including company-owned

In Business Since: 1957

Equity Capital Needed: $40,000 minimum

Financial Assistance Available: Investment would include franchise fee and pre-opening expenses to include—rent deposit, utility deposit, advertising, legal fees, etc. Additionally, $15,000-$20,000 recommended for use as operating capital. Company will give consideration to making financial arrangements.

Training Provided: The owner/manager is required to attend an intensive 2 week pre-opening training session at the company's home office. Additional training is conducted at franchisee's office for both himself and his staff at the time of opening. The operation is then closely monitored, including staff visits, until effectively operating.

Managerial Assistance Available: Gilbert Lane provides continuous guidance and assistance in all areas of agency management. Interchange job openings and applicants throughout the Gilbert Lane network. Annual franchise manager's meetings, issuance of training tapes and operating manuals are part of ongoing program.

Informtion Submitted: May 1987

HAYES PERSONNEL SERVICES, INC.
25 North Cascade
Suite 208
Colorado Springs, Colorado 80903
David Hayes, President

Description of Operation: A total Human Resource Center, nationally scoped. The franchise consists of 3 distinct employment divisions: permanent, temporary, and executive placement services, plus a high tech, high touch consulting/training division allowing full service to clients under one franchise. The Hayes system makes available research, marketing programs and presentation booklets, advertising techniques and materials, complete operational manuals for each division, management and staff reports, and training.

Number of Franchisees: 2 in Colorado and 1 in Arizona

In Business Since: 1974

Equity Capital Needed: Franchise fee is $15,000, we recommend 6 months minimum living and business expense capital.

Financial Assistance Available: Franchise fee includes start-up materials, operational manuals, brochures and sales presentation books. Plus the franchisors reinvest the first 13 weeks royalty into the new franchise to be used at your discretion.

Training Provided: Continual assistance through a complete support system of headquarters management. Assistance starts with a full 3 weeks of high-impact training; 2 weeks at headquarters and the next week within 3 months of start-up. The trainer will return with Hayes exclusive 50-key area check list and spend the week going over those areas needing additional training. Besides those initial 3 weeks, continued assistance provided as reasonably requested.

Managerial Assistance Available: Same as above

Information Submitted: July 1987

HERITAGE PERSONNEL SYSTEMS, INC.
4926 Windy Hill Drive
Raleigh, North Carolina 27609
Robert A. Hounsell, Director of Franchising

Description of Operation: Full service, "across the board" professional personnel service, from entry level positions to top executives in all job categories on a "company-paid fee" basis, offering both advertising and recruiting services with marketing emphasis on a national basis.

Number of Franchisees: 3 in North Carolina and Tennessee

In Business Since: 1974; began franchising in 1977

Equity Capital Needed: $10,000-$30,000 initial franchise fee, plus approximately $3,000 start-up costs.

Financial Assistance Available: Possibility of company-financing of up to 50 percent of franchise fee, and advice and consultation in obtaining other sources of financial assistance.

Training Provided: 2 weeks at company headquarters; 1 week in franchisee's office; continuous consultancy and assistance thereafter.

Managerial Assistance Available: Continuous assistance to franchisee in advertising, marketing, hiring and training of staff, accounting, legal, office expansion and new job market development. Close cooperation in the system's "management by objectives" procedures is maintained by phone, mail and personal visits.

Information Submitted: July 1987

HRI SERVICES, INC.
140 Wood Road
Suite 205
Braintree, Massachusetts 02184
Paul R. Tallino, President

Description of Operation: HRI Services, Inc., is a national executive search and placement organization. HRI assist companies throughout th hospitality industry in meeting their management, executive and professional requirements.

Number of Franchisees: 3 in Florida and Texas

In Business Since: 1977

Equity Capital Needed: $30,000

Financial Assistance Available: None

Training Provided: A 30 day intensive training program held at the corporate office in Boston, Massachusetts is conducted for all new franchisees.

Managerial Assistance Available: Continued management service is available.

Information Submitted: June 1987

INTELLIDEX CONTRAC CORP.
One Sheraton Plaza
Suite 702
New Rochelle, New York 10801
Louis G. Cornacchia, President, Electronic Engineer

Description of Operation: Intellidex is a full service temporary hi-tech personnel company providing industry with state of the art engineering support, computer programmers, technicians, designers, CAE, CAD capabilities and other scientific disciplines. The founder of the franchise has owned and operated two corporations providing primary engineering and other temporary technical support personnel. The franchise is offered to qualified "start up" and existing business owners. Intellidex finances 100 percent of all temporary support personnel payroll, and provides all back office support for payroll documentation taxes, invoicing, etc. Intellidex makes available marketing, research, client support, creative advertising, all support manuals, temporary employee benefits, continuing employee educational materials, newsletter, staff training, national accounting and franchisor -franchisee group events. For further information call (914) 576-6530 collect.

Number of Franchisees: 2 in New York

In Business Since: Collins Consultants International, Ltd. 1967—Charger Tech Services, Inc., 1974. Both still in business and to be joined to Intellidex as company-owned operations. Intellidex Contract Corp., August 1987

Equity Capital Needed: $46,500-$66,500. Franchise fee of $10,000 included in initial capital required.

Financial Assistance Available: Negotiable—will finance portion of franchise fee at no interest.

Training Provided: An initial 2 week program at central home facility. Training includes use of training manuals developed by Intellidex. Franchisor will provide continued training at franchisee office and continuing field support by franchisor professional staff. Seminars, national meetings, newsletters and other publications will be provided in the future for continuous support in all special areas to meet future continuing changing disciplines evolving in the temporary support industry.

Managerial Assistance Available: Intellidex will augment on a national scale, techniques, utilizing data based systems allowing immediate access capabilities by our franchisees to current ongoing engineering and scientific data. Candidate availability, industry information both economic and technical, military and industrial contract awards, and other current data will also be provided via newsletters and bulletins for creating a competitive edge. Intellidex is a highly disciplined organization with a unique concept to the professional approach.

Information Submitted: August 1987

JBS INC.
260 Cochituate Road
Suite 109
Framingham, Massachusetts 01701
G. A. Powers, President

Description of Operation: JBS operates temporary help services in several States. Three offices are company-owned. The balance are franchised.

Number of Franchisees: 4 in 4 States

In Business Since: 1970

Equity Capital Needed: No franchise fee, but successful applicant will need a minimum of $15,000 equity capital.

Financial Assistance Available: Franchisor provides financing for the temporary payroll, which is the major capital outlay in the temporary help business. Franchisor finances workers compensation and liability insurance coverage, charging same back to franchisee on a pay-as-you-go basis. Franchisor also makes timely payroll tax deposits on a charge-back basis.

Training Provided: Applicants must have a minimum of 2 years of hands-on experience in the management and/or sales of temporary help services, in order to qualify.

Managerial Assistance Available: A minimum of 1 week start-up assistance will be provided to franchisee in his market by a staff member. Continuing assistance provided as reasonably requested. Payroll, invoicing, and tax records will be handled entirely by franchisor, although franchisee has option to write payroll locally. Most forms used in the business furnished by franchisor, along with promotional material from time to time.

Information Submitted: May 1987

• J.O.B.S.
2535 Landmark Drive
Suite 201
Clearwater, Florida 33519
Paul Elieff, Vice President, Franchising

Description of Operation: J.O.B.S. is an employment information service which targets the largest U.S. market, those who earn less than $25,000 a year. The unemployed customers are provided with a computer-matched listing of available jobs. In addition, each store is computer-linked to all other stores by a National Computer Network. Revenue is also generated from resume production.

Number of Franchisees: 34 in 21 States

In Business Since: 1981—franchising since 1984

Equity Capital Needed: $35,000 minimum

Financial Assistance Available: Yes

Training Provided: 2 weeks initial training and follow-up visits, if necessary. Continuous telephone contact. Franchisor also receives weekly sales report analysis to help franchisee improve sales.

Managerial Assistance Available: Ongoing assistance. Retraining will be provided, if requested, at a nominal fee. Franchisor continues to research and develop new techniques to benefit each franchisee. Comprehensive operations manual and three months' operating supplies are included.

Information Submitted: May 1987

LLOYD PERSONNEL CONSULTANTS
10 Cuttermill Road
Great Neck, New York 11021
Merrill Banks, President

Description of Operation: A highly respected national placement firm. Major area of specialization are in sales, sales management and marketing staff personnel in the computer, communications, and office products field. Other areas of national specialty are insurance, office services, and graphics. A professional office services temporary operation known as Lloyd Creative Temps is a sister company that is also available.

Number of Franchisees: 2 in New York and New Hampshire

In Business Since: 1971, franchising since 1986.

Equity Capital Needed: $25,000 franchise fee plus $5,000 start-up cost, plus living expenses.

Financial Assistance Available: Yes, payment terms available.

Training Provided: The initial training provided to new franchisee consists of a combination of 15 days in franchisor's office and in the new franchisee's office. The initial training consists of a comprehensive program of management training, including leadership responsibilities, planning, both monetary and performance, personnel selection, retention, compansation and responsibilities, client relations, marketing and advertising techniques, accounting, bookkeeping and financial matters as well as training in all phases of the actual activities of a placement

counselor involved in the recruiting and interviewing of applicants, the solicitation of job orders, the making of referrals and the effecting of placements. After the initial training, additional training is provided on an as needed and requested basis.

Managerial Assistance Available: Assistance begins with site selection, office layout, equipment purchase, and complete office set up including all forms and necessary printing. Franchisor or representative will be on-site for opening of franchise office for the purpose of continued education and rendering assistance. A daily telephone contact program covering everyday operation will take place for as long as franchisee deems necessary. This daily assistance program will be insulated with a written manager's operational guide as well as a situation answer guide to questions.

Information Submitted: May 1987

•MANAGEMENT RECRUITERS INTERNATIONAL, INC.
1127 Euclid Avenue
Suite 1400
Cleveland, Ohio 44115-1638
Alan R. Schonberg, President

Description of Operation: Search and recruiting service business under the names of "Management Recruiters," "Sales Consultants." "OfficeMates/5, and "CompuSearch." Also refer to the listing under Sales Consultants International.

Number of Franchisees: 452 offices including 6 company-owned offices in 44 States, the District of Columbia and Canada

In Business Since: 1957

Equity Capital Needed: Minimum $35,500. Maximum $62,400 depending on location.

Financial Assistance Available: None

Training Provided: The franchisor's staff will provide the licensee with an intensive initial training program of approximately 3 weeks conducted at the franchisor's corporate headquarters in Cleveland, Ohio plus an initial on-the-job training program of approximately 3 additional weeks is conducted in the licensee's first office. In addition to the above, the franchisor's staff will assist and advice the licensee in (a) securing suitable office space and the negotiation of the lease for same, (b) the design and layout of the office, (c) the selection of office furniture and equipment and the negotiation of the purchase or lease agreement for same, and (d) the establishment of a suitable telephone system for the licensee's office.

Managerial Assistance Available: The licensee is provided with a detailed operations manual containing information, procedures and know how for operating the business. In addition, the licensee receives a VCR and a 19" color TV set plus franchisor's complete video training film series (21 cassettes), and a 90 day supply of all necessary operating forms, brochures, etc. The franchisor will furnish the licensee with continuing advice, guidance and assistance through national and regional meetings, seminars, correspondence, video training films, telephone and personal instruction with respect to the licensee's personnel placement service operations and procedures and their improvement and revision.

Information Submitted: May 1987

THE MURPHY GROUP
1211 West 22nd Street
Oak Brook, Illinois 60521
William A. Murphy, President

Description of Operation: Murphy Employment Service offers a unique full service private personnel placement service concentrating on the placement of administrative, executive, sales, professional, secretarial and general office personnel. All offices are currently integrated with a unique computerized interoffice communications system for the exchange of job orders and candidates.

Number of Franchisees: 8 in Illinois and Florida

In Business Since: 30 years

Equity Capital Needed: Franchise fee of $10,000 and $25,000 available capital.

Financial Assistance Available: None

Training Provided: For Illinois franchisees only, placement consultant training is conducted at the Corporate office, primarily classroom in nature, consisting of 5 or more half day sessions. This is followed up with 24 half hour instructional audio tapes covering all facets of actual activities of the personnel consultant, plus a series of video tapes with a thorough analysis of interviewing and marketing. In addition, franchisee will receive periodic analysis of operating statistics. All franchisees in Illinois and other States are furnished with a complete set of training manuals and tapes, and an operations manual. They are also provided with continual management service for the life of the franchise in such areas as operations, analysis and advertising.

Managerial Assistance Available: Manager's training consists of 12 half day sessions over a minimum of 6 days which cover basic management and leadership training, budgeting, all facets of personnel functions from a management prospective, marketing, advertising, client relations, training as well as networking.

Information Submitted: August 1987

* NORRELL TEMPORARY SERVICES, INC.
3092 Piedmont Road, N.E.
Atlanta, Georgia 30305
Dennis A. Fuller, Director of Franchise Development

Description of Operation: Temporary help industry. Catering to all the segments of business. Vertical marketing programs designed for the banking, insurance, financial services and office automation industries. Unique facilities staffing concept to address clients changing personnel needs. Utilize a consultive approach to the temporary help industry.

Number of Franchisees: 115 in 27 States plus 180 units company-owned.

In Business Since: 1963

Equity Capital Needed: $40,000-$70,000 no up front franchise fee.

Financial Assistance Available: Payroll financing and accounts receivable financing.

Training Provided: Initial, both field training and 6 day classroom course are provided. Continuing classroom training and seminars in the franchisee's area are provided quarterly. Cassette tapes, manuals and other written program are available for each individual franchise office.

Managerial Assistance Available: Field dedicated regional managers and district managers assist in making sales calls with the franchisee, teaching proper pricing, assisting in recruiting, etc. Norrell supplies computer payrolling, customer billings, operations manuals, forms, brochures, national advertising and direct mail promotion.

Information Submitted: May 1987

THE OLSTEN CORPORATION
1 Merrick Avenue
Westbury, L.I., New York 11590
Jeffrey A. Gerber, Director of License Development

Description of Operation: A national public company operating branch, franchise and licensed offices. Provides temporary office and industrial personnel for as long as needed by businesses, government, industry and institutions.

Number of Franchisees: 105 franchise offices and 58 licensed offices.

In Business Since: 1950

Equity Capital Needed: $40,000 minimum, includes working capital, required to cover start-up costs and general operating expenses, plus living expenses. No up-front money.

Financial Assistance Available: Temporary payroll funded by The Olsten Corporation.

Training Provided: Comprehensive on-the-job training and field training as well as periodic visits covering every phase of business operations.

Managerial Assistance Available: Full operating manuals, forms, printed sales material and basic supplies provided no charge. In addition, provides continuous, ongoing assistance in all facets of the business including technical assistance, insurance, marketing, sales, advertising and other areas of temporary help. National sales leads also supplied whenever possible.

Information Submitted: May 1987

PARKER PAGE ASSOCIATES, INC.
P.O. Box 6353
Bellevue, Washington 98008
Glenn D. Lindley, President

Description of Operation: Executive recruiting in the specialized fields of chemicals, plastic, paint, ink, adhesives, pulp and paper, food, computers and insurance. Office work together with an interchange system.

Number of Franchisees: 4 in Georgia, Texas, New York and North Carolina

In Business Since: 1972

Equity Capital Needed: $35,000 working capital with reserve to support owner for three months.

Financial Assistance Available: Negotiable

Training Provided: Complete on-the-job training for 1 week. Daily consultation with toll free call to home office. Will aid in staffing and training all staff members.

Managerial Assistance Available: Continued program to develop new specialty categories and training of each office as developed.

Information Submitted: July 1987

* PERSONNEL POOL OF AMERICA, INC.
303 S.E. 17th Street
Fort Lauderdale, Florida 33316

Description of Operation: International provider of supplemental personnel services through two speciality divisions: medical personnel pool furnishing licensed/unlicensed staff relief services to hospitals and nursing homes as well as home health care licensed nursing and unlicensed companion/nurse's aid services; personnel pool furnishing commercial, industrial and governmental clients with skilled, semi-skilled and unskilled personnel in clerical, paralegal, paratechnical, light industrial and industrial work environments. Franchise opportunities available in one or both divisions depending on market size and availability.

Number of Franchisees: Medical Personnel Pool—181, Personnel Pool—121, company-owned—114.

In Business Since: 1946

Equity Capital Needed: Approximately $50,000-$150,000

Financial Assistance Available: Growth capital financing for franchisees after first year in operation.

Training Provided: 2 weeks at company's home office includes owner/management training in financial and back office management and sales/marketing training; plus 2 weeks on-the-job training at franchisees' office after opening. Staff and management training ongoing via seminars, regional training, teletraining, video and audio program training.

Managerial Assistance Available: Franchisor provides consulting services to all franchisees in the areas of advertising, insurance, finance, legal, risk management, sales strategies, market development, national accounts, data processing, recruitment.

Information Submitted: May 1987

PLACE MART FRANCHISING CORP.
1140 Bloomfield Avenue
West Caldwell, New Jersey 07006
M. B. Kushma, President

Description of Operation: Employment agency.

Number of Franchisees: 2 in New Jersey

In Business Since: 1962

Equity Capital Needed: $30,000-$40,000

Financial Assistance Available: No

Training Provided: Intensive training at corporate office from 3 to 6 weeks, then follow-up training at franchisee's location. Periodic systematic supervisory follow-up.

Managerial Assistance Available: Continuous training and supervision from field personnel, seminars, training sessions, newsletters, new ideas and systems constantly introduced. Periodic franchise meeting discussing policies and administrative problems and exchange of ideas for mutual help.

Information Submitted: May 1987

THE REGIONAL NETWORK OF PERSONNEL CONSULTANTS
1211 West 22nd Street
Oak Brook, Illinois 60521
William A. Murphy, President

Description of Operation: A new concept in the private employment business networking existing agencies by a computer integrated local area network allowing all network members to get full exposure to all jobs within the region without losing control of their own accounts and having the opportunity to increase their applicant, job order and placement activity.

Number of Franchisees: 8 in Illinois

In Business Since: Start-up January 1985

Equity Capital Needed: $5,000 for franchise fee, additional $5,000 for computer equipment.

Financial Assistance Available: None

Training Provided: Since this is a conversion franchisor it is sold only to highly selected private employment agencies already in business and the only training needed is in the familiarity of computerization of job orders and placements in the local area network. This training will be given at the corporate offices or on-site and will take no more than 2 half days.

Managerial Assistance Available: None. The Network will be run by regional councils representing each member in the region.

Information Submitted: August 1987

RETAIL RECRUITERS INTERNATIONAL, INC./ SPECTRA PROFESSIONAL SEARCH
84 Paunton Street
Plainville, Massachusetts 02762
Jacques J. Lapointe, President

Description of Operation: Personnel Placement Service Business under the names of "Retail Recruiters," and "Spectra." Specializing in middle to upper level management placement, and executive search. Strong co-broking system within organization.

Number of Franchisees: 20 in 16 States

In Business Since: 1969

Equity Capital Needed: $20,000-$40,000 depending on location.

Financial Assistance Available: None

Training Provided: Complete training in all aspects of operation. Intensive 3-4 weeks training of new franchisee and new employees of initial franchise. Training at home office and at new franchisees first office. Continuous and follow-up triining as needed. Assist in securing suitable office space, help negotiate lease, design layout of office, selection of proper office furniture and equipment, and proper telephone system.

Managerial Assistance Available: Company provides detail training manual and video tapes that contain detailed information and know-how for operating personnel business. We will provide continuing advice, guidance and assistance through meetings, personal visits on a continuous basis to insure proper operation of business.

Information Submitted: July 1987

*ROMAC & ASSOCIATES, INC.
183 Middle Street
P. O. Box 7469 DTS
Portland, Maine 04112
R. N. Nordstrom, Director, Franchise Development

Description of Operation: Romac & Associates is a network of offices which provides personnel placement services to clients in need of professionals in the areas of corporate accounting, public accounting, data processing, finance, and banking. The offices are staffed by executives whose business background is in the fields which they serve. Romac's reputation for success is based on its strict adherence to confidentiality, to the interaction of the offices within the organization, and to a guarantee backed by refunds.

Number of Franchisees: 38 in 24 States

In Business Since: 1966

Equity Capital Needed: $55,000 to $105,000 (depending on market area)

Financial Assistance Available: Yes

Training Provided: All franchisees participate in an intensive training program in the corporate office at which time all phases of the business operation are covered. Follow-up training is conducted at the local office.

Managerial Assistance Available: Interoffice jobs and candidate referrals are maintained through our exclusive electronic mail ROMNET system. Continuous training and support, training sessions, SM seminars, newsletters, and training manuals are provided, as well as preparation and assistance with advertising, marketing, recruiting and screening, and help with financial and accounting procedures. Group plans for insurance and employee benefits, fee schedules, cooperative advertising, etc., are continually updated and maintained.

Information Submitted: July 1987

ROTH YOUNG PERSONNEL SERVICE, INC.
1500 Broadway
New York, New York 10036
David Roth, President

Description of Operation: Contingency and executive search service.

Number of Franchisees: 31 in 24 States

In Business Since: 1964

Equity Capital Needed: Approximately $92,000

Financial Assistance Available: Negotiable

Training Provided: Initial training of 2 weeks at home office, 1 week at licensee's office. Further training as determined by licensor.

Managerial Assistance Available: Office visits, seminars, conventions, bulletins, manuals, etc., all at licensor's discretion.

Information Submitted: May 1987

*SALES CONSULTANTS INTERNATIONAL
A Division of MANAGEMENT RECRUITERS INTERNATIONAL, INC.
1127 Euclid Avenue, Suite 1400
Cleveland, Ohio 44115-1638
Alan R. Schonberg, President

Description of Operation: An opportunity to join an organization involved solely in searching and recruiting of sales managers, salesmen, saleswomen, sales engineers, and marketing people.

Number of Franchisees: 127 offices (including company-owned offices) in 39 States and the District of Columbia

In Business Since: 1957

Equity Capital Needed: $35,500 to $62,400 depending on location.

Financial Assistance Available: None

Training Provided: The franchisor's staff will provide the licensee with an intensive initial training program of approximately 3 weeks conducted at the franchisor's corporate headquarters in Cleveland, Ohio plus an initial on-the-job training program of approximately 3 additional weeks which is conducted in the licensee's first office. In addition to the above, the franchisor's staff will assist and advise the licensee in (a) securing suitable office space and the negotiation of the lease for same, (b) the design and layout of the office, (c) the selection of office furniture and equipment and the negotiation of the purchase or lease agreement for same, and (d) the establishment of a suitable telephone system for the licensee's office.

Managerial Assistance Available: The licensee is provided with a detailed operations manual containing information, procedures and know-how of operating the business. In addition, the licensee receives a VCR and a 19" color TV set plus franchisor's complete video training film series (21 cassettes), and a 90 day supply of all necessary operating forms, brochures, etc. The franchisor will furnish the licensee with continuing advice, guidance and assistance through national and regional meetings, seminars, correspondence, video traning films, telephone and personal instruction with respect to the licensee's personnel placement service operations and procedures and their improvement and revision.

Information Submitted: May 1987

*SANFORD ROSE ASSOCIATES INTERNATIONAL, INC.
265 South Main Street
Akron, Ohio 44308
Doug Eilertson, Vice President

Description of Operation: Executive recruiting. Activities center on recruitment of management level personnel for industry and business with emphasis on companies having high technology products or processes. SRA offices, while autonomous, share the resources of the parent company's Opportunity Center Division, the largest operators of career centers worldwide. Foreign affiliates assist in international market. All offices participate in weekly job order and resume exchange. All offices receive hundreds of professional openings weekly from headquarters national marketing program. Ownership of an SRA office is limited to college graduates with significant business or industrial experience.

Number of Franchisees: 85 in 24 States

In Business Since: 1959

Equity Capital Needed: $50,000 minimum

Financial Assistance Available: $40,000 includes the portion of the license payment due prior to opening, as well as usual start-up costs. Financing is available for the balance of the license fee. Normal operating capital is also included, the amount varying according to the size and type of office selected.

Training Provided: Current program is 15 days of intensive 8 hour days in addition to a minimum of 2 weeks in the new licensees office. This includes classroom as well as "hands-on" work. Extensive training manuals and tapes are furnished to each licensee. Regular 5 day personnel consultant training courses are also furnished on a no charge basis to the licensee's employees.

Managerial Assistance Available: Sanford Rose Associates provides a complete time tested system for personnel recruitment and placement. All forms, routines and procedures are included. National and State laws are taught as a part of training. Complete computerized financial statements are rendered monthly, to each office. Field operations personnel visit offices on a routine and request basis. Sales contests, seminars, and other recruiter incentives are regularly used by Sanford Rose Associates.

Information Submitted: May 1987

*SNELLING AND SNELLING, INC.
Executive Offices
Snelling Plaza
4000 South Tamiami Trail
Sarasota, Florida 33581

Description of Operation: Snelling and Snelling franchisees, depending on location, experience and inclination of owner range in size from 1-15 or more employees. Their fields of placement and recruiting range from highly specialized services in areas such aas: data processing, engineering, marketing, accounting, finance, oil and gas, etc., to the general areas of secretarial, office and clerical, sales, administrative, and technical.

Number of Franchisees: Over 480 in U.S. and Brazil.

In Business Since: 1951

Equity Capital Needed: $40,000 to $80,000

Financial Assistance Available: Yes

Training Provided: Video tapes covering virtually every aspect of the profession are backed up by detailed training manuals for each position in the franchise. Initial training consists of 2 weeks at home office in Sarasota, Florida for owner(s) and staff. The franchisor is available for counselling and at the present time national marketing consultants travel throughout the U.S. offering additional management advice, assistance, and training.

Managerial Assistance Available: Pre-opening aid selection, lease negotiation, phone systems, furniture selection, etc., provided by staff at home office.

Information Submitted: July 1987

SOURCENET INTERNATIONAL
A Division of HEALTHCARE RECRUITERS INTERNATIONAL, INC.
5420 LBJ
Suite 575
Dallas, Texas 75240
Frank A. Cooksey, President

Description of Operation: Contingency and retainer executive recruiting/search specializing only in data processing, accounting, finance, engineering, sales, sales management, and general management. SourceNet International is known as the "National Network for Recruiting Specialists." Each office is owned and staffed by executives whose business background has been in the industry which they specialize in. SourceNet International's success has been established by developing systems that provide a real opportunity for an individual to "control their own destiny" utilizing those proven systems and established computerized client and candidate base.

Number of Franchisee: Newly developed—32 HealthCare Recruiters International offices in 23 states.

In Business Since: 1983

Equity Capital Needed: $60,000 to 80,000—Depending on location.

Financial Assistance Available: Yes

Training Provided: Intensive training program of 2 weeks at the corporate headquarters in Dallas, Texas. Utilizing the latest audio visual training techniques in the industry, including video tapes, training/operation manual, reference guides and client/candidate information. SourceNet International provides training in all aspects of the recruiting and executive search business, including specialized training for owner-managers and account executives. Also, all account executives

employed during the lifetime of the Franchise, are trained, in-house by SourceNet International. On the job taining is conducted by home office representative to provide continuing training through a program of weekly telephone and periodic visits. In addition, SourceNet International conducts bi-annual training seminars and conferences. SourceNet International will assist and advise the licensee in (1) office site selection and lease negotiation, (2) office layout and furniture selection (3) selection of computer equipment system (4) account executive recruitment. In summary, SourceNet International will provide its network franchisees with training, resources and guidance to operate a medical sales management and marketing executive recruiting business.

Managerial Assistance Available: Continuing support thru daily, weekly, monthly phone consultation and periodic management visits covering all aspects of the medical recruiting business. In addition SourceNet International provides collection assistance of Licensee's accounts receivable and detailed analysis of all phases of their operation. SourceNet International also provides national advertising and marketing support programs as well as target account solicitation by headquarter personnel.

Information Submitted: May 1987

*TEMPORARIES, INCORPORATED
3255 K Street
Washington, D.C. 20007
D. Geoffrey John, President

Description of Operation: Temporaries, Inc., supplies temporary office and medical help to business and professional firms, governments, and medical institutions. The franchise program started in November 1973 and will continue in medium to large size markets. Currently has 34 offices in 27 markets.

Number of Franchisees: 5 in 4 States, plus 29 company-owned

In Business Since: 1969

Equity Capital Needed: $100,000 is needed for operating and receivables expense.

Financial Assistance Available: No

Training Provided: A home office training school utilizing audio-visual training techniques offers initial management training for 2 weeks. Then intensive on-site, on-the-job training by franchisor sales and counselor trainers are continued for 2 weeks. consistent field training is ongoing by franchisor to assure profitability quickly.

Managerial Assistance Available: Assistance in all phases of pre-opening and supply of forms and manuals. Continuous management service for the life of the franchise in all phases of an operation, i.e., sales, management, training of employees, accounting, advertising, recruiting, etc. Home office staff works closely via telephone and mail with all franchisees and makes regular visits to assist in these areas.

Information Submitted: May 1987

TEMPOSITIONS
150 Post Street
San Francisco, California 94108
John B. Petersen, Senior Vice President

Description of Operation: TemPositions is a full services temporary help service. Licenses will be trained in the systems and procedures requires to corporate a profitable temporary help firms. Licenses are provided with IBM PC, training, marketing assistance, payroll and accounts received financing as well as management reports and field assistance.

Number of Franchisees: 2 plus 10 company-owned

In Business Since: 1962

Equity Capital Needed: $50,000-$70,000

Financial Assistance Available: TemPosition provides 100 percent of funding for payroll and accounts receivable. Licensee must provide license fee ($15,000) and initial capital.

Training Provided: 1 week in operating TemPositions office. 1 week classroom on systems and procedures, periodic field training seminars.

Managerial Assistance Available: Payroll, billing, government reports, insurance systems assistance is a continuing function of the licensor (TemPositions).

Information Submitted: May 1987

THANK GOODNESS I'VE FOUND...TGIF
P. O. Box 828
Old Lyme, Connecticut 06371
Joanne Kobar, President

Description of Operation: Search Service for Domestic In-Home Help. We are a personal service with affordable fees to appeal to the average-income family. Coast-to-coast offices will work together as a network for mutual matchmaking. Franchisees have potential for in-home offices.

Number of Franchisees: 11 locations including company-owned.

In Business Since: 1982, franchising since 1986.

Equity Capital Needed: $8,500 franchise fee plus $4,700 start-up expenses.

Financial Assistance Available: None

Training Provided: 2-3 day all-expenses-paid training at either home or office or location of franchise.

Managerial Assistance Available: June 1987

Managerial Assistance Available: Coast-to-coast network mutual matchmaking and a system of interviewers; continuous support and guidance with home office and other offices; monthly newsletter and constant updating of new innovations and expanded services to the franchisees.

Information Submitted: May 1987

TIME SERVICES, INC.
6422 Lima Road
Fort Wayne, Indiana 46818
Bruce Bone, President

Description of Operation: A midwestern corporation with company-owned and franchised offices offering a full line of temporary help in the office clerical and light industrial fields and contract help in the technical fields.

Number of Franchisees: 3 in Pennsylvania, and Ohio plus 1 company-owned.

In Business Since: 1982

Equity Capital Needed: $50,000 to $85,000

Financial Assistance Available: Payroll and accounts receivable are financed by franchisor.

Training Provided: Field and classroom training is provided on a continuous basis for both franchisees and their personnel.

Managerial Assistance Available: Managers work in the franchise office and in the field with sales calls on a regularly scheduled basis. Continuous planning, advertising material and copy counsel and marketing assistance is provided. Management also provides periodic visits and seminars to supplement the training programs.

Information Submitted: May 1987

TODAYS TEMPORARY
18111 Preston Road
Suite 850
Dallas, Texas 75252
Kevin W. Roberts, Franchise Marketing Coordinator

Description of Operation: Franchisor operates a full-service, high-quality office clerical temporary employment service, a business in which franchisor's founders have over 20 years experience collectively.

Number of Franchisees: 26 in 9 States

In Business Since: 1982

Equity Capital Needed: No franchise fee, $60,000 to $80,000 working capital to cover start-up and operating expenses.

Financial Assistance Available: Temporary payroll and accounts receivable financing.

Training Provided: Initial training involves a minimum of 2 weeks intensive classroom and field training on all aspects of sales, operations, and management of franchisor's temporary service. Quarterly training seminars along with periodic in-market visits by field coordinators provides franchisees with continued training in all aspects of business operations.

Managerial Assistance Available: Franchisor provides a comprehensive set of manuals detailing start-up, operations and sales procedures. In addition, assistance is provided for temporary recruiting, yellow page advertising, site selection, business development, insurance, and budgeting. Franchisor also provides direct mail and national account leads.

Information Submitted: May 1987

TRANSWORLD TEMPORARIES FRANCHISE CORPORATION
6151 W. Century Boulevard, 1200
Los Angeles, California 90045
Nancy Seyfert, Vice President & General Manager

Description of Operation: Full service quality clerical and light industrial temporary personnel.

Number of Franchisees: 9 in California, Arizona, Nevada, New Jersey, Pennsylvania

In Business Since: 1979

Equity Capital Needed: Franchise fee: $15,000; start up costs; $10,000-$15,000; Operating capital: $30,000—$40,000.

Financial Assistance Available: Finance temporary employee payroll; accounts receivable financing.

Training Provided: 1 week formal classroom training in sales and management. 1 week outlet training in Operations & Administration. Ongoing consulting support and "Hot Line" to Corporate Office.

Managerial Assistance Available: Development of business plan, ongoing consultation on all aspects of temporary services business. Full training manual system, start-up kit of marketing and operational materials.

Information Submitted: May 1987

* TRC TEMPORARY SERVICES, INC.
5600 Roswell Road
Prado East, Suite 350
Atlanta, Georgia 30342

Description of Operation: Franchise opportunity with one of the finest temporary help firms in the country. Business is the placement of temporary workers with clients, in the areas of clerical, secretarial, word processing, marketing and light industrial skills.

Number of Franchisees: 11 in 9 states.

In Business Since: 1980

Equity Capital Needed: $75,000-$125,000 of working capital.

Financial Assistance Available: No financial assistance toward working capital. However, franchisor finances temporary help payroll, credit and collections, taxes, insurance, supplies, field training.

Training Provided: 5 day pre-opening training, formal training for sales, operations and management, 5 days each course. Within 6 weeks of opening, 30 man days of training at the office site. Ongoing communications, newsletter, seminars.

Managerial Assistance Available: 10 days after closing, 3 man days of management consultation. 5 man days per quarter, spent in each office. Ongoing monitoring.

Information Submitted: May 1987

UNIFORCE TEMPORARY PERSONNEL, INC.
1335 Jericho Turnpike
New Hyde Park, New York 11040
John Fanning, President

Description of Operation: A publicly held, national temporary personnel service which offers a complete line of services including all office, light industrial, marketing, accounting, and technical. These services are provided to industry, business and government agencies. In addition to supplying basic temporary personnel services, Uniforce specializes in project staffing, providing large groups of temporaries for long-term special assignments.

Number of Franchisees: 58 in 22 States

In Business Since: 1962

Equity Capital Needed: $40,000 to $50,000 which includes an initial licensing fee of $15,000. The remaining capital is needed for general operating expenses. Regional franchises available with an initial licensing fee of $15,000 and $15,000 in interest bearing notes, additional capital of $50,000-$75,000 is necessary for general operating expenses.

Financial Assistance Available: Temporary employees payroll financing and financing of accounts receivable without any interest charge—ever! Fifty percent of the licensing fee may be financed through promissory notes at current interest rates.

Training Provided: No prior experience is required. Owner will spend one week of training at the company's home office training center. Utilizing the latest audio-visual training techniques, including video tapes, Uniforce will provide training in all phases of temporary help operations, including specialized training for owner-managers, personnel placement, counselor instruction and sales representative training. On-the-job training is conducted by a home office branch service representative assigned to the franchisee's office to provide continuing training and guidance through a program of telephone contact and periodic visits. In addition, Uniforce conducts a series of regional conferences and seminars for owners and their staffs, as well as an annual training seminar and conference.

Managerial Assistance Available: Assistance in initial selection of site and layout of office, negotiation of lease, selection of furniture and equipment and telephone systems. A continuous supply of all forms and materials necessary for the continuous operation of the Uniforce business: manuals, guides, monthly updates, unlimited phone consultation and periodic management visits. In addition, Uniforce prepares and finances the temporary help payroll, billing and accounts receiveable and provides detailed computer analysis to each office on all phases of the temporary help operation. Monthly management guidance tapes are provided in addition to the support by the home office staff. Training tapes provided at no charge. In addition, Uniforce provides marketing and advertising support programs including all necessary promotional materials.

Information Submitted: May 1987

UNI/SEARCH, INC.
P.O. Box
Waterbury, Connecticut 06762
Peter Allvin, President

Description of Operation: Uni/Search is a regional franchised professional employment service with 5 offices principally concerned with the placement of clerical and middle management personnel. A unique job exchange system provides for maximum utilization of the resources of the network. New franchisees would benefit most from being located within reasonable proximity to existing offices in Connecticut.

Number of Franchisees: 6 in Connecticut

In Business Since: 1968

Equity Capital Needed: Franchise cost is $10,000. The only additional money needed is for working capital and varies depanding on location, size of office, personal needs of franchisee, etc.

Financial Assistance Available: Up to $2,500 of the franchise fee may be financed by the franchisor. Franchisee must be willing to incur all of the start-up costs plus 6 months working capital.

Training Provided: Formal training of franchisee prior to start-up date is usually 2 weeks in length, depending on previous experience of franchisee. Training is usually in the form of one on one discussions on all subjects relevant to the management of a private employment agency, and follows closely the training guidelines, provided by the National Association of Personnel Consultants, Post start-up training is continuous through formal meetings, lectures, on sight review of operations, etc.

Managerial Assistance Available: A complete range of managerial assistance is available from site selections, advertising and public relations, legal, accounting, and of course relevant placement techniques. After start-up most assistance is provided on "as needed" basis.

Information Submitted: July 1987

WESTERN TEMPORARY SERVICES, INC.
301 Lennon Lane
P. O. Box 9280
Walnut Creek, California 94598
A. Terry Slocum, Vice President, Corporate
Development

Description of Operation: Western operates nearly 300 offices in the USA and overseas, both company-owned and franchised. We provide a full line of temporary personnel services, including clerical office support, industrial, marketing, technical, medical/dental, pharmacy and Santa/Photo.

Number of Franchisees: 65 in 26 States

In Business Since: 1948

Equity Capital Needed: Initial franchise fee based on population, ranging from $2,500 to $10,000 for most cities; plus sufficient working capital to cover initial operating and living expenses.

Financial Assistance Available: Western finances the temporary payroll and accounts receivable completely. Western also provides a special start-up incentive for the franchised operation for the first six months, and offers additional incentives for volume thereafter.

Training Provided: Western provides initial training in 3 phases: 1) 1 week of operational and sales classroom training at corporate headquarters; 2) 2-3 days supervised hands-on experience in an operating field office; and 3) 2 days on-site training and orientation after the new franchise office has opened.
Ongoing training through annual workshops is also made available.

Managerial Assistance Available: Western supplies complete operating manuals to all franchisees, and provides an experienced manager for on-site sales and operational assistance during training. In addition, franchisees receive ongoing management and technical assistance, which includes field meetings, publications, training tapes, sales bulletins, sales leads and referrals, public relations and direct mail assistance, promotional events, accounting support, credit and collection assistance, and national advertising. Western's corporate staff is always available for advice and consultation.

Information Submitted: May 1987

EQUIPMENT/RENTALS

A TO Z RENTAL CENTERS
3550 Cedar Avenue South
Minneapolis, Minnesota 55407
Orv Klemp, President

Description of Operation: A to Z Rental Centers operate a general purpose rental store. The primary market for a A to Z Rental Store is the homeowner, light contractor and the truck and trailer market including all moving aids for the self-mover.

Number of Franchisees: 63 in 22 States including company-owned.

In Business Since: 1972

Equity Capital Needed: Up to 100 percent inventory financing available upon approval of required financial statement plus working capital.

Financial Assistance Available: A to Z has financing available at this time and will assist franchisee is preparing the required papers.

Training Provided: A 10 day training program at company store. A 5 day on-the-job training program at franchisees store. There is no charge for training program.

Managerial Assistance Available: Accounting and bookkeeping, advertising techniques, business consulting, financial planning, insurance, inventory selection, maintenance program, market testing of new rental items, rate guides, store displays and vendor selection. These services are provided as long as the franchisee remains with the A to Z system.

Information Submitted: July 1987

* ADVENTURENT/CLUB NAUTICO
5450 N.W. 33rd Avenue, 106
Fort Lauderdale, Florida 33309
Nino Martini, President

Description of Operation: Powerboat rental operation and boating club. Franchisee maintains fleet of powerboats and markets club membership. Members receive preferential rates at all Club Nautico rental centers.

Number of Franchisees: 28 in Florida, Texas, Georgia and California.

In Business Since: 1986

Equity Capital Needed: Franchise Fee—$25,000, Capital Requirements—$75,000.

Financial Assistance Available: Equipment leasing

Training Provided: Pre-opening training and continuing training in the field.

Managerial Assistance Available: 5 days of management and/or technical assistance during first year. 1 day for management and/or technical assistance each subsequent year. For additional time, if required, Franchisees are provided management and technical assistance on an out-of-pocket cost remibursed basis.

Information Submitted: May 1987

APPARELMASTER, INC.
10385 Spartan Drive
Cincinnati, Ohio 45215
James R. Wahl, President

Description of Operation: Offers unique business service recommended as a diversification possibility for drycleaning, laundry and/or linen supply establishments. Includes detailed instruction and on-site training of how to utilize existing equpment and personnel to sell, service and process industrial uniform, dust control, and career apparel rental. Other services and benefits include optional data processing invoicing, accounting and inventory control, seminars, workshops, training schools, garment and emblem supply.

Number of Franchisees: 270 in 44 States, Canada, United Kingdom, New Zealand, and Australia

In Business Since: 1971

Equity Capital Needed: License of $17,000

Financial Assistance Available: None

Training Provided: Ongoing

Managerial Assistance Available: Operation and other manuals provided. Managerial and technical assistance provided on every aspect of the industry for life of franchise.

Information Submitted: July 1987

*ASSOCIATED VIDEO HUT, INC.
11 North Pearl Street
4th Floor
Albany, New York 12201

Description of Operations: Drive up video rental stores. Top 30 titles of new releases. Convenience and new movies found in parking lots of stores.

Number of Franchisees: 2 in operation at present in New York, 150 waiting final stages.

In Business Since: 1986

Equity Capital Needed: $80,000 investment, which includes franchise fees, building, computer, 300 tapes, and training process.

Financial Assistance Available: Yes, to qualified applicants.

Training Provided: In depth training program for 5 days at corporation headquarters located in Albany, New York with continuous training and support.

Managerial Assistance Available: Site selection and pre-opening assistance is provided by corporation headquarters. Throughout the term of the franchise, ongoing assistance is provided in accounting, marketing and operations.

Information Submitted: July 1987

GRAND RENTAL STATION
P.O. Box 1510
Butler, Pennsylvania 16003-1510
Bill Bourque, Manager—Rental Program

Description of Operation: Licensed, nationally registered rental program offered by American Hardware Supply Company to its owner/members (over 3800), and to related business entrepreneurs. By taking advantage of its co-op buying leverage, the company can offer members products and services at advantageous pricing. As a buying co-op any product realized, after deducting operating costs, is shared with its owner members.

Number of Franchisees: 55 in 19 states.

In Business Since: 1910

Equity Capital Needed: $500 License fee, $100,000 inventory plus cost of site.

Financing Assistance Available: 3-5-7 year fixed term financing for highly rated accounts.

Training Provided: 7-14 day in-store "hands-on" training provided within reasonable distance of business location. Exposure and participation in all operational aspects of a general rental business are included. Training on specific product lines also available from company or supplier/vendor.

Managerial Assistance Available: Complete managerial assistance is provided both on and off premise during start-up and initial opening priod. Ongoing consulting and management assistance in available via phone from various departments at company headquarters, or on-site when requested.

Information Submitted: June 1987

HOME CALL MOBILE VIDEO LIBRARIES
8233-10 Gator Lane
West Palm Beach, Florida 33411
Mike King, President

Description of Operation: Mobile video rental and refreshment store also carries video cassette recorders for rental purposes. This is a custom built van solely built for the above purposes. Each van has exclusive territorial rights. 10-15,000 population.

Number of Franchisees: 2 in Florida

In Business Since: 1983

Equity Capital Needed: $43,900

Financial Assistance Available: None

Training Provided: 2 days, 1 in main office and 1 day on mobile van.

Managerial Assistance Available: MVL provides complete works manual, accounting procedures, movie exchange program, proved organized system, and continual market research and hot line.

Information Submitted: August 1987

MAJOR VIDEO, INC.
2700 East Sunset Boulevard
Suite 38
Las Vegas, Nevada 89120
W. H. Jebb, Assistant Franchise Director

Description of Operation: Major Video retail store primarily in the business of renting prerecorded cassette movies; secondarily, the franchisee will sell prerecorded cassette movies, and sell and/or rent recorders, related consumer electronics equipment and certain accessories.

Number of Franchisees: 32 in 9 States plus 9 company-owned.

In Business Since: 1981

Equity Capital Needed: $188,000 or more depending on location.

Financial Assistance Available: None

Training Provided: Intensive 1 week training period or more required for each new franchisee at agreed upon location.

Managerial Assistance Available: Provide manuals and materials to assist franchisees in most aspects of the business operation. Assist in selection of appropriate location. Administer with committee of franchisee members a national advertising fund. May assist in various aspects of store operations, provide seminars and other matters pertinent to franchisees' needs.

Information Submitted: June 1987

*MR. MOVIES, INC.
10373 West 70th Street
Suite 130
Eden Prairie, Minnesota 55344
William H. Kaiser, President
Todd D. King, Director of Franchising

Description of Operation: Mr. Movies is one of the nation's fastest growing chains of video cassette rental stores. The stores boast an attractive decor and service representatives help insure expertly merchandised stock. Market research department selects location and provides in-depth market analysis on an individualized basis. Point of sale computer system gives store owner vital stock information.

Number of Franchisees: 45 in Minnesota, Wisconsin, Texas, and Massachusetts.

In Business Since: 1985

Equity Capital Needed: $70,000

Financial Assistance Available: No financing is available in-house at this time. Mr. Movies will assist in preparing loan applications.

Training Provided: 5 day mandatory training program includes 2 days of in-store training and includes complete operations manual. Mr. Movies personnel assist in merchandising and finalize training prior to opening at franchisee's location. Various seminars are conducted on an as-needed basis.

Managerial Assistance Available: Franchisee receives "recommended buy" list each month. Service representatives and/or regional managers visit stores at least once per month. Operational consultants, computer trouble-shooters, and title selection advisors are available via toll free number. Franchisees computer data is analyzed by franchisor monthly. Advertising and promotional material, store supplies, and some pre-recorded cassettes can be obtained from Mr. Movies warehouse.

Information Submitted: May 1987

NATION-WIDE GENERAL RENTAL CENTERS, INC.
1684 Highway 92 West
Suite A
Woodstock, Georgia 30188
I. N. Goodvin, President

Description of Operation: A Nation-Wide General Rental Center operates a full line consumer-oriented rental center including items for the contractor, do-it-yourself home owner—items as baby equipment; camping supplies, contractor's equipment and tools; concrete tools; carpenter tools; invalid needs; lawn and yard tools; mechanics tools; painters equipment; moving needs; party and banquet needs; plumbers tools; sanding machines, trailer hitches; household equipment and local trucks and trailers. Building required is 1,800 to 3,000 square feet with outside fenced storage area, good traffic flow and parking for 6 to 10 cars.

Number of Franchisees: 178 in 36 States

In Business Since: 1976

Equity Capital Needed: $25,000 plus $7,500—$10,000 working capital. No franchise fees.

Financial Assistance Available: With the down payment of $25,000, franchisee will get $98,500 worth of equipment and opening supplies. The balance can be financed over 5 years with local banks—company assistance to qualified applicants. No franchise or royalty fees, down payment goes toward equipment cost. All risk liability, conversion, group health, accident and life insurance coverage available to franchisee. We also have a buy back agreement and exclusive area agreement.

Training Provided: On-the-job training for 5 full days at no charge to the franchisee. Training covers everything you need from familiarization and maintenance of equipment; accounting computerized system; advertising and promotion, purchasing add on equipment; rental rates; insurance; inventory control and operation manual covering much more.

Managerial Assistance Available: Consultation on location and market feasibility studies; assistance in securing and negotiation building lease; a monthly computerized financial report giving balance sheet—income statement and a list of all equipment in inventory with a month rental income per item. A rate guide book giving rental rates for each item and for your area. One hundred percent financing for growth inventory or new equipment. Franchisee can buy all their equipment at 3 to 10 percent over cost which offers great purchasing power and discounts to each store owner. Buy back agreement gives you full credit on equipment. At the grand opening we will be there to help establish the franchisee in the community. We also mail 9,000 promotions to every home around a new center at grand opening time.

Information Submitted: July 1987

PCR PERSONAL COMPUTER RENTALS
300 Sevilla Avenue
Suite 205
Coral Gables, Florida 33134
Robert R. Edmonson, Vice President Franchise Development

Description of Operation: Business oriented rental center operated from office space. Each outlet provides short-term micro-computers and peripherals to all segments of the business community. Owners stress value added customer service and cater to the needs of the client including free delivery, installation and maintenance, extensive training and personal support.

Number of Franchisees: 34 in 8 States plus 1 company-owned unit.

In Business Since: 1983

Equity Capital Needed: $40,000 to $50,000.

Financial Assistance Available: None

Training Provided: Minimum 2 week comprehensive training for owner-operator and assistant manager. additional week available (optional) to strengthen hardware, software knowledge.

Managerial Assistance Available: After initial training, ongoing support and training are provided for the term of the franchise agreement. Complete manuals, forms and instructions are furnished. In addition, franchisees will be informed of new products with evaluations, price changes, and improved software and hardware to market. A continuous research and development program will

thoroughly test and evaluate products before they are recommended. Ongoing advertising will serve to create awareness of franchise and develop preference level.

Information Submitted: July 1987

*REMCO FRANCHISE DEVELOPMENT CORP.
P. O. Box 720259
Houston, Texas 77272
Sam Love, Vice President, Franchising

Description of Operation: Rental, sales, and service of name brand television, stereo, video, and major appliances with rental ownership options. Over 70 company stores in 17 States.

Number of Franchisees: 109 in 29 States

In Business Since: 1969

Equity Capital Needed: $75,000-$250,000 (includes franchise fee).

Financial Assistance Available: Financing arranged through major lending institution for inventory requirements.

Training Provided: Comprehensive 3 week training program in Houston for store managers which includes classroom teaching. On-the-job training in a Remco store for a minimum of 6 weeks. Major training areas are sales management, credit management, administrative management, and store management. Special three day training seminar for investors. Continued weekly traning in the form of printed material and video tapes.

Managerial Assistance Available: Company representatives provide regular on-site assistance in all phases of operations. A complete and highly detailed set of operational policies and procedures are provided to each franchise. All marketing and advertising programs are administered by the corporate office.

Information Submitted: July 1987

RENAPPLI OF AMERICA, INC.
3900 N. Peoria Road
Springfield, Illinois 62702
Lou R. Messervy, President

Description of Operations: Rent-To-Own-Appliances T.V.'s, stero, V.C.R.'s, furniture, computers, satallites. Store consists of 2-3000 square feet, must have off store parking potential, unlimited-anytown 4,000 population or more.

Number of Franchisees: 6 in Illinois and Iowa

In Business Since: 1972

Equity Capital Needed: $60,000

Financial Assistance Available: Contact with National Finance Company. Normally 80 percent of inventory.

Training Provided: Originally 1 week—(home office)—1 week in field continues throughout agreement.

Managerial Assistance Available: Training and procedure manual, audio, video training film's, computer home, software, updated as needed. Profit and loss statements, balance sheets are provided monthly, comparisons with all stores, showing products rented, time rented average income per unit, etc.

Information Submitted: May 1987

RENTAL CENTERS U.S.A., INC.
2224 Dryden Road
Dayton, Ohio 45439
George Gruber, President

Description of Operation: General Equipment Rental Centers. Offers a full line of equipment including automotive, hand and power tools, light contractors equipment, home care, painting, plumbing, lawn and garden equipment. Program is flexible to meet the needs of the individual and the community. Building sizes vary depending on initial program and projected growth.

Number of Franchisees: 29 in 16 states

In Business Since: 1984

Equity Capital Needed: $15,000 to $20,000—no franchise fees, royalty or continuing costs.

Financial Assistance Available: Guidance in securing financial assistance through local lending institutions.

Training Provided: Complete on-the-job training covering all aspects of operations including maintenance, customer relations, accounting, rental rates, business and health insurance and advertising. Follow-up training on location with continual support.

Managerial Assistance Available: Continual follow-up assistance available in all aspects of management, operations and quantity purchasing power which includes special dating and lease programs offered by various manufacturers. Corporate Rental Center constantly evaluating products and procedures to remain current with todays rental market.

Information Submitted: May 1987

SOUNDS EASY INTERNATIONAL, INC.
1030 Atherton Drive
Suite 205
Salt Lake City, Utah 84123

Description of Operation: Retail, rental stores featuring video, stereo, television, home electronics. A complete electronic home entertainment store and concept. Emphasis on video machine and movie rentals. Sounds Easy International, Inc., coordinates and manages local and regional advertising.

Number of Franchisees: 70 in 18 States

In Business Since: 1980

Equity Capital Needed: $70,000 to $100,000 (including franchise fee and start-up capital).

Financial Assistance Available: Assist in loan proposal preparation.

Training Provided: Pre-opening training at national training center—1 week, grand-opening—2 days. Post-opening assistance—yes.

Managerial Assistance Available: Seminars, updated operations manuals, assist in store selection, and leasing. Continued training on customer relations, advertising, buying, accounting, technical training on home electronics, and generally assist owner in operation and management of owners Sounds Easy business.

Information Submitted: July 1987

TAYLOR RENTAL CORPORATION
(Subsidiary of THE STANLEY WORKS)
P. O. Box 8000
New Britain, Connecticut 06050

Description of Operation: A franchised Taylor Rental Center operates a full service general rental business carrying a complete selection of rental items for do-it-yourselfers, homeowner, light contractor, business and party markets

Number of Franchisees: 280 in 43 States

In Business Since: 1963

Equity Capital Needed: Average initial investment $250 million of which $90 million must be in liquid assets

Financial Assistance Available: Guidance in securing financing is provided qualified prospects.

Training Provided: Taylor provides regional and main office dealer service representatives to assist both new and established dealers in all phases of operations. Qualified business management directors are available or at the main office to assist dealers in all phases of management and operations. A computerized monthly status report to franchisees provides current income and inventory data on every piece of rental equipment on a percentage return against original cost basis. Taylor provides all franchisees with a descriptive product book including a suggested rental rate guide which is updated continuously to reflect current equipment and rate changes. Budgets, cash flow and projection assistance are provided to increase current and long-range profitability. Complete operational, health and life and disability insurance are provided in the program as well as support in training, marketing, advertising/promotion and an on-going merchandise support/purchase program. Comprehensive in-store computer system designed to handle virtually all management reports, starting with the customer transaction, is available from Taylor.

Managerial Assistance Available: See above

Information Submitted: May 1987

UNITED RENT-ALL, INC.
6269 Variel Avenue
Suite A
Woodland Hills, California 91367

Description of Operation: General Equipment Rental Stores. The full line of equipment offered includes automotive, hand and power tools, contractors equipment, floor care, party, household and guest, medical, exercise, painting and plumbing. lawn and garden, sporting and camping, moving and towing. The "Total Rental Department Store" concept of rental equipment service categories. Stores have an attractive image and are located in growing metropolitan communities throughout the country. Franchisor surveys market, selects site and prepares store for opening.

Number of Franchisees: Approximately 40 in 20 States

In Business Since: 1948

Equity Capital Needed: Approximately $35,000 to $65,000 plus working capital.

Financial Assistance Available: A portion of the franchise fee can normally be financed. Store location may be sub-leased from franchisor for the term of the franchise.

Training Provided: A comprehensive training program, both classroom style and practical on-the-job implementation at the store location is provided. Included is discussion of rental concepts, equipment familiarization and maintenance, counter systems, cash and accounting methods, inventory control and management, advertising, promotion, customer relations, store security, employment management, telephone techniques, insurance, purchasing, cooperative and commission renting. Subsequent training is also given by regional directors on an ongoing basis.

Managerial Assistance Available: Company provides regularly scheduled in-store business development consultation. Developing topics include budgets and forecasts, inventory management, equipment and merchandise sales, prospective customer business calls, marketing, employee training procedures, and overall business building techniques. Home office support services include equipment purchasing, advertising and operations.

Information Submitted: July 1987

YARD CARDS INC.
1700 Scheel Street
Belleville, Illinois 62221
Michael Hoepfinger, Presdient

Description of Operation: YARD CARDS specializes in the rental of 8' high wooden greeting cards to be placed in yards as well as indoors to recognize special occasions. This can be an excellent opportunity for an add-on business for a florist, balloon business, cake decorating business, or party supply business, as well as an independent business operated from your home.

Number of Franchisees: 3 plus, company-owned in Illinois.

In Business Since: 1983, franchising since 1986

Equity Capital Needed: $5,000-$15,000

Financial Assistance Available: None

Training Provided: Training is provided at the office of franchisor and will not be longer than 3 days. Attendance is optional, and at the expanse of franchisee. A complete, detailed Operations Manual is provided.

Managerial Assistance Available: Ongoing assistance is provided by Yard Cards personnel, this includes all phasis of operation, and is provided readily at the request of franchisee. Complete, detailed Operations Manual is provided, and includes updates as they occur.

Information Submitted: May 1987

ZM VIDEO RENTAL, INC.
3501 Chateau Boulevard
Suite E-3
Kenner, Louisiana 70065
Randall G. Goddick, Executive Vice President

Description of Operation: Fast growing and aggressive Video Rental Stores of movies and equipment. We offer professional ongoing support and group purchasing benefits.

Number of Franchisees: 22 in Louisiana and Mississippi

In Business Since: 1984

Equity Capital Needed: $70,000-$110,000

Financial Assistance Available: Financing is available but must have 1/2 equity.

Training Provided: The initial training is at our training center, for 1 week. Classroom and in-store.

Managerial Assistance Available: Field training at locations during opening and on going consulting.

Information Submitted: July 1987

FOOD-DONUTS

BOSA INTERNATIONAL, INC.
3219 North First Avenue
Tucson, Arizona 85719
Director of Franchise Sales

Description of Operation: BoSa Donuts is a total franchised business concept, with a premium line of donuts, fancy pastries and baked goods. Over 87 varieties of donuts, fritters, fruit pies, muffins, cookies ahd homemade breads are baked fresh on the premises twice each day. Stores are 1,550 to 1,800 square feet—free standing or end locations in line shopping centers. Stores feature counter service, limited seating, carry-out and drive-thru service.

Number of Franchisees: 28 plus 103 company-owned in Arizona, New Mexico, Texas, Illinois, Ohio and Minnesota.

In Business Since: 1975

Equity Capital Needed: $45,000 to $55,000 cash. Balance of funds required $66,700.

Financial Assistance Available: Franchisor offers no direct financial assistance, although sources of lease or loan funds have been developed, and have proven willing to accept qualified borrowers.

Training Provided: 3 weeks intensive training at Tucson facility, teach the franchise owner every phase of business operations, including records, hiring and training personnel, inventory control, managing wholesale accounts, and of course, baking the BoSa product line.

Managerial Assistance Available: Following training period, an operations department staff person will assist and oversee in-store operations during the first critical week to ensure proper procedures and production guidelines are followed to maximize the franchise owner's opportunity to succeed. Operations are monitored by regional and division managers, on ongoing basis, and are as near as the telephone, should their advice or assistance be necessary.

Information Submitted: May 1987

DAWN DONUT SYSTEMS, INC.
G-4300 West Pierson Road
Flint, Michigan 48504
Bill Morin, Director of Franchising

Description of Operation: Franchisor owns, operates and licenses others to own and operate shops under the name "Dawn Donut." All Dawn Donut Shops are required to be built to franchisor's specifications and standards. The majority of existing shops are free-standing, cement block buildings, substantially uniform in design and appearance, with adjoining parking space for 12 to 25 cars. Some franchisees also sell gasoline of major oil companies, which is available to new franchisees only. Some new units will sell convenience items, sandwiches and soup. The typical free-standing Dawn Donut Shop has a production area and a separate eating area, which services generally from 16 to 40 persons. Generally free-standing shops require a minimum of 22,000 square foot lot and a 2,000 square foot building.

Number of Franchisees: 25 with 38 units in Michigan

In Business Since: 1956

Equity Capital Needed: $50,000

Financial Assistance Available: Franchisor will assist franchisee in arranging financing, and in some cases franchisor will finance qualified franchisees.

Training Provided: Franchisor requires that franchise owners and other operating personnel attend a 3 week training course at a designated Dawn Donut Shop. The training course provides instruction in the production, merchandising and/or servicing of food and beverage served in Dawn Shops and also in the financial, administrative and organizational procedures, which the franchisor considers to be essential in operating a Dawn Donut Shop successfully. Franchise owners must satisfactorily complete this training program before being permitted to open their shop.

Managerial Assistance Available: Initial site selection assistance provided; final decision requires our approval. Dawn Donuts maintains a continuing advisory relationship with the franchisor owners, including consultation in the areas of marketing, merchandising and general business operations.

Information Submitted: May 1987

DIXIE CREAM FLOUR COMPANY
P. O. Box 180
St. Louis, Missouri 63166
Attention: Franchise Director

Description of Operation: Franchised privately-owned donut and coffee shops, with both walk-in and drive-thru stores. Retail and wholesale selling of over 50 varieties of freshmade yeast raised and cake donuts, as well as coffee and other beverages.

Number of Franchisees: 68 in 15 States

In Business Since: 1929

Equity Capital Needed: One-time only, franchise fee of $15,000. There are no overrides, royalties, or percentages of any kind. Your franchise agreement also entitles you to a guaranteed territory, the limits of which are negotiable with your Dixie cream representative. The profits are all yours. We will assist you in site selection, as well as supply you with a detailed floor plan of your particular store. New equipment costs for a hand cut donut production shop will be about $25,000.

Financial Assistance Available: Financing may be available through your local lending institutions or leasing companies.

Training Provided: As part of the franchise fee, we have an extensive hands-on in-shop training program of approximately 2 weeks duration. Our company technicians works with you in your shop during this period. A comprehensive training manual is provided for production assistance. Additionally, information concerning new products as well as pertinent new ideas in helping your donut shop operate as efficiently as possible, is available from our St. Louis office.

Managerial Assistance Available: Continuous communication by correspondence, direct toll free phone and in-store visits by qualified home office personnel. There is also a procedures manual provided for everyday use in your donut shop. This manual, along with our technical assistance will help each franchise attain their ultimate goal of profit and success.

Information Submitted: May 1987

THE DONUT HOLE
P. O. Box 1247
Dickinson, North Dakota 58602
Guy Moos, Director of Franchising

Description of Operation: Franchised and company owned shops with sit-down and take-out service with over 50 varieties of donuts, decorated cakes and tortes, home of the Birthday Donut, and pastry items. Majority of products are delivered to The Donut Hole shops on a regular basis from a central commissary in a frozen dough stage. Products are then baked or fried daily in each shop to guarantee freshness. All shops are required to be build to correct specifications and standards.

Number of Franchisees: 19 stores located in North Dakota, South Dakota and Montana

In Business Since: 28-years. Have been franchising for 8-years.

Equity Capital Needed: $25,000 to $35,000

Financial Assistance Available: None

Training Provided: Franchisor requires that franchise owner/manager attend a 3 week training program at a designated The Donut Hole shop. Areas covered will be production, merchandising, administrative and organizational procedures. Franchisee must satisfactorily complete this training before being permitted to open their shop.

Managerial Assistance Available: Franchisor assists in site selection and pre-opening. Franchisee receives comprehensive operational and procedures manuals; with constant updates on new products and procedures and marketing and advertising concepts. A quarterly newsletter on The Donut Hole happenings. Yearly seminar with an awards banquet. Each store has a support manager who services them on a regular basis. Home office has a marketing department, full bookkeeping services and in store sales training programs available.

Information Submitted: May 1987

★ DONUT INN INC.
6355 Topanga Canyon Boulevard
Suite 403
Woodland Hills, California 91367

Description of Operation: Franchised donut and coffee shops—dirve-in and walk-in units. Retail selling of more than 80 varieties of donuts, pastries, cookies and muffins and cheesecake. Drinks are primarily coffee, milk and other nonalcoholic beverages. Each Inn manufactures its own donuts, pastries, cookies and muffins. We offer individual franchises or territory (areas) franchises. We encourage growth through qualified individuals and groups with our sub-franchisor program.

Number of Franchisees: 22 plus 6 company-owned in California

In Business Since: 1975

Equity Capital Needed: Franchise fee: $20,000. Equipment package approximately $45,000 to $65,000.

Financial Assistance Available: We finance up to 75 percent of the equipment package to qualified franchisees.

Training Provided: 3-4 weeks of concentrated training in all phases of the business in our training facility. Continuous updating and retraining as needed, on the newest and most innovative concepts and equipment. 1 week training in your store upon opening.

Managerial Assistance Available: We provide a comprehensive recipe and procedure manual which guides the franchisee in the every day operation relating to product and quality control, service, sales, bookkeeping, inventory, ordering, marketing, etc. Whenever the franchisee has a question or needs advice on anything relating to their Donut Inn shop, there is 24 hours a day, 7 days a week, and a hot line.

Information Submitted: May 1987

DONUTLAND, INC.
23 Twist Road, N.E.
Cadar Rapids, Iowa 52402

Description of Operation: Franchised and company-owned specialty food shops with sit-down, take-out and drive-thru service. Over 65 varieties of donuts and donut-related products are sold retail and wholesale. Each shop serves product that is prepared fresh daily. Deli-sandwiches, soup and salad are also served.

Number of Franchisees: 39 plus 2 company-owned in Illinois, Iowa, North Dakota, Wisconsin and Nebraska.

In Business Since: 1964

Equity Capital Needed: Franchise fee $25,000. Total package, excluding real estate $140,000 approximately.

Financial Assistance Available: Assistance in securing financing is provided.

Training Provided: 6 week training program is provided in Cedar Rapids, Iowa corporate headquarters. The source includes training in production, operations, labor relations, accounting and financial management.

Managerial Assistance Available: Site selection and pre-opening assistance is provided. Throughout the term of the franchise, ongoing assistance is provided in accounting, marketing and operations.

Information Submitted: May 1987

DONUT MAKER
99 Cambridge Street
Charlestown, Massachusetts 02129
James DeVellis, Treasurer

Description of Operation: Retail coffee, donut, muffin stores

Number of Franchisees: 9 in Massachusetts and New Hampshire

In Business Since: 1978

Equity Capital Needed: $60,000-$75,000

Financial Assistance Available: None

Training Provided: Intensive 5-6 weeks of training, in all aspects of operating a donut shop. They include manufacturing of products, financial equipment maintenance, personnel and customer service.

Managerial Assistance Available: Franchisor will assist franchise for 2 weeks on a full time basis at opening of new store and any additional expertise necessary to amke operator operationally sound. Complete manual of operation is provided.

Information Submitted: May 1987

DONUTS GALORE, INC.
115 East Glenside Avenue
Glenside, Pennsylvania 19038
James Samter, President

Description of Operation: Franchised and company-owned coffee and donut shops with drive-in, walk-in units and shopping mall units. Retail selling of more than 50 varieties of donuts, cookies, muffins, brownies, macaroons, cupcakes, cookies and other bakery products, soup, hotdogs, coffee and other beverages. Donut products are centrally made, frozen and shipped to shops on regular basis. No bakers required on premises.

Number of Franchisees: 6 (2 company) in Pennsylvania, New Jersey and Delaware

In Business Since: 1955

Equity Capital Needed: Franchise fee $15,000; working capital approximately $16,000; equipment package approximately $50,000 plus.

Financial Assistance Available: We will assist franchisee in securing financing.

Training Provided: 2 week training program consisting of practical instruction in our stores.

Managerial Assistance Available: Continuous operational assistance is available. The company helps in quality control, new products programs, and marketing programs for all shops.

Information Submitted: May 1987

DONUTS N' COFFEE
2222 State Street
Columbus, Indiana 47201
Larry Stith

Description of Operation: Exclusive donuts and donut related pastries. We offer inside dinning, carryout and drive-thru window service.

Number of Franchisees: 8 in Indiana and Florida.

In Business Since: 1984

Equity Capital Needed: $50,000 to $80,000

Financial Assistance Available: None

Training Provided: Approximately 1 month with ongoing training thereafter. Two weeks company store and 2 weeks in the new franchisee's store.

Managerial Assistance Available: Managerial assistance available at all times.

Information Submitted: May 1987

*DUNKIN' DONUTS OF AMERICA, INC.
P. O. Box 317
Randolph, Massachusetts 02368
Robert M. Rosenberg, Chairman and Chief Executive Officer
Thomas R. Schwarz, President and Chief Operating Officer

Description of Operation: Franchised and company-owned coffee and donut shops with drive-thru and walk-in units. Sales of over 52 varieties of donuts, munchkin donuthole treats, muffins, cookies, brownies, and related bakery items, at retail, along with soup, coffee and other beverages. Franchises are sold for individual shops and, in selected markets, multiple license agreements may be available. Franchisor encourages development of real estate and building by the franchisee, subject to approval of Dunkin Donuts of America, Inc. Franchisor also develops locations for franchising and for company supervisions.

Number of Franchisees: 1,539 (44 company) in 39 States, Canada, Japan, The Philippines, Thailand, Bahamas, Korea, Singapore, Colombia, Venezuela, Chile, Brazil Indonesia, Saudi Arabia and Taiwan.

In Business Since: 1950

Equity Capital Needed: Franchise fee, $27,000 to $40,000, depending on geographical area and whether franchisee owns or controls the real estate. Working capital, approximately $18,000.

Financial Assistance Available: Financing assistance for real estate acquisition and development. Equipment and sign financing assistance is available to qualified franchisees.

Training Provided: 6 weeks training course for franchisees at Dunkin' Donuts University in Braintree, Massachusetts consisting of production and shop management training. Initial training of donutmakers and managers for franchises and retraining is carried out at Dunkin' Donuts University without additional charge.

Managerial Assistance Available: Continuous managerial assistance is avaiable from the district sales manager assigned to the individual shop. The Company maintains quality assurance, research and development and new products programs. The franchisee-funded marketing department provides marketing programs for all shops. The marketing programs are administered by a field marketing manager who develops plans on a market basis.

FOSTER'S DONUTS, INC.
Suite 3J
4685 East Industrial Street
Simi Valley, California 93063
Linda Horn, Franchise Broker

Description of Operation: The Foster's Donuts shop franchise is a retail donut shop usually located in a neighborhood shopping center and sublet to the franchisee by Foster's. The shop sells a complete assortment of Foster's Donuts freshly baked on the premises every day and a complementary variety of hot and cold beverages. Each franchise offers take-out service and some counter seating and is fully equipped to bake and sell donuts. Area franchises available for development in selected areas.

Number of Franchisees: 55 units in California

In Business Since: 1971

Equity Capital Needed: $35,000

Financial Assistance Available: Franchise fee of $35,000 must be in cash. Foster's will finance the equipment package.

Training Provided: The Foster's Donuts training program includes no less than 10 days of pre-opening training covering all phases of Foster's Donuts shop operation, including donut baking, equipment operation, product merchandising, and business management. This is followed up by 10 days of in-shop training and supervision at the franchisee's shop when it opens, during which the franchisee will operate the shop under the guidance of a Foster's field representative.

Managerial Assistance Available: Foster's provides ongoing managerial and technical assistance by having a field representative available for telephone consultation every weekday between 9 am and 5 pm; field representatives also visit the franchise location regularly to check on shop operations and are available for trouble-shooting and problem solving. All shop bookkeeping and tax return preparation is done by Foster's. Foster's also provides the franchisee a confidential operating manual containing technical and managerial advice, forms, guides, directions, and operating tips and techniques and conducts periodic refresher courses, seminars, and other educational programs and continuous market and product research.

Information Submitted: July 1987

HONEY FLUFF DONUTS, INC.
4494 Millbranch Road
Memphis, Tennessee 38116
Lawrence E. Clark, President

Description of Operation: Franchisor of retail and/or wholesale donut shops.

Number of Franchisees: 10 in Tennessee, Mississippi and Arkansas

In Business Since: 1967

Equity Capital Needed: $40,000

Financial Assistance Available: Will finance 40 percent of equipment package.

Training Provided: 30 days on-site training

Managerial Assistance Available: Any and all phases needed to operate a profitable donut shop business.

Information Submitted: July 1987

*JOLLY PIRATE DONUT SHOPS
3923 East Broad Street
Columbus, Ohio 43213
Nick Soulas, President

Description of Operation: Retail sales of donuts, cookies, brownies, baked goods, and coffee and soft drinks.

Number of Franchisees: 24 in Ohio, West Virginia and Kentucky. 19 franchised, 5 company-owned.

In Business Since: 1961, franchising since 1970.

Equity Capital Needed: $25,000 minimum, depending on ability to finance.

Financial Assistance Available: None. Franchise fee $15,000 as of July 1, 1986.

Training Provided: 6 weeks to 3 months on-the-job, learning product preparation and shop management, in an operating shop.

Managerial Assistance Available: 2 weeks in store training for manager, bakers and crew at opening. Periodic visits by company personnel to consult and advise, and as requested by phone.

Information Submitted: April 1987

*MISTER DONUT OF AMERICA, INC.
Subsidiary of INTERNATIONAL MULTIFOODS CORPORATION
Multifoods Tower
Box 2942
Minneapolis, Minnesota 55402

Description of Operation: Franchised doughnut and coffee shops-drive-ins and walk-in units. Retail selling of more than 55 varieties of doughnuts baked goods and nonalcholic beverages, primarily coffee. Located on well traveled streets, near schools, churches, shopping centers, amusements and entertainment. Each shop produces its own doughnuts in its own kitchen.

Number of Franchisees: 616 in 33 states and Canada.

In Business Since: 1955

Equity Capital Needed: In the U.S.A. equipment package $70,000; franchise fee $15,000; working capital $20,000. Cost of real estate and building are responsibility of franchisee, but location is subject to Mister Donut's approval.

Financial Assistance Available: Equipment can be financed by company with 25 percent down payment. Financing over 60 months at current interest rates.

Training Provided: Continuous professional 4 weeks training program, consisting of practical as well as classroom training at company school in St. Paul, Minnesota.

Managerial Assistance Available: An area representative is permanently located at company expense in each area of the United States and Canada for managerial assistance to franchise operators. The company maintains a quality control service as well as a research and development department, marketing and advertising services, to assist franchise owners. Location analysis, lease negotiation and assistance with building design and construction is also provided by Mister Donut personnel.

Information Submitted: May 1987

SOUTHERN MAID DONUT FLOUR COMPANY
3615 Cavalier Drive
Garland, Texas 75042
Doris Franklin, Vice President

Description of Operation: Southern Maid offers a tailored to order operation for each prospect. We have available all technical, managerial, and business information. Southern Maid sells most major brands of donut equipment. We consider our flour blends of the finest quality for the price. Franchises are available nationwide.

Number of Franchisees: 65 in Texas, Kansas, Louisiana, Arkansas, and Florida.

In Business Since: 1937

Equity Capital Needed: A 40 percent down payment is required before equipment is ordered. Franchise fee is $5,000.

Financial Assistance Available: None

Training Provided: In shop technical training for period necessary (time varies with each operation).

Managerial Assistance Available: Continuous advisory information is available.

Information Submitted: May 1987

*SPUDNUTS
A Division of U.S. DESIGN SYSTEMS, INC.
2801 Townsgate Road
Suite 113
Westlake Village, California 91361

Description of Operation: Spudnuts offers franchisees a unique and established product for a retail donut shop. The store is approximately 1,600 square feet and includes drive-thru service whenever possible. The exterior image of the building has a brand new look that blends in any area.

Number of Franchisees: 27 in 18 States plus 4 company-owned stores.

In Business Since: 1937

Equity Capital Needed: $15,000 franchise fee

Financial Assistance Available: Franchisees to arrange their own financing. Franchisor will assist in arrangements.

Training Provided: 3 weeks of in-depth training is provided plus additional training in the new franchised shop at the time of opening and grand opening. This additional training is to give the franchisee confidence in working with the new equipment in his shop and to become familiar with the procedures learned while in training before the shop was completed. Training includes: making Spudnuts unique products; hiring of personnel; record keeping; promotional and advertising concepts; production controls, quality control; marketing ideas and concepts.

Managerial Assistance Available: Spudnuts assistance continues for the length of the franchise agreement. Spudnuts know-how manual will be revised on a continual basis. Field support will visit shops and assist franchisee with complete operation of shops and introduce new products developed from their research and development department.

Information Submitted: July 1987

* TASTEE DONUTS, INC.
2121 Ridgelake Drive
Suite 105
Metairie, Louisiana 70001
Burges E. McCranie, Jr., President

Description of Operation: Tastee Donuts, Inc., offers investment and career opportunities to both multiple unit and single unit licenses. Our concept is to provide a large variety of fresh, high quality donuts, baked goods, and small hamburgers with excellent coffee and other beverages to take-out, sit-down or drive-thru in both free-standing and shopping center locations.

Number of Franchisees: 45 in 3 States

In Business Since: 1965

Equity Capital Needed: $50,000 cash; includes $20,000 licensee fee. $65,000 financed. $125,000 total not including real estate.

Financial Assistance Available: Tastee Donuts, Inc., assist licensee condidates in arranging financing from major credit institutions on both an SBA and conventional loan basis. Real estate assistance is available for qualitative approval of site selection, but licensees are responsible for lease negotiations.

Training Provided: Intensive 6 week training course covering all aspects of production and shop management. The course is taught at the Tastee Donuts training school in New Orleans, Louisiana.

Managerial Assistance Available: Continuous managerial assistance is available from regional supervisors. Advertising and marketing assistance is provided through licensee supported programs.

Information Submitted: July 1987

THE WHOLE DONUT FRANCHISE SYSTEMS, INC.
894 New Britain Avenue
Hartford, Connecticut 06106-3921
Frank S. Gencarelli, President
Joseph J. Algiere, Executive Vice President

Description of Operation: Each store averages 1,700-1,800 square feet with drive through and walk-in units. The Whole Donut sells donuts, pastries, muffins and cookies along with coffee and soft drinks. Some stores have a deli where sandwiches, soups and salads are served. Most stores are open 24 hours a day.

Number of Franchisees: 30 in Connecticut, Massachusetts, New Hampshire, Rhode Island and Vermont.

In Business Since: 1953, started franchising in 1984

Equity Capital Needed: $60,000 cash which includes the $25,000 franchise fee. $75,000 financed. $10,000 working capital. Excluding cost of real estate and buildings which must be approved by The Whole Donut.

Training Provided: 5 to 6 weeks training course in Hartford, Connecticut. Instructions in product preparation, marketing, customer service, hiring, employee training, inventory control, recordkeeping, and other supervisory skills. Instruction is continued at franchisee's location before and immediately after opening for business.

Managerial Assistance Available: Company representatives are at your side assisting you in setting-up and operating your store. The company provides marketing and advertising services to franchisees, along with continued product line evaluation and selection.

Information Submitted: May 1987

* WINCHELL'S DONUT HOUSE
16424 Valley View Avenue
La Mirada, California 90637
Patrick J. Meegan, Vice President, Franchise Development

Description of Operation: Winchell's is an established and highly recognized retail donut shop chain which offers a large variety of donuts, brownies, croissants, muffins, cookies and related bakery items, as well as, coffee and other beverages. Retail units are normally free standing or strip shopping center, walk-in and drive-thru locations.

Number of Franchisees: 745 company-owned and 18 franchised locations in 13 Western States. Also, 34 locations in Japan, Korea, Philippines and Guam.

In Business Since: 1948

Equity Capital Needed: $55,000 minimum with the ability to secure financing for the remaining portion of investment. (Initial franchise fee $25,000-$30,000.)

Financial Assistance Available: Franchisees to arrange own financing. Winchell's provides a list of approved lenders.

Training Provided: A comprehensive 6 week franchisee training course where you'll receive extensive instruction from the production of donuts to retail sales management, as well as, personal development and communication. Additional training and supervision by a qualified company representative for approximately 7 days during store opening.

Managerial Assistance Available: Franchisee will receive operations support through effective operating methods, systems and procedures which begin at the grand opening and continue with periodic store visits throughout the term of the franchise. Also, marketing support, developed by qualified professionals, through high impact advertising materials and promotions. Winchell's television and radio advertising, as well as, research and development of new products, and sales building promotions.

Information Submitted: June 1987

FOOD-GROCERY/SPECIALTY STORES

ALL MY MUFFINS LICENSING, INC.
2147 N. Hudson
Chicago, Illinois 60614
Paul Bernstein

Description of Operation: Gourmet muffin shops featuring over 200 different types of muffins. Also offering fourmet coffees and teas, fresh juices, smoothies and soups.

Number of Franchisees: 3 in Illinois, California and Michigan

In Business Since: 1986

Equity Capital Needed: $100,000-$177,000

Financial Assistance Available: None, however approximately $40,000 of the initial investment is in equipment, which can be leased through various sources.

Training Provided: 1 week of comprehensive training at a company-owned unit followed with additional 1 week of training at franchisee's location.

Managerial Assistance Available: Ongoing periodic on-site assistance, along with continuing updated information from the home office.

Information Submitted: May 1987

ALPEN PANTRY, INC.
1748 Independence Boulevard
Suite C-6
Sarasota, Florida 33580
John Hartnett

Description of Operation: Retail specialty food stores located primarily in major regional shopping malls featuring gourmet foods, domestic and imported cheeses, sausages, wines and "deli board" gourmet sandwiches.

Number of Franchisees: 10 in 11 States

In Business Since: 1975

Equity Capital Needed: Approximately $75,000 plus leasehold improvements

Financial Assistance Available: Assistance in obtaining local bank financing.

Training Provided: Prior to opening, 2 week course in: product knowledge, sales techniques, merchandising, promotional calender, inventory control and managing a successful business.

Managerial Assistance Available: Ongoing program of communication by bulletins, phone and store visits; annual convention, and sales seminars.

Information Submitted: May 1987

AMERICAN BULK FOOD
22451 Michigan Avenue
Dearborn, Michigan 48124
Martin Benson or Jeff English

Description of Operation: American Bulk Food is a bulk food grocery store which stocks over 1100 Gourmet, Exotic, Ethnic, Natural, Diet and Sugar-free products in bulk. Items are displayed in clear plastic bins which allow the consumer to see the colors and quality and smell the aromas of the food. The Consumer may buy as much or as little as needed which makes buying exciting, fun, practical and economical.

Number of Franchisees: 10 plus 3 company-owned in Michigan.

In Business Since: 1983

Equity Capital Needed: $120,000-$200,000

Financial Assistance Available: Financing available to qualified applicants

Training Provided: Training covers all aspects of bulk food market operations, which include: sanitation, inventory procedures, quality control, shelf lift control, pricing strategies, ordering and product selection, display and signage, market environment control, advertising and promotion, ongoing owner staff training in the above, and many other areas.

Managerial Assistance Available: Ongoing support program 52 weeks a year, news letter, field consultant, technical and operating trainers, regular visits by field consultants, ongoing research and development programs; seminars and meetings. Access to centralized buying from Corporate wareshous.

Information Submitted: May 1987

ATLANTIC CONCESSIONS SYSTEMS, INC.
P. O. Box 39359
Ft. Lauderdale, Florida 33339
Dr. Chase Adams, President
Sandy Rasmussen, Franchise Director

Description of Operation: Atlantic Concessions is a unique franchise opportunity. Franchise is granted on an exclusive territorial basis and franchisee has right to operate all concessions within his or her territory. Typical concessions include both food and non-food concessions at national, State, and local parks, beaches, stadiums, arenas, race tracks, airports, country clubs, golf tournaments, tennis tournaments, fairs, concerts, and similar high-traffic locations. Emphasis is on quick, efficient service, high quality products, and cleanliness. In every case, you have access to a captive audience and the odds of success are multiplied tremendously in your favor; also, your profitability is increased because of the "tricks of the trade" available to you as an Atlantic Concessions franchise. Development plan calls for each franchisee to be doing a million dollars in sales volume in your fifth year of operation.

Number of Franchisees: 21 in 6 States

In Business Since: 1977

Equity Capital Needed: Minimum of $25,000, including franchise fee. Could be higher in certain territories.

Financial Assistance Available: Atlantic will finance up to one-third the franchise fee for qualifying franchisees.

Training Provided: Intensive mandatory training course for all new franchisees and key personnel. Minimum 2 weeks. One week of training in the acquisition of new concession locations. One week of training in the operations of your first location prior to opening. At least 1 week of the training is in your home territory, with a key management person working directly with you all day every day.

Managerial Assistance Available: Atlantic provides continued management and technical assistance for the life of the franchise in such areas as bookkeeping, advertising, inventory control, cash control, employee training, etc. Complete manuals of operations, forms, and directions are provided. District and field managers are available in all regions to work closely with franchisees and visit locations to assist in solving problems. Atlantic sponsors meetings of franchisees and conducts marketing and product research to maintain high level of acceptance of Atlantic's products and services.

Information Submitted: May 1987

ATLANTIC RICHFIELD COMPANY
515 South Flower Street
Los Angeles, California 90071
Larry Bittner, Manager, San Francisco Region
Nancy Dicks, Manager, Los Angeles Region
am/pm Franchise Marketing

Description of Operation: The "am/pm" mini market franchise is a system for retail grocery store services and the identification, layout, and operation of retail grocery stores identified principally by the service name and service mark "am/pm," featuring the sale of prepackaged foods, beverages, sundries and convenience store goods.

Number of Franchisees: 519 as of May, 1987 in 5 States

In Business Since: 1979

Equity Capital Needed: $50,000 through $400,000 excluding the cost of acquiring or leasing the real estate and excluding any deposits and any investment required in connection with other businesses conducted from the premises.

Financial Assistance Available: None

Training Provided: 2 to 3 weeks training including basic bookkeeping, accounting, sales promotion, inventory control and retail and management techniques.

Managerial Assistance Available: Complete managerial assistance from franchisor includes the personalized service of an am/pm franchise representative, sales manager, and franchise manager at the field level with assistance from a headquarters staff to create new program and manage sustaining advertising and sales promotion techniques. Additionally, complete manuals detailing systems, forms, accounting and inventory service, and marketing techniques are also provided to the franchisee.

Information Submitted: June 1987

AUGIE'S, INC.
1900 West County Road C
St. Paul, Minnesota 55113
Ray Augustine, President

Description of Operation: Industrial catering. Special equipped trucks to serve hot foods to workers on-the-job.

Number of Franchisees: 54 in Minnesota

In Business Since: 1958

Equity Capital Needed: $5,000, some instances less.

Financial Assistance Available: Weekly payment on amount due.

Training Provided: Approximately 1 week training in driving and sales.

Managerial Assistance Available: Same as above

Information Submitted: July 1987

BALBOA BAKING COMPANY
4686 University Avenue
San Diego, California 92105
Sam Tringali, Owner

Description of Operation: We make quality bread, specializing in sour dough loafs and rolls. Franchising in the San Diego area only.

Number of Franchisees: 6 in California

In Business Since: 1970

Equity Capital Needed: $100,000

Financial Assistance Available: Will help in financing if franchisee is fully qualified.

Training Provided: Training for packers and drivers, packers-slicing, and packing bread for following day. Drivers-learn routes, customer promoting— restaurants, Deli's and markets.

Managerial Assistance Available: Balboa provides continual management service for the life of the franchise. In areas such as bookkeeping advertising and inventory control. Complete manuals of operations, forms and directions are provided. District and field managers are available to work closely with franchisee and assist in solving problems. Balboa sponsors meetings and conducts marketing and product research to maintain high Balboa consumer acceptance.

Information Submitted: July 1987

BARNIE'S COFFEE & TEA COMPANY, INC.
PRIMROSE COFFEE & TEA PURVEYORS
340 North Primrose Drive
Orlando, Florida 32803
B. Philip Jones, Jr., President

Description of Operation: Barnie's is a gourmet coffee and tea store selling imported whole bean coffees, bulk and packaged teas, related accessories, complementary food items and cupped coffee, espresso, cappuccino and specialty baked goods. Store units are located in premiere regional mall locations.

Number of Franchisees: 21 in Florida, Alabama, Louisiana, Illinois, Pennsylvania and New Jersey

In Business Since: 1980, incorporated in 1982

Equity Capital Needed: $80,000 to $150,000

Financial Assistance Available: No financial assistance is available. The franchisor does help coordinate presentation of loan package to lending institutions.

Training Provided: 4 day orientation at home office. Franchisee and staff participates in initial store set and then two days in store orientation. Grand opening week in store supervision. Detailed operations manual provided.

Managerial Assistance Available: During first year frequent visits by franchise operations department. Three franchisee meetings per year during duration of franchise agreement. Access to central buying power and distribution through Primrose Coffee & Tea Purveyors. Ongoing participation in store with promotions and new product introduction.

Information Submitted: July 1987

BLUE CHIP COOKIES, INC.
124 Beale Street
4th Floor
San Francisco, California 94105
Matt Nader, President

Description of Operation: Retail gourmet fresh cookies.

Number of Franchisees: 18 in California, Arizona, Colorado, New Mexico, Ohio, Texas and Minnesota.

In Business Since: 1983

Equity Capital Needed: $90,000-$115,000

Financial Assistance Available: None

Training Provided: All aspects from making the cookie dough to mixing, baking, selling and marketing. 2-3 weeks of training to franchisee and/or management.

Managerial Assistance Available: As needed and when needed for the life of the franchise. Building and architectual design, layout, equipment specs and purchasing.

Information Submitted: July 1987

LE CROISSANT SHOP
dba BLUE MILL ENTERPRISES CORP.
227 West 40th Street
New York, New York 10018
Robert Le Lamer, President
Jacques Pelletier, Vice President

Description of Operation: Retail facilities selling authentic French baked croissants, pastries, breads, salads, soups, beverages and other baked and cooked products.

Number of Franchisees: 8 plus 4 company-owned in New York

In Business Since: 1981, offering franchises since 1984

Equity Capital Needed: $85,000 to $200,000

Financial Assistance Available: None

Training Provided: 4 weeks training baking and sales

Managerial Assistance Available: Operational and managing assistance provided throughout the terms of the contract.

Information Submitted: May 1987

* **BOARDWALK FRANCHISE CORPORATION, INC.**
T/A THE BOARDWALK PEANUT SHOPPE
10th Street and Boardwalk
P.O. Box 936

Ocean City, New Jersey 08226
Leo Yeager, III, President
Patricia Gargone, Franchise Director

Description of Operation: Retail nut and candy shoppe. Featuring "hot" roasted peanuts, freshly prepared nuts and popcorn, dried fruits, health mixes and seeds, chocolates, candy, and gift packages.

Number of Franchisees:

7 (including company-owned stores)

In Business Since: 1972

Equity Capital Needed: Total investment ranges from $94,500-$132,000. This includes a $12,000 franchise fee. Additional working capital and deposits of $15,000 may be required.

Financial Assistance Available: No. Franchisor will assist in preparation of a loan package.

Training Provided: A policies manual is issued and enhanced by a 1 week training program. This on-the-job training provides exact specifications for producing quality products, marketing strategies, management and administrative systems.

Managerial Assistance Available: Start-up assistance provided in opening locations as well as ongoing support. Through a call-line, a franchise can contact the franchisor with a problem or question. Franchisees will receive updates on the latest trends and promotional strategies. There is also periodic field supervision.

Information Submitted: July 1987

THE BREAD BASKET, INC.
P.O. Box 93
Mt. Ephraim, New Jersey 08059
Mark D. Peters, Director of Franchise

Description of Operation: The Bread Basket offers a retail bake shop concept specializing in but not limited to ethnic bread and rolls. Frozen dough is proofed and baked on a daily basis. Most products are made on the premises in view of the customer. Over 50 delicious varieties of breads and rolls are offered for sale, ideal store size is 1,600 square feet.

Number of Franchisees: 11 in New Jersey, Florida, and Delaware including company-owned.

In Business Since: Parent company 1920, franchising since 1974

Equity Capital Needed: Franchise equity varies and is dependent on site, size and location and machinery. Franchise fee is $10,000.

Financial Assistance Available: Financing may be available through lending institutions and leasing companies.

Training Provided: A comprehensive training program in baking and operation of Bread Basket at parent company. Transportation, meals and lodgings are franchisee's responsibilities.

Managerial Assistance Available: Continuous assistance and direction by correspondence, direct phone, in store visits by qualified home office personnel. Location floor plan and equipment evaluation. Assistance with advertising and promotional costs. Company provides managerial and technical assistance to each franchisee with ultimate goal of profit and success.

Information Submitted: May 1987

BREAKTIME, INC.
11616 Kaw Drive
Kansas City, Kansas 66111
Frank L. Norton, President

Description of Operation: Convenience centers located in multitenanted buildings. Each convenience center offers a wide variety of pre-packaged food and personal items. All units operate during normal business hours—no weekends or evenings. A regional warehouse and commissary supports each franchise to maintain the integrity of the profit structure. Area distributorships and local franchisees available in all states.

Number of Franchisees: 23 franchise units, plus 44 company-owned units.

In Business Since:

1984; franchising since May 1986

Equity Capital Needed: Approximately 33,500 (franchise fee included).

Financial Assistance Available: Partial financing available to qualified individuals.

Training Provided: BreakTime, Inc., provides 3 days of intensive classroom and hands-on' training on the locale of the franchisee. The classroom training consists of inventory control, ordering of product, employee relations, management and complete accounting procedures. Additional training is available for multiple unit operation.

Managerial Assistance Available: Areas covered in this assistance include site survey, lease negotiations, convenience center design and equipment purchasing. When a convenience center is scheduled to open, a field representative is available to help oversee the operation and provide back-up support for the owner in areas of employee training and successful opeational procedures. After home-office support is made available to each franchisee. All promotional items and new products are test marketed in the company-owned units prior to introduction to franchisees.

Information Submitted: May 1987

* BULK INTERNATIONAL
31000 Lahser Road
Suite 2
Birmingham, Michigan 48010
Leonard Daitch

Description of Operation: Bulk International is the franchisor of Mister Bulky's Foods and Johvince Bulk Food stores. Bulk International offers turnkey franchises of retail bulk food markets. Each store is between 2,500 and 4,000 square feet, and is located in strip malls or regional malls. These markets are unique as they offer over 1,000 bulk food items to consumers, with the opportunity to buy a pinch or a pound, and in most cases, at considerable savings over normal grocery markets. The products are merchandised out of plexigas bins, and an extremely attractive presentation acts as a strong incentive to Mrs. consumer. Items merchandised are dried fruits and nuts, candies, spices, grains and cereals, pastas, peas and beans, large assortment of flours, sugars, spices of the world, extracts, cake mixes, baking supplies, baking ingredients, and related giftware.

Number of Franchisees: 23 in Michigan, Ohio, Indiana, New Jersey and Pennsylvania

In Business Since: 1983

Equity Capital Needed: $75,000 minimum

Financial Assistance Available: A total investment of between $130,000 (low) to $150,000 (high) is required to open a bulk food franchise on a turnkey basis. This includes the franchisee fee, all fixturing and equipment, shelving, two computerized checkout counters, signage package, and approximately $35,000 of start-up inventory. This figure also includes an estimation for leasehold improvement, first and last months' rent and initial advertising and insurance costs. The franchisor does no direct financing, but will provide the franchisee with assistance to obtain financing, and if the franchisee's credit and security are acceptable, lending institutions will generally advance 50 percent of the required capital.

Training Provided: The franchisor provides assistance in site selection and lease negotiation. Franchisor provides approximately 3 weeks of training for manager, owner, and staff, comprised of 2 weeks prior to store opening at franchisee's location or other designated location, and 1 week of training reinforcement after store has opened. Ongoing supervision is part of the franchisor's program. Training methods include operating manuals, hands-on training, cashier manuals, employee handbook, specifically dealing with care and control of handling foods in bulk, and retail merchandising.

Managerial Assistance Available: Bulk International provides continual supervision through store visits, newsletters, and area meetings, to ensure that the franchisee is kept up to date on seasonal merchandise, new products, new ideas, and new merchandising techniques.

Information Submitted: July 1987

* BUNS MASTER BAKERY SYSTEMS, CORP.
751 Main Street, East
Milton, Ontario, Canada L9T 3Z3
John Mallinick, Franchise Manager (United States)

Description of Operation: Buns Master Bakery is a unique self-service, bake-on premises bakery which offers distinctive quality breads, buns, rolls and other bakery products at factory prices. All bakeries use the same formilae and all are required to have the same name, logo, decor, product bins and product mix.

Number of Franchisees: 13 in Washington, New York, Ohio, Michigan and Arizona. 124 in Canada

In Business Since: 1979 in the U.S.A.; 1976 in Canada

Equity Capital Needed: Minimum $60,000

Financial Assistance Available: None

Training Provided: All initial training program which consists of particpating in the day-to-day operation of another Buns Master Bakery for 2 to 5 days prior to opening his own bakery is offered to the franchisee. In addition, for the first 14 days of operation of the franchisee's bakery, a technical trainer teaches the franchisee and his staff the Buns Master Bakery System's methods of preparing and merchandising products, and standard operating practices, methods and procedures.

Managerial Assistance Available: The franchisor assists the franchisee in site selection, lease negotiations, bakery layout, preparing financial information for financing, purchasing the required equipment package, initial training, initial advertising and promotion, continuing advertising and promotion, product mix and product development.

Information Submitted: May 1987

CHEESE SHOP INTERNATIONAL, INC.
255 Greenwich Avenue
Greenwich, Connecticut 06830

Description of Operation: Retail sale of the fine cheese, gourmet foods, related gift items and wines where permissible. Typically located in a shopping center or on main street of better suburban communities.

Number of Franchisees: 50 in 16 States

In Business Since: 1965

Equity Capital Needed: $50,000-$100,000

Financial Assistance Available: None

Training Provided: 4 weeks; 5 days per week actually working in an existing Cheese Shop under the direction of a company expert.

Managerial Assistance Available: In addition to the training we provide an expert to help during the grand opening week. On a continuous basis we accept collect phone calls to plan and advise on all purchases necessary to run the business. This service includes discussing the following as applies to various suppliers; availability of product, freshness, specials, quality, next arrivals, trucking routes, air freight, costs, etc. It also includes recommending where to place a given order for a certain product at that particular time. This service is optional and typically done on a weekly basis. We also organize promotions, designed to increased sales. Continuous supervision and advice in all phases of retail operations is available.

Information Submitted: July 1987

CHEZ CHOCOLAT
P.O. Drawer 11025
Winston-Salam, North Carolina 27106

Description of Operation: Retail candy and nut shops selling domestic and imported products. Operated primarily in kiosk and store locations in regional malls.

Number of Franchisees: 48 stores in 25 states plus 6 company-owned.

In Business Since: 1972

Equity Capital Needed: Estimated costs include complete turnkey, franchise fee, and inventory, Kiosks range from $30,000—$135,000.

Financial Assistance Available: Outside financing preferred. Some internal financing available under certain circumstances.

Training Provided: Regional supervisors and field operations managers train frnachisees in their respective locations for a time depending on past retail experience. In addition, franchisees may receive on-the-job training with operating units in their area.

Managerial Assistance Available: Field operations managers set up and open stores providing in depth initial training. Afterwards, regional supervisors visit locations as needed to assist in maximizing operations, marketing new, seasonal, and holiday merchandise. Regional meetings are held for operations seminars and holiday product shows in advance of major holidays.

Information Submitted: July 1987

CINNAMON SAM'S, INC.
10890 Benson
Suite 300
Overland Park, Kansas 66210
C. Glynn Culver, Vice President

Description of Operation: A gourmet specialty bakery whose signature product is a half pound gourmet cinnamon roll prepared from all natural ingredients. Also offered are eight to ten additional specialty bakery items served in a coffee shop environment.

Number of Franchisees: 22 in 12 States

In Business Since: 1985

Equity Capital Needed: $80,000 to $100,000

Financial Assistance Available: None

Training Provided: 2 weeks classroom, 1 week on-site and ongoing evaluation.

Managerial Assistance Available: Bakery operations, bookkeeping, marketing, small business management and advertising.

Information Submitted: May 1987

*THE COFFEE BEANERY, LTD.
G-3453 Pierson Place
Flushing, Michigan 48433
JoAnne Shaw, President

Description of Operation: Specializes in groumet coffee and tea, selling coffee by the pound and cup, bulk and packaged tea, related accessories. Stores are located in major malls.

Number of Franchisees: 6 plus 5 company-owned stores in Michigan

In Business Since: 1976

Equity Capital Needed: $45,000 to $75,000 depending upon location, store size and construction.

Financial Assistance Available: A total investment of $95,000 to $150,000 is required to open a Coffee Beanery Ltd. on a turnkey basis. Included would be franchise fee, fixturing, shelving, signage, inventory and some working capital. Franchisor does no direct financing but will provide qualified franchisees assistance in obtaining financing.

Training Provided: 1 week in corporate office, 1 week in company-owned store, and 2 weeks in franchise store. Training manuals include employee manual, management manual and product training manual. Training may include product, inventory control, bookkeeping, daily operations and much more.

Managerial Assistance Available: Assistance available by store visits, training meetings, newsletters, phone, access to group buying through central distribution, a complete monthly marketing program, research and development for new products and marketing techniques.

Information Submitted: July 1987

THE COFFEE MERCHANT
Box 2159
Sand Point, Idaho 83864

Description of Operation: The Coffee Merchant is a specialty retail store providing an exceptional variety of the worlds best coffees, fine teas and related accessories.

Number of Franchisees: 2 in California, 3 in Iowa, 1 in Illinois and 1 in Ohio

In Business Since: 1979

Equity Capital Needed: $65,000 to $95,000 dependent on store size, location and construction need.

Financial Assistance Available: The franchisor will assist the franchisee in applying with local banks for financing.

Training Provided: The prospective franchisee is trained for a 2 week period in a company store with emphasis placed on merchandising and accounting skills.

Managerial Assistance Available: The franchisor provides ongoing managerial assistance and has available accounting services for the franchisee.

Information Submitted: July 1987

THE COFFEE MILL
268 Cavalier Road
Athens, Georgia 30606
Mel J. Witt, President

Description of Operation: The Coffee Mill is a specialty coffee, tea, and mug shop which carries unique blends and specialty imported coffees from all over the world. Exquisite cappuccino machine which provides customary attraction and sales volume.

Number of Franchisees: 3 in Georgia

In Business Since: 1981

Equity Capital Needed: $35,000 to $70,000 depending on location, store size and construction requirements.

Financial Assistance Available: No financial assistance available. Franchisor available to provide consultant to franchisee and lending institutions.

Training Provided: 1 week initial training at an existing location. One to 2 weeks preopening and initial opening training. Periodic store visits.

Managerial Assistance Available: Training and technical assistance in all phases of product merchandising, record keeping and product information and general store operation.

Information Submitted: May 1987

COFFEE, TEA & THEE
c/o Specialty Retail Concepts, Inc.
P. O. Drawer 11025
Winston-Salem, North Carolina 27116

Description of Operation: Gourmet coffee and tea specialty shops located within enclosed shopping malls.

Number of Franchisees: 35 in 19 States, including company-owned.

In Business Since: 1979

Equity Capital Needed: $85,000 to $125,000

Financial Assistance Available: No financial assistance available. However, franchisor is available for consultation with lenders.

Training Provided: Initial training of staff (normally 1 to 2 weeks) and periodic visits thereafter.

Managerial Assistance Available: Initial training at same time staff training takes place. Periodic visits by operations staff thereafer.

Information Submitted: June 1987

COLONIAL VILLAGE MEAT MARKET FRANCHISE CORP.
Manoa Shopping Center
Office #4
Harbertowm, Pennsylvania
C. Robert Blair, President

Description of Operation: Each store is approximately 4,000 square feet with ample store front parking. Our meats are displayed in self-service cases for volume purposes. Our meat rooms are visually displaled to the customer for their inspection. All stores have a full service Deli line with a full or limited line of grocery and product. Our reputation is built on giving our customers quality, cleanliness, service and variety of competitive prices.

Number of Franchisees: 17 in Pennsylvania, New Jersey and Delaware

In Business Since: 1968

Equity Capital Needed: $50,000 to $100,000

Financial Assistance Available: Financial assistance is limited. Third party financial institutions will provide partial financing to acceptable franchisee. Franchisor, in certain situations, may finance all or part of franchisee's equipment requirement.

Training Provided: Prospective franchisee should have at least 5 years managerial experience in retail food industry with working knowledge of meats. Sixteen hours of class training with 2 weeks of in-store training is recommended and sometimes required.

Managerial Assistance Available: We provide ongoing management services for the life of the franchise in all areas of internal and external store operations. Complete manuals of store operations, forms and directions are provided. Field managers are available in all regions to work closely with franchisees and visit stores.

Information Submitted: July 1987

*CONVENIENT FOOD MART, INC.
World Headquarters
9701 West Higgins Road
Suite 850
Rosemont, Illinois 60018
Robert S. Risberg, President

Description of Operation: Grocery stores are 2,400 to 3,600 square feet in size with ample parking. Stores are open 365 days a year from 7 am 'til midnight. Stores stock complete lines of top name national brand merchandise normally stocked in a chain supermarket (except fresh red meat requiring cutting at store level). CFM franchises regional territories to a franchisor under a licensing agreement who, as an independent contractor, in turn, franchises stores to individuals. The regional franchisor selects locations, negotiations with investors to build the store, and takes a long-term lease, subleasing same to CFM owner-operators. There are 48 licensed franchisors (some with multiple franchises) operating in parts of or all of 39 States and Canada. For information about open areas and franchisors for any State may be obtained from national office.

Number of Franchisees: 1,316 throughout the USA and Canada

In Business Since: 1958

Equity Capital Needed: Varies by regional franchisor.

Financial Assistance Available: Varies by regional franchisor.

Training Provided: Program includes, planning, hiring, purchasing, merchandising, advertising, and business management. Easily implemented cash and inventory controls are also taught. Additional training at franchisee's store at time of opening.

Managerial Assistance Available: Continuous communication by bulletins, corresppondence, direct phone, in-store visits by qualified personnel, and ongoing training sessions are conducted.

Information Submitted: May 1987

* **THE COOKIE BIN, INC.**
7684 Sprinkle Road
Kalamazoo, Michigan 49002
M. Charles Kuepfer, President

Description of Operation: Now you can own a business that combines the universal appeal of homebaked cookies with an unparalleled opportunity for financial independence. It's the Cookie Bin, a warm and homey place to shop for cookies that look, smell, and taste like the ones Mom used to make. They're made from the finest ingredients and mixed and baked right on the premises. You needn't be a baker—or even a mom—to own a Cookie Bin. All you need is a Cookie Bin franchise to turn a small space into a bustling exciting new business of your own.

Number of Franchisees: 6 in Michigan, Ohio, Colorado and South Carolina. We are offering franchises in most States, including Alaska and Hawaii.

In Business Since: 1981

Equity Capital Needed: $10,000 to $80,000 or more depending on the location and type of franchise.

Financial Assistance Available: The Cookie Bin does not offer an internal finance program. but we will assist you in whatever way we can in arranging financing. We can in some instances direct you to sources from which other franchisees have successfully obtained loans. However, these are third parties and their decisions are independent of Cookie Bin. A total investment of $40,000 to $135,000 is required to open a Cookie Bin franchise.

Training Provided: All franchisees and one additional employee must attend and successfully complete the 10-day training program provided by Cookie Bin at our headquarters in Kalamazoo, Michigan. The cost of this initial training is included in your franchise fee; **however, those costs connected with travel and lodging will be at your expense.** In addition to your initial training period, an operations specialist will work with you in your market for 3 days during your first month of operation.

Managerial Assistance Available: First of all, you will receive a Cookie Bin operations manual covering the many important facets of your business operation. As the manuals are updated, revisions will be made available to you. Periodically, you will receive company newsletters containing useful management information and bulletins which spotlight important happenings. You will also receive regular visits by our field representatives who will consult with you and offer useful advice and counsel on such system elements as identity, quality, customer convenience, product information, advertising, recordkeeping, communication, training, and incentives. This continues throughout your Cookin Bin franchisee carrier.

Information Submitted: May 1987

* **COOKIE FACTORY OF AMERICA**
500 Park Boulevard
Suite 140
Itasca, Illinois 60143
Contact: Director of Franchising

Description of Operation: Retail selling of cookies, croissants, muffins, and other specialty baked foods. Locations are in regional shopping centers.

Number of Franchisees: 80 in 67 States

In Business Since: 1974

Equity Capital Needed: Total package approximately $125,000.

Financial Assistance Available: None

Training Provided: Training classes at home office. Program includes, planning, hiring, purchasing, merchandising, advertising, and business management. Easily implemented cash and inventory controls are also taught. Additional training at franchisee's store at time of opening.

Managerial Assistance Available: Continuous communication by bulletins, correspondence, direct phone, in-store visits by qualified home office personnel, and ongoing training sessions are conducted.

Information Submitted: June 1987

THE COOKIE STORE
c/o SPECIALTY RETAIL CONCEPTS
P. O. Drawer 11025
Winston-Salem, North Carolina

Description of Operation: Cookies, cookie cakes, brownies, frozen yogurt, and related items.

Number of Franchisees: 33 in 15 States, including company-owned.

In Business Since: 1982

Equity Capital Needed: $75,000 to $100,000

Financial Assistance Available: No financial assistance available. However, franchisor is available for consultation with lenders.

Training Provided: Initial training of staff (normally 1 week) and periodic visits thereafter.

Managerial Assistance Available: Initial training at same time staff training takes place. Periodic visits by operations staff thereafter.

Information Submitted: June 1987

COUNTRY BISCUITS
3131 Atlanta Highway
Athens, Georgia 30606
Mel S. Witt, Vice President

Description of Operation: Specialty biscuit, country ham, sausage, steak and other food type products, prepared and served the old time way. Located in enclosed shopping malls or strategic locations.

Number of Franchisees: 3 in Georgia

In Business Since: 1980

Equity Capital Needed: $29,000 to $65,000

Financial Assistance Available: No financial assistance available. Franchisor is available for consultation with lenders.

Training Provided: Training consists of 2 to 3 days observation at an existing location. One to 2 weeks preopening and initial opening training provided.

Managerial Assistance Available: Ongoing advise and assistance through periodic site visits, technical advise on product preparation, marketing, bookkeeping, pricing and general store operations.

Information Submitted: July 1987

* **DAIRY MART CONVENIENCE STORES, INC.**
240 South Road
Enfield, Connecticut 06082
Leonard F. Crogan, Vice President

Description of Operation: Dairy Mart Convenience Stores, Inc., operates retail convenience stores in Southern New England and the Midwest. Dairy Mart/Lawson stores are open 7 days a week from 18 to 24 hours per day depending upon location. Stores average approximately 1,800 to 2,000 square feet in size. Dairy Mart/Lawson typically provides the physical location and all equipment necessary to operate a convenience store.

Number of Franchisees: 167 in 6 States

In Business Since: 1957

Equity Capital Needed: Minimum of $15,000

Financial Assistance Available: No direct financial assistance is provided by franchisor. However, franchisor will make banking contract and assist franchisee in obtaining bank financing.

Training Provided: Typically, a 2 week traning period is provived, primarily at the store location.

Managerial Assistance Available: After the initial training period, regular store visits are made by Dairy Mart area supervisors. Dairy Mart also sponsors periodic meetings covering various aspects of store management including personnel, merchandising, and theft prevention.

Information Submitted: May 1987

DIAL-A-GIFT, INC.
2265 East 4800 South
Salt Lake City, Utah 84117
Clarence L. Jolley, President

Description of Operation: National gift wire service (like florists). National delivery of fancy gift baskets—fresh fruit, gourmet foods, cheeses, wines and champagne, decorated cakes, bouquets of balloons, steaks, smoked ham, turkey and salmon.

Number of Franchisees: 115 in 28 States

In Business Since: 1980

Equity Capital Needed: $15,000

Financial Assistance Available: None

Training Provided: Intensive 3 days training at home office.

Managerial Assistance Available: Perpetual assistance.

Information Submitted: July 1987

FOOD-N-FUEL, INC.
8500 Lexington Avenue
Circle Pine, Minnesota 55014
Edward Bird, General Manager

Description of Operation: Retail grocery and gasoline.

Number of Franchisees: 76 in Minnesota, Wisconsin, Iowa, North Dakota and South Dakota.

In Business Since: 1978

Equity Capital Needed: $250,000

Financial Assistance Available: None

Training Provided: 1 week prior to opening store, ongoing thereafter.

Managerial Assistance Available: Ongoing

Information Submitted: July 1987

LAURA CORPORATION
dba FRONTIER FRUIT & NUT COMPANY
3823 Wadsworth Road
Norton, Ohio 44203
Alex E. Marksz, Vice President

Description of Operation: The Frontier Fruit & Nut Company offers a unique retail store operation in regional malls featuring the retail sales of bulk dried fruits, nuts, candies and gifts.

Number of Franchisees: 17 franchisees, 56 locations in 16 States

In Business Since: 1977

Equity Capital Needed: $25,000 minimum

Financial Assistance Available: None

Training Provided: On-site training by full-time Frontier Fruit & Nut employee at time of opening.

Managerial Assistance Available: Frontier provides continual assistance for the life of the franchise in such areas as bookkeeping, advertising and inventory control. Complete manual of operations, product knowledge, forms and directions are provided.

Information Submitted: June 1987

GIULIANO'S DELICATESSEN & BAKERY
1117 East Walnut Street
Carson, California 90746
John E. Kidde, President

Description of Operation: Specialty store consisting of a full service delicatessen offering 125-150 imported and domestic meats and cheeses; kitchen with an extensive take-out menu; catering; bread and pastry bakery; gourmet grocery; and extensive selection of imported and domestic wines and beers.

Number of Franchisees: 5 in California

In Business Since: 1953

Equity Capital Needed: Total package including building, leasehold improvements, inventory, initial franchise fee and working capital is between $600,000-$800,000. Equity capital initially required is approximately $150,000.

Financial Assistance Available: Franchisor does not provide direct financial assistance although it is very active in assisting in securing attractive and reasonable terms for its franchisees. Franchisor will act as lessee and sublet to franchisee to assist in securing the best location at an attractive rate. Franchisor extends attractive credit terms on all purchases by franchisee from its central commissary.

Training Provided: 3 months initial training program before commencement of operation.

Managerial Assistance Available: Ongoing assistance from franchisor include site visitations by company representative; classes and training sessions for new products, merchandising, personnel and hiring practices; complete corporate advertising program, etc. Franchisor provides an operations manual, bookkeeping system and promotional assistance.

Information Submitted: June 1987

GLASS OVEN BAKERY
1640 New Highway
Farmingdale, New York 11735
Robert G. Emmett, President
George J. Holzmacher, Vice President

Description of Operation: Retail bakery/cafe where all baked goods are baked directly in view of the customers. One can choose to enter into the retail bakery or combine the retail bakery with the concept of a fast-food service as well. A complete and diversified line of baked goods are offered for sale. The company was purchased by a national franchisor with the intent to develop a nationwide network of franchised units.

Number of Franchisees: 30 in 6 States

In Business Since: 1977

Equity Capital Needed: Franchise fee $19,500. Total investment required will vary dependent upon location, cost of renovations at said location and extent and cost of equipment.

Financial Assistance Available: Financing may be available through lending institutions and leasing companies.

Training Provided: 2 week training program in management, operations, record keeping, employee relations, scheduling, bookkeeping, ordering and other aspects of managing and operating a bakery or a bakery/fast-food business. A company representative will be available on location for 40 hours to assist in grand opening and to work with the owner and employees in helping get the business started.

Managerial Assistance Available: Information of new products, new systems, updated equipment information, advertising and continued guidance and support provided by franchisor.

Information Submitted: July 1987

GLORIA JEAN'S COFFEE BEAN CORP
12C West Colidge
Arlington Heights, Illinois 60004
Edward C. Kvetko, President

Description of Operation: Gloria Jean's Coffee Bean Corp Stores offer for retail sale bulk coffees, teas, beverages, yogurt, ice cream, candies, pastry, groumet foods, housewares, sandwiches, coffee and tea makers and related items. Some stores offer delicatessen type service for immediate consumption of the above products. The stores are generally located in high traffic, high density shopping centers and require approximately 770 square feet of space. The franchisor does not currently lease equipment or premises to franchisees.

Number of Franchisees: 16 stores including company-owned in Illinois Wisconsin and Michigan.

In Business Since: 1979

Equity Capital Needed: From $45,600 and up, depending on premises and equipment, all of which may be financed by a prospective franchisee.

Financial Assistance Available: None at this time.

Training Provided: All new owners and managers are required to complete the Gloria Jean's Coffee Bean Corp Store training program. The program comprises 10 business days of intensive instruction at the Gloria Jean's Coffee Bean Corp corporate offices as well as at neighboring retail stores. The course covers such topics as product knowledge, equipment use and care, store operations and procedures, sales training, erchandising, and in-store training.

Managerial Assistance Available: Gloria Jean's Coffee Bean Corp provides an operations manual to all franchisees containing specifications, standards and operating procedures necessary to successfully manage a Gloria Jean's Coffee Bean Corp Store. In addition, Gloria Jean's Coffee Bean Corp provides refresher training programs, offers advice and assistance on store operations, assists franchisees in obtaining store brands and other approved brands, and formulates and conducts advertising and promotional programs.

Information Submitted: July 1987

GRANDMA LOVE'S COOKIES AND COMPANY
268 Cavalier Road
Athens, Georgia 30606
Mel J.Witt, President
(404) 546-0389

Description of Operation: Specialty cookie store shops located in high traffic shopping malls and downtown locations. Selling high quality freshly baked cookies, cookies, cakes and related items.

Number of Franchisees: 6 in Georgia, Tennessee, Florida and South Carolina

In Business Since: 1978

Equity Capital Needed: $40,000 to $75,000

Financial Assistance Available: No financial assistance available. The franchisor is available for consultation with lenders.

Training Provided: Training consists of 3 days observation in an existing store. One to 2 weeks of pretraining and start-up assistance. Periodic site visits by operations staff.

Managerial Assistance Available: Ongoing support of business operations through periodic site visits. Technical advise on product preparation, marketing, bookkeeping, pricing, and general store operations.

Information Submitted: May 1987

* GREAT EARTH VITAMIN STORES
1801 Parkcourt Place
Building A
Santa Ana, California 92701
Christopher Barr, Executive President

Description of Operation: Great Earth Vitamin stores offer an extensive line of the highest quality vitamin and mineral products, sold at competitive prices by well-trained vitamin specialists. The typical store is 600 square feet.

Number of Franchisees: 160 stores in 16 States

In Business Since: 1971

Equity Capital Needed: Franchise fee $20,000, opening fee $7,500; product inventory, leasehold improvements, equipment, supplies and operating capital typically are an additional $60,000 to $80,000.

Financial Assistance Available: Willing to carry note on a portion of franchise fee for qualified license applicants.

Training Provided: 4 weeks of extensive training in product knowledge, retail sales, systems and procedures, advertising, promotion, and management of the business.

Managerial Assistance Available: Great Earth International (as franchisor) provides assistance in store site selection, lease negotiation, leasehold improvenient supervision, and grand opening. Field representatives provide ongoing assistance in hiring and training of your personnel, and communicating new product and promotion information on a regular basis. A library of video tapes is also maintained for continuing education in all aspects of the business.

Information Submitted: May 1987

* GREAT HARVEST FRANCHISING, INC.
P. O. Box 488
Dillon, Montana 59725
Peter Wakeman, President

Description of Operation: Specialty Whole Wheat Retail Bakery, using premium whole wheat, stone ground daily on premises for fresh flour and highest quality bread.

Number of Franchisees: 17 in 11 States

In Business Since: 1976

Equity Capital Needed: $65,000-$75,000

Financial Assistance Available: Advice only

Training Provided: Approximately 400 hours aid in start-up, including 100 hours training in all aspects of business at franchisee's location.

Managerial Assistance Available: Personal attention to special problems as needed. Newsletter, visits, wheat shipments, coop buying, promo materials, etc.

Information Submitted: May 1987

* THE GREAT SAN FRANCISCO SEAFOOD CO., LTD.
1630 Welton
Denver, Colorado 80202
Ms. Elizabeth Bennett, President

Description of Operation: The Great San Francisco Seafood offers area franchises for the establishment of fresh retail and wholesale seafood markets.

Number of Franchisees: 9 in Colorado, Wyoming, Arkansas, Iowa and Michigan

In Business Since: 1979

Equity Capital Needed: $30,000-$35,000

Financial Assistance Available: Outside only

Training Provided: Comprehensive 3 week traning program in purchasing, handling and displaying of seafood, store promotions, pricing and grand opening assistance.

Managerial Assistance Available: Continuous assistance and direction.

Information Submitted: July 1987

HEAVENLY HAM
365 Northridge Rd
Suite 230
James M. Cook, Vice President

Description of Operation: Heavenly Ham is a high quality specialty food store specializing in fully cooked spiral sliced, honey and spice glazed hams. Heavenly Ham also sells high quality mustards, jams, jellies and other meat products. All stores concentrate on high quality food products, convenience and customer service.

Number of Franchisees: 14 with 20 stores in 10 States

In Business Since: 1984

Equity Capital Needed: $100,000

Financial Assistance Available: Heavenly Ham does not provide any direct financing to franchisees at the present time. However, it does provide assistance in obtaining financing such as assisting the franchisee in preparing his proposal for bank financing and meeting with potential lenders.

Training Provided: 1 week training course in company-owned facility. Ongoing training after store is opened. Managerial assistance provided. Manuals, public relations, sales and promotional strategies and operations assistance.

Managerial Assistance Available: See above.

Information Submitted: June 1987

* HICKORY FARMS OF OHIO, INC.
1505 Holland Road
Maumee, Ohio 43537
Franchise Services

Description of Operation: Retail stores selling packages and bulk specialty food featuring the Hickory Farms Beef Stick Summer Sausage, a variety of imported and domestic cheeses, candies and other related food products under the Hickory Farms label. Locations are usually situated in regional shopping centers. The service and operation is under direct supervision of home office on a continuing basis.

Number of Franchisees: 190 franchise stores, 220 company stores in 49 States

In Business Since: 1951

Equity Capital Needed: $100,000 plus leasehold improvements, inventory and other expenses described in UFOC.

Financial Assistance Available: None. Capital requirements vary by location.

Training Provided: 1 week at home office in planning, purchasing, stocking and merchandising, advertising and business operation. Two weeks prior to opening a new store opening company assists in the direct opening of the store.

Managerial Assistance Available: Continuous communication by bulletins, correspondence, direct phone, in store visits by qualified home office personnel, annual national convention and interim regional meetings and training sessions are conducted.

Information Submitted: May 1987

IN N' OUT FOOD STORES, INC.
19215 West Eight Mile Road
Detroit, Michigan 48219

Description of Operation: Convenience food stores with or without gasoline sales.

Number of Franchisees: 35 in Michigan and California

In Business Since: 1976

Equity Capital Needed: Approximate average $60,000 and $75,000

Financial Assistance Available: The total investment required is from $110,000 to $200,000. Initial fee $15,000. A down payment can range from 60,000 to $75,000 depending on store circumstances. Financing assistance is available through company.

Training Provided: When a 3 day initial evaluation program is passed then a 1 week pre-opening training in a local store is provided by franchisor.

Managerial Assistance Available: Through field reps and other personnel advisory assistance is provided for the life of the franchise in the following areas: accounting, security, merchandising, advertising and inventory control. Also a complete manual of operation is provided. IN N' OUT sponsors franchisee meetings with results of market and product research with emphasis on high consumer acceptance.

Information Submitted: July 1987

INTERNATIONAL AROMAS
P. O. Box 429
New Boston, New Hampshire 03070
William Bradlee, Chief Operating Officer

Description of Operation: Retail coffee, tea and spice shoppes. Located in malls in either patented modular units or as in line shoppers. Merchandise is quality oriented fresh gourmet coffee, teas, spices and all. Types of appliances. Also retailed is the exclusive gift line.

Number of Franchisees: 7 shoppes in New England

In Business Since: 1978

Equity Capital Needed: Varies between $50,000 to $120,000 depending on type of store.

Financial Assistance Available: None. Capital requirements vary by location.

Training Provided: Full training system of approximately 3 weeks initially and 1 week per year thereafter. Training consists of sales and marketing, retailing and general merchandising as well as management.

Managerial Assistance Available: Supervision as needed. Semi-annual management meetings.

Information Submitted: July 1987

JO-ANN'S NUT/HOUSE
P. O. Drawer 11025
Winston-Salem, North Carolina 27106

Description of Operation: Retail candy and nut shops, selling domestic and imported products. Operated primarily in kiosk and store locations in regional malls.

Number of Franchisees: 83 stores in 25 States plus 1 company-owned

In Business Since: 1972

Equity Capital Needed: Estimated costs include complete turnkey, franchise fee, and inventory. Kiosks range from $30,000-$100,000.

Financial Assistance Available: Outside financing preferred. Some internal financing available under certain ciscumstances.

Training Provided: Regional supervisors and field operations managers train franchisees in their respective locations for a time depending on past retail experience. In addition, franchisees may receive on-the-job training with operating units in their area.

Managerial Assistance Available: Field operations managers set up and open stores providing in depth initial training. Afterwards, regional supervisors visit locations as needed to assist in maximizing operations, marketing new, seasonal and holiday merchandise. Regional meetings are held for operations seminars and holiday product shows in advance of major holidays.

Information Submitted: July 1987

JR. FOODMART
440 North Mill Street
Jackson, Mississippi 39207
Danny W. Neal, Vice President, Franchise Sales

Description of Operation: Junior Food Mart Convenience Stores. Stores licensed on a multi-store basis or a single location. All stores are three diminisioned; groceries, fast foods and self-service gasoline. Major concentration and future development geared to rural communities.

Number of Franchisees: 396 units in 17 States

In Business Since: 1919

Equity Capital Needed: Multi-store license; $110,000 needed for inventory, equipment and working capital, initial territory franchise fee is $35,000. Single license; $25,000 needed for inventory and working capital, initial franchise fee is $7,500.

Financial Assistance Available: None; company finds locations, secures leases and constructs buildings.

Training Provided: Operations and food service personnel provide pre-opening assistance, in-store training, pre-opening merchandising, equipment set up, store operations, vendor and distribution contracts and grand opening assistance. New franchisees are required to attend training school, plus management information systems training.

Managerial Assistance Available: Ongoing and periodic evaluations performed.

Information Submitted: July 1987

KATIE MCGUIRE'S OLDE FASHIONED PIE SHOPPE
17682 Sampson Lane
Huntington Beach, California 92647
Jon Walker, Director of Marketing

Description of Operation: Old fashioned, home style, pie and bake shop. Typically located in shopping centers and utilizing space of 1,000 to 1,200 square feet. Stores are able to operate without experienced employees as all of the products are produced at a central location.

Number of Franchisees: 19 in California

In Business Since: 1982

Equity Capital Needed: $65,000-$95,000

Financial Assistance Available: None

Training Provided: Complete training program of 2 weeks that allows a franchisee to operate.

Managerial Assistance Available: Ongoing technical assistance by a professional staff through the term of the franchise agreement.

Information Submitted: May 1987

*KID'S KORNER FRESH PIZZA, INC.
P. O. Box 8863
Madison, Wisconsin 53708
A. E. Brejeha, Vice President, Franchising

Description of Operation: Custom made pizza you take home to bake.

Number of Franchisees: 30 in Wisconsin, Minnesota, Illinois, Georgia and Louisiana.

In Business Since: 1977

Equity Capital Needed: Approximately $25,000 to $30,000 including franchise fee, equipment and inventory.

Financial Assistance Available: None—company can assist in preparing financial presentations for use with lenders.

Training Provided: On-site training at home office and outlet site. Help with site selection, equipment selection, and decor and layout.

Managerial Assistance Available: Help with advertising, promotion, seminars, bookkeeping, and product research.

Information Submitted: May 1987

LI'L PEACH CONVENIENCE FOOD STORES
101 Billerica Avenue
North Billerica, Massachusetts 01862
Francis X. Kearns, President

Description of Operation: Li'l Peach offers fully equipped and stocked convenience food stores averaging approximately 1,800-2,400 square feet. All stores are open seven days a week, most from 7:00 am until 12 midnight.

Number of Franchisees: 12 plus 55 company-owned in Massachusetts

In Business Since: 1972

Equity Capital Needed: Minimum of $8,000

Financial Assistance Available: Financial assistance is available toward purchase of the store inventory. The franchisor does not extend financial assistance in regard to the initial investment.

Training Provided: In-store training totaling 3 weeks in one of our special training stores and in the new franchisee's own store.

Managerial Assistance Available: Continual management service in such areas as accounting, payroll preparation, loss prevention. All manuals and forms are provided. Li'l Peach works closely with its franchisees through regularly scheduled visits by field representatives.

Information Submitted: July 1987

MR. DUNDERBAK
RANCE, INC.
744 Cherry Hill Mall
Cherry Hill, New Jersey 08002
Gene Taylor, President

Description of Operation: Mr. Dunderbak's Old World Deli & Cafe offers a combination of specialty merchandising elements that include a fast food sandwich and specialty restaurant, superior quality delicatessen, and unequaled cheese shop, a unique gourmet food shop, a noteworthy beer and wine shop, and the uncommon gift shop. The shop blends parts of all these elements into an old world atmosphere of fun, service, and quality. Single unit and regional franchises are available.

Number of Franchisees: 19 in 13 States

In Business Since: 1962

Equity Capital Needed: Costs dependent on size.

Financial Assistance Available: Advice and counsel on local bank financing, with or without SBA guarantee.

Training Provided: 5 week formal training in company school, 52 weeks of continued training after shop is open. Two weeks on-site opening assistance by corporate operations staff.

Managerial Assistance Available: Operating manuals with continuous update and bulletins, visits by home office personnel to assist in general operations and specific problems.

Information Submitted: May 1987

*MRS. POWELLS DELICIOUS CINNAMON ROLLS
1970 East 17th Street
Suite 103
Idaho Falls, Idaho 83401
Dick Powell, President

Description of Operation: Retail sales of delicious cinnamon rolls and other specialized bakery items.

Number of Franchisees: 23 in 10 States

In Business Since: 1984

Equity Capital Needed: $90,000-$110,000

Financial Assistance Available: None

Training Provided: 2 week initial training, ongoing support and training.

Managerial Assistance Available: Assistance with lease negotiations, design and blueprints. Complete set of production and operations manuals.

Information Submitted: May 1987

NEAL'S COOKIES
c/o COOKIE CUTTER, INC.
423 Southwest Freeway
Houston, Texas 77002

Description of Operation: Gourmet chocolate chunk cookie and gourmet muffins. Cookie doughs and muffin mixes are prepared at our own plants, then shipped to each franchise store. The franchisee simply scoops and bakes. And, we're the only cookie company which actually makes our own (Swiss style) chocolate for our cookies.

Number of Franchisees: 17 in Texas, California, and Colorado.

In Business Since: 1984

Equity Capital Needed: $90,000-$140,000 total cost, with $25,000 cash minimum.

Financial Assistance Available: Franchisee is responsible for financing, however, the franchisor will assist in financial package preparation and bank submission.

Training Provided: 1 week training at our Houston headquarters and 1 week in-store. Total training, 2 weeks, plus ongoing service during the life of the franchise.

Managerial Assistance Available: On staff, research and development department as well as managerial expertise. We work closely with an agency for public relations and advertising support. We have an 24 hour 1-800 telephone service to answer any questions or to assist in any way.

Information Submitted: July 1987

T F M CO.
dba OKY DOKY FOOD MARTS
1250 Iowa Street—P. O. Box 300
Dubuque, Iowa 52001
John F. Thompson, President

Description of Operation: Stores average from 1,200 square feet to 4,000 square feet—convenient parking required—open daily 7 a.m. to 11 p.m.—inventory selected for maximum turnover—equipment and building may be leased. Regional franchises now available to qualified individuals. Renovating gas stations or other existing good locations our specialty. No franchise fees charged on gas.

Number of Franchisees: 21 in Iowa, Wisconsin and Illinois. Company operations presently centered in the tri-state region of Iowa, and Illinois and Wisconsin. However, other regional franchises are available.

In Business Since: 1947

Equity Capital Needed: Minimum $15,000 plus $25,000.

Financial Assistance Available:

Training Provided: On-job training at home office or on site is required before franchisee is considered. This is at no expense to franchisee.

Managerial Assistance Available: Expertise always available at home office upon request.

Information Submitted: May 1987

*THE ORIGINAL GREAT AMERICAN CHOCOLATE CHIP COOKIE COMPANY, INC.
4685 Fredrick Drive
Atlanta, Georgia 30339
Arthur S. Karp, President

Description of Operation: Retail cookie stores primarily in major regional malls nationwide.

Number of Franchisees: Over 300 franchised units

In Business Since: 1977

Equity Capital Needed: $30,000, total investment is between $100,000-$125,000.

Financial Assistance Available: None

Training Provided: Complete training is provided in all operations of a cookie store.

Managerial Assistance Available: Managerial assistance is provided as long as necessary.

Information Submitted: July 1987

PAPA ALDO'S INTERNATIONAL, INC.
1519 Southwest Sunset Boulevard
Portland, Oregon 97201
John A. Gundle

Description of Operation: Take out pizza. Fresh unbaked pizza to be baked at home.

Number of Franchisees: 85 in 6 States.

In Business Since: 1981

Equity Capital Needed: $15,000-$25,000

Financial Assistance Available: None

Training Provided: 2 weeks total—1 week at corporate company store, 1 week in franchisee's store.

Managerial Assistance Available: Ongoing field support.

Information Submitted: May 1987

PAPA JOHN'S, INC.
199 West Sherman Avenue
Fort Atkinson, Wisconsin 53538
Dave Maurer, President

Description of Operation: We sell fresh unbaked pizza and sub sandwiches and salads. We have no cooking equipment; the customer bakes the pizza at home. Minimum 800-1,000 square feet.

Number of Franchisees: 6 including company stores in Wisconsin

In Business Since: 1981

Equity Capital Needed: $12,500

Financial Assistance Available: Total investment ranges from $45,000-$50,000. This total investment may be reduced through the use of leasing companies, for equipment and an outdoor sign.

Training Provided: There is a 1 week training program provided for up to 2 people.

Managerial Assistance Available: Our assistance is only a phone call away. We have a representative visit each franchise store on a monthly basis. We are able to meet the complete needs of the franchisee in terms of management assistance.

Information Submitted: May 1987

SAUCY'S PIZZA FRANCHISES, INC.
2930 Wetmore
Suite 908
Everett, Washington 98201
Graham S. Haight, Executive Vice President
Gary K. Alcombrack, President

Description of Operation: "We....Make You Bake" pizza stores, selling fresh groumet pizza to be taken home and cooked when ready. Average store size if 1,000 square feet (typically in strip-shopping centers) and minimal hours needed (2 pm-9 pm typical). Very low overhead with no cooking or waiter needed. Counters, sinks and large pizza preparation table are included in total price.

Number of Franchisees: 82 in Washington, Oregon, California, Utah and Hawaii.

In Business Since: 1982

Equity Capital Needed: $45,000-$50,000

Financial Assistance Available: A total investment of $45-$50,000 is necessary to open a Saucy's Pizza franchise and represents all the funds needed for a complete turnkey store. Franchisor does not provide financing but may assist in obtaining outside financing.

Training Provided: 10-14 days intensive, hands-on training in a corporate owned store for all new franchisees as well as 1 week for new franchisees designated manager. Saucy's will have personnel on-site during each opening to guide and assist in supervision.

Managerial Assistance Available: Complete operations manual, cost analysis and break down manual are provided and updated periodically. A file for marketing concepts in maintained by each owner and is updated or added to each month. Quality control personnel visit each sote at least once every 60 days to grade the store and give useful tips to owners. Owners meetings are held and newsletters sent out at least quarterly both covering the latest trends and ideas in the pizza industry.

Information Submitted: May 1987

SAV-A STEP FOOD MART, INC.
4265 Roosevelt Avenue
Louisville, Kentucky 40213
Joseph Pierce, President

Description of Operation: Grocery-convenient type. Floor space approximately 2,000 square feet. Open 8 am til midnight, 7 days a week. Franchisee owns all equipment and inventory and leases building from parent firm. Regional franchises available in most States.

Number of Franchisees: 12 in Indiana and Kentucky and 11 company stores.

In Business Since: 1973

Equity Capital Needed: $40,000

Financial Assistance Available: Help with securing bank loans.

Training Provided: 4 to 6 weeks in-store training.

Managerial Assistance Available: Site selection, equipment installed. On-job training, consistent supervision, accounting service which includes monthly P & L. Sales and tax reports, payroll and paying weekly invoices. Marketing merchandising and promotions. Self-service gasoline.

Information Submitted: July 1987

THE SECOND CUP
293 Church Street
Oakville, Ontario
L6J 1N9
Canada
Paul Embro, Franchise Director

Descriptin of Operation: The Second Cup has become the largest gourmet coffee and tea specialty chain in North America. Our stores offer a wide variety of highest quality coffee, specialty teas and related accessories and gifts. Most stores are in enclosed shopping malls. Stores are approximately 500 plus square feet.

Number of Franchisees: 105 in Canada

In Business Since: 1975

Equity Capital Needed: $40,000-$50,000 cash down payment

Financial Assistance Available: Total cost of new store ranges from $120,000-$150,000. The Second Cup has franchise finance assistance program with the Royal Bank of Canada—full assistance given.

Training Provided: Full training provided including coffee college, in-store and ongoing support.

Managerial Assistance Available: The Second Cup provides retail operations supervisors to assist and develop the owner/operator with sales, merchandising, staffing, and profit attainment. The Second Cup monitors the monthly profit and loss statements and follows with regular visits from their retail operations supervisors to assist in getting the most out of each store for the franchisee. The Second Cup finds locations, negotiates the lease, constructs the store, and provides advertising and promotional assistance on an ongoing basis.

Information Submitted: March 1987

6-TWELVE CONVENIENT MART, INC.
18705-B N. Frederick Road
Gaithersburg, Maryland 20879
George M. Palmer, Franchise Coordinator

Description of Operation: Large "upscale" convenience store featuring groceries, beef loin (zoning permitted) and complete line of fast foods.

Number of Franchisees: 12 in Maryland and Virginia

In Business Since: 1984

2Equity Capital Needed: $50,000-$100,000

Financial Assistance Available: In Mid-Atlantic area franchisors may lease site from owner/landlord and sub lease to franchisee.

Training Provided: 3 weeks of management training and 1 week operation training in store.

Managerial Assistance Available: Ongoing assistance by operational consultants.

Information Submitted: May 1987

* **THE SOUTHLAND CORPORATION**
  2828 North Haskell Avenue
  Box 719
  Dallas, Texas 75204-0719
  Wayne Beeder, Manager Franchise Affairs

Description of Operation: Convenience grocery stores (7-Eleven).

Number of Franchisees: 3,177 in 20 states plus District of Columbia.

In Business Since: 1927, franchised operations since 1964.

Equity Capital Needed: Total Investment Required: The cost of a Store's inventory and cash register fund average $38,806 and $773 respectively. The cost of all necessary business licenses, permits, and bonds is approximately $500. The franchise fee is computed for each store as follows: The initial franchise fee for a store that has not been continuously operated for the preceding 12 calendar months is an amount equal to 15% of the previous calendar year's annualized average per store month Gross profit (excluding Gross Profit from gasoline) for all stores located within the District in which the franchised store is or is to be located. If the store has been continuously operated for at least the preceding 12 calendar months, the franchise fee is an amount equal to 15% of that store's Gross Profit (excluding Gross Profit from gasoline) for the immediately preceding 12 calendar months.

Minimum Initial Investment: The minimum initial investment required includes the franchise fee, the amount of the cash register fund, and a portion of the cost of the initial inventory and of business licenses, permits, and bonds. Except where a franchisee transfers from one 7-Eleven Store to another, the franchisee is required to provide, in cash, as a portion of the cost of the inventory, a down payment of the greater of $12,500 or an amount equal to the average weekly sales of the Store for the prior 12 month period or such shorter time as the Store has been open.

Financial Assistance Available: The remainder of the investment in the inventory and of the cost of business licenses and permits may be financed with Southland, as well as the franchisee's continuing purchases and operating expenses.

Training Provided: 2 weeks in local training store and 1 week in a regional training center are provided.

Managerial Assistance Available: Continuing advisory assistance is provided by Field Consultants and other 7-Eleven personnel. 7-Eleven has been a member of The International Franchise Association (IFA) since beginning Franchised operations.

Information Submitted: May 1987

* **SWISS COLONY STORES, INC.**
  1 Alpine Lane
  Monroe, Wisconsin 53566
  G. Richard Cope, President

Description of Operation: Retail stores offering popularly priced, high quality domestic and imported cheeses, sausage, European style pastries, candy, specialty foods, gifts, and a food service sandwich, deli and bakery program.

Number of Franchisees: 105 stores in 35 States

In Business Since: 1964

Equity Capital Needed: Approximately $100,000 plus leasehold improvements.

Financial Assistance Available: None

Training Provided: 7 day mandatory, thorough training at home office Monroe, Wisconsin, plus 2 weeks in-store training covering all phases of store operation, management and retailing. Advanced programs with incentives also available.

Managerial Assistance Available: Continuous supervision in-store at intervals by highly qualified company personnel.

Information Submitted: May 1987

TIDBIT ALLEY, INC.
Parkway 109 Office Center
328 Newman Springs Road
Red Bank, New Jersey 07701
Robert D. Powers, President, Chief Executive Officer

Description of Operation: Tidbit Alley, Inc. (NASDAQ: TBAI) operates a chain of specialty food retail stores offering a uniquely broad range of domestic and imported foods and other items that are displayed in bins and barrels for self-service by the customer. Tid Bit Alley TM stores are located primarily in regional shopping malls. The average store has approximately 2,000 square feet of space, stocks over 1,400 food items and has had annual sales in excess of $200 per square feet.

Number of Franchisees: 31 company-owned and 7 franchisee units in Pennsylvania, New Jersey, New York, Ohio and West Virginia.

In Business Since: 1983, franchise program began in 1986.

Equity Capital Needed: Company requires a franchisee to provide a minimum of 25 percent of the total investment.

Financial Assistance Available: A total investment of $105,000 (plus leasehold improvements) provides a complete "turnkey" package including a complete level of start-up support services, our custom fixtures package, training and signage, opening inventory, point-of-sale advertising, inventory control and re-ordering system and computerized pricing system. Franchisee must arrange its own financing.

Training Provided: Tidbit Alley requires franchisees to undergo extensive classroom and in-store training which may require 30 days or more before an individual is judged qualified to own, manage and effectively operate a Tid Bit Alley store.

Managerial Assistance Available: Tidbit Alley, Inc., will provide periodic field service visits, provide research and development services, competitive studies, purchasing and distribution services, training, marketing and advertising services and programs and other services deemed to be of interest to the company and its franchisees. As a convenience to its franchisees, Tidbit Alley, Inc., provides comprehensive buying, warehousing and distribution services.

Information Submitted: June 1987

T. J. CINNAMONS, LTD.
555 Plaza Center Building
800 West 47th Street
Kansas City, Missouri 64112
Avery Murray, Vice President/Franchise Sales & Marketing

Description of Operation: T. J. Cinnamons operates and franchises retail bakery operations. These bakeries specialize in cinnamon-related bakery products. Bakeries range from 700 square feet to 1,200 square feet and are located in major shopping malls and strip centers. Units are open 7 days per week, approximately 12-14 hours per day.

Number of Franchisees: 106 in 30 States and Canada

In Business Since: 1985

Equity Capital Needed: Varies by territory, but a minimum of $100,000-$150,000.

Financial Assistance Available: None.

Training Provided: Intensive 12-day mandatory training course is required for each person who will be responsible for the overall day-to-day management of a bakery. This course is held in Kansas City and is tuition-free. A T. J. Cinnamons trainer goes to help open the first two bakeries opening in each territory for a four-day period at each bakery.

Managerial Assistance Available: Assistance includes ongoing managerial, operations, and bakery consultation. Our Vice President/real estate assists with real estate contracts, lease consultation, etc. Complete manuals and specifications for opening and operating a bakery are provided as is assistance in using this material. Advertising and marketing guidance is provided. T. J. Cinnamons also conducts ongoing market research into new products and monitors quality standards of the franchise operations.

Information Submitted: May 1987

* **WHITE HEN PANTRY, INC.**
  660 Industrial Drive
  Elmhurst, Illinois 60126
  Arthur W. Haak, Franchising Manager

Description of Operation: A White Hen Pantry is a convenience food store of approximately 2,500 square feet. There is generally up-front parking for 10 to 15 cars. Stores are usually open 24 hours (some operate a lesser number of hours) 365 days a year. Product line includes a service deli, fresh bakery, fresh produce, and a wide variety of the most popular staples. White Hen Pantry stores are franchised to local residents who become owner/operators of this "family business."

Number of Franchisees: 320 in Illinois, Wisconsin, Indiana, Massachusetts and New Hampshire

In Business Since: 1965

Equity Capital Needed: $20,000-$25,000 (varies by location)

Financial Assistance Available: Total investment averages $41,300-$48,000. Investment includes approximately $24,000 merchandise; $5,000 security deposit; $3,000 supplies; $200 cash register fund; and $10,000 training and processing fee. A minimum investment of $20,000 is required. Financial assistance available.

Training Provided: Classroom and in-store training precede store opening. Follow-up training provided after taking over store. Detailed operation manuals are provided.

Managerial Assistance Available: This is a highly organized and comprehensive program. Other services provided include merchandising, accounting, promotions, advertising, and business insurance (group health and plate glass insurance are optional). Store counselor visits are regular and frequent.

Information Submitted: June 1987

WYOMING ALASKA COMPANY
Box 26
Woods Cross, Utah 84087
Reuel T. Call

Description of Operation: Trailside General Store, a convenience store with general merchandise, gasoline fast food service and inside seating.

Number of Franchisees: 4 in Utah, Arizona and Montana.

In Business Since: 1979

Equity Capital Needed: $300,000-$500,000 depending on land costs.

Financial Assistance Available: Franchisor may co-sign on approved sites. Company may furnish equipment which amounts to about one third of total investment.

Training Provided: Classroom and in store training. A required continuing program conducted with personnel and employees from some 20 company operated stores.

Managerial Assistance Available: Assistance in managing your people, serving the public, inventory control, keeping a clean store and clean yard. Also assistance on the computer in the small store.

Information Submitted: June 1987

ZARO'S AMERICA'S HOME BAKERY
138 Bruckner Boulevard
Bronx, New York 10454
Al Firstman, Franchise Director

Description of Operation: A full line bakery including hot and cold drinks, frozen yogurt, bagels with spreads. Bakery items are prepared in commissary and shipped frozen and baked off in front of consumer. Items include muffins, croissants, pastries, layer cakes, bread, rolls, bagels, etc.

Number of Franchisees: 6 plus 9 company-owned in New York, New Jersey and Connecticut.

In Business Since: 1935

Equity Capital Needed: $100,000 cash. Equity capital approximately $350,000 depending on size and condition of store.

Financial Assistance Available: Assistance offered by introduction to bank.

Training Provided: 4 to 5 weeks training in our plant, in company stores and an additional 2 weeks in franchisees store after opening. Training includes baking off procedures, merchandising, and operating a Zaro's Bakery.

Managerial Assistance Available: Continuous assistance by phone and by periodic visits by our operations manager. Merchandising aids are available for all occasions.

Information Submitted: May 1987

ZIP FOOD STORES, INC.
1200 West 15th Avenue
Gary, Indiana 46407
E. T. Eskilson, President

Description of Operation: Zip stores are approximately 2,500 square feet in size with adjacent parking. Depending on location, open 12-15 hours per day, 7 days per week. Zip provides the building and equipment on leases with renewed options to its franchise operator. Products are name brand merchandise and most stores have deli's and fast food accommodations.

Number of Franchisees: 12 in Indiana (Limited to Northwest Indiana

In Business Since: 1970

Equity Capital Needed: $12,000 minimum

Financial Assistance Available: Franchisee is required to purchase store inventory of approximately $30,000. Nine thousand dollars of the $12,000 minimum capital will be applied to inventory purchase. Franchisee can arrange own financing or Zip, Inc., will finance balance if credit references are acceptable.

Training Provided: 1 week to 10 days of full-time **training on site** with experienced supervisor to acquaint operator and his personnel with policy's and procedures.

Managerial Assistance Available: Continuous management services provided. All bookkeeping, inventory control, payroll and relted services provided at central office for all stores. Monthly profit and loss statements provided on request or suggestion of franchisor.

Information Submitted: May 1987

FOODS—ICE CREAM/YOGURT/CANDY/ POPCORN/BEVERAGES

* **BASKIN-ROBBINS, INC.**
31 Baskin-Robbins Place
Glendale, California 91201
Jim Earnhardt, Vice President of Operations

Description of Operation: High quality, multi-flavored, hand dipped retail ice cream store. Franchisor normally selects site, negotiates a lease, the store is completely equipped, stocked and brought to a point where it is ready to open. This complete store is then sold to a qualified individual under a franchise after intensive training.

Number of Franchisees: Over 3,000 stores in 895 cities throughout the United States, Canada, Japan and Europe.

In Business Since: 1945

Equity Capital Needed: Approximately $50,000 plus depending on retail location.

Financial Assistance Available: Yes

Training Provided: A complete training program is provided plus on-the-job training in operating store under the guidance of experienced supervisors.

Managerial Assistance Available: Continuous merchandising program, accounting procedures, business counsel, and insurance program (source optional).

Information Submitted: July 1987

* **BEN & JERRY'S HOMEMADE INC.**
Box 240, Route 100
Waterbury, Vermont 05676
James A. Rowe, Director of Retail Operations

Description of Operation: Ben & Jerry's offers a super premium ice cream parlor and scoop shoe, featuring 34 flavors, sundaes, fountain sodas, and fresh squeezed juices.

Number of Franchisees: 30 in 8 States

In Business Since: 1978

Equity Capital Needed: $50,000

Financial Assistance Available: None

Training Provided: Extensive, 1 week, mandatory training course scheduled for manager/franchisees. Bookkeeping and office procedures, hands-on operation/waiting on customers, quality and portion control.

Managerial Assistance Available: On-site pre-opening assistance by field personnel for store set up, hiring and employee training. Refresher training by field representative is available upon request.

*BRESLER'S 33 FLAVORS, INC.
999 East Touhy Avenue, Suite 333
Des Plaines, Illinois 60018
Howard Marks, Director of Franchising

Description of Operation: Multi-flavor specialty ice cream shops—featuring ice cream cones, hand-packed ice cream, soft serve yogurt, complete soda fountain and made-to-order ice cream specialty items.

Number of Franchisees: Approximately 350 in 32 States

In Business Since: 1962

Equity Capital Needed: Approximately $40,000.

Financial Assistance Available: A present total investment of approximately $90,000 to $105,000 required plus working capital of which approximately 50 percent is in cash. Franchisee may obtain own financing, or at his request franchisor will attempt to obtain third party financing for qualified applicant.

Training Provided: Classroom and in-store training comprising a minimum of 3 weeks duration.

Managerial Assistance Available: Franchisor assists franchisee in all aspects of shop operation, record keeping, advertising, and promotion and selling techniques. Manuals of operations and counseling are provided. Area licensees and home office field personnel are available to visit stores regularly.

Information Submitted: May 1987

*BRIGHAM'S
30 Mill Street
Arlington, Massachusetts 02174
Bernie Cullen, Director of Operations

Desciption of Operation: Food service, ice cream parlours and restaurants.

Number of Franchisees: 56 in Massachusetts

In Business Since: 1914

Equity Capital Needed: Between $5,000-$20,000

Financial Assistance Available: Partial financing is available through Brigham's.

Training Provided: Approximately 3 to 6 weeks.

Managerial Assistance Available: Area managers (consistent and ongoing assistance), chain-wide advertising, accounting service (full accounting and payroll services), business insurance, and paid training program.

Information Submitted: July 1987

THE CALIFORNIA YOGURT COMPANY
2401 Vista Way
Suite E
Oceanside, California 92054
Jim Swickard, Vice President

Descripton of Operation: The California Yogurt Co., is now offering its sparkling Hi-Tech look stores as a franchise. The stores offer 10 flavors of fresh frozen yogurt daily, 30 toppings and a variety of specialty yogurt items.

Number of Franchisees: 7 company-owned stores in California and 8 franchise stores plus 1 in Norway.

In Business Since: 1982

Equity Capital Needed: $60,000-$75,000.

Financial Assistance Available: Franchisor will assist the franchisee in applying for financial assistance. The company does not make direct loans to the franchisee.

Training Provided: Complete training is provided at the franchisor's training school. The training includes all phases of the stores operation, including equipment maintenance, bookkeeping, inventory control, employee management, and customer relations and an additional 5 day training will be provided in the franchisee's store prior to opening.

Managerial Assistance Available: The California Yogurt Co., franchisees are provided with a confidential operations manual which provides detailed information to all aspects of th CYC system. Site selection, equipment purchase and grand opening activities are also provided by the franchisor.

Information Submitted: May 1987

CARBERRY'S HOMEMADE ICE CREAM FRANCHISE SYSTEMS, INC.
42 Rose Street
Merritt Island, Florida 32953
Stephen R. Carberry

Description of Operation: Carberry's Homemade Ice Cream Parlours offer a complete range of ice cream operation from manufacturing to the sale. Carberry's caters to children of all ages. Birthday parties and field trip showing children how Carberry's makes ice cream are our specialties. Master franchise territories available throughout the United States.

Number of Franchisees: 7 in Florida

In Business Since: 1980

Equity Capital Needed: $75,000-$95,000

Financial Assistance Available: None

Training Provided: 5 days of training at Carberry's training facility in Merritt Island, Florida. 2-5 days training at franchisee's new location.

Managerial Assistance Available: Sales management, cost control, training manual provided. Field supervisors make periodic in store inspections and assist in any way they can.

Information Submitted: May 1987

CARTER'S NUTS, INC.
215 West 34th Street
New York, New York 10001
Robert Rogal, Marketing Director

Description of Operation: Retail nut outlets—containing a full variety of all the world's nuts and dried fruits— where all nuts are freshly roasted every day on the premises, freshly made pop-corn, potato chips, plantain chips, freshly roasted coffee and tea. . .and a full line of fresh-exotic fruits. Mobile truck units are also available.

Number of Franchisees: 3 in New York

In Business Since: 1976

Equity Capital Needed: $35,000

Financial Assistance Available: 50 percent of equipment for stores. 90 percent for mobile truck units.

Training Provided: 100 page operations manual is provided by franchisor to franchisee and an intensive in-store work program of 2 weeks is required. Two weeks assistance is provided upon opening of franchisee's store.

Managerial Assistance Available: Managerial assistance in purchasing and hiring.

Information Submitted: June 1987

*CARVEL CORPORATION
201 Saw Mill River Road
Yonkers, New York 10701

Description of Operation: Retail ice cream shops, featuring both hard and soft ice cream, manufactured by the store owner in the shop for on and off premises consumption. Specializing in full-line of ice cream (36 flavors, 60 varieties) for all occasions. Also cakes and dessert items. Locations include free standing, shopping center, and inner city types.

Number of Franchisees: Over 800 stores operating in 18 States (not including international).

In Business Since: Carvel franchising ice cream stores since 1948. In business since 1934.

Equity Capital Needed: Approximately $60,000-$70,000.

Financial Assistance Available: Yes

Training Provided: 19 day training period covering all facets of store operation and complete standard operating procedure manual, plus assistance in opening store.

Managerial Assistance Available: Continuous in-field counseling covering merchandising, quality control, advertising, promotion, and annual area educational seminars.

Information Submitted: May 1987

CHIPWICH A LA CARTE OF CALIFORNIA
232 Anacapa Street
Santa Barbara, California 93101
Paul D. Waterman, Executive Vice President

Description of Operation: Sales of ice cream novelties from portable ice cream carts.

Number of Franchisees: 2 in California

In Business Since: 1983

Equity Capital Needed: $5,000 minimum

Financial Assistance Available: None

Training Provided: Full training for 2 days.

Managerial Assistance Available: Complete assistance to reform to highest standards.

Information Submitted: July 1987

CREATIVE CORN COMPANY
45-35 39th Street
Long Island City, New York 11104
Dave Lowe, Vice President
Tim Lowe, Vice President

Description of Operation: A New York based gourmet popcorn operation currently offering 18 different flavors of popcorn complimented by a complete line of popcorn related products such as gift tins, home popping kits and specialty seasonings.

Number of Franchisees: 2

In Business Since: 1984

Equity Capital Needed: $50,000-$68,500

Financial Assistance Available: None

Training Provided: A 1 week training program detailing all aspects of running a Creative Corn Company retail outlet. In addition, franchisees can expect continued update training services and support programs.

Managerial Assistance Available: As part of its franchised package Creative Corn will provide assistance with site selection, distribution, inventory control, equipment usage, marketing, store layout and design. Creative Corn Company will also provide a complete operations manual detialing policies and procedures related to running a successful Creative Corn Company retail outlet.

Information Submitted: August 1987

CUSTOM LEASING CO.
233 Diagonal Street
P.O. Box 323
Galenda, Illinois 61036
Norval L. Auman, General Manager

Description of Operation: Ice cream equipment to product high quality, old fashioned ice cream, sherberts, custards, frozen yogurt, old style root beer barrels to dispense old fashion keg style root beer. Displays of hrd candies. Popcorn machine and limited sandwich menu along with some deli items. Old fashioned soda fountain with old "turn of the century ice cream store furnishings."

Number of Franchisees: 17 in Iowa, Illinois and Wisconsin. Only Mid-West inquiries desired.

In Business Since: 1941

Equity Capital Needed: Package price approximately $45,000 depending on amount of used equipment available and if all the various departments are made part of the operation, usually 50 percent bank financing available.

Financial Assistance Available: None. Equipment lease program available.

Training Provided: Full on-the-job training program provided over 2 week period. Follow-up dadvisory letters and bulletins for food and beverage operation. Continual management assistance is provided a long with training for purchasing portion control, cost accounting, manu pricing, bookkeeping and advertising.

Managerial Assistance Available: Continual management assistance and educational programs always available.

Information Submitted: May 1987

DAVIE'S ICE CREAM SHOPPES, INC.
7000 Palmetto Park Road
Boca Raton, Florida 33433
Tom Floyd, President

Description of Operation: The Davie's Ice Cream Shoppe is a traditional ice cream parlour with a wholesome, family orientation and is the retail outlet for Davie's Ice Cream—a premium-quality ice cream manufactured at the Davie's Creamery in Winter Haven, Florida. Each shop is approximately 1,800 square feet and is equipped for counter service and table service. In addition to cones and hand-packed take-home containers, the Davie's menu includes about 75 sundaes and ice cream-related items. Old-fashioned style candies and homemade fudge are also sold. The typical shop is open 10 or 11 hours a day, 7 days a week.

Number of Franchisees: 3 plus 1 company-owned shops in Florida

In Business Since: 1983

Equity Capital Needed: $35,000-$50,000

Financial Assistance Available: Estimated cost to establish a Davie's Ice Cream Shoppe is between $85,000 and $100,000 depending on location, lease arrangements, size of shop etc. (this cost includes the $18,500 franchise fee). The franchisee assumes responsibility for arranging outside financing.

Training Provided: An intensive, 2 week training program for franchisees and their key personnel is provided prior to opening. In addition, training seminars are conducted from time to time to facilitate profitability of the franchise and to ensure quality of product and service to the customer.

Managerial Assistance Available: Davie's provides site selection assistance as well as standard specifications, plans and descriptions for store layout, furnishings, decor, equipment and other items required prior to opening. Assistance is also provided in locating suppliers for equipment and other items. In addition, Davie's provides an operations manual, procedures, policies and other know-how relating to the operation of a Davie's Ice Cream Shoppe as well as ongoing advice and consultation with staff and officers. Assistance is available to the franchisee in planning grand openings, special promotions and local advertising, and an advertising co-op program has been developed. Also available to the franchisee is an accounting package that eliminates the drudgery associated with bookkeeping but allows him virtually total freedom in running his own business.

Information Submitted: July 1987

DIPPER DAN ICE CREAM SHOPPES & SWEET SHOPPES
DIPPER DAN, INTERNATIONAL, INC.
P.O. Box 47068
St. Petersburg, Florida 33743
Leo L. LaBonte, Executive Vice President

Description of Operation: 5 unique concepts each focusing it's marketing into retailing 32 delicious ice cream flavors from cones to mile-high sundaes. In addition to ice cream, our "basic" unit features a food program, cookies and candy. The "basic plus" shoppe also features gorumet popcorn and fudge, both made on premise. There are two "upscale" type shopes, one which features a secondary line into hand-cut doughnuts and the other a full bakery operation, truely a total sweet shoppe. Ne for 1987, a unique concept whereby ice cream is merchandised along with a full muffin program. Space requirements vary between 900 to 1,800 sq. ft., depending on concept.

Number of Franchisees: Over 400 in 13 States, Japan, and Taiwan.

In Business Since: 1955, franchising 1963

Equity Capital Needed: Approximately $70,000 to $100,000, depending on concept and geographic area.

Financial Assistance Available: None

Training Provided: A complete and comprehensive program on every facet of shoppe operations conducted at location.

Managerial Assistance Available: The shoppe owner is continuously assisted in all phases of merchandising and shoppe operations. Special services rendered to assisting lease negotiations, customized mechanical blueprints provided.

Information Submitted: May 1987

* **DOUBLE RAINBOW FRANCHISES, INC.**
275 South Van Ness Avenue
San Francisco, California 94103
Stephen Garfink, President or
Nancy Magdaleno, Vice President of Marketing

Description of Operation: Double Rainbow Gourmet Ice Cream has been voted Best in the USA over 75 brands in the Great American Lick Off. The complete line of all natural super premium ice creams are displayed in a unique dessert cafe concept featuring award-winning architecture. An extensive assortment of gourmet cakes, pastries, coffees are also sold.

Number of Franchisees: 20 operating 23 franchises in California and Oregon (in addition to six company-owned parlors).

In Business Since: 1976, in franchising since 1983.

Equity Capital Needed: Total investment for a typical dessert cafe is $100,000-$150,000. Equity required depends on franchisee's financial strength.

Financial Assistance Available: Franchisor assists in guiding franchisees to third party financing sources.

Training Provided: 2 week training program for owner-operators begins in corporate headquarters in San Francisco. Training includes all phases of the parlor's operation—inventory control, customer relations, personnel training, equipment maintenance. The program continues with "hands-on" experience in an established parlor followed by special support during the franchise opening week.

Managerial Assistance Available: Double Rainbow, backed by 10 years' experience operating its own ice cream parlors, offers the franchisee practical advice and support through a continuous program of management assistance. The program includes merchandising and promotion techniques, and computerized management control systems. A complete operations manual is provided. In addition to the above, the franchisor's staff will assist and advise the franchisee in securing a suitable location, negotiating the lease, and shopping for the equipment and supplies. Customized architectural blue-prints are provided.

Information Submitted: May 1987

EMACK AND BOLIO'S ICE CREAM AND ICE CREAM CAKES FOR THE CONNOISSEUR
9 Babcock Street
Brookline, Massachusetts 02146
Richard Rubino, President

Description of Operation: Emack and Bilio's Ice Cream for the Connoisseur is a gourmet ice cream company. Ice Cream and related products are manufactured by the franchisor and sold retail by the franchisee. The guiding principal behind this company is to produce super premium ice cream with exotic flavors. Flavor selections are changed on a weekly basis. Over 200 recipes for flavors are made throughout the year using seasonal ingredients. The ice cream is served in hand rolled gourmet cones and flavored cones as well as cups, sundaes, etc. Ice cream cakes are also a profitable item for shop owners.

Number of Franchisees: 20 in Massachusetts, Rhode Island, New Jersey, South Carolina, Florida and Virginia, plus 5 company-owned-stores.

In Business Since: 1975

Equity Capital Needed: The total initial investment for the shops located in the United States is approximately $75,000—$125,000. The total initial investment fr shops located out of the country would be in excess of $150,000, not including territorial fees.

Financial Assistance Available: None

Training Provided: An intensive 2 week training program is scheduled for all new franchisees and their personnel at company training stores.

Managerial Assistance Available: Emack and Bolio's provides continual operational support for the life of the franchise.

Information Submitted: May 1987

ERNIE'S WINE & LIQUOR CORP.
305 Littlefield Avenue
South San Francisco, California 94080
James P. Cancilla, Franchise Operations Director

Description of Operation: Retail liquor, beer and wine stores.

Number of Franchisees: 40 in California (only)

In Business Since: 1938

Equity Capital Needed: $120,000

Financial Assistance Available: None

Training Provided: A complete program is provided which includes pre-opening training and on-the-job training.

Managerial Assistance Available: Limited, see training provided.

Information Submitted: May 1987

FOREMOST SALES PROMOTIONS, INC.
5252 North Broadway
Chicago, Illinois 60640

Description of Operation: Foremost is a marketing and consulting service for (1) experienced retail liquor store owners already in business; (2) inexperienced retail liquor store owners who purchase existing stores; and (3) both experienced and inexperienced people who open new retail liquor stores. The service includes but is not limited to information on operating a successful retail package liquor store such as site selection, store layout, inventory control, accounting methods, advertisig, erchandising, sales promotion and liquor by wire service. Each store opeates within the laws of the state in which it does business.

Number of Franchisees: Over 105 in Illinois and Florida. More than 2,000 retail stores affiliated through Foremost Liquor by Wire Network and foremost National Network of Independent Liquor Dealers.

In Business Since: 1949

Equity Capital Needed: Approximately $100,000 to $150,000.

Financial Assistance Available: Available to qualified people.

Training Provided: See Managerial Assistance

Managerial Assistance Available: As package liquor store consultants, full scale assistance is available pertaining to all the information needed to operate a successful package liquor store.

Information Submitted: May 1987

FROSTY FACTORY INTERNATIONAL, INC.
1600 Furman
Ruston, Louisiana 71270
Dolph Williams, President

Description of Operation: The franchise offered consists of the right to sell frozen alcoholic and nonalcoholic beverages in a retail store using recipes and machines provided by franchisor in an approved location under the proprietary mark Frosty Factory.

Number of Franchisees: 4 in Louisiana

In Business Since: 1985

Equity Capital Needed: $150,000 minimum.

Financial Assistance Available: Part of the franchise fee may be financed for a year period. The remaining amount must be provided by franchisee or it may be financed by an outside source.

Training Provided: A 1 week training period is provided by franchisor at a company-owned store. Store opening training is provided by franchisor at franchisee's outlet.

Managerial Assistance Available: As a service, we offer help with detailed drawings, specifications and with site location. We also provide training programs and operational assistance which includes hi-tech electronic cash registers, interfaced with an in-house micro-computer. By using these required components, the owner is provided with management reports, such as daily, weekly, and monthly sales analysis reports, labor productivity reports and inventory variance reports.

Information Submitted: July 1987

FRUSEN GLADSE FRANCHISE, INC.
424 East John Street
Lindenhurst, New York 11757
Director of Franchise Operations

Description of Operation: Ice cream manufacturer and franchisor of ice cream stores.

Number of Franchisees: 57 in 17 States

In Business Since: 1981

Equity Capital Needed: $50,000

Financial Assistance Available: None

Training Provided: Intensive training in all phases of ice cream store operations.

Managerial Assistance Available: Managerial assistance is provided in all areas of store operations.

Information Submitted: July 1987

THE FUDGE CO.
103 Belvedere Avenue
Charlevoix, Michigan 49720
R. L. Hoffman, President
Dennis Crain, Vice President, General Manager

Description of Operation: The Fudge Co., is a retail fudge store. an important part of the operation is cooking in copper kettles, creaming (forming) done on large marble slabs. Only natural ingredients are used and combined with the showmenship of making fudge provides a unique, enjoyable and profitable retail operation. Eahc store requires 400 to 600 square feet. Fudge Co., provides all equipment, franchisee leases or purchases its own building, with guidance from the Fudge Co. ALso includes cookie franchise. Baking and selling fresh chocolate chunk and a variety of six other cookies. Either franchise can be purchased separately.

Number of Franchisees: 7 in Arizona, Alaska, Texas, and Virgin Islands, plus 3 company-owned stores.

In Business Since: 1978, franchising since 1982

Equity Capital Needed: Resort area includes all equipment, training, 3 month starting inventory, cost—$35,000 to $42,000. Regional mall store—equipment, training, 3 month inventory, cost—$75,000 to $85,000.

Financial Assistance Available: None, franchise fee $12,500.

Training Provided: Franchisor trains and educates franchisees 2 to 3 weeks in its home office in Dallas, Texas. Upon opening of franchisee's store, franchisor's general manager supervises and trains personnel for 7 to 14 days.

Managerial Assistance Available: Fudge Co., provides managerial service including inventory control, advertising and assistance for day to day operations during the life of the franchise. Franchisor provdes all necessary forms and documents for daily operation. Provides information regarding new products and how to prepare and merchandise said products. franchisor provides personnel to visit franchisee's outlet to assistin volving problems of cooking and day to day operations.

Information Submitted: May 1987

GASTON'S, INC.
1950 Innes Street
San Francisco, California 94124
Douglas D. Gaston, President

Description of Operation: Gaston's Ice Cream of San Francisco offers a wide selection of ice cream delicacies and fountain items for take out. There are over 100 flavors of ice cream all developed by its founder Doug Gaston. The ice cream is made fresh daily on the premises.

Number of Franchisees: 30 in California and 2 in Indonesia, 1 in Singapore

In Business Since: 1976

Equity Capital Needed: Approximately $120,000 depending on location and type of store.

Financial Assistance Available: The Company will assist the franchisee in applying for financing. The company will not make direct loans to franchisee.

Training Provided: Gaston's training program will consist of a 3 week training period. The franchisee will be trained in manufacturing, preparing all ice cream delicacies and fountain items, in accounting, inventory control, store management, employee management, customer relations, and other additional areas.

Managerial Assistance Available: Gaston's franchisees are given a confidential manual which gives in detail the complete opeations of a Gaston's Ice Cream Shop. Gaston's is available at all times to the franchisee to offer assistance in all problems the franchisee may have.

Information Submitted: May 1987

J. L. FRANKLIN & CO.
dba GELATO AMARE
11504 Hyde Place
Raleigh, North Carolina 27614
John L. Franklin, President

Description of Operation: Gelato Amare is a super-premium ice cream shop which features Italian style homemade ice cream and ices and homemade ice cream cones.

Number of Franchisees: 2 including 2 company-owned in North Carolina.

In Business Since: 1983

Equity Capital Needed: $25,000-$30,000 of total $80,000-$100,000 investment

Financial Assistance Available: Total assistance in preparation of business presentations to banks, lending institutions, etc.

Training Provided: 2-3 weeks intensive training for owners and all management in company-owned retail store. Continuing training in franchisee store.

Managerial Assistance Available: Full assistance is provided in site selection, lending institution presentations, management training, store design, equipment selection, store opening and personnel and administrative procedures. Continuing assistance includes advertising, public relations, market research and new product development. A 24-hour-a-day telephone hotline is available to answer questions as they arise.

Information Submitted: June 1987

* GELATO CLASSICO FRANCHISING, INC.
369 Pine Street, Suite 900
San Francisco, California 94104
Jeanne Heffernan, Vice President

Description of Operation: Gelato Classico Italian ice cream manufactures complete line of Italian ice cream, sorbetto, and yogurt and supplies these products to its franchisees who retail to the public. Franchisees are part of nationwide program for franchised shops.

Number of Franchisees: 30 franchise locations plus 4 company-owned stores in 9 States

In Business Since: 1976

Equity Capital Needed: $50,000 per shop

Financial Assistance Available: No financial assistance provided by franchisor.

Training Provided: Intensive 1 week program prior to opening, and additional training in franchisees shop during first 3 days at opening. Complete operations manual also provided.

Managerial Assistance Available: In addition to above, franchisor visits at least 2 times per year to provide in shop assistance. Other assistance provided on as needed basis.

Information Submitted: May 1987

GORIN'S HOMEMADE ICE CREAM AND SANDWICHES
158 Oak Street
Avondale Estates, Georgia 30002
Robert Solomon, President

Description of Operation: Upscale homemade ice cream and sandwich shop featuring gourmet ice cream and a wide selection of grilled deli sandwiches.

Number of Franchisees: 24 in Georgia, North Carolina and Alabama.

In Business Since: 1981

Equity Capital Needed: $35,000-$50,000, total investment of $100,000-$150,000.

Financial Assistance Available: None

Training Provided: 3-4 weeks of comprehensive training in all aspects of operation for three management personnel per store to be opened.

Managerial Assistance Available: Site selection, equipment lists, preliminary drawings on store, inventory lists and specifications, ongoing supervision for the operation of the business.

Information Submitted: July 1987

THE GREAT MIDWESTERN ICE CREAM CO.
209 North 16th Street
P. O. Box 1717
Fairfield, Iowa 52556
Jamie Robert Vollmer, Director Franchise
Development

Description of Operation: Great Midwestern Ice Cream Company Stores are premium desserts shops featuring 32 flavors of ice cream, fresh croissants, deluxe coffees, homemade soups and sandwiches. Great Midwestern Ice Cream, voted the Best Ice Cream in America by People Magazine, is a super premium, 16 percent butterfat product using all natural ingredients. The stores are approximately 2,000 square feet, seat 40-50 people in an upscale environment of warm, beautiful colors, arches, trellis-work and plants. Ice Cream represents 50 percent of annual sales, pastries 20 percent, and soup and sandwich 30 percent. This is not a restaurant—there is no grill in the store. The simple soups are made from scratch; the sandwiches are light, deli-style and made to order. The ice cream, ice cream novelties and sundae toppings and frozen products are made at the franchisor factory and delivered as ordered. Area franchise development is encouraged.

Number of Franchisees: 9 in Iowa, Nebraska, Missouri, Kansas and Illinois.

In Business Since: 1979

Financial Assistance Available: Great Midwestern has been given the authority by a bank to qualify applicants for fiancial assistance. This program is available only to those who, with aggressive Great Midwestern participation, have been unable to secure financing through a lending institution in their market area. Representatives from Great Midwestern will consult with the applicant and visit local bankers and SBA officials.

Training Provided: 4 weeks total training (w weeks in the company store in Iowa City, Iowa; 2 weeks in the franchisee's store prior to grand opening). Both theoretical and practical training in all areas of franchise store operation including: food preparation; customer service and relations; employee relations and scheduling; financial management and control; product merchandising; sales training; inventory control and equipment maintenance. The operation manual is thorough, organized and highly usable as a ready reference for management.

Managerial Assistance Available: Great Midwestern has franchise support staff that includes retailing and merchandising experts, a promotions and advertising department, financial advisors and cash flow managers, and an in-house product research and development department. The support staff is cooperative and active. At this time a franchisor representative visits each store an average of 1 day every 3 weeks. All members of the support staff including all officers of the company are always available to assist the franchisees in their development.

Information Submitted: July 1987

THE HARDIN GROUP, INC.
325 East Hillcrest
Suite 130
Thousand Oaks, California 91360
Mr. Doug Frank, Director of Franchising

Description of Operation: Penguin's Frozen Yogurt master franchisor. Penguin's sells frozen yogurt. It is a quick serve, convenience restaurant with 36 different toppings and 30 flavors of yogurt served in a clean, black and white, comtemporary environment.

Number of Franchisees: 97 in 7 states

In Business Since: 1983, franchising 1984

Equity Capital Needed: An ability to finance an investment of $180,000-$200,000 or a minimum net worth of about $350,000 is required.

Financial Assistance Available: We do not provide financial assistance for any part of the store costs.

Training Provided: A 6 week program consisting of: a 4 week training in a designated training center; a 5 day classroom program; 1 week spent in 2 or 3 stores with the chains most successful managers.

Managerial Assistance Available: Continuous managerial and technical assistance when needed.

Information Submitted: August 1987

*HEIDI'S FROGEN YOZURT SHOPPES, INC.
24422 Avenida De La Carlota
Suite 290
Laguna Hills, California 92653
Brian L. Pallas, Vice President

Description of Operation: All Heidi's are located in high traffic quality centers and malls. The menu selection and unique store design make it possible to offer a limitless choice of flavors **daily**. All products are developed from low-fat, or non-fat, low-calorie, soft serve frozen yogurt. All shoppes are custom-designed with ceramic tile, oak, custom wallpaper, and premium quality equipment.

Number of Franchisees: 53 in California and Nevada plus 7 company-owned.

In Business Since: 1982

Equity Capital Needed: $150,000-$180,000 per shoppe.

Financial Assistance Available: Approximately $150,000 is necessary to open a Heidi's Frogen Yozurt Shoppe franchise. This pays for equipment, leasehold improvements, inventory, franchise costs, and all permits. Franchisor does not offer direct financing however, has excellent bank and leasing company referrals to obtain the required financing.

Training Provided: A comprehensive, hands-on training course is provided for owners and managers, and the franchisee also receives training guides and manuals for the shopp's employees. 1 week of training is spent in a corporate training facility, and for your second week for trainers come to you to assist you in your first week of business.

Managerial Assistance Available: The franchisor provides technical assistance with all equipment placed in the field. The staff of the franchisor will be providing a substantial amount of follow-up management support and quality control service to the franchisee. The franchisee is also endorsed by Heidi A. Miller, President, and Co-Founder of the franchise, fashion model, actress, and the national bodybuilding champion.

Information Submitted: May 1987

*I CAN'T BELIEVE IT'S YOGURT
5005 LBJ Freeway
Suite 1650
Dallas, Texas 75244

Description of Operation: Our business is serving soft-serv frozen yogurt in cones, sundaes, parfaits and shakes. Our ICBIY "Softie" ® frozen yogurt is a special recipe we manufacture ourselves to ensure the highest of qualify and innovation.

Number of Franchisees: 119 franchise locations, 8 company-owned locations.

In Business Since: 1977

Equity Capital Needed: Total investment approximately $135,000. Equity capital varies due to location and franchisee financial strength.

Financial Assistance Available: Not available at this time.

Training Provided: Shortly before the opening of a franchise store, a 10 day training school will be conducted. A maximum of 2 people representing each franchise store can attend. This school will cover our success formula, accounting and bookkeeping procedures, operations, staffing, cost control, and the basics of management.

Managerial Assistance Available: Our company has an "ICBIY Franchise Consultants" who is a resource person for trouble shooting in all areas of store operation and is readily available for managerial and technical assistance. Such assistance and supervision will be provided in the following ways; mail, phone contacts, visits, conferences, newsletters, clinics and seminars. These methods will remain in affect for the duration of the business partnership between ICBIY and its franchise owners.

Information Submitted: May 1987

ICE CREAM CHURN, INC.
P. O. Box 759
Byron, Georgia 31008
Lee Anderson, Vice President

Description of Operation: "Ice Cream Churn" establishes an ice cream parlour with 28 flavors of dip ice cream, milk shakes, sundaes and banana splits in a current operating business such as convenience stores, deli's, and bakeries. A unit for malls and a new 14'x36' modular unit designed for smaller markets and metropolitan markets are also available.

Number of Franchisees: 901 locations in 35 States

In Business Since: 1978—Franchising since 1981

Equity Capital Needed: (1) Individual franchises for existing locations $3,500-$5,000, (2) Modular concept franchises $24,000-$30,000, and (3) Regional franchises available for Alaska, Hawaii and foreign countries $20,000-$100,000.

Financial Assistance Available: Available for all phases of operation by franchisor.

Training Provided: Complete training of all regional agents who are responsible for the franchise's individual stores training. An agent works with locations on regular visits.

Managerial Assistance Available: Ice Cream Churn furnishes each franchisee with all training, equipment, inside and outside signs, promotions and incentives programs for managers.

Information Submitted: June 1987

I LOVE YOGURT CORP.
12770 Coit Road
Suite 415A
Dallas, Texas 75251
David L. King, Executive Vice President

Description Operation: Frozen yogurt and sandwich shoppes.

Number of Franchisees: 7 in Kansas and Texas

In Business Since: 1980

Equity Capital Needed: $84,000-$126,000

Financial Assistance Available: None

Training Provided: 1 week intensive training at home office and 1 week in-store training at time of opening.

Managerial Assistance Available: Management and operational assistance provided to all franchisees. Computerized accounting system for store evaluation and complete simplified advertising and marketing program.

Information Submitted: May 1987

ISLAND SNOW HAWAII
P. O. Box 364
Kailua, Hawaii 96734
James J. Kodama, President
Lisa M. Sinai, Vice President

Description of Operation: Hawaiian themed dessert shave ice, gourmet ice cream, and yogurt.

Number of Franchisees: 25 in Hawaii, California, Arizona, Nevada, Canada and Australia

In Business Since: 1981

Equity Capital Needed: $50,000-$100,000

Financial Assistance Available: None

Training Provided: The training covers operation and maintenance of the shave ice machine, preparation of the syrup where applicable, inventory control and storage, customer service, sanitation and pest control, employee hygiene, computerized accounting system, procedures, marketing and other miscellaneous subjects pertinent to the operation of an Island Snow Hawaii shop. Generally, the training time covers approximately 20 hours, but the training time may vary depending on the trainee's ability to master the subjects being taught.

Managerial Assistance Available: Ongoing

Information Submitted: May 1987

●J. HIGBY'S YOGURT TREAT SHOPPES
1111 Howe Avenue
Suite 305
Sacramento, California 95825
Mark Moyers, Vice President

Description of Operation: Over 60 flavors of fresh frozen yogurt. Also serve ice cream and a variety of fresh baked cookies, "walk-away sundaes," yogurt fruit salads, hot "Higgy Dogs," drinks and other related items.

Number of Franchisees: 53 with 102 under construction in U.S. and 11 in Japan. Seeking area or regional development in all of the United States.

In Business Since: 1983

Equity Capital Needed: Varies as to location and franchisee.

Financial Assistance Available: Franchisor will assist with third party financing.

Training Provided: A minimum of 2 weeks at the corporate training center and franchisee's store.

Managerial Assistance Available: Management and operational assistance provided to all franchisees. Computerized accounting system for store evaluation and complete simplified advertising and marketing program.

Information Submitted: May 1987

KARA SIGNATURE CHOCOLATES
A-5 University Mall
Orem, Utah 84058

Description of Operation: Kara franchises produce, on their premises, candies and confections using fresh ingredients, no perservatives and special Kara flavorings. All candies and chocolates are sold fresh; retail and wholesale.

Number of Franchisees: 1 company-owned shop, 10 franchised shops.

In Business Since: 1978

Equity Capital Needed: $25,000 franchise fee. Estimated minimum investment required is $35,000 to 4125,000.

Financial Assistance Available: Yes, some on both franchise fee and equipment.

Training Provided: Intensive 5 day training session with operational and classroom instruction covering operations, promotion and control of a franchise. Full operating manual provided, covering manufacture, wholesale and retail sales.

Managerial Assistance Available: Comprehensive operations support after opening and continuing indefinitely.

Information Submitted: July 1987

KARMELKORN SHOPPES, INC.
P. O. Box 35286
Minneapolis, Minnesota 55435
John Hydwke, Vice President

Description of Operation: Karmelkorn Shoppes make and sell Karmelkorn popcorn candy, popcorn, popcorn confections, a variety of kitchen style candies and related snack food items. New Shoppes range in size from 400 to 650 square feet and are mostly located in major shopping centers. Business hours are those established by the shopping center with minor variations. In most cases, the company accepts the primary lease liability and sublets to the owner-operator.

Number of Franchisees: 230 in 44 States

In Business Since: The original Karmelkorn Shoppe was established in 1929

Equity Capital Needed: $75,000 to when standard financing is available.

Financial Assistance Available: The total investment is in a Karmelkorn franchised Shoppe varies according to construction costs. Most Shoppes in 1986 ranged $90,000 to $120,000. They company assists franchisee in applying for his original financing upon request.

Training Provided: A national training center at the Minneapolis office of Karmelkorn Shoppes, Inc., is built as a model Karmelkorn Shoppe to stimulate working conditions during training. The 5 day curriculum is designed for new and existing franchisees, as well as their Shoppe managers and key employees. Grand opening assistance is provided by a company representative.

Managerial Assistance Available: The franchisee receives and is instructed in the use of an operating manual, which is supplemented by business newsletters, that provide updates and operational information. Management and supervisory services are provided for the life of the franchise, and include periodic supervision by training supervisors; annual conference with business, product and advisory seminars; assistance in obtaining sources of supply and equipment, promotional material, and assistance in a planning promotion programs.

Information Submitted: May 1987

●KILWINS CHOCOLATES FRANCHISE
200 Division Road
Petoskey, Michigan 49770
Wayne Rose, President

Description of Operation: Franchise Kilwins Chocolate Shoppes. These stores sell Kilwins handmade chocolates. Fudge and optional ice cream.

Number of Franchisees: 22 in Michigan, Indiana, Ohio, Florida, Wisconsin and North Carolina.

In Business Since: 1981

Equity Capital Needed: $20,000 to $100,000 for turnkey operation.

Financial Assistance Available: $20,000 franchise fee plus initial investment capital of $20,000 to $50,000. Estimates do not include cost of real property or improvements to same. Financing not available from franchise company.

Training Provided: The training program is designed to last 10 business days and will cover all of the basic aspects of the retail candy business including how the candy is manufactured, how it is packaged and sales techniques along with other techniques for opeating the franchisee's business.

Managerial Assistance Available: Regular reports of improvements in business methods developed by franchisor and other franchisees, the services of franchisor's advertising department to assist franchisee in planning local advertising and on franchisee's request, the personal assistance and counsel of a qualified representative of franchisor.

Information Submitted: May 1987

*LARRY'S OLDE FASHIONED ICE CREAM PARLOURS, INC.
14550 McCormick Street
Tampa, Florida 33625
Larry F. Kirian, President

Description of Operation: Larry's Olde Fashioned Ice Cream Parlours serve only the award-winning Larry's Ice Cream. Parlours emit an atmosphere of "yesteryear" offering customers homemade ice cream in cones, sundaes, shakes and malteds, sodas, and cakes and pies. Larry's has received the Award of Excellence from the National Ice Cream Retailers Association, Larry's was named Best Chocolate Ice Cream at the Fountainbleau Chocolate Festival, and is featured in the book, The Very Best: Ice Cream and Where to Find it, by Carol Robbins and Herb Woff

Number of Franchisees: 75 parlours located in 5 States..

In Business Since: 1981

Equity Capital Needed: Minimum $85,000-90,000 investment for complete turnkey operation. Distributorships also available with investments varying according to regional areas desired.

Financial Assistance Available: Franchisor cannot provide financing in developing new parlours.

Training Provided: A comprehensive traning program is provided in an established parlour and is completed in the franchisee's parlour upon opening. Ongoing technical support is provided for the duration of the franchise agreement through a regularly updated operations manual, franchisee meetings and seminars, and a monthly newsletter.

Managerial Assistance Available: (1) The corporate marketing department provides brand awareness and identity through advertising, publicity, and promotions. This department also assists individual franchisees with their particular marketing needs. (2) The corporate operations department works with parlours on a regular basis to improve profitability. (3) Franchisee representatives meet monthly with the company president and executive vice president to maintain lines of communication between franchisees and franchisor.

Information Submitted: May 1987

MARBLE SLAB CREMERY, INC.
3100 South Gessner
Suite 230
Houston, Texas 77063
Therese Clausen, Franchise Sales

Description of Operation: Retail ice cream stores featuring super premium quality ice cream, cones baked fresh daily, fresh frozen yogurt, frozen pies and cakes. Ice cream is custom designed for customer on frozen marble slab (patent pending) and made daily in the store. Open 7 days a week.

Number of Franchisees: 19 in Texas, Louisiana and Iowa

In Business Since: 1983

Equity Capital Needed: $30,000

Financial Assistance Available: None

Training Provided: 10 days training in the company's training facility in Houston, Texas; 6 additional days of training at franchisee's store (3 days before opening, 3 days after opening).

Managerial Assistance Available: Marble Slab Creamery, Inc., maintains an ongoing business relationship with its franchisees, with assistance available in all phases of store operations. A complete operations manual is provided to all franchisees. Company field personnel visit stores on a regular basis to insure that operating standards are being followed to insure the consistency of operations throughout the franchise system. Marble Slab Creamery, Inc., constantly updates advertising programs and evaluates new products for its franchised locations.

Information Submitted: May 1987

M.G.M. LIQUOR WAREHOUSE INTERNATIONAL, INC.
1124 Larpenteur Avenue West
St. Paul, Minnesota 55113

Description of Operation: Retail, off-sale liquor store, specializing in fine wine, spirits and beer. Standard store size 5,000 to 8,000 square feet. Franchises currently available in Minnesota, South Dakota, Wisconsin, California, Arizona.

Number of Franchisees: 21 franchise units in Minnesota, and 1 franchise unit in Wisconsin, 1 in South Dakota, and 2 in Arizona.

In Business Since: 1970

Equity Capital Needed: Total package price exclusive of building $210,000 to $350,000, including franchise fee.

Financial Assistance Available: Financing available at local banks—not available from franchisor.

Training Provided: Company-operated management training school providing extensive and detailed instruction in store operation, management and administration for franchisees, management or both. Instore training.

Managerial Assistance Available: Operational and merchandising assistance is provided as needed through the headquarters office.

Information Submitted: June 1987

MISTER SOFTEE, INC.
901 East Clements Bridge Road
P. O. Box D
Runnemede, New Jersey 08078
James F. Conway, Vice President and General Manager

Description of Operation: Retailing soft ice cream products from a mobile unit, a complete dairy bar on wheels. Dealer is given a franchised area to operate. Mister Softee, Inc., maintains a supply department plus a service and parts department. Franchisees are supported with a merchandising, promotional, and advertising program.

Number of Franchisees: 860 in 20 States

In Business Since: 1956

Equity Capital Needed: $22,000

Financial Assistance Available: Financing can be arranged for qualified individuals.

Training Provided: Franchisee is trained on his mobile unit in his franchised area for 1 week in merchandising, route planning, operation of the mobile unit, sanitation and maintenance.

Managerial Assistance Available: Area representative visits franchisee for continuing assistance periodically and suggesting improvements when needed. Standard operating procedure manual, service manual, accounting ledgers. Inventory control forms are provided to each franchisee.

Information Submitted: July 1987

NIELSEN'S FROZEN CUSTARD
NFC MANAGEMENT CORPORATION
P. O. Box 731
Bountiful, Utah 84010
Doug Nielsen, Director of Marketing
Jeff Dunford, Franchise Development

Description of Operation: Nielsen's Frozen Custard is proud to bring back the goodness and taste of an old-fashioned ice cream product. Our frozen custard is made fresh every few hours right in the store. Our secret recipe, specially designed patented freezing machine, and concern for quality all result in the rebirth of the smooth real dairy taste that America loves.

Number of Franchisees: 5 plus 4 company-owned in 5 States.

In Business Since: 1981

Equity Capital Needed: Franchise fee $12,500. Total investment $70,000 to $90,000.

Financial Assistance Available: None

Training Provided: Nielsen's training personnel will instruct you and your people during the build-out of your store at our training facility. You will receive a Nielsen's "know-how-book" which covers everything from the design and operation of the machine to the recipes and finished products. We also cover accounting procedures, employee management, customer relations, and much more.

Managerial Assistance Available: The people at NFC will make final site approval, supply state of the art marketing ideas, develop special advertising materials to cover from ground breaking to grand opening, provide an ongoing flow of new advertising ideas, and supply a store design package which includes store layout, construction specifications, menu board ideas and information, major and miscellaneous equipment lists, and sign design requirements.

Information Submitted: June 1987

OLD UNCLE GAYLORD'S, INC.
824 Petaluma Boulevard South
Petaluma, California 95942
Gaylord W. Willis, Chairman

Description of Operation: "Uncle Gaylord's Ice Cream Cafes" offer a complete line of super-premium ice creams (recently selected The Best of San Francisco and written up in such prestigious magazines as Gourmet) that are made from original receipes perfected by company founder, Gaylord Willis, in the late 60's. Company stores compliment their unique ice creams with fresh baked sweet butter cookies and cakes (baked on the premises), expresso and other hot drinks and has recently introduced a full line of soups, stews, chili, salads and other quick serve food prepared in the company's central kitchen. Store sizes range from 500 to 2,000 square feet and tend to become a part of neighborhood culture with art shows, classical music and as a meeting place for friends. Store volumes average $250,000. Company now emphasizing licensing for foreign countries and the outright sale of their system in the continental U.S. other than Northern California.

Number of Franchisees: 10 in California and State area licenses in Illinois, Nevada and Idaho.

In Business Since: 1971—selling franchises since 1976

Equity Capital Needed: $75,000 to $125,000 includes all franchise fees and a turnkey business.

Financial Assistance Available: None

Training Provided: Training includes all aspects of ice cream making, baking, food preparation, retailing, merchandising, personnel training and development as well as accounting for small business. Licensees are permitted to bring along a camera and tape recorder for their future referral. Normal training is in-plant for 6-8 days; retail operations 4-6 days; seminars with Baylord for 2-3 days. Company will train two people for each licensee at no additional charge. Prior to the grand opening, Gaylord Willis will spend 40 hours at the new operation training and assisting the management in any way needed. . .including running some ice cream or baking some cookies or stirring a soup pot.

Managerial Assistance Available: On-site follow-up after opening for 40 hours. Thereafter, as required both in plant and on-site.

Information Submitted: June 1987

THE PEANUT SHACK OF AMERICA, INC.
c/o SPECIALTY RETIAL CONCEPTS, INC.
P. O. Box 11025
Winston-Salem, North Carolina 27116

Description of Operation: Specialty nut and candy shops located within enclosed shopping malls.

Number of Franchisees: 197 in 30 States, Puerto Rico, including company-owned

In Business Since: 1975

Equity Capital Needed: $50,000-$125,000

Financial Assistance Available: No financial assistance available. However, franchisor is available for consultation with lenders.

Training Provided: Initial training of staff (normally 1 to 2 weeks) and periodic visits thereafter.

Managerial Assistance Available: Initial training at same time staff training takes place. Periodic visits by operations staff thereafter.

Information Submitted: June 1987

PERKITS YOGURT, INC.
100 Galleria Parkway
4th Floor
Atlanta, Georgia 30339
Kit Evans, Director

Description of Operation: Soft frozen yogurt shops.

Number of Franchisees: 29 in 11 States

In Business Since: 1985

Equity Capital Needed: Approximately $100,000.

Financial Assistance Available: Up to 80 percent thru various lending sources.

Training Provided: 1 to 2 weeks on premises.

Managerial Assistance Available: Same as above.

Information Submitted: May 1987

PHANNY'PHUDGE EMPORIUMS
571 North Poplar Avenue
Suite B
Orange, California 92668
John F. Peace, President

Description of Operation: A non-preparation specialty store selling chocolates, coffee/tea and machines, fresh desserts, food gift baskets with Phanny's labels etc.

Number of Franchisees: 5 in California

In Business Since: Franchisor established 1957—Franchising since 1985

Equity Capital Needed: Approximately $25,000-$100,000. Total investment will vary between $45,000-$225,000 depending upon Emporium size.

Financial Assistance Available: Provides franchisee with assistance in locating financing sources.

Training Provided: 3 weeks of comprehensive training for owner and manager. Training covers all aspects of operational procedures, bookkeeping, employee training, advertising and promotion and management techniques.

Managerial Assistance Available: Prior to opening field coordinator spends 1 week at location assisting franchisee. Continuous ongoing marketing and field support.

Information Submitted: May 1987

POPCORN PALACE AND CANDY EMPORIUM
2146 Michelson
Suite B
Irvine, California 92715

Description of Operation: Popcorn Palace and Candy Emporium is a retail store concept which manufactures and sells 34 gourmet flavors of popcorn in a contemporary boutique setting. The product line also features gift packs, and imported candies.

Number of Franchisees: 11 company-owned in California.

In Business Since: 1982

Equity Capital Needed: Franchise fee $20,000. Total investment $60,000-$100,000.

Financial Assistance Available: None

Training Provided: Initial training includes a formal 3-week training program which is divided between classroom time, on-the-job training in a company-owned store, and pre-opening training at the franchisee's location.

Managerial Assistance Available: Program includes ongoing assistance in product development advertising, promotions, quality control, and accounting systems and controls.

Information Submitted: July 1987

*POPCORN PARLOR FRANCHISE SYSTEMS
4277 Trans Port Street
Ventura Marina, California 93003
Alden Jay Glickman, Franchise Director

Description of Operation: Retail sales of gourmet popcorn, Gelato ice cream, country fudge, gifts and also mail order division and commercial sales.

Number of Franchisees: 5 including company-owned in California

In Business Since: 1984

Equity Capital Needed: $60,000 to $90,000

Financial Assistance Available: Assistance in obtaining lease or loan capital.

Training Provided: 2 weeks before opening plus ongoing.

Managerial Assistance Available: Bi-monthly lists, operations manual, test kitchen, new product development, etc. Full technical assistance and bookkeeping assistance.

Information Submitted: May 1987

REAL RICH SYSTEMS, INC.
1337 F Street, N.W.
Washington, D.C. 20004
Sheldon Fischer, President

Description of Operation: Real-Rich is a full service family ice cream parlor featuring cones, sundaes, shakes, cookies baked on premises, hot and cold sandwiches and platters. Ice cream parlors may be located in malls, stores or free standing buildings. Real-Rich Ice Cream is made to a special receipe and features over 30 flavors.

Number of Franchisees: 12 located in Maryland, Virginia and District of Columbia

In Business Since: 1971

Equity Capital Needed: Varies depending on size and location of store and ranges from $50,000 to $100,000 and whether ice cream only or added food items are offered.

Financial Assistance Available: None directly but source direction available.

Training Provided: On-site training at nearest store prior to opening own store, assistance in site selection, store planning and equipment and continued supervision after opening.

Managerial Assistance Available: Continuous guidance relating to operational control, merchandising, inventory control, advertising and promotions.

Information Submitted: May 1987

ROCKY MOUNTAIN CHOCOLATE FACTORY, INC.
P. O. Box 2408
Durango, Colorado 81302
Kayo Folsom, Vice President, Franchise Development

Description of Operation: Sale of candy.

Number of Franchisees: 38 in 8 States

In Business Since: 1981

Equity Capital Needed: $175,000 which includes $30,000 franchise fee.

Financial Assistance Available: Corporation does not provide financing but does assist in acquiring financing. Provides financial statements, projections and pro-forma statements.

Training Provided: 1 week intensive training in Durango: 1 week training in respective store.

Managerial Assistance Available: Continual support in marketing, merchandising, finance, etc.

Information Submitted: July 1987

STEVE'S HOMEMADE ICE CREAM, INC.
424 East John Street
Lindenhurst, New York 11757
Seymour Deutsch

Description of Operation: Steve's offers the highest quality super premium ice cream in over 50 flavors yet still maintaining the old fashion store look.

Number of Franchisees: 90 franchised plus 11 company-owned stores.

In Business Since: 1974

Equity Capital Needed: 10 percent of total investment of $67,000-$147,000.

Financial Assistance Available: None

Training Provided: A 1 week training program is provided at a company training store in all phases of store operation.

Managerial Assistance Available: Ongoing operational assistance will include visits by an operations representative to monitor quality control, and store appearance. Complete manuals of operations, advertising, and promotion are provided. Other services include site approval, store design, approved suppliers, cooperative advertising assistance, ongoing proven menu enhancements and the availability of a unique equipment package.

Information Submitted: July 1987

SWEETCREAMS FRANCHISE SYSTEMS, INC.
P. O. Box 4098
Waterbury, Connecticut 06704
Gregg Nolan, Franchise Director

Description of Operation: Ice cream shops, featuring 40 flavors of ice cream. Chocolates, coffees and cakes. Premium ice cream in 27 adult flavors including all natural liquors.

Number of Franchisees: 2 in Connecticut

In Business Since: 1985

Equity Capital Needed: $70,000

Financial Assistance Available: None

Training Provided: 2 weeks on-site

Managerial Assistance Available: Weekly visits to stores, sales and management seminars.

Information Submitted: June 1987

*SWENSEN'S ICE CREAM COMPANY
P. O. Box 10245
Phoenix, Arizona 85064-0245

Description of Operation: "Swensen's Ice Cream Stores" offer the complete range of ice cream operations from manufacture to sale. Each "store sells" its own ice cream from manufactured secret formulas developed by the firm's founder, Earl Swensen, who has been in the ice cream business in San Francisco since 1948. Franchisees purchase their supplies from independent suppliers. Swensen's stores vary from 250 to 4,000 square feet and are complete turn-of-the-century ice cream parlors, featuring marble tables and soda fountain, tufted booths, tiffany-style lights and oak woodwork and furnishings. Swensen's stores engage in the retail sale of ice cream, fountain products, and ice cream novelties made to Swensen's specifications. Many stores also offer a sandwich menu.

Number of Franchisees: 274 in 35 States and 16 countries.

In Business Since: 1963

Equity Capital Needed: $120,000 minimum; equity capital requirements may vary depending on size of the store.

Financial Assistance Available: Swensen's consults with franchisees regarding financing of project costs by independent financial institutions.

Training Provided: Training consists of a 4-week program in Swensen's training facility in Phoenix, Arizona, where franchisees learn ice cream making, preparation of fountain items, ice cream specialty and other items, food preparation, store operation, accounting, store maintenance, inventory control and all other aspects of the operation of a Swensen's Ice Cream Store. Extensive operations manuals provided and training films available.

Managerial Assistance Available: In addition to initial training, complete operations manuals and forms are provided. Franchisees are periodically provided with new flavor recipes and related promotional material. Swensen's maintains full-time operations and product personnel who regularly visit stores to assist franchisees. Franchisees submit monthly operating statements to Swensen's home office.

Information Submitted: May 1987

TCBY ENTERPRISES, INC.
dba "TCBY" YOGURT
11300 Rodney Parham, Suite 150
Little Rock, Arkansas 72212
Herren Hickinbotham, President
Don Terry, Senior Vice President, Franchise Development

Description of Operation: Frozen yogurt and yogurt related treats.

Number of Franchisees: Over 400 throughout the United States.

In Business Since: 1981

Equity Capital Needed: $95,000-$145,500

Financial Assistance Available: None

Training Provided: 1 week intensive training at home office (personnel, accounting, operations) and 1 week in-store training at time of opening.

Managerial Assistance Available: Ongoing assistance in all phases of operations. Field supervisors make periodic in-store inspections and assist in any way they can.

Information Submitted: July 1987

TOPSY'S SHOPPES, INC.
6045 Martway
Mission, Kansas 66202
Ronald L. Fiest, Vice President

Description of Operation: Topsy's Popcorn Shoppes are engaged in the sale, for off-premises consumption, popcorn, ice cream, confectionary items and soft drinks.

Number of Franchisees: 5 who have 10 Shoppes in 2 States, 23 total units (company-owned and franchised).

In Business Since: 1966

Equity Capital Needed: $100,000 plus licensed

Financial Assistance Available: None

Training Provided: Topsy's offers a 5-day training program in an actual Shoppe. The training program includes information necessary to operate a Topsy's Popcorn Shoppe, including food preparation, methods of maintaining cleanliness, quality standards, employee training, proper use of accounting forms and business practices.

Managerial Assistance Available: Topsy's approves the site selected for the franchise location, and provides basic layout plans for the franchisee to adapt to the space available. An operations manual, reporting methods and procedures for accounting, and advice with respect to purchasing and selection of suppliers are furnished. Topsy's provides a representative for 4 working days to assist the franchisee during opening of the Shoppe. Topsy's provides advice and consultation with respect to operation of the Shoppe and administers the national advertising fund.

Information Submitted: June 1987

TRA-HANS CANDIES, INC.
2420 Rocky Point Road
Palm Bay, Florida 32950
Paul E. Trahan, President

Description of Operation: Manufacture and retail of complete chocolate and candy products of qualitl excellence, 1,200 square feet required for kitchen and store, with kitchen-view operation. Ice cream optional.

Number of Franchisees: 6 in Florida, Massachusetts, Connecticut and Maine

In Business Since: 1953, franchising since 1978

Equity Capital Needed: Approximately $65,000-$75,000.

Financial Assistance Available: Franchisor assists franchisee thru independent financial institutions.

Training Provided: Candy manufacture—merchandising—bookkeeping; complete operations of 'hand crafted' candy shop. At least 4 weeks with assistance available at all times.

Managerial Assistance Available: Sales management, cost control, sources of supplies etc.; assistance available at all times.

Information Submitted: May 1987

TROPICAL YOGURT, INC.
P. O. Box 537
Los Alamitos, California 90720

Description of Operation: Tropical Yogurt, Inc., offers franchises for the sale of Soft Serve Frozen Yogurt dispensed in various portion sizes, fresh fruits and dry toppings, yogurt sundaes, waffle cones made daily, Aloha fruit boats, and a variety of Tropical protein shakes such as: Kona crunch, Fiji Fantasy, South Pacific and more. Tropical Yogurt offers more varieties of yogurt flavors including: Aloha Chocolate, Macadamia Cafe, Banaa Mauna Loa, Kiwi Kauai, etc. Tropical Yogurt, Inc., have developed certain techniques to control product consistency (PCC). Stores are distinguished by a unique decor.

Number of Franchisees: 3 plus 1 company-owned in California and a partnership in Hawaii.

In Business Since: 1985

Equity Capital Needed: Total investment including franchise fee and working capital ranges from $120,000 to $145,000.

Financial Assistance Available: Franchisor does not offer, directly or indirectly any financing arrangements to the farnchisee. Franchisee is responsible for obtaining all of its own financing arrangements. Advice on possible financing alternatives may be available if requested.

Training Provided: Complete training in all phases of business functions at company-owned facility; ongoing support.

Managerial Assistance Available: Franchisor will provide continuing consultation, supervision and information with regard to the successful operation of the franchised business. The franchisor will also assist in developing and preparing a promotional "grand opening" advertising campaign.

Information Submitted: June 1987

TRUFFLES CHOCOLATIER, INC.
7450 Washington Avenue
Eden Prairie, Minnesota 55344
George Bond, President

Description of Operation: Retail shops selling domestic and imported chocolates and candies and specializing in chocolate truffles.

Number of Franchisees: 3 in Illinois and Minnesota plus 6 company-owned stores.

In Business Since: 1979

Equity Capital Needed: $60,000 to $100,000

Financial Assistance Available: None

Training Provided: 1 week of intensive training with ongoing consultation.

Managerial Assistance Available: Display and presentation, art, keyline, and advertising, buying, design, construction, inventory, all procedures and systems, and marketing, merchandising.

Information Submitted: May 1987

TWISTEE TREAT
TWISTEE TREAT CORPORATION
3434 Hancock Bridge Parkway
North Fort Myers, Florida 33903
Lee Lanktree, President

Description of Operation: Twistee Treat sells its high quality 'Firm Serve' all natural ice cream products through its self-merchandising stores, which are uniquely shaped like giant ice cream cones. 'Firm Serve' has the quality of hard, premium ice cream, but is dispensed from the company's proprietary soft-serve ice cream machines. More than 76 flavors are available and are changed every two weeks as a part of their merchandising. The Company also has developed a non-dairy, all fruit-based Super Lo-Cal product (less than 15 calories per 4 oz. serving) for the growing diet-conscious market. It contains no cholesterol and has the same smooth texture as Twistee's real ice cream. Twistee's building is only 300 square feet and may be erected in shopping center or mall parking lots and other high traffic areas where other buildings may be precluded.

Number of Franchisees: 40 in Florida, including company-owned. Areas available for development.

In Business Since: 1982—became publicly held in 1983

Equity Capital Needed: $35,000-120,000 cash investment, plus operating capital.

Financial Assistance Available: See above and franchisor assists through independent financial institutions

Training Provided: 2 weeks training at corporate headquarters and in company-owned stores. Additional training and continuing supervision at owner's location.

Managerial Assistance Available: Weekly visit to each location. Complete operations manual. All phases of business operation procedures and help as requested. Franchisee participates in non-profit advertising association.

Information Submitted: May 1987

VIC'S CORN POPPER, INC.
4513 South 133rd Street
Omaha, Nebraska 68137
John M. Kuhry, President

Description of Operation: Small retail stores (500 square feet to 1,500 square feet) with old-fashioned decor which feature pre-packaged gourmet white hulless popped popcorn, caramel and cheese popcorn, plus soft drinks and old fashion ice cream. Products are also sold off premises in wholesale outlets. A companion mail order popcorn gift business also out of retail locations. Emphasis is on quality, taste, value and convenience.

Number of Franchisees: 60 franchised and 12 company-owned stores in 12 States.

In Business Since: 1980 under this corporate name, but recipes used go back 50 years.

Equity Capital Needed: Contact company for full information.

Financial Assistance Available: None. Franchisees required to have adequate net worth to qualify.

Training Provided: Separate training courses offered to both owners and operators. Training conducted in model training stores and on-site. Pre-opening store training also provided.

Managerial Assistance Available: Regular consultation and assistance. Detailed operating manuals are provided on each facet of the operation. Company makes available promotional and advertising materials.

Information Submitted: July 1987

> **WHIRLA WHIP SYSTEMS, INC.**
> 11307 "P" Street
> Omaha, Nebraska 68137
> Duke Fischer, Director of Marketing

Description of Operation: The custom blending of vanilla and chocolate ice cream or yogurt with the customer's choice of candy bars, fruits, cookies, nuts or candy. Done in seconds at the point of sale.

Number of Franchisees: 108 in 17 States and Washington D.C., Canada, Japan, and Australia.

In Business Since: 1981

Equity Capital Needed: $13,000 to $80,000.

Financial Assistance Available: None

Training Provided: Initial training 3 days, continued training as needed.

Managerial Assistance Available: Initial training 3 days, opening assistance as needed, continued assistance as needed.

Information Submitted: July 1987

> *WHITE MOUNTAIN CREAMERY
> 1340 Centre Street
> Newton, Massachusetts 02159

Description of Operation: On-site old fashioned manufacturer of ice cream.

Number of Franchisees: 15 in 6 States, plus 9 company stores

In Business Since: 1982

Equity Capital Needed: $60,000 and ability to acquire financing.

Financial Assistance Available: None

Training Provided: 2 weeks corporate training school at corporate headquarters.

Managerial Assistance Available: 2 weeks corporate training school at corporate headquarters.

Information Submitted: July 1987

> **WIZARD ICE CREAM & CONFECTIONERY SHOPPE, LTD.**
> 730 North Franklin
> Suite 700
> Chicago, Illinois 60610
> U.S. Director of Franchising

Description of Operation: Wizards Ice Cream Magic shops offer custom blended ice cream and yogurt products using Wizards patented blending equipment.

Number of Franchisees: 10 open and 129 sold in Illinois, Chicago, Tennessee, Michigan and Florida.

In Business Since: 1984, public since 1987

Equity Capital Needed: $15,000-$75,000

Financial Assistance Available: Equipment leasing.

Training Provided: 1 week with company, and 1 week at franchisee location. Comprehensive programs and ongoing support includes training videos and operations manual.

Managerial Assistance Available: Complete support includes assistance in staffing, advertising, customer service, accounting, administrative, and new product development.

Information Submitted: May 1987

> *ZACK'S FAMOUS FROZEN YOGURT, INC.
> 3850 North Causeway Boulevard
> Metairie, Louisiana 70002
> Sam Holt, President

Description of Operation: Zack's is a manufacturer, retailer, and franchiser in the frozen yogurt industry. Each retail shop offers cups, cones, sundaes, banana splits, milkshakes, smoothies, etc., all made with frozen yogurt.

Number of Franchisees: 150 in 20 States.

In Business Since: 1977

Equity Capital Needed: $110,000

Financial Assistance Available: Advice and counsel as to where and how funds may be obtained. No direct financial assistance provided.

Training Provided: Initial training is of 1 weeks duration at company headquarters. Ongoing training provided at franchisee's location.

Managerial Assistance Available: Franchisees are provided with in-depth training re: shop management, employee relations, inventory control; accounting, product preparation, and a thorough familiarization with all aspects of the business.

Information Submitted: May 1987

FOODS-PANCAKE/WAFFLE/PRETZEL

> **ELMER'S PANCAKE & STEAK HOUSE, INC.**
> 11802 Southeast Stark Street
> P. O. Box 16595
> Portland, Oregon 97216 Herman Goldberg, President

Description of Operation: Full service family restaurant, serving breakfast, lunch and dinner.

Number of Franchisees: 32 in 6 States

In Business Since: 1960

Equity Capital Needed: Minimum $150,000

Financial Assistance Available: Financial assistance is not available.

Training Provided: Training at company location in Portland, Oregon and at franchisee's site.

Managerial Assistance Available: Annual management seminar, ongoing consultations, on-site visitations, newsletters, training manuals.

Information Submitted: May 1987

> *INTERNATIONAL HOUSE OF PANCAKES RESTAURANTS
> 6837 Lankershim Boulevard
> North Hollywood, California 91605
> Richard K. Herzer, President

Description of Operation: Full service family restaurant serving breakfast, lunch, dinner, snacks and desserts including a variety of pancake specialties and featuring cook's daily special. Wine and beer served in some locations.

Number of Franchisees: 450 in 36 States, Canada and Japan

In Business Since: 1958

Equity Capital Needed: Varies depending on location.

Financial Assistance Available: None

Training Provided: 4-6 weeks of classroom and on-the-job instruction. Continued training available.

Managerial Assistance Available: Franchisor provides opening supervision, regular visits and assistance from field coordinators. Complete manual of operations specifies how each menu item is prepared and served, how the business is to be operated profitably.

Information Submitted: May 1987

> *LE PEEP RESTAURANTS, INC.
> 1777 South Harrison Avenue
> Suite 802
> Denver, Colorado 80210
> Mark S. Grabowski, Vice President, Franchise Development

Description of Operation: Le Peep is an upscale breakfast and brunch restaurant, specializing in creative omelettes, frittatas, pancakes, and sandwiches. We offer full table service in a relaxing atmosphere. Our restaurants are open from 6:30 am to 2:30 pm, Monday-Friday and 7:00 am-2:30 pm Saturday and Sunday.

Number of Franchisees: 12 in 10 States

In Business Since: 1981

Equity Capital Needed: Range $100,000-$300,000

Financial Assistance Available: None

Training Provided: Le Peep provides 9 weeks of comprehensive training in all aspects of restaurant operations for three management personnel per restaurant to be opened.

Managerial Assistance Available: Le Peep provides real estate site selection assistance; the preliminary drawings of each restaurant; construction assistance; approved vendors for equipment and food; marketing assistance and grand openings and ongoing promotional activities, and operational consultations for all phases of an ongoing business.

Information Submitted: May 1987

MARY BELLE RESTAURANTS
P. O. Box 706
Orange, New Jersey 07051
George Livieratos, Acting Manager

Description of Operation: Mary Belle Restaurants are complete family-style restaurants with table service, unique style, it combines all types of restaurants in one by featuring full menu—pancake and waffle section with beautiful warm decor. Forty flavors of ice cream made on premises. Stores are approximately 3,000 square feet. Complete construction or remodeling, equipment, seating provided by company.

Number of Franchisees: 28 in New Jersey, New York, Florida, Tennessee and Pennsylvania

In Business Since: 1952

Equity Capital Needed: $30,000 to $60,000 depending on size.

Financial Assistance Available: Company will assist franchisees with locating financing of balance, rate of interest and term of financing dependent of franchisees' financial statement and ability.

Training Provided: Minimum 160 hours training period in operating store and company in-store trainer for as long as needed upon opening.

Managerial Assistance Available: Management and technical assistance included in training period, with continuing support from main company representatives and from area representatives. National and statewide advertising program will be developed by main company for implementation in franchisee's area as needed.

Information Submitted: July 1987

PANCAKE COTTAGE FAMILY RESTAURANTS
P. O. Box 371
Smithtown, New York 11787
Morton Fluhr, President

Description of Operation: Pancake Cottage Family Restaurants are full service restaurants serving all three meals. Our target is the person who is tired of do-it-yourself hamburger stands and $50 per person dinner restaurants. Our menu and prices attract the great middle class of America.

Number of Franchisees: 20 in New York and Maryland

In Business Since: 1971

Equity Capital Needed: $125,000 minimum cash includes $10,000 franchise fee.

Financial Assistance Available: The corporation will finance the balance of approximately $100,000 over 5 years.

Training Provided: Intensive training in an established restaurant is provided with at least 150 hours being mandatory. We also provide a cook and dining room manager for 100 hours just prior to and after opening.

Managerial Assistance Available: A complete operations manual and other printed materials are provided. We are also available on a continuing basis for consultation. The corporation keeps abreast of changes in the market place and adjusts the menu items and prices to reflect them.

Information Submitted: May 1987

*PERKINS RESTAURANTS, INC.
6401 Poplar Avenue
Memphis, Tennessee 38119
Phil Joseph, Director Franchise Development

Description of Operation: 24 hour, family-style restaurant with moderately priced menu items.

Number of Franchisees: 329 in 27 States

In Business Since: 1957

Equity Capital Needed: Estimated initial investment ranges from $914,000 to $1,407,000; equity required varies depending upon lender's requirements.

Financial Assistance Available: No financial assistance is provided by franchisor.

Training Provided: Franchisee and management training in company-owned, operated restaurant for 4-6 weeks. Opening team at restaurant to assist in training of staff for three weeks.

Managerial Assistance Available: Provide designs, plans and specifications for construction, furnishing, equipping restaurant. Advice, consultation and specifications for purchasing food supplies and uniforms. Provide core menu with specifications. Marketing and advertising programs. Quality assurance inspections to ensure compliance with standards of operation. Ongoing operations consultation.

Information Submitted: April 1987

VICORP RESTAURANTS, INC.
Selling: VILLAGE INN PANCAKE HOUSE FRANCHISES
400 West 48th Avenue
Denver, Colorado 80216
Maxine Crogle. Coordinator/Franchise Services

Description of Operation: Village Inn restaurants are family oriented, offering moderately priced menu items for all meal periods.

Number of Franchisees: 53 in 24 States

In Business Since: 1958

Equity Capital Needed: $80,000 not including real estate and equipment.

Financial Assistance Available: Any financial assistance provided by franchisor to franchisee is negotiated on an individual basis depending upon factors such as the availability of financing generally, the credit worthiness of the franchisee, other security that the franchisee may have, and other factors typically considered by commercial lendors.

Training Provided: Recommended 10-14 weeks management training for general manager and kitchen manager's positions, plus ongoing program of instruction.

Managerial Assistance Available: Provides consultation and supervision in the areas of marketing, operations and purchasing. Also, provides traning staff for new restaurant openings, operating manuals and industry updates.

Information Submitted: June 1987

WAFFLETOWN U.S.A. LTD.
2 Koger Center
Norfolk, Virginia 23502
Tim Mathas

Description of Operation: Table service 1-1/4" Belgium waffles, pancakes, eggs, omeletes, sandwiches, entrees, family style restaurant. Also fast food units.

Number of Franchisees: 5 in Virginia, 1 in Singapore and 1 in Taiwan.

In Business Since: 1981

Equity Capital Needed: $75,000 to $125,000 based on type of unit.

Financial Assistance Available: None

Training Provided: All personnel trained 2 week period.

Managerial Assistance Available: Continuous technical assistance.

Information Submitted: May 1987

FOODS-RESTAURANTS/DRIVE-INS/ CARRY-OUTS

*A & W RESTAURANTS, INC.
One Parklane Boulevard
Suite 500 East
Dearborn, Michigan 48126
Larry Kohler, Director of Administration
Anita Smith, Franchise Coordinator

Description of Operation: A & W Restaurants, Inc., is presently offering licenses to operate one or more A & W Restaurants. The Restaurant building is approximately 3,000-3,500 square feet and features a salad bar and drive-thru where feasible. The menu features world-famous A & W Root Beer, 1/6 and 1/3 lb. hamburgers, cheeseburgers, bacon cheeseburgers, hot dog, breast of chicken sandwich, french fries, onion rings, chili, homemade soups and gourmet ice cream.

Number of Franchisees: 486 in 40 States plus 50 international.

In Business Since: 1919—Franchising since 1926

Equity Capital Needed: Approximately $200,000 per unit depending upon financing considerations.

Financial Assistance Available: No direct financial assistance is available at this time.

Training Provided: An intensive 2 week mandatory initial training course is provided for the licensee (or a member of licensees service management staff) and all restaurant managers before the restaurant opens for business. Refresher courses and seminars are also available periodically.

Managerial Assistance Available: In addition to the training mentioned above, the licensee is provided pre-opening and opening assistance in staffing, equipment procurement and layout, inventory and supply procurement, advertising and promotion, as well as periodic visits by field representatives.

Information Submitted: May 1987

ACROSS THE STREET RESTAURANTS OF AMERICA, INC.
United Founders Tower
Suite 300
Oklahoma City, Oklahoma 73112

Description of Operation: Family charcoal hamburger restaurant specializing in 1/4 pound hamburgersin 12 varieties, spaghetti, steaks, shrimps, telephone order system, Americana decor. Atmosphere above other fast food systems and just under a super club theme.

Number of Franchisees: 8 in 3 States

In Business Since: 1964

Equity Capital Needed: $90,000 plus

Financial Assistance Available: Franchisor wil counsel franchisee in obtaining a loan.

Training Provided: Franchisor provides 14 days of training for franchisee's management at training center in Oklahmoa City concerning all phases of operation; food preparation, cooking, make-up, procedures, etc. Franchisor's training personnel sent to franchisee's restaurant to assist for 10 days during restaurant opening.

Managerial Assistance Available: A.I.A. building plans and specifications provided to franchisee. Aid in site selection. Operations manual including policies, procedures, recipes, forms, etc.

Information Submitted: August 1987

• ALL AMERICAN HERO, INC.
2200 West Commercial Boulevard
Suite 100
Ft. Lauderdale, Florida 33309
Steven Shoeman, President

Description of Operation: Fast food franchise specializing in the retail sale of sliced steak and hero sandwiches. Units are primarily located in prime regional shoping malls and high traffic areas.

Number of Franchisees: 80 in 24 States

In Business Since: 1980

Equity Capital Needed: $100,000-$135,000

Financial Assistance Available: None

Training Provided: 2 weeks training at headquarters; 1 week on-site.

Managerial Assistance Available: Ongoing

Information Submitted: May 1987

ALLEN'S SUBS INTERNATIONAL CORPORATION
764 San Souci Parkway
Wilkes-Barre, Pennsylvania 18702
Gregory Allen, President

Description of Operation: Allen's Subs is a submarine sandwich shop specializing in 30 varieties of subs, salads, and side orders. Shops are designed to produce subs made to order from order to counter in 3 minutes or less. Layout and design of the facility is geared toward high volume fast food production. The unit's state-of-the-art system in doing business will give owner/operator and/or multi-unit operation complete managerial controls over day-to-day operations which include, but not limited to, inventory, sales, cost control, payroll and cost projections. Some Franchise units currently offer home delivery. Drive-thru and pasta are currently being test marketed.

Number of Franchisees: 7 in Pennsylvania and North Carolina.

In Business Since: 1977

Equity Capital Needed: $50,000 minimum

Financial Assistance Available: Franchisor does not provide financing; however, financial assistance is available through franchisor's lending institutions to those who qualify. Franchisee has the option to arrange own financing.

Training Provided: Intensive 6 week training program is mandatory for new franchisees and their top level management. This training program will take place at franchisor's training center. Franchisor will provide complete personnel training program for franchisee's opening crew at franchisor's training center or franchisee's unit.

Managerial Assistance Available: Allen's Subs will provide continual management services for the entire term of the franchisee's contract. Complete manuals of operation, forms, and form stencils are provided. Area field supervisors will be available to frequently visit franchisee's unit and assist owner/operator and/or store managers in solving their problems and offering them ways and methods of improving the franchisee's unit. Research and development into new products and methods of doing business are constantly taking place to improve and strengthen the entire Allen's Subs franchise system.

Information Submitted: June 1987

ALL-V'S, INC.
5200 S. Quebec
Suite 504
Greenwood Village, CO 80111
Kenneth K. Cox, President

Description of Operation: Quick service primarily hot sandwiches freshly and individually prepared for each customer. 44 sandwiches from Italian cold cuts, steak, pastrami and sausage, etc.

Number of Franchisees: 4 in Colorado and 1 in Wyoming

In Business Since: 1973

Equity Capital Needed: $100,000-$160,000

Financial Assistance Available: Yes

Training Provided: Minimum training 4 weeks before the franchisee's unit opens, consisting of all food preparation, management, inventory, handling co-workers, bookkeeping, budget and monetary control. A representative of All-V's, Inc., will spend 2 weeks in franchisee's unit, or more, if needed, to assist in opening of store.

Managerial Assistance Available: Training for at least 4 weeks in management, inventory, training, food preparation, bookkeeping and monetary control. Ongoing.

Information Submitted: May 1987

AL'S BAR BQ, INC.
AL'S CHICAGO'S 1 ITALIAN BEEF
22 West 140 North Avenue
Glen Ellyn, Illinois 60137
Terry G. Palelli, President

Description of Operation: Fast food, Italian beef, sausage and hot dogs.

Number of Franchisees: 3 in Illinois

In Business Since: 1985

Equity Capital Needed: $110,000

Financial Assistance Available: None

Training Provided: 6 weeks in all phases of operation.

Managerial Assistance Available: Continual management service for the life of the franchise.

Information Submitted: May 1987

ANDY'S OF AMERICA, INC.
206 Louisiana
Little Rock, Arkansas 72201

Description of Operation: Fast food restaurant featuring a complete breakfast with fresh biscuits and cooked-to-order eggs. A variety of quality sandwiches and related items. Salad and baked potato bars. Andy's own delicious frozen yogurt completes the menu.

Number of Franchisees: 3 stores in Arkansas, Louisiana, Oklahoma, Kansas, and Missouri plus 13 company stores.

In Business Since: 1977

Equity Capital Needed: Approximately $50,000

Financial Assistance Available: None

Training Provided: A 5 week training program including 2 week in-store orientation and 3 week training school in company.

Managerial Assistance Available: Building and equipment plans and specifications, complete operations sytstem and manual. national accounts buying power, ongoing training and supervision programs. Business forms and financial control systems available. In-house financial control systems available. In-house advertising agency available to franchisees.

Information Submitted: August 1987

APPETITO'S, INC.
4747 North 7th Avenue
Phoenix, Arizona 85013
Richard L. Schnakenberg, Chairman and President

Description of Operation: Appetito's, Inc., is a fast service Italian restaurant. The average store size is 1,800 square feet although restaurant sizes range from 900 square feet to 3,000 square feet and are in-line, in shopping centers or stand alone buildings. The menu consists of hot and cold submarines, pizza by the slice or pie, salads and hot dinners of spaghetti, lasagna and ravioli. The company stresses quick service including drive through, take-out and delivery, cleanliness and high quality food products. Total turnkey operation. Selling individual restaurants and multiple unit territory franchises.

Number of Franchisees: 17

In Business Since: 1974

Equity Capital Needed: $40,000 to $50,000

Financial Assistance Available: Equipment financial package.

Training Provided: Minimum of 160 hours of training at company facility in Phoenix, Arizona for franchisees managers and assistant managers.

Managerial Assistance Available: Operations, training, maintenance, accounting and financial planning. Company provides grand opening package, multi-franchise territory package, central advertising and promotion.

Information Submitted: May 1987

APPLEBEE'S
1801 Royal Lane
Suite 902
Dallas, Texas 75229

Description of Operation: Applebee's is positioned as a neighborhood pub, where consumers can obtain a high value experience through attractively prices food and alcoholic beverages. The principles of fast food (convenience, quality and service, coupled with limited time and money) can be applied to an adult consumer.

Number of Franchisees: 31 plus 13 company-owned in 10 States

In Business Since: 1983

Equity Capital Needed: $3,000,000 net worth and $500,000 liquid assets.

Financial Assistance Available: None

Training Provided: Training is provided for general manager, kitchen manager and franchisee's restaurant managers in operations training facility for such period of time as franchisor shall deem reasonably necessary, and shall complete that course to franchisor's reasonsable satisfaction.

Managerial Assistance Available: Applebee's basically provides management training, preopening assistance, ongoing and follow-up assistance. Additionally, they help find site locations, and offer assistance with purveyors for purchasing; marketing programs and format assistance provided.

Information Submitted: August 1987

*ARBY'S, INC.
Ten Piedmont Center, Suite 700
3495 Piedmont Road, Northeast
Atlanta, Georgia 30305
Russell S. Johnson,
Senior Vice President/Franchising

Description of Operation: Fast food restaurant specializing in roast beef sandwiches.

Number of Franchisees: 337 in U.S. and internationally, 1,686 stores open as of February 28, 1987.

In Business Since: 1964

Equity Capital Needed: Minimum of $100,000 (assuming land and building are leased) and ability to acquire financing.

Financial Assistance Available: No direct assistance—however, Arby's will guide franchisees in obtaining financing.

Training Provided: 4 weeks training to include classroom and in-store training. Ten days of on-site pre/post opening training.

Managerial Assistance Available: Manuals, advice and counseling available covering all aspects of Arby's operation.

Information Submitted: May 1987

ARTHUR TREACHER'S, INC.
5121 Mahoning Avenue
Youngstown, Ohio 44515
Ed Hamrock, Director of Information

Description of Operation: Offers franchises for the operation of Arthur Treacher's Fish & Chips Restaurants. Arthur Treacher Fish & Chip Restaurants have a fast food format located in buildings or store fronts which project the Arthur Treacher image. Franchisee offers all items on the standard menu, which features seafood and chips specialties, and also includes such items as chicken, salad, soup, batter dipped hot dogs, and other complements.

Number of Franchisees: 90 franchise units plus 35 company-owned units in 14 States

In Business Since: 1969

Equity Capital Needed: Franchise fee $15,000. Total investment depends on location.

In Business Since: 1969

Equity Capital Needed: Franchise fee $15,000. Total investment depends on location.

Financial Assistance Available: None

Training Provided: The Arthur Treacher training program consists of 3 segments and last approximately 5 weeks. Both of the five week programs consist of on-site training at an Arthur Treacher restaurant selected by the company. There is also a minimum of 4 days in-classroom training. Franchisee is supplied operational and other appropriate manuals at the training session. Franchisee is required to satisfactorily complete the course prior to opening of his restaurant.

Managerial Assistance Available: There is no tuition charge for the initial training course, however, franchisee must bear the cost of room, board, travel and other personal expenses. Arthur Treacher's at all times make available to the franchisee advice with regard to the management and operation of his restaurant. It also makes available to the franchisee changes and improvements in its' menu, products, food preparation techniques and business methods.

Information Submitted: August 1987

AUNT CHILOTTA SYSTEMS, INC.
1125 West Main
Anoka, Minnesota 55303
Robert W. Schachtschneider, President

Description of Operation: Limited menu Mexican fast food, featuring carry-out, drive-thru and inside seating for approximately 30. The restaurant is 28' x 36' and it is build on-site. Also available are plans for malls or remodeling existing structures. The total charge, including the franchise fee, is $55,000, and it includes everything needed in the kitchen, from the freezer and refrigerator down to the pans and spoons.

Number of Franchisees: 6 in 4 States

In Business Since: 1976

Equity Capital Needed: It varies, but generally $25,001 to $50,000.

Financial Assistance Available: We give information and assistance that should help in securing your own local financing.

Training Provided: In a comprehensive 14-day training program you receive on-the-job training in a company-owned restaurant that includes food preparation, product knowledge, inventory, purchasing, portion control, shift scheduling, daily reports, cash register procedures, staff appearance and hygiene, public relations and success motivation.

Managerial Assistance Available: One of our operations directors will assist in the actual opening of your new business and on a continuing as is, we will supply monthly promotions and advertising materials, make periodic inspections, and continue our ongoing resarch and development to help increase profits.

Information Submitted: May 1987

AURELIO'S PIZZA FRANCHISE LTD.
18162 Harwood Avenue
Homewood, Illinois 60430
Joseph M. Aurelio, Director

Description of Operation: Aurelio's Pizza restaurants engaged in the retail sale of pizzas, sandwiches and liquid refreshments. Options for sit-down restaurant or a carry-out type of operation. Franchises are independent owners.

Number of Franchisees: 25 in Illinois, Indiana, and Minnesota plus 5 company-owned stores.

In Business Since: 1959

Equity Capital Needed: $130,000-$400,000

Financial Assistance Available: Assistance in obtaining financing and advice.

Training Provided: 72 hour training program for start-up. Continuous training as desired/required.

Managerial Assistance Available: Continuous assistance and advice as required/desired for all phases of operations during life of contract.

Information Submitted: April 1987

BACALLS CAFE FRANCHISES, INC.
Suite 200
6118 Hamilton Avenue
Cincinnati, Ohio 45224

Description of Operation: Bacalls is a comfortable, neighborhood-oriented, full service restaurant and bar, seating between 100 and 125. The design of each unit is tailored to the individual community, yet each location utilizes the standardized strengths of the Bacalls system.

Number of Franchisees: 4 in Ohio and Florida

In Business Since: 1982

Equity Capital Needed: $50,000 minimum

Financial Assistance Available: A total minimum investment of $165,000 will be needed to open a Bacalls Cafe. No direct financing is offered. However, full assistance is average to complete presentations for financial institutions or government agencies offering financing.

Training Provided: All franchisees, and if they choose, 2 other employees, must attend and successfully complete 4 weeks of training at the company head-quarters.

Managerial Assistance Available: An operational specialist works with the franchisee during the first month of operation. A Bacalls operations manual covering all facets of the business is provided and updated as needed. A field representative regularly visits each unit to consult with teh franchisee and offer useful advice and counsel on such system elements as identity, quality, customer convenience, product information, advertising, record keeping, training, communication, and incentives.

Information Submitted: May 1987

BAGEL NOSH, INC.
70 West 36th Street
New York, New York 10018

Description of Operation: Manufacturing of bagels and sale of delicattessen meats, salads, smoked fish on bagels— no bread used-light hot meals-health salads-cafeteria style with average unit seating 100.

Number of Franchisees: 35 in 14 States

In Business Since: 1973

Equity Capital Needed: $100,000 cash including $25,000 franchise fee.

Financial Assistance Available: $275,000 needed to build and equip a Bagel Nosh. Equipment leasing available to qualified individuals—franchisee may select own bank or SBA.

Training Provided: 6 to 8 week mandatory in-store for training under supervision of company instructors for all owners, managers and personnel that franchisee wishes trained.

Managerial Assistance Available: Bagel Nosh provides continual management service for term of agreement in quality controls. Company supervisors work closely with franchisees and visit all units on regional basis. Operational manuals are provided for all phases of Bagel Nosh operations and standards.

Information Submitted: May 1987

BALDINOS GIANT JERSEY SUBS, INC.
760 Elaine Street
Hinesville, Georgia 31313
Henry T. Gerould, President

Description of Operation: Seventeen hot and cold submarine sandwiches. Rolls baked on-premises twice daily. Quality ingredients are sliced fresh as ordered on every sub. Everything is done in full view of the customer(s).

Number of Franchisees: 4 in Georgia and North Carolina

In Business Since: 1975

Equity Capital Needed: $50,000—$10,000 franchise fee.

Financial Assistance Available: Equipment leasing and financing programs available to qualified investers.

Training Provided: Complete training—30 days

Managerial Assistance Available: For duration of agreement: follow-up supervision, periodical on-site inspections and assistance and continuous update of technical data and operations manual.

Information Submitted: July 1987

* BANANAS
EVERYTHING YOGURT NEW JERSEY, INC.
Franchise Division
204 Port Richmond Avenue
Staten Island, New York 10302
Richard Nicotra, Chairman

Description of Operation: Bananas restaurants are fast service kiosk operations featuring whipped frozen fruit drinks, fresh fruit cups, fresh fruit (by the piece) and fresh baked pretzels with assorted toppings.

Number of Franchisees: 54 in New York, New Jersey, Pennsylvania, Maryland, Massachusetts, California, and Washington, D.C. Expansion projects planned for 1986-87 include Texas, Georgia, Viriginia, Florida, Missouri, Arizona, and California.

In Business Since: 1976, offering franchises since 1981

Equity Capital Needed: $50,000—cash or equivalent equity.

Financial Assistance Available: No company financing offered. Administrative assistance offered by company in providing necessary information to local banks for financing.

Training Provided: 2 week initial training program provided at company head-quarters and at other stores in chain. Additional on-site training at franchisees store for one week prior to opening. follow-up training provided on a continuing basis as directed by company.

Managerial Assistance Available: Operational and merchandising assistance provided as needed through headquarters office. Area representatives visit franchisees for continuing assistance periodically suggesting improvements when needed. Comprehensive operations manual provided.

Information Submitted: May 1987

BARN'RDS INTERNATIONAL
307 First National Bank Building
Council Bluffs, Iowa 51501
Samuel B. Marvin

Description of Operation: Fast food restaurant specializing in baked, natural, lite foods featuring beef, ham, turkey, chicken, cod, salads, soup and chili.

Number of Franchisees: 11 in 6 States

In Business Since: 1980

Equity Capital Needed: $40,000-$80,000 depending on the size and location of restaurant.

Financial Assistance Available: Complete counciling service.

Training Provided: Initial training period—4 weeks technical and people skills. Store opening assistance—2 weeks technical and people skills.

Managerial Assistance Available: Continuous in all phases of operation.

BARBACOA ENTERPRISES, INC.
6724 Patterson Avenue
Richmond, Virginia 23226
Dr. Robert J. Filer

Description of Operation: Barbacoa offers three unique franchises: Bagel L'oven—a bagel bakery, deli and restaurant which includes take-out; The Paddock—specializing in a variety of smoked meats; The Round-up—a combination of Bagel L'oven and The Paddock. All restaurants are fast-food concepts that seat from 60-100 people.

Number of Franchisees: 1 franchise, 2 joint ventures and 1 company-owned in Virginia. Expanding to other States.

In Business Since: 1983

Equity Capital Needed: $145,000-$240,000 less equipment of $55,000-$100,000 if leased.

Financial Assistance Available: Will assist with leasing equipment package.

Training Provided: Minimum 2 weeks training in Richmond restaurant and 1 week training at franchise location.

Managerial Assistance Available: Start-up and operational manuals are provided for follow-up procedures. Technical assistance is provided for site selection, restaurant layout, equipment purchase, personnel training, supplier selection and opening ceremonies. Continuous update procedures and new innovations are passed on to franchisee.

Information Submitted: August 1987

BARRO'S PIZZA, INC.
15848 Halliburton Road
Hacienda Heights, California 91745
John Barro, President

Description of Operation: Making and selling of Pizza, sandwiches and other complimentary items. Beer and wine at our larger eat in locations.

Number of Franchisees: 53 in California, Arizona, Georgia and Illinois.

In Business Since: 1969

Equity Capital Needed: $15,000 take out, $25,000 eat in.

Financial Assistance Available: Equipment leasing and equipment packages.

Training Provided: 2 weeks to 1 month training.

Managerial Assistance Available: 2 week, owner's manual and on-the-job training. Operation is so simplified training is required as a on-the-job process.

Information Submitted: August 1987

BASH RIPROCK'S RESTAURANTS, INC.
275 South Lind Drive
Suite 202
Lexington, Kentucky 40523
Paul M. Hilliard, Vice President/Franchising

Description of Operation: Full service restaurant, specialty menu, general seating in 75 to 150 range, alcoholic beverages.

Number of Franchisees: 12 in 11 States

In Business Since: 1981

Equity Capital Needed: $50,000 to $75,000

Financial Assistance Available: None

Training Provided: Initial 10 day intensive training course in all phases of operations followed by on-site additional training for a minimum of 1 week and usually running for 3 weeks. Additional periodic refreshers and seminars.

Managerial Assistance Available: Franchisor provides complete operational package encompassing all aspects from marketing and promotion to complete accounting system. Franchisor is available to meet needs of the franchisee for the entire term of the agreement and also makes periodic calls to franchise unit for evaluation and assistance.

Information Submitted: August 1987

BEEFY'S, INC.
107 Music City Circle
Suite 208
Nashville, Tennessee 37214
Charles R. Montgomery, President

Description of Operation: Beefy's Hamburgers is a double drive-thru only, fast food restaurant, specializing in 100 percent pure beef hamburgers, French fried and soft drinks.

Number of Franchisees: 23 plus 3 company-owned in Tennessee, Kentucky, South Carolina, Alabama, and Georgia. Units are under construction in Louisiana, Illinois, and North Carolina.

In Business Since: 1984

Equity Capital Needed: $25,000-$150,000 excluding land.

Financial Assistance Available: None

Training Provided: A mandatory pre-opening 2 week training course is conducted in Nashville, Tennessee. Course is 2 days classroom, and remainder, extensive on-the-job training in a corporate-owned store.

Managerial Assistance Available: Managerial and technical assistance is provided for site selection, layout, equipment purchases, training of personnel, selection of suppliers and the opening. A general manual and manual of operations, covering restaurant operations, quality standards, financial control, etc., is provided. Additional ongoing assistance is provided through periodic on-site inspection and review of operational procedures.

Information Submitted: June 1987

BEN FRANKS FRANCHISING CORPORATION
1300 Hancock Street
Redwood City, California 94063
Stephen S. Hiller

Description of Operation: Ben Franks Restaurants are 216 square feet, free-standing, drive thru/walk-up with limited menu facilities.

Number of Franchisees: 6 in California and Nevada

In Business Since: 1979

Equity Capital Needed: Less than 428,000. Franchise fee for first restaurant is $15,000. Additional restaurants $10,000 per location. Site location fee: $10,000 first site, $7,500 each additional site. Miscellaneous expenses (lease, deposits, fees) generally less than $8,000 per site. Building, equipment and leasehold improvement package approximately $115,000.

Financial Assistance Available: None. Independent financing is available to qualified individuals.

Training Provided: 2 week courst—1 week classroom 1 week company store plus 1 week assistance on-site.

Managerial Assistance Available: Continuing technical assistance provided throughout life of franchise. Including site review, advertising, product development.

Information Submitted: May 1987

BENIHANA OF TOKYO
8685 N.W. 53rd Terrace
P. O. Box 520210
Miami, Florida 33152
Michael W. Kata, Director of Licensee Operations

Description of Operation: Benihana is a Japanese style steakhouse. But what immediately sets Benihana apart from other restaurants, is its method of food preparation. All foods are prepared on the same table around which guests are seated. Each table seats eight, leaving room for a Japanese chef to do slicing, seasoning and cooking in full view of everyone.

Number of Franchisees: 7 in 6 States and Canada

In Business Since: First company-owned restaurant opened 1964, first franchise restaurant opened 1970.

Equity Capital Needed: $350,000

Financial Assistance Available: A total investment of at least $850,000 is necessary to build and open a Benihana restaurant. A substantial protion of this cost can normally be financed, depending on the franchisee's financial soundness. However, Benihana does not provide any financing to its franchisees.

127

Training Provided: An intensive 12 week training course is available for all restaurant management staff. An intensive 8 to 12 week training course is available for all chefs. All training is performed at a company restaurant under the supervision of a full-time Benihana employee.

Managerial Assistance Available: Benihana provides free consultation for the life of the franchise in all phases of the restaurant operation including bookkeeping, inventory control and menu development. Complete manuals of operations, forms, recipes are provided. District and field managers are available in different regions to work with each franchisee if requested.

Information Submitted: May 1987

* BIG BOY FAMILY RESTAURANTS MARRIOTT CORPORATION
Marriott Drive, Department 868.53
Washington, D.C. 20058
Attention: Franchise Department

Description of Operation: Big Boy is a full service, moderately priced family restaurant serving a high quality basic American menu at breakfast, lunch and dinner in a 5,000 square foot building open seven days a week from 6 a.m. to 12 midnight.

Number of Franchisees: 25 franchisees operating over 600 Big Boy restaurants in 30 States, Canada, Japan and Indonesia.

In Business Since: 1936

Equity Capital Needed: Minimum net worth of $1,000,000 plus franchise fee per unit of $25,000.

Financial Assistance Available: None

Training Provided: Intensive training conducted at Big Boy headquarters in Washington, D.C. Executive, unit management and hourly training encompasses site selection, construction management, pre-opening hiring, training, opening procedures, operating management and control.

Managerial Assistance Available: Full resources of the Marriott Corporation in marketing, procurement, personnel, operations, training, maintenance, accounting, design and construction.

Information Submitted: June 1987

BIG CHEESE PIZZA CORPORATION
1877 North Rock Road
P. O. Box 8087
Wichita, Kansas 67208
Andre Job, President

Description of Operation: Pizza franchise system offering a heavy topping, high value pizza product to customers. Unit size range between 1,800 to 4,000 square feet. Free standing image building plans for 2,700 square feet are available.

Number of Franchisees: 66 in 7 States and Puerto Rico

In Business Since: 1977

Equity Capital Needed: $250,000

Financial Assistance Available: None

Training Provided: Classroom and on-job training for a 14 day period conducted at home office and company units. Seven day training period the first week of franchisees store opening.

Managerial Assistance Available: Big Cheese Pizza provides periodic training seminars for franchisees and operations personnel. Complete operations and management manuals are also provided. Franchise field representative inspects units periodically and assists franchisee with operational and marketing problems.

Information Submitted: May 1987

BIG ED'S HAMBURGERS FRANCHISE SYSTEMS
P. O. Box 32165
Oklahoma City, Oklahoma 73120
Ed Thomas, President

Description of Operation: Family restaurant specializing in hamburgers.

Number of Franchisees: 26 in Oklahoma and Kansas

InBusinessSince: 1964 Franchising since 1982

Equity Capital Needed:

Financial Assistance Available: None

Training Provided: 3 weeks management and operations prior to opening. Training of employees prior to opening (approximately 4 days) and supervision/training during first days open (4-8 days as needed).

Managerial Assistance Available: Big Ed's provides continuing consultation throughout the term of the contract. Short-term workshops are provided to upgrade and improve operational skills. Areas included are bookkeeping, cooking procedures, supervision of employees, marketing skills and more. Operations consultants makes periodic visits to aid in helping franchisee maintain procedures consistent with established procedures.

Information Submitted: May 1987

* BOARDWALK FRIES
9051 Baltimore National Pike
Ellicott City, Maryland 21043
David DiFerdinando, President

Description of Operation: Fast food—French fries, fried veggies, fresh cut potatoes, fried in hot peanut oil, served with toppings of cheese or gravy, sold with sodas.

Number of Franchisees: 50 in 15 States and Washington, D.C.

In Business Since: 1981

Equity Capital Needed: Initial franchise fee with down payment on location—total to amount to between $60,000 and $145,000 total.

Financial Assistance Available: Through commercial lending institution, possibly in house assistance.

Training Provided: 14 days training.

Managerial Assistance Available: 3 days, longer if necessary.

Information Submitted: May 1987

* BOBBY RUBINO'S USA, INC.
5353 North Federal Highway
Suite 306
Ft. Lauderdale, Florida 33308
Gerald Moniz, Director of Operations

Description of Operation: Bobby Rubino's Place for Ribs is a full service restaurant specializing in barbequed ribs and chicken. Each store is approximately 7,600 square feet.

Number of Franchisees: 9 plus 10 company affiliated in Florida, Pennsylvania, New York, New Jersey, Illinois, Canada, California, and Indiana.

In Business Since: 1978

Equity Capital Needed: $500,000 plus

Financial Assistance Available: None

Training Provided: 28 day intensive management training program at home office and in home market restaurants for key people. Two to 5 weeks training on-site from pre-opening until all franchisees and staff is confortable with the system.

Managerial Assistance Available: Continual management for the life of the franchise in bookkeeping, advertising (franchiser controls a flat 2 percent of annual gross). Complete operation manuals, forms and materials are provided. Excellent marketing support.

Information Submitted: May 1987

BO-JAMES SALOON
188 South Clinton
Suite 300
Iowa City, Iowa 52240
Leah Cohen, National Franchise Director

Description of Operation: The sale of gourmet burgers, steaks, and seafood restaurants and their services. Also the sale of liquor where feasible.

Number of Franchisees: 3 in Iowa, Colorado, Wisconsin, and Illinois.

In Business Since: 1983

Equity Capital Needed: $150,000 to $450,000

Financial Assistance Available: Partial financing of equipment.

Training Provided: Full training in food preparation, food service, management and bookkeeping. Training 1 to 2 weeks.

Managerial Assistance Available: Ongoing

Information Submitted: June 1987

BOJANGLES' OF AMERICA, INC.
c/o BOJANGLES' CORPORATION
P. O. Box 240239
Charlotte, North Carolina 28224-8837
A. N. Rudelic
Director, Franchise Development

Description of Operation: Bojangles' is a fast-service food operation featuring Cajun style cooking, offering Cajun mild southern style fried chicken and home-made biscuits. The units offer a 3-plus meal opportunity for the consumer. All products are fresh and prepared at each location. The majority of the locations are free-standing facilities offering 40 to 100 seats and drive-through windows.

Number of Franchisees: 46 in 15 States, (151 Franchise Units)

In Business Since: 1977

Equity Capital Needed: Cash requirements: $120,000-$150,000 range.

Financial Assistance Available: Recommendations available.

Training Provided: 5 weeks management training. Continuous training at unit level.

Managerial Assistance Available: Continuous service from our field service department. Real estate site selection assistance. equipment purchasing assistance. Product evaluation continuously. Complete marketing program for advertisement.

Information Submitted: May 1987

BONANZA RESTAURANTS
Division of USA CAFES
8080 North Central Expressway
Suite 500Dallas, Texas 75106-1666
Ronald Parker, Senior Vice President, Finance and Franchise Development
Brian Beach, Director, Franchise Development
Ken Myres, Director, Franchise Development

Description of Opeation: Franchisor of Bonanza Restaurants.

Number of Franchisees: 585 in 43 States, Canada, and Puerto Rico

In Business Since: Bonanza International, Inc. from 1966 to October 1983; Bonanza restaurants since 1983

Equity Capital Needed: Amounts vary depending on structural locale, etc. Contact company for full particulars.

Financial Assistance Available: Contact company

Training Provided: 5 days training in company classrooms plus minimum of 30 days on-the-job training. 5 to 7 days spent in unit by company representative and/or representative of area developer if applicable.

Managerial Assistance Available: Continuous guidance by all company personnel when and as needed; calls via telephone and in person on continuous basis during life of license agreement. Special visits in person when and as conditions required.

Information Submitted: July 1987

BOWINCAL INTERNATIONAL, INC.
421 Virginia Street West
Charleston, West Virginia 25302
Buford Jividen, President

Description of Operation: Bowincal offers franchises for its family fast-food restaurants featuring "simply delicious" olde fashioned hot dogs and Bowincal soft-serve ice cream. Each store is free standing or store-front (most remodelled existing structures), with approximately 1,100-1,500 square feet. Bowincal provides a complete set of specs and drawings for the standardized equipment and decor.

Number of Franchisees: 11 in West Virginia

In Business Since: 1973

Equity Capital Needed: $25,000

Financial Assistance Available: A total investment of $55,000 to $75,000 is required to open a Bowincal franchise. The $25,000 cash required represents the franchise fee of $9,500, down payments on equipment and remodeling, security deposits, licenses and opening inventory. Bowincal provides no financing.

Training Provided: 10 day training program at the company training center and Bowincal opening crew spends 2 weeks training franchisee's and opening inventory. Bowincal provides no financing.

Managerial Assistance Available: Bowincal offers franchisees its expertise in all phases of day to day operations; including employment, training, systems, sadvertising and sales promotion, inspection, retraining, uniforms and accounting systems.

Information Submitted: May 1987

BOY BLUE OF AMERICA, INC.
10919 West Janesville Road
Hales Corners, Wisconsin 53130

Description of Operation: Franchising of soft serve, and limited menu stores.

Number of Franchisees: 14 in 2 States

In Business Since: 1963

Equity Capital Needed: Over $40,000

Financial Assistance Available: Boy Blue of America, Inc., will assist the operator in finding sources of financing and will assist in the preparation of the necessary financial statements.

Training Provided: The operator is required to complete a 2 week training program and pass all the tests connected with the course.

Managerial Assistance Available: Semi-annual advertising meetings and profit seminars for the franchisees.

Information Submitted: August 1987

BOZ HOT DOGS
770 East 142nd Street
Dolton, Illinois 60419
Don Hart, PresidentHarry Banks, C.B.

Description of Operation: Fast food carry-out—no grills or fryers. All steam-table operations. Limited menu.

Number of Franchisees: 20 in Indiana, and Illinois plus 6 company-owned.

In Business Since: 1969

Equity Capital Needed: $40,000

Financial Assistance Available: None

Training Provided: New franchisee trained on location for 1 month, assistance from then on.

Managerial Assistance Available: Assistance from day one, stands are checked weekly for freshness, and cleanliness.

Information Submitted: May 1987

BREAD & COMPANY, LTD.
THE INTERNATIONAL CAFE
9023 Frankford Avenue
Philadelphia, Pennsylvania 19114
Jack Perlman, General Manager

Description of Operation: A modular bakery/pastry/food operation specializing in high quality breads, croissants, European pastry, and international foods in an up-scale atmosphere. Full service and self-service configuration. Store size from 1,200 square feet to 1,200 square feet to 2,500 square feet

Number of Franchisees: 3 master franchises in Pennsylvania.

In Business Since: 1980

Equity Capital Needed: Total unit costs vary from $125,000 to $285,000.

Financial Assistance Available: None by franchisor directly. Other sources will finance on individual credit worthiness.

Training Provided: 2 weeks for administration, 4 weeks in company's units and 1 week during opening.

Managerial Assistance Available: Complete support system from location finding, layouts, design criteria, equipment and product specifications, pre-opening hiring and training. Periodic visits to store and operation guidance.

Information Submitted: August 1987

BRIDGEMAN'S RESTAURANT, INC.
3706 Enterprise Drive, S.W.
Rochester, Minnesota 55902
Wayne Thede, President

Description of Operation: Bridgeman's is a chain of ice cream parlours and restaurants. They feature quality family style food and specialize in ice cream creations.

Number of Franchisees: 25 units in Minnesota, Iowa and Wisconsin including company-owned.

In Business Since: 1941

Equity Capital Needed: $90,000-$100,000

Financial Assistance Available: None

Training Provided: 3 weeks intensive classroom and on-sight training. Help in selecting and training workforce.

Managerial Assistance Available: Complete manuals of operation, forms, and directions are provided. District managers are available to work closely with franchisees and assist in solving particular store problems. Quarterly franchise meetings are held.

Information Submitted: June 1987

BROWNS CHICKEN
2311 West 22nd Street
Oak Brook, Illinois 60521
Frank Portillo, Jr.

Description of Operation: Combination sit down/carry-out restaurants. Specialty "chicken."

Number of Franchisees: 123 (including 32 company-owned) in Midwest and Florida.

In Business Since: 1965

Equity Capital Needed: $100,000 to $150,000 and ability to obtain financing on a additional $300,000 to $350,000.

Financial Assistance Available: Franchisees must obtain their own financing

Training Provided: 6 weeks training school plus continual training on an inspection basis or request from franchisee.

Managerial Assistance Available: Training school, monthly field inspections, special assistance upon request, annual franchise seminar and spring and fall advertising meetings.

Information Submitted: May 1987

BUBBA'S BREAKAWAY FRANCHISE SYSTEMS, INC.
PFG Building, Suite
102270 Walker Drive
State College, Pennsylvania 16801
Joseph I. Shulman, Executive Vice President,
Franchise Development

Description of Operation: Bubba's Breakaway offers the franchisee a unique opportunity in the area of home delivery of subs and cheesesteaks. Quality, variety and free delivery are the fundamentals stressed in each store unit. A complete menu of sandwiches, cheesesteaks, pierogies, tacos, chips, salads, and soups are offered the the public through free home delivery.

Number of Franchisees: 13 with 22 stores in 6 States

InBusiness Since: 1981

Equity Capital Needed: $28,500 minimum

Financial Assistance Available: A total investment of approximately $70,000 is necessary to open a Babba's Breakaway store unit. Bubba's Breakaway Franchise Systems, Inc., provides no direct financing. However, the corporation will assist the franchisee in securing outside financing through the franchisee's own sources or one suggested by the franchise corporation.

Training Provided: Intensive, 21-day, mandatory training course is scheduled for all new franchisees and their personnel. 14 days are conducted at the home office school and at corporately-owned stores; 7 days at franchisee's store unit under the supervision of full-time Bubba's Breakaway Franchise Systems, Inc. employees.

Managerial Assistance Available: Bubba's Breakaway Franchise Systems, Inc., provides continual management service for the life of the franchise in such areas as recordkeeping, advertising, inventory control and store operations. A complete manual of operations, forms, directions and advertising is provided. District operations managers are available in all regions to work closely with franchisees and visit stores regularly to assist solving problems. Bubba's Breakaway sponsors a franchise advisory council and conducts marketing and product research to maintain high Bubba's Breakaway consumer acceptance.

Information Submitted: May 1987

BUN N BURGER INTERNATIONAL, INC.
370 Lexington Avenue
New York, New York 10017

Description of Operation: Hamburger shops.

Number of Franchisees: 4 in New York and New Jersey plus 7 company-owned.

In Business Since: 1968

Equity Capital Needed: Over $70,000

Financial Assistance Available: None

Training Provided: As long as required.

Managerial Assistance Available: As much technical assistance as is needed for as long a period as is necessary.

Information Submitted: August 1987

BURGER BARON
9725 East 46th Place
Tulsa, Oklahoma 74146
Bob Waller

Description of Operation: Drive thru fast food.

Number of Franchisees: 2 in Oklahoma

In Business Since: 1985

Equity Capital Needed: $135,000

Financial Assistance Available: None

Training Provided: 3 month store and classroom training.

Managerial Assistance Available: Supervisor assistance in local area.

Information Submitted: May 1987

*BURGER KING CORPORATION
P. O. Box 520783 (M.S. #1643)
Miami, Florida 33152
Oliver P. Brown, Vice President, Franchise Affairs

Description of Operation: Limited menu restaurants specializing in hamburgers. The company's operating philosophy is to consistently serve quality food, reasonably priced with fast courteous service in clean, pleasant surroundings.

Number of Franchisees: More than 5,240 restaurants, including approximately 788 company operated units, located in all 50 States, Puerto Rico, and 28 international markets.

In Business Since: 1954

Equity Captial Needed: $500,000 net worth of which $250,000 must be in liquid assets.

Financial Assistance Available: Franchisees must arrange their own financing which can usually be obtained from local banks and national finance or leasing companies.

Training Provided: Preopening training consists of a comprehensive restaurant operations training program at regional training centers and operating restaurants, and a management course at Burger King University in Miami, Florida.

Managerial Assistance Available: Restaurant development, operations, marketing, human resource, accounting and training. Operations, equipment and accounting manuals are loaned to the franchisee.

Information Submitted: August 1987

BUSCEMI'S INTERNATIONAL
30362 Gratiot Avenue
Roseville, Michigan 48066
Anthony Buscemi

Description of Operation: Fast food—pizza, submarines, steak sandwiches. Dine in, carry out, drive thru window.

Number of Franchisees: 22 in Michigan including 8 company-owned.

In Business Since: 1975

Equity Capital Needed: $50,000

Financial Assistance Available: None

Training Provided: 4 week training program at operating location.

Managerial Assistance Available: 2 week in-store training by supervisor, company policy book and operating manual.

Information Submitted: August 1987

* **CALIFORNIA SMOOTHIE**
  1033 Clifton Avenue
  Clifton, New Jersey 07013
  Robert B. Keilt, President

Description of Operation: Limited menu 'healthy foods' featuring "California Smoothies" frozen yogurt with unlimited toppings, quiche, pita lites, salads, soup, and other fresh juice beverages. Typically located in mall food courts or in-line stores between 500 and 1,200 square feet.

Number of Franchisees: 10 in 6 States

In Business Since: 1973

Equity Capital Needed: Investment between $129,000 and $197,000 total.

Financial Assistance Available: Franchisor does not provide financing but will assist franchisee in preparing package for presentation to financing institutions.

Training Provided: Minimum of 8 days in company store and home office plus 2 weeks with opening team on franchisee's premises. Longer training available at no additional cost to franchisee if requested by franchisee.

Managerial Assistance Available: In addition to preopening traning, franchisor provides assistance with supplier selection, employee training, complete design and construction, equipment selection, and ongoing supervision through franchisor's regional operations managers for the entire term of the initial agreement (typically 10 years).

Information Submitted: May 1987

CALLAHAN'S INTERNATIONAL, INC.
520 Main Street
Fort Lee, New Jersey 07024
Leonard J. Castrianni

Description of Operation: Mention the name Callahan's to any hot dog lover and you will most likely hear "Biggest" and "Best Hot Dog Around." Since its establshment in 1950 as a fast food restaurant. Callahan's has stood second to none in strict quality control. Meat for hot dogs, hamburgers, and sausage sandwiches has always been of the highest quality. The potatoes for the French fries have always been prepared fresh, never frozen. That same uncompromising insistence upon quality control has been the guiding principle for the owners of Callahan's over thirty years.

Number of Franchisees: 3 plus 1 company-owned in New Jersey

In Business Since: 1950

Equity Capital Needed: $150,000 to $500,000

Financial Assistance Available: A $2,500 security deposit is necessary atr time of consideration. The balance of the franchise fee $32,500 is payable in full at time of signing contracts. No additional financing is provided.

Training Provided: A 3 month training program at the company-owned store plus 2 weeks at franchisee's store is necessary. After this program is completed, constant supervision from company is conducted on a weekly and monthly basis.

Managerial Assistance Available: Callahan's International provides constant management and technical assistance for the duration of the franchise. District managers are constantly available to help in supervision of the stores and readily available on a daily basis to help involving problems that may arise.

Information Submitted: August 1987

* **CAPTAIN D'S**
  P. O. Box 1260
  1727 Elm Hill Pike
  Nashville, Tennessee 37202
  Attention: Franchise Director

Description of Operation: Seafood and hamburger restaurant with carry-out of self-service dining room. Menu features variety of seafood served in a pleasant, nautical theme atmosphere.

Number of Franchisees: 210 stores in 23 States

In Business Since: 1969

Equity Capital Needed: $100,000 and up depending on operators' ability to finance.

Financial Assistance Available: Franchisee is responsible for land, building and equipment.

Training Provided: 4 weeks formal and in-store training plus continuing on-the-job supervision.

Managerial Assistance Available: Captain D's is a division of a multi-state restaurant chain. This program first opened in 1969 and now have over 400 stores open. All operational and technical services of the parent company are available to the franchisee.

Information Submitted: May 1987

CARBONE'S PIZZA
680 East 7th Street
St. Paul, Minnesota 55106
Thomas Carbone, President

Description of Operation: Family restaurant specializing in pizza and Italian food.

Number of Franchisees: 14 in Minnesota and Wisconsin

In Business Since: 1953—franchising since 1967

Equity Capital Needed: $20,000

Financial Assistance Available: No direct financial assistance is provided.

Training Provided: 4 weeks including on-the-job training and opening assistance.

Managerial Assistance Available: Ongoing assistance in advertising and other business aspects. Periodic visits and guidance as needed.

Information Submitted: June 1987

* **CARL KARCHER ENTERPRISES, INC.**
  1200 North Harbor Boulevard
  Anaheim, California 92803
  Frank Karcher, Vice President of Franchising

Description of Operation: Carl Karcher Enterprises operates a chain of fast food restaurants which offers moderately priced, high quality food in attractive and comfortable surroundings. A diversified menu features hamburgers, specialty sandwiches, salad bar, dessert items and breakfasts.

Number of Franchisees: 81 plus 350 company-owned in California, Arizona, and Nevada

In Business Since: 1956

Equity Capital Needed: $250,000 net worth of which $175,000 must be in liquid assets from non-borrowed funds.

Financial Assistance Available: Interim financing for land and construction with third party committment to assume franchisors position.

Training Provided: 1 week of classroom and an additional 9 weeks of in-restaurant training at CKE corporate headquarters in Anaheim, California.

Managerial Assistance Available: Site selection, real estate construction and orientation course, prior to opening. Opening assistance. Thereafter, CKE will provide franchise operations personnel to assist the franchise operator during the entire term of the franchise.

Information Submitted: May 1987

* **CASA LUPITA RESTAURANTS, INC.**
  P. O. Box 578
  Dayton, Ohio 45401
  Richard E. Hillesheim

Description of Operation: An upscale, full-service Mexican dinnerhouse operation.

Number of Franchisees: 27 including company-owned in 9 States.

In Business Since: 1982

Equity Capital Needed: Approximately 1 million dollars.

Financial Assistance Available: None

Training Provided: We offer a 6 and a 1/2 week course which prepares store level management for the proper operation of a Cash Lupita. We also offer additional, on-the-job training for supervisors and a week-long course geared specifically to franchisees.

Managerial Assistance Available: In addition to that mentioned above, we offer ongoing assistance from all facets of the business—operations, marketing, purchasing, menu development, etc.

Information Submitted: May 1987

CASSANO'S, INC.
1700 East Stroop Road
Dayton, Ohio 45429-5095
Richard O. Soehner, Senior Vice President

Description of Operation: Cassano's, Inc., a wholly owned subsidiary of Greyhound Food Management, Inc., operates and franchises Cassano's Pizza & Subs, specializing in the sale of pizzas, subs, and beverages. The business specializes in home delivery, carry-out, and has some units with limited seating. There are 71 operating units.

Number of Franchisees: 17 in 4 States including Ohio, Kentucky, Missouri, and Illinois

In Business Since: 1953

Equity Capital Needed: $250,000 net worth with 250,000 in liquid assets. Total investment (excluding building and land) approximately $105,000 to $250,000.

Financial Assistance Available: No direct finaincing, but third party commitments available with no franchisor guarantees.

Training Provided: 4 weeks in unit/classroom in home office facility. Ongoing training provided.

Managerial Assistance Available: Ongoing assistance for all facets of the business—regular visits and consultation from franchisor's field representatives.

Information Submitted: July 1987

CASTLEBURGER INTERNATIONAL, CORP.
1500 N.W. 49th Street
Suite 605
Ft. Lauderdale, Florida 33309
Linda D. Biciocchi, President

Description of Operation: Fast food hamburger chain.

Number of Franchisees: 5 in Florida

In Business Since: 1985

Equity Capital Needed: $100,000

Financial Assistance Available: Having financing company for equipment, no other financing is available.

Training Provided: 2 week training program

Managerial Assistance Available: Ongoing operations, marketing, purchasing, finance, accounting, real estate and construction.

Information Submitted: May 1987

CATFISH SHAK
RESTAURANT DEVELOPMENT, CORP., OF AMERICA, INC.
353 Courthouse Road
Gulfport, Mississippi 39507
J. R. Rick Carter

Description of Operation: Seafood restaurant franchise with rustic decor, featuring farm raised catfish, cajun style dishes and country cooking.

Number of Franchisees: 9 in Texas, Florida, Mississippi and Louisiana.

In Business Since: 1982

Equity Capital Needed: $850,000-$1,000,000

Financial Assistance Available: None

Training Provided: 4-6 weeks training at headquarters.

Managerial Assistance Available: Provide manuals, training program at headquarters, periodic visits as needed by field representatives.

Information Submitted: May 1987

CATFISH STATIONS OF AMERICA, INC.
2834 Airways Boulevard
Memphis, Tennessee 38116
Charles E. Parnell, President

Description of Operation: Fast food restaurants featuring Mississippi farm raised, grain fed catfish.

Number of Franchisees: 2 in Tennessee

In Business Since: 1985

Equity Capital Needed: ,000

Financial Assistance Available: Will provide lease for portable building and equipment at cost of $225,000.

Training Provided: 2 weeks in headquarters store, 1 week in franchisee's location.

Managerial Assistance Available: Building and equipment is a turnkey operation, plus thorough training in hiring of employees, sales techniques, counter operations, cash registers and computer accounting procedures; preparation of recipes and other menu items and interpretations of the operation manual, continued supervision throughout the term of the agreement.

Information Submitted: May 1987

CHEESE VILLA
INTERNATIONAL SERVICES COMPANY, LTD.
One Bowen Place
126 East Sixth Street, Suite 301
Cincinnati, Ohio 45202
Carlton C. Perin, President

Description of Operation: Non-cooking, limited menu food service for on-premise consumption and carry-out. Deli-style sandwiches featured plus gourmet soups, salads, desserts and soft serve yogurt. Primary locations are in downtown high traffic areas, major office buildings and commercial retail plazas. Format breakfast items. Typical hours of operation 7 am to 6 pm and limited Saturday operaton depending upon location.

Number of Franchisees: 10 franchises in 6 States

In Business Since: 1975

Equity Capital Needed: $30,000 to $70,000 depending upon total cost of project and strength of your financial statement. Total cost can range from $75,000 to $250,000.

Financial Assistance Available: No direct financing provided. Assistance is provided in preparing presentations to lending institutions. SBA guaranteed loans have been obtained for several Cheese Villas.

Training Provided: 1 week of home study, 2 weeks of training in a Cheese villa shop. Training includes stocking, food preparation, store management, advertising and promotion. One week prior to opening a supervisor handles receipts of inventory, stocking of store, and grand opening preparations. Supervisory personnel on hand during first week of opening.

Managerial Assistance Available: Location evaluation, lease negotiation, grand opening allowance, and continuing assistance. Inspection, financial and administration consultation, and protected operating territory. communication by correspondence, telephone and visitation.

Information Submitted: August 1987

CHELSEA STREET PUB
c/o RANKEN INC.
8802 Shoal Creek
P. O. Box 9989
Austin, Texas 78766
Norman Crohn, President

Description of Operation: Chelsea Street offers a quick service seated food and drink operation in a English Pub atmosphere serving deli type sandwiches, salads, and a unique limited menu requiring no cooking. Also serving fancy alcoholic drinks of all types as well as beer and wine. Live entertainment nitely. Primarily located in major enclosed malls of high traffic, hours 11 am until 2 am six days a week.

Number of Franchisees: 9 plus 12 company-owned in Texas, New Mexico, Louisiana, Florida and Tennessee.

In Business Since: 1973

Equity Capital Needed; $150,000

Financial Assistance Available: Total investment is approximately $280,000 the franchisee is required to arrange own financing however Chelsea Street will assist in obtaining franchising by providing background information, projections, references etc., to the bank of franchisee's choice.

Training Provided: Mandatory 45 day intensive training program including 15 days in Chelsea Street's home office school plus 30 days in on-the-job supervised training encompassing every phase of running a successful Cehlsea Street Pub.

Managerial Assistance Available: Chelsea Street provides both technical and managerial assistance throughout the life of the franchise. Chelsea street will supply site selection and build a complete pub as well as assist in opening the unit plus training all personnel. Continued assistance in advertising, supply, bookkeeping and entertainment and controls are provided in addition complete manuals of operations as well as forms and directions are provided and updated. 24 hour direct line consultation as well as periodic visits by Chelsea Street supervisors are provided to assist in maximizing income and quality.

Information Submitted: August 1987

CHICAGO'S PIZZA, INC.
9060 Crawfordsville, Rd.
Indianapolis, Ind. 46234
Robert L. McDonald

Description of Operation: Pizza, sandwiches, salad bar.

Number of Franchisees: 2 in Indiana.

In Business Since: 1979

Equity Capital Needed: $80,000 to $200,000

Financial Assistance Available: None

Training Provided: Complete 4 week opening, 2 weeks on site after opening and quarterly inspection.

Managerial Assistance Available: Consult in all areas.

Information Submitted: May 1987.

* CHICKEN DELIGHT OF CANADA, LTD.
395 Berry Street
Winnipeg, Manitoba
Canada R3J 1N6
Otto Koch, President
Robert J. Ritchie, Director of Marketing

Description of Operation: Inside dining and/or carry-out and delivery restaurant plus catering; some units also have drive-through windows. All facilities feature chicken, shrimp, fish, BBQ ribs and pizza. Area franchises also available.

Number of Franchisees: 87 in 6 States, Canada and Trinidad

In Business Since: 1952

Equity Capital Needed: $101,000 to $275,000 (Exclusive of land costs), depending on size of unit, and ability to acquire additional financing.

Financial Assistance Available: None directly.

Training Provided: On-the-job training which includes all phases of operations.

Managerial Assistance Available: Continual assistance in all phases of operations.

Information Submitted: May 1987

CHICKEN UNLIMITED ENTERPRISE, INC.
1531 North Federal Highway
Hollywood, Florida 33020
Bob Fullen, Executive Vice President

Description of Operation: Quick service dining featuring fried chicken. Menu consists of chicken sold by the individual part as well as dinners and boxes of large orders. Menu variety features fish, shrimp dinners, apple puffs, French fries and cole slaw, as well as soft drinks. A typical restaurant is a free standing building featuring a 50 seat dining area and carry-out section.

Number of Franchisees: 33 in 2 States and the Bahamas including company-owned

In Business Since: 1964

Equity Capital Needed: $50,000

Financial Assistance Available: None

Training Provided: An operations specialist is present to work with the operator and most importantly, to assist in the training of the new personnel.

Managerial Assistance Available: Chicken Unlimited has a field operations specialists who visit each restaurant frequently for continuing management guidance, training, and assistance with promotions.

Information Submitted: May 1987

CHILI GREAT CHILI, INC.
215 West Franklin Street
Suite 307
Monterey, California 93940
Vernon W. Haas, President

Description of Operation: Restaurant, original chili, vegetarian chili, and new hothead chili, served in one hundred ways. Salad bar, beer and wine.

Number of Franchisees: 2 in California

In Business Since: 1984

Equity Capital Needed: $100,000

Financial Assistance Available: None.

Training Provided: 1 month training provided in all aspects of operations.

Managerial Assistance Available: Turnkey operation

Information Submitted: August 1987

CHOWDER POT INTERNATIONAL
2 Market Yard
Freehold, New Jersey 07728
Robert Dehl, Vice President

Description of Operation: Family seafood restaurants.

Number of Franchisees: 6 in New Jersey

In Business Since: 1971

Equity Capital Needed: $85,000 start-up cash; $300,000 total investment.

Financial Assistance Available: No financing assistance available.

Training Provided: 8 weeks in-store training covering all areas of operation.

Managerial Assistance Available: Ongoing training, on-site inspections monthly, managerial communications and organizational tools.

Information Submitted: May 1987

CHURCH'S FRIED CHICKEN, INC.
P. O. Box BH001
San Antonio, Texas 78284
George Samaris, Vice President, Franchising

Description of Operation: Fast food restaurant.

Number of Franchisees: 160 in 22 States including the District of Columbia, Canada, Mexico, Puerto Rico, Indonesia, and Oman, Panama, Taiwan, Singapore, and Jakarta.

In Business Since: 1952

Equity Capital Needed: Varies

Financial Assistance Available: None

Training Provided: Store and classroom training in a CFC Management Development Center for 4 weeks.

Managerial Assistance Available: Real estate/construction consultant assistance during site selection and construction of all stores. Operations field consultant assistance during opening of all new stores and duration of the store thereafter.

Information Submitted: May 1987

CIRCLES INTERNATIONAL NATURAL FOODS, INC.
310 Bay Ridge Avenue
Brooklyn, New York 11220
John Fahy, Franchise Manager

Description of Operation: Large menu with mixed ethnic specialities from all over the world and inexpensive groumet fish and chicken dishes. Baked goods on premise and natural beverages.

Number of Franchisees: 8 in New York

In Business Since: 1976

Equity Capital Needed: Over $260,000 to open a store.

Financial Assistance Available: None

Training Provided: 2 weeks in home store and 2 weeks in franchisee's store.

Managerial Assistance Available: Daily checks on operations, five days. Ongoing development.

Information Submitted: August 1987

CLUCK IN A BUCKET INTERNATIONAL, INC.
2335 Honolulu Avenue
Montrose, California 91020
Robert R. Baird, President

Description of Operation: Fast food restaurant featuring skinless chicken only. Take-out and dine-in facilities. Restaurant offers side dishes with chicken that generally complement the lower cholesterol/lower calorie content of the skinless chicken.

Number of Franchisees: 3 in California

In Business Since: 1985

Equity Capital Needed: $215,000

Financial Assistance Available: None

Training Provided: 5 weeks in training facility and 1 full week in franchisee's restaurant. Training provided for 2 management persons per franchise. Franchisee pays for own travel to training site and food and lodging during training.

Managerial Assistance Available: On-site guidance, telephone "hot-line," manuals and training materials. On-site guidance provided by operational directors assigned to each franchise area, who are available to the franchisee as needed.

Information Submitted: May 1987

COCK OF THE WALK
P. O. Box 806
Natchez, Mississippi 39120
George Eyrich, President

Description of Operation: Cock of the Walk is a restaurant concept which serves mainly catfish fillet in a rustic style family restaurant, seating from 175 to 250. We furnish training.

Number of Franchisees: 16 in 7 States

In Business Since: 1977

Equity Capital Needed: Franchise cost $18,000 to $25,000 plus enough to get financing for $400,000 to $750,000 depending on size and area.

Financial Assistance Available: Franchisee is to arrange own outside financing.

Training Provided: 1 week training at restaurant of our choice for owner or manager and 2 or 3 key personnel and cooks. 1 weeks opening assistance in all phases of the operation, or longer if required.

Managerial Assistance Available: Manuals for construction and materials to be used, operational manual for bookkeeping, forms, day-to-day operation, cooking, pre-mix and recipes. A field representative is available to assist in solving problems. At least one annual meeting for franchisees plus training for any new products.

Information Submitted: August 1987

COLONEL LEE'S ENTERPRISES, INC.
3080 East 50th Street
Vernon, California 90058
Colonel John C. Lee, President

Description of Operation: Specialty fast service restaurant offering limited menu of individually prepared Monoglian barbeque of beef, lamb, pork and turkey meats and a variety of vegetables, Colonel Lee's special sauces, and other complimentary items. Emphasis is on efficient service with inside seating service. Restaurant is operated under the trade name of Colonel Lee's Mongolian Bar-B-Q. The concept and menu line dates back to beyond the 13th century of ancient China.

Number of Franchisees: 4 in California

In Business Since: 1967, franchise operation began in 1976.

Equity Capital Needed: $165,000 to $195,000 and ability to acquire financing.

Financial Assistance Available: None

Training Provided: 20 days on-the-job training mandatory. Complete opera tional manuals and handbook provided.

Managerial Assistance Available: Regular visits by field supervisors. Advertising program, accounting system, management training provided by home office throughout the operatins of the business. Advice and consultation with home office available on request.

Information Submitted: May 1987

COOKER CONCEPTS, INC.
2440 Gainstead Drive
P. O. Box 4999
Louisville, Kentucky 40204

Description of Operation: Fast food restaurant sales products—fresh made, non-fried foods, salads, sandwiches, natures pasta and soups.

Number of Franchisees: 6 in Kentucky and Tennessee plus 4 company-owned.

In Business Since: 1981

Equity Capital Needed: To open a fine unit location requires a combination of equity and credit approximately $175,000.

Financial Assistance Available: None

Training Provided: Extensive training over 8 weeks starting at training center located in Louisville, to in-store training with continuous training at franchisee's location.

Managerial Assistance Available: Continuous assistance provided via advertising, new products development and monthly in-store inspections and advice with a 100 point checklist for franchisees, each location is visited at minimum one time each month by franchisor staff. A complete operations manual is developed for each franchisee's use.

Information Submitted: August 1987

•COUNTRY KITCHEN INTERNATIONAL, INC.
7800 Metro Parkway
Minneapolis, Minnesota 55420
Richard B. Hohman, President and Chief Executive Officer

Description of Operation: Sit down service restaurant; family type, full-line menu offering home style cooked meals; modestly priced. 16-24 hour operation; high quality oriented; breakfast, lunch, dinner, sandwiches, desserts and beverages.

Number of Franchisees: 250 in 24 States and 2 Provinces in Canada

In Business Since: 1939

Equity Capital Needed: $55,000 plus

Financial Assistance Available: No direct financing available, but possible third party financing.

Training Provided: Classroom and on-the-job training, plus 1 to 2 weeks training during opening featuring complete manuals and audio visual training system.

Managerial Assistance Available: Supervision for the life of the contract, special menu service, programming advertising, purchasing programs, training up-dates, seminars, conventions, research and development, franchise committee meetings, and consulting services.

Information Submitted: May 1987

•COUSINS SUBMARINE SANDWICH SHOP SYSTEMS, INC.
N93 W16112 Megal Drive
Menomonee Falls, Wisconsin 53051
Ronald W. Hammel, Franchise Director

Description of Operation: Cousins Submarine Sandwich Shop Systems, Inc., offers a unique fast food restaurant operation. It specializes in a wide variety of submarine sandwiches which are served on bread baked fresh right on the premises. The ambience consists of clean, attractive facilities, fast, friendly service, great food at even greater value. The shops range from 1,700-2,500 square feet and are open from 10:30 a.m. to 11:30 p.m., 7 days per week.

Number of Franchisees: 1 in Wisconsin

In Business Since: 1972

Equity Capital Needed: $50,000 minimum

Financial Assistance Available: None

Training Provided: An intensive 20 day, mandatory training course is scheduled for all new franchisees and their designated manager. Following this training course an additional 5 days of on-site assistance is given for the purpose of facilitating the opening of the new operation and giving aid in establishing and standardizing procedures and techniques essential to the operation.

Managerial Assistance Available: Cousins Submarine Sandwich Shop Systems, Inc., provides advice and guidance on all material aspects of operating a Cousins Sandwich Shop for the life of the franchise. Complete manuals of operations, forms, and directions are provided. A field representative will work closely with franchisees and visit stores regularly to assist solving problems.

COZZOLI PIZZA SYSTEMS, INC.
555 N.E. 15th Street
Suite 33-D
Miami, Florida 33132
Merrill I. Lamb, President

Description of Operation: Regional Mall in line or food court units. dough only. We now ship a complete equipment package for an individual to go into business anywhere in the world. 750 to 1,200 square feet.

Number of Franchisees: 46 in Florida, Texas, California, Colorado, Tennessee, Virginia and Guatemala.

In Business Since: 1951

Equity Capital Needed: $40,000 cash—cost of units $60,000 to $125,000 depending on size.

Financial Assistance Available: Complete financial assistance above the minimum amount of $40,000.

Training Provided: 2 weeks in existing store and at least 1 week in his store under supervision. Training center is in Miami, Florida.

Managerial Assistance Available: We are available on any problem for as long as he wishes.

Information Submitted: May 1987

* CRUSTY'S PIZZA
Division of DINO'S USA, INC.
20700 Greenfield Road, Suite 500
Oak Park, Michigan 48237
John E. Ray, President
Paul C. Wolbert, Vice President

Description of Operation: Crusty's Pizza, offers one concept. This concept consists of a carry-out and delivery pizza unit which was the foundation for Crusty's overall success. All products are the best quality obtainable.

Number of Franchisees: 161 in 14 States

In Business Since: 1961

Equity Capital Needed: Total investment is in the range of $55,000 to $250,000, depending upon number of units.

Financial Assistance Available: Total investment depends on location from $50,000-$150,000. Will direct but will not guarantee financing through normal banking channels. Referral is made to developers who will develop locations for qualified franchisees.

Training Provided: Franchisees are required to attend a training program for a minimum of 300 hours which includes on-the-job training in designated units. The training includes all phases of the business with continuing assistance to open the franchised unit.

Managerial Assistance Available: Franchise relations personnel are on call if needed and will visit all locations on a regularly scheduled basis.

Information Submitted: May 1987

CUCOS INC.
3009 25th Street
Metairie, Louisiana 70002
Dennis Staub, Vice President, Franchise Development

Description of Operation: Cucos is an upscale Mexican restaurant, specializing in Sonoran-style cuisine which is less pepper-dominated, slightly spicy, and more flavorful. All ingredients are fresh and of the highest quality. Our menu offers a wide selection from steaks to seafood and traditional Mexican favorites like Fajitas, Chimichangas, and enchiladas.

Number of Franchisees: 12 in Alabama, Arkansas, Florida, Louisiana, Mississippi, Virginia and Wisconsin

In Business Since: 1981

Equity Capital Needed: $300,000 estimated

Financial Assistance Available: The capital requirement to open a Cucos restaurant will vary depending on local real estate values and costs to either lease or purchase the facility. Cucos Inc., estimates the total capital requirements will range between $295,000 to $745,000. Cucos Inc., does not provide any financing.

Training Provided: Comprehensive management training program must be completed before restaurant opening. Hourly training program is provided in the restaurant by franchisor prior to restaurant opening.

Managerial Assistance Available: Cucos provides continued assistance and training throughout the term of the franchise agreement. A regional supervisor periodically visits each restaurant. Each franchisee receives a set of operations manuals, along with assistance in site selection, marketing and advertising, food and equipment procurement, design and architectural services, staffing and training.

Information Submitted: May 1987

DAIRY BELLE FREEZE DEVELOPMENT COMPANY, INC.
570 Valley Way
Milpitas, California 95035
Steven H. Goodere, Executive Vice President

Description of Operation: Fast food restaurant featuring a complete line of soft-serve products, hamburgers, fries, specialty sandwiches, and much more.

Number of Franchisees: 17 in California

In Business Since: 1957

Equity Capital Needed: Depends upon the demographics of the area, landlord's requirements, and franchisee's financial statement.

Financial Assistance Available: Franchisor does not provide a finance program.

Training Provided: A minimum of 2 weeks training in company-owned stores. In-store assistance for additional time, as necessary.

Managerial Assistance Available: Continued assistance in all phases of the "Dairy Belle" restaurant operation, including food preparation, cost controls, marketing, accounting, insurance, new product development, purchasing programs, in-store inspections and evaluations, employee development, and customer service educational information.

Information Submitted: May 1987

DAIRY CHEER STORES
2914 Forgey Street
Ashland, Kentucky 41101
W. H. Culbertson

Description of Operation: Fast food, sandwiches, chicken, fish, soup, beans, soft-serve and hard ice cream and serve yourself desserts, salad bar. Available for most States.

Number of Franchisees: 10

In Business Since: 1949

Equity Capital Needed: $5,000 franchise fee, building $85,000; equipment $70,000 and signs $18,000. Approximately

Financial Assistance Available: Local bankers are usually very helpful.

Training Provided: On-the-job training before and after opening.

Managerial Assistance Available: Instructions in technical operations, inspections, advertising, formulas and recipes.

Information Submitted: May 1987

* DAIRY ISLE CORPORATION
P. O. Box 273
Utica, Michigan 48087
David K. Chapoton, President
Shirley Chapoton, Corporate Secretary

Description of Operation: Soft ice cream stores and fast food operation.

Number of Franchisees: 42 in 7 States

In Business Since: 1942

Equity Capital Needed: Minimum $35,000

Financial Assistance Available: Dairy Isle Corporation, does not provide direct financing to franchisees at the present time. However, it does provide assistnce in obtaining financing such as, assisting the franchisee in preparing his proposal for bank financing, and meeting with potential lenders.

Training Provided: 3 days or more depending on individuals being trained plus calls during the operating season.

Managerial Assistance Available: Operations of unit and follow up promotional ideas and equipment purchasing.

DAIRY SWEET CORPORATION
P. O. Box 35092
Des Moines, Iowa 50315
George Olson, President

Description of Operation: Fast food drive-in and carry-out restaurants featuring sandwiches, shrimp, chicken, soft drinks, and soft serve products. Franchisee should have enough capital for down payment plus ground improvements. sewer, water and cement slab on which to set the building. We provide the building plans, and all the equipment. New 1981 phase includes eat-in area seating up to 60 people.

Number of Franchisees: 82 in Illinois, Iowa, Kentucky and Nebraska.

In Business Since: 1952

Equity Capital Needed: $25-$35,000 franchisee responsible for land and building financing.

Financial Assistance Available: None

Training Provided: On-the-job training at time of installation. Time depends on the individual and how much is necessary.

Managerial Assistance Availble: Continuous as long as franchisee is in business and wants assistance.

Information Submitted: August 1987

DALY FRANCHISE COMPANY
31460 Myrna
Livonia, Michigan 48154
Gary Grace

Description of Operation: Daly restaurants feature a full service, moderately priced menu including breakfast, lunch and dinner items, featuring our 'gourmet Dalyburger," foot long "Daly Dog" and "Daly-Maid" ice cream.

Number of Franchisees: 6 in Michigan

In Business Since: 1948

Equity Capital Needed: $30,000 and up.

Financial Assistance Available: None

Training Provided: 2 weeks at company-owned store and 3 weeks at franchisee's store.

Managerial Assistance Available: Continuous technical assistance.

Information Submitted: August 1987

DAMON'S FRANCHISE CORP.
(DAMON'S THE PLACE FOR RIBS)
Building B, Suite 6
Village At Wexford
Hilton Head, SC 29928
Irving Rossman, Chairman of the Board

Description of Operation: Sit down family style barbecue restaurant with cocktail lounge. Featuring BBQ ribs, shrimp, BBQ chicken, steaks and seafood. Approximately 5,000-8,000 square feet. Number of seats 130-180. Either free standing building or shopping center store. can convert existing restaurant.

Number of Franchisees: 23 8 States, 5 company-owned stores.

In Business Since: 1979

Equity Capital Needed: $250,000-$350,000 total package.

Financial Assistance Available: None

Training Provided: 2 weeks at one of our locations and 2 weeks at your location at opening.

Managerial Assistance Available: Damon's provides continual management service for the life of the franchise in such areas as bookkeeping, advertising, inventory control. Complete manuals of opeations, forms, and directions are provided. District and field managers are available in all regions to work closely with franchises and visit stores regularly to assist district and field managers are available in all regions to work closely with franchises and visit stores regularly to assist problems.

Information Submitted: May 1987

DANVER'S INTERNATIONAL, INC.
P. O. Box 41379
Memphis, Tennessee 38174
T. L. Berry, Director of Franchising

Description of Operation: Quality fast food restaurants featuring charbroiled hamburgers, fresh roast beef sandwiches, 30 item salad and baked potato bar.

Number of Franchisees: 16 in 6 States

In Business Since: 1973

Equity Capital Needed: $200,000

Financial Assistance Available: None

Training Provided: 8 week training program for owner and managers.

Managerial Assistance Available: Continuing support of franchise field team.

Information Submitted: May 1987

DEL TACO MEXICAN CAFE
1801 Royal Lane
Suite 902
Dallas, Texas 75229
Claire D. Wright, Director of Franchising

Description of Operation: Del Taco is a Mexican, fast food restaurant with an upscale family appeal. Its new conversions offer table seating, featuring a wide variety of Mexican selections plus the standby hamburger and fries.

Number of Franchisees: 43 in 8 States.

In Business Since: 1965

Equity Capital Needed: For a single unit—liquid assets of $100,000 and a net worth of $250,000. For multi-units—liquid assets of $175,000 and a net worth of $500,000.

Financial Assistance Available: Financing available through Franchise Finance Corp. of America.

Training Provided: Training is provided for general manager, kitchen manager and franchisee's restaurant managers in operations training facility for such period of time as franchisor shall deem reasonably necessary, and shall complete that course to franchisor's reasonable satisfaction.

Managerial Assistance Available: Del Taco basically provides management training, preopening assistance, ongoing and follow-up assistance. Additionally, they help find site locations, and offer assistance with purveyors for purchasing; marketing programs and format assistance is provided.

Information Submitted: May 1897

DIAMOND DAVE'S TACO CO., INC.
118 South Clinton
Suite 300
Iowa City, Iowa 52240
Stanley White, National Franchise Director

Description of Operation: The sale of fast food Mexican restaurants and their services. Also the sale of liquor where feasible.

Number of Franchisees: 37 in Iowa, Illinois, Wisconsin, Missouri and Indiana.

In Business Since: 1978

Equity Capital Needed: $75,000 to $175,000

Financial Assistance Available: Partial financing of equipment.

Training Provided: Full training in food preparation, food service, management and bookkeeping. Training 1 to 2 weeks.

Managerial Assistance Available: Ongoing

Information Submitted: August 1987

DIETWORKS OF AMERICA, INC.
30 West Mount Pleasant Avenue
Livingston, New Jersey 07039
Leonard S. Torine, President

Description of Operation: Reduced calorie, gourmet, full service restaurants complete with retail department. Emphasis on fresh, quality contemporary cuisine. Average unit 2,000 square feet with 60-70 seats. We provide training and turnkey operation. Very timely concept. We have interest in going national with territories and individual units.

Number of Franchisees: 10 in New Jersey

In Business Since: First unit 1975; Dietworks of America formed 1982.

Equity Capital Needed: Total investment $150,000-$200,000—cash required depends on franchisee.

Financial Assistance Available: Possible guidance or assistance depending on financial background of franchisee.

Training Provided: Complete training in all phases of operation, 4-8 weeks at our training unit (New Jersey).

Managerial Assistance Available: Continuous ongoing management and support—new methods, recipes, technical assistance, marketing, etc.

Information Submitted: August 1987

* **DOG N SUDS RESTAURANTS**
  P. O. Box 162
  Utica, Michigan 48087
  David Chapoton, President

Description of Operation: Franchise company of drive-in and family sit-down restaurants, limited menu, specializing in a variety of hot dogs, hamburgers and special sandwiches.

Number of Franchisees: 57 in 12 States

In Business Since: 1953

Equity Capital Needed: $35,000 to $45,000. Franchisee responsible for land and building financing.

Financial Assistance Available: Dog n Suds, does not provide direct financing to franchisees at the present time. However, it does provide assistance in obtaining financing such as, assisting the franchisee in preparing his proposal for bank financing, and meeting with potential lenders.

Training Provided: Complete training and opening assistance.

Managerial Assistance Available: Continued assistance by field department.

Information Submitted: May 1987

* **DOMINO'S PIZZA, INC.**
  3001 Earhart Road
  P. O. Box 997
  Ann Arbor, Michigan 48105
  Deborah S. Sargent, National Director of Franchise Services

Description of Operation: Pizza carry-out and delivery service.

Number of Franchisees: Approximately 683 in the United States, Canada, West Germany, Australia, Hong Kong, Japan and the United Kingdom.

In Business Since: 1960

Equity Capital Needed: $84,700 to $135,500.

Financial Assistance Available: Domino's Pizza does not directly provide financing but can refer to lending institutions who will consider providing financing to qualified franchisees.

Training Provided: Potential franchisees must complete the company's current training program which shall consist of both in-store training and classroom instruction.

Managerial Assistance Available: Domino's Pizza only franchises to internal people, and the kinds and duration of managerial and technical assistance provided by the company is set forth in the franchise agreement.

Information Submitted: May 1987

DOSANKO FOODS, INC.
440 West 47th Street
New York, New York 10036
Mac Hidaka, Vice President

Description of Operation: Dosanko Restaurants operate Japanese fast service food restaurants serving moderately priced menu. Emphasis on quick, efficient service, high quality and freshly cooked food, and cleanliness. The standard menu consists of four varieties of Japanese soup and noodles, dumplings, stir-fried noodles with beef and crisp-fried noodles with beef smothered in sauteed vegetables, Japanese style fried chicken, and assorted beverages.

Number of Franchisees: 7 plus 4 company-owned in New York and New Jersey. Company also has 1,200 franchisees plus 25 company-owned units in Japan.

In Business Since: 1975

Equity Capital Needed: $150,000 minimum and ability to acquire outside financing of $150,000 to $20,000.

Financial Assistance Available: None

Training Provided: 2 week training course in Dosanko Restaurant. 1 week course to study accounting procedures in Dosanko.

Managerial Assistance Available: Technical assistance on special kitchen equipment which are not available tin the United States as well as for special seasoning. Operations, training, maintenance, accounting and equipment manuals provided. Company makes available promotional advertising material plus field representative consultation and assistance.

Information Submitted: August 1987

* **DRUTHER'S INTERNATIONAL, INC.**
  P. O. Box 4999
  2440 Grinstead Drive
  Louisville, Kentucky 40204
  Thomas L. Hensley, President

Description of Operation: Fast food restaurant.

Number of Franchisees: 102 in 7 States plus 54 company-owned units.

In Business Since: 1963

Equity Capital Needed: $50,000 plus or less depending upon franchisee's financial capabilities.

Financial Assistance Available: Assistance in acquiring equipment loan or lease, joint venturing opportunities for qualified candidates.

Training Provided: Development training program—5 weeks—combined unit and classroom work at special training unit—follow-up visits at franchisees unit by training director during next 25 weeks and continued visits by area supervisor.

Managerial Assistance Available: Continued assistance regarding operations and accounting through field and office staff.

Information Submitted: August 1987

EL CHICO CORPORATION
12200 Stemmons Freeway
Suite 100
Dallas, Texas 75234
Robert P. Flack, Vice President, Corporation
Development/Franchise

Description of Operation: El Chico Restaurants are full-service, mid-priced Mexican restaurants with bar facilities. Store sizes approximate 5,100 square feet to 6,000 square feet, requiring 45,000 square feet to 50,000 square feet of land adequate to accommodate building, signage and parking for 100-110 cars. Units operate 7 days per week, 10-12 hours daily. Product quality, customer service, menu variety, product presentation key elements of business. Many items are unique and proprietary.

Number of Franchisees: 25 in Texas, Louisiana, Arkansas, Mississippi, Oklahoma, Kentucky, Tennessee and Alabama.

In Business Since: 1940

Equity Capital Needed: $80,000 net worth—$300,000 liquid.

Financial Assistance Available: None

Training Provided: Intensive 10-week training in designated training unit of franchisor. Required: 2 management representatives of franchise for full-term of training, which includes O.J.T. training in operations, service, product and administration.

Managerial Assistance Available: Ongoing franchise service for term of license, including franchise consultant, field service visitation program, standards maintenance, progress monitoring, periodic training updates offered, marketing materials available, access to corporate accounting system and operations manual, forms and newsletter services.

Information Submitted: August 1987

* **EL POLLO ASADO, INC.**
  3420 East Shea Boulevard
  Suite 150
  Phoenix, Arizona 85028
  Ed Kosan, Vice President, Franchise Development

Description of Operation: Fast food business—we sell char-broiled Mexican style chicken that is marinated.

Number of Franchisees: 25 in 6 States

In Business Since: 1983

Equity Capital Needed: $150,000 cash.

Financial Assistance Available: Total investment ranges from approximately $300,000 to $700,000. Franchise has option to arrange own outside financing.

Training Provided: Intensive 6-week training program. Mandatory training course is required for all new franchisees and 2 additional people. Training will be conducted at home office in Phoenix and on-site at company training store.

Managerial Assistance Available: E.P.A. provides continual management service for the franchisee in such areas as bookkeeping, advertising, purchasing and inventory control, complete manuals for operations, advertising forms and directions are provided. E.P.A. sponsors meetings of franchisees and conducts marketing and research to maintain high customer acceptance.

Information Submitted: May 1987

ETR, INC.
EL TACO RESTAURANTS
7105 South Paramount Boulevard
Pico Riviera, California 90660

Description of Operation: Mexican food drive thru restaurants—inside seating for 50 people. 20 percent of the business through the drive thru.

Number of Franchisees: 34 in 2 States

In Business Since: 1959

Equity Capital Needed: $150,000 cash required

Financial Assistance Available: None

Training Provided: 6 weeks in-store training.

Managerial Assistance Available: None

Information Submitted: May 1987

ESTEBAN INTERNATIONAL, INC.
903 Marquette Avenue South
Minneapolis, Minnesota 55402
R. Stephen Tanner, Chairman
Richard Tourand, President

Description of Operation: Mexican full service with liquor, family atmosphere and mid-priced menu.

Number of Franchisees: 2 in Minnesota plus 5 company-owned.

In Business Since: 1976

Equity Capital Needed: $190,000 cash

Financial Assistance Available: None

Training Provided: 8 weeks full on-site training for staff with manuals. Complete training of restaurant operations with updating of training on an ongoing basis.

Managerial Assistance Available: Accounting-statements, manuals and various materials, franchise director for guidance, full access to upper level management for support (operational), and sound/profitable business ideas.

Information Submitted: May 1987

* EVERYTHING YOGURT
EVERYTHING YOGURT NEW JERSEY INC.
Franchise Division
304 Port Richmond Avenue
Staten Island, New York 10302
Richard Nicotra, Chairman

Description of Operation: Everything Yogurt restaurants are fast service retail operations featuring soft frozen yogurt sundaes and shakes, salads, Quiche, hot and cold vegetable entrees; assorted pasta salads, fresh squeezed fruit juices and realted healthful food and beverage items.

Number of Franchisees: 63 in New York, New Jersey, Pennsylvania, Maryland, Michigan, Massachusetts, Washington, D.C. Expansion projects planned for 1986-87 include, Texas, Georgia, Virginia, Florida, Colorado, and Missouri.

In Business Since: 1976, offering franchises since 1981.

Equity Capital Needed: $60,000-$75,000 cash or equivalent equity.

Financial Assistance Available: No company financing offered. Administrative assistance offered by company in providing necessary information to local banks for financing.

Training Provided: 2 week initial training program provided at company headquarters and at other stores in chain. Additional on-site training at franchisee's store for one week prior to opening. Follow-up training provided on a continuing basis as directed by company.

Managerial Assistance Available: Operational and merchandising assistance provided as needed through headquarters office. Area representatives visit franchisees for continuing assistance periodically suggesting improvements when needed. Comprehensive operations manual provided.

Information Submitted: May 1987

RANDALL ENTERPRISES, INC.
dba FAMILIES ORIGINAL SUBMARINE
SANDWICHES
5376 Tomah Drive #200
Colorado Springs, Colorado 80918
Randall Smith, President

Description of Operation: Families delivers a menu of 27 basic submarine sandwiches with complimentary salads, soups, chili, desserts, and other specialties. Breakfast menu available in some shops. Success is based on unique methods of portion control using Families recipes and formulas, emphasizing nutritional quality and quantity of product delivered in a fast service "take-out" or "sit-down" setting. Shop size is 1,000 to 2,500 square feet and can be incorporated in a "Shoppette" or in a free-standing facility depending on site availability and business potential. Shops are open 12 hours per day, seven days per week. Families offers tailored cost-effective design and special equipment package resulting in a relatively low initial capital investment.

Number of Franchisees: 31 in Colorado, Indiana, South Dakota, and New Mexico.

In Business Since: 1972

Equity Capital Needed: Approximately $55,000-$60,000 will provide franchise fee, equipment, fixtures, inventory, start-up capital, etc., depending on the extent of necessary or desired leasehold improvements or property ownership.

Financial Assistance Available: Families will assist franchisee in developing projections and proposals for financing agencies, including SBA, and may meet with such representatives on yuour behalf, but provides no financial assistance as such.

Training Provided: A mandatory 80 hour training period for each of 2 persons is conducted in Colorado Springs or at a place approved by the franchisor. The course for owners and managers covers the entire operation including necessary accounting, record keeping, marketing, advertising, and personnel management. Also covered are food preparation, sandwich making, and the use and maintenance of standard equipment. Additional instruction for owners, managers, and subordinate personnel will be provided during the opening and grand opening of franchisee's shop.

Managerial Assistance Available: Ongoing training, education, and assistance is provided regularly during the lifetime of the franchise agreement. The franchisee will be kept abreast of new developments in company and industry-wide advertising and marketing techniques as well as economic trends that affect profits. Franchisor will conduct periodic quality control surveys and evaluation shop operations, to include monthly financial management, costs, profits, use of personnel, governmental reporting, continuing education, and other pertinent areas of concern.

Information Submitted: August 1987

FAMOUS RECIPE CORPORATION
1727 Elm Hill Pike
P. O. Box 1260
Nashville, Tennessee 37202
Joseph Wilder, Franchise Director

Description of Operation: Famous Recipe Fried Chicken take-home and sit-down restaurants. Menu includes specialty prepared fried chicken with creamy mashed potatoes and gravy, fresh salads made daily in the units and other complementary items. Home made buttermilk biscuits.

Number of Franchisees: 222 units in 20 States.

In Business Since: 1965

Equity Capital Needed: $100,000—total cost exclusive of real estate is approximately $300,000.

Financial Assistance Available: The franchisor does not provide financial assistance. franchisees with good credit ratings have been successful in obtaining financing for a substantial portion of the initial investment.

Training Provided: A 5 week formal training and management course is required for all new franchisees or their managers; and is conducted by qualified instructors at the franchisor's training facilities. Supervision and training at franchisee's location during initial start-up period is provided.

Managerial Assistance Available: Famous Recipe provides standard building plans, advertising, oeprations and equipment manuals. assistance in lease negotiations is also available. Regular visits by regional supervisors to assist in any problem areas. Advertising Division provides promotional and advertising materials and recommends programs for local markets. Annual national convention is conducted for exchange of new ideas, food preparation methods, and promotional programs. Localized regional markets are also conducted periodically twice each year.

Information Submitted: August 1987

FAT BOY'S BAR-B-Q FRANCHISE SYSTEMS, INC.
1550 West King Street
Cocoa, Florida 32922

Description of Operation: Fat Boy's Bar-B-Q Franchise Systems offers franchises in one of the country's most successful barbeque restaurants. The restaurant serves breakfast, lunch and dinner based on a complete menu. Seating ranges from the 64 seat to the 197 seat restaurant with optional banquet facilities.

Number of Franchisees: 40 franchised, 10 company and family-owned.

In Business Since: 1958

Equity Capital Needed: $100,000-$150,000

Financial Assistance Available: Company will provide full bank and credit references to assist franchisee in obtaining his own outside financing. Assist in acquiring financing through established contacts.

Training Provided: Intensive "in-restaurant" training program. No prior restaurant experience necessary. Will completely train franchisee in operation of restaurant from cooking to purchasing and bookkeeping in an existing Fat Boy's. Training will continue until company and franchisee feel confident of franchisee's readiness for success in opening his own restaurant. Mandatory 400 hours

Managerial Assistance Available: In addition to the complete training program, company will send a start-up team to each grand opening to aid the franchisee in both the kitchen and floor areas. Bookkeeping service is provided if requested. Company continually assists in all aspects of operation from promotion thru menu pricing and purchasing. Establishes national purchasing accounts and provides distribution through a national distributing company. All secret recipes and cooking knowledge is passed on to the franchisee. Quality control is maintained on a regular basis throughout the chain.

Information Submitted: May 1987

FATBURGER, INC.
1801 Avenue of the Stars
Suite 322
Los Angeles, California 90067
Lovie Yancey, President

Description of Operation: Fast food hamburger stand started over 30 years ago. The high quality custom burger and the homemade chili has established a very successful customer following. The meat is the best fresh beef available and the meat patties are hand made. Food is made to order for each customer. Grill is visable for customer to view food preparation.

Number of Franchisees: 36 in California

In Business Since: 1952

Equity Capital Needed: $120,000-$150,000

Financial Assistance Available: $30,000 of the franchise fee may be financed.

Training Provided: Training up to 1 week at the franchisor's location. Supervision at the franchisee's store for up to 2 weeks, for opening.

Managerial Assistance Available: The franchisee and manager will be trained for up to 1 week at a company store. A company supervisor will be at the franchisee's store for up to 2 weeks of supervision.

Information Submitted: August 1987

FLAP JACK SHACK, INC.
3980 U.S. 31 South
Traverse City, Michigan 49684
Virginia Burley, President

Description of Operation: Food service restaurant (family type operation).

Number of Franchisees: 9 in Michigan

In Business Since: 1975

Equity Capital Needed: $500,000 plus. Call franchisor for prospectus and franchise offering circulars.

Financial Assistance Available: None

Training Provided: Provide classroom and on-the-job training for 7 employees of the franchise owner. Such training to be at one of the Flap Jack Shack restaurants owned by the franchisor located in traverse City, Michigan. Provide opening assistance starting 7 days prior to opening of the franchise owners opening, and continuing until 30 days thereafter, as needed.

Managerial Assistance Available: Make available to the franchise owner— individual group advise, consultation and assistance, rendered by personal visit or telephone, as the franchisor may deem necessary and appropriate. General manager and an assistant or kitchen manager shall be able to receive assistance from 7 days prior to franchise owner opening, and continued for 17 days thereafter. Continuous help and assistance by consultation thereafter. Handbooks and employee manuals are furnished to franchise owner.

Information Submitted: August 1987

FLETCHER'S INDUSTRIES, INC.
14651 North Dallas Parkway
Suite 710, Box 37
Dallas, Texas 75240
Franchise Operations Manager

Description of Operation: Fletcher's Original Corny Dogs operates and franchises innovative drive-thru and mall fast food units that offer a distinctive and unique menu that features corny dogs, hot dogs, curly Q fries, and chunky chicken nuggets. Fletcher's modular drive-thru unit is approximately 370 square feet and the mall operations are typically 400-600 square feet in size. The units typically operate 12 to 14 hours per day, 7 days per week. Fletcher's offers an opportunity to address a void in the market with a concept that emphasizes uniqueness of product tast, convenience, and mobility of consumption. A full dressed 1/4 lb. hamburger has been added to the concept.

Number of Franchisees: 16 in Texas, and Oklahoma, and will be implemented in the maturity of the drive thru units in 1987.

In Business Since: 1982

Equity Capital Needed: $100,000 and up depending on operators' ability to finance.

Financial Assistance Available: Typical investment range is $115,000 to $125,000 per retail food service outlet. (Excluding cost of land.) Franchisees arrange own outside financing for building, equipment, and fixtures.

Training Provided: The training program consists of a 6 day, combination of on-site and classroom instruction with major emphasis placed on product preparation, customer service, and daily operational procedures and policies. Additional "certified trainer" instruction is provided to insure that each franchisee has at least one certified trainer on staff. Ongoing follow-up training programs are provided.

Managerial Assistance Available: Fletchers offers assistance to its franchisees in site evaluation, human resources, accounting procedures, and inventory control. The franchise operations manual and handbook cover operational procedures and policies. Fletcher's corporate staff is available to franchisees to assist problem solving and in implementing new Fletcher's programs. Fletcher's sponsors meetings of franchisees and conducts marketing and product research to promote customer patronage and acceptance.

Information Submitted: June 1987

FLUKY FRANCHISE SYSTEMS INTERNATIONAL, INC.
6821 North Western Avenue
Chicago, Illinois 60645
Jack Drexler, President

Description of Operation: Fast food restaurants.

Number of Franchisees: 3 in Illinois

In Business Since: 1929

Equity Capital Needed: $100,000 to $300,000

Financial Assistance Available: None

Training Provided: 1 month in company store and 2 months in franchisee's store.

Managerial Assistance Available: 2 months full supervision at franchisee's unit.

Information Submitted: August 1987

FOSTERS FREEZE INTERNATIONAL, INC.
1052 Grand Avenue, Suite C
Box 266
Arroyo Grande, California 93420
Cliff Hiatt, President
Contact: Charlie Boatright, Operations Officert

Description of Operation: Fosters Freeze International, Inc., is a franchisor of the unexcelled Fosters Freeze soft serve desserts plus a variety of high quality food items.

Number of Franchisees: 182 in California.

In Business Since: 1947

Equity Capital Needed: Estimated initial investment to commence operation of the franchised business may be 4425,000-$645,000. This includes the initial franchise fee of $25,000. The continuing franchise license fee is 4 percent of gross sales and the sales promotion fee is 3 percent of gross sales.

Financial Assistance Available: None

Training Provided: All in California including at company headquarters and company stores for franchisee and store managers.

Managerial Assistance Available: Provided assistance in the areas of menu, private label products, advertising, store openings, operations manuals, regular systemwide meetings, ongoing communications and support staff to provide continued support of the franchisee.

Information Submitted: May 1987

FOUR STAR PIZZA
(Franchise Corporation)
P. O. Box 1370
Washington, Pennsylvania 15301
George Chavel, Franchise Director

Description of Operation: Four Star Pizza specializes in the free home delivery of their special recipe pizza. Each pizza is made to order from the finest quality ingredients, and is delivered to the customers door within 30 minutes. Although the majority of people prefer our free home delivery service, take-out service is also available. Many stores offer dining facilities as well. In addition to pizza, many units offer specialty sandwiches and non-alcoholic beverages.

Number of Franchisees: 16 in 7 States and Ireland

In Business Since: 1981

Equity Capital Needed: $65,000 to $165,000

Financial Assistance Available: Currently, no financing is offered directly to franchisees. Four Star Pizza does, however, work closely with several leasing companies and can help franchisees in securing financing.

Training Provided: The Four Star Pizza operations department provides an extensive training program including a minimum of 24 days of classrroom nd hands-on training. The fundamental knowledge of operating a Four Star Pizza business is gained by completing this program.

Managerial Assistance Available: Four Star Pizza provides direction and assistance in the following phases of franchising: store development; site selection, lease negotiation, store lay-out, construction and equipment package. Marketing and advertising; grand opening, advertising programs, marketing techniques, media recommendations. In addition, Four Star Pizza offers ongoing support with the franchisee liaison program, seminars and company newsletters.

Information Submitted: May 1987

FOX'S PIZZA DEN INC.
3243 Old Frankstown Road
Pittsburgh, Pennsylvania 15239
James R. Fox, President

Description of Operation: Small home town pizza den operation. Open 7 days a week 8 hours per day. Specializing in professional home delivery service. Ideal size 500 to 800 square feet. Ideal for home town individuals to work in business in their home town. Own and operate its own commissary and trucks. Private labeling on all food products.

Number of Franchisees: 98 in Western Pennsylvania, Ohio, Maryland, West Virginia and Virginia.

In Business Since: 1971

Equity Capital Needed: $40,000

Financial Assistance Available: Will assist in bank financing in local towns.

Training Provided: 10 days of training

Managerial Assistance Available: Fox's Pizza Den, Inc., provides continual management service for the life of the franchise in such areas as bookkeeping, advertising, inventory control. Complete manuals of operations, forms, and directions are provided. District and field managers are available in all regions to work closely with franchisees and visit stores regularly.

Information Submitted: May 1987

FRANKIE'S FRANCHISE SYSTEMS, INC.
643 Lakewood Road
Waterbury, Connecticut 06704
Frank Caiazzo, President

Description of Operation: Fast food restaurants called Frankie's Family Restaurants offers a variety of cooked to order foods, specializing in hot dogs with a variety of toppings. Also seafood, hot oven grinders, and hamburgers.

Number of Franchisees: 8 plus 4 company-owned in Connecticut and Florida

In Business Since: 1934—started franchising in 1978

Equity Capital Needed: $35,00-$60,000

Financial Assistance Available: None

Training Provided: Complete training is provided at a company store for franchisee and store managers.

Managerial Assistance Available: Continuous assistance and supervision are provided. Franchisee is given an operations manual for all phases of operation.

Information Submitted: August 1987.

FRENCHY'S INTERNATIONAL, INC.
6830 Mykawa Road
Houston, Texas 77033
Vice President, Franchise Development

Description of Operation: Fast food restaurant operations serving creole style chicken, and a wide variety of fresh side items and fresh desearts.

Number of Franchisees: 15 stores including company-owned in Texas.

In Business Since: 1970

Equity Capital Needed: Approximately $80,000

Financial Assistance Available: None

Training Provided: 6 weeks of extensive training is provided in all phases of operations.

Managerial Assistance Available: Ongoing assistance is provided in phrases of operation including continuous consultation.

Information Submitted: May 1987

FUDDRUCKERS, INC.
Fuddruckers Centre
3636 Medical Drive
San Antonio, Texas 78229
Gil Russell, Vice President of franchising

Description of Operation: Fuddruckers, Inc., operates and franchises restaurants which specialize in high-quality, up-scale hamburgers cooked to order and which emphasis fresh ingredients and moderate prices in a self-serve atmosphere. The key menu items are the 1/2 and 1/3 pound hamburger, however, the menu also includes rib-eye steak sandwiches, hot dogs, wurst, chicken sandwiches, taco salad, French fries, pinto beans, grilled onions, cookies, brownies, soft drinks and ice cream. Each restaurant has a condiment bar where customers may add lettuce, tomatos, onions, pickles, relish, sauerkraut, melted cheese and barbeque sauce to their sandwich. All of the restaurants serve beer and wine and many serve other alcoholic beverages. Each restaurant has a butcher shop in which fresh quarters of beef are cut and ground daily and a bakery in which hamburger buns, cookies and brownies are baked daily. Each restaurant has an indoor dining area from which diners may observe the preparation of hamburgers and other foods, as well as an additional dining area under a yellow awning simulating a patio motif, and many restaurants have outdoor patios. The size of the prototypical restaurant is approximately 6,600 square feet.

Number of Franchisees: There are 77 franchised restaurants in 20 States and Canada. Franchisor is currently franchhsing and developing restaurants in foreign markets such as Europe, Japan and Australia..

In Business Since: 1979

Equity Capital Needed: Estimated initial pre-opening investment between $450,000-$750,000 (including $50,000 initial franchise fee) depending on method of financing for improvements and equipment and cost of real estate. Royalties and advertising contributions based on a percentage of annual gross sales.

Financial Assistance Available: Franchisees bear all costs involved in development, construction and operation of their restaurant.

Training Provided: 6 week comprehensive training for 3 to 4 of franchisee's managers. Also provide experienced opening crew for 3 days prior and 3 days after opening to assist in training franchisee's employees. Continuing inspections and evaluations of franchisee's restaurant made during the year.

Managerial Assistance Available: Franchisor will provide assistance in evaluation of sites proposed by franchisee, standard set of plans and specifications for adaptation to franchisee's site, updated confidential policies and procedures manual. Assistance in planning promotions and advertising relating to restaurant opening, periodic financial analyses or reports, continuing advice and consultation regarding restaurant operation.

Information Submitted: July 1987

FUZZY'S, INC.
P. O. Box 151
Madison, North Carolina 27025
Fred H. Nelson, Senior Vice President

Description of Operation: A fast food Bar-B-Q restaurant with sit down/drive-thru service. The standard menu consists of chopped/sliced Bar-B-Q sandwiches, plates, trays, Fuzzy burger, hush puppies, French fries, home made banana pudding and assorted beverages.

Number of Franchisees: 2 in North Carolina

In Business Since: 1954—Fuzzy's, Inc. since 1978

Equity Capital Needed: Approximate initial investment—$150,000 cash minimum with sufficient net worth.

Financial Assistance Available: None

Training Provided: 2 weeks of on-the-job training at one of our company operated stores. Two weeks of supervision at franchisee's outlet by a full-time representative from Fuzzy's, Inc., to assist in solving problems.

Managerial Assistance Available: Continuous assistance in areas such as quality contol, inventory, advertising, etc. Ooerations manual provided. An ongoing inspection program designed to evaluate the individual store and advise to the physical and technical aspects of the operation.

Information Submitted: August 1987

GIFF'S SUB SHOP FRANCHISE SYSTEM, INC.
134 Pamela Ann
Ft. Walton Beach, Florida 32548
Lance H. Arnette

Description of Operation: Custom made submarine sandwiches specializing in steak subs.

Number of Franchisees: 15 in Florida

In Business Since: 1977

Equity Capital Needed: $25,000-$35,000

Financial Assistance Available: None

Training Provided: 1 week at corporate headquarters and 1 week on location.

Managerial Assistance Available: Giff's provides ongoing assistance to all outlets. We help set up bookkeeping, inventory and opening equipment.

Information Submitted: May 1987

GIORDANO'S INTERNATIONAL FRANCHISE SYSTEM, INC.
521 South La Grange Road
La Grange, Illinois 60525
Joe Bogho, President

Description of Operation: Acclaimed as Chicago's best pizza and originators of famous stuffed spinach pizza. Giordano's also serve famous stuffed sandwiches, stuffed pasta and a wide variety of salads, other products and desserts.

Number of Franchisees: 16 in Illinois and Iowa including company-owned.

In Business Since: 1974—franchising since 1980

Equity Capital Needed: Minimum $100,000 to $150,000.

Financial Assistance Available: Will assist in finding financing.

Training Provided: 6 weeks complete training course at one of the company-owned restaurants for the franchisee and their personnel. Two week supervised help on the opening of franchisee's outlet.

Mangerial Assistance Available: Provides management training, kitchen training, cooperative advertising, manual of operation and employees handbook. Field supervision is available to fully assist in all problem areas. Meetings are held to discuss marketing, restaurant operation and product quality.

Information Submitted: August 1987

*GODFATHER'S PIZZA
9140 West Dodge Road
Omaha, Nebraska 68114
Bill Methven, Vice President, Operations

Description of Operation: Godfather's Pizza offers franchises for the development and operation of Godfather's Pizza restaurants. Each restaurant sells a variety of pizza products as well as salads, a limited number of sandwiches and beverages. Most restaurants have approximately 3,000 square feet and are located in shopping centers. Products are available for consumption in the restaurant or take out. Delivery is available.

Number of Franchisees: 65 in 39 States

In Business Since: 1973

Equity Capital Needed: $200,000 to $285,000 per unit.

Financial Assistance Available: The franchisor in certain situations may provide financial assistance to a franchisee in the development and operation of Godfather's Pizza restaurants. The duration and terms of this financing will depend upon the amount and type of financing, available collateral security and the credit standing of the franchisees.

Training Provided: Training is provided to key personnel of a franchisee at a company operated Godfather's Pizza restaurant geographically proximate to the franchisee. This training normally lasts for 7 days. Additional training programs in the form of videotapes and/or slide presentations are available for use in training other personnel of the franchisees.

Managerial Assistance Available: In addition to the training program described above, the franchisor assigns a regional manager of franchise operations ("RMFO") to provide assistance to the franchisee in operational matters. The franchisor's field marketing staff provides marketing assistance in the development of new products and the enhancement of existing products. A real estate staff provides assistance in site selection.

Information Submitted: August 1987

GOLDEN BIRD FRIED CHICKEN
P. O. Box 5354
Newport Beach, California 92662-5354
Albert A. Garey, Director of Franchise Development

Description of Operation: Franchise offers a unique restaurant format which serves primarily fried chicken, catfish, together with additional items as french fried potatoes, coleslaw, potato salad, sweet potato pie, apple pie and soft drink beverages. Golden Bird restaurants have developed certain trade secret recipes in connection with a unique method of food preparation, service of menu items, marketing techniques and operational procedures relevant to the successful operation of each restaurant. The food is now served primarily on a take-out basis, with a dining area provided with table service in some facilities. The furniture, fixtures and decorative items are designed to be comfortable and serviceable.

Number of Franchisees: 6 plus 11 company-owned in California.

In Business Since: 1981

Equity Capital Needed: Total investment, including initial franchise fee, ranges from $134,500 to $238,000.

Financial Assistance Available: On a case-by-case, franchisor may guarantee a part of the franchisee's financing of the investment.

Training Provided: Franchisee is provided with 4 weeks of intensive instruction prior to taking possession of the facility. The training includes theory, instruction, testing and on-the-job training in a selected Golden Bird restaurant. In addition, franchisee may require further training of 1 week per year.

Managerial Assistance Available: The franchisor may inspect the franchise premises and operations periodically and will offer advice and operational assistance as necessary. Franchisor's field representative will work with franchisee to review costs, purchasing, and marketing programs to build community support and attract customers. The franchisor will also assist in developing and preparing a promotional "grand opening" advertising campaign.

Information Submitted: May 1987

GOLDEN CHICKEN FRANCHISES
3810 West National Avenue
Milwaukee, Wisconsin 53215
Robert L. Bloom, President

Description of Operation: Fast food offering both carry-outs and home delivery. Specializing in chicken, pizza and seafood. Open minimum of 6 days per week for 7 hours each day open. Each store requires approximately 800 square feet of space. Franchisee provides own space and equipment. Stores are located in store fronts and preferably strip shopping centers.

Number of Franchisees: 15 in Wisconsin and Minnesota plus 1 company-owned.

In Business Since: 1959

Equity Capital Needed: $3,500 for franchise fee plus net cost for equipment and setup.

Financial Assistance Available: A total investment of approximately $30,000 is needed. Franchisor does no financing but will assist franchisee in securing sources. Primary source of financing has been leasing company. Franchisee puts up $6,000 for franchise fee, lease and security deposits and working capital. Balance usually financed over 60 month period.

Training Provided: Franchisee must spend 7 days at a company store. Franchisor spends 14 days with franchisee in his own unit after opening.

Managerial Assistance Available: Golden Chicken provides continual management service for the life of licensing agreement in such areas as bookkeeping, advertising and promotions. Franchisor visits stores a minimum of once a year, sponsors meetings of franchisees and keeps franchisee informed of new products and promotions via news letters.

Information Submitted: August 1987

*GOLDEN CORRAL FRANCHISING SYSTEMS, INC.
5151 Glenwood Avenue
Raleigh, North Carolina 27612
Robert B. Heyward, Director of Franchising

Description of Operation: Franchisor of Golden Corral Family Steakhouse Restaurants.

Number of Franchisees: 2 in Washington and North Carolina

In Business___ince: 1986

Equity Capital Needed: $110,000-$225,000

Financial Assistance Available: None

Training Provided: 2 weeks classroom training and 8 weeks on-the-job training in the managerial training program will be completed approximately 8 weeks prior to opening.

Managerial Assistance Available: We provide extensive training program, operations manual, supplemental training program and accounting forms and procedures.

Information Submitted: May 1987

GOLDEN FRIED CHICKEN OF AMERICA, INC.
1016 LaPosada
Suite 139
Austin, Texas 78752
Steven G. Neeley, President

Description of Operation: Golden Fried Chicken of America, Inc., is a franchisor of fast food restaurants, specializing in quality fried chicken and appropriate side orders. A typical restaurant requires 2,000 square feet and a drive-thru window.

Number of Franchisees: 28 operating 61 restaurants in Texas.

In Business Since: 1968

142

Equity Capital Needed: Minimum liquid net worth is $75,000. Typical restaurant costs: under $300,000 including land, building, equipment, and working capital.

Financial Assistance Available: None

Training Provided: Extensive 3-week classroom and hands-on training, mandatory for franchisee/store manager. Training on system and updates available on a continuous basis via national training program.

Managerial Assistance Available: GFCA provides continuous support for the life of the franchise, including pre-opening assistance, marketing programs, negotiation of national purchase contracts, operations manuals, regular visits by field personnel, and product, equipment, and market research.

Information Submitted: May 1987

GOLDEN SKILLET INTERNATIONAL, INC.
P. O. Box 35815
Minneapolis, Minnesota 55435
Charles Cocotas, Executive Vice President

Description of Operation: Golden Skillet International, Inc., operates and franchises a chain of fast food restaurants featuring a nique fried chicken. Restaurants are free-standing with 'country kitchen' decor. Golden Skillet promotes friendly, and courteous service, high standards of restaurant cleanliness, and top quality food products. The fried chicken cooking process and cooker are patented. Golden skillet is a subsidiary of International Dairy Queen, Inc.

Number of Franchisees: Over 73 in 8 States, Puerto Rico and Trinidad.

In Business Since: 1963

Equity Capital Needed: The franchise fees are $25,000 for plan A plus $15,000 for initial sales promotion. All prospective franchisees must meet certain financial requirements.

Financial Assistance Available: Qualified franchisees may purchase equipment on a conditional sales contract over a 5 year payment period with the required down payment.

Training Provided: Franchisees are required to complete an 3 week scheduled first phase training session in basic operations held in Minneapolis, Minnesota. Support training, second phase, by operations department at franchisee's new restaurant.

Managerial Assistance Available: Golden Skillet provides full-range support services including: real estate consultation, buildingplans and specifications, equipment training, maintenance, accounting, marketing. The company provides an operations manual, marketing handbook, real estate/architecture/construction guide, plus field representative consultations and assistance.

Information Submitted: May 1987

GOLD STAR CHILI, INC.
2244 Beechmont Avenue
Cincinnati, Ohio 45230
Raymond P. Peterson, Franchise Manager

Description of Operation: Gold Star Chili is a specialty restaurant, featuring our Chili. The single item menu concept assures the highest quality control and at the same time permitting a high volume of sales with a minimum of employees. Locations are fee standing (2,100 square feet), mall food courts 450 to 600 square feet.

Number of Franchisees: 76 in Ohio, Kentucky, Florida, and Missouri

In Business Since: 1964

Equity Capital Needed: $12,000 franchise fee, equipment approximately $50,000.

Financial Assistance Available: None

Training Provided: On-the-job training provided for operations. Personnel for a minimum of 2 weeks.

Managerial Assistance Available: Site location, equipment layout, consulting assistance for installation of equipment, opening—specialized field consultant up to 1 week, advertising and promotional materials and continuing unit inspection.

Information Submitted: May 1987

GOOD EARTH CORPORATION
23945 Calabasas Road
Suite 107
Calabasas, California 91302
E. R. Wilson, President

Description of Operation: The Good Earth Corporation offers restaurant franchises which sell health-oriented foods, substantially free of preservatives, artificial flavors and colors.

Number of Franchisees: 15 in California

In Business Since: 1986

Equity Capital Needed: Approximately between $579,000 and $775,000

Financial Assistance Available: None

Training Provided: The following positions are required to pursue and complete the franchisor's operations training course: franchisee and/or general manager, 1 assistant manager, 1 kitchen manager and 1 baker. This course lasts approximately 1 month.

Managerial Assistance Available: Franchisor will make available to the franchisee: names of approved suppliers; consultation on-site adaptation equipment; opening supervision and consultation at the franchisee's premises during not less than 30 days; standard chart of accounts, cashier's training systems and portion control systems; marketing research and advice; recipes, food preparation instructions; also additional services, facilities, rights and privileges used in the program will be made available from time to time.

Information Submitted: May 1987

* GRANDY'S, INCORPORATED
997 Grandy's Lane
Lewisville, Texas 75067
Franchise Department

Description of Operation: Fast food chicken restaurant.

Number of Franchisees: 100 units in 21 States

In Business Since: 1973

Equity Capital Needed: $750,000-$900,000

Financial Assistance Available: No financial assistance available through Grady's, Inc.

Training Provided: 5 weeks, 6-days a week, classroom and on-the-job training in all facets of the restaurant. 6 day overview course of study available for owners and their executive officers.

Managerial Assistance Available: Complete line of operational training, real estate construction and marketing services.

Information Submitted: May 1987

THE GREAT GYROS
7311 Player Drive
San Diego, California 92119
Stewart L. Green, President

Description of Operation: Greek fast food.

Number of Franchisees: 2 in California and Arizona plus 2 company-owned.

In Business Since: 1980

Equity Capital Needed: Varies depending on location.

Financial Assistance Available: None

Training Provided: 2 weeks

Managerial Assistance Available: Managerial assistance provided as long as necessary.

Information Submitted: August 1987

GREENSTREETS NATIONAL CORPORATION
7765 Mitchell Road
Eden Prairie, Minnesota 55344
Gordon Weber, President

Description of Operation: Hamburger grill and bar.

Number of Franchisees: 5 in Minnesota

In Business Since: 1982

Equity Capital Needed: $30,000-$120,000

Financial Assistance Available: None

Training Provided: 1 month initial training plus ongoing in all phases of operation.

Managerial Assistance Available: 1 month initial managerial assistance plus ongoing.

Information Submitted: August 1987

HAPPY JOE'S PIZZA & ICE CREAM PARLORS
1875 Middle Road
Bettendorf, Iowa 52722
Lawrence J. Whitty, President and Chairman of the Board

Description of Operation: Happy Joe's Pizza & Ice Cream Parlors specialize in delivery, take-out, and catering to families and feature supurb pizza and premium quality ice cream creations. Family appeal is emphasized with birthday party celebrations a house specialty.

Number of Franchisees: 87 in 9 States and Cairo, Egypt.

In Business Since: 1972

Equity Capital Needed: Approximately $80,000-$500,000

Financial Assistance Available: None

Training Provided: Extensive on-the-job training including all facets of the operation lasting up to 30 days.

Managerial Assistance Available: Complete assistance and supervision in opening the business and an ongoing program of managerial and operational training and assistance from field supervisors. Additional assistance in advertising and promotion is also available.

Information Submitted: May 1987

HAPPY STEAK COMPANIES, INC.
2246 East Date Avenue
Fresno, California 93706
Randy Brooks, Vice President

Description of Operation: Family style budget steakhouse.

Number of Franchisees: Happy Steak, Inc. (28), Perko's, Inc. (41) in California and Nevada.

In Business Since: 1969

Equity Capital Needed: $95,000

Financial Assistance Available: None

Training Provided: Complete on-the-job restaurant training prior to opening—then as needed.

Managerial Assistance Available: Minimum monthly scheduled visits of 4 hours.

Information Submitted: August 1987

* HARDEE'S FOOD SYSTEMS, INC.
P. O. Box 1519
1233 North Church Street
Rocky Mount, North Carolina 27801-1619

Maurice M. Robbins, President,
Franchise Development and Planning

Description of Operation: Fast food limited menu restaurant.

Number of Franchisees: 250 operating 2,724 Hardee's units in 40 States, Central America and the Middle East (includes 897 company units).

In Business Since: 1962

Equity Capital Needed: $250,000 plus land and building

Financial Assistance Available: No financial assistance available. Require licensee to finance, land, building, equipment, working capital and license fee.

Training Provided: 4 weeks training in learning center (combination restaurant and classroom). Ten days training and supervision at restaurant upon opening.

Managerial Assistance Available: Hardee's provides continued supervision on a scheduled basis and also provides bookkeeping methods, advertising direction, operating controls, complete operating manual, basic forms, continued advice and counseling.

Information Submitted: May 1987

HARTZ KRISPY CHICKEN
dba HARTZOG, INC.
14409 Cornerstone Village Drive
Houston, Texas 77014
W. Lawrence Hartzog, President

Description of Operation: Hartz Krispy Chicken is a fast food operation maintaining excellence of quality and providing the utmost in customer service. Kripsy fried chicken the main menu item. Side orders include potato salad, cole slaw, french fries, and corn on the cob. All food is served in an Early American atmosphere or may be taken out.

Number of Franchisees: 20 franchisees in Texas, Mississippi, Alabama and Georgia operating 33 locations.

In Business Since: 1972

Equity Capital Needed: $200,000 not including land and building. Acquisition of real estate is a franchiseee responsibility.

Financial Assistance Available: None. Franchisee is responsible for obtaining all financing.

Training Provided: Hartz requires at least 200 hours training at the franchisee's expense. Training facilities are provided by Hartz in Houston, Texas. Assistance and guidance, but not labor, is supplied during pre-opening stages.

Managerial Assistance Available: Hartz personnel continuously inspects and overseas franchise stores in order to maintain uniformity and quality. Discourse and correspondence is maintained with franchisees on a daily basis.

Information Submitted: August 1987

HOUSE OF YAKITORI JAPANESE RESTAURANTS
3-Y Corp.2120 Hollowbrook Drive
Suite 200
Colorado Springs, Colorado 80918
Frederick S. Reamer, President

Description of Operation: House of Yakitori offers franchises for both full service and food court style Japanese restaurants. The specialty dish is flame broiled skewered chicken, ("yakitori") cooked in a proprietary sauce. The restaurants were developed to cater to and be owned by Americans. No professional oriental help is required. Prepared foods, accounting services, management, site selection and training are all provided by the franchisor.

Number of Franchisees: 3 in Colorado

In Business Since: Franchising since 1983. Company-owned restaurants since 1980.

Equity Capital Needed: A minimum of $50,000.

Financial Assistance Available: The total investment ranges from $90,000 to $180,000 depending on whether a food court of a full service restaurant franchise is purchased. No financing is provided by the franchisor.

Training Provided: Full training for 6 to 8 weeks is provided by the franchisor to include all aspects of restaurant operations and management. Training is normally conducted in Colorado Springs. Follow on training and an opening team is provided at the franchisee's location.

Managerial Assistance Available: House of Yakitori provides continual management and advisory services for the life of the franchise. This includes but may not be limited to accounting, payroll, budgetary tools for food costs and labor costs, quality assistance visits, product research, menu analyses, consumer surveys, advertising and promotions.

Information Submitted: May 1987

HUBB'S PUB
P. O. Box 279
Altamonte Springs, Florida 32701
Fran Ungar

Description of Operation: Pub restaurant with a specialty in draft imported beer (30 kinds) and deli sandwiches.

Number of Franchisees: 2 in Florida

In Business Since: 1983

Equity Capital Needed: Minimun $50,000

Financial Assistance Available: Will help secure financing.

Training Provided: Required 3 weeks, optional 3 weeks added.

Managerial Assistance Available: Constant

Information Submitted: May 1987

* HUDDLE HOUSE, INC.
2969 East Ponce De Leon Avenue
Decatur, Georgia 30030
Douglas Kley, Executive Vice President

Description of Operation: 24 hour convenience restaurant service, breakfast, steaks, seafood items and sandwiches.

Number of Franchisees: 128 in 9 States

In Business Since: 1964

Equity Capital Needed: $25,000 franchise licensing fee and $21,000 operating capital.

Financial Assistance Available: None

Training Provided: 2 weeks at training unit, 2 weeks at units and additional pre-opening and opening training.

Managerial Assistance Available: Training, continuous supervision, commissary food purchasing, restaurant equipment and supplies, operation manuals, daily accounting forms, district supervisors work closely with owner/operators to solve problems and promote profits.

Information Submitted: May 1987

THE HUNGRY HOBO
5306—23rd Avenue
Moline, Illinois 61265
Ray Pearson, Vice President-Sales

Description of Operation: Fast food restaurant specializing in deli sandwiches. We also bake our own bread. Sell 6 food party sandwiches and cater party buffet trays. Baked potatoes and taco salads.

Number of Franchisees: 9 and 10 company-owned in Illinois and Iowa

In Business Since: 1969

Equity Capital Needed: $55,000 to $100,000

Financial Assistance Available: Legal assistance in negotiating a loan.

Training Provided: On-the-job training in sandwich making, portion control of meats and cheeses. Cost controls, advertising, purchasing, inventory control, financial statements—2 weeks.

Managerial Assistance Available: Start-up crew provided for the opening of new location until new employees are properly trained. Weekly reports, monthly financial statements and other records monitored by franchisor. Scheduled and unscheduled visits to franchisee on a monthly basis.

Information Submitted: August 1987

INTERNATIONAL BLIMPIE CORPORATION
740 Broadway
6th Floor
New York, New York 10003
Charles Leaness, Vice President, Franchise Development

Description of Operation: Limited menu operation featuring "America's Best Dressed Sandwich" and marketing concept. No cooking, eat-in and take-out units. Also features 3 and 6 food party sandwiches and customized catering for special occasions.

Number of Franchisees: 275 in 16 States

In Business Since: 1964

Equity Capital Needed: $50,000

Financial Assistance Available: Total investment ranges from $70,000-$100,000. Company may assist with the arrangement of financing.

Training Provided: Comprehensive 2 week training program includes on-the-job training in sandwich preparation, purchasing, inventory control, cost controls, financial staements and advertising.

Managerial Assistance Available: Continuous managerial assistance for the duration of the franchise provided by area representatives. Areas of assistance include: management, menu pricing, cost of sales, inventory control, problem solving and advertising/marketing. Operation and construction manuals provided.

Information Submitted: July 1987

INTERNATIONAL DAIRY QUEEN, INC.
P. O. Box 35286
Minneapolis, Minnesota 55435
John Hyduke, Vice President, Franchise Development

Description of Operation: International Dairy Queen, Inc., is engaged in developing, licensing and servicing a system of franchised retail stores which offer a selected menu of soft dairy products, hamburgers and beverages marketed under "Dairy Queen," "Brazier" and "Mr. Misty" trademark.

Number of Franchisees: There are currently over 4,800 "Dairy Queen" and "Dairy Queen/Brazier" stores located in all 50 States and 12 foreign countries.

In Business Since: The soft serve dairy product was first offered to the public in 1938 with the first "Dairy Queen" store being opened in 1940. In 1962 certain territorial operators formed international Dairy Queen, Inc., by contributing their respective "Dairy Queen" territorial franchise rights.

Equity Capital Needed: The franchise fees are $30,000. All prospective franchisees must meet certain financial requirements.

Financial Assistance Available: Qualified franchisees may purchase equipment on a conditional sales contract over a 5 year payment period with the required down payment.

Training Provided: International Dairy Queen, Inc.'s national training center in Minneapolis, Minnesota offers an intensive 2 week training course to all new and existing franchisees. The course covers sanitation, sales promotion, inventory control and basic functions of management. The company also offers new franchisees the services of a special opening team that assists operators in opening their new "Dairy Queen" or "Dairy Queen/Brazier" store.

Managerial Assistance Available: International Dairy Queen, Inc., maintains an operations specialty division in addition to regional and district managers, who provide continuing assistance involving store operatin, product quality, customer convenience, product development, advertising, financial control, traning, communication and incentives. a research and development department is engaged in developing new products, cooking methods and procedures. Sales promotion programs are conducted through newspapers, radio, television and billboards.

Information Submitted: August 1987

INTERNATIONAL SHORT STOP, INC.
1101 Capital of Texas Highway South
Building D, Suite 210
Austin, Texas 78746
John Barclay, Vice President

Description of Operation: "Short Stop" sells franchises for the operation of drive thru restaurants featuring the sale of high quality hamburgers, French fries and soft drinks.

Number of Franchisees: 31 in Texas, Florida, Louisiana and Colorado

In Business Since: 1984

Equity Capital Needed: $180,000 per store

Financial Assistance Available: None

Training Provided: 30 days training school

Managerial Assistance Available: Pre-opening assistance, operating assistance, site selection and training programs.

Information Submitted: May 1987

INTERNATIONAL YOGURT COMPANY
5858 N.E. 87th Avenue
Portland, Oregon 97220
David Hanna, Marketing Director

Description of Operation: The Yogurt Stand/Healthy Deli Restaurants are based on a growing concern for diet and nutrition. Thick, mouthwatering sandwiches, delicious home-made soups and salads compliment the fine frozen yogurt in an atmosphere of warm, natural cedar and subdued earth-tone colors. Locations are in busy urban centers, malls and shopping centers. Size varies from 600 square feet to 1,600 square feet, and seating from 20 to 70.

Number of Franchisees: 8 franchisees and 48 licensed outlets in Oregon and Washington; area licensees in Missouri, Alaska, British Columbia and Hawaii.

In Business Since: 1977

Equity Capital Needed: $15,000 minimum for franchise—$25,000 minimum for area licensees.

Financial Assistance Available: Investment ranges from $65,000 to $110,000 depending on size and location of The Yogurt Stand/Healthy Deli Specialty Restaurant Franchise. Franchisee arranges outside financing with assistance from the International yogurt Company which has a very successful history with conventional and SBA loan procurement.

Training Provided: 1 week intensive training in headquarters mall restaurant, 1 week opening and start-up training and assistance by operations manager and regional field supervisors in all operational functions. Regular individual sessions with operations manager and our CPA evaluating monthly profit and loss.

Managerial Assistance Available: International Yogurt Company provides full counseling in all operational areas including menu planning, purchasing assistance and profit integrity. Our operations manual covers in depth day to day operation procedures with periodic updating and revision. Continuous visitations and communication, updating of methods of procedures are maintained throughout the life of the franchise.

Information Submitted: May 1987

ITALO'S PIZZA SHOP, INC.
3560 Middlebranch Road, N.E.
Canton, Ohio 44705
Italo P. Ventura

Description of Operation: Italo's Pizza franchise is designed for the small investors. Any store over 900 square feet can be turned into a profit making operation. For the next two years Italo's Pizza Shop, Inc., is concentrating expansion only in Ohio.

Number of Franchisees: 18 in Ohio, California and West Virginia

In Business Since: 1966, franchising since 1975

Equity Capital Needed: $12,000

Financial Assistance Available: A total investment of $62,250 for carry-out only and about $95,500 with dining room. Franchisee must provide outside financing.

Training Provided: Intensive 2 months on-the-job training in our main location, 2 weeks of assistance at the time of opening, and continuing assistance as needed.

Managerial Assistance Available: Italo's Pizza provides continual assistance and recommendations in any area. Forms and manuals are provided for the smooth performance of the business. Weekly or monthly visits by franchisor to help solve any problem and continued assistance by phone for any emergency.

Information Submitted: May 1987

• **JACK IN THE BOX FOODMAKER, INC.**
9330 Balboa Avenue
P. O. Box 783
San Diego, California 92112
Helen M. Trent, Division Vice President-Franchise Development

Description of Operation: Jack in the Box is a popular fast food chain in the Western States with hamburgers as a mainstay, but best known for the variety in menu. THe first to have remote-entry drive-through ordering, five years ago Jack in the Box also revolutionized the fast food menu from "hamburger and fries" to bacon cheeseburgers, chicken supreme sandwiches, breakfasts, Mexican food, and salads to go.
Jack in the Box is offering a unique chance to buy existing restaurant units in many major market areas. This assists new franchisees to become knowledgeable in the fast food business quickly. Also offered are new-store development possibilities and some exclusive territory agreements. Jack in the Box is searching for the experienced businessperson who wants multiple store ownership.

Number of Franchisees: Over 200 locations. The company operates 665 restaurants, all west of the Mississippi.

In Business Since: 1951

Equity Capital Needed: Existing restaurants: $140,000 liquid assets minimum; much higher net worth required to construct new units and obtain development rights.

Financial Assistance Available: Existing restaurant: The cost of a unit is estimated to be in the range of $275,000-$400,000 excluding the land and building. Franchisee will be required to invest 40 percent of actual investment at the onset of the venture. New restaurants: Franchisees are required to have adequate net worth to obtain land, building and equipment. Foodmaker prefers any needed financing be obtained from outside sources in both instances.

Training Provided: Comprehensive 8 weeks field training program in 4 major cities plus 3 days classroom time in San Diego. Within 6 months after taking over restaurant, franchisee will be required to return to San Diego for 1 week of advanced management training.

Managerial Assistance Available: Franchise operations consultants are available in the field to work closely with franchisees and visit stores regularly to assist in solving problems.

Information Submitted: May 1987

JAKE'S INTERNATIONAL, INC.
1204 Carnegie Street
Rolling Meadows, Illinois 60008

Description of Operation: Jake's International is a franchised pizza operation. Emphasis is on high quality food, cleanliness and efficient service in the carry-out and delivery food industry. Pub type operations with full dining rooms and cocktail lounges are also available.

Number of Franchisees: 23 in Illinois

In Business Since: 1962

Equity Capital Needed: $70,000 minimum and the ability to acquire financing.

Financial Assistance Available: Equipment leasing if elected by the franchisee and if qualified.

Training Provided: Minimum of 200 hours in actual operations. Additional management training is provided on-the-job and throughout the duration of the franchise.

Managerial Assistance Available: Training, operations management, on-site field consulting and quality control assistance and market available promotional advertising material. Access to central commissary, if desired.

Information Submitted: June 1987

JERRY'S SUB SHOP
15942 Shady Grove Road
Gaithersburg, Maryland 20877
George M. Palmer, Franchise Director

Description of Operation: The chain is famous for its "overstuffed" subs and pizza. The self-service concept is placed in high volume, high traffic locations in very pleasant, up scale surroundings, beer and wine complement the menu.

Number of Franchisees: 95 in 13 States and Washington, D.C.

In Business Since: 1952

Equity Capital Needed: $19,500 franchise fee and approximately $30,000 additionally for deposits, etc.

Financial Assistance Available: Assistance in loan preparation as well as contacts to particular S.B.A. programs that franchise qualifies.

Training Provided: Extensive training both in classroom as well as unit operation. Follow-up training in franchisee's own site is also provided.

Managerial Assistance Available: When a new store opens, Jerry's places a start-up team of trained supervisors in the store to help with the opening. The franchisor then has site supervisors visit the store twice a month, more if necessary, to assist the franchisee in running an efficient operation.

Information Submitted: August 1987

JIMBOY'S TACOS
JIMBOY'S MARKETING, INC.
1560 B. Juliesse Avenue
Sacramento, California 95815
Don D. Rapisura, President

Description of Operation: Jimboy's Marketing, Inc., offers franchises in California and Nevada. Mexican restaurants serving a limited menu for both in-house dining and take-out orders.

Number of Franchisees: 27 units in California and Nevada.

In Business Since: 1977

Equity Capital Needed: $150,000

Financial Assistance Available: No financing is available from franchisor at this time.

Training Provided: Operations manual is provided to franchisee, in-store training followed by ongoing assistance to the franchise through periodic store inspections and visits. Continuous promotional and advertising campaigns.

Managerial Assistance Available: See above.

Information Submitted: May 1987

JO ANN'S CHILI BORDELLO, INC.
1919 Landon Avenue
Jacksonville, Florida 32207
Leonard Doctors, President

Description of Operation: A specialty restaurant serving 15 varieties of gourmet chili, gourmet hamburgers, plus a selection of fancy sandwiches in an operation designed to run with a minimum of labor and food costs.

Number of Frnchisees: 10 in Florida, Nevada and Arizona

In Business Since: 1981

Equity Capital Needed: $60,000-$150,000

Financial Assistance Available: Franchisees to provide their own financing.

Training Provided: Training at franchisee site, 2-3 weeks and home office.

Managerial Assistance Available: Training at franchisee site and home office.

Information Submitted: August 1987

JOHNNY ROCKETS
7507 Melrose Avenue
Los Angeles, California 90046
Ronn Teitelbaum, President
Cynthia Uanos, Assistant to the President

Description of Operation: Johnny Rockets is a retro diner with a bold contemporary flair. Each store is approximately 900-1,500 square feet and house a 20-28 stool counter. Stores are open 13 to 15 hours daily, 7 days a week. A lean, well defined menu is maintained.

Number of Franchisees: 6 in California, Minnesota and Georgia

In Business Since: 1986

Equity Capital Needed: $250,000 minimum

Financial Assistance Available: None

Training Provided: Intensive 30 day mandatory training course is scheduled for all new franchisees and their personnel. Training program is conducted at the home office school and on-site at the company store.

Managerial Assistance Available: Johnny Rockets provides continual management service for the life of the franchise in such areas as operations, inventory control, promotion and/or advertising. Complete manuals of operations, forms, and directions are provided. Field managers are available in all regions to work closely with franchisees and visit stores regularly to assist solving problems.

Information Submitted: July 1987

JOYCE'S SUBMARINE SANDWICHES, INC.
1527 Havana Street
Aurora, colorado 80010
David Meaux, President

Description of Operation: Fast food franchise consisting of submarine and deli sandwiches, soup, chili, salad bar, soft drinks, snacks and desserts. Operate in 1,000-1,500 square feet leased space. Open 7 days per week.

Number of Frnchisees: 41 in Colorado and Wyoming.

In Business Since: 1971

Equity Capital Needed: $25,000 minimum down payment for "turnkey" store operation.

Financial Assistance Available: The total cost of a Joyce's Sub Shop operation is $50,000. $25,000 is required for a down payment. Joyce's Submarine Sandwiches, Inc., will carry back note for balance of $25,000 to acceptable persons with good credit references. Franchisee has option to arrange own outside financing.

Training Provided: Joyce's Subs provides 3 weeks free, intensive training for up to 2 persons at company-owned training store. Franchisee trained in menu preparation, inventory ordering and portion control, customer and employee relations, expense control, and fast food marketing techniques.

Managerial Assistance Available: Periodic monitoring of store operations by Joyce's Corporate staff to assure product quality control, hygene, customer relations, inventory and portion control, expense control, marketing techniques, and development of advertising and promotion programs. Joyce's provides complete training manual and conducts periodic owners' meetings to assist in problem solving and assure quality in its operations.

Information Submitted: May 1987

JRECK SUBS, INC.
P. O. Box 6
Watertown, New York 13601
H. Thomas Swartz, President

Description of Operation: Sit-down and carry-out of submarine sandwiches in all stores. Stores vary in size and volume depending on market area.

Number of Franchisees: 34 in New York

In Business Since: 1967

Equity Capital Needed: $30,000

Financial Assistance Available: Franchisor will aid in securing outside financing in an advisory role.

Training Provided: 3 weeks of intensive in-store training; including sandwich preparation, store management, bookkeeping, personnel management and operational procedures.

Managerial Assistance Available: Marketing, advertising, operational assistance on a continuous basis.

Information Submitted: May 1987

JR.'S HOT DOGS INTERNATIONAL
Lake Arrowhead Village
28200 Highway 189, Suite 02-240
P. O. Box 1875
Lake Arrowhead, California 92352
M. N. Joe Camp, Jr.

Description of Operation: Carry-out and sit-down fast food. Hot dogs, chili dogs, cheese dogs, beef sandwiches, cold drinks, French fries and Polish sausage.

Number of Franchisees: 12 franchisees in Illinois, 8 regional franchises sold; 3 company-owned stores.

In Business Since: 1969

Equity Capital Needed: If you have property; building costs range from $60,000 to $125,000. Banks require 25 percent down. Build-to-suits available. $15,000 franchise fee.

Financial Assistance Available: SBA loan packaging available with acceptable credit.

Training Provided: Complete on-the-job and classroom training.

Managerial Assistance Available: We will assist in site selection, hiring, set-up of new location, and overall operation for the first few weeks of operation.

Information Submitted: August 1987

J-SYSTEMS FRANCHISING, INC.
3134 Lehigh Street
Allentown, Pennsylvania 18103
Harold G. Fulmer, President

Description of Operation: J's Steaks and Subs is a fast food submarine sandwich shop featuring steak sandwiches, a variety of cold and hot subs, salads, and side orders for eat-in or take-out.

Number of Franchisees: 40 in Pennsylvania, New Jersey and Indiana

In Business Since: 1968

Equity Capital Needed: $50,000 minimum

Financial Assistance Available: None

Training Provided: Training program is held 2 weeks prior to opening covering all aspects of the operation. A J's representative will spend 2 weeks, or more as needed, at the franchisee's premises to facilitate opening.

Managerial Assistance Available: Provide ongoing training and supervision of franchisee's unit. Provide to franchisee advancements and new developments through the operating manual, bulletins, and other promotional material J-Systems will administer and direct a national advertising fund for group advertising.

Information Submitted: May 1987

J. T. MCCORD'S RESTAURANTS
13020 Preston Road
Suite 201
Dallas, Texas 75240
Dennis Staub, Vice President, Franchise Development

Description of Operation: J. T. McCord's is a full service restaurant and bar that specializes in "gourmet style hamburgers," assorted finger foods, and a variety of sandwiches and dinners. It is medium priced dining in a casual atmosphere with large quantities of tasty food.

Number of Franchisees: 10 including company-owned in Texas.

In Business Since: 1978

Equity Capital Needed: $350,000 estimated

Financial Assistance Available: The capital requirements to open a J. T. McCord's will vary depending on local real estate values and costs to either purchase or lease the facility. Flagship estimates the total capital requirements will range between $500,000 and $1,500,000. Flagship does not provide any financing.

Training Provided: A comprehensive training program must be completed by all members of management. A minimum of 8 weeks is spent at the company training store in Dallas, Texas. Hourly training is also provided in the restaurant by the franchisor, prior to restaurant opening.

Managerial Assistance Available: J. T. McCord's continues to provide assistance to each franchisee throughout the term of the agreement. A regional manager visits each restaurant periodically to assist in operations. Each franchisee receives a set of operations manuals and constant assistance in areas of marketing, menu development, food and equipment procurement, real estate, architectural services, staffing and training.

Information Submitted: August 1987

K-BOB'S, INC.
5757 Alpha Road
Suite 716
Dallas, Texas 75240
Vice President of Development

Description of Operation: Family western style steakhouse, full sit down service, steaks, salad wagon, chicken, fish, hamburgers and Mexican. Each restaurant is approximately 5,000 to 6,000 square feet. Open 11 am to 10 pm, 7 days a week.

Number of Franchisees: 102 with a total of 110 franchises sold in Texas, Oklahoma, New Mexico, Kansas, Colorado and Arizona.

In Business Since: 1966

Equity Capital Needed: $175,000

Financial Assistance Available: None

Training Provided: 6 to 8 weeks of management training, standard building plans and equipment package, site selection and marketing analysis. On-site opening assistance, 2 weeks. Continual operational assistance.

Managerial Assistance Available: Continual operational assistance.

Information Submitted: August 1987

*KEN'S PIZZA
4441 South 72nd East Avenue
Tulsa, Oklahoma 74145
Robert C. Taft

Description of Operation: The Ken's Pizza concept entails an integrated system utilizing an attractive free-standing building with a drive-thru window, a unique limited menu and a simplified operating concept. Taken all together, the system combines a profitable menu with confortable table service format. Ken's Pizza is owned by Ken's Restaurant Systems, Inc., which has been in business for 23 years.

Number of Franchisees: 44 locations plus 41 company-owned in 11 States.

In Business Since: 1961

Equity Capital Needed: Initial franchise fee—$20,000. Land, building and equipment must be financed by franchisee.

Financial Assistance Available: None

Training Provided: Training program provided in Tulsa, Oklahoma training restaurant. Program is extensive and follows a formal "management training" manual. Time required varies between 4-15 weeks depending upon capabilities and previous experience of franchisee.

Managerial Assistance Available: 3 full-time employees travel among franchise stores offering operational assistance, further training and inspections. Company regularly conducts new product and training seminars in its Tulsa facilities. All franchisees are invited to these seminars.

Information Submitted: August 1987

*KETTLE RESTAURANTS, INC.
dba KETTLE RESTAURANTS
P. O. Box 2964
Houston, Texas 77252
Philip W. Weaver, Director of Franchise

Description of Operation: Full service 24-hour family restaurants.

Number of Franchisees: 108 in 17 States (95 company-owned)

In Business Since: 1968

Equity Capital Needed: $139,000

Financial Assistance Available: None

Training Provided: On-the-job training from 2 to 16 weeks.

Managerial Assistance Available: Managerial instruction given during the normal on-the-job training. Technical assistance given by franchisor to key personnel prior to opening for business and after opening until the operation stabilizes. Periodic visits thereafter, approximately every quarter or more often if deemed necessary or requested.

Information Submitted: May 1987

*KFC CORPORATION
P. O. Box 32070
Louisville, Kentucky 40232
Harold G. Dunford, Vice President, Franchising, Domestic

Description of Operation: Sale of Colonel Sanders' Kentucky Fried Chicken and related products.

Number of Franchisees: 896 in all States except Montana and Utah, and 230 Internationally.

In Business Since: March 1964 (purchase of Kentucky Fried Chicken, Inc., which was begun in 1952 by Colonel Harland Sanders).

Equity Capital Needed: Variable. $20,000 initital franchise fee. Land, building and equipment must be financed by franchisee.

Financial Assistance Available: Commercial sources available based on franchisee's own merits.

Training Provided: Required of all new franchisees and recommended for key employees—12 day training seminar covering proper store operation including management, accounting, sales, advertising, catering and purchasing. Ongoing training provided in areas of customer service, general restaurant management and quality control. Also available—sales hostess instruction and seminars for instruction on specific KFC programs and equipment such as the automatic cooker. Franchisees are also provided with confidential operating manual.

Managerial Assistance Available: Engineering assistance regarding best suited building, blueprints, recommended floor plan lay-out, placement of selected equipment—field services assistance including site selection, store opening, periodic visits to assist including store opening, periodic visits to assist in matters dealing with daily store operation, quality control standards—corporation offers regional and local seminars and workshops.

Information Submitted: May 1987

*KOOR'S SYSTEMS, INC.
Franchisor of KOOR'S DELI
9 Linwood Avenue
Melrose, Massachusetts 02176
Jan L. Koor, President

Description of Operation: Koor's Deli offers custome "made to order" sandwiches, using only quality ingredients on freshly baked breads and rolls. Steak sandwiches and our own soups are also offered. The company stresses quick service, cleanliness and a pleasant atmosphere. Units are located in high traffic shopping malls and downtown locations, and are of standard construction, design and color scheme. Individual and multi-unit franchises are available.

Number of Franchisees: 4 units including company-owned

In Business Since: 1974

Equity Capital Needed: $80,000-$125,000 including $20,000 franchise fee.

Financial Assistance Available: Koor's Systems Inc., will assist franchisee in arranging needed financial assistance.

Training Provided: 4 weeks in-store and classroom instruction. Manuals of the operation and direction are provided.

Managerial Assistance Available: Koor's provides continual management service for the life of the franchise in areas such as bookkeeping, advertising, inventory control and food preparation and handling. District and field persons are available to work closely with franchisees and visit stores regularly to assist in solving problems.

Information Submitted: August 1987

LAMPPOST PIZZA
1585 Sunland
Costa Mesa, California 92626
Dominic Petrossi, Vice President

Description of Operation: Family style pizza restaurant serving Italian food, appealing to families and large groups.

Number of Franchisees: 61 in California.

In Business Since: 1976

Equity Capital Needed: $250,000 ($75,000 cash minimum)

Financial Assistance Available: Assistance in seeking financing is provided.

Training Provided: Management and employee training for 30 days located at company headquarters and company-owned restaurants.

Managerial Assistance Available: Assistance by management staff and field representatives in site selection, financial assistance, restaurant start-up, staffing, cost control, marketing and advertising.

Information Submitted: August 1987

LANDIS FOOD SERVICES, INC.
Suite 210
104 Carnegie Center
Princeton, New Jersey 08540
Mitchell Landis, President

Description of Operation: Landis Food Services, Inc., is the franchisor of five operating Mexican full service restaurants. Our "Marita's Cantina" dinnerhouses serve Mexican favorites such as tostadas, fajitas, grilled fish dishes, chimichangas, and other specialties in a well developed, casual atmosphere. Our "Cantina," or lounge, offers many Mexican beers, over 17 types of tequila, large frozen Margaritas, and red and white Sangria.

Number of Franchisees: 7 in New Jersey, Pennsylvania

In Business Since: 1977

Equity Capital Needed: Pre-opening costs range from $125,000 to $275,000 of which past franchisees have been able to borrow up to 70 percent.

Financial Assistance Available: Franchisor, although not providing financial assistance, will consult with franchisee on possible avenues of financing.

Training Provided: Training is as follows: franchisee and/or manager will train at existing locations until proficient in the Marita's Cantina operating system. Then, upon opening of franchisee's restaurant, the field supervisor will remain in the restaurant for up to two weeks. Additional help is available as required.

Managerial Assistance Available: Franchisor will instruct franchisee as to Marita's operating systems including the computerized register system, sales recording, employee timekeeping and payroll, food and beverage inventories, in addition to consulting on employee hiring, training, staffing, scheduling, and advertising and promotion. Franchisor will also consult with franchisee on site selection, lease negotiation, interior and exterior design, and equipment purchasing.

Information Submitted: May 1987

LAROSA'S, INC.
5870 Belmont Avenue
Cintinnati, Ohio 45224
Stewart A. Smetts, Franchise Director

Description of Operation: A full service, full menu, Italian style family restaurant especially known for pizzas. Most locations offer beer and wine.

Number of Franchisees: 40 in Ohio and Kentucky

In Business Since: 1954—franchising began in 1967

Equity Capital Needed: $50,000 minimum

Financial Assistance Available: Prospective franchise owner must secure own financing.

Training Provided: Mandatory training for franchise owner in a corporate facility. Management and supervisory personnel to be trained in corporate facility at franchisees expense—duration of training depends on the experience and capabilities of the personnel.

Managerial Assistance Available: An opening supervisory crew trains employees for 1 week prior to opening and stays approximately two weeks after opening. After the first 6 months, franchise operations personnel spend a day at all locations approximately once every 30 days.

Information Submitted: May 1987

LIFESTYLE RESTAURANTS, INC.
11 East 26th Street
New York, New York 10010
Robert G. Everett, Executive Vice President

Description of Operation: Lifestyle Restaurants, Inc., owns and operates restaurants throughout the Eastern Seaboard. Our restaurants are best known for their dining package consisting of a complete dinner with unlimited salad and shrimp, plus beer, wine, and sangria, has a loyal following attracted by good food at excellent value.

Number of Franchisees: 27 in 9 States

In Business Since: 1969

Equity Capital Needed: Initial $25,000

Financial Assistance Available: None

Training Provided: We train their owners, managers and staff. We provide: marketing, advertising, promotions, assistant purchasing, and cost project analysis.

Managerial Assistance Available: Consulting and assist managers in making restaurants as profitable as possible.

Information Submitted: May 1987

LITTLE BIG MEN, INC.
2110 Overland Avenue
Suite 126
Billings, Montana 59102
Steven W. Arntzen, Executive Vice President

Description of Operation: Pizza restaurant chain emphasizing relaxed family dining. Units are approximately 3,500 square feet and set 100-150 people.

Number of Franchisees: 9 units plus 1 company owned units in Montana, and Wyoming.

In Business Since: 1972

Equity Capital Needed: $40,000 cash with a net worth of approximately $150,000.

Financial Assistance Available: Financing presentation aid only.

Training Provided: An intensive 2 week training course is offered to each franchisee and/or their manager candidates prior to each unit's opening. In addition, a training group is provided at each opening to supervise the training of the unit's crew members. The training group is made up of the training director and at least one other qualified training assistant.

Managerial Assistance Available: Little Big Men provides continual management assistance in areas such as cost analysis and inventory control, menu mix, bookkeeping, advertising, and all related marketing areas including service and promotional analysis. Complete manuals are furnished for operations and accounting as well as support manuals for managers and employees, field consultatnts visit each unit every 60 days to determine problem areas and to assist in problem solving. Little Big Men also sponsors meetings of franchisees on semi-annual basis.

Information Submitted: August 1987

*LITTLE CAESAR ENTERPRISES, INC.
24120 Haggerty Road
Farmington Hills, Michigan 48024
Robert Massey, Vice President-Franchise Sales

Description of Operation: Little Caesars is the world's largest carry-out pizza chain in the country and the third largest pizza chain overall. Aggressive expansion plans provide investors with an excellent opportunity for growth and profit.

Number of Franchisees: 1,240 franchised and 390 company-owmed.

In Business Since: 1959

Equity Capital Needed: Approximately $50,000 per unit.

Financial Assistance Available: Third party financing available.

Training Provided: Little Caesars Human Resource Center provides all necessary training. The initial intensive training program includes classroom and in-store sessions. Classes are provided for all levels of management.

Managerial Assistance Available: Little Caesars corporate staff of professionals provide its franchisees with ongoing managerial assistance for all phases of operations.

Information Submitted: August 1987

*LITTLE KING RESTAURANT CORPORATION
11811 I' Street
Omaha, Nebraska 68137
Sidney B. Wertheim, President
David K. Kilby, Vice President, Franchise Development

Description of Operation: The Little King Restaurant Corporation operates and directs a successful chain of company and franchised-owned submarine/deli-style sandwich and pizza outlets. Emphasis is on fresh-foods-fast, with the products being prepared from the freshest of ingredients directly in full-view of the customers, fresh bread baked on the premises, and a special 300 calorie or less "lite menu." Product quality, customer service, and store cleanliness are the standards of the Little King operation for over 18 years.

Number of Franchisees: 38 units in 14 States plus 26 company-owned outlets.

In Business Since: 1968—franchising began in 1978

Equity Capital Needed: $85,000-$125,000 (approximate) single restaurant. Multi-unit development program available to qualified candidates.

Financial Assistance Available: Equipment lease programs available through non-affiliated sources. Differed payment of multi-unit development program franchise fee.

Training Provided: Total 4 weeks. 2 week course in company head-quarters, Omaha, Nebraska, which includes in-store and classroom studies of operations, managerial methods, accounting procedures, marketing techniques. 2 weeks training and supervision is provided by field representatives in franchisee's restaurant prior to and during initial opoening.

Managerial Assistance Available: Field representation and consultation is provided at franchisee's restaurant quarterly, in addition to weekly communications, verbal and written materials. Company provides promotional and marketing ideas and concepts to franchisee's through monthly marketing report. Each facet of the operation is supported by detailed manuals.

Information Submitted: May 1987

LONDON FISH N'CHIPS, LTD.
306 South Maple Avenue
South San Francisco, California 94080

Description of Operation: Fast food service for both eat in and take out.

Number of Franchisees: 41 in California

In Business Since: 1967

Equity Capital Needed: $78,000

Financial Assistance Available: None

Training Provided: In shop training and in company shop training. Direct supervision in franchisee shop as needed.

Managerial Assistance Available: Help with bookkeeping. Advise on new methods and products and selling procedures for duration of franchise. Provide periodic inspection and instruction as needed.

Information Submitted: August 1987

*LONG JOHN SILVER'S, INC.
JERRICO, INC.
P. O. Box 11988
Lexington, Kentucky 40579
Eugene O. Getchell, Vice President, Franchising

Description of Operation: Fast food restaurants-self-service-carry-out or seating in a wharf-like atmosphere. Menu includes fish and fryes. Shrimp, clams, chicken, hush puppies, cole slaw, desserts, sea salads and a variety of hot and cold beverages.

Number of Franchisees: 532 franchised plus 884 company-owned.

In Business Since: Founder started in 1929. Parent company, Jerrico, Inc., incorporated in 1946. Long John Silver's started 1969.

Equity Capital Needed: Contact company for full information.

Financial Assistance Available: None: franchisees required to have adequate net worth to obtain real estate and equipment on their own.

Training Provided: 7 weeks formal training course for management.

Managerial Assistance Available: Continuous training and supervision program in all phases of management through training academy, field supervisors and home office personnel.

Information Submitted: May 1987

LOSURDO FOODS, INC.
20 Owens Road
Hackensack, New Jersey 07601
Michael Losurdo, President

Description of Operation: Italian restaurant with accent on pizza.

Number of Franchisees: 4 in New Jersey, and Pennsylvania.

In Business Since: 1973

Equity Capital Needed: $50,000

Financial Assistance Available: None

Training Provided: 2 week training period plus regular monthly training session.

Managerial Assistance Available: Continual assistance in product preparation and advertising assistance.

Information Submitted: August 1987

LOVE'S WOOD PIT BARBEQUE RESTAURANTS
568 East Lambert Road
Brea, California 92621
Ronald C. Mesker, President

Description of Operation: Complete full service barbecue restaurant featuring barbecued ribs, beef, port, chicken, steak, seafood and salads. Love's is a medium priced lunch and dinner house located in the Western United States. Love's Restaurants also offer late evening suppers and cocktail lounge service. Breakfast now being served at some locations.

Number of Franchisees: 21 franchised units plus 2 company-owned in California.

In Business Since: 1948

Equity Capital Needed: Varies as to location.

Financial Assistance Available: None

Training Provided: Formal training as required by individual franchisee.

Managerial Assistance Available: Franchisor provides opening supervision, assists in hiring of personnel plus regular visits and assistance from field coordinators. Complete manual of operations specifies how each menu item is prepared and served, how the business may be operated effectively.

Information Submitted: May 1987

MACAYO MEXICAN RESTAURANTS, INC.
4001 North Central
Phoenix, Arizona 85012
Stephen C. Johnson, President

Description of Operation: Full service Mexican restaurants with lounges.

Number of Franchisees: 10 company-owned in Arizona and Nevada.

In Business Since: 1940

Equity Capital Needed: $300,000

Financial Assistance Available: None

Training Provided: 3-6 weeks for management training course, and at store location 2-3 weeks for hands on supervision.

Managerial Assistance Available: Manuals; 6 week training for general management at Phoenix, Arizona unit. Lodging and transportation provided by franchisee. Opening team for 2 weeks at initial opening, and monthly supervisory trips to monitor store.

Information Submitted: May 1987

MAID-RITE PRODUCTS, INC.
536—36th Street
Des Moines, Iowa 50312
P. Maxheim, President

Description of Operation: Fast food—limited menu sandiwch type operation with take-out or set down—suitable in towns of population 2,000 to 2 million. Restaurant in free-standing buildings, strip malls or shopping centers.

Number of Franchisees: 160 in 18 States

In Business Since: 1928

Equity Capital Needed: $50,000-$65,000 average. Varies with size of operation, site and location, including initial franchise fee, equipment package, sign, opening inventory and working capital. Lease hold improvements or construction costs will vary with site and size.

Financial Assistance Available: None

Training Provided: On-the-job training and classroom—operations manual on food preparation, personnel management and cost control.

Managerial Assistance Available: Continuing assistance by home office personnel in regards to operation, operations manual, recommended floor plan layout, product development cooking methods, bookkeeping and architectural services availble when requested, ongoing assistance in advertising.

Information Submitted: August 1987

MARCO'S, INC.
dba MARCO'S PIZZA
5254 Monroe Street
Toledo, Ohio 43623
Pasquale "Pat" Giammarco, President
Samuel B. Morrison, Secretary and General Counsel

Description of Operation: Pizza and submarine sandwich carry-out and home delivery, serving premium quality pizza at an affordable price.

Number of Franchisees: 18 in Ohio, plus 15 company stores

In Business Since: 1978

Equity Capital Needed: $59,000 to $88,000 total, including initial franchise investment—equity needed depends on franchisee's financing capabilities.

Financial Assistance Available: Marco's does not provide direct financing to franchisees at the present time. However, it does provide assistance in obtaining financing such as assisting the franchisee in preparing his/her proposal for bank financing, and meeting with potential lenders.

Training Provided: Minimum of up to 4 months, dpending upon the rate of progress of the franchisee.

Managerial Assistance Available: Continued service for the life of the contract, including forms, advertising, trademarked paper goods, special training if needed, and a manual for the manager and staff covering food preparation, personnel management and cost control, plus periodic visits, inspections and assistance.

Information Submitted: June 1987

MAVERICK FAMILY STEAK HOUSE, INC.
1752 West Jefferson
Springfield, Illinois 62702
Cliff Crispens

Description of Operation: Semi-cafeteria style family steak house.

Number of Franchisees: 4 company-owned stores in Illinois plus 2 franchises in 2 States.

In Business Since: 1983

Equity Capital Needed: Approximately $100,000 to $150,000.

Financial Assistance Available: No direct financial assistance.

Training Provided: Training on-the-job at company-owned stores and training facility. Supervision prior to and during opening.

Managerial Assistance Available: Continuous assistance when and as needed. Operations manuals furnished and updated. Special training and visits in person as conditions require.

Information Submitted: July 1987

∗ MAZZIO'S PIZZA
4441 South 72nd East Avenue
Tulsa, Oklahoma 74145
Robert C. Taft

Description of Operation: Mazzio's Pizza concept is an integrated concept that features a high value pizza product. Mazzio's restaurants are primarily free-standing buildings, but include in-line shopping center locations or remodeled existing buildings. Mazzio's Pizza is owned by Ken's Restaurant Systems, Inc., which has been in business since 1961.

Number of Franchisees: 26 with 107 locations plus 69 company-owned in 13 States.

In Business Since: 1979

Equity Capital Needed: Varies. Initial franchise fee—$20,000. Land, building and equipment must be financed by franchisee.

Financial Assistance Available: None

Training Provided: Management training program provided in Tulsa, Oklahoma training restaurant. Program is extensive and requires between 4-15 weeks, depending upon capabilities and previous experience of franchisee.

Managerial Assistance Available: Operational assistance for 2 week minimum following opening. Continued assistance from assigned representatives in areas of training, operations, inspections, and marketing. Company conducts training seminars in Tulsa and is always available for whatever assistance is needed. Company also provides confidential training manual.

Information Submitted: August 1987

∗ MCDONALD'S CORPORATION
1 McDonald's Plaza
Oak Brook, Illinois 60521
Licensing Department

Description of Operation: McDonald's Corporation operates and directs a successful nationwide chain of fast food restaurants serving a moderately priced menu. Emphasis is on quick, efficient service, high quality food, and cleanliness. The standard menu consists of hamburgers, cheeseburgers, fish sandwiches, French fries, apple pie, shakes, breakfast menu, and assorted beverages.

Number of Franchisees: Over 1,800 in the United States

In Business Since: 1955

Equity Capital Needed:

Conventional Franchise: $160,000 minimum from nonborrowed funds and ability to acquire outside financing for an additional $218,000 to $293,000.

Business Facilities Lease: $66,000 from nonborrowed funds.

Financial Assistance Available: None

Training Provided: Prospective franchisees are required to complete a structured training program which includes approximately 12-18 months of in-store training (on a part-time basis) and 5 weeks of classroom training.

Managerial Assistance Available: Operations, training, maintenance, accounting and equipment manuals provided. Company makes available promotional advertising material plus field representative consultation and assistance.

Information Submitted: May 1987

MCFADDIN VENTURES
1900 Yorktown #100
Houston, Texas 77056

Description of Operation: McFaddin Ventures is presently offering its concept: Studebaker's, a 50's and 60's bar/diner serving alcoholic drinks of all kinds including beer and wine. A limited late night snack menu is offered. Sites can be free-standing or in shopping malls located in city or suburban areas.

Number of Franchisees: 12 in 9 States including company owned.

In Business Since: 1982

Equity Capital Needed: $300,000 and up depending on operators ability to finance.

Financial Assistance Available: Franchisee is responsible for land, building and equipment.

Training Provided: Training at corporate office.

Managerial Assistance Available: The company provides ongoing assistance on a regular basis for the management, operational and promotional program.

Information Submitted: August 1987

MELVIN'S, INC.
1602 Savannah Highway
Charleston, South Carolina 29407
Melvin Bessinger, President

Description of Operation: Restaurant specializing in barbeque.

Number of Franchisees: 4 in South Carolina

In Business Since: 1964

Equity Capital Needed: $150,000

Financial Assistance Available: None

Training Provided: Franchisee will receive on-the-job training of 4 weeks prior to the opening of a unit, with 2 weeks of close supervision to be provided by the franchisor staff at initial opening of a unit.

Managerial Assistance Available: Franchisor will provide franchisee a technical manual of complete instructions for operating each individual unitl. In addition, technical support will be provided by the franchisor as needed.

Information Submitted: July 1987

MILTON'S PIZZA HOUSE, INC.
810 Kempsville Road
Suite 6
Virginia Beach, Virginia 23462
George P. Kotarides, Senior, President

Description of Operation: Milton's Pizza Restaurant system is a distinctive, highly competitive operation featuring an Italian-type menu offering a menu of pizza, spaghetti, lasagna, subs and desserts. The stores are approximatelyl 3,000 square feet, seating 100, set in a standarized, unique atmosphere.

Number of Franchisees: 18 units in Virginia and North Carolina

In Business Since: First unit opened 1977 chartered by Commonwealth of Virginia September 1979.

Equity Capital Needed: $140,000-$380,000 depending on location.

Financial Assistance Available: Total investment depends on location from $50,000-$200,000. Will direct but will not guarantee financing through normal banking channels. Referral is made to developers who will develop locations for qualified franchisees.

Training Provided: Orientation training at corporate headquarters for franchisee and/or key person 2-5 days. Initial training for manager, assistant manager, assistant manager and head waitress prior to opening 2-7 days.

Managerial Assistance Available: Opening team for new unit from 1-2-1/2 weeks. Franchise representatives will assist and advise for term of agreement. Access to all corporate directors and officers. Complete oerations manual which is periodicallyl updated.

Information Submitted: August 1987

MINSKY'S PIZZA, INC.
10550 Barkley, Suite 100
Overland Park, Kansas 66212
Arrow A. Wilson

Description of Operation: Comprehensive pizza restaurant concept. Menu ranges from gourmet pizza to sandwiches and salads. All items are made from fresh, natural ingredients.

Number of Franchisees: 9 in Kansas and Missouri.

In Business Since: 1975

Equity Capital Needed: $150,000 to $350,000

Financial Assistance Available: None

Training Provided: 4 weeks management training program at Kansas City area training store.

Managerial Assistance Available: Systems consultations on a continuous basis by full-time franchise representatives.

MINUTE MAN OF AMERICA, INC.
P. O. Box 828
Little Rock, Arkansas 72203
John Jenkins, President

Description of Operation: Fast food specialty restaurant—free standing building (3,000 square feet)—carry-out and eat in featuring broiled hamburgers, 12 types of sandwiches and hot pies. At this time not interested in franchising any units over 450 miles from headquarters.

Number of Franchisees: 5 company-owned and 2 franchisee.

In Business Since: 1965

Equity Capital Needed: $75,000 turnkey-lease by franchisee on ground and building.

Financial Assistance Available: Advice and counsel only.

Training Provided: 6 weeks at home office at the expense of franchisee—required. Trainee will receive $200 weekly while training.

Managerial Assistance Available: Real estate selection based on computer test volume. Help in lease negotiation and equipment purchasing. Manager manual and on-the-job help in hiring and training first crew. Complete advertising programs through national advertising committee. Continuous visitation and invitational meetings.

Information Submitted: August 1987

MOUNTAIN MIKE'S PIZZA
2797 Park Avenue #102
Santa Clara, California 95050
Ernest L. Stewart, President

Description of Operation: Pizza restaurant with oven baked sandwiches, hamburgers, salad bar, beer and wine. Rustic theme and decor.

Number of Franchisees: 46 in California, Nevada and Florida

In Business Since: 1978

Equity Capital Needed: $60,000

Financial Assistance Availble: None

Training Provided: 5 weeks in-store training.

Managerial Assistance Available: Ongoing operational and advertising assistance. A franchise representative is on hand for 10 days at the opening of the restaurant.

Information Submitted: May 1987

MR. BURGER, INC.
P. O. Box 8248
Amarillo, Texas 79109
Robert Coleman, Franchise Director

Description of Operation: Fast food hamburger, chicken, ice cream. Seating for 52 to 72 people. Franchises availble in Texas, Oklahoma, New Mexico, Colorado and Louisiana.

Number of Franchisees: 31 in Texas, Oklahoma, New Mexico, Arkansas, Colorado, Louisiana and Kansas. Plus 30 company-owned in same States.

In Business Since: 1969

Equity Capital Needed: $150,000 net worth of which $75,000 must be in liquid assets.

Financial Assistance Available: Franchisee must arrange own financing.

Training Provided: 6 weeks training in unit and class covering unit operation, equipment and administration.

Managerial Assistance Available: Operational and marketing assistance is provided on an ongoing basis.

Information Submitted: August 1987

*MR. CHICKEN NATIONAL, INC.
29025 Lakeshore Boulevard
Willowwick, Ohio 44094
Michael Simens, Director of Franchise Operations

Description of Operation: Mr. Chicken is a fast food, sit-down and take-away operation, specializing in high quality fried chicken and accompanying products.

Number of Franchisees: 12 company-owned in Ohio.

In Business Since: 25 years.

Equity Capital Needed: $25,000 initial franchise fee. Land, building, and equipment must be financed by franchisee.

Financial Assistance Available: No financial assistance available.

Training Provided: A minimum 14 day training course is required of all franchisees, and is strongly recommended for their key employees. The course is conducted at the Mr. Chicken training facility, and entails both classroom and hands-on instruction in the areas of accounting, advertising, cooking procedures, store operations, quality control, purchasing, and employee management. Mr. Chicken also makes available regional training seminars to instruct franchisees on the most up-to-date programs.

Managerial Assistance Available: Franchisor provides assistance in site selection as well as providing standardized building plans. Franchisor also helps in start up of operation, as well as providing regional representatives to make periodic visits to locations to review and retrain franchisees and their staff. Representative will evaluate the operations in the field. Franchisor will continue to upgrade all locations with the latest products and procedures as they become available.

Information Submitted: May 1987

*MR. GATTI'S, INC.
220 Foremost Drive
Austin, Texas 78745

Description of Operation: Mr. Gatti's is a pizza restaurant concept concentrating on qualityl products with fast service in a facility with an average of 125 seats. Pick-up window and delivery service is also available.

Number of Franchisees: 183 franchises; 150 company-owned in 10 States.

In Business Since: 1964, franchising began 1969.

Equity Capital Needed: $40,000 to $50,000 (minimum)

Financial Assistance Available: Franchisee is responsible for obtaining own financing. Total investment is approximately $450,000-$500,000.

Training Provided: 2 weeks at company operated school; 1 week in-store training.

Managerial Assistance Available: Field consultation, purchasing methods, cost control procedures, operations and equipment manuals; provided on a current basis.

Information Submitted: July 1987

MR. JIMS PIZZERIA CORPORATION
2817 Regal Road #108
Plano, Texas 75075
Chris Bowman, Executive Director-Franchise Operations

Description of Operation: Pizza carry-out and delivery restaurants.

Number of Franchisees: 40 franchisees, 6 company owned

In Business Since: 1976

Equity Capital Needed: $65,000

Financial Assistance Available: Franchisees must arrange own financing

Training Provided: 300 hours in store training required.

Managerial Assistance Available: Ongoing managerial and technical assistance is available to franchisee's corporate representatives will be in the store for the first 10 days.

Information Submitted: May 1987

MR. PHILLY
Sub. of RESTAURANT DEVELOPERS CORP.
6902 Pearl Road
Cleveland, Ohio 44130
Joseph M. McClellan, Vice President of Franchise Marketing

Description of Operation: Mr. Philly, a total fast food restaurant, features Philadelphia style cheese steaks, Romanburgers, fresh potato fries, fresh salads and delicious cheesecake.

Number of Franchisees: 85 units in Ohio

In Business Since: 1965

Equity Capital Needed: Minimum of $100,000 plus construction, building and/or land costs.

Financial Assistance Available: Franchisee is responsible for obtaining his own financing with assistance from franchisor.

Training Provided: 5 weeks intensive program on-the-job in a training unit and in classroom sessions.

Managerial Assistance Available: Restaurant Developers Corp., will provide assistance and advice in selection and securing of a location. Advisory services will be rendered relating to operations, preparation and development of recipes and food products, equipment needed and layout. Supporting services such as advertising, portion control systems, and opening assistance will be provided. Supervisory staff will visit stores on a regular basis to assist in solving problems.

Information Submitted: August 1987

MR. STEAK, INC.
International Headquarters
P. O. Box 9006
Littleton, Colorado 80160

Description of Operation: Mr. Steak, Inc. is a full service, sit down family type restaurant with seating facilities for up to 220 persons. The store hours are normally 11 am to 9 pm. We specialize in USDA Choice steaks, as well as seafood, chicken and sandwiches. Alcohol permitted.

Number of Franchisees: 159 in 36 States and Canada including company-owned.

In Business Since: 1962

Equity Capital Needed: $75,000 to $100,000

Financial Assistance Available: None

Training Provided: Comprehensive 7 weeks mandatory training is provided with the franchise fee for the restaurant manager. Travel, food and lodging is the responsibility of the trainee while in training.

Managerial Assistance Available: Opening and continuing assistance is provided by the company. Site approval, lease assistance, building plans with specifications, construction inspection and opening assistance is provided by franchisor. Continued assistance in marketing and advertising product planning is also available. The franchisor also has franchise regional directors in the field. Restaurant accounting, equipment and many food items can be purchased with franchisor assistance. The company provides operational assistance in new techniques developed by the company.

Information Submitted: August 1987

• NATHAN'S FAMOUS, INC.
1515 Broadway
New York, New York 10036

Description of Operation: Nathan's Famous, Inc., franchised units offer a variety of foods, featuring the world famous all-beef frankfurter, in a nostalgic atmosphere, serving to its standards, moderately prices. It is essentially a restaurant and fast food establishment. Nathan's Famous, Inc., has variety of size of stores that fit various marketing areas.

Number of Franchisees: 4 in New York, New Jersey and Maryland plus 13 company owned

In Business Since: 1916

Equity Capital Needed: Variable, depending upon size and location.

Financial Assistance Available: None

Training Provided: Intensive, mandatory training for key personnel. Training could be up to 5 weeks at company's location. Training is under the direction of franchisor and is formalized in nature.

Managerial Assistance Available: Continual management supervision. Specifications as to operations, food preparation, food specifications, accounting, advertising. Complete manual of operations is provided and field supervision is conducted by franchisor to assist franchisee.

Information Submitted: August 1987

NEW MEIJI FRANCHISE CORPORATION
dba NEW MEIJU TAKE OUT
435 East 149th Street
Gardena, California 90248
Bob Endo, General Manager

Description of Operation: A fast food oriental restaurant serving hot food items in combinations or in individual portions in addition to a wide variety of Sushi (Japanese style raw fish and rice).

Number of Franchisees: 16 in California

In Business Since: 1976

Equity Capital Needed: $100,000 to $120,000

Financial Assistance Available: None

Training Provided: 3 weeks intensive training for the franchisee and personnel in management, hot food and Sushi preparation. Complete set of manuals are provided in addition to hands on training.

Managerial Assistance Available: Franchisee will receive information regarding site selection, store design and equipment specifications. Opening week assistance will be provided in addition to periodic visits providing managerial and technical assistance in advertising, merchandising and quality control. Franchisor helps in advertising and promotion. Continuous research and development of new food items and combinations.

Information Submitted: July 1987

NEW ORLEANS' FAMOUS FRIED CHICKEN
OF AMERICA, INCORPORATED
P. O. Box 700
Greenwood, Mississippi 38930

Description of Operation: New Orleans Famous Fried Chicken of America, Inc., is a fast food operation that specializes in specially seasoned chicken and biscuit breakfast. New Orleans also sells many side orders like baked beans, cole slaw, mashed potatoes, gravy and onion rings.

Number of Franchisees: 22 in Mississippi, Tennessee. Texas and Idaho plus 20 company-owned

In Business Since: 1974, franchising since 1979

Equity Capital Needed: $50,000

Financial Assistance Available: None—total investment of $85,000 excluding real estate.

Training Provided: 4-8 weeks training for manager or operator in classroom and on-the-job training at New Orleans Famous Fried Chicken's Management Institute in Columbus, Mississippi.

Managerial Assistance Available: We provide oprational manuals. Every franchise is inspected frequently to insure that the continued quality is maintained. All franchises are constantly informed on new products and techniques to improve their productivity and profitability. Bookkeeping and accounting services available.

Information Submitted: August 1987

NOBLE ROMAN'S INC.
P. O. Box 1089
Bloomington, Indiana 47402
John West, Vice President

Description of Operation: Noble Roman's is a restaurant business specializing in 4 types of pizzas, salads, and sandwiches for on premises and off premises consumption.

Number of Franchisees: 110 in Midwest and Florida as of April 30, 1987.

In Business Since: 1972—franchising since 1972.

Equity Capital Needed: Franchise fee $12,500, approximately $235,000 to $375,000 for total package.

Financial Assistance Available: None

Training Provided: Training is provided at a company training center. The standard training period is approximately 4 weeks.

Managerial Assistance Available: Managerial, technical and marketing assistance provided.

Information Submitted: April 1987

NORTH'S FRANCHISING CORPORATION
1005 North Riverside Avenue
Medford, Oregon 07501
John F. North, Jr., President

Description of Operation: NRI is a unique, buffet style restaurant chain. The restaurants vary in size, from approximately 6,000 square feet to 12,000 square feet, with approximately 125 parking spaces. The restaurants are open 7 days a week and serve lunch and dinner, except Sunday, on which day dinner only, is served.

Number of Franchisees: 14 in California, Idaho, Oregon and Washington plus 8 company-owned.

In Business Since: 1959

Equity Capital Needed: $100,000 minimum

Financial Assistance Available: None

Training Provided: Extensive 60 day mandatory training program, which covers all aspects of restaurant operation, with additional on-site supervision by company personnel during the initial opening, plus extensive follow-up during the first few months of operation.

Managerial Assistance Available: NRI provides continual management service for the life of the franchise on a minimum of once a quarter visit to outlet. All accounting and payroll functions are done by the home office. Complete operations, accounting and employee manuals are provided, district management personnel are available to work clsoely with franchisees and to visit outlets on a regular basis to assist in solving problems. NRI sponsors meetings and work shops for the franchisees and their management personnel.

Information Submitted: August 1987

NUGGET RESTAURANTS
4650 Brightmore Road
Bloomfield Hills, Michigan 48013
Gordon R. Eliassen, President

Description of Operation: Short order—full menu restaurant.

Number of Franchisees: 10 in Michigan

In Business Since: 1962

Equity Capital Needed: $60,000

Financial Assistance Available: None

Training Provided: Training is provided as necessary.

Managerial Assistance Available: Managerial and technical assistance is provided when needed.

Information Submitted: May 1987

*NUMERO UNO FRANCHISE CORPORATION
20335 Ventura Boulevard
Suite 430
Woodland Hills, California 91364
Rodney Reed, Director of Franchising

Description of Operation: Pizzeria full menu—full service restaurant.

Number of Franchisees: 62 in California, Hawaii and Louisiana

In Business Since: 1973

Equity Capital Needed: $100,000-$125,000 cash minimum. Total investment $200,000-$300,000.

Financial Assistance Available: None

Training Provided: 4 weeks extensive training.

Managerial Assistance Available: Continuous and ongoing.

Information Submitted: August 1987

O! DELI
One Van Noss Avenue
San Francisco, California 94102
Mike Kilck, Director of Franchising

Description of Operation: O! Deli offers quality sandwiches, salads, breakfast and desserts at fast food prices. Customers are primarily working people during working hours, with O! Deli's often open only 5-1/2 days per week. O! Deli quality and value build a loyal repeat clientele. Catering and delivery are used. O! Deli's are approximately 1,000 square feet.

Number of Franchisees: 7 in California and Massachusetts

In Business Since: 1985

Equity Capital Needed: $35,000-$50,000

Financial Assistance Available: O! Deli assists franchisees, when requested, in preparing business plans and obtaining financing.

Training Provided: O! Deli provides 2 weeks training for 2 people in an operating O! Deli. O! Deli staff provides training and assistance during franchisee store opening week. An extensive operations manual covers portion control, hiring and training, financial controls, and food preparation.

Managerial Assistance Available: O! Deli helps with site selection, lease negotiation, restaurant layout, discounts on equipment and food purchases, training in operations management and control. Ongoing assistance involves frequent contact with O! Deli operations people to fine tune your operation, analyzes sales trends and help the business prosper.

Information Submitted: May 1987

THE OLDE WORLD CHEESE SHOP
3333 South Pasadena Avenue
South Pasadena, Florida 33707
Bob Ross, President

Description of Operation: The Olde World Cheese Shop offers a unique family restaurant which has designed gourmet sandwiches using our own breads and dressings. In addition we serve our own unique omlete and appetizers, we are open seven days a week for breakfast, lunch and dinner.

Number of Franchisees: 16

In Business Since: 1975

Equity Capital Needed: $150,000 for in line unit.

Financial Assistance Available: We will assist the franchisee in arranging the balance of the investment with our bank or the Small Business Administration. Our complete total turnkey cost is approximatelyi $400,000 for a line unit and $1,000,000 for a free standing restaurant.

Training Provided: We have a mandatory 12 week training course which is accomplished at our headquarters in South Pasadena, Florida. During these 8 weeks the franchisee is trained by our specialists in very facet of our operation. We then go with franchisee and assist them in the opening of their new store.

Managerial Assistance Available: The Olde World Cheese Shop provides management service for the entire life of the franchise in all areas of operation. Complete operation manuals, visits by our staff regularly, and a monthly newsletter are provided. We are always available to help the franchisee with any problems. The Olde World Cheese Shop conducts constant research for new products and new marketing techniques.

Information Submitted: May 1987

*OLGA'S KITCHEN LICENSING, INC.
1940 Northwood Drive
Troy, Michigan 48084
Robert H. McRae, Vice President-Franchise Operations

Description of Operation: Specialty restaurant, table service at moderate prices, featuring The Olga, with secret recipe bread, cooked fresh to order.

Number of Franchisees: 40 in operation and 8 franchised.

In Business Since: Olga's Kitchens in operation since 1976. Franchising since January 1984.

Equity Capital Needed: Approximately $100,000 to $150,000 (providing that financing is obtainable) with total investment ranging from $289,000 to $490,000 depending upon size and type of outlet.

Financial Assistance Available: None

Training Provided: Comprehensive "PRO" training program of approximately 5-6 weeks duration at our Detroit area training center, and restaurant opening assistance of approximately 2 weeks.

Managerial Assistance Available: Our specialists will provide recommended locations or location evaluations, store development and employee training for opening the restaurant. After start-up the operation will continue to benefit from our follow up systems. We can supply services in areas such as operations, quality control, advertising, marketing, insurance, bookkeeping and cost analysis.

Information Submitted: May 1987

OMAHA STEAKSHOPS, INC.
8420 West Dodge Road, Suite 525
Box 3300
Omaha, Nebraska 86103
Joseph M. Alfieri, Vice President & General Manager

Description of Operation: Omaha Steakshops, Inc., an affiliate of Omaha Steaks International, is a national franchisor of retail stores that sell high quality frozen beef products and a variety of high quality veal, pork, lamb, seafood, dessert items and hard-to-find food delicacies. The red meat products are carefully aged, trimmed and handcut by Omaha Steaks International, exclusive supplier for the franchise system. Other products are supplied by companies which are carefully screened by Omaha Steaks International.

Number of Franchisees: 4 plus company-owned in Colorado, Texas and Nebraska.

In Business Since: 1985. Affiliate, Omaha Steaks International, in business since 1917.

Equity Capital Needed: $125,000-$150,000

Financial Assistance Available: None

Training Provided: 2 week course in product knowledge, sales techniques, merchandising, promotional calendar, inventory control and managing a successful business. Approximately 1 week at corporate headquarters and one week on-site, including the grand opening.

Managerial Assistance Available: Ongoing advice and assistance through site visits, technical advice on product knowledge and preparation, marketing, pricing and store operations. Complete operations manual provided along with an ad source book.

Information Submitted: August 1987

THE ONION CROCK, INC.
4485 Plain Field N.E.
Grand Rapids, Michigan 49505
E. T. LaCroix, President

Description of Operation: Limited menu full service restaurant franchise specializing in homemade soups, salads, sandwiches and light dinners.

Number of Franchisees: 1 in Michigan and 1 in Wisconsin.

In Business Since: 1974

Equity Capital Needed: Estimated $75,000 minimum, $300,000 minimum net worth.

Financial Assistance Available: None

Training Provided: 2 weeks or more, as needed on-the-job training for franchisee and store manager in corporate stores and at corporate headquarters.

Managerial Assistance Available: On-site opening assistance, periodic visits and continuous consultation availability by corporate staff or designates.

Information Submitted: May 1987

ORANGE BOWL CORPORATION
227 N.E. 17th Street
Miami, Florida 33132
Leonard Turkel, President

Description of Operation: A bright, colorful snack bar designed exclusively for operation in shopping centers, having the advantage of a limited menu offering popular food products such as pizza, hot dogs, hamburgers, soft ice cream and fruit drinks.

Number of Franchisees: 63 nationwide plus 35 company-owned and operated.

In Business Since: 1965

Equity Capital Needed: Approximately $50,000 to $60,000—total cost $95,000 to $135,000.

Financial Assistance Available: The franchisor does not directly offer any financing to the franchisee; however, it does assist the franchisee in securing bank financing and/or SBA guaranteed financing.

Training Provided: 2 weeks of on-the-job training and orientation at the franchisor's training center for the franchisee, his designee or manager.

Managerial Assistance Available: Complete turnkey opening provided, with continual home office and area assistance in every aspect of store operations, promotions, and store review.

Information Submitted: May 1987

THE ORIGINAL WIENER WORKS, INC.
8290 Hubbard Road
Auburn, California 95603
Harold G. Ackerman, President

Description of Operation: The Original Wiener Works is a unique fast food sit down restaurant that serves 49 different hot dogs, 6 hamburgers and over 50 different domestic and imported beers. One of the other unique products sold are fresh cut French fries. Each unit is decorated like an old hot dog restaurant. Size of units vary from 1,200 square feet to 1,500 square feet. Units are open 7 days a week from 11 a.m. til 10 p.m. THe company provides site selection, plans, bookkeeping system and advertising assistance.

Number of Franchisees: 1 plus 1 company-owned in California.

In Business Since: 1983

Equity Capital Needed: $87,500 to 93,000

Financial Assistance Available: Although company provides no financing the Original Wiener Works, Inc., will provide help in compiling and presenting loan package to various financial institutions.

Training Provided: Extensive 3 weeks hands on training at a training store prior to opening of franchisee's unit. 1 week or more as needed after unit is opened.

Managerial Assistance Available: The Original Wiener Works, Inc., provides extensive ongoing help with bookkeeping, management, food cost control, advertising, employee relations and all other aspects of the business that relates to the continuing success of the franchisee and the unit.

Information Submitted: May 1987

O'TOOLE'S FOOD CORP. OF AMERICA
8808 Centre Park Drive
Suite 207
Columbia, Maryland 21045
Peter C. Martucci, President

Description of Operation: Full service restaurant/bar theme style operation.

Number of Franchisees: 3 in Maryland

In Business Since: 1984

Equity Capital Needed: $250,000

Financial Assistance Available: None

Training Provided: Classroom and on-hands training of 6-12 weeks.

Managerial Assistance Available: Policies and procedures, menu development, quality assurance, costing programs, hiring and training.

Information Submitted: May 1987

PACIFIC TASTEE FREEZ, INC.
721 Brea Canyon Road
Suite 3
Walnut, California 91789
Lowell Meyer, President
Loy Coon, General Manager

Description of Operation: Fast food drive-in restaurant featuring hamburger, Mexican food, ice cream and beverages.

Number of Franchisees: 34 in California and Oregon.

In Business Since: 1955

Equity Capital Needed: Approximately $120,000-$180,000 plus land and building.

Financial Assistance Available: Equipment financing and or leasing assistance available.

Training Provided: 4 weeks in actual store.

Managerial Assistance Available: Duration of franchise, assistance through field representation.

Information Submitted: May 1987

PANTERA'S CORPORATION
11933 Westline Industrial Drive
St. Louis, Missouri 63146

Description of Operation: The company manages Pantera's Pizza restaurants, grants franchises and area development licenses, sells supplies to franchisees, and renders services to franchisees in developing opening and operating units.

Number of Franchisees: 126 in 9 States

In Business Since: 1978

Equity Capital Needed: $175,000 total capital for restaurant or $65,000 total capital for delivery unit.

Financial Assistance Available: Franchisees usually invest 25 percent of capital needed and borrow balance.

Training Provided: 6 weeks training of general manager; 2 weeks training of restaurant employees.

Managerial Assistance Available: Consultation advice and training prior to restaurant opening; one week on premises consultation prior to opening, one week on premises consultation and training after opening, implementation of grand opening, periodic revisions of approved product list and approved supplier list, advertising and marketing assistance, occasional promotions and new products introductions.

Information Submitted: August 1987

PARIS CROISSANT NORTHEAST CORP.
670 Point Road
Little Silver, New Jersey 07739
Gaston A. Schmidt

Description of Operation: French cafe bakery.

Number of Franchisees: 4 in Connecticut

In Business Since: 1984

Equity Capital Needed: $150,000

Financial Assistance Available: None

Training Provided: 3 weeks in all phases of operation

Managerial Assistance Available: Managerial and technical assistance up to 30 days during first year.

Information Submitted: June 1987

PASQUALE FOOD COMPANY, INC.
19 West Oxmoor Road
Birmingham, Alabama 35209

Description of Operation: Prepare and serve to the public pizza, pasta, and a line of Italian-style sandwiches. Meat, bread and pizza doughs are manufactured and baked under strict quality control complete with chemist and laboratory.

Number of Franchisees: 84 plus 4 company-owned in 13 States.

In Business Since: 1955

Equity Capital Needed: Approximately $70,000 $100,000.

Financial Assistance Available: None

Training Provided: Initial 2 weeks training and periodically thereafter.

Managerial Assistance Available: Managerial and technical assistance provided.

Information Submitted: May 1987

THE PASTA HOUSE COMPANY FRANCHISES, INC.
1924 Marconi
St. Louis, Missouri 63110
John Ferrara, President

Description of Operation: Our concept is to offer the public delicious Italian foods, with a complete menu of gourmet pastas, appetizers, salads, sandwiches, soups, deserts, pizzas, etc. For the family at affordable prices. 80 percent of gross income from food, 20 percent from beer, wine and liquor. ($1,000,000 average gross per store.)

Number of Franchisees: 15 plus 10 company-owned in Missouri, Illinois, Tennessee, and Florida.

In Business Since: 1967

Equity Capital Needed: $45,000 franchise fee. Total costs exceeds $500,000.

Financial Assistance Available: Franchisor does not finance any portion of the total investment; its franchise broker (American Marketing Group, Inc.) assists in packaging the financial portfolio for the bank and SBA.

Training Provided: 12 to 14 weeks of basic training for key personnel covering all aspects of the business plus kitchen, dining room and bar training. Two to 4 weeks of on-the-job site "store opening" training.

Managerial Assistance Available: Managerial assistance in basic training (13 weeks), store opening training (3 weeks), financial packaging, site selection, furniture, fixtures, equipment, architectural design, decor and construction. Ongoing support, audits and reviews, public employee surveys, advertising assistance, and menu additions and testing and expansion or resale assistance.

Information Submitted: August 1987

PENGUIN POINT FRANCHISE SYSTEMS, INC.
P. O. Box 975
Warwaw, Indiana 46580
W. E. Stouder, Jr., Vice President

Description of Operation: Fast food restaurants.

Number of Franchisees: 2 in Indiana

In Business Since: 1949

Equity Capital Needed: $125,000

Financial Assistance Available: None

Training Provided: 6 weeks training in company-owned training store and 2 weeks assistance during opening.

Managerial Assistance Available: Continuing support in operation including bookkeeping, inventory and labor cost control, advertising and technical assistance.

Information Submitted: May 1987

* PEPE'S, INCORPORATED
1325 West 15th Street
Chicago, Illinois 60608
Robert C. Ptak, President
Mario Dovalina, Jr., Secretary

Description of Operation: Pepe's, Incorporated franchises Pepe's Mexican restaurants. The restaurants are a combination carry-out and family dining. A full menu of Mexican meals is our specialty. Most restaurants offer beer and wine. Seating capacity is from 75-150 seats.

Number of Franchisees: 49 in Illinois, 11 in Indiana, and 1 in Wisconsin.

In Business Since: 1967

Equity Capital Needed: $75,000-$150,000

Financial Assistance Available: A total investment of from $75,000-$200,000 is necessary to open a Pepe's Mexican Restaurant. This is for the cost of remodeling, purchasing equipment and signs, paying deposits of utilities and insurance, and payment of franchise fee.

Training Provided: A new franchisee is required to train for a period of 4 weeks at one of our existing restaurants.

Managerial Assistance Available: Pepe's Incorporated provides continuing management service during the entire franchise period in the area of quality control, advertising, inventory control, and new product development. A manual of operations and menu preparation is provided.

Information Submitted: May 1987

PETER PIPER PIZZA
2321 West Royal Palm Road
Phoenix, Arizona 85021
Frank A. Cavolo, Executive Vice President

Description of Operation: Peter Piper Pizza operates and directs a chain of Family Pizza Restaurants, offering "great pizza about half the price." Menu is limited to pizza, salads, soft drinks and beer.

Number of Franchisees: 15 with 70 units plus 44 company-owned units in Arizona, Colorado, Oklahoma, Texas, Utah, California, Nevada, New Mexico and Virginia.

In Business Since: 1973

Equity Capital Needed: $100,000 to $150,000

Financial Assistance Available: A total investment of $275,000 to $450,000 is necessary to obtain a suitable shopping center location, complete leasehold improvements, purchase equipment, furniture and fixtures. Franchisor will help in obtaining financing, but does not provide direct assistance.

Training Provided: Franchisee and/or managers must attend and complete a minimum 2 week training session at franchisors training center in Phoenix, Arizona.

Managerial Assistance Available: Manual of operations on all aspects of restaurant operations, financial control, employee training and equipment maintenance is provided franchisee. Franchisor conducts periodic seminars to update franchisee training and skills.

Information Submitted: May 1987

THE PEWTER MUG
207 Frankfort Avenue
Cleveland, Ohio 44113
Stanley Morganstern

Description of Operation: English pub and restaurant, serving luncheon and dinner.

Number of Franchisees: 9 in Ohio

In Business Since: 1962

Equity Capital Needed: Approximately $375,000—depending on location.

Financial Assistance Available: Limited

Training Provided: Training of all personnel in parent restaurant in Cleveland and on premises by training staff.

Managerial Assistance Available: Assistance given in lease negotiations, general contracting, hiring of employees and coordination of kitchen and bar operation. We have our own man on premises 1 week before opening and 1 week after opening.

Information Submitted: August 1987

PEWTER POT, INC.
211 Middlesex Turnpike
Burlington, Massachusetts 01803
Bruce R. Butterworth, President

Description of Operation: Pewter Pot Family Restaurants, we believe, offer a more "total experience" than any similar chain in the country. Pewter Pot offers a warm, early American atmosphere with real wood, carpeting and hand painted murals; a varied menu of high quality foods including main courses, endless omelettes, hearty breakfasts, all-American sandwiches, and bounteous desserts. Plus an extra measure of hospitality served up New England style.

Number of Franchisees: 16 including company-owned units in Massachusetts, and Connecticut.

In Business Since: 1964

Equity Capital Needed: Approximately $100,000.

Financial Assistance Available: A total investment of approximately $350,000 is needed to build and equip a Pewter Pot Family Restaurant. Pewter Pot does not finance any of the package.

Training Provided: Intensive 6 week mandatory training course is scheduled for all new franchisees and their manager. This course is conducted at the home office school and on-site company store under the supervision of a Pewter Pot supervisor.

Managerial Assistance Available: Pewter Pot Family Restaurants provide continual management services for the life of the franchise in such areas as operations, menu planning, advertising, inventory control, and food cost control.

Information Submitted: June 1987

PHILADELPHIA STEAK & SUB COMPANY
1033 Clifton Avenue
Clifton, New Jersey 07013
Robert B. Keilt, President

Description of Operation: Limited menu featuring Philly-style cheesesteak and submarine sandwiches, primarily located in regional shopping malls in either food court or in-line adaptations. Store size is between 600 and 800 square feet.

Number of Franchisees: 15 in York and Florida.

In Business Since: 1977

Equity Capital Needed: Total investment averages $165,000.

Financial Assistance Available: Franchisor does not provide financing but will assist franchisee in preparing package for presentation to lending institutions.

Training Provided: Minimum 8 days in company operated store and home office plus 2 weeks with opening team in franchisee's premises.

Managerial Assistance Available: In addition to preopening training, franchisor assists with selection of suppliers, complete design and construction, equipment selection, employee training, and ongoing regional supervision through company supervisors for the entire duration of the agreement (tyupically 10 years).

Information Submitted: May 1987

PIETRO'S PIZZA PARLORS, INC.
407 Cernon Street
Vacaville, California 05688

Description of Operation: Family style restaurant—pizza, Italian/dinners, open 7 days a week 11 am to 12 pm.

Number of Franchisees: 6, plus 1 company-owned in California.

In Business Since: 1960

Equity Capital Needed: $75,000 to $150,000 depending on size of operation.

Financial Assistance Available: None

Training Provided: 8 weeks and then whatever is necessary.

Managerial Assistance Available: Continuous service as needed.

Information Submitted: August 1987

PIONEER TAKE OUT CORPORATION
3663 West 6th Street
Los Angeles, California 90020

Description of Operation: Pioneer provides a unique fast food service operation featuring an exciting variety menu. In addition to its Gold Metal winning golden fried chicken there's Pioneer crispy chicken, Pioneer oven baked chicken, Pioneers famous chicken chili, as well as fish fillets, home baked biscuits, all the great side dishes and for desert, fresh baked chocolate chip cookies. There's even a brand new building design that needs only a smidgen of land to offer drive-thru service or on premise dining. When you talk about getting it all together—you talk Pioneer Chicken!

Number of Franchisees: 335 in California, Hawaii and Arizona including company-owned.

In Business Since: 1961

Equity Capital Needed: $65,000 to $175,000

Financial Assistance Available: Pioneer does not provide direct financing however, we have a list of sources from whom financing is available for franchise fees, equipment, signs, and even land and building if desired.

Training Provided: 10 weeks intensive and complete training program; 3 weeks on-the-job training in special training units; 2 weeks management training; 2 weeks management intership and 3 weeks in your restaurant when it opens. Our training program is college accredited.

Managerial Assistance Available: Pioneer Take Out Corporation provides continuous management services for the life of the license in such areas as bookkeeping, advertising, quality, service, food preparation and control. Complete manuals of operations, food preparation and field marketing are provided. Field coordinators work closely with licensees; visit stores regularly to assist solving problems. Pioneer conducts licensee seminars and market and product research to maintain high volume, profitable locations.

Information Submitted: May 1987

PIZZA CHALET FRANCHISE CORPORATION
P. O. Box 7100
Redlands, California 92374
Donald F. Frisbie, President

Description of Operation: Pizza parlor done in a Swiss decor with family dining.

Number of Franchisees: 18 in California

In Business Since: 1972

Equity Capital Needed: $150,000

Financial Assistance Available: Assist in getting loans from bank.

Training Provided: In store training 6 weeks.

Managerial Assistance Available: Ongoing managerial and technical assistance.

Information Submitted: August 1987

*PIZZA INN, INC.
2930 Stemmons Freeway
P. O. Box 660193
Dallas, Texas 75266-0193

Description of Operation: Pizza Inn is a $265 million company that operates and franchises over 720 pizza restaurants in 29 States and 12 foreign countries. The vertically integrated company 3 cheese plants and its own distribution company that supplies every item essential to the successful opeation of a Pizza

Inn. Both 2,990 square feet 125 seat free-standing Inns and low cost 2,500 square feet 95 seat storefront Inns feature dine in, take out an home delivery capabilities. Two classes of franchises are offered: (1) full service Pizza Inn with optional delivery and (2) home delivery Pizza Inns that feature pizza and chicken, the two most popular take away and home delivery foods.

Number of Franchisees: 166 franchisees.

In Business Since: 1959 with stock traded on the American Stock Exchange.

Equity Capital Needed: $75,000 liquidity and $150,000 net worth per Inn.

Financial Assistance Available: Will assist by providing a loan package for presentation to receptive lenders.

Training Provided: A highly structured 5 week training program consists of video, classroom and hands-on training. Each new unit is equipped with a learning center for hourly employees. Opening assistance is provided by certified trainers using a state-of-the-art video hourly operations training program. Ongoing training is provided by literally hundreds of seminars conducted at convenient locations each year. The company believes the training program are among the best in the restaurant industry.

Managerial Assistance Available: Development stage management assistance is provided for site selection and construction. A professional operations specialist offers periodic on-site support. Manuals are furnished covering all basic functions including operations, marketing and advertising, personnel, real estate and construction, accounting, management and production skills development. Voluntary one-stop shopping at competitive prices is available with weekly delivery from company-owned distribution centers.

Information Submitted: August 1987

PIZZA MAN "HE DELIVERS"
6930-1/2 TuJunga Avenue
Los Angeles, California 91605
Vance E. Shepherd, President

Description of Operation: Pizza Man offers a fast food home delivery operation. Each store is approximately 1,000 square feet, does 80 percent of its business in home delivery and is open 7 days a week 12 noon to midnight. Limited menu, low rent leases, turnkey operation.

Number of Franchisees: 50 in California

In Business Since: 1973

Equity Capital Needed: $50,000

Training Provided: Complete training given, 2 weeks mandatory for franchisee with 2 or more weeks available. All training at no charge to franchisee. Training at Hollywood, California. Training for franchisee's employees given at franchisee's outlets.

Managerial Assistance Available: Pizza Man provides continual management assistance for the life of the franchise. Complete operation manuals, bookkeeping forms and direction are provided. Supervisor visits stores regularly to assist franchisee. Pizza Man provides advertising and promotional designs and research.

Information Submitted: May 1987

PIZZA PIT INVESTMENT ENTERPRISES, INC.
DBA PIZZA PIT
2154 Atwood Avenue
Madison, Wisconsin 53704
Kerry P. Cook, Vice President and Director

Description of Operation: Pizza Pit restaurants feature free, fast and hot home delivery of pizza and sandwiches, and catering, with optional inside seating, pizza-by-the-slice and salads.

Number of Franchisees: 6 plus 13 company-owned in Wisconsin and Iowa.

In Business Since: 1969

Equity Capital Needed: $88,835-$161,335

Financial Assistance Available: None

Training Provided: 4-6 week course covering all aspects of the operation of a Pizza Pit unit.

Managerial Assistance Available: Managerial and technical assistance is provided continuously from 60 days prior to opening and throughout the life of the unit. Marketing and training support is continuous and periodically updated via-on-site visits and regular interactive communication.

Information Submitted: May 1987

PIZZA RACK FRANCHISE SYSTEMS, INC.
2130 Market Avenue North
Canton, Ohio 44714
William Cundiff, President

Description of Operation: Operate and franchise pizza, French bread pizza, chicken and submarine sandwich carry-outs, with delivery. Franchise is designed for the small investors. Stores are designed with a victorian atmosphere for family dining or carry-out.

Number of Franchisees: 12 Stores in Ohio

In Business Since: 1975

Equity Capital Needed: $25,000-$35,000

Financial Assistance Available: Assistance with bank presentation. Company will carry back part of franchise fee with a qualified individual.

Training Provided: A new franchisee is required to train for a period of 6 weeks at one of our existing stores.

Managerial Assistance Available: Pizza Rack provides continuing management service during the entire franchise period in the area of quality control, advertising, inventory control and new product development. A manual of operations and menu preparation is provided.

Information Submitted: May 1987

PLUSH PIPPIN RESTAURANTS, INC.
10320 S.E., Highway 12
Clackamas, Oregon 97015
Dan Dyer, President

Description of Operation: Family-oriented restaurants specializing in freshly-baked pies of over 30 varieties. Also have full line of ice cream and fountain favorites, making a Plush Pippin the place "where dessert becomes the main course."

Number of Franchisees: 8 plus 5 company-owned units in Oregon, Washington, Idaho, Minnesota, Colorado and Hawaii.

In Business Since: 1974

Equity Capital Needed: $100,000 minimum and ability to acquire financing.

Financial Assistance Available: None

Training Provided: A minimum of 14 weeks of on-the-job training and instruction is required in the preparation and merchandising of Plush Pippin and in the procedures to be followed in operation and managing a Plush Pippin Restaurant.

Managerial Assistance Available: Continuous management assistance for the life of the franchise in such areas as management, bookkeeping, menu pricing, food costing. Operations manuals, recipes, forms and directions are provided. Computerized accounting with financial statements available also for a reasonable monthly fee.

Information submitted: August 1987

PO FOLKS, INC.
P. O. Box 17406
Nashville, Tennessee 37217
John A. Scott, Vice President, Franchising

Description of Operation: Full service family restaurants with country cooking and down home atmosphere.

Number of Franchisees: 130 in 19 States

In Business Since: 1975

Equity Capital Needed: $500,000 plus

Financial Assistance Available: None

Training Provided: 4 month manager training in restaurants which also includes a 2 week classroom training course at corporate headquarters. Four days prior and 2 weeks after opening of each restaurant.

Managerial Assistance Available: Inspection and advise during term of the franchise agreement. Co-operative purchasing available through distributors. Regular meetings with franchise advisory committee. Annual franchise meeting.

Information Submitted: May 1987

*PONDEROSA, INC.
P. O. Box 578
Dayton, Ohio 45401
Edward J. Day, Director, Franchise Sales/Administration

Description of Operation: Waitress assisted family steak house featuring limited menu, moderate priced selection ranging from steaks, chicken, fish, salad buffet and breakfast.

Number of Franchisees: 246 units (plus 407 company-owned units) in 30 States, Canada, Puerto Rico, Singapore, Taiwan and the United Kingdom.

In Business Since: 1965

Equity Capital Needed: Over $125,000 plus $500,000 net worth.

Financial Assistance: None

Training Provided: 4 weeks of formal training in classroom in steak house with training instructor. Follow-on training in steak house as required to develop necessary skills.

Managerial Assistance Available: Complete operations manual detailing methods of scheduling labor, maintenance of equipment, training of employees, hiring practices, ordering supplies and recording and controlling expenses. Field consultants provided on regular basis to help resolve operational problems. Seminars held to give advertising, promotional, and other managerial support to franchisee.

Information Submitted: May 1987

PONY EXPRESS PIZZA
931 Baxter Avenue
Louisville, Kentucky 40204
Kenneth Lamb, President

Description of Operation: Pizza delivery chain.

Number of Franchisees: 16 in Kentucky and Indiana.

In Business Since: 1982

Equity Capital Needed: $2,500 minimum

Financial Assistance Available: Relative to location selection and financial stability.

Training Provided: Area supervisor provides complete training in the art of pizza making and business related paperwork for all new franchisees and their personnel.

Managerial Assistance Available: Pony Express provides continual management service for the life of the franchise in such areas as bookkeeping, advertising, food cost and inventory control. Complete manuals of operation, recipes, paperwork forms and directions are provided. Area supervisors are available in all regions to work closely with franchisees and visit stores regularly to assist in solving problems.

Information Submitted: August 1987

*POPEYES FAMOUS FRIED CHICKEN AND BISCUITS
International Headquarters
One Popeyes Plaza
1333 South Clearview Parkway
Jefferson, (New Orleans) Louisiana 70121
William A. Copeland, Executive Vice President-Franchise Division

Description of Operation: Fast food operations specializing in sales of specially seasoned products conducting business from single units with drive-thru and sit-down facilities.

Number of Franchisees: 560 in 40 States and 14 international units.

In Business Since: 1972

Equity Capital Needed: Approximately $125,000 per unit with $1,500,000 net worth.

Financial Assistance Available: None

Training Provided: 7 weeks.

Managerial Assistance Available: Accounting, operational, marketing, advertising and real estate.

Information Submitted: May 1987

PORT OF SUBS, INC.
100 Washington street
Suite 200
Reno, Nevada 89503
Edward R. Baird, Director of Franchise Sales

Description of Operation: Port of Subs, Inc., is a submarine sandwich restaurant operation. Sandwiches are made-to-order with highest quality ingredients. Typical stores are approximately 12-1,500 square feet and seat 30-35 people.

Simplicity of operation and efficiency are cornerstones of the Port of Subs system. A nautical theme with blue, yellow and white interiors presents a crisp, clean environment.

Number of Franchisees: 22 in Nevada and California

In Business Since: 1975

Equity Capital Needed: $35,000-$40,000

Financial Assistance Available: A total investment of $85,000-$90,000 is estimated for a Port of Subs franchise. Port of Subs, Inc., assists potential franchisees in preparing documents for financing and maintains relationships with several banking institutions. Port of Subs, Inc., does not provide any internal financing.

Training Provided: Port of Subs, Inc., provides a mandatory, intense 13-day training course that will give the skills, the knowledge and the confidence franchisee needs to manage the business effectively and efficiently. Training is conducted at corporate headquarters and at a company-owned store location and covers all material aspects of the operation of a Port of Subs franchise.

Managerial Assistance Available: Port of Subs, Inc., provides franchisees with reference manuals, business forms, purchasing power, accounting service (optional), and the benefits of insurance programs and creative advertising campaigns. Port of Subs, Inc., also provides opening assistance during the initial opening for at least 5 days, and provides guidance in creating an attention-getting grand opening. Ongoing support includes monthly visits by representatives who will provide new up-dates, merchandising concepts, idea exchanges and two-way communication. The corporate staff is always available between visits to provide assistance.

Information Submitted: May 1987

PRIMO, INCORPORATED
21622 North 14th Avenue
Phoenix, Arizona 85027
Franchise Director

Description of Operation: Primo's delicafes. Compact stylish sidewalk cafes riding the crest of "The Deli Boom." Serving highest quality deli style sandwiches, salads, soups and pasta with rapid counter service.

Number of Franchisees: 103 in 28 States, located in major malls, shopping centers and business districts.

In Business Since: 1972

Equity Capital Needed: $35,000 to $50,000

Financial Assistance Available: Preparation of complete financial plans. Assistance in securing financing through commercial loans and for leases.

Training Provided: Comprehensive training at national training center, and direct assistance in opening and initial operation of restaurant.

Managerial Assistance Available: Direct assistance in site location, leasing, design construction and procurement of equipment, food and supplies. Ongoing technical and operational guidance. Periodic on-site assistance.

Information Submitted: August 1987

PUB DENNIS INTERNATIONAL, INC.
369 Park East Drive
Woonsocket, Rhode Island 02895
Jerry Buck, Director of Franchising

Description of Operation: Pub Dennis is a full service family style restaurant. Our restaurant system is a distinctive, highly competitive operation featuring steak, seafood, chicken, daily specials, a childrens menu and a Sunday (only day) breakfast buffet. The restaurants are approximately 5,000 square feet, seating 180, set in a standardized, unique free standing building. The decor includes distinctive carousel horses, natural oak and lots of brass.

Number of Franchisees: 13 in Rhode Island and Massachusetts

In Business Since: 1983

Equity Capital Needed: $250,000 to $350,000 plus ability to acquire financing for an additional $350,000 to $600,000 depending on location.

Financial Assistance Available: Franchisee obtains own financing. Advice available.

Training Provided: Training at corporate headquarters and nearby Pubs. A minimum of 4 weeks training for franchisee. A minimum of 8 weeks training for the franchisee's 2 senior managers. Ongoing assistance on all aspects of the business.

Managerial Assistance Available: The company provides ongoing assistance on a regular basis for the management and operation of the Pub Dennis. Operations and equipment manuals provided.

Information Submitted: May 1987

PUDGIES PIZZA FRANCHISING, INC.
524 North Main Street
Elmira, New York 14901
Francis J. Cleary

Description of Operation: New York and Siclian style pizza and a variety of hot and cold submarine sandwiches, burgers, French fries and standard soft drinks. 3,000 square feet free standing units with 72 and 82 seats and drive-in window. Pudgies is presently considering expansion into other Northeastern States under multi-unit development agreements.

Number of Franchisees: 36 units in New York and Pennsylvania plus 1 in South Carolina.

In Business Since: 1963 started franchising in 1973.

Equity Capital Needed: $125,000, excluding building and leasehold improvements, minimum capital requirements—$50,000.

Financial Assistance Available: No direct financing available. Pudgies does, however, assist in the preparation of the financing application and the structuring of the bank presentation. Company also makes available, to qualified franchisees, a list of potential developers who have expressed interest in investing in leasehold improvements.

Training Provided: 6 week program of classroom and in-store instruction at the company's schooling facilities in Elmira, New York.

Managerial Assistance Available: Pudgies has an ongoing inspection program designed to evaluate the individual store and advise as to physical and technical aspects of the operation. Pudgies also has a continued product development program and test markets various related products for chain wide introduction to the menu.

Information Submitted: May 1987

RANELLI FRANCHISE SYSTEMS, INC.
dba RANELLIS DELI AND SANDWICH SHOPS
2134 Warrier Road
Birmingham, Alabama 35208
Frank A. Ranelli, President

Description of Operation: Ranellis a deli and sandwich shop operation specializing in deli type sandwiches and pizza. Feature products is a 16" Poboy called a Richman. Also featured is homemade lazagna served every Thursday. Stores have a specialty grocery section as well as a by the pound deli case.

Number of Franchisees: 5 in Alabama

In Business Since: 1949 started franchising in 1979.

Equity Capital Needed: $7,500 franchise fre.

Financial Assistance Available: Total investment is approximately $35,000 including franchise fee. Franchisor offers no financial assistance.

Training Provided: 2 weeks in company unit, 1 week at location. Continuing assistance with problems thereafter.

Managerial Assistance Available: Opeations manual provided, and assistance with problems. Continuing inspections to avert problems.

Information Submitted: August 1987

RAX RESTAURANTS, INC.
1266 Dublin Road
Columbus, Ohio 43215
William J. Dolan, Vice President/Franchising Operations

Description of Operation: Rax Restaurants, Inc., is headquartered in Columbus, Ohio. Rax Restaurants serve a wide menu, featuring sandwiches, salad bar, and baked potatoes with toppings. The Rax Restaurant is an upscale concept in menu and building design.

Number of Franchisees: 370 franchise stores and 155 company operated units in 35 States.

In Business Since: 1978

Equity Capital Needed: $100,000 plus net worth for lease.

Financial Assistance Available: None

Training Provided: Currently a 5 week program, 3 weeks of in-resturant training, beginning with production and service training, and basic management functions. Two weeks of classroom training focus on supervisory skills and administration.

Managerial Assistance Available: Rax provides initial standard specifications and plans for the building, equipment, furnishings, decor, layout and signs, together with advice and consultation concerning same. Franchise area supervisors offer guidance and assistance beginning in the early stages of planning. A variety of company resources are available to franchisees in areas such as marketing, development and purchasing. Company training instructors are provided to train employees several days prior to opening, and remain in store two days after opening.

Information Submitted: August 1987

RED ROBIN INTERNATIONAL, INC.
3123 Eastlake Avenue East
Seattle, Washington 98102
Ida Church

Description of Operation: Franchising full service restaurant with emphasis on gourmet hamburgers and specialty drinks.

Number of Franchisees: 27 locations in Washington, California, Idaho, Arizona, Colorado and Maryland.

In Business Since: 1969

Equity Capital Needed: $500,000

Financial Assistance Available: None

Training Provided: Support manuals on all aspects of project development and operations. As well as in-depth training at headquarters and on-the-job training in the stores.

Managerial Assistance Available: See above.

Information Submitted: August 1987

*RITZY'S AMERICA'S FAVORITES
4660 Kenny Road
Columbus, Ohio 43220
Franchise Sales Department

Description of Operation: Upscale decor, premium quality food and ice cream restaurant characterizing the soda shop or road side diner of the 1940's era. Featuring fresh grilled hamburgers, coneys, chicken, light menu.

Number of Franchisees: 45 in 11 States

In Business Since: 1980

Equity Capital Needed: $250,000

Financial Assistance Available: None

Training Provided: 3 weeks initial, then ongoing training for "refresher."

Managerial Assistance Available: Periodic visits to franchised store for advice and update. Assistance with training, operations, expansion planning.

Information Submitted: May 1987

*ROCKY ROCOCO CORPORATION
340 West Washington Avenue
Madison, Wisconsin 53703
Raymond Baker

Description of Operation: Pizza Restaurant providing full dining, carry-out, drive-thru, delivery service and featuring pizza by the slice.

Number of Franchisees: 115 units including company-owned in Illinois, Iowa, Minnesota, Wisconsin, Colorado, Ohio and Missouri, Florida and Indiana.

In Business Since: 1974

Equity Capital Needed: $75,000

Financial Assistance Available: None

Training Provided: 6 week manager training, combination of classroom and in-restaurant, various 1-2 day seminars.

Managerial Assistance Available: Continuous business assistance in areas: real estate, construction, operations (from restaurant opening to regular visits), marketing, finance, quality assurance.

Information Submitted: May 1987

ROMA CORPORATION
9400 North Central Expressway
Suite 1520
Dallas, Texas 75231
Larry Zimmerman, Vice President

Description of Operation: Full service restaurant operation specializing in bar-becued ribs and chicken. ALI stores have separate dining and lounge facilities with full service bar.

Number of Franchisees: 50 in 13 States and Canada, Japan, and Bahamas and London.

In Business Since: 1972 under private ownership—corporation since 1976.

Equity Capital Needed: $400,000

Financial Assistance Available: None—Roma corporation does not lend or guarantee the financial responsibilities of its franchisees.

Training Provided: Training of general manager, and chef supervisor. Training program ranges over a period of 6 to 8 weeks with refresher courses available.

Managerial Assistance Available: Training program in company-owned stores. In-store supervision and assistance offered before and after opening.

Information Submitted: May 1987

ROUND TABLE FRANCHISE CORPORATION
601 Montgomery Street
5th Floor
San Francisco, California 94111
Kathleen A. Low, Director of Franchise Sales

Description of Operation: Round Table Pizza franchises are restaurants offering a distinctive atmosphere serving a superior pizza product, sandwiches, hamburgers, salads and beverages. Appealing to a broad spectrum of the public, we're known as "The Last Honest Pizza."

Number of Franchisees: Over 517 restaurants in 12 States.

In Business Since: Round Table originated in 1959—began franchising in 1962.

Equity Capital Needed: $320,000 ($100,000 cash minimum).

Financial Assistance Available: Assistance in seeking financing is provided.

Training Provided: Extensive 4 week training course required at our training facility in Culver City, California. Cost of training included in initial investment.

Managerial Assistance Available: Headquarters staff and field representatives provide comprehensive assistance and direction in site generation, financial assistance, restaurant start-up, staffing, cost control, maintenance, sanitation and quality control, local and regional marketing and system-wide advertising.

Information Submitted: May 1987

ROYAL GUARD FISH & CHIPS, INC.
4 Apple Tree Drive
Stamford, Connecticut 06905
Henry R. Parente, President, Franchising

Description of Operation: Fish & chips, etc., self-service seating or take-out.

Number of Franchisees: 3 in Connecticut, 1 in Florida and 1 company-owned.

In Business Since: 1970

Equity Capital Needed: Contact company for full information.

Financial Assistance Available: None

Training Provided: 4 weeks company shop training.

Managerial Assistance Available: Bookkeeping, etc. Complete operation is supported by company manuals.

Information Submitted: August 1987

*MARRIOTT CORPORATION
ROY ROGERS DIVISION
1803 Research Boulevard, Suite 101
Rockville, Maryland 20850
Franchise Sales

Description of Operation: Roy Rogers fast food restaurant serving fresh roast beef, chicken, burgers, salad bar, fixings bar, shakes, soft drinks and fries.

Number of Franchisees: 45 franchisees with 206 units in 13 States.

In Business Since: Marriott since 1927, Roy Rogers since 1967.

Equity Capital Needed: $150-$175,000 plus real estate.

Financial Assistance Available: None

Training Provided: 10 weeks hands-on training for owner/operator and 8 weeks training for each assistant manager.

Managerial Assistance Available: Assistance in site selection, assistance in opening unit, franchise consultant required to visit unit on a regular basis to advise franchisee and to assist in whatever way possible.

Information Submitted: May 1987

S.A.F. CALIFORNIA/LETTUCE PATCH
333 Bristol Street
Costa Mesa, California 92626

Description of Operation: Salad bar restaurant.

Number of Franchisees: 4 in California

In Business Since: 1976

Equity Capital Needed: $200,000 to $250,000

Financial Assistance Available: Total financial assistance available after extensive training program (approximately 1 year).

Training Provided: A franchiseee will work in a new or existing unit, training in all phases of operation for approximately 1 year or until he has proven he can totally run the operation.

Managerial Assistance Available: Total assistance both managerial and technical for duration of franchise agreement.

Information Submitted: August 1987

THE SALAD BAR CORPORATION
(A Division of PRIMO, INCORPORATED)
21622 North 14th Avenue
Phoenix, Arizona 85027
Franchise Director

Description of Operation: Jan Drake's Garden Cafes & Drake's Salad Bars "The Food Concepts of the 80's." Bright garden restaurants featuring fresh, light healthy foods (salads, pasta, soups and quiche). No cooks, no grills, no grease!

Number of Franchisees: 83 in 25 States, located in major shopping centers and business districts.

In Business Since: 1975

Equity Capital Needed: $40,000 to $60,000

Financial Assistance Available: Preparation of complete financial plans. Assistance in securing financing through commercial loans and for leases.

Training Provided: Comprehensive training at national training center, and direct assistance in opening and initial operation of restaurant.

Managerial Assistance Available: Direct assistance in site location, leasing, design construction and procurement of equipment, food and supplies. Ongoing technical and operational guidance. Periodic on-site assistance.

Information Submitted: August 1987

SAMURAI SAM JR., LTD., INC.
6151 Miramar Parkway
Miramar, Florida 33023
Sid Shane, President

Description of Operation: Samurai Sam Jr., Take-Out and Delivery restaurants with limited counter seating operate fast food restaurants specializing in Oriental stir-frying, teppanyaki grilling and char-broiling. Emphasis on speedy delivery via radio dispached vehicles. A moderately priced menu serving high quality and freshly cooked foods. Bright, attractive and clean, designed for strip centers. Fresh food display with all cooking in view of customer. Quality control by companys special sauces.

Number of Franchisees: 7 in 3 States

In Business Since: 1985

Equity Capital Needed: $25,000 cash—cost of unit, equipment and construction ready to open $85,000-$100,000 depending on size.

Financial Assistance Available: None

Training Provided: Intensive 14 day training course is scheduled for all franchisees and their personnel. On-the-job training is conducted at a training location to cover all phases of operation.

Managerial Assistance Available: On-site opening week assistance, periodic visits and continuous consultation. Complete manual of operations, forms and directions are provided.

Information Submitted: May 1987

SBARRO, INC.
763 Larkfield Road
Commack, New York 11725
Mario Sbarro, President

Description of Operation: Italian style restaurant chain, featuring pizza, calzone, sausage rolls, and other Italian specialty items.

Number of Franchisees: 53 in 12 States

In Business Since: 1977

Equity Capital Needed: $250,000-$400,000

Financial Assistance Available: None

Training Provided: 4 weeks training in all phases of operating a Sbarro restaurant.

Managerial Assistance Available: Managerial and technical assistance is given during training.

Information Submitted: May 1987

SCHLOTZSKY'S, INC.
200 West 4th Street
Austin, Texas 78701

Description of Operation: Limited menu sandwich shop concept featuring unique sandwiches served on daily fresh baked bread, also salads and soup.

Number of Franchisees: 210 in 14 States

In Business Since: 1971

Equity Capital Needed: Approximately $110,000.

Financial Assistance Available: Shlotzsky's, Inc., does not offer any financing arrangements.

Training Provided: Pre-opening training program in company-owned stores addressing all operational aspects of sandwich production and store management.

Managerial Assistance Available: Supply complete and detailed operations manual covering every aspect of shop operations. Immediate response to all significant operational problems encountered by licensee. Diagnostic business reviews and quality controls subject to check on a regular and consistent basis. Established elected-franchisee committee interfaces on a regular basis with Schlotzsky's, Inc.

Information Submitted: August 1987

SCOTTO MANAGEMENT CORPORATION
P. O. Box 1319
Highstown, New Jersey 08520
John Scotto

Description of Operation: Sales of pizza by slice or by pie, Italian style sandwiches, specialty dishes.

Number of Franchisees: 50 Nationwide

In Business Since: 1977

Equity Capital Needed: $180,000-$209,000 approximately.

Financial Assistance Available: Scotto Management Corporation does not offer any financing arrangements nor does it recommend any particular financing institution.

Training Provided: Provide pre-opening training program at a Scotto Pizza Restaurant which would include food preparation, special recipes, advertising promotion, hiring and training of personal and bookkeeping procedures. It is anticipated that the training program will be approximately 6 weeks.

Managerial Assistance Available: Assist licensee in selecting location and negotiating lease. Prepare and provide initial plans for building, equipment, furnishings, decor and signs, together with advise and consultation concerning them. Provide opening supervision with regard to promotion, merchandising, marketing and special techniques.

Information Submitted: May 1987

*SEAFOOD AMERICA
645 Mearns Road
Warminster, Pennsylvania 18974

Description of Operation: Seafood America is a retail seafood carry-out franchise. Approximately 1,600 square feet is needed to operate a Seafood America carry-out. The site may be located in either a viable shopping center or a free-standing building.

Number of Franchisees: 24 plus 2 company-owned in Pennsylvania and New Jersey.

In Business Since: 1971

Equity Capital Needed: $40,000 start-up, total $110,000.

Financial Assistance Available: No financing assistance available.

Training Provided: A 2 phase traning program. The first takes place over a period of 6 to 8 weeks and requires 15 to 20 hours a week in an existing Seafood America restaurant. The second phase is post-opening and includes further training of franchisee and initial employees at franchisee's actual location lasting usually 6 weeks, with trainers gradually diminished during this period.

Managerial Assistance Available: Seafood America Franchise, Inc., provides a wide range of services designed to help the franchisee. These including one-time services such as site and building development as well as ongoing services such as purchasing, training, marketing and equipment engineering when needed. The company maintains trained employees to answer questions and lend assistance when needed.

Information Submitted: May 1987

*SEA GALLEY STORES, INC.
6920 22nd Street, S.W.
Mountlake Terrace, Washington 98043
Suzanne M. Scharz, Vice President, Franchising

Description of Operation: Sea Galley operates 48 full-service seafood restaurants which feature fresh fish, oyster bar with exotic appetizers, prime rib and specialty drinks. The majority of restaurants are free-standing and will seat approximately 250 guests.

Number of Franchisees: 7 plus 41 company-owned.

In Business Since: 1975

Equity Capital Needed: Per agreement, multi-territorial agreements only.

Financial Assistance Available: None

Training Provided: Support manuals on all aspects of project development and operations. Intensive 6 week training program for all new franchisees.

Managerial Assistance Available: Continuous assistance provided in areas of: real estate, construction, operations, marketing, research and development, and quality assurance. District managers and regional chefs are also available to work closely with franchisees.

Information Submitted: May 1987

SERGIO'S INTERNATIONAL, INC.
Suite 212
Broadway Park Office Complex
16 Broadway
Fargo, North Dakota 58102
Russell D. Maring

Description of Operation: Franchising Mexican restaurants.

Number of Franchisees: 4 in Wisconsin and North Dakota

In Business Since: 1981

Equity Capital Needed: Varies from $145,000 to $220,000 per restaurant depending on the nature of the financing.

Financial Assistance Available: None

Training Provided: Franchisee and kitchen manager must attend a formal training program provided for at a corporate store. Normally lasting from 10 to 30 days.

Managerial Assistance Available: All types of managerial and technical assistance is provided by the franchisor to franchisee, including but not limited to training, marketing, accounting, quality control, site selection assistance, etc.

Information Submitted: April 1986

*SHAKEY'S INCORPORATED
Suite 600
1320 Greenway Drive
Irving, Texas 75062
Dale Ross, Vice President, Franchise Development

Description of Operation: Shakey's new look is a turn of the century motiff featuring stained glass, tiffany lamps, hanging plants and natural woods. Customer dining areas have raised levels to create a comfortable atmosphere for the entire family. Menu features thick, thin and super pan pizza, chicken, sandwiches, pasta, salad bar, domestic and imported beers, wine and soft drinks. Shakey's is currently developing shopping center locations, conversion of existing structures as well as free standing restaurants.

Number of Franchisees: 400 in the United States, Canada, Mexico, Japan, The Phillippines, Guam, Singapore, Taiwan, West Indies, Malaysia and Thailand.

In Business Since: 1954

Equity Capital Needed: Varies—$100,000 working capital.

Financial Assistance Available: None

Training Provided: Complete training consisting of classroom and in-restaurant curriculum provided. Training at company facilities for a period of 3 weeks and grand opening assistance.

Managerial Assistance Available: Shakey's provides continual management service in such areas as marketing, quality control, and operations. Complete operating manuals are provided. Regional managers and dealer consultants work closely with franchisees and visit restaurants to assist in any problem area. Franchisees meet generally 2-3 times a year to exchange views and opinions with Shakey's advisory staff. Shakey's also provides site selection counseling and assistance prototype plans and specifications and sources for F.F.&E.

Information Submitted: June 1987

*SHOWBIZ PIZZA TIME, INC.
A Subsidiary of BROCK HOTEL CORPORATION
4441 West Airport Freeway
Irving, Texas 75062
Franchise Sales

Description of Operation: dba ShowBiz Pizza Place and Chuck E. Cheese's Pizza Time Theatre are entertainment centers featuring life-sized animated floor shows; a menu of quality pizza, deli sandwiches and salad bar; plus games and rides for the entire family.

Number of Franchisees: 122 company-owned units and 149 franchised units.

In Business Since: Parent company 1969, ShowBiz 1980.

Equity Capital Needed: Varies, contact company for complete information.

Financial Assistance Available: None

Training Provided: Instruction for managers and electronic specialists is provided at ShowBiz Pizza Time College in Irving, Texas. Training in all phases of entertainment center operations is accomplished through classroom lectures, group exercises, and hands-on teaching.

Managerial Assistance Available: Site selection counseling and assistance; prototype plans; on-site opening assistance and supervision at franchisee's expense; installation of animated entertainment components at franchisee's expense; specifications and sources for FF & E; continuing advisory assistance on the oeration of the franchised restaurant; periodic evaluation of the restaurant and of the products sold and used in its operation.

Information Submitted: June 1987

SIR BEEF, INC.
P. O. Box 5623
Evansville, Tennessee 47715
Jon K. Fink, Vice President

Description of Operation: Fast food restaurant with British atmosphere. Inside seating for 90 with a drive-up window. Limited menu with roast beef a feature item (55 percent of sales is roast beef). Fresh meat, not a processed loaf, roasted on site continually. Full salad bar, 15 different varieties of sandwiches, 18 side orders varieties (baked potatoes, desserts, onion rings, etc.).

Number of Franchisees: 2 in Indiana

In Business Since: 1967

Equity Capital Needed: $150,000

Financial Assistance Available: None

Training Provided: Minimum 6 weeks on-job-training needed.

ManagerialAssistance Available: Field consultant works in unit with management to insure that the operation manual, which details system, procedures and control are being followed.

Information Submitted: June 1987

*SIRLOIN STOCKADE INTERNATIONAL, INC.
Nine Compound Drive
Hutchinson, Kansas 67502
Judy Froese, Director of Franchise Development

Description of Operation: Sirloin Stockade family steadhouses feature a selection of top quality steaks, chicken and fish, served quickly and attractively, and a self-service salad bar, hot food and dessert bar, at affordable prices. Restaurant facilities are free standing buildings of 4,000-7,000 square feet, seating 150 to 300 persons. Approximately 1 acre of land is required.

Number of Franchisees: 57 units plus 4 company-owned units in 11 States

In Business Since: Sirloin Stockade restaurants since 1966; Sirloin Stockade International, Inc., since 1984.

Equity Capital Needed: $100,000 minimum; must be able to obtain financing for land and building.

Financial Assistance Available: SSI estimates the total capital requirements to open a Sirloin Stockade franchise will range between $750,000 and $1 million, depending on the cost of real estate and the method of financing for improvements and equipment. Sirloin Stockade International provides no financing.

Training Provided: A comprehensive 6-week training program in all phases of operation is provided for store management at a company training facility. The franchisee receives a complete set of confidential operation manuals, including recipes and food pre procedures, employee training, marketing and equipment manuals.

Managerial Assistance Available: In addition to pre-opening assistance, SII proves ongoing training, education and assistance during the lifetime of the franchise agreement. Regular visits by SII operation field consultants offer assistance, in solving field problems, conduct quality control surveys and evaluate store operations. Franchisees are informed of new development in the company and the industry, as well as techniques to improve productivity and profitability. A nation-wide marketing program is administered by the Franchise Marketing Advisory Council. Competitive food prices with weekly delivery is offered from the product distribution center.

Information Submitted: May 1987

SIR PIZZA INTERNATIONAL, INC.
700 South Madison Street
Muncie, Indiana 47302
R. W. Swartz

Description of Operation: Retail and commissary operations, selling pizza, sandwiches, etc., for both on-premise consumption and carry-out.

Number of Franchisees: 26 in 11 States

In Business Since: 1958

Equity Capital Needed: $50,000 to $100,000

Financial Assistance Available: None. Land acquisition is franchisee's responsibility.

Training Provided: Complete on-the-job training program provided. Training covers all aspects of the business-operational procedures, bookkeeping, employee training, advertising and promotion and management techniques, menu selection.

Managerial Assistance Available: Regional managers continue to counsel franchisee in advertising, merchandising and quality control. Parent company assists with local advertising and promotion.

Information Submitted: August 1987

SIZZLER STEAK-SEAFOOD-SALAD
5400 Alla Road
Los Angeles, California 90066
WIlliam R. Hobson, Director, Franchise Development

Description of Operation: Popular priced family steak house featuring a carefully planned menu, quality food, contemporary surroundings and customer participation format.

Number of Franchisees: 550 in 35 States and 5 countries including company-owned.

In Business Since: 1959

Equity Capital Needed: Must be able to obtain financing for land and building; additional minimum cash requirement of approximately $225,000.

Financial Assistance Available: None

Training Provided: 12 weeks "on-the-job" and classroom training at regional training stores.

Managerial Assistance Available: Sizzler Steak-Seafood-Salad provides continued field and management services for life of the franchise in areas of marketing, advertising, and training of key personnel, accounting, purchasing, restaurant management and scheduled training schools and seminars. The Sizzler Restaurant Management Guide, a confidential plan for successful management, is provided each new licensee. Field representatives contact periodically to review progress and help institute new policies and procedures to improve service, sales and profits.

Information Submitted: May 1987

SKINNY HAVEN, INC.
190 West Cerritos Avenue
Anaheim, California 92805

Description of Operation: Restaurants that cater to special diets in a healthy way of eating.

Number of Franchisees: 9 in California, Texas and Arizona plus 6 company-owned.

In Business Since: 1970

Equity Capital Needed: Depends on type of size of unit.

Financial Assistance Available: None

Training Provided: 4 to 8 weeks—dependant on franchisee's previou experience.

Managerial Assistance Available: Daily assistance in all phases from start to approximately 2 weeks after opening. District managers are available thereafter for any assistance required.

Information Submitted: August 1987

*SKIPPER'S, INC.
14450 N.E. 29th Place
Suite 200
Bellevue, Washington 98007
Chris R. LeSourd, President
Jim Jones, Director, Franchise Sales and Administration

Description of Operation: Skipper's offers a limited menu of fish, shrimp, oysters, clams, chicken, salad bar, salads, and clam chowder in a "casual, quick service" moderately priced restaurant with a fishermans wharf motif. Approximately 2,100 square feet of restaurant, with beer and wine, open 7 days a week. Currently we have a total of 215 restaurants open.

Number of Franchisees: 40

In Business Since: 1969

Equity Capital Needed: $75,000-$100,000 and ability to acquire outside financing depending upon location, and if property is leased or purchased.

Financial Assistance Available: None, except in the Minneapolis area.

Training Provided: 8 weeks of classroom and in-restaurant training at specified Skipper's training restaurants. Further training will be provided at the opening of the franchisee's new restaurant. This program is designed for the individual with no restaurant background.

Managerial Assistance Available: Skipper's, Inc., will provide representatives who will visit a franchisee's restaurant periodically for inspections and assistance in the areas of operations, cost control, marketing, accounting, real estate and construction. Franchisee will be supplied with complete sets of manuals of operations, all necessary forms, standard specifications and building plans, site selection assistance, marketing support and purchasing support.

Information Submitted: May 1987

SKYLINE CHILI, INC.
109 Illinois Avenue
Cincinnati, Ohio 45215
Joseph E. Novosat, Director of Franchising

Description of Operation: Manufacturer of chili and franchisor of restaurants serving a limited menu specializing in chili related food products.

Number of Franchisees: 53

In Business Since: 1949

Equity Capital Needed: $30,000-$150,000 depending on nature of intended site.

Financial Assistance Available: None

Training Provided: 5 week in-depth training program consisting of 4 weeks on-the-job training (in company stores) and 1 week management workshop.

Managerial Assistance Avaialble: Comprehensive management training program, restaurant opening assistance, and periodic quality assurance reviews, and updates on techniques, equipment, etc.

Information Submitted: May 1987

*SONIC INDUSTRIES, INC.
120 Robert S. Kerr
Oklahoma City, Oklahoma 73102
Roy S. Lemaire, Senior Director of Development

Description of Operation: Fast food drive-in restaurant specifically designed for speed of service and freshness of food. Emphasis on hamburgers, hot dogs, onion rings.

Number of Franchisees: 900 plus 64 company-owned in 20 States

In Business Since: 1959

Equity Capital Needed: $30,000 to $50,000, includes $7,500 franchise fee.

Financial Assistance Available: None

Training Provided: Franchisor requires classroom and on-location training and provides management seminars and periodically updates on new techniques and profit making.

Managerial Assistance Available: Specifically designed and tested equipment; certain expertise in site selection; quality control recommendations and testing of food products; requirements of proper training, chain wide inspection program; and helps to provide voluntary chain wide advertising programs and purchasing co-ops. Sonic Industries, Inc., provides time tested managerial and technical assistance to each franchise with the ultimate goal of profit and success.

Information Submitted: July 1987

SONNY'S REAL PIT BAR-B-Q, INC.
3631 S.W. Archer Road
Gainesville, Florida 32608
Marion Whitescarver, Director of Operations

Description of Operation: Sonny's Real Pit Bar-B-Q, Inc., offers a licensing program for the south's most successful and finest barbeque restaurants. We serve lunch and dinner with a complete barbeque menu and the south's finest salad bar. Seating ranges from 100 up to 196 seats.

Number of Franchisees: 75 currently open, 10 stores under contract for 1987. Area of operations includes Florida, Georgia, North Carolina, South Carolina, Tennessee, Mississippi, Louisiana, Alabama, Kentucky, Virginia, Southern Ohio, and Illinois.

In Business Since: 1968, licensing since 1977.

Equity Capital Needed: $25,000 for the franchise rights, and approximately $295,000 for building, excluding real estate.

Financial Assistance Available: None

Training Provided: In one of our restaurants, licensee will be fully trained in all departments (cooking, service, purchasing and bookkeeping) usually 750 man-hours or until company and licensee are sure of licensee's readiness to open their own restaurant.

Managerial Assistance Available: In addition to manager training we also train assistant manager or head cook additional 500 hours in kitchen operations. Company will send an opening team to aid the licensee in both the kitchen and dining area to help start the restaurant. The company will continue to assist licensee in all areas after they are in operation, with regards to quality and service. ALl recipes and years of knowledge will be given to the licensee so they can be assured of a success.

Information Submitted: May 1987

SOUP AND SALAD SYSTEMS, INC.
2645 Financial Ct.
Suite A
San Diego, California 92117
Don Boensel, President

Description of Operation: Owner and operator of Soup Exchange restaurants. These are modern self-service soup, salad, bakery, and dessert bar operations that offer a wide variety of fresh, healthful, high quality foods in an up-scale dinner-house dining environment. Size ranges from 5,000 to 6,500 square feet and seating from 175 to over 300 with patios. Average meal price is $5.50 to $6 in an "all-you-can-eat" format; a 50 item salad bar, 6 fresh soups per day, and freshly baked muffins, breads and pastries are featured, along with fresh fruits.

Number of Franchisees: 6 including company-owned in California.

In Business Since: 1978, including predessors.

Equity Capital Needed: $120,000 to $150,000 depending on location.

Financial Assistance Available: Assistance in preparation of forecasts and plans for securing third-party financing through leasing and loan arrangements. Direct loans or equity seed financing is also available in some limited special circumstances.

Training Provided: Intensive training of up to 5 key personnel for 30 days at one of the existing Soup Exchange locations is a requirement for each franchise location.

Managerial Assistance Available: A complete and comprehensive operating manual is provided, along with a library of training video segments for each of the job functions in a Soup Exchange restaurant. Assistance is also provided for site selection, lease/purchase analysis and negotiation, design and construction of the facility, recruitment, interview, and hiring of the initial work crew, and the presence of an on-site supervisor for at lease 1 week before and 1 week after the scheduled opening. In addition, ongoing guidance and direction as well as on-site assistance is provided through area representatives via visits twice per month at each franchise store; these are supplemented by daily accumulation of sales, labor, and food cost data from each franchise location through a modern point-of-sale data acquisition system linked to a home office computer.

Inforamtion Submitted: May 1987

THE STEAK ESCAPE
ESCAPE ENTERPRISES, INC.
392 East Town Street
Columbus, Ohio 43215
Kennard M. Smith, Chairman

Description of Operation: The Steak Escape typically operates in 600 to 900 square feet located in retail mall food courts or in specialty retail projects. We specialize in Genuine Philadelphia Cheesesteak Sandwiches and fresh cut French fries. Outstanding performance record and industry reputation.

Number of Franchisees: 35 in 13 States

In Business Since: 1982

Equity Capital Needed: Total investment approximately $180,000 to $230,000

Financial Assistance Available: None

Training Provided: Management training—4 to 6 weeks and store opening training—3 weeks.

Managerial Assistance Available: Store planning and design. Architectural drawing development. Ongoing weekly and monthly support with regard to all aspects of store operations.

Information Submitted: May 1987

STEWART'S RESTAURANTS, INC.
114 West Atlantic Avenue
Clementon, New Jersey 08021
Michael W. Fessler, President

Description of Operation: Drive-in restaurants, with or without dining room with car-hop service.

Number of Franchisees: 68 in 7 States

In Business Since: 1931

Equity Capital Needed: $35,000-$50,000

Financial Assistance Available: Land acquisition is franchisee's responsibility.

Training Provided: Complete on-the-job training program provided. Training covers all aspects of the business-operational procedures, bookkeeping, employee training, advertising and promotion and management techniques, menu selection.

Managerial Assistance Available: Regional managers continue to counsel dealer in advertising, merchandising and quality contrl for the life of the franchise. Parent company helps with local advertising and promotion.

Information Submitted: May 1987

STUCKEY'S CORP.
2135 Wisconsin Avenue, N.W.
Suite 403
Washington, D.C. 20007

Description of Operation: A one-stop center for the traveler on the interstates and main U.S. highways. Specializing in unique pecan candies, a broad-based food service program, restaurant seating, novelties, gifts, and souvenirs, gasoline service and sparkling clean restrooms. Open 7 days per week, approximately 12-14 hours per day.

Number of Franchisees: 117 in 25 States

In Business Since: 1931

Equity Capital Needed: Amount varies dependent upon individual situation. Determined during discussions.

Financial Assistance Available: Limited—dependent upon individual situation.

Training Provided: 3 week program in zone training stores. This includes business operation procedure, bookkeeping procedures, management techniques, on-the-job experience in our local shoppe and concepts and procedures of the administrative functions of the corporate office. Periodic region meetings for continuous updating on procedures and oprations are held.

Managerial Assistance Available: Managerial and technical assistance is provided in site location, site preparation and building construction. Company representatives also visit units periodically for inspection and assistance in all phases of the business. Home office personnel are always available to assist the franchisee in all areas of the business. A complete accounting and retail auditing service is available at a nominal monthly fee. Stuckey's sponsors meetings of franchisees and meets with the franchise advisory board. A newsletter is also sent to all franchisees.

Information Submitted: August 1987

STUFT PIZZA FRANCHISE CORPORATION
26875 Calle Hermosa
Capistrano Beach, California 92624
John S. Bertram

Description of Operation: Stuft Pizza operates 5 company stores and has an additional 25 franchises. This chain's award winning pizza features fresh dough, hand-formed and tossed to develop a fine and tender crust. Incorporating a special sauce and the finest cheeses available, Stuft Pizza selects vegetables fresh each day and uses only the choicest meats. This outstanding pizza can be enjoyed in a relaxed and pleasant atmosphere, suitable for all ages.

Number of Franchisees: 25 in California

In Business Since: 1976

Equity Capital Needed: $105,000 to $250,000

Financial Assistance Available: Franchisee obtains own financing.

Training Provided: Training includes 2 weeks intense management and operation experience in existing store plus full-time consultant first 5 days of operation on new franchise. Continuing advisory services provided including consultation on promotions, business problems and analysis of business.

Managerial Assistance Available: Stuft Pizza will provide, at no charge to franchisee, assistance in site selection, business format, operations manual, standardized record keeping techniques, and continuing consultation services.

Information Submitted: May 1987

SUB & STUFF SANDWICH SHOPS, INC.
Suite 412, First National Center
Hutchinson, Kansas 67501
Louis Stoico, President, CEO

Description of Operation: Specialty sandwich shop operation including Italian style submarine sandwiches, and steak sandwiches.

Number of Franchisees: 6 in Iowa and Kansas

In Business Since: 1977

Equity Capital Needed: $60,000-$100,000

Financial Assistance Available: No.

Training Provided: 3 week comprehensive on-the-job management training program in one of franchisor's units prior to store opening. Pre opening and opening week assistance in training part-time employees.

Managerial Assistance Available: Ongoing opeational assistance and appraisal. Location selection and lease negotiation assistance. Store development guidance and standard building plans for free-standing units. Operative and advertising manuals. Guidance and assistance in all aspects of advertising and promotion. Ongoing product review and new product testing.

Information Submitted: May 1987

SUB STATION II, INC.
P. O. Box Drawer 2260
Sumter, South Carolina 29151-2260
Richard W. Reid, Vice President

Description of Operation: Sub Station II sandwich shops offer a variety of over 25 submarine sandwiches. We have developed an efficient method of preparing each sandwich to the customers' request. Emphasis is on high quality food and cleanliness.

Number of Franchisees: 93 in 11 States

In Business Since: 1975, first franchise began opration in January of 1976.

Equity Capital Needed: Minimum of $65,000

Financial Assistance Available: Provides franchisee with financial counseling and assistance in locating financing sources.

Training Provided: Owner/operator must complete a minimum of 7 consecutive full days at a designated training unit. A representative of the training department is avaiable for a period of up to 7 days prior to opening to assist with installation of equipment and decor and 7 days after opening to assist in training additional staff and follow-up on the progress of the trainee.

Managerial Assistance Available: Operations, maintenance, equipment, public relations, and food safety manual is provided. ALso availble is promotional and advertising material and field representation, consultation and assistance.

Information Submitted: May 1987

* SUBWAY
25 High Street
Milford, Connecticut 06460
Richard T. Pilchen, Franchise Director

Description of Operation: Freshly prepared foot-long specialty sandwiches (submarines) and salads. Present menu includes 10 varieties of hot and cold sandwiches. No grilling is involved other than in a microwave oven. All stores have a take-out service and many stores have eat-in facilities. Stores are open late 7 nights per week. All franchisees make freshly baked bread and whole wheat bread.

Number of Franchisees: 1,500 in 44 States, Washington, D.C., England, Canada, Puerto Rico, Bahrain, the Bahamas, and Austria.

In Business Since: 1965 (franchising since 1974

Equity Capital Needed: Approximately $25,000. Total investment $29,500 to $79,000.

Financial Assistance Available: Equipment leasing available depending on analysis of financial statements.

Training Provided: Subway provides 2 weeks of comprehensive classroom and practical training at Subway headquarters for store owners and store managers. The classroom curriculum includes training in location selection, store construction, accounting procedures, management theory as well as instruction in business analysis, product formulas and control mechanisms specific to Subway System. In addition to classroom study, practical training is provided in one of the local Subway stores to develop skills in sandwich making along with the day to day operation and management of a successful Subway store. Upon successful completion of this 2 week training course, all owners are eligible to attend a graduate training course. This graduate course is a week long seminar which deals more in depth with management theory and multiple unit opration. At any time during the life of the franchise any franchisee or designated manager may enroll in either of these training courses.

Managerial Assistance Available: During store construction, which takes between 20 to 60 days, managerial and technical assistance is provided for each franchisee by a development agent and an office coordinator assigned to handle their file. Areas covered in this assistance include site selection, store design and layout, interior construction, equipment purchasing, arrangement of suppliers and initial inventory ordering. When a store is scheduled to open, a development agent is available to help oversee the operation and provide back-up support for the store owner in areas of employee training and successful operational procedure. After store opening, periodic inspections and field visits are conducted in each unit by the assigned development agent. Continual office support is made available to each franchisee through frequent contact with one's assigned coordinator. The coordinator development agent system for service provides continual assistance and support for each franchisee through the life of the franchise (20 years). Weekly, a newsletter, comprised of articles written by department heads is sent to all franchisees. With receipt of this newsletter, all franchisees are kept continually apprised of new company policies and developments across the country. Also included in this publication are sections dealing with store management. Ongoing assistance in advertising is provided by the franchise advertising fund which is directed by a board of directors comprised of 11 store owners elected by the franchisees.

Information Submitted: May 1987

* TACO BELL CORPORATION HEADQUARTERS
17901 Von Karman Avenue
Irvine, California 92714
Attention: Manager, Franchise Development

Description of Operation: Taco Bell is the nation's largest operator and franchisor of fast service Mexican food restaurants with over 1,370 units operating in over 47 States, as well as internationally. Franchised restaurants total 1,106 to date.

Number of Franchisees: 261 in 39 States

In Business Since: 1962 (franchising since 1965)

Equity Capital Needed: Minimum requirement of $300,000 net worth, $150,000 of which needs to be liquid assets.

Financial Assistance Available: None currently being provided.

Training Provided: 30 hour restaurant orientation is part of the initial orientation program. After qualifying, training is a four-step process beginning with a pre-opening 2 to 6 week intensive training program for the franchise owner and manager. Additional training programs for management personnel are held at division training centers during the course of the year, with crew training programs available at company cost.

Managerial Assistance Available: Real estate orientation and site selection process is provided. A pre-opening and post-opening program puts a Taco bell regional franchise oprations professional in the restaurant to assure a truly "grand" opening. Regional managers, franchise oeprations also provide ongoing assistance, as required.

Information Submitted: May 1987

TACO CASA INTERNATIONAL, LTD.
P. O. Box 4542
Topeka, Kansas 66604
Alan Ward, President

Description of Operation: Taco Casa International, Ltd., is the operator and franchisor for Taco Casa restaurants. Taco Casa is a fast food Mexican restaurant featuring a limited menu and quick, courteous service in an attractive atmosphere. Taco Casa International, Ltd., operates both free-standing and enclosed mall locations. Normal operating hours are from 11 am to 12 midnight, 7 days a week.

Number of Franchisees: 17 in 8 States plus 2 company-owned.

In Business Since: 1963

Equity Capital Needed: The total franchise package is approximately $45,000 which includes equipment, inventory, start-up costs, starting capital, plus leasehold improvements.

Financial Assistance Available: May assist in methods for arranging financing.

Training Provided: An initial 2 week training school for new licensee's at our training school. One week opening assistance upon opening the new unit. Complete operations manual provided to unit. Continuous counseling and assistance with routine inspections by company representative. Monthly newsletter updating current events in Taco Casa and restaurant industry.

Managerial Assistance Available: Open line for licensee's inquiries and assistance. Purusal of weekly reports by Taco Casa headquarters and appraisal given. Routine inspections and assistance by company representatives. Bulletins concerning important legislation. Continuing research in products and procedures. Assistance in advertising. Regional or national advertising when minimum level of units make it possible.

Information Submitted: May 1987

TACO DEL SOL (T.D.S., INC.)
101 North 4th
Suite 8
Norfolk, Nebraska 68701
Dick Drummond, President

Description of Operation: Mexican fast food featuring extensive menu for both carry-out and semi-cafeteria sit down. All food prepared for dining room service is served on china using silverware. Full service concept with waitress service and liquor license also available.

Number of Franchisees: 25 in 4 States

In Business Since: 1978

Equity Capital Needed: $25,000-$35,000 cash

Financial Assistance Available: None

Training Provided: 2 weeks, in-store and classroom

Managerial Assistance Available: Continuing management and consulting services will be provided for the life of the franchise agreement. During construction, equipment installations and the first week of operation, home office personnel are available for assistance. A complete operations manual including forms, adveritising formats, employee handbook and recipes is provided to each unit.

Information Submitted: April 1987

TACO GRANDE, INC.
P.O. Box 12062
Wichita, Kansas 67277
John Wylie, President

Description of Operation: Mexican limited menu restaurants.

Number of Franchisees: 35 plus 6 company stores in 12 States.

In Business Since: 1961

Equity Capital Needed: $150,000 net worth, $45,000 cash requirement.

Financial Assistance Available: None

Training Provided: 4 to 6 weeks in company store.

Managerial Assistance Available: Operations manual also, training manual and franchise development guidelines manual provided. Consultation on operations, marketing, real estate, construction and menu development.

Information Submitted: August 1987

TACO HUT, INTERNATIONAL, INC.
P. O. Box 692
Joblin, Missouri 64802
Ralph L. Gray, President

Description of Operation: Taco Hut, Inc., is the franchisor for Taco Hut Restaurants, featuring Mexican-style fast food prepared from top quality ingredients and special blended spices. Taco Hut's unique and recognizable building design allows the convenience of comfortable inside seating, take-out, drive-thru service and specializing in Mexican dinners.

Number of Franchisees: 30 in 9 States.

In Business Since: 1965

Equity Capital Needed: $55,000 minimum

Financial Assistance Available: None

Training Provided: Training and orientation begins in selected Taco Hut Restaurants and continues as necessary. Prior to and after opening of your restaurant, Taco Hut, Inc., personnel will continue training until you are sufficiently familiar with all aspects of operation.

Managerial Assistance Available: Franchisees will be supplied with information regarding site selection, store design, and after opening of your restaurant, Taco Hut, Inc., representatives make periodic visits providing managerial and technical assistance needed.

Information Submitted: August 1987

MAHAN'S TACO INN, INC.
dba TACO INN
224 North Story Road
Suite 148
Irving, Texas 75061
L. S. Mahan, President

Description of Operation: Operates and grants franchises to operate high quality, popular priced, limited menu Mexican fast food restaurants.

Number of Franchisees: 21 plus 4 company-owned in Texas, Arizona, Louisiana and Mississippi

In Business Since: 1973

Equity Capital Needed: $25,000

Financial Assistance Available: Taco Inn does not provide direct financing but does assist the franchisee in preparing loan applications for lending institutions or SBA financing.

Training Provided: A comprehensive training program of 4 weeks is provided at the corporate headquarters and in corporate stores located in the Dallas area. A corporate team assists in pre-opening and opening of new franchise restaurants.

Managerial Assistance Available: A Taco Inn representative conducts in-store inspections periodically and an operations manual is furnished to franchisees containing full details on the operation of the restaurant, including food preparation, quality control, cost control, etc. A training reveiw program is provided at the corporate stores in the Dallas area as needed. All franchisees are given a test before certified to operate a Taco Inn.

Information Submitted: May 1987

*TACO JOHN'S INTERNATIONAL
808 West 20th Street
Cheyenne, Wyoming 82001
Harold Holmes and James F. Woodson

Description of Operation: Taco John's is a fast food, carry-out, limited menu, Mexican food operation. Restaurants are between 800 and 2,200 square feet. The locations can be free-standing, in line or a food court. Most units have drive-thrus where available.

Number of Franchisees: 392 in 28 States

In Business Since: 1969

Equity Capital Needed: $70,000 minimum

Financial Assistance Available: A minimum total investment of $150,000 is necessary to open a Taco John's unit. The ideal method of financing is at a local bank, and Taco John's International is availble to provide background information, projections, references, etc., to the bank to enable them to make a decision on the loan. A number of SBA loans have been obtained and a few units have been leased. If the franchisee desires to lease the building and equipment, Taco John's has sources available for them to contact.

Training Provided: An intensive 15 day mandatory training course is scheduled for all franchisees, or their managers in Cheyenne, Wyoming. The training consists of a combination of classroom and actual production at an operating Taco John's unit.

Managerial Assistance Available: Taco John's International provides technical and managerial assistance through the life of the franchise. When the new Taco John's is open, we provide opening personnel for approximately 1 week thereafter, periodical calls by Woodson-Holmes field personnel, complete manuals of operation, forms, and directions are provided and are continually up-dated. In addition, advertising materials are provided periodically, a monthly newsletter gives operating tips and general information, and regional and national meetings are held throughout the year and provide additional assistance.

Information Submitted: July 1987

THE TACO MAKER, INC.
P. O. Box 9519
Ogden, Utah 84409
Gil L. Craig, President

Description of Operation: Mexican fast food, American style, franchising. Great menu, inside seating and drive-thru window, quick service, quality products.

Number of Franchisees: 55 in 8 States and Puerto Rico.

In Business Since: 1977 (with 18 years in other Mexican fast food under different names).

Equity Capital Needed: $50,000 to $60,000

Financial Assistance Available: Open for discussion.

Training Provided: 30 day training. Great store opening program with marketing.

Managerial Assistance Available: Continual ongoing follow-up in advertising, research and development; operational and other. Preopening and grand opening detail assistance.

Information Submitted: July 1987

TACO MAYO FRANCHISE SYSTEMS, INC.
10405 Greenbriar Place
Suite B
Oklahoma City, Oklahoma 73159
Randy Earhart, President

Description of Operation: Taco Mayo is a fast food Mexican restaurant with an ever increasing broad range of customers. All of our products are prepared fresh daily with only the finest ingredients. We have recently completed construction of our new 2,000 square foot prototype building designed to provide our customers with pleasant inside dining and a fast, efficient drive-thru service.

Number of Franchisees: 35 franchise units plus 20 company units in Oklahoma, Texas, Arkansas, Kansas, and New Mexico.

In Business Since: 1978

Equity Capital Needed: $80,000 to $300,000

Financial Assistance Available: None

Training Provided: We offer an extensive, comprehensive training program of approximately 6 to 8 weeks that is designed to familiarize each individual with basic operational skills necessary to operate a successful operation.

Managerial Assistance Available: To provide a continuing advisory service including, but not limited to, consulting on franchisee's promotional business or operational problems. To provide analysis of franchisee's sales, marketing and financial data. To provide franchisee informational bulletins on sales, marketing, developments and suggested operational techniques.

Information Submitted: May 1987

*TACO TICO, INC.
3305 East Douglas
Wichita, Kansas 57218
Director of Licensing

Description of Operation: Taco Tico, Inc., is engaged in the business of operating and granting licenses to operate high quality, limited menu, Mexican style fast food restaurants.

Number of Franchisees: 35 units in 7 States (plus 75 company-operated units).

In Business Since: 1962

Equity Capital Needed: Over $50,000.

Financial Assistance Available: No direct financial assistance is available. Company may be however, able to direct franchisee to prospective financing sources or assist in preparing financial presentations to lending institutions or investors.

Training Provided: A pre-opening training course is conducted in a designated restaurant by a company training instructor.

Managerial Assistance Available: Complete operation manual detailing product preparation, quality control, cost control and other key areas. Field assistance to help resolve operational problems. Advisory service available on all functional areas of the business.

Information Submitted: May 1987

*TACO TIME INTERNATIONAL, INC.
P. O. Box 2056
3880 West 11th
Eugene, Oregon 97402
Jim Thomas, Vice President, Franchise Sales

Description of Operation: Taco Time is a dynamic leader in the Mexican fast food business. Outstanding food products feature quality fresh ingredients and exciting menu items. New 1,700 square foot solarium enhanced prototype unit is

highly efficient and attractively designed to encourage high volume sales and lower break even point. High quality food and new product development has made Taco Time a favorite in U.S. and Canada.

Number of Franchisees: 245 operating units (164 U.S. franchises, 62 Canada franchises, 2 Venezuela, and 17 company-owned).

In Business Since: 1960

Equity Capital Needed: $70,000-$100,000 recommended minimum

Financial Assistance Available: Taco Time International, Inc., does not finance franchised units directly, but does provide assistance in preparing bank loans or SBA financing. Outside funding options for franchises are currently being explored.

Training Provided: Taco Time International, Inc., conducts an intensive 3 week management training program at its corporate headquarters in Eugene, Oregon. The program focuses on overall TacoTime restaurant operations. Taco Time International's preopening team assists in the actual store opening, followed by continued support.

Managerial Assistance Available: Franchise operations personnel conduct in-store visitations and facility inspections periodically. Trouble-shooting and pre-opening assistance for new stores are additional services provided. Franchisees are kept up-to-date through bulletins, training seminars, and conventions. Research and development on new products is a continuing process carried on at corporate headquarters. Computer software for accounting and food cost explosion programs are also available for franchisee purchase.

Information Submitted: May 1987

TARK ENTERPRISES, INC.
2116 Sherman Street
Hollywood, Florida 33020
Gary Tarquinio, President

Description of Operation: Tark Enterprises offers a unique seafood and chicken menu under the trade name of Tark's Clam Stand.

Number of Franchisees: 6 in Florida

In Business Since: 1966

Equity Capital Needed: $50,000-$125,000

Financial Assistance Available: None

Training Provided: Intensive 3 week program prior to opening. All 3 weeks are spent in company-owned store. After opening Tark Enterprises personnel available for ongoing training.

Managerial Assistance Available: Continual management service in all areas including bookkeeping, advertising and inventory control. Complete manual of operations is provided.

Information Submitted: June 1987

TASTEE FREEZ INTERNATIONAL, INC.
8345 Hall Road, P. O. Box 162
Utica, Michigan 48087
David K. Chapoton, President
Shirley Chapoton, Executive Vice President

Description of Operation: Year-round fast food services family restaurants, and seasonal ice cream stores. The menu includes a variety of foods, such as the Tastee Burger Family, Tastee Crisp Chicken Family, fish and salad bar. Also features the complete line of Tastee-Freez soft ice cream desserts plus new homemade premium ice cream. Seeking individuals or investor groups capable of multi-unit as well as single unit development in reserve market areas. Subfranchise areas are available.

Number of Franchisees: Over 500 throughout 38 States and overseas.

In Business Since: 1950

Equity Capital Needed: Total investments for restaurant equipment and license run from $55,000 to $125,000, which does not include sales tax if applicable, or operating capital and food inventory.

Financial Assistance Available: T.F.I. does not provide direct financing to franchisees at the present time. However, it does provide assistance in obtaining financing such as, assisting the franchisee in preparing his proposal for bank financing, and meeting with potential lenders.

Training Provided: Training course for all new licensees conducted at company training center and or licensee's own store. Source covers managerial, accounting, promotional, food preparation and operational phases under actual operating conditions. Continuous in-field counseling thereafter, covering merchandising, quality control, advertising and promotion by company regional store-supervisors.

Managerial Assistance Available: Regional territorial franchisees and/or State supervisors, continue to counsel licensee in cost controls, new operational methods, advertising, merchandising and quality control. In addition, company conducts national convention once each year for all licensees to exchange ideas on merchandising, advertising, management and new food preparation methods.

Information Submitted: May 1987

TEXAS TOM'S, INC.
714 Tracy
Kansas City, Missouri 64106
Tom Nigro, President

Description of Operation: Offer a wide variety of food items on the menu and homemade recipes. Both sit down and carry-out service is available and also call-in service. We also feature several "basket" combinations, unique to the fast food industry. Western decor.

Number of Franchisees: 9 in Missouri and Kansas

In Business Since: 1953

Equity Capital Needed: $50,000

Financial Assistance Available: Company assists qualified applicants in arranging financing. Assistance in obtaining equipment financing, equipment lease, sign lease and specifications.

Training Provided: 3 weeks in-store traning. Company also will send qualified representative after store opens for 2 weeks (minimum).

Managerial Assistance Available: Provide assistance in-site selection, building financing, lease negotiations, accounting referral, and continuous advisory assistance. Also, inspection of premises and advertising aids.

Information Submitted: August 1987

TIPPY'S TACO HOUSE,INC.
P. O. Box 665
Winnsboro, Texas 75494
W. L. Locklier, President

Description of Operation: Fast food to take home—using drive-thru and inside seating—Mexican food.

Number of Franchisees: 17 in 5 States

In Business Since: 1967

Equity Capital Needed: Cash and credit, approximately $80,000.

Financial Assistance Available: None

Training Provided: Pre-opening training on location at operating unit and opening week training.

Managerial Assistance Available: Continuing assistance by personal visitations, letters, bulletins, telephone.

Information Submitted: May 1987

*TODDLE HOUSE RESTAURANTS, INC.
1541 Cherry Road
Memphis, Tennessee 38117
Ronald A. Artzer, President

Description of Operation: 24 hour diner style full service coffee shop.

Number of Franchisees: 6 in Connecticut, Pennsylvania, Virginia, FLorida and Illinois

In Business Since: 1931

Equity Capital Needed: $100,000 liquid assets, $250,000 net worth.

Financial Assistance Available: None

Training Provided: A centralized training course for management, duration of 2 weeks. On-site training of crew 10 days.

Managerial Assistance Available: Visits o units approximately every 30-45 days to access maintenance of established standards and investigations of opportunities from a marketing, sales and profitability basis.

Information Submitted: May 1987

*TOGO'S EATERY
M.T.C. MANAGEMENT INC.
900 East Campbell Avenue, Suite 1
Campbell, California 95008
Ross Woodard, Vice President

Description of Operation: Fast food sandwiches.

Number of Franchisees: 88 in California, Florida and Hawaii.

In Business Since: 1977

Equity Capital Needed: $90,000 to $150,000

Financial Assistance Available: None

Training Provided: 2 weeks on-site with periodic follow-up.

Managerial Assistance Available: Purchasing, cost control, sanitation, product development, promotion, and general management for the life of the franchise.

Information Submitted: March 1987

TUBBY'S SUB SHOPS, INC.
34500 Doreka Drive
Fraser, Michigan 48026
Tom Paganes, Director of Franchising

Description of Operation: A unique fast food concept serving 25 varieties of submarine sandwiches competitively priced. Sandwiches offered consist of steak, burger, ham and traditional Italian meats. All sandwiches are custom made to order either grilled or steam tabled using only high quality ingredients. Customer services offered are sit down, drive-thru and call-in. **Area franchises currently available.**

Number of Franchisees: 37 in Michigan, 2 in Georgia (plus 12 company-owned units).

In Business Since: 1968

Equity Capital Needed: Cash and credit, approximately $100,000 to $150,000.

Financial Assistance Available: None

Training Provided: 8 week training program for franchisee-owners includes indoctrination in all upper management functions, plus orientation in every phase of store operation at an operating unit.

Managerial Assistance Available: Continual accessibility to company headquarters. Development of public, employee and community relations. services of company supervisor in assembling an opening staff for unit operation plus others.

Information Submitted: May 1987

2 FOR 1 PIZZA ENTERPRISES
1122 East Lincoln
Orange, California 92665
John T. Murray, President

Description of Operation: 2 for 1 Pizza Company, take-out and delivery pizza. With buy 1 and get 1 free offer, always in effect. We require approximately 1,100 square feet with ample store front parking and open 12-14 hours per day.

Number of Franchisees: 19 franchised and 24 units company-owned in California, South Carolina and Hawaii.

In Business Since: 1982

Equity Capital Needed: $35,000

Financial Assistance Available: A total or $70,000 is necessary to open a "2 for 1 Pizza Co." franchise. We offer assistance in locating lenders.

Training Provided: 6 weeks in training store.

Managerial Assistance Available: Location and construction assistance, store supervision, bookkeeping, and Q.S.C. supervision.

Informatin Submitted: May 1987

UNCLE TONY'S PIZZA & PASTA FAMILY RESTAURANT
Suite 17 I
1800 Post Road
Warwick, Rhode Island 02886
Edward A. Carosi, President

Description of Operation: Family style Italian restaurant, dining room and take out service.

Number of Franchisees: 9 in Massachusetts and Rhode Island.

In Business Since: 1970

Equity Capital Needed: Approximately $55,000.

Financial Assistance Available: Preparation of bank proposals and SBA applications.

Training Provided: Will be trained in every phase of the Uncle Tony's systems; training will be both classroom and on-the-job for about 3 months.

Managerial Assistance Available: Ongoing assistance in day-to-day operations and administration.

Information Submitted: July 1987

UNO RESTAURANT CORP.
100 Charles Park Road
W. Roxbury, Massachusetts 02110
William F. Suessbrick, Jr., Vice President, Development

Description of Operation: A "Pizzeria Uno Restaurant and Bar" is a full-service restaurant with a complete bar serving a variety of menu items and featuring Chicago's original deep-dish pizza. There are over 36 units throughout the world.

Number of Franchisees: 17 in 8 States, Washington, D.C., England, Australia and New Zealand.

In Business Since: 1979

Equity Capital Needed: Fully capitalized, it costs approximately $1,250,000 to open a 5,000 square foot restaurant.

Financial Assistance Available: None

Training Provided: Intensive 7 weeks program in Boston.

Managerial Assistance Available: Quarterly visits to all units by company field consultants. Detailed operations manuals are provided along with supplementary manuals on marketing, recipes, etc.

Information Submitted: May 1987

VISTA FRANCHISE, INC.
1911 Tuttle Creek Boulevard
Manhattan, Kansas 66502
Bradley C. Streeter, President

Description of Operation: Fast food operation specializing in quality hamburgers and dairy items.

Number of Franchisees: 7 in Kansas

In Business Since: 1964

Equity Capital Needed: Total capital needed—$150,000 equipment, $250,000 building.

Financial Assistance Available: Possible building lease available.

Training Provided: Initial training program 3 months. Continuous training available as needed.

Managerial Assistance Available: All necessary work methods, building plans, accounting, and training procedures available.

Information Submitted: August 1987

*WARD'S INTERNATIONAL, INC.
P. O. Box 870
Hattiesburg, Mississippi 39403
Kenneth R. Hrdlica, President

Description of Operation: Fast food restaurant with high food quality. Standard menu consists of hamburgers, chili dogs, chicken nuggets, fries, shakes, root beer in frosted mugs and breakfast menu.

Number of Franchisees: 50 in Texas, Louisiana, Mississippi, Alabama, Florida and Tennessee.

In Business Since: 1978

Equity Capital Needed: $75,000 to $100,000

Financial Assistance Available: None

Training Provided: Mandatory on-job-training.

Managerial Assistance Available: Regular visits by Ward's field consultants, employee training, new merchandising techniques, financial reviews, seminars and other support personnel are available for consultation upon request.

Information Submitted: June 1987

WCF OF AMERICA, INC.
423 Hillcrest Landing
Omaha, Nebraska 68127
Robert R. Blank, President

Description of Operation: Fast food restaurant with integrated amusement area. Our menu consists primarily of frank and sausage items.

Number of Franchisees: 15 units including company-owned in 5 States.

In Business Since: 1980

Equity Capital Needed: Minimum of $25,000 cash and credit.

Financial Assistance Available: None

Training Provided: Training is provided in Omaha for a period of at least 6 days. Training is also provided in the franchisee's store at the time of opening of that store for a period of 3 days prior to opening and 3 days after opening. Additional training is available as needed.

Managerial Assistance Availble: Franchisor provides ongoing assistance in the operation of stores through information sharing and periodic inspections. Workshops and franchisee meetings are also held throughout the year.

Information Submitted: May 1987

*WENDY'S OLD FASHIONED HAMBURGERS
c/o WENDY'S INTERNATIONAL, INC.
P. O. Box 256, 4288 West Dublin-Granville Road
Dublin, Ohio 43017
Franchise Application Specialist
Franchise Sales and Development Department

Description of Operation: Fast service restaurant with quality food. Limited menu centered around fresh-cooked 1/4 pound hamburgers, chili, breast of chicken sandwich, hot stuffed baked potatoes, and salad bar, featuring plus dining rooms and "pick-up" window.

Number of Franchisees: 2,442 units (3/31/87) plus 1,324 company restaurants located throughout the United States, Bahamas, Belgium, Canada, England, France, Germany, Japan, Luxemborg, Malaysia, Netherlands, Puerto Rico, Spain, Switzerland, Australia, Italy, South Africa, SIngapore, Korea, Mexico, Philippines, Guam, and the Virgin Islands.

In Business Since: 1969

Equity Capital Needed: $250,000 net worth,$200,000 liquid assets

Financial Assistance Available: None. Total investment varies.

Training Provided: Intensive 14 week in-restaurant and classroom structured program for new owners.

Managerial Assistance Available: Provide manuals, field service, and consultation at regular intervals to provide support and insure compliance to company standards.

Information Submitted: May 1987

WESTERN SIZZLIN STEAK HOUSE
1537 Walton Way
Augusta, Georgia 30904
Nick Pascarella, President

Description of Operation: Semi-cafeteria style family steak house.

Number of Franchisees: 600 in 30 States

In Business Since: 1962

Equity Capital Needed: Approximately $100,000-$150,000.

Financial Assistance Available: No direct financial assistance.

Training Provided: Training on-the-job at our company-owned stores. Supervision at time of opening.

Managerial Assistance Available: Available as assistance is needed. Operating and accounting manuals furnished.

Information Submitted: August 1987

*WESTERN STEER-MOM 'N' POP'S, INC.
Ham House Drive
P. O. Box 399
Claremont, North Carolina 28610
Marshall E. Digh, President and CEO
Charles F. Connor, Jr., Executive Vice President

170

Description of Operation: Western Steer-Mom 'N' Pop's, Inc., operates family style restaurants as well as fast service steak houses and fish restaurants. The company also franchises Western steer Family Steakhouses. There are presently 57 company-owned units and 184 franchised units. The most popular franchise being the fast service steak houses operated under the tradename "Western Steer Family Steakhouse."

Number of Franchisees: 142 Western Steers in 13 States and 42 company-owned Steers.

In Business Since: 1970

Equity Capital Needed: $75,000, if building and equipment are leased and franchisee credit sufficient.

Financial Assistance Available: Franchisor will offer trained assistance to franchisee to put together total franchise package. Franchisor does not offer direct financial assistance.

Training Provided: Franchisor will train managers, cooks, meat slicers and all other personnel necessary for staffing franchised unit.

Managerial Assistance Available: Western Steer provides extensive and continual assistance to franchisee in all areas of restaurant operation including, but not limited to, bookkeeping, inventory control, purchasing, operations manuals and constant field supervision.

Information Submitted: May 1987

WESTSIDE DELI, INC.
2420 Grand River Avenue
Williamston, Michigan 48895
Martin Dunleavy, Marketing Director

Description of Operation: A variety of options are available, from take-out to seating inside and drive thrus—featuring a large sandwich, sweet shop and pizza menu.

Number of Franchisees: 18 in Michigan

In Business Since: 1981

Equity Capital Needed: $80,000

Financial Assistance Available: None

Training Provided: 6 weeks starting out in the corporate bakery-to classroom-to in store-back to classroom-intensive training-applicant must pass corporate criteria or franchisee will be denied.

Managerial Assistance Available: Baking, cooking of all menu items, store management, bookkeeping, advertising, custom controls, computerization, inspection process, receipes/formulas, marketing and personnel management.

Information Submitted: June 1987

•WHATABURGER, INC.
4600 Parkdale Drive
Corpus Christi, Texas 78411
Joseph A. Middendorf

Description of Operation: Fast food restaurant with dining room and drive through facilities featuring four sizes of made-to-order hamburgers. Also serve fish and chicken sandwiches, FAJITA TACO plus breakfast menu. Most units open 24 hours. Emphasis on quality.

Number of Franchisees: 375 units operating in Sunbelt States, including company operations. Franchises being offered in Texas, New Mexico, Arkansas, Louisiana, Tennessee, Florida and Oklahoma.

Equity Capital Needed: Minimum $75,000 cash. Total investment per unit is $500,000-$800,000 (depending on the location).

Financial Assistance Available: None

Training Provided: Instruction on all phases of restaurant operations—4 to 8 weeks.

Managerial Assistance Available: Ongoing operational real estabe, marketing, and administrative assistance provided throughout the term of the franchise.

Information Submitted: May 1987

WIENER KING SYSTEMS, INC.
P. O. Box 149
Easton, Pennsylvania 18044-0149
Richard Dennis

Description of Operation: Fast food restaurant specializing in hot dogs and chili. Also features hamburgers. Seating capacity for 38 or 80 people depending on size of unit.

Number of Franchisees: 18 in 9 States and multiple unit franchisee in Singapore.

In Business Since: 1970

Equity Capital Needed: $50,000 to $80,000

Financial Assistance Available: Development based on individual's net worth.

Training Provided: It is mandatory that franchisee spend 2 weeks plus in training at company designated location.

Managerial Assistance Available: Continuous assistance provided throughout the term of franchise agreement. Each unit is visited periodically by a consultant to assist in maximizing income and by the quality department to assure maintenance of high uniform standards.

Information Submitted: July 1987

WIENERSCHNITZEL INTERNATIONAL, INC.
4440 Von Karman Avenue
Newport Beach, California 92660

Description of Operation: Fast food restaurant specializing in hamburgers and hot dogs. Drive thru service plus patio or inside seating.

Number of Franchisees: 275 in 11 Southwestern States

In Business Since: 1961

Equity Capital Needed: $60,000-$180,000

Financial Assistance Available: CGI does not generally guarantee or assist in financing, however, consultation and referrals are available.

Training Provided: 6 weeks of in-store and classroom training required. New store training team, and ongoing seminars and workshops available.

Managerial Assistance Available: Continuous ongoing consultation, periodic restaurant inspections, marketing and operational consultation.

Information Submitted: May 1987

WINNERS CORPORATION
101 Winners Circle
P. O. Box 184
Brentwood, Tennessee 37027

Description of Operation: Winners Corporation is a 170 unit chain of Mrs. Winner's Chicken House with interior dining area designed to provide a comfortable, soft atmosphers appointed with live plants. The restaurants are open for all 3 meal occasions, offering a variety of breakfast items, whipped potatoes, hash browns, baked beans, country gravy, and strawberry shortcake.

Number of Franchisees: 42 in 8 States

In Business Since: 1971

Equity Capital Needed: $100,000-$200,000

Financial Assistance Available: None.

Training Provided: The required training program consists of a 200 hour comprehensive course both in classroom and on-the-job experience.

Managerial Assistance Available: In addition to assistace in site selection, the company provides opening supervision, frequent operational assistance, marketing assistance, and support "kits" in accounting and operations functions. Single unit and multi-unit operations are considered.

Information Submitted: May 1987

YANKEE NOODLE DANDY, INC.
817-A Slaters Lane
Alexandria, Virginia 22314-1219
Ed Goldberg, Vice President of Operations

Description of Operation: Yankee Noodle Dandy offers a unique concept in the fast food industry...fresh pasta cooked in approximately 1 minute, before your eyes! Each store is approximately 2,200 square feet. An extensive inventory of Cardullo's Food Products including pastas, sauces, and desserts is maintained.

Number of Franchisees: 2 in Virginia

In Business Since: 1986

Equity Capital Needed: $15,000 minimum

Financial Assistance Available: A total investment of $300-$400,000 is necessary to open a Yankee Noodle Dandy franchise. A $15,000 franchise fee pays for a license, permit and training. Yankee Noodle Dandy will provide a contact to arrange financing.

Training Provided: An intensive 2 week training course will cover everything from operations to marketing. Training will take place in the factory, in a store unit and the main office.

Managerial Assistance Available: Yankee Noodle Dandy provides a continual support service for the life of the franchise. Complete manuals of operations, forms, and directions are provided. Initial assistance will consist of a home office supervisor on-site at the new franchise for 4 days during its opening. After then opening, supervisors will always to available to assist franchisees with any problems that arise. Regular field inspections to insure quality, service, and sanitation will be made on a monthly basis.

Information Submitted: August 1987

YOUR PIZZA SHOPS, INC.
1177 South Main Street
North Canton, Ohio 44720
John Purney, Jr., President

Description of Operation: Carry-out, dining room operation with salad bar and or smorgasbord available.

Number of Franchisees: 20 in Ohio, Arizona and Florida.

In Business Since: 1949

Equity Capital Needed: $40,000-$60,000

Financial Assistance Available: None directly but source information available.

Training Provided: 1 month training in one of our operating shops, then training in franchisee's own shop until we feel franchisee can handle their own operation.

Managerial Assistance Available: We are always available to our franchisees if they have any problems or questions of any kind, be it legal, accounting, managerial or operational, for as long as they remain a franchisee.

Information Submitted: July 1987

YUMMY YOGURT, INC.
1337 "F" Street, N.W.
Washington, D.C. 20004
Sheldon Fischer, President

Description of Operation: Yummy Yogurt offers two concepts—Concept 1 relates to a carry-out, mall or store front location. Yummy Yogurt Feastery Concept 2 related to a full service cafeteria restaurant. Both Yummy Yogurt's feature hard and soft yogurt made on the premises and a menu ranging from chicken, pizza, salads, sandwiches, subs featuring pita bread and bagels.

Number of Franchisees: 3 franchised stores and 3 company-owned stores in Washington, D.C.

In Business Since: 1976

Equity Capital Needed: Varies depending on size and location of store from $85,000 to $125,000

Financial Assistance Available: None directly but source information available.

Training Provided: On-site training at our Washington, D.C. training center prior to franchisee opening own store. continued assistance after opening.

Managerial Assistance Available: Continuous guidance relating to operational control, purchasing, merchandising, products, inventory control, promotions, advertising.

Information Submitted: May 1987

ZAB'S DEVELOPMENT CORP.
RT. 6
Andover, Connecticut 06232
J. M. Zabkar, President

Description of Operation: Zab's is a quick service concept specializing in premium formula hot dogs prepared over real charcoal. In addition to restaurant and food court style locations, Zab's also offers a line of upscale pushcarts for street vending. Two varieties of hot dogs are offered: (1) traditional red hots and (2) "all natural" white hot dogs. The hot dog formulas are a proprietory recipe of Zab's.

Number of Franchisees: 12 in Rhode Island, Virginia, Connecticut, New York, California and Florida.

In Business Since: 1980

Equity Capital Needed: $4,000 minimum for pushcarts; $25,000 minimum for stores.

Financial Assistance Available: A total investment of $19,000 is required for a pushcart, and $105,000 for a restaurant. Financing up to 75 percent of the investment is available through third-party sources with appropriate credit. Zab's does not finance directly.

Training Provided: Pushcart: 1 day classroom, 2 day operation/cart training. Restaurant: intensive 15 day, mandatory training course is scheduled for all new franchisees and store managers. The training is conducted at the company's training facilities in Rochester, New York. An additional 5 day program is offered at the franchisee's location before, during, and after initial store opening.

Managerial Assistance Available: Zab's provides continual management service for the life of the franchise agreement in such areas as customer service, food preparation and service, store operations and advertising. Complete manuals of operation, site location, consultation, employee orientation, forms and directions are provided. Supervision is available to work with franchisees and visit locations regularly to assist solving problems. Zab's sponsors meetings, elective training programs and research and development to maintain a high consumer acceptance.

Information Submitted: May 1987

GENERAL MERCHANDISING STORES

• BEN FRANKLIN STORES, INC.
500 East North Avenue
Carol Stream, Illinois 60188

Description of Operation: Ben Franklin Stores is a general merchandise division of Fox Meyer, which provides both merchandise and retailing assistance to franchisees in 50 States. The franchisee operates a private business with the advantages of chain-store buying, merchandising and promotional expertise, with a nationwide reputation for professional service to the public.

Number of Franchisees: 1,320 in 50 States

In Business Since: 1877

Equity Capital Needed: $80,000-$120,000—may be less for existing stores.

Financial Assistance Available: Financing is arranged through local and regional commercial lending institutions.

Training Provided: The new franchisee is required to attend one week of classroom instruction in headquarters, and two weeks in-store training at one of our training stores.

Managerial Assistance Available: Assistance is available in site selection, lease negotiations, sales promotion and all phases of operation by regular visits of trained field and headquarters personnel.

Information Submitted: May 1987

• COAST TO COAST STORES
CENTRAL ORGANIZATION INCORPORATED
501 South Cherry Street
Denver, Colorado 80222

Description of Operation: Retail "total hardware" store that features national brands plus private-level merchandise structured in 12 basic departments: hardware, electrical, plumbing, automotive, sporting goods, housewares/giftwares, materials, and lawn/farm/garden supplies. Stores are designed to be dominant in their markets.

Number of Franchisees: 1,023 in 31 States

In Business Since: 1928

Equity Capital Needed: $70,000 to $150,000, depending on store size. Equity investment is secured by inventory and fixtures; there is no initial payment for the franchise. There is a monthly franchisee fee of $50. Entire investment goes for inventory and store operations.

Financial Assistance Available: Franchisee normally furnishes half the initial capital needed; the company's division finance manager and district managers help negotiate additional term financing through local community sources.

Training Provided: New store owners attend a training school (with sessions, loading and meals at company expense) that thoroughly covers, all phases of store operations. Project and district managers help and new store owner with layout, display, set up and grand opening; thereafter, district manager makes continuing visits to give store owner additional training and counsel. This assistance is part of an ongoing program for the store owner.

Managerial Assistance Available: So that the store owner can devote his time to building his business. Coast to Coast offers a wide range of services that eliminate many tedious details. These services include complete bookkeeping and tax accounting, layout and display ideas to maximize inventory turnover, inventory control, pre-printed price tickets; electronic order entry system; group insurance program; sales circulars and merchandising helps; two merchandising meetings a year; training clinics; and continuing advice and assistance from the district manager and other store-operations personnel. Many of these are furnished without charge.

Information Submitted: May 1987

HEALTH AIDS/SERVICES

AMERICAN HEALTH & DIET COMPANY
475 Park Avenue South
34th Floor
New York, New York 10021
Craig A. Reynolds, President

Description of Operation: American Health & Diet Company sells and operates professional weight management workshops. Nutritional, fitness, and behavioral components of the program are individualized to each member. In addition to metabolic gas monitoring by the exclusive Calometer, all program participants are tested for body fat composition, food sensitive reactions through IgE and IgG Rast tests, as well as physical and cardiovascular fitness levels. All tests and workshops are conducted and taught by expertly trained, licensed professionals. Further, this program has all of the components necessary for the first fully reimbursable nutritional/weight management program ever available.

Number of Franchisees: 4

In Business Since: 1977 (as American Diet Counselors, Inc.)

Equity Capital Needed: $100,000-$120,000

Financial Assistance Available: No financial assistance available.

Training Provided: An extensive 1 week training program at corporate head-quarters is included in the cost of the franchise in areas such as diet, nutrition, menus, counseling, advertising and basic business techniques, together with an exercise program.

Managerial Assistance Available: In addition to training at our national headquarters, franchisee will receive continuing assistance from headquarters personnel trained in individual fields of bookkeeping, inventory control, operations, individual dieter needs, monthly newsletter and direct telephone communication.

Information Submitted: May 1987

AMERICAN PHYSICAL REHABILITATION NETWORK, INC.
4050 Talmadge Road
P. O. Box 8864
Toledo, Ohio 43623-0864
Richard R. Leffler, Chairman

Description of Operation: Complete business system for out-patient physical therapy service—free standing clinic.

Number of Franchisees: 2 in Ohio including company-owned

In Business Since: 1958, franchising since 1987

Equity Capital Needed: $25,000 for franchise; $25,000 for EDP system; $25,000 to $50,000 for working capital.

Financial Assistance Available: None

Training Provided: 2 weeks initial, 1 week annually thereafter.

Managerial Assistance Available: Monthly site visits, prototype contractual arrangements, interpretation of medical regulations and preparation of cost reports. Management consultation and all general accounting (financial statement preparation).

Information Submitted: May 1987

BETA OSTEOPOROSIS DIAGNOSTIC CENTERS OF AMERICA
7922 Ewing Halsell
Suite 100
San Antonio, Texas 78229
Gordon L. Bilbrey, MD, Chairman & Chief Executive Officer

Description of Operation: 600-800 square feet, free-standing, outpatient center for testing of patients for decreased bone density and education of patient in ostoporosis.

Number of Franchisees: 12 in 8 States

In Business Since: 1984

Equity Capital Needed: $59,000

Financial Assistance Available: All materials (brochures, manuals, video tapes, etc.) provided to franchisee at Beta Diagnostics Inc., cost. All equipment provided at cost. No financing on equipment provided.

Training Provided: Extensive training of physicians and technicians in technical, administrative and marketing procedures.

Managerial Assistance Available: As above.

Information Submitted: July 1987

BODY BEAUTIFUL BOUTIQUE
5118 Park Avenue
Suite 103
Memphis, Tennessee 38117
Liz or Bob Anderson

Description of Operation: Personal care figure salon using European body wrap, nutritional weight loss, passive exercise toning tables, and European facials and skin care.

Number of Franchisees: 6 in Tennessee and Mississippi

In Business Since: 1984

Equity Capital Needed: $36,000

Financial Assistance Available: None

Training Provided: Intensive 5 day instruction in all areas of operation.

Managerial Assistance Available: For life of contract, continuing development of new ideas and methods, area training and sales seminars, advertising advice for local markets.

Information Submitted: May 1987

CLAFLIN HOME HEALTH CENTERS
1070 Willett Avenue
East Providence, Rhode Island 02915
Ted Almon, President

Description of Operation: Claflin Home Health Centers are designed specifically to serve the needs of the home health care market. They are an integral part of their communities. Personnel are professionally trained in all aspects of the field. Products available for sale or rental in a Claflin Home Health Center include durable medical products such as wheelchairs and hospital beds; surgical and medical supplies; respiratory and physical therapy equipment, and self-care items. All are of the highest quality available.

Number of Franchisees: 6 in Rhode Island and Massachusetts

In Business Since: 1982

Equity Capital Needed: Franchise fee $25,000, total investment $150,000.

Financial Assistance Available: None

Training Provided: Thorough, in-depth traning is vital to the success of our franchise program. Our training staff comprised of experts in the many aspects of running a Claflin Home Health Center, will guide you through 3 weeks of intensive training in our model store. We will cover such areas as: hiring and training your staff, developing controls and projections, buying procedures, professional sales techniques, bookkeeping methods, and personnel management.

Managerial Assistance Available: Continual management service is provided.

Information Submitted: May 1987

CONCEPT 90 PERSONAL FITNESS STORES
685 N.W. 4th Avenue
Fort Lauderdale, Florida 33311
Michael J. Shea, President

Description of Operation: Concept 90 Personal Fitness Stores offers a unique retail store operation. Concept 90 stores offer a broad selection of quality exercise products for the home, together with professional advice and service. Each store is approximately 2,000 square feet.

Number of Franchisees: 5 in Alabama, South Carolina, Connecticut and New Jersey.

In Business Since: 1983

Equity Capital Needed: $50,000 minimum

Financial Assistance Available: None

Training Provided: Intensive, 14 day mandatory traning program covers the basics of anatomy and exercise physiology, demonstration procedures for all equipment, sales techniques, marketing, oerations, accounting and personnel. A combination of classroom instruction and on-the-job training in one of the franchisor's stores is used.

Managerial Assistance Available: The franchisor provides continual advice and support services for the life of the franchise in areas such as advertising, equipment selection, layout, etc. A complete manual covering all areas of the business is provided at training and is updated regularly.

Information Submitted: May 1987

CONTEMPO WOMEN'S WORKOUT
2540 West Lawrence Avenue
Chicago, Illinois 60625
Audrey Sedita, President

Description of Operation: Complete women's health and fitness club.

Number of Franchisees: 5 units in Illinois

In Business Since: 1968

Equity Capital Needed: $35,000 initial franchise fee. Approximately $120,000 for equipment and leasehold improvements.

Financial Assistance Available: None

Training Provided: The franchisee is given a mandatory comprehensive 4 week training program. 2 weeks in a company-owned club and 2 weeks in their own club.

Managerial Assistance Available: Franchisee receives complete manuals of operation, form's, advertising, marketing—franchisor provides ongoing management and technical service on a continual basis.

Information Submitted: May 1987

CORPORATE CHIROPRACTIC SERVICES, INC.
5214 Pinemont Drive
Murray, Utah 84123
Donald L. Stokes, D.C.

Description of Operation: Franchising the chiropractic profession—conducting seminars, national advertising, national promotion of chiropractic—video tapes both educational and marketing—creating a research foundation, etc.

Number of Franchisees: 100 in 7 States

In Business Since: 1986

Equity Capital Needed: Approximately $1,500

Financial Assistance Available: None

Training Provided: None

Managerial Assistance Available: Managerial if any, varies according to chiropractor's need—no technical

Information Submitted: May 1987

*DIET CENTER, INC.
P. O. Box 160
Rexburg, Idaho 83440
Raymond Lindstrom, General Manager of Franchise

Description of Operation: The Diet Center business includes administration of the 5-phase Diet Center Weight Control Program through private, daily counseling and weekly classes; and sales of various vitamin, food, and nutritional products generally under the Diet Center brand name. The Diet Center organization has grown, since its inception, to become the number-one franchised weight-control program in North America. With more than 2,200 locations throughout the United States and Canada, Diet Center continues to expand the scope of its organization to meet the needs of today's market.

Number of Franchisees: There are over 2,200 in all States of the United States and Canada

In Business Since: 1972

Equity Capital Needed: Initial franchise fee is $12,000 U.S. and $24,000 U.S. (includes starter kit, complete training program, necessary equipment, and franchise rights in exclusive territory). Minimum $10,000 additional operating capital essential.

Financial Assistance Available: None

Training Provided: A 1-week training seminar is provided to prepare operators for responsibilities of administering the Diet Center program and running a Diet Center business. Included in the seminar are courses providing instruction in every aspect necessary to the successful operation of a Diet Center.

Managerial Assistance Available: In addition to refresher courses provided at counselor training school at the corporate headquarters, continuing education is conducted throughout the year at regional counselor-training seminars across the country and at annual international Diet Center conventions. Counselors and franchisees are also informed of new information through the monthly publications of the

AdVantagemagazine, the franchisee forum newsletter, and the Diet Center newsletter.

Information Submitted: May 1982

FORTUNATE LIFE WEIGHT LOSS CENTERS
P. O. Box 5604
Charlottesville, Virginia 22905
Richard Beslin, Vice President

Description of Operation: The Fortunate Life Center is a supervised weight control program. The program is scientifically based and focuses in on the key ingredients of successful weight control—controlling caloric intake, modifying behavior and working with a committed individual. The program is unique within the weight control industry.

Number of Franchisees: 45 in 15 States

In Business Since: 1984 JenDale Inc., purchased franchise in June 1986

Equity Capital Needed: $6,000 plus working capital and initial franchise fee

Financial Assistance Available: JenDale may provide financing with 80 percent down at our discretion.

Training Provided: 3-5 days extensive marketing and clinical training.

Managerial Assistance Available: Physician and consulting dietician at home office. Marketing and clinical training updates provided through field visits and conventions.

Information Submitted: May 1987

HEALTHCARE RECRUITERS INTERNATIONAL, INC.
5420 LBJ
Suite 575
Dallas, Texas 75240
Frank A. Cooksey, President

Description of Operation: Contingency and retainer executive recruiting/search specializing only in medical sales, marketing, and management positions. HealthCare Recruiters is known as the "National Network for Medical Sales and Marketing." Each office is owned and staffed by executives whose business background has been in the healthcare industry, only. HealthCare Recruiters International's success has been established by developing systems that provide a real opportunity for an individual to "control their own destiny" utilizing those proven systems and established computerized client and candidate base.

Number of Franchisees: 32 in 23 states

In Business Since: 1983

Equity Capital Needed: $60,000 to $80,000—Depending on location.

Financial Assistance Available: Yes

Training Provided: Intensive training program of 2 weeks at the corporate headquarters in Dallas, Texas. Utilizing the latest audio visual training techniques in the industry, including video tapes, training/operation manual, reference guides and client/candidate information. HealthCare Recruiters provides training in all aspects of the recruiting and executive search business, including specialized training for owner-managers and account executives. Also, all account executives employed during the lifetime of the Franchise, are trained, inhouse by HealthCare Recruiters International. On the job training is conducted by home office representative to provide continuing training through a program of weekly telephone and periodic visits. In addition, HealthCare Recruiters conducts bi-annual training seminars and conferences. HealthCare Recruiters International will assist and advise the licensee in (1) office site selection and lease negotiation, (2) office layout and furniture selection (3) selection of computer equipment system (4) account executive recruitment. In summary, HealthCare Recruiters will provide its network franchisees with training, resources and guidance to operate a medical sales management and marketing executive recruiting business.

Managerial Assistance Available: Continuing support thru daily, weekly, monthly phone consultation and periodic management visits covering all aspects of the medical recruiting business. In addition HealthCare Recruiters International provides collection assistance of Licensee's accounts receivable and detailed analysis on all phases of their operation. HealthCare Recruiters International also provides national advertising and marketing support programs as well as target account solicitation by headquarter personnel.

Information Submitted: May 1987

HEALTH CLUBS OF AMERICA
Box 4098
Waterville, Connecticut 06714
Gregg Nolan, Franchise Director

Description of Operation: Health and slenderizing salons with separate facilities for men and women.

Number of Franchisees: 18 in Connecticut, New York and New Jersey.

In Business Since: 1961

Equity Capital Needed: Minimum of $35,000, depending on equipment.

Financial Assistance Available: Financing may be arranged through Horizons of America, Inc., parent company.

Training Provided: 1 week management training in main office in New York. At least 3 weeks of day-to-day operational training at own club.

Managerial Assistance Available: Company is always available for counseling.

Information Submitted: May 1987

HEALTH FORCE
1600 Stewart Avenue
Westbury, New York 11590
William O'Keefe, Vice President

Description of Operation: Company provides staff-relief in hospitals and nursing homes, home health care for the elderly and convalescents. Company funds weekly outside payroll for nurses, aides and homemakers. Company handles receivables and billings, in turn freeing franchisee for marketing.

Number of Franchisees: 42 in 13 States

In Business Since: 1960

Equity Capital Needed: $50,000-$60,000

Financial Assistance Available: Unlimited funding of weekly temporary payroll.

Training Provided: 2 weeks home office, 1 week franchisee's office, periodic field service throughout the year, and plus ongoing help as needed.

Managerial Assistance Available: Aid in surveying the market, setting rates, site selection, training of permanent staff. A complete set of oprations manuals. Field servicing throughout the year. Computer processing of payroll and receivables. Franchisor does all billing and collections to accounts, provides continual back up services including administrative and marketing assistance.

Information Submitted: August 1987

HOMECARE HELPING HAND, INC.
Subsidiary of PHARMACEUTICAL INNOVATORS, LTD.
116 Franklin
West Union, Iowa 52175
Ronald Garceau, President
Robert Johnson, Vice President

Description of Operation: Selling and renting of durable medical equipment and supplies to the homebound patients, nursing homes, hospitals and medical clinics plus serving public and private health organizations.

Number of Franchisees: 3 in Iowa

In Business Since: 1983

Equity Capital Needed: $25,000 to $50,000

Financial Assistance Available: None

Training Provided: Intensive 2 weeks training at the home office for all new franchisees and their personnel. Additional training is conducted at the franchisees place of business as an ongoing educational program and updated.

Managerial Assistance Available: Homecare Helping Hand, Inc., provides continual management service for the life of the franchise in such areas as bookkeeping, computer service, advertising, inventory buying and control, assistance with claims control and marketing of the services. Home office personnel are available per toll

free call 24 hours daily and make visits to stores regularly to assist solving problems. Home office also seek out the latest in medical equipment by attending national and international buying shows and give report to franchisees.

Information Submitted: June 1987

INFOMED CORPORATION
13 Inverness Way South
Englewood, Colorado 80112
Paul W. Shatusky, President

Description of Operation: Infomed Corporation offers a unique medical outreach program for pulmonary function and other medical capabilities to hospitals, clinics and specialty practices for the purposes of increasing revenue flow and generating referrals.

Number of Franchisees: 12 in California, Colorado, Texas, Illinois and Pennsylvania.

In Business Since: 1981

Equity Capital Needed: $250,000

Financial Assistance Available: A total investment of $250,000 is necessary to open an Infomed franchise. The down payment of $5,000 pays for license security deposits and training. Financing is available through LeaseAmerica on a 60 month payment basis. Franchise has option to arrange own financing.

Training Provided: Intensive 13 day mandatory training course is scheduled for all new franchisees and their personnel. 3 days are conducted at the home office; 10 days at the franchise outlet under supervision of a full-time Infomed employee.

Managerial Assistance Available: Infomed provides management and software for billing and analysis. Complete manuals and directions are provided. Standard forms and supplies are available from Infomed, as well as, extended service warranties on equipment. The Infomed main computer center is available to archive records and back up the franchise for the life of the franchise if desired.

Information Submitted: May 1987

JAZZERCISE, INC.
2808 Roosevelt Street
Carlsbad, California 92008

Description of Operation: Jazzercise is a dance fitness program utilizing choreographed dance fitness routines to music. The franchisee must successfully complete a training workshop and be proficient in dance and exercise in order to qualify for a franchise.

Number of Franchisees: 3,499 franchised instructors in the USA plus 29 foreign countries.

In Business Since: 1974

Equity Capital Needed: Approximately $3,000.

Financial Assistance Available: None

Training Provided: A 4 day workshop.

Managerial Assistance Available: Jazzercise provides the services of agents who supervise and assist franchisees in all facets of their business on an ongoing basis.

Information Submitted: May 1987

JENEAL INT. SKIN CORRECTION AND HEALTH CENTERS
2721 Hillcroft
Houston, Texas 77057
Dr. Jerry O'Neal, Ph. D., President

Description of Operation: Jeneal is a system of skin correction which utilizes certain methods, techniques and products to provide skin analysis, dietary recommendations and surface exfoliation of the dead cells of the skin and the promotion of rapid reproduction of normal skin cells. This system ultimately results in smooth, blemish-free skin. Janeal also is a system of superfluous hair removal which utilize an organic enzyme.

Number of Franchisees: 13 in 6 States.

In Business Since: 1965

Equity Capital Needed: $15,000-$60,000

Financial Assistance Available: None

Managerial Assistance Available: An intensive 14 day mandatory training course is scheduled for all new franchisees and their managers at Jeneal Corporation offices in Houston, Texas. An additional 7 days of training is conducted at the franchisee's outlet under the supervision of a full-time Janeal employee (usually the company president).

Information Submitted: May 1987

LEAN LINE, INC.
151 New World Way
South Plainfield, New Jersey 07080
Antonia Marotta, President

Description of Operation: A weight reduction organization. The people who join become members and they are expected to attend one meeting each week. The length of time or membership depends upon the amount of weight the individual needs to lose. A member may terminate his or her relationship at any time and not be penalized financially. The program teaches the member how to lose weight using a nutritionally sound diet and university tested behavioral techniques aimed at changing poor eating habits.

Number of Franchisees: 4 in 2 States plus 3 company-owned.

In Business Since: 1968

Equity Capital Needed: Approximately $10,000.

Financial Assistance Available: None

Training Provided: Training takes franchisee through all phases necessary to operate a successful business. Emphasis is placed upon class procedures and presentations which include the nutritional and psychological understanding necessary to indoctrinate the membership. Training manuals are also provided.

Managerial Assistance Available: The managerial and technical assistance is provided as part of the ongoing relationship. After their initial training, franchisees are at liberty to call upon us at any time for any assistance they may need. If there are any changes in policy or form, franchisees are thoroughly indoctrinated.

Information Submitted: August 1987

* LIFE TIME MEDICAL NURSING SERVICES, INC.
1171 Main Avenue
Warwick, Rhode Island 02886
Stephen A. Brassard, Franchise Sales Director

Description of Operation: Life Time Medical is a regional nursing service that provides staffing relief, private duty nursing and in-home care. Major users of the services are hospitals, nursing homes, physicians, offices, emergency rooms, and private industry. The staff provided by the agency are registered nurses (including specialists in intensive care, pediatrics, pychiatric, neonatal) and other licensed practical nurses, nurse's assistants and homemakers.

Number of Franchisees: 5 in Connecticut and Massachusetts

In Business Since: 1979

Equity Capital Needed: $40,000-$60,000 which includes a $15,000 franchise fee.

Financial Assistance Available: The franchisor offers no financial assistance.

Training Provided: The franchisor offers 1 week training for each franchisee at their home office. This is followed up by additional training at the franchisees site. Support will be provided on a continuous basis.

Managerial Assistance Available: The franchisor will provides supervision to assist franchisees from the corporate office on an ongoing basis. Assistance will be provided in recruiting, training, advertising, marketing, sales, closings, office management, etc. Support via telephone, computer, and office visits will be ongoing.

Information Submitted: May 1987

* MEDICAL NETWORKS, INC.
10203 Birchridge
Suite 400
Humble, Texas 77338

Description of Operation: Franchisor of freestanding primary/urgent healthcare clinics. Also provides emergency department and other services to hospitals, trains medical and paramedic personnel, provides physician recruiting and management services. Provides healthcare consulting services.

Number of Franchisees: 20 in Illinois, Pennsylvania, Texas and Wisconsin.

In Business Since: 1974

Equity Capital Needed: Varies—minimum $250,000.

Financial Assistance Available: None

Training Provided: Management systems, operating policies and procedures, operations and application—1 week, and data processing, accounting, sales, marketing—various schedules.

Managerial Assistance Available: Site selection, architecture, facilities development, pre-opening marketing, supplies and inventory purchasing, grand opening, marketing, advertising and promotion, creative development, operations, accounting and data processing, sales, and significant other assistance available at option of franchisee.

Information Submitted: May 1987

MED-WAY MEDICAL WEIGHT MANAGEMENT
11303 Chevy Chase
Houston, Texas 77077
Jerry O. Cooksey, Executive Vice President

Description of Operation: The Med-Way Medical Weight Management franchise is a proven weight loss program offering sound nutrition, education and behavior modification to the general public. The program is administered by physicians and nurses in a professional, clinical atmosphere. Franchise ownership is available to nurses and non-medical investor owners. MED-WAY provides complete assistance with site selection, center layout, personnel selection, training, advertising support and comprehensive on-going support.

Number of Franchisees: 8 in Texas, 35 additional agreements have been signed. Franchising in other states also.

In Business Since: 1987

Equity Capital Needed: The total capital requirements to get a typical Med-Way Weight Management center open is from a low of $27,000 to $40,000, which includes the franchise fee. Average $36,000

Financial Assistance Available: Franchisor does not provide financial assistance at this time.

Traininng Provided: Franchisor provides free training to the franchisee and franchisee's employees at Franchisor's headquarters in Houston, Texas. Franchisor will train franchisee's employee's at not cost to franchisee for as long as franchisee owns the franchise. The franchisee is responsible for paying all costs of travel, food and lodging to and from Houston, Texas. Franchisor provides five days training in Houston and up to 5 days training at franchisee's center.

Managerial Assistance Available: In addition to the above training at Franchisor Headquarters, Franchisor provides ongoing advice and assistance with advertising, promotions, seminars, written advisories, bulletins and meetings at Franchise Headquarters. Franchisor has staff available during normal working hours to assist all Franchisee's with routine questions. Franchisor has "Area Nurse Managers" to advise and assist all franchise locations. Franchisor provides all Franchisee's with an Operations Manual, supply lists and pre-printed forms lists. Franchisor can supply all items used in each center, but Franchiee's do not have to purchase anything from Franchisor.

Information Submitted: May 1987

NATIONAL HEALTH ENHANCEMENT
SYSTEMS, INC.
3200 N. Central Avenue
Suite 1750
Phoenix, Arizona 85012
Jeffrey T. Zywicki, Vice President of Finance

Description of Operation: National Health Enhancement Systems, Inc. offers health care providers, through a business system, an innovation way of generating additional revenue, through the marketing of health evaluations to prevention-conscious consumers. Its comprehensive medical assessment program, designed to determine the relative health of an apparently well individual, was developed in 1979 by Dr. Edward B. Diethrich, and has evolved into five distinct systems that may be utilized as stand-alone or complementary products. Each program analyzes life-style, nutritional habits and physical condition as they related to cardiovascular disease risk factor and overall fitness.

Number of Franchisees: 115 in 31 states

In Business Since: 1983, formerly AHI, Limited

Equity Capital Needed: Approximately $22,200, including initial fee.

Financial Assistance Available: In certain situations the initial license fee is payable 1/3 down upon execution of a franchise agreement with the balance (plus interest) due in 12 equal monthly payments. The investment pays for all start up materials and software product. (Does not include personal computer hardware equipment).

Training Provided: An intensive 4-day mandatory training program held in Phoenix, Arizona; subsequent and follow-up training as often as franchisee requests under the direct supervision of full time NHES employees.

Managerial Assistance Available: National Health provides continual marketing and technical support for the life of the franchise in the administration of the medical assessment and evaluation programs it provides to its franchisees.

Information Submitted: May 1987

NU-CONCEPT BODY WRAP, INC.
607 Cleveland Street
Elyria, Ohio 44036
Arlene S. Doman, President
Dennis S. Doman, Vice President

Description of Operation: 750-2,000 square feet, ladies figure salon. Loss of unwanted inches using elastic bandages soaked in special mineral solution (pat. pend.) and special wrapping techniques to compact body tissue and tighten skin. Reduces or remove celulite. Good results with men also.

Number of Franchisees: 3 in Ohio

In Business Since: 1981

Equity Capital Needed: $5,000

Financial Assistance Available: A total investment of $10,000 to $15,000. Depending on size of operation. Franchise fee is $3,750 (outside financing only).

Training Provided: 1 week at authorized training center.

Managerial Assistance Available: Ongoing assistance to franchised salon, home office bulletins on latest wrapping techniques, new products, sales ideas and methods, improved business management techniques, sales promotion, etc. Very low prices on products and materials needed for body wrapping.

Information Submitted: August 1987

NURSEFINDERS
1400 North Cooper Street
Arlington, Texas 76010
Larry M. Carr

Description of Operation: NURSEFINDERS is a national supplemental nursing service and home care agency that provides registered nurses, licensed (Voc./Prac.) nurses, nurses ads and other nurse specialists as supplemental staffing in health care facilities and as private duty staff in both health facilities and in the home. Each franchise is for an exclusive territory agreed upon by the franchisor and franchisee.

Number of Franchisees: 49 in 16 States

In Business Since: 1975

Equity Capital Needed: $70,000-$140,000

Financial Assistance Available: The franchisor offers no financial assistance to franchisees when they start operations. In situations where a franchise shows outstanding growth, the franchisor may offer short-term loans of expansion capital.

Training Provided: The franchisor provides a 2-week training period for each franchisee at one of its established offices and 2 weeks' additional training at the franchise site before the franchise begins operations. Additional training includes on-site training visits and periodic management workshops.

Managerial Assistance Available: The franchisor assists the franchisee with site analysis and selection and office decor and layout. Regional service directors visit franchise sites at least annually to consult with franchisees about business operations and to offer suggestions for implementing NURSEFINDERS policies and procedures.

Information Submitted: May 1987

* NUTRA BOLIC WEIGHT REDUCTION SYSTEMS
OF AMERICA, INC.
4790 Douglas Center N.W.
Canton, Ohio 44718
Dennis Kline, National Marketing Director

Description of Operation: We offer unique franchise opportunities throughout the United States in the field of weight loss.

Number of Franchisees: 95 in 9 States

In Business Since: 1982

Equity Capital Needed: $32,000

Financial Assistance Available: None

Training Provided: 2 day owner training, 1 week long owner/employee training and 1 week grand opening assistance.

Managerial Assistance Available: Weekly and monthly meetings.

Information Submitted: June 1987

* NUTRI/SYSTEM, INC.
Willow Wood Office Center
3901 Commerce Avenue
Willow Grove, Pennsylvania 19090

Description of Operation: Nutri/System Weight Loss Centers offers the consumer a comprehensive, professionally-supervised weight reduction program utilizing medical and professional treatment, individualized personal care and maintenance. Using Nutri/System 2000, an exclusive pre-packaged natural food program. Nutri/System Weight Loss Centers provides rapid, safe weight loss without drugs, injections or diet pills.

Number of Franchisees: 731 (120 company) in all 50 states plus 12 in Canada.

In Business Since: 1971

Equity Capital Needed: $89,500 minimum.

Financial Assistance Available: None available.

Training Provided: Franchisor provides complete training for franchisees, medical personnel and entire office staff through training seminars, on-site instruction and training guides. Periodic training seminars and area coordinators provide continual follow-up supervision.

Managerial Assistance Available: Franchisor provides continual management and technical service is such areas as client treatment, bookkeeping, advertising, sales, inventory control and business management. Complete manuals of operations are provided along with printed and electronic aids. National and district advisors work closely with franchisees to analyze and evaluate operations.

Information Submitted: August 1987

OMNI HEALTH INTERNATIONAL, LTD.
6666 Security Boulevard
Baltimore, Maryland 21207
Irvin Mordes, President

Description of Operation: Omni Health International, Ltd., offers an effective way to lose weight, stop smoking, overcome negative habits and control stress through an original technique using subliminal hypnosis. Each professional operation consists of an office, waiting room, control room and induction room. Services are rendered in a classroom setting or on a one to one basis. Control room and induction room come completely furnished.

Number of Franchisees: 4 in Maryland, 1 in Pennsylvania and 1 in Virginia.

In Business Since: 1970

Equity Capital Needed: $50,000-$60,000

Financial Assistance Available: The company does not offer financing, but assistance in arranging financing is provided.

Training Provided: Training in hypnosis and in the operation of the hypnosubliminal equipment for a period of 2 weeks or longer if necessary. Instructions in running the business, client relations, advertising programs and all record keeping procedures necessary for a smooth operation preliminary to the inception of the operation, so franchisee starts totally prepared and confident. Continuous follow-up supervision is provided.

Managerial Assistance Available: Periodic check-ups (especially at conception of the business) to ascertain the satisfactory progress being made and availability of Omni Hypno-Health Centers. FOr assistance whenever necessary regarding conducting of the business, planning advertising, entertaining new ideas or solving any problems that may possibly arise.

Information Submitted: May 1987

**OPTIMUM HEALTH SYSTEMS
SHARE/CONCERN**
2368 Victory Parkway
Cincinnati, Ohio 45206
Peter Crotty, Vice President of Marketing & Sales

Description of Operation: Offers the CONCERN®: Employee Assistance Program and SHARE®: Occupational Health Program. Franchises are hospitals. Hospitals sell these programs to business and industry in their local markets.

Number of Franchisees: 41 in 14 States.

In Business Since: 1985

Equity Capital Needed:

Financial Assistance Available: None.

Training Provided: Intensive, 10 day training at the home office in sales, marketing and operations. On site training includes: sales, marketing and operations.

Managerial Assistance Available: Optimum provides ongoing sales marketing and operations assistance throughout the life of the contract. Complete manuals of operations and sales are provided. Account Executives are assigned to each Franchisee. All marketing, promotional and operational materials are provided.

Information Submitted: May 1987

OUR WEIGH
3340 Poplar
Suite 136
Memphis, Tennessee 38111
Helen K. Seale, President

Description of Operation: A unique weight control group consisting of: thirty minute meetings, behavior modification, exercise, and most important a nutritional diet that allows members to eat what they like and not have to eat foods they don't like. First in the field to introduce "food rewards" and free weekly weigh in upon reaching desired weight.

Number of Franchisees: 4 in Tennessee and Mississippi.

In Business Since: 1974

Equity Capital Needed: $1,500.

Financial Assistance Available: None

Training Provided: 7 to 10 working days training on-the-job at national headquarters plus visit from national headquarters executive opening week, on the site training. Monthly letter sent to individual franchisees with latest nutritional, advertising, promotions, group leading, personal information.

Managerial Assistance Available: 24 hours a day, 365 days a year open communication with national headquarters executives plus as mentioned above. Constant telephone calls, letters sent and visits to keep franchisees up to date on all aspects of their business.

Information Submitted: May 1987

PHYSICIANS WEIGHT LOSS CENTERS OF AMERICA, INC.
30 Springside Drive
Akron, Ohio 44313
Franchise Division

Description of Operation: A Physicians Weight Loss Center franchise consists of a high volume, medically supervised weight reduction business, offering the consumer a comprehensive, medically supervised program utilizing medical and professional treatment, individualized personal care, counseling, and maintenance. The program consists of a safe, nutritionally sound medical method of weight reduction and control for both men and women with the use of vitamin and mineral supplements, in conjunction with behavior modification counseling and comprehensive maintenance programs.

Number of Franchisees: 235 in 20 States (23 company-owned).

In Business Since: 1979

Equity Capital Needed: $42,600 to $56,000.

Financial Assistance Available: The company does not offer financing.

Training Provided: Physicians Weight Loss Centers of America Institute provides franchisees with comprehensive educational development programs and technical knowledge in the areas of business management, successful operations of a Physicians Weight Loss Center, record and bookkeeping procedures, media advertising, and staffing and training of medical and office personnel. Additional instruction is provided in the area of sales and marketing, enrollments, telephone

presentations, and motivation. Complete procedures and methods of counseling of patients, and the handling of dietary problems are provided as an integral part of patient services.

At Physicians Weight Loss Centers of America Institute mandatory attendance of all new franchisees is required for a period of 13 days for certification.

Managerial Assistance Available: Physicians Weight Loss Centers of America, Inc., provides continued management and technical support in such areas as patient treatment, accounting, bookkeeping, multi-media advertising, sales and marketing, inventory control, and motivational and business management. Comprehensive manuals for operatins, medical staffing, behavior modification, and advertising are provided. In addition, regional field service operations personnel work closely with franchisees to analyze and evaluate center operations. Regional and local update seminars and development programs are provided for increased effectiveness and productivity on a quarterly basis.

Information Submitted: July 1987

PREGNAGYM
St. Anthony's Ancillary Services
P.O. Box 12588
St. Petersburg, Florida 33733
Rosemary Colombo, Managing Director

Description of Operation: Pregnagym is a medically supervised exercise program designed specifically for pregnant women. Pregnagym requires about 1,200 square feet and the weight based machines are purchased by the franchise. As this is a medically supervised program, the purchaser must be affiliated with a physician or hospital. Pregnagym provides a start up materials, operational procedures, promotional package and a training program for the staff.

Number of Franchisees: 16 in 8 states

In Business Since: 1984

Equity Capital Needed: Total investment of $90,000 which includes franchise fee of $19,750, $40,000 for equipment, $30,000 for leasehold improvement and signage.

Financial Assistance Available: Leasing of equipment possible.

Training Provided: 3 days of on site intensive training is provided with an instructor who goes thru the assessments and methods of the program. A workbook and video with step by step guidance also is a part of training. Follow-up and consultation available.

Managerial Assistance Available: Policy and procedure manual, camera ready of all forms and operational procedures taught. Telephone consultation available as well as an on site visit by physician who developed the model of this program. Research continues and as new advances are made, franchises are kept current.

Information Submitted: May 1987

RESPOND FIRST AID SYSTEMS
3850 J. Nome Street
Denver, Colorado 80239
James G. Plouffe, Chairman of the Board

Description of Operation: Respond franchisees operate van-oriented, route sales business offering quality first aid and emergency medical supplies, service and training to the commercial market.

Number of Franchisees: 27 outlets in 16 states

In Business Since: 1979, franchising since 1984

Equity Capital Needed: $20,000

Financial Assistance Available: In certain circumstances.

Training Provided: 5-7 days of classroom training, 2 days field training and support in the franchisee's area, and ongoing support. We will also provide additional operations visits plus seminars and meetings.

Managerial Assistance Available: See above

Information Submitted: May 1987

SLENDER CENTER, INC.
9 Odana Court
Madison, Wisconsin 53719
Jean Geurink, President

Description of Operation: Weight loss consultation on individual basis. Use of normal, regular foods in unique rotation system called 3-step breakthrough program. Increased calories throughout weight loss to jolt metabolism. No drugs, no exercise, no products. Each client receives informative manual including cookbook and self-taught behavior management exercises. Clients are seen twice a week and given a guarantee on projected loss.

Number of Franchisees: 43 Centers plus 5 company-owned in Michigan, Rhode Island, Illinois and Wisconsin.

In Business Since: 1979

Equity Capital Needed: $4,500-$9,000 plus franchise fee $12,000-$27,000.

Financial Assistance Available: None

Training Provided: Initial 5 day training at corporate headquarters at lake retreat near Madison, Wisconsin. Training manuals, on-site grand opening support, visitation, newsletters monthly and seminars.

Managerial Assistance Available: Training manuals, field staff, full advertising campaigns, and "hands-on" experience at company-owned sites prior to grand openings. Newsletters monthly and seminars available on district basis.

Information Submitted: August 1987

SUTTER MEDICAL MANAGEMENT CO., INC.
1154 Sutter Street
San Francisco, California 94109
Jackie Gallman

Description of Operation: Option I: Turnkey urgent care center. SMMC selects site, does all lease improvements, instal computers, pre market, and train staff. Option II: Existing clinic: computerize joint marketing already operating clinic. Infuse capital when needed.

Number of Franchisees: 3 in California

In Business Since: 1984

Equity Capital Needed: Option I: $60,000 Option II: $ 5,000

Financial Assistance Available: Variable

Training Provided: 1 month training.

Managerial Assistance Available: Continuing computer service bureau, payroll, payables, general ledger services and medical peer review.

Information Submitted: July 1987

THERMOGRAPHIC MEDICAL ASSOCIATES, INC.
1950 Lee Road
Suite 103
Winter Park, Florida 32789
Dr. Harry Rein, J.D., M.D.

Description of Operation: Computerized electrodiagnostic testing with thermography.

Number of Franchisees: 2 in Florida.

In Business Since: 1982

Equity Capital Needed: $75,000

Financial Assistance Available: None

Training Provided: Training of physician and technician, continued. Two day comprehensive thermography training course for physician.

Managerial Assistance Available: Review and analysis of site location. Continuous information regarding use of thermography. Assistance in present and future acquisition of equipment. Advertising provided by franchisor including franchise offices. Expertise in billing and collection.

Information Submitted: July 1987

THIN LIFE CENTERS
151 New World Way
South Plainfield, New Jersey 07080
Lorraine Wurtzel, President

Description of Operation: Thin Life Centers is a medically oriented rapid weight loss facility which also deals with the psychological aspects of the clients personality. Each Center occupies approximately 1,500 square feet and is located typically, in a professional complex or shopping mall with ample parking. The Centers are open five and one half days per week.

Number of Franchisees: 2 in Pennsylvania plus 5 company-owned.

In Business Since: 1977 (parent company Lean Line in business since 1968).

Equity Capital Needed: $30,000-$90,000 plus franchise fee.

Financial Assistance Available: Assistance in obtaining SBA loan.

Training Provided: Intensive 2 week classroom and clinical experience.

Managerial Assistance Available: Support constantly available.

Information Submitted: August 1987

T.L.C. NURSING, INC.
15 Dunwoody Park
Suite 100-C
Atlanta, Georgia 30338
Bill Wimbish, President

Description of Operation: The TLC Nursing Center is a locally owned nurse-placement service which arranges nurses, homemakers, sitters, live-ins, etc., catering primarily to the home health care market, but is fully capable to furnish the same to hospitals and institutions.

Number of Franchisees: 10 in Pennsylvania, New Jersey and Georgia.

In Business Since: 1984

Equity Capital Needed: $5,000 to $20,000 plus franchise fee.

Financial Assistance Available: Franchisor will finance up to 50 percent of the franchise fee of $20,000 which includes all material and training necessary to initiate business.

Training Provided: In addition to a complete manual for the business, a trained operator will work with franchisee in a hands on manner until he capable of working alone. Additional training is provided later by field people and franchisee may work at an existing center at no charge other than his own expenses.

Managerial Assistance Available: Same as above.

Information Submitted: June 1987

TONNING & TANNING CENTERS
c/o FITNESS SYSTEMS, INC.
P.O. Box 266
Independence, Missouri 64051
Glen Henson

Description of Operation: We feature Toning Tables, Tanning Beds and Isokinetic treadmills, bicycles with a line of Isokinetic exercises for muscle toning. The program is designed for all ages of women and men alike. Our centers are priced so they may be adapted to any town of 5,000, to 10,000, or 20,000, as well as the larger communities. Our phone number is 816-765-3303

Number of Franchisees: 150 in 15 states

In Business Since: 1975

Equity Capital Needed: $10,000 and up

Financial Assistance Available: Limited

Training Provided: 1 week optional in Independence, Missouri and on site training when opening at no charge.

Managerial Assistance Available: Total training on all aspects of the business at no charge. Managerial and technical assistance provided in use of all equipment, office forms, bookkeeping, etc.

Information Submitted: May 1987

TOTAL LIFESTYLE CORPORATION
1835 Nonconnah Boulevard
Suite 169
Memphis, Tennessee 38132
David Wolfe, National Franchise Sales Manager

Description of Operation: Local, franchising Total LifeStyle Centers, physician-owned and directed, and operated by a trained nurse. Offering comprehensive weight-loss care. This includes one-on-one nurse counseling, behavior-modification training, individualized diet and exercise programs, education and motivation, and one year of maintenance once the target weight has been reached. Programs are provided women, men and children, with the average weight loss 18-20 pounds in 6 weeks. No drug injections or pills are used.

Number of Franchisees: 66 in 16 states

In Business Since: 1985

Equity Capital Needed: Initial franchise fee $12,500 for a population area of up to 12,500; $25,000 for a population of up to 25,500. (Fee includes exclusive territory, initial nutritional product order, training, bookkeeping system, marketing and advertising assistance, ongoing visits and monitoring at least monthly, etc.)

Financial Assistance Available: Up to 50 percent of franchise fee.

Training Provided: Complete initial training and continuing advanced seminars on regional basis. Initial training held in Memphis.

Information Submitted: August 1987

UNITED SURGICAL CENTERS
380 Warwick Avenue
Warwick, Rhode Island 02888
Stevan Datz, President

Description of Operation: Home health care—sales and rentals of durable medical equipment and convalescent aids.

Number of Franchisees: 3 plus 1 company-owned.

In Business Since: 1973—franchising since 1980.

Equity Capital Needed: $100,000

Financial Assistance Available: None

Training Provided: Hands on training (our training school, our store and in franchisees store).

Managerial Assistance Available: Our staff at our location and also at franchisee's. Continual support.

Information Submitted: May 1987

VICTORY INTERNATIONAL, INC.
dbaSUDDENLY SLENDER, THE BODY WRAP & HEALTH CENTER
THE BODY WRAP
SUDDENLY SLENDER
VICTORIA M. COSMETICS
1231 South Parker Road
Suites 104 & 105
Denver, Colorado 80231
Catherine M. Cooper, President

Description of Operation: A safe, effective way to lose inches (in the right places) in only 70 minutes utilizing the original Victoria Morton formula and process. Body compacting, reshaping method—loss of unwanted inches and cellulite using bandages soaked in special mineral solution (patent pending) and special wrapping techniques (patent pending) with two written guarantees; minimum 6" overall loss for women (4" for men) on the first wrap; inches lost will not return if you don't gain weight. Face sculpturing (taping plus mineral wrap process)—radically tightens skin, smooths wrinkles, cuts in cheekbones and raise eyebrows, eliminates jowls and double chins. Special bra for increasing, decreasing, firming bust. Natural product line for control of water-retention, aging-reversal, energy, skin-tightening and weight loss. Skin care line for smoothing wrinkles and refining skin. A system for diminishing scars is available as part of the operation. Considered the only permanent inch-loss process in the industry.

Number of Franchisees: 272 in 20 States, Mexico and Canada

In Business Since: 1969, franchising since 1981.

Equity Capital Needed: $60-$90,000 depending upon size of center, area and elegance. Franchise fee is $20,000, balance of cost is $22,000 for a 2-station center, $29,900 for a 4-station center, and $37,500 a 6-station center. Includes equipment, furniture, supplies, training and protected territory. The balance of suggested capital is for operating capital, salaries, start up costs, and leasehold improvements.

Financial Assistance Available: Yes, franchisee must have equity to cover loan.

Training Provided: 3 weeks of intensive training. Comprehensive manual must be learned before attending class. Through lectures, classroom discussion, audio-visual presentations and extensive practical applications, trainees master wrapping techniques, shop procedures, sales techniques, employee selection and training, bookkeeping systems and management techniques. Frequent up-dates on new technology, techniques, newsletters and annual seminars. Training is held at the Denver, Colorado, training center. 2-5 day seminars are available. Phone consulting always available with inventor of process, Victoria Morton. (Personal figure improvement is an added benefit.)

Managerial Assistance Available: Ongoing assistance available by phone or by field personnel, 2-5 day seminars available designed to develop strong managerial and training skills; annual seminars feature improved management methods, sales promotion techniques, improved body shaping techniques, body builder techniques and face sculpturing techniques.

Information Submitted: May 1987

WEIGH TO GO, INC.
2435 Colt Road
Rancho Palos Verdes, Louisiana 90274
Annette Y. Dahlman, Ph.D., President

Description of Operation: Medically supervised weight management program developed exclusively for hospital/clinic operation.

Number of Franchisees: 1 in New Jersey and 7 in California

In Business Since: 1983

Equity Capital Needed: $75,000

Financial Assistance Available: Varies

Training Provided: Didactic training for 3 days, on-the-job training monthly.

Managerial Assistance Available: Weigh to Go Inc., provides complete manuals of operations, forms, programs, and administrative procedures. Continual consultation is provided in areas of marketing, promotion, training, systems and medical updating and research developments. Site representatives work with individual franchisees and maintain close working relationships with staffs. Weigh to Go, Inc., sponsors meetings of franchisees to conduct marketing and product research and update franchisees of recent research developments relating to the Weigh to Live System. Marketing and advertising services are provided and regional programs offered.

Information Submitted: July 1987

WOMEN AT LARGE SYSTEMS, INC.
1020 South 48th Avenue
Yakima, Washington 98908
Sharlyne R. Powell, President & C.E.O.

Description of Operation: Women at Large is a unique physical fitness/image enhancement program designed exclusively for large and extra-large women, providing a support system through support groups and behavior modification. Self-esteem is elevated by providing make-up, hair design, fashion, and other related workshops geared to helping the large and extra large woman re-enter the mainstream of today's life as a healthy, beautiful, well-adjusted, vital force, full of positive energy, self-assurance and determination, for the first time, to live life to the fullest!

Number of Franchisees: 10 in Nevada, Washington, Alaska, Georgia and Tennessee.

In Business Since: 1983 franchising since 1986.

Equity Capital Needed: Approximately $35,000-$50,000.

Financial Assistance Available: None

Training Provided: 2 week intensive training at our home office with fitness beginning before coming for training, franchisee returns home with a video to continue the fitness training and polishing until her opening day. Training provided for owner and 4 other people. 2 days assistance at grand opening by Women at Large representative.

Managerial Assistance Available: New routines are sent via video tape on a continuing basis. Visits by a trained Women at Large representative to be a support system between franchisee and home office. Regional seminars and yearly conventions provide a continual education on industry updates. Continuous contact through newsletters and direct phone correspondence.

Information Submitted: May 1987

HEARING AIDS

*MIRACLE-EAR
DAHLBERG, INC.
Interchange Tower, Suite 701
600 South County Road 18
St. Louis Park, Minnesota 55426
Norman L. Blemaster, Vice President of Franchising

Description of Operation: The franchisor is in the business of designing, manufacturing, and distributing a complete line of hearing aids and in franchising MIRACLE-EAR Hearing Aid Centers.

Number of Franchisees: 140 in 48 States

In Business Since: 1948

Equity Capital Needed: Approximately $17,500.

Financial Assistance Available: None

Training Provided: 5-day training course in all technical and sales aspects of the hearing aid industry, license application course, advanced technical seminar, and advanced sales seminar.

Managerial Assistance Available: Network of regional managers available at all times to provide ongoing technical and managerial assistance to the franchisee.

Information Submitted: May 1987

HOME FURNISHINGS/FURNITURE—RETAIL/ REPAIR/SERVICES

ABBEY CARPET COMPANY
425 University Avenue
Suite 200
Sacramento, California 95825

Description of Operation: Specialty store—retail carpets. Franchises are only available to people already in the retail carpet business.

Number of Franchisees: 200 throughout the U.S.

In Business Since: 1967

Equity Capital Needed: $5,000

Financial Assistance Available: None

Training Provided: None

Managerial Assistance Available: None

Information Submitted: Auguat 1987

* AMERICLEAN
Americlean Franchising Corporation
6602 South Frontage Road
Billings, Montana 59101
James L. Pearson, Vice President

Description of Operation: Liquid dry cleaners of carpenting; drapery; and upholstery; disaster restoration services; acoustical celling cleaning; specialty cleaning services. Seeking responsible owners to manage high volume operations. Must be able to co-ordinate several crews at once and be customer service oriented.

Number of Franchisees: 20 in 8 states

In Business Since: 1979

Equity Capital Needed: $20,000

Financial Assistance Available: Assistance seeking financing through standard lending institutions.

Training Provided: 1 week initial business training plus 1 week in-field training. Grand opening and installation. Operations manuals, newlsetters, conventions and seminars. Periodic phone calls and personal visits by support department personnel.

Managerial Assistance Available: See above

Information Submitted: May 1987

AMITY, QUALITY RESTORATION SYSTEMS, INC.
410 Atlas Avenue
P. O. Box 7204
Madison, Wisconsin 53707
L. O. Alexander, President

Description of Operation: Amity offers a unique "furniture stripping and restoration system" of equipment and chemicals for the stripping and restoration of antiques and furniture. The system to be located in purchasers rented shop. There are no purchase requirements. No fee, all funds paid are for equipment and merchandise. All chemicals non-flameable. Also sells paint remover, spray equipment and finishers, wholesale to the trade.

Number of Franchisees: 700 in all States except Alaska and Hawaii.

In Business Since: 1971

Equity Capital Needed: $1,800 to $10,000

Training Provided: Training provided at home office for 2 days on use and application. Free consulting advice, conventions, seminars, newsletters. Training includes stripping, finishing and repair.

Managerial Assistance Available: Technical advice provided on restoration, stripping, finishing, repairing, business management.

Information Submitted: May 1987

CARPET BEAUTY
P. O. Box 2
Fair Haven, New Jersey 07701
Ray Costa

Description of Operation: Carpet Beauty offers franchising of on location residential carpet cleaning.

Number of Franchisees: 3 in New Jersey

In Business Since: 1985

Equity Capital Needed: $4,995

Financial Assistance Available: Yes

Training Provided: Carpet Beauty provides a 3 day training period with a successful work schedule formula.

Managerial Assistance Available: Periodically home personnel will visit each franchise to continue guidance and support.

Information Submitted: July 1987

CARPETERIA, INC.
1122 North Vine Street
Hollywood, California 90038
Bryan Haserjian, Executive Vice President

Description of Operation: Franchising and/or operating retail carpet outlets.

Number of Franchisees: 35 in California, Nevada and Washington plus 27 company stores.

In Business Since: 1973

Equity Capital Needed: $100,000 to $400,000, depending on size and scope of operation contemplated.

Financial Assistance Available: $0-$25,000

Training Provided: 4-8 weeks depending on prior business and industry training and experience.

Managerial Assistance Available: Managerial and technical assistace is available from the franchisor.

Information Submitted: May 1987

CARPET TOWN, INC.
937 North Citrus Avenue
Hollywood, California 90038

Description of Operation: Floorcovering retail and wholesale.

Number of Franchisees: 8 in California plus 16 company-owned stores.

In Business Since: 1954

Equity Capital Needed: Negotiable

Financial Assistance Available: None

Training Provided: In franchisor's main office in Hollywood, California; in franchisor's warehouse in Hollywood, California; in one or more operatings Carpet Town Stores. Training program covers both administrative and merchandising matters, also includes one or more tours of carpet mills, instructors for the training program are key employees of frachisor with 5 or more years of experience. The training is free of charge. Duration: 10-20 full days for franchisees having a basic familarity with retail sales operations; more if not.

Managerial Assistance Available: After the initital training shown above, continued assistance (free of charge) in the following areas: accounting, record keeping; inventory control; purchasing; sales; collections; merchandise display; advertising and promotion; price techniques; fiber content, colors and textures; installation; current market trends; etc.

Information Submitted: August 1987

CENTER THIRD MATTRESS STORES
13601 Hawthorne Boulevard
Hawthorne, California 90250
Al Heller

Description of Operation: Center Third Mattress Stores offer a unique franchise opportunity in the bedding specialty industry. Center Third stores feature an exclusive line of mattress and boxspring with add-on sales of brass and white iron beds. Each store is 1,500-1,800 square feet and is open 7 days a week.

Number of Franchisees: 10 in California including company-owned.

In Business Since: 1983

Equity Capital Needed: $48,500, includes franchise fee

Financial Assistance Available: No direct financing assistance.

Training Provided: Intensive 2 week mandatory training divided between corporate headquarters and franchisee's facility.

Managerial Assistance Available: Center Third Inc., will provide ongoing assistance and counseling in areas such as inventory, promotion, customer relations, accounting, etc. Center Third also sponsors annual and quarterly franchisee meetings and new product testing and development.

Information Submitted: May 1987

CHEM-CLEAN FURNITURE RESTORATION CENTER
P. O. Box 787
Rock Stream, New York 14878
Dr. R. G. Esposito, President

Description of Operation: Patented Non-Water Systems for furniture stripping and refinishing.

Number of Franchisees: 77 in 16 states, Canada and Europe.

In Business Since: 1967

Equity Capital Needed: $7,000-$25,000 total required.

Financial Assistance Available: Lease purchase or financing plans available. No royalties, licensee owns all equipment outright. Equipment and solvents covered by U.S. and Canadian patents.

Training Provided: Up to 2 weeks of complete instruction in licensee-owned shop, plus follow-up. Environmental assistance.

Managerial Assistance Available: Complete operating procedures, including technical and managerial techniques. Annual meetings of licensees. Newsletters.

Information Submitted: May 1987

CHEM-DRY CARPET CLEANING
HARRIS RESEARCH, INC.
3330 Cameron Park Drive, #700
Cameron Park, California 95682
Robert Harris, President

Description of Operation: Chem-Dry offers a unique, patented (#4219333) cleaning process utilizing a completely safe, nontoxic solution in conjunction with carbonation. The carbonated cleaner has opened the door for innovative approach to carpet cleaning and franchising. Carpets are guaranteed against damage, are left with no dirt-attracting residues, and generally dry in less than one hour.

Number of Franchisees: 1,100 in 50 States, and ten countries.

In Business Since: 1977

Equity Capital Needed: $4,900

Financial Assistance Available: The $4,900 down payment pays for equipment and solutions, office supplies, an advertising package, and training. Balance financed at zero interest.

Training Provided: A 2 day training program includes on-the-job training where carpet cleaning skills will be taught, as well as the necessary business management aspects. A franchisee, his managers, or employees may obtain as much additional training as they desire at no charge. Training can also be done by the purchase of a video tape program which includes a written test.

Managerial Assistance Available: A franchisee, his managers or employees may obtain as much additional training as they desire at no charge.

Information Submitted: May 1987

CLEANMARK CORPORATION
185 Greens Farms Road
Westport, Connecticut 06880
Helmuth W. Krause, President

Description of Operation: Cleanmark specialists provide Cleanmark brand name commercial and residential cleaning service for carpets and furniture, drapes, walls. Smoke and flood restoration. Office cleaning. Carpet and furniture cleaning utilizes company-developed patented equipment and methods.

Number of Franchisees: 2 in Connecticut

In Business Since: 1966, in franchising since 1979.

Equity Capital Needed: $12,000

Financial Assistance Available: Company assists franchisee in obtaining local financing of up to 2/3 of total.

Training Provided: 5 day on-the-job and in-office training. Continuous information service by bulletin, correspondence, and verbal communication.

Managerial Assistance Available: Cleanmark provides continued marketing, management, and technical assistance to franchisee.

Information Submitted: August 1987

*DECORATING DEN SYSTEMS, INC.
4830 Montgomery Avenue
Bethesda, Maryland 20814
Jim Bugg, President

Description of Operation: The retailing of custom-made draperies, window treatments, floor coverings, wallcoverings, furniture, and other related decorating products. All merchandise sold from samples and catalogues in the customer's home on an appointment basis. Business does not require inventory or a retail store. This is a professional service business with competitive pricing on quality products.

Number of Franchisees: 610

In Business Since: 1970

Equity Capital Needed: Franchise fee of $16,900 plus working capital of $5,000-$10,000.

Financial Assistance Available: Franchise fee cash. Lease available on ColorVan.

Training Provided: Decorating Den's initial training takes approximately 6 months. It combines classroom work, home study, meetings, seminars, on-the-job experience and an internship with an experienced decorator. Secondary, advanced and graduate training continue throughout the owner's career with Decorating Den. Decorating Den decorators are trained to identify lifestyle, personality, color preferences and a comfortable budget. Emphasis is on the "feelling," the way people live more than historical period stylings.

Managerial Assistance Available: Grand opening preparation and attendance. Planning and sales projection meeting. Post opening progress checks. Ongoing services in marketing, sales, business operations and business expansion as part of fee.

Information Submitted: June 1987

DIP 'N STRIP, INC.
2141 South Platte River Drive
Denver, Colorado 80223
E. Roger Schuyler, President

Description of Operation: Franchised and company-owned operations providing the household community, antique dealers, furniture refinishers, industrial and commercial accounts in the removal of finishes from wood and metal. Operation requires approximately 2,000 square feet of warehouse space with concrete floor, drain, cold water tap, 220 single-phase power, overhead door, and small office space. The removal is accomplished with a cold stripping formula in chemical solutions. Dip 'N Strip is a federally registered trademark since April 13, 1970. Dip 'N Strip trademark is registered in France, Germany, the Belulux Countries, and in the United Kingdom.

Number of Franchisees: 194 in 38 States, Canada and 42 in Europe.

In Business Since: 1970

Equity Capital Needed: $12,500—no franchise fee required.

Financial Assistance Available: $3,000 will be financed up to 3 years, simple 10 percent interest, and will be carried by the franchisor for those who qualify.

Training Provided: A complete traning program is provided for 5 days of actual job and office training in all aspects of the business at the franchisee's own location prior to the grand opening. In Europe, the same training is provided at the master licensee pilot location.

Managerial Assistance Available: A complete operations manual and technical assistance is supplied during the training program, and in order to keep the franchisees current on the corporation and other franchisee's activities, a monthly newsletter Dip 'N Script, is published. All advertising mats, layouts, and slicks are provided without charge to the franchisees on request.

Information Submitted: August 1987

*DURACLEAN INTERNATIONAL
2151 Waukegan Road
Deerfield, Illinois 60015
Paul Tarman, Franchise Sales Director

Description of Operation: On-location cleaning of carpet, rugs, upholstery and drapery fabrics using exclusive, patented processes; plus ceiling cleaning, stain repelling, soil-retarding, static removal, spot removal, mothproofing and minor carpet repair.

Number of Franchisees: 800 in all 50 States, throughout Canada and 20 countries overseas.

In Business Since: 1930

Equity Capital Needed: Standard dealership price is $16,800. Two other dealershp options, up to $25,900.

Financial Assistance Available: For standard dealership Duraclean will finance balance of cost after $6,900 down payment, for qualified applicants. Financing also available for other options.

Training Provided: 1 week resident training school, transportation, tuition, room and board at no cost to new dealers. Also, training with experienced dealer.

Managerial Assistance Available: Advertising, sales promotion, bookkeeping, laboratory services on cleaning and technical spotting. Regional meetings throughout the U.S. and Canada. International conventions.

Information Submitted: May 1987

*EXPRESSIONS
3212 West Esplanade
Metairie, Louisiana 70002
Eric Aschaffenburg, President

Description of Operation: Expressions is a specialty furniture store featuring custom order upholstered furniture. Expressions stores have been developed to maximize sales in a small store using a very limited inventory. This is accomplished by displaying samples of over 100 frame styles for sofas, sofa sleepers, and chairs along with a unique wall display of 500 fabric samples. Customer chooses frame style and fabric and delivery is scheduled within six weeks.

Number of Franchisees: 19 in 14 States plus 8 company-owned stores.

In Business Since: 1978

Equity Capital Needed: approximately $130,000, which includes $15,000 franchise fee.

Financial Assistance Available: None

Training Provided: Expressions has developed a comprehensive and intensive training program that covers all phases of the furniture industry and in particular the techniques and methodology of running a successful Expressions store. The training program, which is administered by our highly qualified and professional training staff, consists of 6 days at our home office in New Orleans, one day at our manufacturing facility in Tupelo, Mississippi and 1 week at franchise location to include the period of grand opening. An Expressions training manual is provided.

Managerial Assistance Available: Site Selection and Lease Negotiation—Provide site selection guidelines based on traffic count, resident demographics, storefront visibility, and general location layout. Also, assistance in lease ngotiations. **Merchandising**—Design department assists with opening inventory and floor layout with great attention to correlation of fabrics and styles. Ongoing recommendations are made. **Advertising**—Advertising department furnishes franchisee with effective advertising campaigns and materials. Particular attention is paid to budgeting media selection and advertising material. **Financial Analysis**—Expressions will review your financial statements on a quarterly basis. **Continued Training**—Training staff is available with adequate notice to provide review or update training to any personnel. **General**—Expressions' staff of accountants, designers, sales consultants, advertising and production personnel stand ready to assist at all times.

Information Submitted: May 1987

FABRI-ZONE OF AMERICA, INC.
375 Bering Avenue
Toronto, Ontario, Canada M823B1
David Collier, President

Description of Operation: Establish cleaning service franchisees, total service including, carpet, upholstery, drapery, ceiling, smoke and fire damage, water resturation, odor removal, and retail product sales.

Number of Franchisees: 8 in 7 States

In Business Since: 1985

Equity Capital Needed: $23,000

Financial Assistance Available: Complete business plan for start-up, territory study, complete program, financing to qualified individuals.

Training Provided: 1 week at corporate office, then field training.

Managerial Assistance Available: Complete technical and systems support, advertising and marketing promotions, monthly newsletters, regional seminars, management support, and monthly bulletins.

Information Submitted: April 1987

THE FLOOR TO CEILING STORE
c/o FCS DISTRIBUTORS, INC.
4909 Highway 52 North
Rochester, Minnesota 55901
George Scheer, President

Description of Operation: The Floor to Ceiling Stores are a retailer of interior decorating products including floor coverings, wallcoverings, kitchen and bathroom products and related accessories.

Number of Franchisees: 36 in 8 Midwestern States plus 5 company-owned.

In Business Since: 1981—acquired franchise division from Plywood Minnesota, Inc.

Equity Capital Needed: $165,000-$445,000, depending on store size, which includes an initial franchise fee of $25,000.

Financial Assistance Available: Franchisee normally furnishes a third of the initial capital needed. Franchisor will assist in negotiating additional term financing through local community sources.

Training Provided: Company provides assistance in site development: layout; remodeling; pre-opening advertising, merchandising and display and accounting. The company also has an ongoing training program both locally and system-wide.

Managerial Assistance Available: Company provides ongoing assistance in store operations, product selection, distribution, advertising, accounting, and group insurance to allow franchisee to concentrate on building his business.

Information Submitted: May 1987

G. FRIED CARPETLAND, INCORPORATED
800 Old Country Road
Westbury, New York 11590
Al Fried, President

Description of Operation: Retail floor covering stores. Stores vary in size from 2,500 feet to 15,000 feet. Smaller stores are purely sample operations. Larger stores show samples and rolls.

Number of Franchisees: 24 in New York, New Jersey, Connecticut and Florida.

In Business Since: Parent Corporation—1889. Franchising Corporation—1969.

Equity Capital Needed: Cash minimum $15,000 per individual. We suggest two partners in each franchise. In large stores cash requirements would be proportionately more.

Financial Assistance Available: We have been able to arrange loans.

Training Provided: There is no definite training period required. We only want experienced floor covering professionals to apply.

Managerial Assistance Available: Franchisor constantly supervises franchisee's operation.

Information Submitted: August 1987

GROUNDWATER, INC.
3942 North 76th Street
Milwaukee, Wisconsin 53222
Larry Labensky, Vice President

Description of Operation: Waterbeds and furniture retail store.

Number of Franchisees: 9 in Wisconsin

In Business Since: 1972

Equity Capital Needed: Varies—ranges $40,000

Financial Assistance Available: Co-ordinate bank financing through parent bank.

Training Provided: Varied

Managerial Assistance Available: Whatever is needed.

GUARANTEE SYSTEM
CARPET CLEANING & DYE COMPANY
2953 Powers Avenue
Jacksonville, Florida 32207
Stan Minkoff, Sales Director

Description of Operation: The Guarantee System offers an excellent opportunity in the carpet and upholstery cleaning business. The ability to successfully dye and tint carpeting on location is a unique part of the process. Specially formulated products have been thoroughly tested and proven. Guarantee System also offers a water damage restoration process, smoke and ordor elimination and also specializes in drapery and oriental rug cleaning.

Number of Franchisees: 563 in 39 States and Washington, D.C.

In Business Since: 1969

Equity Capital Needed: $10,000 minimum excluding van type truck.

Financial Assistance Available: Franchise fees are based on population. $5,000 per 100,000 population. Minimum franchise fee $10,000 for 200,000 or less. We require 1/4 down and balance payable weekly on 12 percent note retained in our office. Franchise fee may be paid in full at anytime without penalty. Complete equipment (less van) and initial expendable materials $8,500. Materials will produce $7,000 to $9,000 gross sales.

Training Provided: 2 weeks traning in Jacksonville. Includes management, marketing and technical both in the classroom and in the field. Advanced training available on specialty services.

Managerial Assistance Available: Guarantee provides continuous follow-up training for the duration of the franchise via nationwide toll free Wats line, at least two regional meetings each year in all areas and an annual national meeting and convention. Field assistance for specific problems at no charge to the franchisee. Marketing and technical manuals are provided and continually updated.

Information Submitted: May 1987

HILLSIDE BEDDING
65 South Street
Mont Vernon, New York 10550
Frank Prato, Director of Franchising

Description of Operation: Largest chain of bedding shops offers franchised stores featuring matresses, brass headboards, convertible safas, and most other sleep products. National brand names such as Seally sold at discount prices.

Number of Franchisees: 50 in New York, New Jersey, Connecticut and Pennsylvania.

In Business Since: 1973

Equity Capital Needed: $39,150-$54,000

Financial Assistance Available: Will assist in obtaining financing.

Training Provided: 1 week of formal classroom training and 1 week with store manager of a company store. 1 week quarterly and 2 day monthly refresher courses available as continuing education.

Managerial Assistance Available: Each region has a local supervisor of operations available at all times. Each month, a vice president of operations visits each store for an entire day to assist owner with problem solving and implementation of new products and promotional campaigns. Monthly marketing meeting in local areas and quarterly franchise meeting at company headquarters.

Information Submitted: June 1987

HOWARD KAPLAN'S FRENCH COUNTRY STORE
35 East 10th Street
New York, New York 10003
Pearl Bedell

Description of Operation: Howard Kaplan's French Country Store is a retail home furnishings store carrying a full line of wallpapers, fabrics, furniture and tabletop accessories. Many of the items carried by the store have been designed by Howard Kaplan.

Number of Franchisees: 2 stores in New York and Indiana

In Business Since: 1985 Franchise corp., prototype store has been in existence since 1970.

Equity Capital Needed: $175,000-$300,000 depending on location.

Financial Assistance Available: None

Training Provided: 2-3 day training at company-owned store.

Managerial Assistance Available: Ongoing assistance—Mr. Kaplan will be available to provide creative assistance and advice as well as provide the services of his staff.

Information Submitted: August 1987

INDOOR MAGIC, INC.
555 South 19th
Blair, Nebraska 68008
B. Dean Ellis, President

Description of Operation: Indoor Magic franchise systems offers a unique decorating business. Specializing in draperies and all other window treatments also carpets and wallcovering. Franchise owner need no inventory, no workrooms, no sewing machines, no employees, no labor, no retail location, very low investment, do business from your home and car.

Number of Franchisees: 6 in Missouri, Nebraska and Iowa.

In Business Since: 1972

Equity Capital Needed: $4,300

Financial Assistance Available: 50 percent can be carried by indoor Magic Inc., for 18 months.

Training Provided: Training program, usually it takes years to become a skilled decorating consultant, with Indoor Magic professional training you do it in months, and you build a successful business at the same time, drapery and decorating is only part of what you learn. You will learn sales skills, business management, and the technical aspects of measuring and ordering. It is all available to you in a planned progression so you learn just what you need, when you need it.

Managerial Assistance Available: Indoor Magic provides continual management service for the life of the franchise in such areas as bookkeeping, advertising, and sales, complete manuals of operations, forms, and directions are provided. District managers are available to work closely with franchisees to assist in solving problems. Indoor magic sponsors meetings with franchisees and conducts marketing and product research to maintain tight Indoor Magic acceptance.

Information Submitted: August 1987

INTERNATIONAL HOME MARKETING SYSTEMS, INC.
1450 Mitchell Boulevard
Schaumburg, Illinois 60193
John Beltramo, President

Description of Operation: Buyers club concept whereby members are enabled to purchase home furnishings and related goods and services through the club at dealer's wholesale prices.

Number of Franchisees: 2 in Illinois and Missouri

In Business Since: Franchisor was incorporated in 1986 and is a wholly-owned subsidiary of International Home Marketing Inccorporated in 1972.

Equity Capital Needed: Total investment $126,000 to $153,500; which includes: franchise fee of $37,500, showroom display material $12,500, leasehold improvements, office furniture $4,500 to $15,000. Working capital (including insurance and related premiums) $69,000 to $83,500.

Financial Assistance Available: None

Training Provided: Franchisor shall furnish to the initial manager, a training program of such duration as determined by franchisor's sole discretion, based on the initial manager's prior business experience and other relevant factors.

Managerial Assistance Available: Franchisor may, in its sold distretion, provide from time to time, refresher training programs. Franchisor shall furnish guidance for the operation of the franchised business.

Information Submitted: May 1987

JOHN SIMMONS GIFTS
c/o STS, INC.
1503 Union Avenue
Suite 216
Memphis, Tennessee 38104

Description of Operation: Franchised John Simmons and The Shop of John Simmons gift shops. These are retail gift operations specializing in home furnishings and unique gifts. Company also offers its own import operation for incorporation into the franchised stores.

Number of Franchisees: 9 in 5 States

In Business Since: 1960

Equity Capital Needed: $100,000-$135,000

Financial Assistance Available: None

Training Provided: Management training in Memphis 3 to 4 day-cover start to finish of 1 day out of operation. Operating manual is given and high lights are covered. When we supervise setting up of store, we work with personnel in display, sales, and maintenance.

Managerial Assistance Available: We continue to work with franchise by sending a representative from the home office twice a year. We work with franhchisee at 2 markets, talk with each by telephone when needed (as long as the franchise is in effect).

Information Submitted: May 1987

KING KOIL SLEEP PRODUCTS
KING KOIL BEDQUARTERS FRANCHISE DIVISION
770 Transfer Road, Suite 13
St. Paul, Minnesota 55114
Ernest L. Friedman, President

Description of Operation: King Koil BedQuarters offers an opportunity to enter the retail sleep products business with a limited investment and is designed especially for the individual with some prior retail experience, preferably, but not necessarily in the household consumer goods area. The franchisee will be responsible for precuring his own location and commitment to real estate or lease. Inventory requirements are flexible with a minimum King Koil start up inventory of $12,000. King Loil must represent 51 percent or more of the total floor sampling and inventory.

Number of Franchisees: 179 in 22 States and 2 countries

In Business Since: 1982, franchising since 1982.

Equity Capital Needed: $60,000, limited one time franchise fee of $2,500.

Financial Assistance Available: The franchisor has developed an outstanding display package—partially supplied at no cost.

Training Provided: The franchisor has designed exclusive advertising and sales promotion materials including television and radio commercials, newspaper ads, collateral P.O.P. material and a sales training manual and marketing manual. Several sales training films will also be available. In addition, new materials will be developed on an ongoing basis. A unique cooperative preplanned advertisig program has been developed to maximize penetration. A BedQuarters franchisee will receive continuous sales training, merchandise counselling and long-range promotional planning.

Managerial Assistance Available: A tight system of inventory control will be maintained jointly by King Koil and the franchisee enhanced by the BedQuarters Rapid delivery System. A national advertising program for bedquarters was initiated in the Spring of 1984. In addition to standard nationally advertised King Koil products, the BedQuarters franchise will have exclusive "made by BedQuarters merchandise" available to them.

Information Submitted: June 1987

LANGENWALTER-HARRIS CHEMICAL CO., INC.
4410 East LaPalma Avenue
Anaheim, California 92807
Roy Langenwalter, President

Description of Operation: Langenwalter-Harris Chemical Co., Inc., offers a unique carpet and upholstery dle process franchise. a breakthrough in dye chemistry in which the liquid dye is solubolized to produce a stable color. A dye which "sets" instantly and permanently and allows the dyer to guarantee the color against color fade or lift from cleaning, etc., for two years. The dyer can control any color (an array of 18 brillant colors) with perfect uniformity over extreme large areas of carpet and upholstery. Langenwalter-Harris Chemical Co., Inc., offers two distinct franchises. One, for the businessman who would enjoy providing the dye service for carpet and upholstery. The other entrepreneur who would like to become a sub-franchisor in a region and/or territory whreby he supplies all dye, chemicals and equpment to the dyers in that region. Both franchises now available for marketing overseas.

Number of Franchisees: 243 and 32 sub-franchises in 24 States.

In Business Since: 1972

Equity Capital Needed: $12,500.

Financial Assistance Available: None

Training Provided: An intensive, comprehensive, 5 days mandatory training course. The training program is held in the Langenwalter Dye Concept School facility in Anaheim, California. Franchisor provides testbook, operational and technial manuals.

Managerial Assistance Available: Franchisor provides continual technical, chemical and management update seminars and workshops for all franchisees. A continuous marketing and product research and development program for all franchises.

Information Submitted: August 1987

LAURA'S DRAPERIES & BEDSPREADS SHOWROOM, INC.
11 Greenway Plaza
Suite 1200
Houston, Texas 77046
Harold Nedell

Description of Operation: Laura's Draperies & Bedspreads Showrooms, Inc., is a unique retail approach to the custom drapery and bedspread business. "Affordable elegance" is the idea behind Laura's with a storng emphasis on service. An inventory of ready-made draperies, bedspreads, and decorator pillows is maintained, but the main thrust of the business is the custom market. Each store is no more than 1,500 square feet and are located in strip centers near major malls, open 6 days a week from 10 a.m. to 6 p.m.

Number of Franchisees: 9 in Arizona, Texas and New York

In Business Since: 1986

Equity Capital Needed: Total capital required $68,500.

Financial Assistance Available: None

Training Provided: 3 weeks in design, fabric selection, management, customer relations, finance, sales and prospecting techniques.

Managerial Assistance Available: Laura's provides continual management service for the life of the franchise in such areas as bookkeeping, advertising, inventory control. Complete manuals of operations, forms, and directions are provided. Operation managers are available in all regions to work closely with franchisees. Laura's sponsors meetings of franchisees and conducts marketing and product research to maintain high Laura's consumer acceptance.

Information Submitted: May 1987

MODERNISTIC CARPET CLEANING
1816 Star Batt Drive
Rochester, Michigan 48063
Robert McDonald, President

Description of Operation: Clean carpet; upholstery; draperies; accoustical ceiling tile cleaning.

Number of Franchisees: 2 in Michigan

In Business Since: 1973

Equity Capital Needed: $10,000

Financial Assistance Available: Leasing and possible financial help from local Michigan bank.

Training Provided: 1 week on our shop; training includes video; one-on-one instruction; and in the field training.

Managerial Assistance Available: Complete operational manual; heavy instruction on marketing and telephone. Computer instruction available; bookkeeping available ongoing support 1-800 in Michigan for support over phone. They can come in for additional training at anytime.

Information Submitted: June 1987

MURPHY BEDS OF CALIFORNIA, INC.
6904 Miramar Road
San Diego, California 92121
Harry Adler, President

Description of Operation: Murphy Beds of California, Inc., is the exclusive distributor for the trade marked MURPHY (concealed metal wall bed) BED in California. The franchises are retail operations located in stratigic areas of California. 1,600 to 2,000 square feet of retail space is required. Murphy Beds of California provides the brand name bed and the custom cabinets which surround the bed.

Number of Franchisees: 5 stores in California including company-owned.

In Business Since: 1984

Equity Capital Needed: $50,000—additional $10,000 needed for start-up costs.

Financial Assistance Available: None. Franchise fee is $50,000. Down payment of $25,000 pays for inventory, sign and carpet. Balance of $25,000 payable upon completion by franchisor of turnkey store. an additional $10,000 needed for start up expenses. There is a 5 percent royalty of all gross sales due franchisor.

Training Provided: Up to 3 months training period either at company stores or on franchise site. Complete "how to" manual. Bookkeeping and sales techniques are taught.

Managerial Assistance Available: Original contract calls for a 10 year association with optional renewal clause for another 10 years. Relationship and training is ongoing with all technical assistance provided.

Information Submitted: May 1987

NAKED FURNITURE, INC.
1099 Jay Street
Building 5
Rochester, New York 14611
Patrick V. Lippa, Director of Franchise Sales

Description of Operation: A Naked Furniture store franchise is a specialty retail store selling better quality solid wood ready-to-finish furniture, custom finishing service and custom tailored upholstery.

Number of Franchisees: 50 including company-owned in 15 States

In Business Since: 1972

Equity Capital Needed: $40,000 required investment; total package $96,000-$156,000

Financial Assistance Available: Franchisor will assist in preparing financing proposal for presentation to lending institutions.

Training Provided: Complete operator training and support provided through intensive 1 to 2 week training program as well as full field support on a continuing basis.

Managerial Assistance Available: Naked Furniture, Inc., provides continual management service for the length of the franchise and provides an operations manual, a full bookkeeping package, forms, inventory selection assistance, regional warehousing, advertising and professional floor display plan. Periodic visits from regional field representatives will provide help in every area of store management and operation.

Information Submitted: May 1987

NETTLE CREEK INDUSTRIES, INC.
Peacock Road
Richmond, Indiana 47374

Description of Operation: Home furnishings retail stores specializing in semi-custom bedspreads, window treatments and decorative pillows. These are located in high income shopping areas and cater to people that need advice and assistance in interior decorating. The stores are about 1,500 square feet, and feature Nettle Creek products.

Number of Franchisees: 48 in 25 States

In Business Since: 1950

Equity Capital Needed: $50,000—investment including one time franchise fee of $5,000.

Financial Assistance Available: None

Training Provided: Manuals and operating systems, on-site training of 1 week's duration, in factory training of 2 to 3 days duration and continuing support and advice after the franchise is opened.

Managerial Assistance Available: Nettle Creek provides bookkeeping systems, omplete stationery supplies, advertising materials and operating manuals. Full-time franchise coordinators assist in location research, store layout, set-up, merchandise selection, and co-op advertising. Our entire executive staff is available for consultation.

Information Submitted: August 1987

OFF-TRACK BEDDING
P.O. Box 3240
Providence, Rhode Island 02909
Thomas A. Barron, President

Description of Operation: Retail bedroom furniture showrooms.

Number of Franchisees: 11 in Rhode Island, Massachusetts, Connecticut and New Hampshire including company-owned.

In Business Since: 1980

Equity Capital Needed: $68,000-$99,000, total investment.

Financial Assistance Available: None

Training Provided: 2 weeks on floor training at an active Off-Track Bedding location. Two weeks training on-site at the franchised location.

Managerial Assistance Available: All training is ongoing. Site search and selection, complete system of merchandise and operating manuals that are constantly updated. Warehouse distribution center.

Information Submitted: June 1987

PROFESSIONAL CARPET SYSTEMS, INC.
5250 Old Dixie Highway
Forest Park, Georgia 30050
Joseph R. Lunsford, President

Description of Operation: Professional Carpet Systems is the leader in "on-site" carpet redyeing, servicing thousands of apartment complexes, hotels, and motels, worldwide services also include carpet cleaning, rejuvention, repair, water and flood damage restoration and "guaranteed odor control" for pet odor removal. "A total carpet care concept," members: American Association Textile Chemists and Colorists.

Number of Franchisees: 125 offices in 34 States, franchises available in remainder of States, Canada and abroad.

In Business Since: 1978

Equity Capital Needed: Total cost of franchise $30,000, franchisor requires $12,000 down, balance financed after the $12,000 down.

Financial Assistance Available: The balance of $18,000 is company financed, using territory as collateral. No percentage royalties, no advertising fees.

Training Provided: 60 hours intensive technical/sales training; and 20 hours office and bookkeeping managerial skills. Total training 2 weeks at our company headquarters.

Managerial Assistance Available: Our franchise includes equipment package, supplies, printing, hotel, airfare, and lodging cost. Continual ongoing assistance thru upgraded training sessions, monthly newsletters, toll free hot lines, and national accout acquisition and sales program.

Information Submitted: May 1987

RAINBOW INTERNATIONAL CARPET DYEING AND CLEANING COMPANY
1010 University Park Drive
Waco, Texas 76707
Donald J. Dwyer, President

Description of Operation: Carpet and upholstery dyeing and tinting—carpet and upholstery cleaning, deordorization services, fire and water restoration, fire retardant—fiber guard.

Number of Franchisees: 1,000 in United States, Canada, France, Nassau, St. Croix and Grand Caymon.

In Business Since:

Equity Capital Needed: $12,000

Financial Assistance Available: Will finance 70 percent.

Training Provided: 1 week classroom and on-the-job-ongoing training via WATTS line—mailing—regional seminars.

Managerial Assistance Available: Continuous back up and support via toll free telephone number.

Information Submitted: May 1987

RECROOM SHOPPE OF OMAHA, INC.
Corporate Offices
980 South 72nd Street
Omaha, Nebraska 68114
William Grant, National Franchise Manager

Description of Operation: High volume retailer of waterbeds, spas, jetted bathtubs, saunas, above ground pools, billiard tables, game tables, exercise equipment, tramplines, patio furniture. Product lines balanced for consistant monthly volume.

Number of Franchisees: 2 including company-owned in Nebraska.

In Business Since: 1971

Equity Capital Needed: $150,000-$750,000 or more depending upon market size, demographics, and available bank financing.

Financial Assistance Available: Financing of initial franchise fee to qualified individuals. Normal credit terms. Possible joint ventures in large markets.

Training Provided: Mandatory 30 day training program for a minimum of 3 key persons, which includes on-the-job training at company-owned store in Omaha, Nebraska.

Managerial Assistance Available: Aggressive advertising and marketing programs. Site selection, training, grand opening, accounting, inventory control, volume purchasing and technical support programs, complete operations and standards manuals.

Information Submitted: July 1987

REPELE INTERNATIONAL
219 Newbury Street
Boston, Massachusetts 02116
Philip W. Sweeney, Vice President

Description of Operation: Repel International is a service-product company that treats carpets, upholstery, and wall coverings with a proprietary silicone-based fabric finish that protects them against permanent staining. Repele is applied by its licensed fabric technicians. Repele deals with the high end of the residential and commercial marketplace through its unique system of interior designer referrals. The company also markets a complete line of fabric maintenance products.

Number of Franchisees: 8 in California, Texas, Colorado, Florida, New Jersey, New Hampshire and Massachusetts.

In Business Since: 1983

Equity Capital Needed: $8,000 minimum

Financial Assistance Available: The company requires a minimum down payment of $8,000 which pays for training, inventory, technical manuals and documentation.

Training Provided: 1 week, of intensive training is conducted at the home office; instruction includes, on-site application of Repele, technical instructions on fabric finishes, marketing and sales, stain removal and cleaning seminar.

Managerial Assistance Available: Repele provides management, accounting, sales, marketing, and technical assistance for the life of the franchise. The company also conducts periodic seminars for the franchisees. Repele maintains a product research group and a technical advisory service.

Information Submitted: July 1987

*SCANDIA DOWN CORPORATION
7617 South 180th Street
Kent, Washington 98032
Stephen B. Cuthrell, Director of Franchise Development

Description of Operation: Scandia Down Shops are a full-range bedding shops retailing products such as: down comforters and pillows, European linens, wool bed pads, classic brass beds, and contemporary designer beds. The stores range from 500-1,400 square feet. They may, but need not, be located in covered retail shoping malls. Work hours are subject to lease negotiations. Stores must maintain representative samples of all Scandia Down trademarked items. They may stock a variety of bedding related non-trademarked items subject to Scandia Down approval. Franchisor participation in lease negotiations, if the franchisee requests.

Number of Franchisees: 90 stores

In Business Since: 1980

Equity Capital Needed: $35,000-$50,000 minimum.

Financial Assistance Available: A total investment of between $117,500-$222,000 is necessary to open a Scandia Down Shop Franchise. The franchise fee is $25,000. Additional investment requirements include inventory ($35,000-$45,000), store buildout (usually $25,000-$80,000) and operating capital ($20,000-$40,000). Financial assistance available.

Training Provided: Franchisor conducts an intensive 14-day training period at the corporate headquarters. The training is conducted along the outline of the operations manual. In addition, a field representative is provided for the initial five days of a new store opening.

Managerial Assistance Available: Scandia Down Corporation provides continuing management services for the life of the franchise in such areas as inventory control, bookkeeping, advertising, continuing marketing research and development,

and general store operations. A corporate operations manual guides the full aspects of store operations. District managers and field representatives are available in all regions to work closely with franchisees in all aspects of store operations.

Information Submitted: July 1987

SIESTA SLEEP, INC.
386 Lindelof Avenue
Stoughton, Massachusetts 02072
Manual or Alan Gilickman

Description of Operation: Retail specialty mattress outlets carrying brand name bedding, brass beds, and related specialty exclusive items.

Number of Franchisees: 5 plus 7 company-owned in Massachusetts and New Hampshire. Two Sleep Specialty Stores.

In Business Since: 1953

Equity Capital Needed: $15,000 to $25,000 or arrange for a 'turnkey' existing and proven shop. Partner often available on financial help.

Financial Assistance Available: Yes

Training Provided: 6 to 8 weeks intensive training plus continuous follow-up supervision plus as needed.

Managerial Assistance Available: Very close contact and sincere assistance.

Information Submitted: August 1987

SLUMBERLAND, INC.
630 Pierce Butler Route
St. Paul, Minnesota 55104
Kenneth R. Larson

Description of Operation: Slumberland operates retail specialty stores. Slumberland features name brand mattresses, sleep sofas and reclining chairs.

Number of Franchisees: 12 in Minnesota, Iowa, Wisconsin, South Dakota and Nebraska.

In Business Since: 1967

Equity Capital Needed: $50,000 to $100,000

Financial Assistance Available: Limited

Training Provided: Extensive training covering marketing, sales and advertising.

Managerial Assistance Available: An ongoing relationship includes marketing assistance, long range planning, site selection, delivery and warehousing.

Information Submitted: June 1987

*SPRING CREST COMPANY
505 West Lambert Road
Brea, California 92621
Jack W. Long, Executive Vice President

Description of Operation: Spring Crest Drapery Centers, retail draperies, drapery hardware and accessories.

Number of Franchisees: 300 in 39 States, Canada, New Zealand, Australia, South Africa, Saudi Arabia, United Kingdom and Trinidad.

In Business Since: 1955, franchising since 1968.

Equity Capital Needed: $40,000 to $50,000 for total package.

Financial Assistance Available: Yes

Training Provided: Initital training at headquarters with additional training at franchise location.

Managerial Assistance Available: Operations manual. One area meeting and one national convention per year. Monthly newsletter. Consultation from regional managers or home office staff.

Information Submitted: May 1987

*STANLEY STEEMER INTERNATIONAL, INC.
5500 Stanley Steemer Parkway
P. O. Box 156
Dublin, Ohio 43017
Wesley C. Bates, President

Description of Operation: A complete franchise system for on location carpet and furniture cleaning, water damage cleanup and odor removal services. Company manufactures patented intruct and portable equipment—maintains complete supplies to provide backup for franchises.

Number of Franchisees: Over 200 in 31 States; plus 15 company operations.

In Business Since: 1947 carpet and furniture cleaning. 1972 manufacturing and franchise sales.

Equity Capital Needed: Variable, minimum $15,000.

Financial Assistance Available: Lease program available on equipment and new truck.

Training Provided: 2 weeks or longer, depending on need at company headquarters. Training conducted by training director with a great amount of on-the-job training with experienced cleaning crews. Periodic review and retraining provided where necessary. All manuals are provided.

Managerial Assistance Available: Bi-monthly newsletter and periodic technical and service bulletins issued. Specific department head help available on an individual basis. A complete advertising department is maintained for franchise support. Annual convention and regional meetings for franchisees. Group liability insurance and major medical and hospitalization insurance programs are available. Continuous research and development for improvement of cleaning methods and equipment.

Information Submitted: May 1987

* **STEAMATIC INCORPORATED**
  1601 109th Street
  Grand Prairie, Texas 75050
  Lindy Berry, General Manager

Description of Operation: Controlled-heat carpet cleaning service and portable in-home drycleaning service for upholstery and drapes. Also insurance work, fire restoration, odor removal, water removal and wood restoration. Air duct cleaning, corrosion control.

Number of Franchisees: 186 in 27 States, Germany, Canada, Japan, Mexico, Ecuador, Australia, Guam, Nigeria, West Indies and Jordan.

In Business Since: 1968

Equity Capital Needed: $14,0000 to $35,000

Financial Assistance Available: If franchisee qualifies, one-third of franchisee fee can be financed through Fort Worth bank.

Training Provided: 2 weeks at headquarters at Grand Prairie.

Managerial Assistance Available: Continuous assistance in sales, equipment service, advertising materials, research and development, computer management system.

Information Submitted: May 1987

* **STOREHOUSE, INC.**
  2403-D Johnson Ferry Road
  Chamblee, Georgia 30341
  Mark K. Mayerhoff, Vice President, Director of Stores

Description of Operation: Contemporary home furnishings stores specializing in butcher block tables, custom built sofas, classic design chairs, bedroom furniture, storage systems, and outdoor furniture.

Number of Franchisees: 5 in South Carolina, Texas, Florida and North Carolina plus 23 ompany-owned stores.

In Business Since: 1969

Equity Capital Needed: Total capital required ranges from $115,000-$205,000.

Financial Assistance Available: No financial assistance available however a inventory repurchase agreement is offered which can be assigned to a lender to assist franchise in acquiring financing.

Training Provided: 1 week in corporate office, 2 weeks in company store and 2 weeks in franchise store.

Managerial Assistance Available: Operating manual and product information manual, site selection, lease negotiation, store design and construction, approximate monthly visits first 6 months, periodic thereafter, monthly advertising program and merchandising program, and merchandise avaialble through company distribution centers.

Information Submitted: July 1987

UNITED CONSUMERS CLUB
8405 South Broadway
Merrillville, Indiana 46410
Anthony G. Foster

Description of Operation: United Consumers Club offers a private service utilizing an alternative to the conventional distribution system, allowing merchandise to be shipped from manufacturers and distributors directly to a local address, thus avoiding the costly expense of the "middlemand." Each catalog center is approximately 4,00-5,00 square feet and is open 5 days a week. A minimum inventory of brand name merchandise and a wide variety of catalogs representing several hundred manufacturers are available to the membership allowing easy ordering of furniture, carpeting and appliances.

Number of Franchisees: 60 franchised units in 23 States; 5 company-owned units in 5 States.

In Business Since: 1971

Equity Capital Needed: Approximately $43,000, excluding working capital.

Financial Assistance Available: A minimum franchise fee down payment of $15,000 is necessary to open a UCC franchise. UCC will finance the balance of the $50,000 franchise fee for qualified candidates.

Training Provided: The UCC provides 4 weeks of initial classroom and on-site training. Major emphasis is placed on understanding and implementing the Club's business plan, operational guidelines and the marketing system to achieve a high level of profitability. Transportation to and from Merrillville, plus lodging, is provided to the new franchise owner and one other person.

Managerial Assistance Available: UCC provides continual management service for the life of the franchise in the areas of accounting, sales, personnel, etc. Complete sales and general operation manuals, audio-visual support programs, forms and directives are provided. Field supervision is also available to work with franchisees and conduct marketing and product information seminars.

Information Submitted: May 1987

* **WALLPAPERS TO GO**
  Division of WNS, INC.
  P. O. Box 4586
  Houston, Texas 77210-4586
  Houghton B. Hutcheson, Vice President, Franchise Development

Description of Operation: Wallpapers To Go is the nation's largest chain of retail stores specializing in in-stock wallcoverings and related home decoration products, including coordinated fabrics, window treatments and trim paints. Stores present a distinctively feminine image appealing to women, the primary consumer of residential wallcoverings. Wallpapers To Go targets the do-it-yourselfer with extensive in-store training materials.

Number of Franchisees: 10 plus 73 company-owned in Arizona, California, Missouri, Texas and Washington

In Business Since: 1977; franchising since 1986

Equity Capital Needed: $100,000 liquid for multi-unit territory.

Financial Assistance Available: Total investment for the development of a typical multi-store franchise may exceed $500,000. WNS, Inc., assists qualified candidates in locating institutions which may provide SBA-guaranteed or other financing.

Training Provided: Intensive 5 day classroom training prepares franchisees for the operation of their stores. Field staff assists in store takeover/opening to ensure successful transition.

Managerial Assistance Available: Market research, furnishings, fixtures and equipment. Wallpapers To Go provides assistance with site selection, market research, construction specs; furnishings, fixtures and equipment; merchandising and visual presentation. Field staff work closely with franchisees on an ongoing basis. Franchisees participate in national and regional marketing programs. More than 1,000 name-brand designer wallcoverings are furnished exclusively to franchisees through the Wallpapers To Go distribution center.

Information Submitted: May 1987

* **WASH ON WHEELS—VAC II**
  5401 South Bryant Avenue
  Sanford, Florida 32771
  Robin Keeley

Description of Operation: Carpet, furniture and drapery cleaning.

Number of Franchisees: 2

In Business Since: 1987

Equity Capital Needed

Financial Assistance Available: Financial assistance available to those with good credit.

Training Provided: 5 days intensive training, then constant ongoing manuals, seminars, newsletters, hot lines and direct mail.

Managerial Assistance Available: Ongoing

Information Submitted: May 1987

WFO FRANCHISES
222 Banta Place
Fairlawn, New Jersey 07410
Arnold Hershbain

Description of Operation: Retail furniture stores specializing in wall systems, bookcases, audio cabinets, etc.

Number of Franchisees: 2 in New York and New Jersey plus 11 company-owned stores.

In Business Since: 1965, franchising since 1984.

Equity Capital Needed: $49,000-$69,000

Financial Assistance Available: None

Training Provided: 2 weeks training on-site in all phases of operation.

Managerial Assistance Available: Ongoing in all aspects of managerial and technical assistance.

Information Submitted: August 1987

*WINDOW WORKS, INC.
7301 West Palmetto Park Road
Suite A-205
Boca Raton, Florida 33433

Description of Operation: Window Works offers retail stores set up as showrooms in high-volume shopping plazas. Window Works specializes in the sale and installation of custom window treatments. Products are national brands in vertical blinds, mini-blinds, woven woods, shades, draperies and interior shutters. Customers are from the residential and commercial sectors.

Number of Franchisees: 70 in 10 States.

In Business Since: 1978

Equity Capital Needed: $42,000

Financial Assistance Available: $42,000 fee includes complete training, complete store set-up, securing of all tools and licenses, and initial lease payments on the mall location and business vehicle.

Training Provided: Training consists of both classroom and in-field instruction. The training program is designed to give the franchisee complete working knowledge of product, installation, systems, accounting, sales and work-flow. Training lasts no more than 3 weeks.

Managerial Assistance Available: With extensive computer capability, Window Works, Inc., provides continuous monitoring of each franchise operation. Each store is provided monthly analysis of sales, margins, product distribution, media effectiveness, profit analysis, expense monitoring, etc. Window Works, Inc., also provides complete management service for the life of the franchise.

Information Submitted: May 1987

*WORKBENCH, INC.
470 Park Avenue, South
New York, New York
Odessa Alexander, Franchise Coordinator

Description of Operation: A contemporary retail furniture store with a mix of imported and domestic products.

Number of Franchisees: 11 with 26 stores in 12 States, plus 34 company-owned stores.

In Business Since: 1956

Equity Capital Needed: $50,000

Financial Assistance Available: A total investment of $400,000 is necessary to open a Workbench store. This pays for inventory, design charge, store set up and training. Workbench, Inc., does not provide financial assistance, but does provide support materials to develop financing.

Training Provided: 2 weeks training at corporate office and stores for two people. Additional 2 weeks training around the date of the store opening.

Managerial Assistance Available: Workbench provides complete manuals of operation, forms, direction and basic inventory program. Stores are visited regularly to give support in display and operations. Workbench constantly reviews new products and updates basic inventory program.

Information Submitted: May 1987

INSURANCE

AMERICA ONE, INC.
6035 Executive Drive
Lansing, Michigan 48910
Joanne F. Dillman, Vice President of Operations

Description of Operation: America One, Inc., sets up independent insurance agencies for licensed salespeople. Extensive training, licensing with insurance companies, advertising and continuing assistance in marketing, etc., are provided.

Number of Franchisees: 23 in Michigan

In Business Since: 1980

Equity Capital Needed: $6,000

Financial Assistance Available: $6,000 down payment. Balance of $4,000 due upon opening of business.

Training Provided: 12 to 15 days training for franchisee and employees in all aspects of operating an insurance agency. Continuing training in franchisee's office after opening of business. All manuals, forms, etc., provided.

Managerial Assistance Available: America One provides continual management services in areas of bookkeeping, marketing, money management, advertising, sponsors monthly meetings of franchisees, does marketing research for additional services that will help franchisees be successful.

Information Submitted: August 1987

*ISU INTERNATIONAL
633 Battery Street, #450
San Francisco, California 94111
Susan Mead, Manager, Communications Services

Description of Operation: An ISU franchise provides a select group of insurance independents with the marketing rights which arise from the strengths and resources of size and industry awareness. It entitles these independent agents to access exclusive insurance products, programs, systems, and company relations.

Number of Franchisees: 465 throughout the United States.

In Business Since: 1979

Equity Capital Needed: Initial franchise fee of $3,000/monthly service fee of $300.

Training Provided: Formal classroom traning, on premises training in the exclusive ISU/1084 Sales and Marketing System.

Managerial Assistance Available: ISU provides continual management and technical support through the use of a toll-free number. Complete manual of operations is provided. Regional managers are available to work closely with franchisees. ISU organizes regional meetings and yearly national management conferences.

Information Submitted: August 1987

PRIDEMARK CORPORATION
23002 Lake Center Drive
Suite 100
Lake Forest, California 92630
Wayne R. Weld, President

Description of Operation: Franchising independent insurance agencies. Thru the company's distribution system of regional offices, services are delivered to franchisees in the areas of: management, internal operations, sales, programs and products and image.

Number of Franchisees: 190 in 8 States and Washington, D.C.

In Business Since: 1981

Equity Capital Needed: $5,000

Financial Assistance Available: None

Training Provided: Management training/sales training/staff training are provided continuously at the Regional Institute of Insurance.

Managerial Assistance Available: Sales seminars in area of commercial lines and personal lines of insurance. Complete manuals of operations are provided. Regional personnel work closely with franchisees and consult with agent in his agency to assist in solving problems.

Information Submitted: August 1987

SYSTEMS VII
14110 East Firestone Boulevard
P. O. Box 2117
Santa Fe Springs, California 90670
Pat W. Mazzotta, President

Description of Operation: Systems VII is a franchise company establishing a network of independently owned and operated insurance agencies. The franchise is directed to the development of the new local neighborhood insurance agency; that has a uniform image; mass media advertising; recruiting; training and ongoing insurance education. Also, providing a referral system, centralized purchasing sources; assistance with insurance company appointments and insurance programs.

Number of Franchisees: 192 in California—and nationally throughout the United States.

In Business Since: 1980

Equity Capital Needed: Franchise fee is $799. Additional cost based on office size.

Financial Assistance Available: Local financing where applicable.

Training Provided: Initial 3 day "orientation" seminar. Constant training for the agent and broker. Programs designed to make the NEW agent productive as soon as possible. This is followed up with workshops, periodic sales rallies and ongoing sales training programs.

Managerial Assistance Available: In additional to providing complete standards, procedures, operations and tradename manuals to all franchisees, Systems VII corporate staff makes field visits providing evaluations, assistance, progress reports, on a continuing basis.

Information Submitted: August 1987

LAUNDRIES, DRY CLEANING-SERVICES

A CLEANER WORLD
ACW MANAGEMENT CORP.
2334 English Road
High Point, North Carolina 27260
Ray W. Edwards, President

Description of Operation: Dry cleaning and shirt laundry featuring drive around service. Selling franchises in the State of North Carolina only.

Number of Franchisees: 29 franchised and 16 company-owned stores in North Carolina, Virginia, Tennessee and Georgia.

In Business Since: 1961

Equity Capital Needed: $50,000

Financial Assistance Available: None

Training Provided: All necessary training provided at a company-owned store.

Managerial Assistance Available: Continuous managerial and purchasing assistance provided. Also complete equipment and maintenance department provided for franchisees.

Information Submitted: June 19876

BRUCK DISTRIBUTING COMPANY, INC.
9291 Arlete Avenue
Arleta, California 91331
Julius Bruck, President

Description of Operation: Eldon Drapery Drycleaning Franchisees: Servicing draperies for both commercial and residential building. Forty percent of business done under name of major department stores.

Number of Franchisees: 45 in 18 States

In Business Since: 1966

Equity Capital Needed: $50,000 to $100,000

Financial Assistance Available: None

Training Provided: Complete production, installation, sales and office procedures. First portion in our training facility. Second portion in franchisee's. We train for as long as franchisee feels is needed.

Managerial Assistance Available: Ongoing program.

Information Submitted: May 1987

CACHE CLEANERS INTERNATIONAL, INC.
1333 West 120th Avenue
One Park Center
Suite 304
Denver, Colorado 80234
Chuck Yerbic

Description of Operation: Discount drycleaning using the tried and true retail concept of high volume, low price and efficient operation. Cache Cleaners strategy is based on two principles: 1. Discount pricing that has great public appeal resulting in large volume sales, 2. State of the art, high tech drycleaning equipment that provides quality cleaning, low operating costs and high employee efficiency.

Number of Franchisees: 6 in Colorado

In Business Since: 1985

Equity Capital Needed: $30,000-$60,000

Financial Assistance Available: Will assist in locating finance sources.

Training Provided: 1 week on-the-job training. 1 day home office business procedures and systems.

Managerial Assistance Available: Operations manual provided. Coordinator of franchise development available in area of franchises. Ongoing assistance all phases of business operation.

Information Submitted: May 1987

* CLEAN 'N' PRESS FRANCHISE, INC.
8020 North 35th Avenue
Phoenix, Arizona 85051-9981
Robert J. Gottschalk

Description of Operation: The fundamental components defined operations as follows: (1) dramatic discount pricing policies (generally 60-70 percent below market); (2) multi unit structure (each franchise begins with 3 locations, including a plant, with an option for a fourth) this allows for rapid volume build-up and immediate visibility in the community, (3) the productive capability to successfully process garments in a quantitative and qualitative manner. All services are offered from clean, fresh, eye-appealing locations.

Number of Franchisees: 10 affiliate owned locations in Arizona.

In Business Since: 1982

Equity Capital Needed: $75,000 minimum; Total investment—$195,000 to $226,000

Financial Assistance Available: The franchisor offers no financing but will assist with providing sources.

Training Provided: Within our 120 day pre-opening period, we provide 4 weeks of intensive training split between trade skill instruction, a complete orientation to the Clean n' Press operation and business system, and on-site opening training.

Managerial Assistance Available: Within the 120 day pre-opening period, we provide assistance in site selection, leasing, equipment purchasing and installation, tenant improvement, ordering supplies, hiring and training of employees, and the initiation of a unique grand opening promotional and advertising campaign. After grand opening, financial analysis, operational assistance, volume purchasing, periodic field visits, "800" Hot Line connection are all a part of our ongoing support program.

Information Submitted: May 1987

COIT DRAPERY & CARPET CLEANERS, INC.
897 Hinckley Road
Burlingame, California 94010

Description of Operation: Professional maintenance of draperies, window furnishings, carpets, and upholstery.

Number of Franchisees: 60 in 35 States, Canada, Europe and South Africa.

In Business Since: 1963

Equity Capital Needed: Minimum $15,000-$125,000

Financial Assistance Available: Will extend credit to qualified individuals, but encourages outside financing.

Training Provided: Initial training at franchisor's plant in California or Monarch headquarters in Chicago or at Cleanol Services, Toronto, Canada. Additional training at franchisee's plant.

Managerial Assistance Available: Refresher training at regional meetings, manual of operating instructions, continuous managerial and technical assistance, quality control and research and development programs. Regional meetings, bulletins, a house journal, and revisions to the franchise manual are used to disseminate information to franchisees.

Information Submitted: May 1987

• DRYCLEAN-U.S.A., INC.
9200 South Dadeland Boulevard
Penthouse #25
Miami, Florida 33156

Description of Operation: Dryclean-U.S.A. has won many plant design awards in the drycleaning industry, based on efficient planning, first-rate equipment, quality work, inviting and attention-getting decor, personal service, attractive packaging, and creative merchandising.

Number of Franchisees: 116 in the United States

In Business Since: 1975

Equity Capital Needed: $50,000-$85,000

Financial Assistance Available: Assistance in financing from financial institutions.

Training Provided: 4 to 6 weeks intensive training in franchisor's training school, and 2 weeks supervisory training upon the opening of the franchisee's store.

Managerial Assistance Available: Dryclean-U.S.A. provides procedural manuals for operation, sales forms and advertising for all franchises. Periodic visits and/or calls are made to assist in any problems and/or questions, and recommendations are made to help retain the high-quality standards Dyrclean-U.S.A. strives for.

Information Submitted: July 1987

• DUDS 'N SUDS CORPORATION
R.R. 3 West Lincoln Way
P. O. Box B Welch Station
Ames, Iowa 50010
Philip G. Akin

Description of Operation: Self-serve laundry, snack bar, and cleaning services. We call it "Good, Clean, Fun." A full service laundry that is energy efficient and also has a soda fountain that serves pop, coffee and even beer. It also has a big screen TV, pool table and video games. Approximately 3,000 square feet.

Number of Franchisees: 85 in 27 States

In Business Since: 1983

Equity Capital Needed: $60,000 total system price $80,000

Financial Assistance Available: We have a loan guide and loan proposal that we present to financial institutions. We also work with the SBA. Limited financial assistance available. Equipment lease programs.

Training Provided: On-site training in store during the opening. Also a week training prior to opening at Ames, Iowa. Also operations manuals and instructional video tapes are provided.

Managerial Assistance Available: Full promotional and management support, manuals, design and layout of store, all signage, video tapes, financial evaluations, inspections, maintenance program, regional and national franchisor meetings.

Information Submitted: May 1987

GOLDEN TOUCH CLEANERS, INC.
8237 North Kimball Avenue
Skokie, Illinois 60076
David B. Lieberman, President

Description of Operation: Drycleaning plants.

Number of Franchisees: 9 in Illinois

In Business Since: 1985

Equity Capital Needed: $30,000

Financial Assistance Available: No financial assistance provided other than introducing prespective franchisee to banks familiar with our operation.

Training Provided: Comprehensive training in all phases of operation. Training period lasts up to 1 month.

Managerial Assistance Available: Franchisor is available for assistance during the entire franchise period at no cost to franchisee.

Information Submitted: August 1987

HIS AND HERS IRONING SERVICE, INC.
6511 West 94th Terrace
Overland Park, Kansas 66212
Kenneth Mairs, Vice President

Description of Operation: His and Hers Ironing Service, Inc., offers a unique service business specializing in hand ironing and laundry, with virtually no competition. Residential and commercial customers are served through a pick-up and delivery system.

Number of Franchisees: 2 in Kansas and Missouri

In Business Since: 1983

Equity Capital Needed: $20,000 to 425,000 which includes franchise fee of $10,000.

Financial Assistance Available: The total investment listed above includes start-up supplies, security deposits, cash fund, licenses, permits, and training for an exclusive territory. Franchisor offers no financial assistance at this time.

Training Provided: Training for 5 days conducted at the franchisor's home office. This training covers office organization, bookkeeping, routes, methods, and promotion.

Managerial Assistance Available: On-going assistance is available on a continual basis. Special on-site assistance is available upon request.

Information Submitted: May 1987.

LONDON EQUIPMENT COMPANY
2243 Bryn Mawr Avenue
Philadelphia, Pennsylvania 19131
Ronald London, President

Description of Operation: Offering complete professional drycleaning plants and coin laundry stores. All stores are custom designed for maximum efficiency and profitability.

Number of Franchisees: 265 in 6 States and Washington, D.C.

In Business Since: 1963

Equity Capital Needed: $25,000 minimum

Financial Assistance Available: Up to 90 percent financing of equipment thru financial institutions.

Training Provided: In-house training as required, service clinics.

Managerial Assistance Available: Field inspection and assistance in all phases of management on a continuing basis.

Information Submitted: May 1987

• MARTIN FRANCHISES, INC.
2005 Ross Avenue
Cincinnati, Ohio 45212

Description of Operation: National recognized, One Hour Martinizing Drycleaning. Selected stores have shirt laundries and offer alterations.

Number of Franchisees: 1,016

In Business Since: 1949

Equity Capital Needed: Minimum capital—$40,000-$65,000. Total investment—$127,000-$216,000.

Financial Assistance Available: Must arrange own financing but assistance available.

Training Provided: A 7 week mandatory training program is scheduled for the franchisee or his designated employee. The first five weeks of training are scheduled as follows in a regional or national training center: 1 week of orientation; 2 weeks of operations/management classroom and hands-on training; and, 2 weeks of supervised application. The final 2 weeks of the training consists of 2 weeks of implementation in the franchisee's own plant under the supervision of a franchise representative.

Managerial Assistance Available: Supervision and guidance provided by local representative and franchisor.

191

WASH-BOWL, INC.
4101 Southwest 73rd Avenue
Miami, Florida 33155
Ralph F. Geronimo, Sales Manager

Description of Operation: Wash-Bowl, Inc., is an independent factory authorized Maytag Distributor—we procure suitable locations in South Florida for the installation of Maytag Home Coin Op Laundries. Wash-Bowl, Inc., negotiates the lease, provides mechanical plans and blueprints, offers factory trained service technicians. These businesses are all independently owned. They pay no royalties, residuals or percentage fees of any kind. Completely turnkey.

Number of Franchisees: 212 in Florida. Soliciting for Florida only.

In Business Since: 1959

Equity Capital Needed: $40,000-$60,000 for a turnkey operation.

Financial Assistance Available: Financing for approximately 2/3 of the selling price of the equipment is presently available.

Training Provided: Wash-Bowl, Inc., trains our clients re: merchandising, store operations and maintenance. Free subscriptions to trade magazines are provided as well as bookkeeping materials. Expert CPA advice is also available as this business provides an attractive depreciation schedule.

Managerial Assistance Available: Ongoing throughout the life of the business if so desired. We believe we should be available at no charge for consultation. Our clients provide outstanding unsolicited testimonials on our behalf because of our attitude toward them.

Information Submitted: May 1987

LAWN AND GARDEN SUPPLIES/SERVICES

BAREFOOT GRASS LAWN SERVICE, INC.
1018 Proprietors Road
Worthington, Ohio 43085
John E. Dunham, Vice President for Franchising

Description of Operation: Barefoot Grass provides professional granular lawn care to residential and commercial lawns. Fertilizers, weed controls, insect controls and disease controls are applied on a scheduled basis following prescribed programs. Enjoyable outdoor work environment.

Number of Franchisees: 31 in 17 States

In Business Since: 1975

Equity Capital Needed: Minimum $25,000.

Financial Assistance Available: None

Training Provided: Technical agronomic training, sales training and business training are provided. Training is conducted at the franchisee's site or at the franchisor's headquarters in Worthington, Ohio, a Columbus, Ohio suburb. Formal introductory training programs last at least 4 days, with follow-up provided as needed.

Managerial Assistance Available: Barefoot Grass provides continuing management services for the duration of the franchise in such areas as computer services, including customer records; bookkeeping, including accounts receivable, payroll; marketing and advertising; purchasing and inventory control. Operating and technical manuals and updates are provided. Forms and supplies are available. Regional managers are available to work closely with franchisees and visit regularly to assist with problem solving and quality control. Barefoot Grass sponsors meetings of branch and franchise managers to maintain high levels of training and performance.

Information Submitted: May 1987

CHEMLAWN SERVICES CORPORATION
5000 McGinnis Ferry Road
Alpharetta, Georgia 30201
Russell E. Favorite, Vice President, Franchise Division

Description of Operation: ChemLawn has originated and developed, through extensive time and effort, unique programs for providing lawn care service, consisting of periodic applications of fertilization, weed and insect control materials ("Lawn Care Program") and for providing tree and shrub care service, consisting of periodic applications of fertilization, insect and disease control materials ("Tree and Shrub Care Program") through the use of distinctive types of equipment, supplies, ingredients, business techniques and methods, and sales promotion programs.

Number of Franchisees: 62 in 28 States

In Business Since: 1969, franchising since 1977

Equity Capital Needed: $30,000

Financial Assistance Available: None

Training Provided: Business planning, sales, office, service, equipment, safety and agronomic. Field trining progams provided at no extra charge; these include a leader's guide, video tape and student workbook. 4 weeks of training required prior to start-up.

Managerial Assistance Available: Annual technical/agronomic visit and review at location (2 days), annual operations visit and review at location (2 days), annual owners' meeting off location (3 days), annual agronomic training either at or off location (2 days) and annual operations training either at or off location (2 days).

Information Submitted: August 1987

GREEN CARE LAWN SERVICE, INC.
3708 8th Avenue North
Birmingham, Alabama 25222
Ronnie L. Zwiebel, President

Description of Operation: Chemical lawn and shrub care programs for southern and transition zone areas. Program of 4 to 6 applications, depending on grass type, assures year round revenues.

Number of Franchisees: 4 in Alabama

In Business Since: 1973

Equity Capital Needed: $30,000

Financial Assistance Available: Long term financing available on equipment, and short-term on some supplies to qualified buyers.

Training Provided: 2 weeks for 2 persons consisting of classroom and on-the-job training at corporate facilities in Birmingham, Alabama. Includes all technical aspects of lawn and shrub care plus application methods and equipment. Care. All aspects of record keeping is covered at this time, also. A week is spent at franchisee's location to assist with start-up.

Managerial Assistance Available: An operating manual is provided for all franchises. Additionally, seminars are held each year for new technical training. Managers updates are held twice each year to address subjects such as interviewing and hiring, asset management, controlling expenses, etc. Ongoing consultation is available for the term of the agreement.

Information Submitted: June 1987

JOHNSON HYDRO SEEDING CORP.
13751 Travialah Road
Rockville, Maryland 20850

Description of Operation: Johnson Hydro Seeding specializes in installing new lawns for builders and erosion control for developers. This is not a lawn maintenance company.

Number of Franchisees: 4 in Maryland and Virginia

In Business Since: 1964

Equity Capital Needed: Approximately $30,000.

Financial Assistance Available: Total investment $50,000-$85,000. No direct financial assistance available, however bank financing is available to qualified buyers.

Training Provided: "On-the-job" training program is conducted at the home office in Rockville, Maryland. Additional field and management training is provided at franchisee's location on an as needed basis. For those purchasers, seeking a partner, we have a "trainee" program which is producing qualified production managers.

Managerial Assistance Available: Continuous throughout the life of the franchise.

Information Submitted: May 1987

*LAWN DOCTOR INCORPORATED
P. O. Box 512142 Highway #34
Matawan, New Jersey 07747
Ed Reid, National Franchise Sales Director

Description of Operation: Professional automated lawn services.

Number of Franchisees: Over 300 in 27 States.

In Business Since: 1967

Equity Capital Needed: Minimum of $27,500.

Financial Assistance Available:

Training Provided: Extensive 2 week managerial, sales and technical training at the home office. Technical training for each employee at the home office. Weekly workshops. Management seminars.

Managerial Assistance Available: All necessary initial bookkeeping, advertising, and sales promotional materials supplied. Close follow-up after initial training with service representatives available for both telephone and in the field assistance whenever required. Public relations consultation available. Extensive TV advertising campaigns in major markets.

Information Submitted: August 1987

* LAWN SPECIALTIES, INC.
5 North Conahan Drive
Butler Industrial Park
Hazelton, Pennsylvania 18201
Neal A. DeAngelo, President

Description of Operation: Franchisees provide professional lawn care services (fertilizing, week control, insect and disease control), and tree and shrub care services, to residential and commercial accounts. Franchisee should have good public relations skills with preferred agronomic, sales or business background.

Number of Franchisees: 2 in Pennsylvania

In Business Since: 1978

Equity Capital Needed: Franchise fee: $4,000. Total capital requirement: $18,000.

Financial Assistance Available: Financing assistance available to qualified persons.

Training Provided: 1 week initial training at home office/3 days at franchise. Includes advertising, managerial and technical training. Ongoing training programs, monthly newsletters, and field support.

Managerial Assistance Available: See above.

Information Submitted: May 1987

LIQUI-GREEN LAWN CARE CORPORATION
9601 North Allen Road
Peoria, Illinois 61615
B. C. Dailey, President

Description of Operation: Lawn spraying of fertilizer and week control, plus many additives; each one is owner operated, consisting of a new Ford 1-ton truck, mounted with 200 and 500 gallon tank with injectors for special products.

Number of Franchisees: 25 in Illinois, Iowa, Pennsylvania, and Texas.

In Business Since: 1953

Equity Capital Needed: $36,500

Financial Assistance Available: Possible to qualified persons.

Training Provided: Extensive on-the-job training in technique, material handling, sales and advertising.

Managerial Assistance Available: Liqui-Green sponsors two seminars a year to introduce new ideas, products and advertising ideas. Liqui-Green is staffed with turf and tree experts for counsel to all it's franchises.

Information Submitted: August 1987

NITRO-GREEN CORPORATION
P.O. Box M
Fort Collins, Colorado 80522
Roger Albrecht, President

Description of Operation: Lawn fertilizing, week control, insect control, disease control for turf. Tree and shrub care.

Number of Franchisees: 36 in 11 States

In Business Since: 1977

Equity Capital Needed: $25,000

Financial Assistance Available: On equipment only.

Training Provided: 10 days traning and ongoing. Seminars at various times during the year. Monthly newsletters, toll free telephone assistance.

Managerial Assistance Available: Bookkeeping, and related lawn technology.

Information Submitted: May 1987

* SERVICEMASTER LAWN CARE
2300 Warrenville Road
Downers Grove, Illinois 60615
Richard White, Vice President

Description of Operation: Professional lawn care for residential and commercial lawns.

Number of Franchisees: 200 in USA

In Business Since: 1985

Equity Capital Needed: $18,000

Financial Assistance Available: $12,500 financing through ServiceMaster and leasing arrangements.

Training Provided: Technical agronomic, licensing preparation and marketing training is provided during 6 day academy. On-site training at licensee's business is provided through the regional manager and master franchise coordinator.

Managerial Assistance Available: Continuous support is available throughout the franchise agreement. This support is provided through the master franchise coordinator for the area.

Information Submitted: August 1987

* SPRING-GREEN LAWN CARE CORP.
P. O. Box 908
Naperville, Illinois 60566
William R. Fischer, President

Description of Operation: Professional lawn, tree and shrub care service to residential and commercial customers. Spring-Green uses state-of-the-art equipment and techniques in a modern and rapidly growing industry. Extremely high annual customer renewal plus complete marketing programs help franchisee to realize solid growth. Customer programs generally include 4-5 applications per year.

Number of Franchisees: 128 in 18 States

In Business Since: 1977

Equity Capital Needed: Total initial investment of roughly $20,000 plus $8,000 working capital.

Financial Assistance Available: In addition, a national equipment lease program is available. Assistance is provided in obtaining financing through private sources.

Training Provided: 1 week intensive modular training at beginning of franchise operation with ongoing guidance and support. Periodic instructional meetings as well as seminars are provided at various times during the year. Bi-weekly newsletter and toll-free telephone assistance is available to all franchisees.

Managerial Assistance Available: S-G provides managerial and technical assistance to the franchisees on an ongoing basis. Training manuals as well as various publications are provided for each franchise. Field representatives visit each franchisee on a regular basis to provide assistance in an area where the franchisee may need help. Seminars are also held during the year covering such items as cash flow projections, selling skills and technical assistance. S-G also provides assistance in advertising, marketing and business management, using video and other modern training techniques.

Information Submitted: May 1987

SUPER LAWNS, INC.
P. O. Box 34278
Bethesda, Maryland 20817
Ron Miller, General Manager

Description of Operation: Super Lawns offers a modern, profitable, realistic approach to the lawn care service industry. Our automatic methods of applying chemicals and seeds while aerating and rolling lawns is fast, easy and efficient. This method reduces labor costs while generating higher gross daily sales per operator.

Number of Franchisees: 23 in Maryland, New Jersey, Virginia and the District of Columbia.

In Business Since: 1976

Equity Capital Needed: From $33,000 plus operating capital of $5,000.

Financial Assistance Available: Limited financing may be available to qualified persons.

Training Provided: Comprehensive training at the home office, in the field and on-the-job. This training includes advertising methods, business systems and accounting, office procedures, sales, turf management and agronomy and general operations.

Managerial Assistance Available: Constant communication and cooperation by parent company to aid franchisee to become a better business person through understanding of advertising concepts, sales, customer relations, bookkeeping, general operatiions and service industry concepts, quality control, inventory controls, small business management and technical training for as long as required by franchisee. Assistance is only a phone call away.

Information Submitted: May 1987

MAID SERVICES/HOME CLEANING/ PARTY SERVICING

CLASSY MAIDS U.S.A., INC.
722 Acewood Boulevard
Madison, Wisconsin 53714
William K. Olday, President

Description of Operation: Classy maids is a fast growing professional home cleaning service with a proven franchisee training and sales system. Franchise investment includes protected sales territory, classroom type sales marketing, and business training for two people at home office for 1 full week. Also, on-the-job training, and equipment and supplies, a training film for maids, coming is software for accounting and records. Even a franchisee with no business experience can learn to manage our business after completing our training program.

Number of Franchisees: 15.

In Business Since: 1980 and began franchising 1985

Equity Capital Needed: $9,000 to $15,000

Financial Assistance Available: None

Training Provided: Complete managerial and operational training starting with 5 day classroom style program covering all facets of sales promotion, advertising, proven methods of getting customers market study, recruiting profile and know-how, brochures, how to train maids one to one and via film, quality control, accounting and record keeping, tax and license requirements, pricing for competitive edge, plus management training in all facets of runing a well disciplined cleaning company for profits. Regional seminars and meetings in franchisee area. Workshops and managerial help on request.

Managerial Assistance Available: Seminars and workshops put on by management and professionals, telephone for immediate help, updated traaning materials, film type training for new maids, updated programs as developed by franchisor, software availability and consulting services as requested.

Information Submitted: May 1987

DAISY FRESH, INC.
10840 Old Mill Road
Suite 6
Omaha, Nebraska 68154
Louis E. Lomberty, President

Description of Operation: Daisy Fresh offers a professional approach to the home cleaning industry. Our comanies service approach is geared to three areas, quality, professionalism, and personalization. These factors provides a unique and opportunity for growth in this fast moving industry.

Number of Franchisees: 2 plus 1 company-owned in Nebraska, Iowa, Minnesota, New Mexico and Arizona.

In Business Since: 1982

Equity Capital Needed: $8,500 for franchise fee plus $10,000 to $15,000 working capital.

Financial Assistance Available: None.

Training Provided: Daisy Fresh provides an intensive 5 day training course at the home office. This comprehensive training includes, marketing, estimating, cleaning techniques, administrative services and employee relations. This training is mandatory for all franchise owners.

Managerial Assistance Available: Daisy Fresh provides continued support with home office staff available to assist. The company provides ongoing updates to operations, and marketing manuals, newsletters, service bulletins, and seminars.

Information Submitted: May 1987

DAY'S EASE, INC.
473 Charing Cross Drive
Grand Blanc, Michigan 48439
Sally Tartoni
Jeanette Stewart

Description of Operation: A house cleaning service. Four Daisy Girls, insured and bonded, work as a team, cleaning thoroughly a home in less than 2 hours—allowing the lady or the man of the house to have a day of ease.

Number of Franchisees: 3 in Michigan and 1 in Ohio

In Business Since: 1976; active franchising 1986.

Equity Capital Needed: Franchise fee $7,000.

Financial Assistance Available: A total of $15,000 is recommended. the franchise fee includes equipment, cleaning materials, and training. Company does not provide financial assistance at this time.

Training Provided: Complete training in every aspect of this business which usually takes 5 days to 1 week. This is intense and is done at our home office.

Managerial Assistance Available: We, as the franchisor, will always offer our assistance to the franchisee, as we want them to succeed. Complete manuals, forms and directions are provided. We will work closely with all franchisees in order that all Day's Ease companies uphold the highest of standards. Newsletters, operations systems and seminars will be provided on a regular basis.

Information Submitted: August 1987

DIAL-A-MAID
D. M. Coughlin, Inc.
7531/2 Harry L. Drive
Johnson City, New York 13790
Dennis M. Coughlin, President

Description of Operation: Dial-A-Maid was developed and is headed by Dennis M. Coughlin, who offers over 25 years of experience in the cleaning industry. The service includes both regular clientele and special project cleanings. Maids arrive at each location with all necessary equipment and supplies.

Number of Franchisees: 2 in New York

In Business Since: 1983

Equity Capital Needed: $9,500 additional capital required approximately $10,000-$15,000.

Financial Assistance Available: Franchise fee may be financed

Training Provided: 1 week at franchisor headquarters, opening assistance, ongoing assistance, and periodic field visits. Manuals and other training materials provided.

Managerial Assistance Available: Continual managerial support for franchisees. Periodic on site visits by franchisors and 24 hour call line.

Information Submitted: July 1987

DOMESTICAIDE, INC.
8717 W. 110th
Suite 750
Overland Park, Kansas 66210

Description of Operation: DomesticAide is genuinely unique in the housecleaning industry in taking a "big-business" approach to the service. In doing so we have made our service affordable to the customer and very profitable to the franchisee. We spent 7 years developing the program before franchising. The thoroughly systematized management program that has been developed enables us to handle large customer counts and take advantage of mass-media advertising. Available to our franchisees is an individually designed advertising campaign which may include TV, radio, newspaper, and direct mailer. We gear our service towards the rapidly increasing market of working women. We are also successful in replacing the individual maid in the upper income market.

Number of Franchisees: 64 in 15 States

In Business Since: 1976, began franchising in 1984.

Equity Capital Needed: $15,000 to $25,000 approximate total investment.

Financial Assistance Available: Limited.

Training Provided: We provide a 1 week traning session covering all areas of this business with emphasis on crew development and customer communication. Included is a thorough video training program to facilitate the training of your crews.

Managerial Assistance Available: Weekly phone consultation to assist you in successful development of your business. Seminars twice a year, two personal visits to your franchise annually.

Information Submitted: May 1987

MAIDAY SERVICES CORPORATION
620 N. Craycroft Road
Suite 204
Tucson, Arizona 85711
Anthony J. Lehrman, President
Louis Kahn, EVP & Director of Marketing

Description of Operation: Maiday Services Corporation franchisees offer to their customers a private, individualzed maid service. The customer gets the same maid each time. Maids will do chores not done by other services. Besides typical housecleaning chores, maids will do dishes, laundry, polich silverware, iron, grocery shop, do windows, and almost anything the customer desires. Most customers use the service on a regular basis.

Number of Franchisees: 4

In Business Since: Original service started in 1975. Offering franchises since January 1987.

Equity Capital Needed: Our franchise fee is $14,000. This includes computer package and all start-up materials. Additional operating capital is approximately $3,000 to $10,000.

Financial Assistance: Is available to qualified franchisees.

Training Provided: Maiday Services Corporation provides an all-intensive week-long training program which covers all aspects of the operations on a Maiday Services Corporation franchise, plus 2-3 days on-site training at the franchisee's location.

Managerial Assistance: We offer continual and ongoing assistance throughout the franchisee/franchisor relationship to assure our franchisee's success, including computer assistance, all training manuals, recordkeeping systems, marketing tools, and complete support via toll-free telephone.

Information Submitted: May 1987

THE MAIDS INTERNATIONAL
5015 Underwood Avenue
Omaha, Nebraska 68132

Description of Operation: The Maids has developed a unique system of cleaning and marketing maid service as well as household project cleaning. Services are segmented to include 4 household market areas with 40 functions performed in the home. The Maids provides a detailed, well tested system that includes everything you need to know to tap the lucrative home cleaning market. Our thorough program is the only professional one developed by experts in cleaning management. Qualified franchise buyers will be particularly interested in our area development program.

Number of Franchisees: 160 in 31 States and Canada

In Business Since: 1980

Equity Capital Needed: Franchise fee $7,500-$11,500; equipment package $3,500; operating expenses $30,000 to $100,000.

Financial Assistance Available: For multiple offices.

Training Provided: The Maids has developed an extensive training program complete with manuals covering sales, administrative, technical, operations, pricing, advertising and bookkeeping. Each franchisee will be required to complete a period of training at the home office. A one-of-a-kind videotape training system, custom made the The Maids, provides the finest training in the industry.

Managerial Assistance Available: The Maids provide continual management support for the life of the franchise. In depth ongoing services are outlined in the training program. The home office personnel make periodic visits to the field. Regional meetings and annual meetings are also scheduled.

Information Submitted: August 1987

MAIDS-ON-CALL
Suite 328-D2
1401 Johnson Fery Rd.
Marietta, Georgia 30068
Theresa Asano, President

Description of Operation: Maids-On-Call is a unique maid service specializing in residential cleaning with commercial cleaning such as commercial window washing, new home construction cleaning and janitoral as a side line.

Number of Franchisees: 30 units in 6 States

In Business Since: 1978

Equity Capital Needed: $9,500-$15,000 determined by size of territory plus $3,000 start up fee.

Financial Assistance Available: With $10,000 down company will assist franchisees terms of financing dependent of franchisees' financial statement and ability.

Training Provided: 3 weeks training (2 weeks in home office or regional office plus 1 week on-the-job training) also continual ongoing program of instructions. Including work manuals, seminars and in service programs.

Managerial Assistance Available: Provides consultation and supervision in the areas of marketing, hiring, training, cleaning and ongoing operations.

Information Submitted: May 1987

MCMAID, INC.
10 W. Kinzie Street
Chicago, Illinois 60610
Andrew Wright, President

Description of Operation: McMaid offers affordable, efficient residential cleaning services. Our team cleaning concept features uniformed teams of well-trained maids that provide the customer with thorough, highly professional cleaning services.

Number of Franchisees: 4 company-owned units in Illinois, New York and Massachusetts, and one franchise unit in Illinois.

In Business Since: 1975 and franchising since 1986

Equity Capital Needed: Equity capital ranges from $10,000-$30,000 and includes the franchise fee.

Financial Assistance Available: McMaid offers financing for part of the franchise.

Training Provided: Prior to the opening of the franchise business, the franchisor will instruct the franchisee in the total management of the business. This will be accomplished during the 7 day training and continuing support programs.

Managerial Assistance Available: McMaid provides continuing managerial assistance through its confidential operating manual, periodic visits by home office personnel as well as ongoing advisory services in all aspects of the franchise business such as financial controls, marketing techniques, advertising and promotional programs and instruction in maintaining professional standards.

Information Submitted: May 1987

* MERRY MAIDS
11117 Mill Valley Road
Omaha, Nebraska 68154
Dale Peterson, Executive Vice President

Description of Operation: Merry Maids is the largest professional home cleaning service in the nation. With over 400 franchise offices, the company dominates important metropolitan markets. Compared with others, Merry Maids has the strongest business control system, the lowest cost structure on equipment and supplies, the most comprehensive employee recruiting and training tools, highly agressive marketing and PR programs, and an unmatched depth of corporate office management and staff.

Number of Franchisees: 450

In Business Since: 1980

Equity Capital Needed: Affordable $15,500 franchise fee plus $10,000-$15,000 to cover start-up expenses including office furnishings, required IBM computer and video equipment, and working capital.

Financial Assistance Available: None

Training Provided: Comprehensive, all-inclusive 5 day training program at Merry Maids' Omaha training center is included in the franchise fee. Curriculum covers all the necessary procedures, program and tools necessary to develop, manage and operate a successful franchise.

Managerial Assistance Available: No one in the industry provides a greater commitment—and ongoing support—to new and established franchise owners. A network of regional coordinators, a corporate staff and the company's unique "Franchise Buddy System" of established owners all contribute to monitoring, counseling and guiding the growth and success of each Merry Maids franchise operation. Individual support is further enhanced through regional franchise owners' meetings, specialized field siminars and the company's national convention which is annually attended by more than 90 percent of Merry Maids franchise owners.

METRO MAID HOUSEKEEPING SERVICES, INC.
4336 Gorman Avenue
Englewood, Ohio 45322
Glenn S. Harper, President

Description of Operation: Metro Maid provides customers with uniformed and trained "cleaning technicians." Metro Maid service is either programmed light housekeeping by a team. . or individuals meeting specific seasonal or personal cleaning needs of residential customers during normal business hours on a regular basis.

Number of Franchisees: 2 in Ohio and Indiana

In Business Since: 1978

Equity Capital Needed: $15,000-$25,000

Financial Assistance Available: None

Training Provided: Initially, either the franchisee or designated manager is given 3 to 5 days home office training. Whether the investor buys a "single" or "multiple" franchise package or is a "present" or "absentee" owner is not important. Metro Maid wants the people responsible for operations to be well trained and capable. Actual on-the-job cleaning, advertising, promotions, banking, bookkeeping, hiring employee relations, scheduling, and maintenance of equipment and supplies are among the many items to be covered.

Managerial Assistance Available: Follow-up training or simply relearning the basics is available at the home office at any prearranged time at no additional cost to franchisees except living and traveling costs during the life of the franchise. Answers to day-to-day operating problems are as close as the telephone. Periodically, home office personnel will visit each franchise. Initial start-up equipment and supplies furnished.

Information Submitted: May 1987

MINI MAID SERVICES, INC.
1855 Piedmont Road
Suite 100
Marietta, Georgia 30066
Leone Ackerly

Description of Operation: Franchisees contract specific cleaning task for residential clients on a regular basis. Professional team cleaning concept and franchise development program.

Number of Franchisees: 110 territories

In Business Since: 1973—first franchised in 1976.

Equity Capital Needed: $15,000-$20,000

Financial Assistance Available: None

Training Provided: Initial 5 days, then recurrent on an annual basis, quarterly seminars, and in service programs.

Managerial Assistance Available: Ongoing training, consultation, initial equipment, forms, procedures, newsletters and seminars, for operating managers and staff development training. Complete supervisory certification program.

Information Submitted: June 1987

*MOLLY MAID, INC.
707 Wolverine Tower
3001 South State Street
Ann Arbor, Michigan 48104
Frank W. Flack, President

Description of Operation: A team of two uniformed maids arrive in their company car with their own cleaning supplies and equipment at the customer's home and with drill-team precision, dust baseboards, pictures, lampshades, nic-nacs, window sills, furniture, fixtures and vacuum throughout. The kitchen and bathrooms are sanitized, walls are spotcleaned, cabinet fronts and floors professionally washed. The maids are bonded and insured.

Number of Franchisees: 257

In Business Since: Started in Canada in 1978 and licensing in the United States in 1984.

Equity Capital Needed: $14,900

Financial Assistance Available: Yes

Training Provided: Prior to the commencement of the Molly Maid business by the franchisee, the franchisor will provide a 5 day training program guiding through methods, procedures, standards and techniques of the Molly Maid system and in the basic marketing, management and bookkeeping system. Training day starts in the early morning and continues through the evening with lectures, discussions, assignments, and actual hands-on training.

Managerial Assistance Available: The franchisor will from time to time hold training seminars, workshops and conferences concerning sales techniques, cleaning techniques, purchasing, training of personnel, performance standards, advertising and promotion programs and merchandising procedures for the franchisee and the franchisee's managerial staff. Continuing help, guidance and support direct from the home office and in the field through visits by home office-staff and regional mangers as long as the franchisee owns the Molly Maid business is the ongoing responsibility of Molly Maid, Inc.

Information Submitted: May 1987

*SERVICEMASTER RESIDENTIAL AND COMMERCIAL CORPORATION
2300 Warrenville Road
Downers Grove, Illinois 60515
D. V. Horsfall, Vice President

Description of Operation: ServiceMaster Residential and Commercial Corporation, a subsidiary of The ServiceMaster Company, offers franchising in On Location Services, Contract Services and Carpet/Upholstery Services. This encompasses carpet, rug, furniture, smooth-floor surface, housewide cleaning, wall cleaning, disaster restoration and ordor removal in homes and commercial buildings, as well as complete janitorial services.

Number of Franchisees: 3,367 in 50 States and worldwide

In Business Since: 1948

Equity Capital Needed: Initial franchise fee for the On Location franchise is $13,600 including training manuals and aids plus an additional $8,400 for a recommended package of promotional materials, professional equipment, supplies and tools and professional chemicals for a total of $22,000. Initial franchise fee for the Contract Services franchise is $16,500, including manuals and aids plus an additional $8,500 for a recommended package of promotional materials, professional equipment, supplies and tools and professional chemicals for a total of $25,000. Initial franchise fee for the Carpet/Upholstery franchise is $6,000 including training manuals and aids plus an additional $5,700 for a recommended package of professional materials, professional equipment, supplies and tools and professional chemicals for a total of $11,700.

Financial Assistance Available:

Training Provided: Home study course, 2 weeks on-the-job training with established franchisee, 1 day in the field with counselor, 1 week resident training school. Continuous training program provided for all licensees.

Managerial Assistance Available: Managerial assistance is available on a continuous basis, from the company and from the master franchise coordinator of franchisees in the field. The company makes available advertising, sales promotions, formal training laboratory services, regional and international meetings.

Information Submitted: May 1987

*SERVPRO INDUSTRIES, INC.
11357 Pyrites Way
P. O. Box 5001
Rancho Cordova, California 95670
Ted A. Isaacson, President

Description of Operation: Multi profit center franchise offering carpet, furniture and drapery cleaning. Also, fire and flood damage restoration, janitorial and maid services, carpet dyeing, ceiling cleaning and deodorizing services to residential, retail and commercial clientele.

Number of Franchisees: Approximately 640 in 48 States.

In Business Since: 1967

Equity Capital Needed: Approximately $15,000. Breakeven budget projection provided prior to purchase.

Financial Assistance Available: A total investment of $32,000 is necessary. Servpro will finance 60 percent. Cash discount available.

Training Provided: Servpro provides a complete set of training manuals for documentation. Also, 2 weeks on-the-job with a local general trainer. 10 days at the national training classroom and 2-day franchise start-up training in your franchised area. Also, continuous area and regional seminars, and a national convention.

Managerial Assistance Available: Principles of management and principles of success courses. Accounting and cash flow budgeting, sales and sales management. Production management, office procedures, advertising and public relations. Trainers are set up throughout the country to provide ongoing managerial assistance. Monthly newsletter also provided.

Information Submitted: May 1987

WRIGHT-WAY CLEANING SERVICES, INC.
P. O. Box 8654
Tyler, Texas 75711
Wally Schovanec, Marketing Director

Description of Operation: Wright-Way is a truly unique home care service system. We dust, of course, but in addition we shampoo carpeting, clean windows, care for lawns, do maintenance, and more.

Number of Franchisees: 2 in Texas

In Business Since: 1982

Equity Capital Needed: $15,000 to $25,000

Financial Assistance Available: Franchisor will carry on a note up to one-half of the $7,900 franchise fee.

Training Provided: 5 days of intensive training in our corporate headquarters in such diverse areas as sales, marketing, public relations, personnel, scheduling, etc. Time will be spent in the field learning to make quotations, do all types of cleaning, carpet shampooing, window cleaning, etc. An additional 5 days will be spent with the franchisee in his or her operation between 30-90 days following opening. A comprehensive operation manual describes in detail how everything is done at Wright-Way.

Managerial Assistance Available: We have an 800 number oustide of Texas and are on 24 hour call for any help as needed. We will also continue to support the franchise with visits from our training staff when needed or requested.

Information Submitted: May 1987

MAINTENANCE-CLEANING/SANITATION-SERVICES/SUPPLIES

ALL-BRIGHT INDUSTRIES CORPORATION OF AMERICA
488 Parque Drive
Ormond Beach, Florida 32074

Description of Operation: Effective professional method of cleaning commerical kitchen exhaust systems. All-Bright uses automated sealed, heat injected, chemical cleaning.

Number of Franchisees: 3 in Florida and Virginia.

In Business Since: 1975.

Equity Capital Needed: $28,570.

Financial Assistance Available: Total investment is $28,570. All-Bright will help find a lending institution if franchise has good credit. Franchisor has option to arrange own outside financing.

Training Provided: Intensive 14 day mandatory training course is scheduled for all new franchisees; 14 days are conducted at the home office and on-site training under supervision.

Managerial Assistance Available: All-Bright provides continual management service for the life of the franchise in such areas as bookkeeping, advertising, inventory, complete manual of operations forms, and directions are provided. A 24 hour hotline, field managers are available to work closely with franchisees, with visits to franchisees solving all problems. All-Bright will conduct marketing and product research to maintain high All-Bright consumer acceptance.

Information Submitted: August 1987.

AMERICORP
24 Hill Road
Parsippany, New Jersey 07054
Joel Santoro, President

Description of Operation: Commercial and industrial maintenance.

Number of Franchisees: 7 in New Jersey

In Business Since: 1975—franchising since 1980

Equity Capital Needed: $10,000 plus working capital.

Financial Assistance Available: None

Training Provided: Classroom and on-the-job training.

Managerial Assistance Available: Continuous in all operations of the company.

Information Submitted: August 1987

CHEMAN MANUFACTURING CORPORATION
5679 Monroe Street #208
Sylvania, Ohio 43560
J. Morgan Crossland, President

Description of Operation: The name "CHEMAN" is a combination of two words: "CHEmical" and "MANufacturing." They describe the function of CHEMAN frachisees, which is to manufacture a line of nearly 50 of the most popular, fastest selling and highest profit maintenance and industrial products; which include all types of detergents, waxes, floor and carpet cleaners, glass cleaners, degreasers, bowl cleaners etc.

Number of Franchisees: 8 in 4 States and Puerto Rico.

In Business Since: 1978 (Parent company, Crossland Laboratories, Inc., in business since 1944.)

Equity Capital Needed: $26,520 minimum

Financial Assistance Available: A total investment of $52,000 to $60,000 is necessary to open a CHEMAN manufacturing business. However, the parent company will finance 49 percent ofthe total investment on a joint venture arrangement for those who qualify. This permits qualified individuals to get started in this high profit business with an initial investment of only $26,520.

Training Provided: Complete and intensive training is provided in all phases of the business, including the compounding of all products, management, sales and marketing, hiring of personnel, bookkeeping etc. This training includes a manual of operations and is continuous during the life of the agreement in order to keep owners abreast of new developments etc., in order to assure continued success.

Managerial Assistance Available: CHEMAN provides continual assistance in every phase of the business, with advice and personal assistance in developing new business and adding new and/or improved products, together with the development of new or special products for customers. In short, everything is done to assist all CHEMAN operations to meet constantly changing conditions and develop successful, thriving businesses.

Information Submitted: August 1987

CHEM-MARK INTERNATIONAL
635 East Chapman Avenue
P. O. Box 1126
Orange, California 92668
Darol W. Carlson, President

Description of Operation: Market commercial dishwashing machines, glass washing equipment, filtered air cleaners, cleaning and sanitation products for restaurants and institutions.

Number of Franchisees: 89 in 46 States, Canada, Northern Europe and Singapore.

In Business Since: 1959

Equity Capital Needed: $18,000

Financial Assistance Available: None

Training Provided: 1 week in home office, field help in own territory.

Managerial Assistance Available: Continued managerial and technical assistance.

Information Submitted: May 1987

CLEANSERV INDUSTRIES, INC.
3403 10th Street
Suite 810
Riverside, California 92501
Thornton E. Tongue

Description of Operation: Janitorial franchise.

Number of Franchisees: 3 in California

In Business Since: 1986

Equity Capital Needed: $10,000

Financial Assistance Available: Will work with franchisee to obtain direct business.

Training Provided: 1 week comprehensive administrative and work oriented training.

Managerial Assistance Available: Continuous, operations manual.

InformationSubmitted: May 1987

CLENTECH-ACOUSTIC CLEAN
2901 Wayzata Boulevard
Minneapolis, Minnesota 55405

Description of Operation: Franchise is turnkey operation with equipment, training and solutions to clean acoustic tile ceiling. Cleaning is many times superior to painting and only about 25 percent of cost of replacing. (State of the art equipment and techniques.)

Number of Franchisees: There are 109 franchises in the U.S. and foreign countries.

In Business Since: 1976

Equity Capital Needed: $19,700

Financial Assistance Available: Subject to negotiation.

Training Provided: Full and complete training with cleaning techniques, marketing methods and introductory business managing. Clentech-acoustic-clean trade marks.

Managerial Assistance Available: General over sight is given to franchisee as needed, as long as contract is in effect.

Information Submitted: August 1987

* COUSTIC-GLO INTERNATIONAL, INC.
7111 Ohms Lane
Minneapolis, Minnesota 55435
Everett C. Smith, President

Description of Operation: The Coustic-Glo concept offers a unique opportunity for an individual to achieve a high degree of financial independence in a virtually untapped industry. The need for ceiling cleaning is all around you in every structure you enter on a daily basis and as a Coustic-Glo franchisee you will be provided with all the equipment, products, chemicals and training necessary to prosper in this field.

Number of Franchisees: 180 throughout the United States, Canada, and Europe.

In Business Since: 1980

Equity Capital Needed: $9,750 to $25,000 dependent upon area assigned.

Financial Assistance Available: None

Training Provided: Each new franchise is provided with a very intensive 2-3 day training program which takes place in their respective exclusive areas under the direct supervision of an experienced franchisee that is brought in from their area to assist in the establishment of the new franchisees business. Also available to the new franchisee is option of training course provided at home office under direct supervison of home office personnel.

Managerial Assistance Available: The home office of Coustic-Glo International, Inc., provides continual support in all areas of this business, toll free phones are maintained to give direct and constant access to the home office and assistance with field problems, technical questions, etc. Complete test reports on all products are provided with updating as necessary. A very aggressive national advertising campaign is pursued. Local and mats and all product identification provided. Complete manuals, forms, and customer lists are supplied each new franchisee. New national accounts are being added and you will have available to you a field man to assist in your area with questions. Company also sponsers meetings of franchisees and continues to maintain market and research and development departments to find further outlets for its products and services.

Information Submitted: May 1987

HIGHLAND'S MAINTENANCE SYSTEMS
A Division of BELSHIRE INDUSTRIES, INC.
P. O. Box 12073
Portland, Oregon 97212
Steve Shirey, President

Description of Operation: The Highland's Maintenance Systems is a specialized floor maintenance program for supermarkets and other large self-service stores. Highland's reputation for quality among large national and regional chains assists new franchisees in gaining acceptance.

Number of Franchisees: 17 in Washington, Oregon, Idaho, Nevada, California, Arizona and Ohio

In Business Since: 1978, original Highland's Building Maintenance since 1959.

Equity Capital Needed: $10,000 plus approximately $2,000 in working capital. Total investment: $27,000.

Financial Assistance Available: Belshire will finance $17,000 with note.

Training Provided: Initial training at either an ongoing franchise and/or at start-up location. Training at start-up location includes production, administration, sales, and equipment maintenance.

Managerial Assistance Available: Belshire provides ongoing marketing, production and management assistance.

Information Submitted: August 1987

* JANI-KING, INC.
4950 Keller Springs
Suite 190
Dallas, Texas 75248
James Cavanaugh

Description of Operation: World's largest janitorial franchisor. Franchisee's provide professional cleaning programs to commercial and industrial buildings on a long-term contract basis. Franchisees follow proven business plan and benefit from national advertising, excellent references coast-to-coast and support from the industry leader.

Number of Franchisees: 1,100 in the United States and Canada

In Business Since: 1969

Equity Capital Needed: $10,000-$16,500

Financial Assistance Available: A total investment of $10,000 is necessary to start a Jani-King franchise. Jani-King will finance part of the total investment depending on the location desired.

Training Provided: Training is provided for all new franchisees through a designated center. Training is conducted under the supervision of a full-time Jani-King employee.

Managerial Assistance Available: A complete manual of operations, forms and directions are provided for each new franchise. Jani-King also provides continual management service for the life of the franchise. In areas such as contract negotiations, bookkeeping, hiring and training procedures, securing new business and public relations. Regional and service managers are available to work closely with franchisees and visit service locations to provide technical advice and assist in solving problems.

Information Submitted: May 1987

JANI-MASTER
JANI-MASTER INTERNATIONAL, INC.
44 Pine Knoll Drive
Suite B
Greenville, South Carolina 29609
James T. Saxion

Description of Operation: The most professional system for commercial janitorial cleaning. Offering a low cost investment with enormous earning potential. Easy financing. Consistant advertising that provides Top of the Mind Awareness by projecting an image of a professional, high quality modern janitorial service. Rigorous certification and ongoing education help insure Jani-Master owners continued success. Extensive equipment, chemical, promotional and training package included.

Number of Franchisees: 5 in Florida and South Carolina

In Business Since: 1986

Equity Capital Needed: Franchise package 50 percent down, $4,997 financed; 20 percent discount/cash price $7,996.

Financial Assistance Available: 3 options available: 1) cash $7,996; 2) $4,995 down and $4,997 financed over 24 months; and 3) $6,997 cash with heavy equipment (buffer, wet vac).

Training Provided: Intensive 4 day classroom at corporate headquarters (travel & lodging included), followed by 2 weeks territorial (home) training plus monthly progress review visitations. Field seminars, hot line, additional profit centers. Ongoing assistance, newsletter and initial revenue assistance.

Managerial Assistance Available: Same as above.

Information Submitted: May 1987

198

LIEN CHEMICAL COMPANY
501 W. Lake Street
Elmhurst, Illinois 60126
Rick Geu, Vice President

Description of Operation: The Lien Restroom Risk Management System employs original and unique methods for selling and performing a program of continuous infection control in commercial, industrial, retail, and institutional restrooms and for the administration and management of the sale and delivery of such services. Lien's service is performed by a skilled service technician visiting a customer's restrooms at a designated frequency to rejuvenate the quality of the restroom environment and furnish an atmosphere conducive to the health and safety of the restroom user.

Number of Franchisees: 42 franchises in 28 States

In Business Since: 1929

Equity Capital Needed: A minimum of $20,000 which includes a basic $10,000 franchise fee.

Financial Assistance Available: None

Training Provided: Complete training in all facets of franchise operation including management, administration, sales and service. Training includes classroom style, manuals, on-the-job experience, and ongoing consulting assistance. Group training meetings are held periodically on topics essential to successful franchise management.

Managerial Assistance Available: In addition to the above, franchise owner is given assistance during the start-up period of the operation. Ongoing consulting service include sales, service, financial analysis, pricing, compensation, personnel recruiting and selection, routing, and cost-control.

Information Submitted: May 1987

MR. MAINTENANCE
21401 South Norwalk Boulevard
Hawaiian Gardens, California 90716
Philip A. Syphers, President

Description of Operation: ABC Maintenance development Corporation has developed a complete system for providing commercial building maintenance services under the tradename of Mr. Maintenance. The company sales force develops as many customers as is desired by the franchisee. Customers are located in an area chosen by the franchisee. Area sub-franchising rights are avaiable to qualified individuals who wish to sell Mr. Maintenance franchises in selected regions of the country.

Number of Franchisees: 53 plus 13 company-owned units in California.

In Business Since: 1971

Equity Capital Needed: $2,000 to $25,000 (proportional to the $ volume of customers provided)

Financial Assistance Available: Partial financing available.

Training Provided: Complete training is provided which lasts from 3 days to 2 weeks for the service franchisee to 1 month for area sub-franchisors. In either program the training consists of both classroom and field training.

Managerial Assistance Available: The company provides complete ongoing managerial services including computerized bookkeeping systems, billing, collecting, employee referals; technical advice, sales assistance, company supervision and continuous management counciling. Payroll services tax deposit and full computerized accounting services are an available option to the franchisee.

Information Submitted: August 1987

MR. ROOTER CORPORATION
8130 West Reno
Oklahoma City, Oklahoma 73127

Description of Operation: Mr. Rooter has developed improved equipment and marketing materials and techniques in the sewer and drain cleaning business. Each licensee has access to the management skills of generations of master plumbers, the use of five U.S. patent office registered servicemarks and an extensive national advertising program designed to increase business. Mr. Rooter is a step by step integrated business system geared for success.

Number of Franchisees: 47 in 15 States

In Business Since: 1968, incorporated 1970

Equity Capital Needed: Initial license fee $25,000 for area under 500,000 but more than 100,000 population, $50,000 for an area over 500,000 population, and $12,500 for area less than 100,000 population. License fee includes equipment for one or two trucks. Working capital suggested at least $10,000. Dealers are also required to have a white van or truck.

Financial Assistance Available: None by company. Applicants who qualify should be able to finance their equipment and truck at their local bank.

Training Provided: Complete training in sewer and drain cleaning and office procedures and business management is available. Company provides transportation and lodging during training period. Length of training depends on prior experience of new dealer.

Managerial Assistance Available: Mr. Rooter corporation maintains a continuous home office advisory service for the lifetime of the agreement. This includes guidance in both managerial and technical aspects of the business. Dealers may take refresher training at any time at their convenience.

Information Submitted: August 1987

NATIONAL MAINTENANCE CONTRACTORS, INC.
4024—148th Avenue Northeast
Redmond, Washington 98052
Lyle R. Graddon, President

Description of Operation: National Maintenance Contractors is an association of independent janitorial contractors. These contractors purchase their accounts from "NMC" and are supported, for a fee, by "NMC's" administrative services. These services include a guarantee of lost account replacements, bonding, insurance, invoicing, collections, training, etc.

Number of Franchisees: 153 in Washington and Oregon.

In Business Since: 1973

Equity Capital Needed: $1,000 minimum

Financial Assistance Available: Total investment is dependent on the volume of accounts purchased. National Maintenance Contractors will carry one-half of the total investment on a note for 1 year.

Training Provided: Initial on-the-job training is conducted in franchisee's accounts and optional additional training is handled in periodic classroom seminars.

Managerial Assistance Available: National Maintenance handles nearly all administrative services for life of the franchise. National also has additional staff for filling in for illness or vacations in all areas.

Information Submitted: August 1987

OK SERVICES
P. O. Box 3146
Waco, Texas 76707
Jeffry S. Hepple, President

Description of Operation: Subscription home maintenance and repair service including appliances, plumbing, electrical, mechanical, glazing and lock repair. Subscribers are entitled to an unlimited number of calls for a low monthly fee.

Number of Franchisees: 2 in Texas

In Business Since: 1987

Equity Capital Needed: $20,000

Financial Assistance Available: None

Training Provided: 1 week classroom. Regional periodic. Continuous telephone and data link training.

Managerial Assistance Available: Continuous backup and support via toll free telephone and computer data link.

Information Submitted: July 1987

PROTECH RESTORATION, INC.
26 East Cota Street
Santa Barbara, California 93101
Mark Knight, Vice President
Arlen Knight, President

Description of Operation: Protech Restoration franchises deal in insurance disaster restoration. The type of work preformed for insurance companies varies from drying water damage carpets, replacing all types of flooring, paint, fire damage and smoke damage.

Number of Franchisees: 14 in California

In Business Since: 1980

Equity Capital Needed: $20,000

Financial Assistance Available: Protech Restoration can lease or finance to those with a good credit background the necessary equipment and 1 large commercial van. This amount comes close to $30,000.

Training Provided: Franchisee's must train at the company-owned location for a minimum of 3 weeks. Two additional weeks are spent in management training. Training covers operations, marketing, bookkeeping, business planning, and general management.

Managerial Assistance Available: Training programs are always open to existing franchises. And a field representative is sent out to each location when they open to help in marketing strategy. Protech holds quarterly meetings and yearly conventions, designed to be informative and filled with information that will benefit each location.

Information Submitted: August 1987

ROOF-VAC SERVICES, INC.
2143 Morris Avenue
Union, New Jersey 07083
Steven H. Adler, President

Description of Operation: Most commercial, industrial, office and institutional buildings have flat roofs covered with gravel to protect the roofing membranes from the harmful ultra-violet rays of the sun. When these roofs need repair the gravel must be removed by the roofing contractor's personnel using brooms, shovels, wheelbarrows and chutes to convey the gravel from the roof to the ground. That need no longer be true. Our Roof-Vac Service companies, using one trained man and a trailor-mounted power vacuum system designed especially for the purpose, can easily remove 10,000 square feet and more of gravel per day. This provides the roofing contractor with a fixed cost for this phase of the roof repair plus greater productivity and profitability and has made the use of our equipment and personnel very desireable.

Number of Franchisees: 5 with 4 pending in New Jersey, Connecticut, Massachusetts and Florida.

In Business Since: 1977

Equity Capital Needed: The franchisee fee is $25,000. The equipment (power vacuum system) is $75,000. The franchisee should plan to have an additional $25,000 in working capital.

Financial Assistance Available: Yes

Training Provided: Field training and complete instructions on equipment operation are given at New Jersey home office location. Further training at franchisee's location including on-the-job assistance is available at a very nominal cost.

Managerial Assistance Available: Marketing and production consultation, national and local direct-mail advertising, trade show exhibits, etc., will be provided on a continuing basis.

Information Submitted: May 1987

*ROTO-ROOTER CORPORATION
300 Ashworth Road
West Des Moines, Iowa 50265
M. B. McCoy, Vice President, Marketing

Description of Operation: Sewer and drain cleaning service.

Number of Franchisees: 740 in all 50 States

In Business Since: 1935

Equity Capital Needed: $7,000 to $60,000

Financial Assistance Available: None

Training Provided: Training available at home office, but most new franchisees prefer training at an operating franchise near their homes.

Managerial Assistance Available: Continued assistance in all phases of operation through field staff, manuals, bulletins, advertising, etc.

Information Submitted: August 1987

SPARKLE WASH, INC.
26851 Richmond Road
Bedford Heights, Ohio 44146
W. T. Sullivan, President

Description of Operation: Sparkle Wash, Inc., operates and directs successful international network of mobile power cleaning licensees. These individuals, partnerships, and corporations provide power cleaning services for a diverse market, including: truck fleets, mobile and residential homes, commercial, governmental and industrial buildings, industrial and farm machinery, boats, etc. Power cleaning services are provided utilizing the company developed patented mobile cleaning units and marketing programs. Services include: washing, waxing, historical restoration, masonry cleaning and sealing, paint and graffitti removal, etc.

Number of Franchisees: 157 in 49 States, Canada, Japan and Austria.

In Business Since: 1965

Equity Capital Needed: $10,000 minimum initial, $37,000-$55,000 total.

Financial Assistance Available: Various financing plans available through company assisted, GMAC and FMC unit financing plans. Cost includes complete start up package, mobile equipment, van and training program.

Training Provided: Initial training in equipment operation, maintenance, chemicals, marketing and sales provided at company headquarters or regional offices. In field training utilizes licensee's unit and operators. Company representative visits licensees area to conduct training and generate initial accounts.

Managerial Assistance Available: Company provides regular publications containing up to date marketing and technical information. Company also provides computer printouts of truck fleet operators, market surveys, advertising materials, sales and business consultation on general or specific needs. Company provides technical assistance programs and periodic regional and international meetings.

Information Submitted: June 1987

SUPER MANAGEMENT SERVICES
1935 Friendship Drive
El Cajon, California 92020
Thomas Magee, President

Description of Operation: Super Management Services offers a unique service franchise, each franchise is a one call, computer assisted property maintenance management service whose subcontractors perform a variety of janitorial, cleaning, landscaping, painting and maintenance services on industrial, commercial and retail buildings and offices.

Number of Franchisees: 4 in Colorado and Oregon

In Business Since: 1977

Equity Capital Needed: $20,000 minimum

Financial Assistance Available: A total investment of $45,000 to $55,000 is required. An additional $5,000 in working capital is recommended. Super Management may finance a portion of the start up costs

Training Provided: Intensive 1 month mandatory training course for all new franchisees and their personnel. 2-2-1/2 weeks are conducted at the corporate training center followed by 2-2-1/2 weeks of in-field training. Franchisee may obtain return of franchise fee up until the end of the initial phase of training.

Managerial Assistance Available: Super provides continuing consultation, advice, research and development regarding advertising, bookkeeping, operations, pricing, sales, etc. Operations manual and forms are provided. Regional meetings are held.

Information Submitted: May 1987

U.S. ROOTER CORPORATION
17023 Batesville Pike
North Little Rock, Arkansas 72116
Troy L. Ratliff, President

Description of Operation: U.S. Rooter sewer and drain cleaning service franchise offers a set of patented sewer machines, accessories, a copyrighted name and service marks, a protected area, a 5 year contract with option to renew at the end of the 5 year.

Number of Franchisees: 10 in California, Louisiana and Arkansas

In Business Since: 1968

Equity Capital Needed: $3,500 minimum

Financial Assistance Available: A minimum of $3,500 will buy the use of 1 set of machines and accessories. Small monthly payments (on a 5 year contract) both payments based on population or telephone book coverage.

Training Provided: Unless he is already experienced, a franchisee may at his option come to the home office for a minimum of 2 weeks traning or more if desired, or to the nearest franchised area.

Managerial Assistance Available: U.S. Rooter Corporation will provide advise verbal or written on different modes of advertising, how to solicit business, we provide a manual of operation.

Information Submitted: May 1987

VALUE LINE MAINTENANCE SYSTEMS
A Division of WESTERN MAINTENANCE COMPANY
3801 River Drive North
Great Falls, Montana 59401
William D. Blackhall, Vice President

Description of Operation: Value Line Maintenance Systems offers a unique service business, specializing in flexible cleaning programs for supermarkets, large retail outlets and other type facilities. Franchise areas are protected within the Value Line operations.

Number of Franchisees: 68 in 18 States

In Business Since: 1959, franchising since 1982

Equity Capital Needed: $23,000 minimum

Financial Assistance Available: A total minimum investment of $42,200, consisting of $25,000 franchise fee, $8,800 equipment, $3,000 inventory, $5,400 working capital and miscellaneous is required. A minimum down payment of $13,000 for franchise fee, plus $10,000 certifiable investment capital, is required. Financing arrangements are available for $12,000 of the franchise fee, and equipment purchases. The inventory can be financed on a 30-60-90-day interest free payment plan.

Training Provided: An intensive 5 day mandatory training course is scheduled for all new franchisees, at the home office. An additional 14 days training is provided in the field, on-site at the franchisees contracts.

Managerial Assistance Available: Value Line provides continuing management and technical assistance as required for the life of the franchise. An operating guide, employee handbooks, video training tape and many other management aids are provided. Regional marketing representatives are available to assist in marketing and problem solving. Value Line also conducts national and regional marketing and product research. The MASCO Sales Division provides supplies and equipment at specially reduced prices.

Information Submitted: May 1987

*WASH ON WHEELS INDOOR
5401 South Bryant Avenue
Sanford, Florida 32771
Robin Keeley

Description of Operation: Clean acoustical tile/vinyl/painted ceilings and walls.

Number of Franchisees: 14 nationwide

In Business Since: 1986

Equity Capital Needed: $7,500

Financial Assistance Available: Financial assistance available to those with good credit.

Training Provided: 5 days intensive training, then ongoing. Manuals, seminars, newsletters, hot lines and direct mail.

Managerial Assistance Available: Ongoing

Information Submitted: May 1987

*WASH ON WHEELS—WOW
5401 South Bryant Avenue
Sanford, Florida 32771
George Louser

Description of Operation: Mobile power cleaning franchise providing cleaning services for a diverse market, including government, industrial, commercial buildings, residential homes and more.

Number of Franchisees: 44 nationwide

In Business Since: 1965, franchising since 1987

Equity Capital Needed: $7,495 to $30,495

Financial Assistance Available: Financial assistance to qualified persons with good credit.

Training Provided: 5 days intensive training, then ongoing. Manuals, seminars, newsletters, hot lines, and direct mail.

Managerial Assistance Available: Ongoing

Information Submitted: May 1987

WESTERN VINYL REPAIR, INC.
3000 South Jamaica Court
Suite 225
Aurora, Colorado 80014
William E. Gabbard, President

Description of Operation: Specializing in repairing, cleaning and redying of vinyl, naughahyde, leather, utilizing technicians and salespersons for total operation. Dash repair and dash covers included. Optional training: pinstripping, bodyside moldings, wheel well and dooredge guards. All vinyl repairs guaranteed with lifetime warranty. National accounts established. Franchise fee includes supplies and equipment.

Number of Franchisees: Over 100 throughout the United States.

In Business Since: 1980

Equity Capital Needed: $13,500 to $40,000

Financial Assistance Available: None

Training Provided: Comprehensive training provided at company headquarters in Denver, Colorado and assistance in sales openings at location of franchise. Technical, managerial, accounting all provided. A-Z package. Continual services provided, systems manuals, trouble-shooting, ordering hotline of chemicals and products.

Managerial Assistance Available: Continual services provided. Advertising, national accounts, and sales training. Technical product knowledge, accounting systems, W.V.R. systems manual, troubleshooting, toll-free number for the assistance and ordering of chemicals and products.

Information Submitted: July 1987

WEST SANITATION SERVICES, INC.
25100 South Normandie Avenue
Harbor City, California 90710
G. M. Emery, President

Description of Operation: Route sanitation service people.

Number of Franchisees: 25 in 8 States

In Business Since: Franchise operations since 1978—wholly owned subsidiary of West Chemical Products Inc., formed in 1882 up to August 1984 when the subsidiary was sold to present owners.

Equity Capital Needed: $9,600 (maximum)

Financial Assistance Available: Franchisor will finance approximately 80 percent of total cost, except inventory and supplies.

Training Provided: Full operational training on-the-job including accounting, administration, customer relations, etc.—1 to 2 weeks duration.

Managerial Assistance Available: Continuous

Information Submitted: May 1987

HOTELS, MOTELS

AMERICA'S BEST INNS, INC.
1205 Skyline Drive
R.R. #3, Box 1719
Marion, Illinois 62959-7719
Robert N. Brewer, President

Description of Operation: For the establishment, construction, equipping and operation of a high grade economy motel concept.

Number of Franchisees: 25 Inns in Missouri; Oklahoma, Illinois, Kentucky, Texas and Florida including company-owned.

In Business Since: 1982

Equity Capital Needed: In addition to an initial franchise fee, the franchisee's investment will consist of the cost of the land, buildings, furniture, fixtures, equipment and inventory to conduct the business.

Financial Assistance Available: The franchisor does not intend to offer nor provide any financing arrangements directly or indirectly itself or through any affiliated company or agent.

Training Provided: Prior to opening—evaluation and approval of site, specification for existing Best Inns, cost estimates, training of key employees, provide operations manual and employee handbooks, furnish projections, during operations— provide a person on premises for 1 week/semi-annual inspections, recommendations on purchasing, copy of necessary forms and provide Best Inns approved credit list.

Managerial Assistance Available: See above.

Information Submitted: May 1987

AmericInn INTERNATIONAL
1501 Northway Drive
P. O. Box 1595
St. Cloud, Minnesota 56302
James J. Graves, President
Rodney L. Lindquist, Director of Marketing

Description of Operation: AmericInn International offers a refreshing, warm contemporary concept to the moderately priced luxury budget motel industry. The primary market of the AmericInns has been the travelling commercial guest. With that in mind, AmericInns have tried to present a very upscale, yet comfortable image. AmericInn has a goal of providing moderately priced rooms, yet top quality construction and furnishings.

Number of Franchisees: 14 in Arizona, Illinois, Iowa, Minnesota, and Wisconsin

In Business Since: 1984

Equity Capital Needed: Approximately $250,000.

Financial Assistance Available: Will assist in compiling a loan application. No direct financial assistance is available.

Training Provided: A 1 to 2 week training period is provided.

Managerial Assistance Available: Ongoing communication via newsletters and workshops.

Information Submitted: May 1987

CLUBHOUSE INNS OF AMERICA, INC.
1080 East Central
Suite 110
Wichita, Kansas 67206
William M. Teich, President

Description of Operation: High quality, garden-style hotel with a "club-like" atmosphere. Included in the room rate is a complimentary, full hot breakfast, plus two hours of complimentary cocktails each evening. 120 to 150 rooms, this is a "cookie cutter type" development and is particularly well-known for the warmth between guests and hotel staff.

Number of Franchisees: 12 in 7 states.

In Business Since: 1983

Equity Capital Needed: Approximately 20 percent of construction cost.

Financial Assistance Available: Franchisor will be happy to point out potential financial sources, but will not do the financing itself.

Training Provided: 2 weeks training at ClubHouse Inns' home office, on-site training by ClubHouse Inns of America to basic staff, and ongoing training for all three key employees each year.

Managerial Assistance Available: Quarterly visits and inspections of the property, problem-solving, continuing training as stated above. Full set of operations manuals, ongoing assistance by request.

Information Submitted: June 1987

*COMPRI HOTEL SYSTEMS, INC.
6225 North 24th Street
Suite 200
Phoenix, Arizona 85016
Kevin W. Holt

Description of Operation: The Compri Hotels is a unique mid-price hotel concept featuring an airline-style club room, four-star quality facilities and a complimentary breakfast and complimentary cocktail reception. The hotels typically range between 150-225 rooms.

Number of Franchisees: 15 in 10 States

In Business Since: 1984

Equity Capital Needed: $2,000,000-$5,000,000

Financial Assistance Available: None

Training Provided: Comprehensive training program relating to operating the hotel pursuant to the Compri System standards.

Managerial Assistance Available: Management and technical services provided.

Information Submitted: May 1987

*DAYS INNS OF AMERICA, INC.
2751 Buford Highway, Northeast
Atlanta, Georgia 30324

Description of Operation: Days Inns of America, Inc., is the operator and franchisor of 550 hotels and motels linked by a toll-free computerized reservation system throughout 46 States and Canada. Profit centers include Inns, Lodges (family suites), restaurants, and lounges.

Number of Franchisees: 500 open in 46 states and Canada plus 46 company-owned.

In Business Since: 1970

Equity Capital Needed: Land (approximately 1 acre) over $500,000.

Financial Assistance Available: Will assist in preparation of loan applications.

Training Provided: Management training—classroom as well as on-the-job training formalized programs; also handbooks and manuals.

Managerial Assistance Available: Continual consulting privileges with franchisor's executives. Semi-annual franchise meetings. Franchisor will help franchie owners find qualified operating managers. Quarterly quality assurance visitations.

Information Submitted: May 1987

*ECONO LODGES OF AMERICA, INC.
6135 Park Road, Suite 200
Charlotte, North Carolina 28210
Robert N. Weller, President
Clarence Johnson, Senior Vice President, Franchise Development
Corinne Simmons, Senior Vice President, Franchise Services

Description of Operation: National owner and/or management operator, international franchisor and supplier of Econo Lodges. (Budget and full service budget hotels and motels.)

Number of Franchisees: Over 400 licensed or owned in 35 States (operational) and Washington, D.C.

In Business Since: 1967

Equity Capital Needed: (a) New construction—one-fourth of total capital investment (could possibly be paid for or with leased subordination land). (b) on conversion of an existing property the equity would be nothing.

Financial Assistance Available: None directly. Indirectly we help obtain mortgage financing. Also have mass purchasing savings to franchisee on furniture and supplies.

Training Provided: Bookkeeping system, site selection, analyization, economics of housekeeping and maintenance, motel inspection periodically by regional operations directors; owner orientation; advertising, marketing and public relations expertise. Will also furnish complete management package if desired. Training provided for owner/managers or managers.

Managerial Assistance Available: Bookkeeping system, site selection, analyzation, economics of housekeeping and maintenance, motel inspection periodically by regional operations directors; owner orientation; advertising, marketing and public relations expertise. Will also furnish complete management package if desired. Training provided for owner/managers of managers.

Information Submitted: June 1987

FAMILY INNS OF AMERICA, INC.
P. O. Box 10
Pigeon Forge, Tennessee 37863
Kenneth M. Seaton, President

Description of Operation: Motels with optional food and beverage facilities. Specializing in delux budget accommodations.

Number of Franchisees: 30 in 8 States

In Business Since: 1971

Equity Capital Needed: Between $100,000 and $250,000 depending upon size desired. One to two acres.

Financial Assistance Available: Feasibility studies, plans, guidance and counseling with financial institutions, national contracts for lower construction cost. Investment opportunities thru limited partnerships.

Training Provided: Complete training covering all phases of motel business, room renting, restaurant and lounge set up and planning as long as needed.

Managerial Assistance Available: Guidance and counseling on company policies, complete audit and accounting forms. Complete insepctions by company, annual meetings and other help will be given at any time. Toll free reservation system, national sales force to increase occupancy.

Information Submitted: August 1987

FORTE HOTELS INTERNATIONAL, INC.
1973 Friendship Drive
El Cajon, California 92090
Jere M. Hooper, Vice Preident

Description of Operations: Motor hotels with full facilities and motels.

Number of Franchisees: 180 in 45 States and worldwide.

In Business Since: 1947

Equity Capital Needed: $500,000 to $1,000,000.

Financial Assistance Available: Will assist franchisee in finding funds.

Training Provided: 1 week training at home office.

Managerial Assistance Available: Area meetings and seminars are held periodically. Quarterly inspections are standard procedure. Franchise services personnel also render assistance and coordination.

Information Submitted: May 1987

* FRIENDSHIP INNS INTERNATIONAL, INC.
2627 Paterson Plank Rd.
North Bergen, N.J. 07047
Al Olshan, President
Gary Turner, Vice President

Description of Operation: Hotel and motel franchising throughout the U. S., Canada and Latin America.

Number of Franchisees: 131 in all 50 states.

In Business Since: 1961

Equity Capital Needed: N/A

Financial Assistance Available: None

Training Provided: 5 training seminars—2 days

Managerial Assistance Available: Consulting available in all aspects of hotel-motel industry.

Information Submitted: May 1987

* HAMPTON INN HOTEL DIVISION
HOLIDAY INNS, INC.
6799 Great Oaks Road
Suite 100
Memphis, Tennessee 38138
Ray E. Schultz, President

Description of Operation: Hotels.

Number of Franchisees: 108 franchise groups in 35 States, 176 approved projects.

In Business Since: 1983

Equity Capital Needed: $300,000 to $1,500,000.

Financial Assistance Available: No direct assistance. Lender referrals are made upon request.

Training Provided: Mandatory general manager's training program. Optional department head training.

Managerial Assistance Available: Hampton Inn division does not offer direct managerial assistance but does make available consultation and advise in connection with operation, facilities and marketing.

Information Submitted: May 1987

HA'PENNY INNS OF AMERICA
630 South Glassell
Orange, California 92666
Joseph T. Mazzola, Franchise Director

Description of Operation: Franchising economy extended stay motels.

Number of Franchisees: 2 in California

In Business Since: 1986

Equity Capital Needed: Conversion 60 rooms, $37,000 to $147,000/new development 120 rooms $3,101,000 to $5,832,000.

Financial Assistance Available: None

Training Provided: 2 weeks initially

Managerial Assistance Available: Assistance on an ongoing basis throughout length of contract.

Information Submitted: May 1987

* HILTON INNS, INC.
9336 Santa Monica Boulevard
Beverly Hills, California 90210
Lloyd S. Farwell, Executive Vice President

Description of Operation: Subsidiary of Hilton Hotels Corporation for the purpose of franchising hotel properties within the United States.

Number of Franchisees: Over 225 in 44 States

In Business Since: 1965

Equity Capital Needed: 20 percent of cost for land, building and furnishings.

Financial Assistance Available: Referral to lendors who franchise lodging facilities.

Training Provided: Pre-opening training of management and department heads.

Managerial Assistance Available: Quarterly on-site reviews of operation—ongoing communications between regional office and franchise.

Information Submitted: May 1985

* HOLIDAY INNS, INC.
3796 Lamar Avenue
Memphis, Tennessee 38195
David B. Jones, Senior Vice President, System Division,
Hotel Group

Description of Operation: Hotels and restaurants.

Number of Franchisees: Over 1,422 franchises worldwide plus 206 company-owned.

In Business Since: 1954

Equity Capital Needed: Varies depending on the size of the project.

Financial Assistance Available: None—direct consultation available.

Training Provided: 3 week course at HOliday Inn University and periodic training seminars.

Managerial Assistance Available: Continuing guidance as needed. Franchise district director assistance program.

Information Submitted: May 1987

MASTER HOSTS INNS
c/o HOSPITALITY INTERNATIONAL, INC.
1152 Spring Street, Suite A
Atlanta, Georgia 30309
Richard H. Rogers, President

Description of Operation: Franchising and operation of motels for Master Hosts Inns.

Number of Franchisees: 27

In Business Since: 1969

Equity Capital Needed: 30 percent of total cost.

Financial Assistance Available: Assistance is rendered in preparation of mortgage package and introduction to financial institutions.

Training Provided: Field training assistance, management orientation/training given at home office in Atlanta.

Managerial Assistance Available: Management company for the purpose of managing franchised motels.

Information Submitted: May 1987

MIDWAY HOSPITALITY CORPORATION
1025 South Moorland Road
Brookfield, Wisconsin 53005
Peyton A. Muehlmeier, President

Description of Operation: Franchise affiliate of Midway Motor Lodges, et al, operators of motor lodges, restaurants and showroom lounges.

Number of Franchisees: 7 in Indiana, Iowa, Michigan, Minnesota, Missouri and Wisconsin.

In Business Since: 1963

Equity Capital Needed: 20 to 30 percent of cost of the project.

Financial Assistance Available: Assistance in preparation of mortgage application.

Training Provided: The franchisee's general manager is required to be trained at another Midway Motor Lodge prior to property opening. A continuing education program for lodge management personnel is provided to the franchisee at cost.

Managerial Assistance Available: Operations and construction standards manuals, an institutional advertising program and a reservation system are provided. Property inspections and on-site consultations are made to insure that quality standards are maintained and operating procedures followed. Complete management and accounting services may be contracted separately with affiliated companies.

Information Submitted: June 1987

PRIME RATE, INC.
3335 West St. Germain
Box 1228
St. Cloud, Minnesota 56301
Merlyn Jerzak, Vice President

Description of Operation: Moderate, mid-priced type motels.

Number of Franchisees: 5 in Minnesota, South Dakota, Montana and Wyoming plus 3 company-owned.

In Business Since: 1976

Equity Capital Needed: Approximately $220,000-$750,000.

Financial Assistance Available: Consulting assistance available.

Training Provided: 1 to 2 weeks.

Managerial Assistance Available: Management contracts available.

Information Submitted: August 1987

*COMFORT INNS, QUALITY INNS,
Clarion Hotels & Resorts
QUALITY INNS INTERNATIONAL, INC.
10750 Columbia Pike
Silver Spring, Maryland 20901
Frederick W. Mosser, Senior Vice President, Franchise Development

Description of Operation: Hotels, resorts, motor inns.

Number of Franchisees: Over 1,000 in the U.S., Canada, Mexico, Europe, and Far East.

In Business Since: 1941

Equity Capital Needed: Variable

Financial Assistance Available: Assistance in preparing and presenting mortgage application.

Training Provided: Orientation program for owners or managers prior to property opening. Employee training programs.

Managerial Assistance Available: Complete operations manuals provided. Continuing seminar programs. Sales and marketing workshops. Property inspections and on-site consultations. Complete management contract services capability.

Information Submitted: May 1987

*RAMADA INNS, INC.
3838 East Van Buren Street
Phoenix, Arizona 85008
Attention: Senior Vice President
System Develoment

Description of Operation: Hotels and motels.

Number of Franchisees: 518 in the United States and 574 worldwide.

In Business Since: 1959

Equity Capital Needed: A minimum 35 percent of total gross investment.

Financial Assistance Available: None

Training Provided: Field workshops for hotel managers and department heads. Additional specializing training at the Ramada Management Institute.

Managerial Assistance Available: Continual counseling privileges with licensees and corporate executives. Assistance in marketing and in local level sales, as well as guidance in regional sales and promotion effort. Field personnel are available to work with and assist licensees with on-site operations and development problems.

Information Submitted: May 1987

RED CARPET INN
c/o HOSPITALITY INTERNATIONAL, INC.
1152 Spring Street
Suite A
Atlanta, Georgia 30309
Richard H. Rogers, President

Description of Operation: Franchising and operation of motels for Red Carpet Inn.

Number of Franchisees: 88

In Business Since: 1969

Equity Capital Needed: 30 percent of total cost.

Financial Assistance Available: Assistance is rendered in preparation of mortgage package and introduction to financial institutions.

Training Provided: Field training assistance, management orientation/training given at home office in Atlanta.

Managerial Assistance Available: Management company for the purpose of managing franchised motels.

Information Submitted: May 1987

*THE RESIDENCE INN COMPANY
257 North Broadway
Wichita, Kansas 67202
Jack P. DeBoer, Chairman of the Board

Description of Operation: All-suite hotels featuring sleeping quarters, living rooms, fireplaces, fully-equipped kitchens and breakfast bars, recreational facilities and swimming pools.

Number of Franchisees: 109 in 34 States.

In Business Since: On January 10, 1985 purchased franchise System from Brock Residence Inns, Inc.

Equity Capital Needed: No minimum required.

Financial Assistance Available: Advisory assistance only.

Training Provided: Initial training program of approximately 2 weeks for franchisee's general manager; ongoing conferences and seminars.

Managerial Assistance Available: Coordinate plans, designs, and layouts for the hotel; provide reservation system; administer a marketing and advertising program; conduct quality evaluation services; provide advisory and consultation assistance in management and operations; publish location directories.

Information Submitted: May 1987

SCOTTISH INNS
c/o HOSPITALITY INTERNATIONAL, INC.
1152 Spring Street
Suite A
Atlanta, Georgia 30309
Richard M. Rogers, President

Description of Operation: Franchising and operation of motels for Scottish Inns.

Number of Franchisees: 97

In Business Since: 1973

Equity Capital Needed: 30 percent of total cost.

Financial Assistance Available: Assistance is rendered in preparation of mortgage package and introduction to financial institutions.

Training Provided: Field training assistance, management orientation/training given at home office in Atlanta.

Managerial Assistance Available: Management company for the purpose of managing franchised motels.

Information Submitted: May 1987

★SHERATON INNS, INC.
Sixty State Street
Boston, Massachusetts 02109
Michael F. Bloomer, Executive Vice President

Description of Operation: Franchising subsidiary of The Sheraton Corporation Inc., is a system of hotels and inns worldwide.

Number of Franchisees: 312 in operation in 43 States and 30 in operation in 13 other countries.

In Business Since: 1962

Equity Capital Needed: Approximately 20 to 30 percent of total cost.

Financial Assistance Available: Will assist in preparing mortgage presentation.

Training Provided: Seminars are periodically scheduled around the country and are open to both new and existing franchisees.

Managerial Assistance Available: Professional management assistance by regional directors of operation: various manuals; sales; advertising and marketing guidance; inspections, regional and national meetings.

Information Submitted: May 1987

★SUPER 8 MOTELS, INC.
1910 8th Avenue, NE
Aberdeen, South Dakota 57402-4090
Loren Steele, President

Description of Operation: Super 8 Motels, Inc., is a franchisor of "Economy Motels" which offer a full size room with free color TV, direct dial phones and attractive decor.

Number of Franchisees: 414 in 41 States and Canada

In Business Since: 1972

Equity Capital Needed: $100,000 to $400,000 depending upon size of motel and arrangements with lender.

Financial Assistance Available: Will assist franchisee in seeking mortgage financing.

Training Provided: Complete management training program is provided, including training films, classroom study, examinations, and on-the-job training.

Managerial Assistance Available: Day-to-day managerial, advertising and accounting services provided. Complete front office procedures and accounting systems are included.

Information Submitted: May 1987

TOURWAY INNS OF AMERICA, INC.
P. O. Box 2057
2230 Chisholm Road
Florence, Alabama 35630
Roy S. Graves, Vice President, Franchise Division

Description of Operation: Hotel/motel.

Number of Franchisees: 5 company-owned

In Business Since: 1964

Equity Capital Needed: $200,000-$300,000

Financial Assistance Available: No direct assistance—lender referrals are made upon request.

Training Provided: Mandatory training period for all new franchisees covering all aspects of motel business.

Managerial Assitance Available: Quarterly inspections provided as well as full management contracts. Consultation and advise as on an as needed basis.

Information Submitted: May 1987

TREADWAY INNS CORPORATION
50 Kenney Place
P. O. Box 1912
Saddle Brook, New Jersey 07662-1912

Description of Operation: Charming inns, fun and productive commercial hotels and destination resorts. All with "free-standing type" full food and bar operations.

Number of Franchisees: 4 plus 5 company-owned Inns in 7 States

In Business Since: 1912

Equity Capital Needed: Negotiable.

Financial Assistance Available: Will assist franchisee in locating financing.

Training Provided: Treadway assists franchisee in selection of manager and department heads, who may attend on-the-job training for up to 6 weeks at one or more Treadway Inns.

Managerial Assistance Available: Full service management including turnkey. Food and beverage industry leaders.

Information Submitted: June 1987

WOODFIN SUITES, INC.
110 South Main
Wichita, Kansas 67202
William Vickrey, Senior Executive Vice President

Description of Operation: Woodfin Suites offers an unique all-suite hotel concept. The guest rooms include one to two bedrooms, kitchens and living rooms with fireplace. Suites are fully furnished, including kitchen appliances, televisions, radio, VCR and linens. Common areas include swimming pool and other recreational facilities, a guest laundry room, one or more meeting rooms, guest business center which provides complete secretarial services, and a clubhouse. Typical Woodfin Suites contains 88 to 225 suites with adjacent parking facilities.

Number of Franchisees: 10

In Business Since: 1985

Equity Capital Needed: $500,000 minimum

Financial Assistance Available: None

Training Provided: General training is required for all general managers hired by franchisee. This training will generally be at another operating hotel designated by franchisor and may be conducted in whole or part at franchisor's offices. Franchisor may require that other employees complete such additional training as directed by franchisor in the areas of marketing and sales, front desk operation, accounting and cash control, housekeeping, maintenance, landscaping and purchasing and inventory control.

Managerial Assistance Available: Woodfin Suites provides management assistance in such areas as accounting, marketing and sales, inventory control and purchasing. Policy and procedures manuals, forms and instructions are provided. Qualitiy assurance evaluations are conducted by Woodfin Suites Inc., in order to maintain a high standard of quality.

Information Submitted: June 1987

OPTICAL PRODUCTS/SERVICES

AMERICAN VISION CENTERS, INC.
138-49—78th Avenue
Flushing, New York 11367
Marvin Convissar, Vice President-General Manager

Description of Operation: The Company franchises and operates "American Vision Center" retail stores specializing in the sale of eyeglasses, contact lenses and related optical items. They offer a unique operational system as well as related merchandising and advertising programs. The Company also owns and operates National contact Lens Distributors, Inc., a wholesale supplier of optical products.

Number of Franchisees: 46 plus 25 company-owned.

In Business Since: 1977

Equity Capital Needed: $25,000

Financial Assistance Available: The total investment in an American Vision Center will run from $75,000 to in excess of $100,000 depending upon store size and physical store improvements required. This investment includes a franchise fee of $10,000; approximately $23,000 in optical and lab equipment; approximately $20,000 in inventory with the balance for fixtures and improvements. Company will assist in obtaining outside financing.

Training Provided: An intensive training program is provided by the Company for all of its franchisees and their personnel. Training in sales, internal procedures, management, product knowledge and financial analysis is conducted at its home office and at a Company operated training store. There is no charge for the training program, however all travel and living expenses are paid by the franchisee.

Managerial Assistance Available: The American Vision Center system provides the support, buying power and merchandising expertise of a major optical chain and provides continuing operational assistance and supervision to its franchised stores. A detailed operations manual is proivded and full supervision is available in all areas to work closely with franchisees to solve problems and improve store operations.

Information Submitted: August 1987

AMERICA'S DOCTORS OF OPTOMETRY, INC.
200 South Street
Tracy, Minnesota 56175
Dr. Jack Von Bokern, CEO

Description of Operation: Develop and distribute a marketing program for professional services of members of ADO, Inc.

Number of Franchisees: 36 in 8 States

In Business Since: 1982

Equity Capital Needed: $3,000 for established practitioner.

Financial Assistance Available: None

Training Provided: As needed.

Managerial Assistance Available: As needed.

Information Submitted: August 1987

D.O.C. OPTICS CORPORATION
19800 West Eight Mile Road
Southfield, Michigan 48075
Richard S. Golden, Vice President, Franchise Marketing

Description of Operation: D.O.C. Optics Corporation operates optical centers staffed by licensed optometrists to provide eye examinations and retailing eye glasses, contact lenses and retail accessories. The company also owns and operates 3 optical laboratories where selected frames are drawn from inventory for fabricating.

Number of Franchisees: 100 company-owned units in 8 States and Canada plus 12 franchisees in Michigan and Missouri.

In Business Since: 1961

Equity Capital Needed: None

Financial Assistance Available: There is an initial franchise fee of $7,500. Additional costs vary. Contact company for complete information.

Training Provided: Initial intensive training program of up to 2 weeks prior to opening of an office. It consists of instruction in the operation of a D.O.C. retail optometric center, a detailed explanation of D.O.C. systems, and training in clinic management, accounting, sales and marketing techniques.

Managerial Assistance Available: Marketing, site and lease negotiation assistance; standard plans and specifications for the development of a franchise location; pre-opening promotion and advertising support. detailed operations manuals are provided, as well as, advertising programs for a percentage of sales. Additional support includes laboratory services and merchandise purchasing; annual seminars and optional training programs concerning new products, services, sales and display techniques and guidance related to the proper operation of a D.O.C. clinic.

Information Submitted: August 1987

FIRST OPTOMETRY EYE CARE CENTERS, INC.
31503 Gratiot
P. O. Box 286
Roseville, Michigan 48066
D. M. Borsand, O.D.

Description of Operation: Marketing, advertising, practice management and volume purchasing and participation in industrial eyecare and capture third party eyecare programs (P.P.O.'s), for the professional practicing doctor of optometry.

Number of Franchisees: 35 in Michigan

In Business Since: 1980

Equity Capital Needed: Typical requirements for optometric office.

Financial Assistance Available: Yes

Training Provided: 40 hours at headquarters. Ongoing reinforcement; sales seminars, contact lens, educational, etc.

Managerial Assistance Available: Motivation, in office marketing, para-optometric training, dispensing and sales, contact lens technician training and general management training.

Information Submitted: May 1987

*NUVISION, INC.
2284 South Ballenger Highway
Flint, Michigan 48503
Jonathan Raven, Senior Vice President Sales

Description of Operation: NuVision, Inc., markets prescription eyeware, contact lenses, sunglasses and related optical products and accessories. The company also owns and operates a modern ophthalmic laboratory and distribution facility which provides laboratory services and eyecare products to company-operated and franchised offices. Optometric services are also provided in all locations.

Number of Franchisees: 44 in Michigan and Indiana.

In Business Since: 1956

Equity Capital Needed: Minimum $50,000.

Financial Assistance Available: Financing of the purchase of existing company-owned locations is available in some situations.

Training Provided: Initial training prior to opening an office consists of a 3-day program designed to treach standardized methods of administrative, merchandising and marketing techniques. Ongoing regular training is also provided.

Managerial Assistance Available: Guidance in connection with methods, sales techniques, procedures, management techniques, services and products, purchasing optical and ophthalmic products, formulating and implementing advertising and promotional procedures for the proper operation of a NuVision office.

Information Submitted: May 1987

*PEARLE VISION CENTERS
2534 Royal Lane
Dallas, Texas 75229
William T. Clark, Vice President-Franchising

Description of Operation: Pearle Vision Centers franchises full-service optical retail outlets.

Number of Franchisees: 500 in 40 States

In Business Since: 1962

Equity Capital Needed: $30,000-$60,000

Financial Assistance Available: Franchisor will provide financing.

Training Provided: Franchisee must be a qualified optician or optometrist with a background in optical management. Franchisor will provide a 3 day orientation program in Pearle Center operations plus optional training programs for franchisees' employees.

Managerial Assistance Available: Franchisor will provide ongoing advice and counsel to franchisee on managerial and technical problems related to the running of a Pearle Vision Center. Franchisor provides advertising support program for a percentage of unit sales and provides marketing support, laboratory services (eyeglass fabrication) and merchandise in accordance with a published price list.

Information Submitted: May 1987

*SITE FOR SORE EYES OPTICIANS
100 Hegenberger Road
Oakland, California 94621
Paul Licht, President

Description of Operation: 1 hour eye glasses and contact lenses. Each store is approximately 2,000 square feet with on-site lab facilities providing discount eyewear in 1 hour. Stores open to to 7 days per week depending on location.

Number of Franchisees: 8 in California

In Business Since: 1979

Equity Capital Needed: $225,000

Financial Assistance Available: None—can assist with local banks.

Training Provided: Training provided for store manager, lab technician, sales people and receptionists. Training is 3 weeks continuous. Training conducted at Site for Sore Eyes training facility at company stores under the direction of full-time trainer.

Managerial Assistance Available: Assistance by phone and on-site for management, technical and sales. Continuous phone consultation and on-site as required. Determined by franchisor assistance is available Monday thru Friday 8:30 a.m. to 6:00 p.m. Other hours by special arrangement. Complete manuals for all operational phases included.

Information Submitted: May 1987

* TEXAS STATE OPTICAL (TSO)
2534 Royal Lane
Dallas, Texas 75229
Patrick H. Fitzsimmons, Senior Vice President/Franchising

Description of Operation: The franchisor (TSO) grants the right to qualified licensed optometrists or experienced opticians to operate a high-quality retail optical dispensing office and an associated optometric office under the proprietary service mark (TSO) Texas State Optical and such other trademarks, service marks and trade names as Texas State Optical, Inc., may license. The retail dispensing office will sell prescription eyewear, contact lenses, high-quality frames and accessories as may be approved by Texas State Optical, Inc. The franchisee has the right to certain advertising and marketing techniques, business methods, procedures and other expertise supplied by TSO, collectively the "TSO system." Optometric examinations and services are offered at an optometric office adjacent to the retail dispensing office.

Number of Franchisees: 139 plus 82 associates and 47 company-owned.

In Business Since: 1935

Equity Capital Needed: $25,000 to $40,000 depending on qualifications and location.

Financial Assistance Available: TSO has working arrangements with several banks and lending institutions which will provide up to 90 percent financing to qualified, licensed optometrists or experienced opticians. Average total investment for a turnkey TSO franchise including equipment, furniture, fixtures, inventory, sign and leasehold improvements is approximately $125,000 to $175,000, depending on the location.

Training Provided: Initial start up assistance provided. Optical training programs, including correspondence courses and on-site training are available to franchisee and employees.

Managerial Assistance Available: Area meetings and seminars are held periodically.

Information Submitted: May 1987

PAINT AND DECORATING SUPPLIES

DAVIS PAINT COMPANY
1311 Iron Street
North Kansas City, Missouri 64116
Julius Hammel, Sales Manager

Description of Operation: Retail paint and wallpaper stores. Also handle drapes, picture framing, unfinished furniture, floor coverings and decorative gifts.

Number of Franchisees: 60 in 10 States. Only Midwestern States served.

In Business Since: 1944

Equity Capital Needed: $40,000 to $50,000

Financial Assistance Available: Will assist in locating financing.

Training Provided: Training at franchisor's plant. Field training by factory personnel and regional sales meetings.

Managerial Assistance Available: Complete assistance in-site location, lease arrangements, store layout, advertising, sales promotion, bookkeeping, insurance, and management techniques. Franchisor personnel and field representatives make regular calls.

Information Submitted: August 1987

PET SHOPS

* DOCKTOR PET CENTERS, INC.
355 Middlesex Avenue
Wilmington, Massachusetts 01887
Leslie Charm, ChairmanClyde H. Treffeisen,
Director/Franchise Development

Description of Operation: Retail pets, supplies, and pet accessories in regional shopping malls.

Number of Franchisees: 245 stores in 32 States, 3 company-owned.

In Business Since: 1966

Equity Capital Needed: Approximately $40,000-$60,000.

Financial Assistance Available: Yes, in certain cases.

Training Provided: 3 weeks at franchisor's headquarters, subjects covered include store operations, care and maintenance of pets, accounting management, inventory, personnel selection, merchandising, promotions, advertising, etc.

Managerial Assistance Available: Advise on stocking, fixture arrangement, receipt of livestock, maintenance procedures, and profit control, site selection, lease negotiation, store planning, etc. On-the-site advisor guides franchisee during first 2 weeks of operations. Advertising materials, accounting forms and seasonal signs furnished. Counselors make frequent visits to stores to assist franchisees.

Information Submitted: May 1987

DOG N' CAT PET CENTERS OF AMERICA, INC.
P. O. Box 38282
Denver, Colorado 80238
Steven L. Hintgen, President

Description of Operation: Dog n' Cat Pet Centers are full-line, full-service retail pet stores, featuring pets, and pet supplies. Our state-of-the-art animal enclosures and store design offer a unique odor free shopping environment to our customers.

Number of Franchisees: 9 plus 1 company-owned in 7 States

In Business Since: 1984

Equity Capital Needed: $40,000 to $60,000 depending on location. Total investment including franchise fee $90,000 to $175,000.

Financial Assistance Available: Franchisor will prepare a financial package, and assist in the presentation to various financial sources.

Training Provided: Minimum of 2 weeks (6 days per week) at home office. Additional 1 week in store. Training covers business management, livestock care, products, sales and advertising.

Managerial Assistance Available: Franchisor assists in all areas of retail pet store management. Franchisor provides; all business forms, guarantees, and operations manuals. All ongoing assistance provided by the home office team.

Information Submitted: May 1987

LICK YOUR CHOPS, INC.
299 Main Street
Westport, Connecticut 06880
Susan J. Goldskin, President

Description of Operation: Lick Your Chops is a complete department store for animals specializing in optimum nutrition, care and services for the pet.

Number of Franchisees: 2 in Pennsylvania and Connecticut.

In Business Since: 1979

Equity Capital Needed: $135,000 turnkey/$15,000 licensing fee.

Financial Assistance Available: None

Training Provided: 1 week training in Westport, Connecticut. Specializing in pet nutrition, retailing, public relations and computer training.

Managerial Assistance Available: Continuous

Information Submitted: July 1987

* PETLAND, INC.
195 North Hickory Street
P. O. Box 1606
Chillicothe, Ohio 45601-5606
Edward R. Kunzelman, President
Linda H. Heuring, Director, Franchising/Marketing

Description of Operation: Full-service retail pet stores carrying pets and pet supplies, specializing in innovative pet care, housing, and customer education.

Number of Franchisees: 118 plus 2 company-owned stores in the U.S. and Canada.

In Business Since: 1967

Equity Capital Needed: $40-$60,000 depending on store size and location. Total investment $125,000-$400,000.

Financial Assistance Available: Franchisor will assist in preparation of financial presentation package.

207

Training Provided: Complete classroom at Ohio main office plus in-store training. Additional assistance in-store after opening. Ongoing training on specific topics related to business management, livestock care, product knowledge, advertising, and sales.

Managerial Assistance Available: Assistance in merchandising, livestock management, and maintenance procedures. On-site advisor guides franchisee during first week of operation. Advertising materials and standardized accounting and reporting forms furnished. Areas field supervisors make regular visits and provide assistance in problem areas. Advertising manual, operations manual, counter reference book, all forms for operations provided.

Information Submitted: May 1987

PETS ARE INN, LTD.
12 South 6th Street
Suite 950
Minneapolis, Minnesota 55402
Harry Sanders-Greenberg, President/Franchising Division

Description of Operation: Pets Are Inn, Ltd. (TAI) was developed and established to meet the needs of a great many consumers who have sought alternatives to pet bording in traditional kennels. Utilizing a completely novel approach to pet boarding. PAI has, within the past two years tapped a high, previously untouched market. Growth in this area is astronomical and there is virtually no competition...yet. Purchase of a PAI franchise guarantees the buyer: exclusive sales territory, advertising and marketing assistance, a comprehensive operations manual along with consulting and training seminars.

Number of Franchisees: 9 in 6 States

In Business Since: 1982

Equity Capital Needed: $1,600-$8,000, varies according to population of exclusive territory.

Financial Assistance Available: Limited financing may be available to qualified persons.

Training Provided: Intensive training program at home office in Minneapolis. Includes on-the-job training and in-field placement, classroom training conducted in conjunction with the operations manual, and computer training (all forms and internal paperwork have been computerized).

Managerial Assistance Available: A step by step operations manual is provided to the franchise owner which covers marketing, promotion, advertising, organization, sales and daily operations. Newsletter, ongoing improvements, toll free hot line for immediate assistance all available to no charge for franchise term.

Information Submitted: May 1987

PRINTING

AIC INTERNATIONAL
200 Mouse Mill Road
P. O. Box N-177
Westport, Massachusetts 02790
Arthur Sansoucy, Chairman and CEO

Description of Operation: ACCU Copy Printing Centers.

Number of Franchisees: 4 including company-owned in Massachusetts and Rhode Island.

In Business Since: 1980

Equity Capital Needed: $37,500

Financial Assistance Available: Lease arrangements. SBA loan application assistance and local bank loan application assistance.

Training Provided: 2 week initial training classes. Ongoing assistance for term of agreement.

Managerial Assistance Available: Technical skills, business management skills, financial management skills and promotional and sales skills.

Information Submitted: June 1987

* ALPHAGRAPHICS PRINTSHOPS OF THE FUTURE
Department Y
845 East broadway
Tucson, Arizona 85719
Rodger G. Ford, President

Description of Operation: AlphaGraphics Printshops Of The Future operate Electronic Graphic Centers and Satellite Centers. By taking advantage of advanced technology, we provide quality laser typeset originals, offset printing, high speed duplicating, and binding for professionals and businesses.

Number of Franchisees: 250 in 30 States, plus 6 company stores in Arizona. and 2 in Texas. Also franchising in Canada and Hong Kong.

In Business Since: 1970

Equity Capital Needed: Approximately $66,500 Satellite Center; $85,000-$105,000; Electronic Graphic Center (including working capital).

Financial Assistance Available: Total investment is approximately $188,000 for a Satellite Center and $264,000 for an Electronic Graphic Center, with approximately $125,000 financible for a Satellite Center and $180,000 financible for an Electronic Graphic Center. Alternatively, you may qualify for SBA financing of up to 80 percent of the total investment.

Training Provided: 3 weeks of intensive training is provided at company headquarters in Tucson, Arizona. There is an additional 10 days of on-site training before and after opening. The curriculum includes: LazerGraphics, customer relations, employee relations, equipment operation, planning and budgeting, accounting, marketing and advertising.

Managerial Assistance Available: Ongoing assistance is provided to all franchisees through monthly scheduled visits by field support managers, as well as troubleshooting over our toll-free line, or in person by company executives. National accounts buying plan, monthly merchandising and advertising programs, equipment reviews, up-dated procedures, and annual planning and budgeting are all part of the AlphaGraphics Printshops Of The Future support package.

Information Submitted: May 1987

* AMERICAN SPEEDY PRINTING CENTERS, INC.
Corporate Offices
32100 Telegraph Road, Suite 110
Birmingham, Michigan 48010
Vernon G. Buchanan, President

Description of Operation: American Speedy Printing Centers, Inc., offers franchise owners an outstanding profit potential in the fast growing quick printing industry. A center is set up with all the necessary equipment for offset printing, bindery and photo copying as well as all other accessories needed to operate a successful quick printing center. For additional information call 800-521-4002 (in Michigan 800-482-0421; in Canada 800-544-8405).

Number of Franchisees: Approximately 500 in 37 States.

In Business Since: 1977

Equity Capital Needed: $30,000 minimum cash requirement; financing available to qualified applicants.

Financial Assistance Available: Franchisor will assist the franchisee in financing equipment package either through a 5-year lease purchase or a 5-year bank loan.

Training Provided: Completion of an extensive 4-week training course which includes bookkeeping and reporting system, equipment operation and maintenance, marketing, pricing, work scheduling and management of employees. Franchisor's representative assists franchisee in his or her location during his or her first week of operation.

Managerial Assistance Available: American Speedy Printing Centers provides a continuing support system to all of its franchisees through the home office as well as several regional offices for the life of the franchise agreement. This includes national conventions, conferences and mini-seminars, advertising; management consultation; employment services; negotiation of national contracts for supply and equipment discounts; equipment, maintenance and repair seminars; sales seminars; press and camera services; technical and supply bulletins; monthly newsletter; and continuing research of new equipment and supplies. The home office staff is available for personal assistance and counselling by telephone and in person.

Information Submitted: May 1987

* AMERICAN WHOLESALE THERMOGRAPHERS, INC.
12715 Telege Road
P. O. Box 777
Cypress, Texas 77429
Patricia Paddy, President

Description of Operation: The American Wholesale Thermographers franchise is a business which offers thermographed (raised letter) printing and attendant services, at the wholesale level. The services and products of the American

Wholesale Thermographers Center will be used by retail establishments, such as printers, office supply stores, and stationers who will subsequently offer the product to the general public.

Number of Franchisees: 17 in 12 States; also in Canada.

In Business Since: 1982

Equity Capital Needed: Approximately $40,000 minimum.

Financial Assistance Available: $23,000 of the $38,500 franchise fee may be financed through an 96-month commercial note. Equipment package, approximately $91,000 can be financed through third party leasing companies.

Training Provided: American Wholesale Thermographers training program encompasses 5 weeks. Two weeks of training are conducted at the corporate headquarters in Cypress, Texas, 2 weeks of training at an operating center and 1 additional week of assistance at the franchisee's AWT Center at the time of opening for business.

Managerial Assistance Available: American Wholesale Thermographers provides continual support service in such areas as operations, advertising, sales, and computer support. Complete manuals of operations, forms, and directions are provided. American Wholesale Thermographers may occassionally hold seminars on subjects of interest to franchisees. Monthly newsletters are issued on various promotional techniques, as well as valuable informatoin about management systems and equipment.

Information Submitted: May 1987

* **BUSINESS CARD EXPRESS**
  31500 Northwestern Highway
  Suite 175
  Farmington Hills, Michigan 48018
  C. S. Derry, Executive Vice President

Description of Operation: Business Card Express is building a network of 100 to 150 fully automated and computerized production facilities to serve the needs of the exploding commercial quick printing market (over 70,000 shops nationwide). Only one Business Card Express will be located in each major market area of 500 printers producing only wholesale thermographed (raised ink) business cards and stationery specialties. Our specialized technology, "captive" market, and simplicity of operation have created a high volume business with outstanding growth potential.

Number of Franchisees: 15 in 12 States

In Business Since: 1982

Equity Capital Needed: $100,000

Financial Assistance Available: BCE will assist franchise owners with collatoral loans and equipment financing. Amounts will be determined by franchise owner's needs and credit history.

Training Provided: Intensive 4 weeks of training: computer opeations, sales and marketing, bookkeeping, typesetting, keylining, proofreading, order processing, stat work, purchasing, inventory, on-site training.

Managerial Assistance Available: Site selection and lease negotiations, layout design, coordinated equipment installation, initial supply packages, research and development of new products, ongoing training and seminars, group insurance packages, one week on-site training, technical bulletins and updates, weekly calls through the first 90 days, 90 day marketing and operational plan of action, computer networking for daily information flow, software updates, national contract pricing for equipment and supplies.

Information Submitted: May 1987

BUSINESS CARDS OVERNIGHT
8 East Henshaw Street
Woburn, Massachusetts 01801
Kenneth Hannan, President

Description of Operation: Business Cards Overnight is a wholesale thermographic (raised) printing center. We provide business cards within 24 hours and also do raised printing on stationery and letterheads.

Number of Franchisees: 6 in 5 States

In Business Since: 1980

Equity Capital Needed: $50,000 minimum

Financial Assistance Available: The purchase price of a Business Cards Overnight center is $90,000. An initial $25,000 franchise fee pays for site location, market survey and research, lease negotiation assistance if needed and

training of center personnel by franchisor prior to opening of the center. The franchisor has made arrangements with a leasing company for financing for the equipment package of $65,000. Franchisee mayl·obtain his own outside financing.

Training Provided: Franchisor will provide franchisee and one other person with training and instruction in the operation and promotion of the Center for 5 business days at the home office or other designated site. Also the franchisor will provide an additional 3 weeks (15 business days) training and instruction in the operation of the BCO system and equipment at franchisee's center.

Managerial Assistance Available: Franchisor will provide a continuing assistance program which shall include consulting and assistance by BCO representatives, accounting and marketing assistance, advising the franchisee of new developments and techniques in the thermographic and reproduction industry. In addition franchisor provides a production facility for franchisee to send difficult and/or undersirable work for distributor purposes. Franchisee gets returned completed work for mark-up and resole.

Information Submitted: August 1987

* **BUSINESS CARDS TOMORROW, INC.**
  3000 N.E. 30th Place
  Suite 102
  Fort Lauderdale, Florida 33306
  Joe Seplow, Vice President Franchise Development

Description of Operation: Business Cards Tomorrow, Inc., is an international franchise organization which offers a wholesale business concept by providing a wide range of quality themographic printing for both commercial and retail printers. Unique to the industry is the specialized service operation—24 hour turnaround for business card printing; 5 business days for other thermographic printing. Free pick-up and delivery is provided with all orders.

Number of Franchisees: 89 in 29 States plus 4 in Canada

In Business Since: 1975

Equity Capital Needed: $75,000

Financial Assistance Available: Initial cash investment $50,000 plus working capital. The initial cash investment of which $25,000 is the franchise fee pay for site location and research, market survey and lease negotiation assistance, training, supervision and assistance provided by franchisor for opening of the center, and general sales and administration expenses of franchisor. The franchisor has made arrangements with finance companies for financing of the equipment package which is approximately $110,000. Franchisee may obtain his own outside financing.

Training Provided: A mandatory training program is scheduled prior to any center opening. This training is for 2 weeks and consists of equipment orientation and operation, business management and marketing, sales technique in the thermography industry. In addition, the franchisor will furnish a qualified representative for a period of 10 business days after opening of the center to instruct the franchisee in operation of his center and to aid in the hiring of personnel and to assist in establishing standard procedures.

Managerial Assistance Available: Throughout the term of the agreement, the franchisor shall provide the franchisee with continuous sales, marketing and technical assistance, consultation and advice on operations and procedures, and accounting and administrative guidance. In addition, the franchisor will apprise the franchisee of new developments in the thermographic printing field.

Information Submitted: May 1987

* **FRANKLIN'S COPY SERVICE, INC.**
  135 International Boulevard
  Atlanta, Georgia 30303
  Hal Collins, President

Description of Operation: Full-service quick printing and office supply stores featuring printing, typesetting, high speed copy reproduction and a complete line of office supplies.

Number of Franchisees: 83 stores in Southeastern United States

In Business Since: 1971

Equity Capital Needed: $30,000 to $40,000 which includes working capital.

Financial Assistance Available: Franklin's will assist franchise owner in obtaining bank financing.

Training Provided: 3 weeks and ongoing as necessary.

Managerial Assistance Available: Franklin's provides support to the franchisee in hiring, marketing, advertising, purchasing and receivables control. The franchisor is available for assistance in any area necessary for the operation of the stores.

Information Submitted: August 1987

*THE INK WELL, INC.
2323 Lake Club Drive
Columbus, Ohio 43232
Ronald L. Strahler, President

Description of Operation: Sales and marketing of fast, quality printing and related services. The Ink Well "business system" is the most complete and most competitively priced offering in the instant printing industry. All aspects of establishing and developing the new owner's printing center are considered and all costs associated with the start-up phase are clearly defined. The experienced manager is equipped with a "business system" for easy transition into the world of instant printing.

Number of Franchisees: 40 plus 1 company-owned.

In Business Since: 1972, Franchising since 1981.

Equity Capital Needed: $25,000 plus working capital.

Financial Assistance Available: Yes, to qualified buyers. Leasing programs are available for all furniture, fixtures, equipment and signage.

Training Provided: Training is conduced in a variety of settings to ensure all phases of the printing business. Classroom sessions are coupled with corporate store exposure for 2 weeks. Complete on-site opening assistance follows the formal training.

Managerial Assistance Available: Complete training manuals—administration, accounting, employee, and technical (all covered in training classes). On-site visits by franchisor supervisors.

Information Submitted: May 1987

INSTANT COPY
232 West Wayne Street
Fort Wayne, Indiana 46802
John M. Thistlethwaite, Director of Franchising

Description of Operation: Instant copy printing, copying and communications centers, are fully equipped with top of the line equipment and communications hardware to provide full service quick printing and desk top publishing service. Each center utilizes the Instant Copy attitude and Instant Copy guarantee. Typical center is approximately 1,500 square feet.

Number of Franchisees: 5 in Indiana

In Business Since: 1969, franchising began in 1985

Equity Capital Needed: $125,000

Financial Assistance Available: A total investment of $250,000 to $300,000 is necessary to open an Instant Copy Center. Instant Copy provides no financial assistance to the franchisee. Approximately $125,000 in cash is needed if franchisee leases equipment and building.

Training Provided: Complete store operations training for franchisee and employees at the Instant Copy offices for 5 weeks; and 2 weeks on-site training.

Managerial Assistance Available: During store set-up Instant Copy provides complete facilities preparation assistance; equipment and inventory assistance as well as opening sales marketing and advertising functions. Ongoing facilities operation analyses; educational seminars, and introduction to new market developments; technical assistance with Instant Copy commercial services plant for business cards, webb press type (high volume) printing, and process printing.

Information Submitted: May 1987

*INSTY-PRINTS, INC.
1215 Marshall Street, N.E.
Minneapolis, Minnesota 55403
Kevin P. Keane, President

Description of Operation: Insty-Prints instant printing centers offer high-quality printing services on a wide range of paper stocks, plus cutting, folding, stapling, collating, drilling and padding, with the emphasis on fast, convenient service. Franchisees receive a package of services including 4 weeks training, site selection and lease negotiation, store design, comprehensive advertising program, bookkeeping system, computerized pricing and cost ratio programs, and continuing management counselling. An equipment and fixture package is provided to fit each location, and one week's opening supervision is provided in franchisee's unit and after the unit has been open 6 months.

Number of Franchisees: 397 locations in 41 States, Washington, D.C., Puerto Rico, Israel and Canada.

In Business Since: 1935

Equity Capital Needed: $35,000 minimum cash requirement. Financing available to qualified applicants on remainder of $82,500.

Financial Assistance Available: $85,500 of total investment may be financed by qualified applicants. $35,000 minimum cash requirement covers (a) $15.000 franchise fee down payment, (b) $20,000 working capital retained by franchisee.

Training Provided: 4 weeks at Minneapolis headquarters, covering use of equipment, advertising, estimating, paper, freight, bookkeeping, counter procedures, inventory and cost control, and general unit management. Fifth week in franchisee's own unit, under home office field supervision. Additional personnel training in Minneapolis headquarters at no additional charge throughout term of agreement.

Managerial Assistance Available: Annual regional workshops, continuing management and technical advice, instant in WATS telephone communication, continuing advertising and promotion programs, complete operations and sales manuals, periodic bulletins, national advertising fund, annual convention.

Information Submitted: May 1987

*KWIK-KOPY CORPORATION
1 Kwik-Kopy Lane
P. O. Box 777
Cypress, Texas 77429
Director—Marketing

Description of Operation: A Kwik-Kopy Center franchise offers a system for production and sale of high quality printing, duplicating, copying, bindery and attendant services on rapid time schedules tailored to meet the customers' desire. The franchise includes volume buying discounts on the purchase of equipment, microcomputer hardware with specialized business systems software, furniture, fixtures and supplies, market research, site selection, negotiation of real estate leases, equipment operation, public relations, sales and advertising programs, start-up assistance, continued support service in technical and business management problems over the entire 25-year term of the franchise agreement.

Number of Franchisees: Approximately over 1,000 in 42 States, Canada, United Kingdom, Australia, South Africa and Israel.

In Business Since: 1967

Equity Capital Needed: Minimum cash requirement of approximately $46,500.

Financial Assistance Available: In addition to the minimum cash requirement, an investment of approximately $76,500 is necessary to open a Kwik-Kopy Center. This amount can be financed for credit-worthy applicants.

Training Provided: Completion of an intensive 2 week training course is provided by Kwik-Kopy Corporation at its management training center and is required prior to opening a Kwik-Kopy Center. Additional one-week on-the-job traning in the franchise owner's place of business during and after start-up is also provided. Training includes equipment operation, accounting, advertising sales and business methods in Kwik-Kopy Center opeations. Pre-and post-training video tapes on business procedures, operation and maintenance of equipment, sales and advertising programs are supplied to each franchise owner.

Managerial Assistance Available: The company provides continued support services to its franchise owners for the term of the franchise agreement, including management counsel, advertising and training of new employees. Assistance and counseling is available to all franchise owners by telephone through nationwide toll-free WATS lines available to all franchise owners.

Information Submitted: June 1987

*MINUTEMAN PRESS INTERNATIONAL, INC.
1640 New Highway
Farmingdale, New York 11735
Roy W. Titus, President

Description of Operation: Minuteman Press International, Inc., offers a unique approach to the instant printing franchise through its full service printing centers. Not only the ability to produce high quality instant printing, butthe versatility of the equipment enables the owners with no previous printing or graphics experience, to product multi-color printing, photostats, overhead visuals and the screening of half-tones. A complete package is offered which includes all the necessary equipment for printing, cutting, folding, padding, collating, stapling, plus the initial supply of ink, film, paper, stationery and promotional materials for marketing. Also included in the package is the research of the proposed area, securing an acceptable location and assistance in the negotiation of the lease as well as overseeing the complete renovations of the location, including the installation of fixtures, signs, furniture and all accessories needed to operate a successful Minuteman Press Full Service Printing Center.

Number of Franchisees: Over 600 in 38 States and Canada

In Business Since: 1973

Equity Capital Needed: Approximately $22,500 to $32,500.

Financial Assistance Available: $67,500 to $77,500 total investment, with financing available through the 3M Company (Minnesota Mining and Manufacturing Company).

Training Provided: There is an intensive 2 week training program held at the Minuteman Press Training Center in Farmingdale, New York, covering all aspects of the business, plus a minimum of 40 hours continued training at the franchisees own location under home office field supervision. Training covers use of all equipment, advertising, pricing, bookkeeping, sales promotion, counter procedures, inventory, and cost control and general management. The owner is also trained in a marketing program developed by the company, which has been one of the keys to the success of the Minuteman Press franchises.

Managerial Assistance Available: The company has regional offices under the supervision of an officer of the company in Atlanta, Baltimore, Boston, Chicago, Cleveland, Dallas, Denver, Ft. Lauderdale, Los Angeles, Louisville, New York, Philadelphia, Pittsburgh, San Francisco, Seattle, St. Louis, and Canada to provide continued support services and guidance to its franchisees, including management, marketing, advertising, and training of new employees. Franchise owners are kept current with results of research and new equipment through periodic meetings and seminars and visits by field representatives who provide assistance as required. Continuous guidance and support is available to all franchise owners through the regional or home office.

Information Submitted: August 1987

* (PIP) POSTAL INSTANT PRESS
8201 Beverly Boulevard
Los Angeles, California 90048
Thomas C. Marotto, President, Chief Executive Officer

Description of Operation: World's largest printing franchise. Pioneers in the instant printing field. PIP services the rapidly growing printing and business needs of companies, professionals, universities, civic groups and individuals. In addition to black and white as well as multi-colored printing, PIP stores offer high-speed duplicating, forms, business cards, collating, binding and more. Owners are provided a comprehensive opening package, including equipment, initial supplies and marketing materials to promote sales. PIP Corporate also assists with the installation of all equipment and provides electrical and plumbing specifications.

Number of Franchisees: Over 1,100 locations in 48 States, Washington, D.C., Canada and United Kingdom. About 25 percent of franchisees are multiple location owners.

In Business Since: 1965

Equity Capital Needed: $15,000 down payment plus $17,500 operating capital (kept in franchisee's account). Total estimated cost, exclusive of working capital: $89,200.

Financial Assistance Available: Franchisor will finance qualified applicants.

Training Provided: 2 weeks of intensive training at PIP's national training center by skilled operations, technical and marketing experts. Training covers the use of all equipment, advertising, marketing, public relations, business management, estimating, record keeping, inventory and cost control, sales, customer relations and employee relations.

Managerial Assistance Available: Immediately following initial training, field support representative spends 1 week assisting with the opening of the store. This is followed by a 3-day visit after 30 days, a 2-day visit after 60 days and another 2-day visit after 90 days of operation. Ongoing field and marketing support and educational seminars year-round. biennial Conclaves conducted for owners during the "even" numbered years. The 1988 Conclave is scheduled for Nashville.

Information Submitted: May 1987

PRINTMASTERS, INC.
370 South Crenshaw Boulevard
Suite E-100
Torrance, California 90503

Description of Operation: PrintMasters, Inc., offers an opportunity for enthusiastic and motivated people to achieve their management and promotional potential in the field of high volume quality instant printing. The Printmaster package includes a complete line of equipment, material and supplies, plus the major items of office furniture required to operate an effective instant printing center.

Number of Franchisees: 85 in California, 1 in Texas

In Business Since: 1977

Equity Capital Needed: Cost of franchise package $79,000. Minimum cash investment $24,500. Working capital $20,000-$30,000.

Financial Assistance Available: Financing available $79,000 (to qualified individuals) on the total package of $79,000.

Training Provided: Technical, managerial and promotional training provided. Minimum of 2 weeks at the franchise training center. Minimum of 2 weeks at the franchisee's location. Managerial and promotional imput continues, as well as technical assistance, through quality control visits and direct contact with franchisee. All aspects of owning and operating an instant printing center are covered in detail.

Managerial Assistance Available: Each franchisee undergoes a CPA consultation for the purpose of setting up the center's books and record keeping system. The franchisee receives continued management, marketing and promotional guidance and support for the duration of the franchise license agreement. Supply sources, pricing techniques and group purchasing discounts are provided on a constant basis. Periodic quality control visits review current and introduce new technical, managerial and marketing skills and products. PrintMasters emphasizes the need for ongoing interaction between the franchisee and the company headquarters. Direct lines of communication are always open to assist, guide and offer support.

Information Submitted: May 1987

* PRINTNET LASER PRINTING CENTERS, INC.
3600 West Commercial Blvd.
Suite 106
Fort Lauderdale, Florida 33309

Description of Operation: Printnet Laser Printing Centers, Inc., offers an instant print center that produces services ranging from duplicating to four color work utilizing latest state of the arts computer and laser technology operating primarily in retail sales.

Number of Franchisees: 4 including company-owned.

In Business Since: 1986

Equity Capital Needed: $180,000

Financial Assistance Available: None

Training Provided: 3 weeks of training at Printnet training facility in Fort Lauderdale, Florida and 3 days training at franchisees new location.

Managerial Assistance Available: Sales management, cash control, training manual provided. Field supervisors make periodic in store inspections and assist in any way they can.

Information Submitted: August 1987

PRINT SHACK
500 North Westshore Boulevard
Suite 610
Tampa, FLorida 33609-1924
Al Slusarchuk, Vice President, Marketing

Description of Operation: Print Shack has established itself as the most unique franchise opportunity in the instant printing industry. Our centers market a full range of printed paper products including multi-color work at discount prices, full typesetting services and related services. Additionally, Print Shack centers offer over 50,000 different advertising specialty products to the same customer base, combining the 3 billion dollar instant printing industry with the 4 billion dollar advertising specialty industry. We offer single store, multi-store and regional opportunities.

Number of Franchisees: 116 in 29 States

In Business Since: 1982

Equity Capital Needed: Franchise fee $26,500 no charge for second franchise, $56,000 total cash.

Financial Assistance Available: Financing available for all equipment and a portion of the franchise fee to qualified individuals. SBA also available.

Training Provided: All franchisees receive a full 3 weeks of comprehensive training at our home office in Tampa, Florida and 1 week on location. In addition, training classes are continuous and you may enroll members of your staff or yourself in any ongoing class at no extra charge for the term of the franchise. Instruction covers every aspect of equipment training, marketing, accounting procedures, personnel, advertising, public relations, proper management and systems control.

Managerial Assistance Available: Continuous, ongoing and comprehensive for the life of our agreements. Your success is our success!

Information Submitted: May 1987

> **PRONTO PRINTER**
> 97 Pratt Street
> Hartford, Connecticut 06103
> Peter Oudheusden, President

Description of Operation: Pronto Printer is a quick printing franchise servicing the printing needs of businesses and organizations. Emphasis is placed on image and professionalism in dealing with our customers, providing offset printing, copying, typesetting, laser printing, and other related services.

Number of Franchisees: 11 in Connecticut and New York

In Business Since: 1969

Equity Capital Needed: $80,000 to $120,000. Total to open, including working capital and grand opening advertising.

Financial Assistance Available: Will assist in locating financing.

Training Provided: 3 weeks of training including operating equipment, sales counter procedures, and business procedures. An additional 3 weeks on in-store training during the first 6 months of operation.

Managerial Assistance Available: Ongoing advertising and marketing guidance and materials, educational seminars, and on-site visitation program.

Information Submitted: August 1987

> **QUIK PRINT, INC.**
> 3445 North Webb Road
> Wichita, Kansas 67226
> Jim Pirtle, Vice President, Franchise Operations

Description of Operation: Quik Print has established itself as an organization with a high standard of customer service and image in mind. A Quik Printing franchise is not only a visable asset in the market place, but a complement to the Quik Print Corporation.

Number of Franchisees: 126 franchisee-owned, 62 company-owned in 24 States.

In Business Since: 1963

Equity Capital Needed: Complete franchise package $72,500 plus suggested $20,000 for working capital, initial investment as low as $32,5000.

Financial Assistance Available: Financing available to qualified individuals.

Training Provided: 4 to 6 weeks at franchisor's headquarters, plus 2 weeks on-the-job at franchisee's new location.

Managerial Assistance Available: Management services in the area of bookkeeping, advertising, equipment and production techniques.

Information Submitted: August 1987

> *****SIR SPEEDY, INC.**
> 23131 Verdugo Drive
> LaGuna Hills, California 92653
> Harold C. Lloyd, Vice President-Franchise Sales and Development

Description of Operation: Sir Speedy, Inc., is a leading franchisor of printing centers. Providing full service printing and the highest average gross sales volume per store in the industry. Centers are franchisee-owned utilizing established system, procedures and techniques. Franchise prackage includes equipment, supplies, signage, graphics, market survey and training programs. Prior printing experience not required.

Number of Franchisees: Approximately 800 in 46 States.

In Business Since: 1968

Equity Capital Needed: Total franchise package is $92,500 plus working capital of $35,000. Initial investment as low as $42,500.

Financial Assistance Available: Financing available for entire package to qualified individuals, excluding working capital.

Training Provided: Total of 4 weeks intitial training. This in-depth initial training includes advertising and marketing strategy, bookkeeping and record keeping, graphic design, shop organization and work flow, pricing, employee relations, and more. Ongoing regional and national seminars conventions to keep franchisees informed of trends in the industry.

212

Managerial Assistance Available: In-depth market surveys, site selection, assist in lease negotiations, national contract purchasing power, marketing and advertising support, accounting system, communication with all franchisees, profit management seminars, equipment evaluations, plus royalty rebate program.

Information Submitted: May 1987

> **STOP & GO PRINTING FRANCHISES, INC.**
> 848 Broadway
> Denver, Colorado 80203
> Lana Lindsey, National Marketing Director

Description of Operation: A Stop & Go Printing Franchise is a full service graphic arts center offering a complete range of quick printing, copying and high quality commercial printing. Desktop Publishing is an available option. Our comprehensive training program and extensive equipment package, including a darkroom, a two-color press and large format cutter, enables the franchisee to operate a high production, high quality center. Our full range of services places us a step ahead of the competition. No previous printing experience is required.

Number of Franchisees: 5 plus 1 company-owned in Colorado

In Business Since: 1974, franchising since 1982

Equity Capital Needed: $22,000 franchise fee, plus $20,000 minimum working capital.

Financial Assistance Available: Financing of 460,000 equipment package is available to qualified applicants.

Training Provided: 3 weeks of comprehensive training for 2 people is provided at company headquarters in Denver, Colorado, plus 40 hours on-site assistance. Our program includes equipment orientation and operation, graphic design, customer relations, management of employees, pricing, work scheduling, order processing, purchasing, inventory control and record keeping, as well as business management, sales and marketing.

Managerial Assistance Available: Site selection, lease negotiation and store layout. Assistance in purchase and installation of equipment, furniture, fixtures and inventory items purchased through national contracts for maximum discounts. Development of advertising, public relations and promotional programs for your center. Ongoing assistance is provided to all franchisees through visits by support specialists, newsletters and telephone consultation. Continuing support includes sales, marketing and technical assistance and consultation and advice on operations and procedures.

Information Submitted: May 1987

> *****TRANSAMERICA PRINTING, INC.**
> 1286 Citizens Parkway
> Suite F
> Morrow, Georgia 30260
> Patrick Koehler, President

Description of Operation: TransAmerica Printing offers a full service printing operation including a two color press in the initial package necessary for high quality registration work. Experienced pressmen are hired as no training on the press is given nor recommended. The franchise package includes assistance in site selection, lease negotiation, store layout, ordering all equipment and supplies and promotional material.

Number of Franchisees: 14 in four states.

In Business Since: 1985

Equity Capital Needed: $35,000 plus $30,000 working capital.

Financial Assistance Available: Equipment ($40,000) can be set up on 60 month lease, one third of $14,900 franchise fee can be financed.

Training Provided: Assistance in hiring of pressman and 3 full weeks on-site training after opening. This procedure permits opening in as little as 3 weeks. No training in running the press is given as an experienced pressman is recommended and required for high quality work. Training is concentrated on management and marketing. The franchise founder had a shop exceed one million dollars in the fifth year (1983) before a buyout.

Managerial Assistance Available: Following the on-site training on 3 weeks, ongoing assistance is available by phone. Monthly art work for advertising and promotion is made available. TransAmerica Printing has quarterly regional seminars on marketing, advertising, financial data and new equipment review.

Information Submitted: May 1987

REAL ESTATE

**ART FELLER AUCTION AND REAL
ESTATE COMPANY**
Garfield Avenue
Box 267
Cissna Park, Illinois 60924
Arthur Feller, Broker

Description of Operation: A real estate franchise. Where each office is independently owned and oprated. Where the Feller Real Estate handles all major advertising, with monthly publicatons of all listings and all offices work together.

Number of Franchisees: 15 in Illinois and Indiana

In Business Since: 1938—auctioneering—1982—real estate.

Equity Capital Needed: None—all franchise office work on percentage sold.

Financial Assistance Available: All literature, brochures of all offices listings of real estate are promoted and advertised throughout area at no cost to franchisee.

Training Provided: Sales meetings held regularly.

Managerial Assistance Available: Sales person visits office when needed to give guidance and advice as needed. District and field managers available to work closely with all franchisees, referral's giving by franchisor.

Information Submitted: August 1987

NORRED REAL ESTATE, INC.
dba BELL REALTY
3922 East Florence Avenue
Bell, California 90201
Frank Ortiz, Vice President

Description of Operation: Complete real estate service.

Number of Franchisees: 4 including company-owned in California.

In Business Since: 1959

Equity Capital Needed: None

Financial Assistance Available: None

Training Provided: Franchisor will provide 3 months at the beginning of acquisition.

Managerial Assistance Available: Ongoing

Information Submitted: August 1987

*BETTER HOMES AND GARDENS REAL ESTATE SERVICE
2000 Grand Avenue
Des Moines, Iowa 50312
George Bruns, Vice President—Member
Development

Description of Operation: A national marketing program licensing the Better Homes and Gardens trademarks to selected real estate firms in assigned exclusive market territories. The variety of programs available to licensees includes a national and local advertising program, a referral service, mortgage origination capability (in states where available), a corporate relocation program, a concurrent licensing program, management seminars, training materials, a home warranty program (in states where available), client promotion materials, a building support program, and the benefits of belonging to a national network of professional real estate firms.

Number of Franchisees: Over 500 in all 50 States

In Business Since: 1978

Equity Capital Needed: The initial joining fee is an applied percentage of the annual residential gross commission income of each firm. The minimum joining fee is $7,338.

Financial Assistance Available: A down payment of 50 percent of the joining fee is due when the contract is executed. The remaining 50 percent is due at the opening date. The opening date is the date that the firm first publicly uses the Better Homes and Gardens marks or 120 days after the effective date of the contract, whichever is earlier.

Training Provided: Better Homes and Gardens Real Estate Service provides a management orientation asession for members at Better Homes and Gardens corporate headquarters. In addition, Better Homes and Gardens provides an orientation for the agents of each new firm at its primary office without charge. Better Homes and Gardens provides periodic regional training seminars for the management of its members at reasonable cost.

Managerial Assistance Available: Better Homes and Gardens maintains a service staff with assigned territories to provide each firm with personal contact and consultation on the effective use of the programs. Toll free inbound WATS lines access the service department for improved communication. Regional groups have been established and sponsored by Better Homes and Gardens to provide for periodic meetings of all members in each geographic area to discuss common ideas.

Information Submitted: August 1987

BETTER HOMES REALTY
710 South Broadway
Suite 200
Walnut Creek, California 94596
Clifford R. Fick, Senior Vice President

Description of Operation: Better Homes Realty is a network of independently owned and operated real estate offices. A dual-identity program allows brokers to retain their established identity, plus combine with Better Homes Realty brand-name awareness, mass marketing, national relocation services, continuous management and associate training and education programs, and consumer-service preferred treatment programs, including a unique in-house Preferred Financing program. Bethom Corporation is the franchisor of Better Homes Realty.

Number of Franchisees: Better Homes Realty currently has 900 associates in over 100 offices.

In Business Since: Founded in Walnut Creek, California, as an all-broker cooperative during the 1960's, Better Homes Realty began franchise expansion in 1974.

Equity Capital Needed: Under the Better Homes Realty franchise agreement, a one-time initial franchise fee of $7,500 allows a franchisee to assume the established Better Homes Realty trademark and support services. A substantial amount of the initial franchise fee is returned to the franchisee in office set-up materials. Service fees are equal to 6 percent of the gross commissions for transactions requiring a real estate license. No additional advertising fees or assessments are charged.

Financial Assistance Available: Franchisor may agree to accept $2,500 down payment and monthly installments of $335 or more until a total fee of $8,530 is paid.

Training Provided: The Better Homes Realty Institute of Real Estate programs begin with recruitment career nights, and cover a sales training course at no cost to associates, a continuing education program for license renewal credit, and regular management and associate conferences over a four to 10-day period.

Managerial Assistance Available: Representatives of the Better Homes Realty business development department make regular visits to Better Homes Realty associate offices to discuss the uses of all business development materials, and to counsel management decisions. Bethom Media, the professionally staffed in-house advertising agency, prepares and produces continuous advertising and marketing campaigns within each regional area.

Information Submitted: July 1987

*CENTURY 21 REAL ESTATE CORPORATION
International Headquarters
Century Centre, 2601 S.E. Main Street
P.O. Box 19564
Irvine, California 92713-9564
Richard Hogue, Vice President, Franchise Sales

Description of Operation: World's largest real estate franchising organization, established to provide a marketing support system for independently owned and operated real estate brokerage offices, offering international advertising, VIP referral system, residential and commercial sales trainng, management training, national accounts center, client follow-up, and other real estate related services. Insurance, mortgage brokerage, and securities and syndication services are available in selected regions through subsidiary companies in Century 21 Real Estate Corporation. Subsidiary of Metropolitan Insurance Company.

Number of Franchisees: Over 6,500 offices in United States, Canada and Japan.

In Business Since: First offices opened in 1972.

Equity Capital Needed: Initial fee—$9,500-$14,000 (varies regionally).

Financial Assistance Available: Some financing may be available.

Training Provided: The exclusive Century 21 CareerTrak program offers training and accreditation in all major real estate disciplines: office management, investment and residential sales, sales management and relocation services. The program links educational standards with productivity for a system-wide method of motivation and career development.

Managerial Assistance Available: New franchisees attend the international management academy, a 3-1/2 day orientation/management training seminar held in Irvine, California. Other courses offered through the regions include the property management support system, principles of sales management and commercial property series.

Information Submitted: June 1987

COAST TO COAST PROPERTIES, INC.
1975 Hamilton Avenue
Suite 1
San Jose, California 95125
George J. Rockson, General Manager

Description of Operation: Coast to Coast Properties franchise is a full service real estate organization offering training programs for both management and sales personnel. Additionally the franchisor provides standards as to brochures, forms, advertising and promotional activities.

Number of Franchisees: 5 in California

In Business Since: 1981

Equity Capital Needed: There is initial franchise fee of $1,500. Additional costs will be determined by the size-type of and location of the individual office. It is estimated that costs for existing independent brokerages to join the franchise in addition for signage, printing and incidental supplies.

Financial Assistance Available: None

Training Provided: An intensive 4 day, mandatory management training program for all new franchisees. The training is conducted at company training facilities. The franchisor also provides training for sales personnel which is conducted at the franchisor's facilities and consists of 32 hours of personal one-on-one trining plus outside work assignments.

Managerial Assistance Available: Coast to Caost Properties provides continual management and sales personnel training in such areas as sales techniques, advertising, management techniques, and other related areas concerning the latest development in the field of real estate. Complete operations manual, advertising manuals, public relations, recruiting techniques, problem solving sessions. The corporation conducts marketing, advertising and selling technique research to maintain and promote the high consumer awareness of the Coast to Coast Properties organization.

Information Submitted: August 1987

COMREAL INTERNATIONAL, INC.
8725 Northwest 18th Terrace
Suite 200
Miami, Florida 33172
Stephen H. Smith, President

Description of Operation: The franchise offered is a format system for operation of a full-service, computerized, commercial real estate brokerage operation including property/asset management, mortgage brokerage, syndication and marketing services.

Number of Franchisees: 7 in Florida

In Business Since: 1983

Equity Capital Needed: $225,000

Financial Assistance Available: None

Training Provided: 1 week for each salesperson and certain staff members; 2 weeks for owners and operators.

Managerial Assistance Available: Continual assistance to franchisee and their staff.

Information Submitted: May 1987

EARL KEIM LICENSING COMPANY
1740 W. Big Beaver
Suite 200
Troy Michigan 48084
William E. McCullen, President

Description of Operation: Real estate franchise, with complete range of services including financial services.

Number of Franchisees: 100 office in Michigan and Florida.

In Business Since: 1958

Equity Capital Needed: Franchise agreement fee $7,000.

Financial Assistance Available: Finance packages available through Colonial Central Savings Bank, and affiliated company.

Training Provided: Through the real estate school which provides pre-license and post-license training. The post-license program, called 'Fast Start' is designed to make the new salesperson productive as soon as possible. Monthly newsletters, special workshops and periodic sales rallies round out the ongoing sales training program.

Managerial Assistance Available: Beginning with a realistic budget and sales forecast, the managerial assistance gives specific guidance in recruiting, interviewing, training, goal setting, motivating, and equipping a salesperson, so as to obtain a highly profitable business. Management development workshops are held 3 times per year. Other services provided include; a national referral service, Guardian Home Warranty programs, relocation department (works on corporations and handles third party listings and buyer referrals), in-house advertising agency, state-wide commercial/investment computer listings, Guarardian Financial Services, (a source of residential and commercial financing), client follow-up program, full array of marketing brochures.

Information Submitted: May 1987

*ELECTRONIC REALTY ASSOCIATES, INC.
4900 College Boulevard
Overland Park, Kansas 66211
Edward R. Gresham, President

Description of Operation: Electronic Realty Associates, Inc. (ERA), is a membership organization for licensed real estate brokerage firms offering its services and programs for use by its members. ERA grants the use of its registered trademarks and service marks and designs, logos, colors and color patterns, and business methods to its members to promote identification with the products and marketing services of ERA and to permit coordination of advertising programs. ERA members participate in a national referral program, a national advertising program, an equity advance program, and a national residential service contract program. ERA services also include advertising materials, training programs, and management and educational programs for the member's real estate brokerage operations. ERA is the exclusive corporate sponsor from the real estate industry of the Muscular Dystroply Association (MDA).

Number of Franchisees: Approximately 2,000 franchisees operating from approximately 2,300 offices in the United States, Australia and Japan as of April 1, 1986.

In Business Since: 1971, and is now a wholly-owned subsidiary of ERA Financial Corporation.

Equity Capital Needed: The initial franchise membership fee is $12,900 plus $500 for each branch office. If paid in a lump sum, the initital fee is $11,900 plus $500 for each branch office.

Financial Assistance Available: ERA does have a financial assistance program to aid new members in the payment of the initital membership fees. New members who qualify may, upon payment of $4,500, finance $8,400 by payment of $2,800 within 60 days, $2,800 within 90 days, and $2,800 within 120 days. Other financing arrangements may be available from time to time, at the sole option of ERA.

Training Provided: A new member must participate in an orientation training program to familiarize the broker with the ERA services and programs. Other training programs believed by ERA to be beneficial to members and to be important for the full and effective implementation of the ERA system are available.

Managerial Assistance Available: ERA provides continuing management service to members in many areas including training, advertising, insurance, and residential service contract administration. Complete manuals of operations, forms, and directions are provided. ERA representatives are available in all regions to work closely with members and to assist in problem solving. ERA sponsors brokers councils in each locality and conducts marketing and product research to maintain high ERA consumer acceptance.

Information Submitted: May 1987

FINANCIAL PARTNERS INTERNATIONAL, INC.
625 Broadway
Suite 1111
San Diego, CA 92101
Carl Anderson, CRS, CRB, President

Description of Operation: A full service network of real estate brokerages serviced state by state by savings and loan associations whose service corporations service the accounts. Residential, agricultural, commercial, and financing services.

Number of Franchisees: Approximately 130 in California, Iowa, Illinois, and Nebraska.

In Business Since: 1979

Equity Capital Needed: $10,000

Financial Assistance Available: Yes

Training Provided: Sales associate, management development, office staff, financial innovations.

Managerial Assistance Available: Intensive during start-up and continuous through operation.

Information Submitted: May 1987

GALLERY OF HOMES, INC.
20 South Orange Avenue
Orlando, Florida 32801
David Boggs, Vice President of Sales

Description of Operation: Gallery of Homes, Inc., an affiliate of Empire of America, Federal Savings Bank, franchises existing experienced real estate brokers of good reputation and proven ability and provides national image, referral services, home warranty, recruiting, training and education, national advertising, corporate relocation and in-field service assistance in return for fees as specified in the agreement. Preference is given to brokers with membership in professional real estate organizations. Standards are high. Applicants should contact headquarter's office for information.

Number of Franchisees: 375 offices in the Continental United States

In Business Since: 1950

Equity Capital Needed: An existing business plus $9,900.

Financial Assistance Available: Yes

Training Provided: A 4 day orientation program and staff assistance and participation of new franchisees in local council of franchisees. Additional professional courses (sales, management, fiscal control) available.

Managerial Assistance Available: In addition to the above manuals are provided that cover general Gallery of Homes techniques, office layout, referrals and corporate business leads, supplies, catalogues, image program, advertising format guide.

Information Submitted: May 1987

GOLDEN RULE REALTY OF AMERICA
10336 Reseda Blvd.
Northridge, California 91326

Description of Operation: Real estate offices.

Number of Franchisees: 15 in California.

In Business Since: 1970

Equity Capital Needed: Approximately $4,000.

Financial Assistance Available: None

Training Provided: Complete real estate training provided.

Managerial Assistance Available: Complete management assistance is provided.

Information Submitted: August 1987

* **HELP-U-SELL, INC.**
57 West 200 South, Suite 200
Salt Lake City, Utah 84101
Greg Farley

Description of Operation: Help-U-Sell is a merger of real estate counseling, marketing and traditional real estate. The Help-U-Sell counseling method is to assist buyers and sellers of real property for a set fee payable at closing. All Help-U-Sell franchisees are real estate brokers and membership in local multiple listing services is recommended. We believe our concept provides more benefits to buyers and sellers and brokers than traditional real estate and is ideally suited to the changing real estate market. Our marketing system has created thousands of buyers calls and listings without walk canvassing, call canvassing or holding open houses. Free packet of information including sample advertising and questions and answers is available. Call (800) 647-4747 (outside California) or (800) 453-2323 (California).

Number of Franchisees: 190 covering 15 States—now proceeding with nationwide expansion program.

In Business Since: 1976

Equity Capital Needed: Real estate $275 per 1,000 population minimum $4,500.

Financial Assistance Available: Terms may be available depending on location (exclusive territory) and qualification.

Training Provided: Up to 10 days at corporate or regional headquarters (or other mutually agreed location) in the Help-U-Sell method and ongoing support.

Managerial Assistance Available: Full training in the Help-U-Sell method and continued assistance for the term of the franchise.

Information Submitted: July 1987

HER REAL ESTATE, INC.
4656 Executive Drive
Columbus, Ohio 43220
Eleanor B. Bailey, President

Description of Operation: A personalized approach to real estate franchising. The brokers keep their own identity for marketing purposes. The identifying marks of the franchisor do not detract or dominate. Franchise owners enjoy "on-location" educational opportunities. Other traditional real estate benefits are offered: an exclusive territory, test-marketed award winning marketing tools and techniques, a superb support program through field representation, continuing education (also "on-location") and other unique educational opportunities.

Number of Franchisees: 33 company and franchised offices in Ohio.

In Business Since: In the real estate industry for over 30 years. Started offering franchises in August 1981.

Equity Capital Needed; Costs of conversion: yard signs, office sign, general office supplies plus the franchise fee. The franchise fees vary with the size and population of the exclusive territory. The minimum frnchise fee is $4,900.

Financial Assistance Available: None

Training Provided: Orientation, on-location—ongoing education, continuing education, regional and state-wide programs.

Managerial Assistance Available: The parent company, HER, Inc., is a source for management assistance with 17 managers, relocation division managers, Marketing Manager and Director of Career Development—all full-time.

Information Submitted: May 1987

HOME MASTER REALTY, INC.
28444 Joy Road
Livonia, Michigan 48150
Christopher L. McDonald, President

Description of Operation: Home Master (a registered trademark) is the "2 percent solution" to satisfy the need of independent real estate brokers of having national name recognition but not siphoning the broker's profit margin for that advantage. State-wide master franchise offered to qualified real estate brokers with good track records in major cities.

Number of Franchisees: 3 in Michigan

In Business Since: 1977

Equity Capital Needed: Net worth of $20,000 for State-wide master franchises.

Financial Assistance Available: Local financing where applicable or terms available with franchisor.

Training Provided: Training for broker and sales associate where applicable.

Managerial Assistance Available: Management training where applicable.

Information Submitted: August 1987

215

HOMEOWNERS CONCEPT, INC.
3508 W. Galbraith Road
Cincinnati, Ohio 45239
Jeffrey C. Knab, President

Description of Operation: Alternative avenue in selling real estate. Homeowner, shows their own property and pays flat fee for professional real estate consulting. Homeowners Concept is a corporation in Ohio.

Number of Franchisees: 47 in 13 States

In Business Since: 1982

Equity Capital Needed: $25,000—initial fee $7,500.

Financial Assistance Available: Neither the franchisor nor any affiliated persons offer direct or indirect financing to franchisees.

Training Provided: 14 hours on-the-job training.

Managerial Assistance Available: Continuous consulting from franchisor and periodic seminars.

Information Submitted: May 1987

HOMETREND, INC.
3600 South Beeler Street
Suite 300
Denver, Colorado 80237

Description of Operation: Hometrend, Inc., is a second generatoin real estate franchisor. In addition to the usual services normally offered, we include a total business management and consulting service to broker-members through a district agent, allow our members to maintain their identity through 50/50 name participation, and an incentive service fee program rewarding greater performance. We provide a computer and computer services as part of our franchise package.

Number of Franchisees: 5 regions, 27 districts, 26 member brokers, operational in 19 States.

In Business Since: 1979, acquired by new owner in 1982.

Equity Capital Needed: Master $50,000, Broker $7,500.

Financial Assistance Available: Total investment of $7,500 initial fee plus $300 for each branch office. In addition, a cost of approximately $1,500 to convert to our signs, etc. Financing available on an individual basis.

Training Provided: Intensive 2-3 day program to instruct district franchise agent in the operations and selling techniques in operating a franchise. Training conducted at home office in Denver. In addition, member-brokers receive extensive management and sales training through the district agent.

Managerial Assistance Available: Management training, consulting and servicing continues for the life of the district franchise agent and member-broker.

Information Submitted: May 1987

IOWA REALTY COMPANY, INC.
3501 Westown Parkway
West Des Moines, Iowa 50265
Gene Knepper, Franchise Director

Description of Operation: Training, management assistance, name recognition, advertising insurance department securities. Allows smaller companies in small communities to have large company name recognition, market support materials and management expertise. National referral network offered as part of membership.

Number of Franchisees: 38 in Iowa (restricted to Iowa).

In Business Since: 1980

Equity Capital Needed: Member must be in the real estate business with offices open to the public. There is a franchise fee for membership.

Financial Assistance Available: Assistance in obtaining financing for customers through our local mortgage company and other local companies on purchase of real estate.

Training Provided: Ongoing monthly training for brokers and sales agents includes pre-license, post license and continuing education classes and seminars.

Managerial Assistance Available: Technical assistance is offered for members through all our department managers and legal staff, including residential, commercial, and farm sales. Rental and property management, closing department securities sales and training department, pre-license and post license training provided by our staff training department.

Information Submitted: May 1987

KEY ASSOCIATES, INC.
Highway 66, P. O. Box 495
Rockport, Indiana 47635
Donald R. Schulte, President

Description of Operation: Real estate.

Number of Franchisees: 34 in Indiana and Kentucky

In Business Since: 1977

Equity Capital Needed: $5,000

Financial Assistance Available: None

Training Provided: 4 days audio video training at cost.

Managerial Assistance Available: None

Information Submitted: May 1987

REAL ESTATE ONE LICENSING COMPANY
29630 Orchard Lake Road
Farmington Hills, Michigan 48018
Gary L. Pownall, President

Description of Operation: Real Estate One Licensing Company, franchises real estate brokers into a network using Real Estate One trademark properties, systems, training methods, and referral programs.

Number of Franchisees: 46 in Michigan

In Business Since: 1972

Equity Capital Needed: Franchise fee is $9,800.

Financial Assistance Available: Yes

Training Provided: Real Estate One provides ongoing seminars and training courses for both brokers and sales associates.

Managerial Assistance Available: In addition to training courses, Real Estate One provides management consultation by visits, telephone, franchise manuals, advertising aids, supplies and forms.

Information Submitted: August 1987

REALTY EXECUTIVES
4427 North 36th Street
Phoenix, Arizona 85018
William Powers, Marketing Director

Description of Operation: The original 100 percent commission concept in real estate. Realty Executives is designed to assist individuals and entities in the development of strong, multi-office companies operating general real estate brokerages using the Realty Executives 100 percent concept as the foundation.

Number of Franchisees: 65 offices in 12 States

In Business Since: 1965

Equity Capital Needed: $10,000 initial fee. Will need minimum of $20,000 for working capital.

Financial Assistance Available: Yes

Training Provided: Intensive 2 day individual instruction, given by national staff, teaching new owners how to operate the Realty Executives 100 percent concept using methods with over 20 years of proven success. A comprehensive operations manual, coupled with the instant accessibility of a national staff, who also administer company-owned offices, provide ongoing assistance. New accounting software is available at additional expense.

Managerial Assistance Available: Unlimited consultation in proven successful accounting procedures, recruiting techniques, clerical hiring, and advertising methods is provided. National and regional meetings cover topics of vital interest to owners. Operation of national referral network and volume purchasing available to our brokers and associates.

Information Submitted: May 1987

REALTY 500
1539 Vassar Street
Suite 101
Reno, Nevada 89502

Description of Operation: A regional marketing program available to select real estate firms. a variety of educational and functional programs designed to increase production and disseminate the most recent marketing and management methods to our member firms. Examples of programs are Brokers' Council, Quarterly

Network meeting, management seminars and retreats. Initial and continual sales training and training aids and client presentation materials all provided at no additional cost to the member. Savings on opeating materials (signs, brochures, business cards, stationery, promotional items, etc.) available through corporate volume purchase.

Number of Franchisees: 30 in Nevada

In Business Since: 1979

Equity Capital Needed: $7,500

Financial Assistance Available: Yes

Training Provided: Extensive initial sales training for sales associates and management and management retreats are provided. (At no charge to member firms.)

Managerial Assistance Available: On-site management consultation provided to member firms from the corporate office. Management workshops, seminars, and retreats are also available.

Information Submitted: June 1987

REALTY WORLD CORPORATION
12500 Fair Lakes Circle
Suite 300
Fairfax, Virginia 22033
Doug Finney, Vice President

Description of Operation: Realty World Corporation is a subsidiary of Southmark Corp., of Dallas, Texas. As a full-service network, Realty World Corporation provides the independent real estate broker with international name and image research and development, educational training, a nation-wide referral system, a national home warranty plan, corporate relocation training, a national advertising program, errors and omissions insurance, national awards programs and marketing assistance.

Realty World Corporation serves as a national distribution network through regional licensees to local independent franchisees. (Licenses and franchises are available and information will be furnished on request.)

Number of Franchisees: Over 1,600 in 49 States, District of Columbia and Canada.

In Business Since: 1974 in United States.

Equity Capital Needed: No specific equity capital required since the franchise is generally already engaged in the real estate business. Initial single office franchise fee ranges from $7,900 to $12,900 with a lower cost for additional branch offices.

Financial Assistance Available: Yes.

Training Provided: Training is supplied to the local franchisee on an ongoing basis by the regional licensee. Subjects include: prelicense training, introduction to real estate, listing, selling, corporate relocation, commercial real estate, administrative assistant training, developing human potential, introduction to management, business planning, financing and many other specialized programs.

Managerial Assistance Available: An exclusive management and business planning course called RealStart. Full-time training and business development directors to instruct and provide counseling in an ongoing manner. Broker councils in each provide communicative link to the corporation. Special training is provided for new programs and products.

Information Submitted: May 1987

RED CARPET REAL ESTATE SERVICES, INC.
P. O. Box 85660
San Diego, California 92138
Scott Lindberg, Vice President of Marketing

Description of Operation: Red carpet Real Estate Services, Inc., is the "oldest but newest" full service real estate franchise in the U.S. Red Carpet offers regional and national training programs; comprehensive training materials; regional and national marketing and television advertising; an exclusive computer software package; relocation assistance and referrals through a national network of over 3,000 member offices; and the unique linkage with a lender who pledges its excellence of service in a performance contract with the franchisee.

Number of Franchisees: 500 in 37 States

In Business Since: 1976

Equity Capital Needed: $9,500 initial franchise fee; capital needed varies.

Financial Assistance Available: 50 percent down, financing balance for up to 2 years.

Training Provided: Regional and national training programs: training classes held on an ongoing basis—at least once a month in each region (4 day class); self-help tapes; professional communication skills; financing methods and skills, etc.

Managerial Assistance Available: Series of national and regional management training courses backed by management computer software system. Ongoing monthly broker services assistance to aid in recruiting, selecting, training, motivating and managing sales associates.

Information Submitted: May 1987

RE/MAX INTERNATIONAL
P. O. Box 3907
Englewood, Colorado 80155
Daryl Jesperson, Vice President, Operations

Description of Operation: An international network of independent real estate brokerage offices, operating under the RE/MAX concept, located throughout the United States and Canada. The concept is based upon a fair exchange: the highest possible compensation for the sales associate in return for shared common overhead expenses. Offering the seasoned professional a full service relocation company, a R.E.O. (asset management) company, an international insurance franchising outlet, in addition to the real estate network; RE/MAX is designed to compliment both franchise owner and sales associate by use of trademarks, international identity and product continuity, management consulting and technical assistance.

Number of Franchisees: 1,320 in 46 States and 10 Canadian Provinces.

In Business Since: 1973

Equity Capital Needed: $10,000 to $20,000 (varies from region to region).

Financial Assistance Available: RE/MAX International provides no financial assistance.

Training Provided: Mandatory attendance to the 5 day course in Denver. The course covers tested techniques directed toward the successful implementation of the concept. From organizational establishment and development to retention and recognition; all are examples of course content and the optional semi-annual executive level seminars. In-depth individual management consulting and technical assistance is available upon request.

Managerial Assistance Available: Ongoing consulting services and managerial guidance are provided on a regular basis to all individuals within the system. Each broker-owner is contacted individually through the regional director network to discuss his/her development and any encountered problems. Regional directors are strategically located throughout the United States and Canada, and along with their staff, provide on-site assistance needed by the franchisees. Broker-Owner Councils and Sales Advisory Councils are developed within each area and provide continuity of effort and consistency in operations throughout the organization.

Information Submitted: May 1987

RENTAL SOLUTIONS, INC.
417 Main Street
Bangor, Maine 04401
Michael H. Round, President

Description of Operation: A service firm devoted to the over one-third of U.S. households that rent. Rental Solutions offers exposure and limited management assistance to property owners, and information to tenants. Computer technology has been developed to store and search the vast universe of data in rental property, and create usable, manageable choices on an individual tenant basis.

Number of Franchisees: 2 in Maine

In Business Since: 1983: As a franchisor since 1987.

Equity Capital Needed: $25,000 plus operating capital.

Financial Assistance Available: None

Training Provided: Up to 5 days in Bangor, Maine, concentrating on computer familiarity and marketing techniques and store operations.

Managerial Assistance Available: The contract calls for continual assistance in all aspects of the franchise operation, excluding legal and accounting expertise usually found on a local basis. Telephone, mail and personal communication will be used as the situation warrants. A growing system will provide greater use of in-the-field visitation. Computer experts provide assistance in that area.

Information Submitted: September 1987

SKI & SHORE MICHIGAN, INC.
200 East Huron (M-72)
P. O. Box 808
Grayling, Michigan 49738
Wayne H. Everett, General Manager

Description of Operation: Northern Michigan recreational oriented real estate franchise assisting real estate offices in resort areas. Offering printed materials, forms and bulk purchasing.

Number of Franchisees: 16 franchisee offices.

In Business Since: 1969—current owners since 1982

Equity Capital Needed: $4,000 to $8,000

Financial Assistance Available: On supplies to get started during transition.

Training Provided: Continuing sales and management programs, broker's meetings and educational and motivational seminars.

Managerial Assistance Available: Franchisor supplies complete set of secretary, office manuals, ongoing improvement program offering new products, techniques, and information. Referral program, management meetings annual awards and monthly awards, corporation advertising promotion and a semi-annual real estate catalog of highest quality available featuring recreational properties of all kinds.

Information Submitted: August 1987

STATE WIDE REAL ESTATE, INC.
1801 7th Avenue North
Escanaba, Michigan 49829
Hugh D. Harris, President
Richard J. Langley, Vice President,
Planning and Development

Description of Operation: State Wide Real Estate, Inc., is a national network providing full service real estate franchises to independent real estate brokerage. State Wide provides marketing programs, education systems, full range creative advertising techniques, sales aids, referral programs, monthly and annual sales awards programs, and staff assistance to qualified franchisees. The National Association of Realtors Real Estate residential success series course is intricate part of education.

There are two types of franchises available:

1. **Master Franchise:** Available in selected large areas (States or larger), on a partnership basis with the home office.

2. **Office Franchise:** Available from the Master franchisee or State wide Real Estate, Inc., depending on the area in which the franchise will be operated.

Number of Franchisees: 110 throughout Michigan, Wisconsin, and Iowa.

In Business Since: 1944

Equity Capital Needed: $10,000 to $20,000

Financial Assistance Available: State Wide Real Estate, Inc., does not directly provide financial assistance for new franchisees, but will assist the franchisee to locate sources of financial assistance.

Training Provided: All new brokers and sales associates are required to attend a 3 day orientation within 6 months of joining State wide Real Estate, Inc. Seminars and courses are offered throughout each year on a regional basis. Courses taught in the past include: "Getting Listings is the Name of the Game," "Legal Awareness and Pitfalls," "Residential Taxation," "Property and Investment Analysis," "Keys to Successful Real Estate Sales," "Business Opportunities," "How to Obtain Commercial Listings," "Agricultural Brokerage," "Tax Planning," "Nuts and Bolts of Real Estate Financing."

Managerial Assistance Available: In addition to training courses, State Wide Real Estate, Inc., maintains a full corporate staff for consultation by telephone, franchise manuals, a full library of tapes and books, advertising aids provided on a monthly basis, supplies and forms.

Information Submitted: May 1987

RECREATION/ENTERTAINMENT/ TRAVEL-SERVICES/SUPPLIES

AIR & STEAMSHIP TRAVEL OF FLORIDA, INC.
260 Sunny Isles Boulevard
North Miami Beach, Florida 33160
Reto Lingenhag, President

Description of Operation: Complete travel arrangements by air, sea, ground, hotel reservations, vehicles rentals, special cruises, turnkey operation.

Number of Franchisees: 2 in Florida

In Business Since: 1983

Equity Capital Needed: $66,000

Financial Assistance Available: Financing available.

Training Provided: Initial training and ongoing consultation.

Managerial Assistance Available: Consultation as needed.

Information Submitted: July 1987

ASK MR. FOSTER ASSOCIATES, INC.
7833 Haskell Avenue
Van Nuys, California 91406
Kelly Nelson, Chief Operating Officer

Description of Operation: Licensing opportunities to established travel agencies in geographical areas not presently covered by Ask Mr. Foster's 274 owned and operated branch offices.

Number of Franchisees: 250 in 36 States

In Business Since: 1984 (parent company since 1888)

Equity Capital Needed: None

Financial Assistance Available: None

Training Provided: Initial orientation and ongoing consultation; specific training programs available at an additional cost.

Managerial Assistance Available: License ("Associate") becomes a part of the Ask Mr. Foster branch network and thereby participates in all company marketing programs and proprietary service systems. Licensees have a dedicated company staff to assist them in utilizing company programs to their fullest.

Information Submitted: May 1987

BATTING RANGE PRO
5954 Brainerd Road
Chattanooga, Tennessee 37421-3598
E. K. Magrath, Jr.

Description of Operation: Indoor and outdoor batting ranges with 6 to 9 JUGS Coin Operated Pneumatic Tire, Variable Speed, Baseball and Softball Pitching Machines. A ball is pitched every 6 seconds at a charge of $1.00 for 15 to 20 balls.

Number of Franchisees: 95 in 26 States

In Business Since: 1979

Equity Capital Needed: $45,000 to $90,000, depending on the number of baseball pitching machines installed.

Financial Assistance Available: None

Training Provided: Complete operational kit is provided to instruct operators that will cover most questions asked.

Managerial Assistance Available: Site selection advice, complete batting range construction plans available, assistance in construction planning.

Information Submitted: May 1987

CHAMPIONSHIP MINIATURE GOLF
CMG FRANCHISE SYSTEMS, INC.
111 South Allen Street
Suite 2A
State College, Pennsylvania 16801
Debbie Williams, Vice President/Franchise Development

Description of Operation: Unique in the miniature golf industry! We've taken a new approach to an old favorite. Interesting designs using mounding, bushes, trees, flowers, water features. . .features from the real game of golf scaled down to a size everyone can enjoy! Each course is individually designed.

Number of Franchisees: 2 in Pennsylvania

In Business Since: 1984, franchising since 1987

Equity Capital Needed: Average investment $75,000 (including $10,000 franchise fee).

Financial Assistance Available: None

Training Provided: 1 week training session including, classroom instruction, discussion, observation, and "hands-on" training. Extensive owner operations manual.

Managerial Assistance Available: Complete franchise system, assistance in site selection (complete feasibility study), individually designed courses, construction supervision, 1 week training, grand opening assistance, advertising/promotions program, newsletters, computerized sales analysis, visits from home office and telephone communication.

Information Submitted: July 1987

CINEMA 'N' DRAFTHOUSE, INC.
2204 North Druid Hills Road
Atlanta, Georgia 30329
John J. Duffy, Owner/Franchise Director

Description of Operation: Motion picture theatres designed in an art deco lounge atmosphere that provides pizza, beer, wine and deli-type food, in addition to being a multi-media facility for seminars and teleconferencing.

Number of Franchisees: 38 in 14 States

In Business Since: 1975

Equity Capital Needed: $15,000 franchise fee, 3 percent royalty fee.

Financial Assistance Available: None

Training Provided: Projection, operation in theatre, bar and restaurant management—2 weeks initial and ongoing refresher courses.

Managerial Assistance Available: Continuous operational assistance in problem solving and promotional direction. Franchisor provides booking service for obtaining films on a weekly basis.

Information Submitted: August 1987

*CORNER POCKETS OF AMERICA, INC.
1445 Broadwater
P. O. Box 20878
Billings, Montana 59104
George Frank, President

Description of Operation: National franchisor of Doc & Eddy's featuring a restaurant/entertainment concept which includes a "sunny" solarium, casual dining, elevated cocktail lounge, big screen TV, sunken billiard area, darts, custom music system and video dancing featuring Top 40 and modern country music.

Number of Franchisees: 15 in 12 States

In Business Since: 1973

Equity Capital Needed: $75,000/$100,000 with satisfactory financial background.

Financial Assistance Available: None

Training Provided: Approximately 2 weeks of formal training at the corporate office and on-the-job training when the facility is opened.

Managerial Assistance Available: Managerial and technical assistance provided on a continuing basis. Tournament and league organizations and intermitent pocket billiard exhibitions. Pre-designed plans and specifications for standard building, assistance in site selection, construction, opening and grand opening.

Information Submitted: May 1987

CRUISE HOLIDAYS INTERNATIONAL, INC.
4740 Murphy Canyon Road
Suite 200
San Diego, California 92123
Joseph F. Ewart, President

Description of Operation: Cruise Holidays offers a retail travel agency franchise selling only cruises.

Number of Franchisees: 11 in California

In Business Since: 1984

Equity Capital Needed: $45,000 including franchise fee.

Financial Assistance Available: None

Training Provided: 1 week training course is conducted at corporate headquarters and at the company-owned store. Advanced seminars and training classes are held periodically.

Managerial Assistance Available: Cruise Holidays provides ongoing management consulting, cruise line negotiation and advisory services. Manuals, forms, data control systems and inventory control guidance is provided. Centralized purchasing of printing supplies is available. advertising on a regional basis is coordinated by the corporate office.

Information Submitted: June 1987

CRUISE SHOPPES AMERICA, LTD.
115 Metairie Road
Suite E
Metairie, Louisiana 70005
Bill Worden, CTC/Admiral
Gary Brown, Vice Admiral

Description of Operation: Franchisor of "cruise-only" travel agencies offering initial entry and conversion of existing travel agencies programs. Each store is approximately 1,000 square feet with designated motif.

Number of Franchisees: 7 in Florida, Missouri and North Carolina

In Business Since: 1985

Equity Capital Needed: $18,500 minimum

Financial Assistance Available: A total investment of $65,000 (including working capital) is needed—outside financing with good credit available.

Training Provided: Intensive 4 day home office training for owner and one manager, quarterly 3 day seminars, numerous on ship 3-4 day seminars/inspections.

Managerial Assistance Available: C.S.A. provides continual managerial services, i.e., advertising, quarterly news letters; accounting support. C.S.A. provides complete sales and operational manuals, regional managers to assist in local problems.

Information Submitted: May 1987

CRUISES ONLY, INC.
Forest Hills Plaza
21 Yost Boulevard
Pittsburgh, Pennsylvania 15221
Gail E. Cortese, President

Description of Operation: Cruises Only, Inc., are retail cruises centers which are service-oriented establishments devoted solely to the sale of retail cruise packages, cruise travel arrangements and other related services. This is an adult market of people in the middle and upper income brackets. A cruise center generally requires 550 square feet of usable commercial space.

Number of Franchisees: 2 in Pennslyvania

In Business Since: 1985

Equity Capital Needed: Minimum $15,000

Financial Assistance Available: Minimum total investment of 43,300 is sufficient to open a franchise center. The initial down payment is used to defray expenses for assistance, training and supervision; legal and accounting services; compliance fees; general and administrative expenses; and selling and promotional expenses prior to franchise opening.

Training Provided: The franchisor requires the successful completion of 5 days administrative training for owners and managers; 8 days of sales training and office procedures for sales personnel. Training program to take place at home office site prior to franchise opening.

Managerial Assistance Available: Continual management assistance in accounting, marketing and advertising will be provided throughout the franchise term; plus the updating of operational manuals and procedures together with product knowledge and trends. Also provided will be problem solving on-site assistance and supervision by company coordinators. The franchisor will schedule periodic product seminars and conferences.

Information Submitted: May 1987

CUE BALL FAMILY POOL COURSES
Route 5 Box 48
Scottsboro, Alabama 35768
Philip Love, President

Description of Operation: Miniature pool courses— similar to miniature golf. Course consist of 18 beautifully molded fiberglass tables. Can be installed indoor or outdoor for year round income. You are challenged along the way with a variety of bends and obstacles in the tables. The course is played with a cue stick and cue ball. Don't miss this new concept in recreational business.

Number of Franchisees: 2 in Massachusetts

In Business Since: 1985

Equity Capital Needed: Approximately $62,000/$89,500 pays for building; prints, all construction cost (does not include land).

Financial Assistance Available: None

Training Provided: 1 week training at operating units.

Managerial Assistance Available: Operational manual, course design and continuing management, service and advice.

Information Submitted: August 1987

EMPRESS TRAVEL FRANCHISE CORPORATION
5 Penn Plaza
New York, New York 10001
Jack Cygielman, President

Description of Operation: Express Travel offers a unique retail travel agency operation, in an existing, stimulating, year-round business, which gives its participants great pleasure and financial reward. An Empress Travel franchise has full support and assistance at all times, from management.

Number of Franchisees: 70 in New York, New Jersey, Connecticut, Pennsylvania, Washington, D.C., Maryland and Virginia.

In Business Since: 1958

Equity Capital Needed: $75,000 including working capital.

Financial Assistance Available: No

Training Provided: Intensive training course for all new franchisees and their personnel at the home office and on-site at company offices, also at franchisee's outlet.

Managerial Assistance Available: Empress Travel provides continual management service with advertising, complete manuals of operations, forms, and directions, etc. Management works closely with franchisees, and assist solving all problems. Empress Travel sponsors meetings of franchisees and conducts marketing research to maintain high Empress Travel consumer acceptance.

Information Submitted: May 1987

FUGAZY INTERNATIONALL FRANCHISE CORP.
555 Madison Avenue
New York, New York 10022
Maria Muccio, Director of Operations

Description of Operation: Full service travel agency.

Number of Franchisees: 42 in 15 States

In Business Since: 1870

Equity Capital Needed: $30,000 and up franchise fee plus $35-$40,000 working capital.

Financial Assistance Available: Yes

Training Provided: Fugazy will aid licensee in leasing and furnishing of a travel office, secure necessary approvals from IATA and ARC, provide trained account executives to establish factors necessary in opening a fully appointed travel agency.

Managerial Assistance Available: Fugazy will assist licensee in recruitment of staff and provide personnel of licensee with training, marketing, sales and advertising handled through corporate office.

Information Submitted: May 1987

FUN SERVICES, INC.
221 East Cullerton Street
Chicago, Illinois 60616

Description of Operation: Fun Services franchisees provide a service of professional Fun Fairs for the leisure time and recreational industries. The primary market in fund raising organizations, such as elementary school P.T.A.'s, churches, youth and fraternal organizations. Entertainment is also provided to industrial picnics and Christmas parties, as well as programmed to insure profits for the organization and fun to the participants. all equipment and supplies needed to perform multiple events simultaneously are proved as part of the franchisee package, as well as a cargo van for delivery and warehousing. In addition, programs have been developed in th fund raising service field involving candy sales, door to door merchandise sales and gift programs through the schools.

Number of Franchisees: 66 in 26 States

In Business Since: 1966

Equity Capital Needed: Over $20,000.

Financial Assistance Available: Fun Services, Inc., finances up to 75 percent of initial franchise cost over a 5-year contract. No payments are required during the first 2 months of operation.

Training Provided: 4 day formal school at Fun Services headquarters. Room, board and local transportation provided as part of training school. Field assistance provided as needed.

Managerial Assistance Available: Complete manuals of operation, forms and directions are provided. Complete promotional program with brochures, letters mail folders, enclosures and stamps provided. Continual top management support, newsletters, regional and national meetings of franchisees. Continual research and periodic introduction of new items, programs, games and fund raising concepts.

Information Submitted: August 1987

GO-KART TRACK SYSTEMS
5954 Brainerd Road
Chattanooga, Tennessee 37421-3598
Jay Grant

Description of Operation: 12 to 15 concession type go-karts which are rented for a 4 to 5 minute ride on approximately 800' curved track at a speed of 18-20 mph.

Number of Franchisees: 82 in 20 States

In Business Since: 1972

Equity Capital Needed: $45,000-$70,000

Financial Assistance Available: None

Training Provided: Training on-the-job until operator is completely satisfied he can handle the job. Manager's manual will cover most questions that come up.

Managerial Assistance Available: Site selection, complete track and building layout, and construction planning.

Information Submitted: May 1987

GOLF PLAYERS, INC.
5954 Brainerd Road
Chattanooga, Tennessee 37421
Earl Magrath, President

Description of Operation: Miniature golf courses with very large, colorful, and distinctive figures and caricatures—some animated. Operation under the name "Sir Goony Golf."

Number of Franchisees: 49 in 12 States

In Business Since: 1964

Equity Capital Needed: $36,800

Financial Assistance Available: None

Training Provided: Training at home office and on-the-job. Continuing help by personal visits, newsletters and phone calls. A complete operational manager's manual is provided.

Managerial Assistance Available: Course design and construction planning, continuing management service and advice.

Information Submitted: May 1987

GRAND SLAM USA ACADEMY
9011 Southeast Jannsen Road
P. O. Box 451
Clackamas, Oregon 97015
Jim McNeill Franchise Coordinator

Description of Operation: Grand Slam USA Baseball/Softball Academies. Completely automatic batting cages. Instruction in such aspects as hitting, fielding, pitching, etc. Machines are coin or token operated. Will throw baseballs or softballs at push of a button. Pro Shop.

Number of Franchisees: 62 in 29 States

In Business Since: 1976

Equity Capital Needed: $150,000

Financial Assistance Available: None

Training Provided: 3 day training at home office in marketing, business, operations, and technical is mandatory. Complete detailed operations manual given to each trainee.

Managerial Assistance Available: Ongoing with field men calling on franchisees every 6-8 weeks.

Information Submitted: May 1987

INTERNATIONAL TOURS, INC.
5001 East 68th Street
Suite 530
Tulsa, Oklahoma 74136
Sales Manager

Description of Operation: The company represents itself as the oldest, most successful franchisor of travel agencies in U.S. and offers two types of franchises: (1) for new agencies, and (2) for conversion of established agencies. The franchise package includes 24 key points, i.e., site selection, selection of office manager, bookkeeping system, office forms, operations manuals, open house assistance, budget preparation, advertising and marketing plans. International Travel Institute, a travel agency training school with locations in Houston, Texas and Tulsa, Oklahoma is a subsidiary of the company.

Number of Franchisees: 212 in 36 States

In Business Since: 1970

Equity Capital Needed: $55,000 to $85,000

Financial Assistance Available: None

Training Provided: Choice of 4 week or 6 day technical training; 3 day management training session at home office; 7 days on-site management assistance and in-house training.

Managerial Assistance Available: Complete set of operations manuals for operation of travel agency; set up bookkeeping system and preparation of first six months financial reports, including monthly profit and loss statements and balance sheets; two company-owned travel agent training schools available for franchisees and their employees (located in Houston, Texas, and Tulsa, Oklahoma); legal counsel to advise on tax and financial considerations; preparation of franchisees' applicatoins for airline and cruise line conference appointments; find qualified and experienced manager to be employed by franchisee; assist with franchisee's grand opening and advertising plans; provide qualified management consultants for on-site visitation and by phone during open office hours of agencies.

Information Submitted: August 1987

LOMMA ENTERPRISES, INC.
1120 South Washington Avenue
Scranton, Pennsylvania 18505
R. J. Lomma, President

Description of Operation: The Lomma Miniature Golf Company, the world's oldest and largest designer and builder of miniature golf courses, offers a dynamic non-commodity, easily run, high cash flow recreational business. The modular golf courses are designed for maximum flexibility of layout and the portability allows usage indoors and outdoors for year round revenue.

Number of Franchisees: 4,808 in 50 States and 15 countries around the world.

In Business Since: 1960

Equity Capital Needed: $3,900

Financial Assistance Available: As little as 10 percent down payment is needed and the balance payable up to 5 years. Complete and concise free franchise program with no franchise or royalty fees to pay.

Training Provided: We conduct seminars at our offices for small groups and/or regionally at your location.

Managerial Assistance Available: We supply a detailed manager's guide and operating manual as well as State, national and international tournaments, and a Miss Lommagolf Contest. Also competition for the Guiness Book of Hall Records.

Information Submitted: May 1987

MINI-GOLF, INC.
202 Bridge Street
Jessup, Pennsylvania 18434
Joseph C. Rogari, Marketing Director

Description of Operation: Prefabricated miniature golf courses—themes also available—minimum space needed. Huge obstacles with plenty of challenge and beauty. No labor problem and non-commodity item. Tournaments and promotions included along with course operator's manual.

Number of Franchisees: Over 450 in 47 States, Canada, and Aruba.

In Business Since: 1981

Equity Capital Needed: $4,900

Financial Assistance Available: 20 percent discount is offered if own financing is arranged. Otherwise a token down payment of 25 percent with up to 3 years to pay.

Training Provided: Invitation to home office in Jessup, Pennsylvania for lectures and concise training.

Managerial Assistance Available: Newly published operator's manual with local, State and national tournaments, along with precise methods of operational and promotional material.

Information Submitted: August 1987

PAY N PLAY RACQUETBALL OF AMERICA
11770 E. Warner, Suite 129
Fountain Valley, California 92708
Charles L. Hohl, President

Description of Operation: Pay N Play Racquetball of America builds convenient, low cost automated racquetball/handball/tennis practice centers that are open to the public 24 hours per day in most locations. There are no memberships, monthly dues, or reservations. Players purchase the amount of court time they want using the automated dollar bill acceptor at each center. Pay N Play provides the building/equipment on long-term lease to franchisees.

Number of Franchisees: 7 in California

In Business Since: 1978

Equity Capital Needed: $60,000 minimum investment.

Financial Assistance Available: Pay N Play Racquetball of America does not finance itself, however company will assist the franchisee in obtaining financing. Basic franchise fee is $15,000 per court. (Minimum $60,000.)

Training Provided: An intensive 1 week mandatory training course is scheduled for all new franchisees. All training is conducted at company headquarters in Westminster, California.

Managerial Assistance Available: Pay N Play provides continual management service for the life of the franchise in areas facility maintenance, advertising, marketing, programming, and bookkeeping. Field managers are available to work closely with franchisee to provide assistance. Pay N Play sponsors meetings of franchisees and conducts marketing and product research to maintain high Pay N Play consumer acceptance.

Information Submitted: May 1987

PHOTON ENTERTAINMENT, INC.
12610 East Northeast Highway
Dallas, Texas 75228

Description of Operation: Photon is a unique experience where a mere earthling is transformed into a Photonian Warrior. It is a fast-paced adventure where you suite up in space-age battle gear and compete on one of two teams of up to 10 people in a heavily-mazed extraterrestrial planet enhance with futuristic lighting and sound effects. The object: score as many points as possible with your phaser pistol and destroy the opponents base goal.

Number of Franchisees: 28 in 31 States, Canada, Japan, Australia, New Zealand, Hong Kong and Taiwan.

In Business Since: 1983

Equity Capital Needed: $650,000

Financial Assistance Available: Payment schedule for fees for multi-market franchises. Time dependent on number of units purchased.

Training Provided: 2 weeks at franchisor's facility to include thorough operational, technical and marketing training including OTJ, films and manuals. On-site technical/operational assistance at opening.

Managerial Assistance Available: Toll-free number provided for any assistance needed at any time. Monthly newsletter with up-dates on operational/marketing plans. Franchise seminars twice a year.

Information Submitted: May 1987

PUTT-PUTT GOLF COURSES OF AMERICA, INC.
P. O. Box 35237
Fayetteville, North Carolina 28303
Bobby Owens, National Franchise Director

Description of Operation: Franchised miniature golf facilities with standardization of color scheme, construction, and putting surface as designed by Putt-Putt Golf Courses of America, Inc. Also franchised video gamerooms in conjunction with miniature golf.

Number of Franchisees: Over 400 in 40 States, and 4 foreign countries.

In Business Since: 1954

Equity Capital Needed: $25,000 to $125,000

Financial Assistance Available: No financing provided by company, however, assistance in obtaining financing through banks and SBA is available.

Training Provided: 1 week annually at international convention. Five regional, 2-day seminars each year from March 1st thru July 1st. ON-site training is available any time at no additional charge from the national training director.

Managerial Assistance Available: Complete computer accounting. Complete manager's manual. Complete promotional program provided including radio, TV, and newspaper advertising, etc., for the duration of the length of the contract.

Information Submitted: May 1987

PUTT-R-GOLF, INC.
Box 5445
Akron, Ohio 44313
Donald C. Nelson

Description of Operation: Supply plans and equipment for family fun centers concentrating on miniature golf, baseball batting ranges, slo-pitch softball batting ranges.

Number of Franchisees: 8 in 2 States and Canada

In Business Since: 1952

Equity Capital Needed: $45,000

Financial Assistance Available: Plans, material lists and consulting.

Training Provided: Informal

Managerial Assistance Available: As needed basis.

Information Submitted: August 1987

*TRAVEL AGENTS INTERNATIONAL, INC.
8640 Seminola Boulevard
Seminole, Florida 33542
James A. Sahley, Senior Vice President

Description of Operation: Travel Agents International offers potential franchisees a retail, turnkey, start-up, full service travel agency. Through negotiations, franchisees can earn higher commissions.

Number of Franchisees: 285 in 35 States and Canada

In Business Since: 1980, franchising since 1982

Equity Capital Needed: $90,000 includes franchise fee and working capital.

Financial Assistance Available: Yes

Training Provided: 3 week initital training program.

Managerial Assistance Available: Assistance provided during start-up, site location, interior design, reservation system. Ongoing support in management, personnel, operations, accounting and sales techniques for both corporate and leisure business.

Information Submitted: May 1987

TRAVEL ALL ENTERPRISES, CORP.
108 North State Street
Suite 910
Chicago, Illinois 60602
Dr. Ibrahim Y. Elgindy, Franchise Manager

Description of Operation: Travel all/shipping all systems off unique and complete transportation services agency, travel, air cargo and freight forwarder on stages. Also offers much higher than normal incentive commissions on many international carriers and much lower cost on air cargo and ocean freight plus training, location selection, lease negotiation, assistance in licensing support in operation, cooperative advertising and assistance in marketing.

Number of Franchisees: 2 in Illinois

In Business Since: 1983

Equity Capital Needed: $65,000

Financial Assistance Available: A total investment of $65,000 is needed to open Travel All franchise. Travel may finance franchisee up to $25,000 depending on credit references of franchisee. Franchisee may provide his financing.

Training Provided: Franchisee shall have 2 weeks of training in Chicago, 1 week in Texas on Sabre computers. For travel, 2nd phase air cargo, franchisee will be trained in Chicago for 1 week ocean freight, franchisee will be trained in chicago for 1 week.

Managerial Assistance Available: Travel provides continual management service for the life of the franchise in such areas as bookkeeping, accounting, marketing, advertising. Complete managing of operations.

Information Submitted: May 1987

TRAVEL PROFESSIONALS INTERNATIONAL, INC.
Suite 360
10172 Linn Station Road
Louisville, Kentucky 40223
James C. Vernon, President

Description of Operations: Travel Professionals International, Inc. (TPI) offers franchises to investors interested in establishing or converting travel agencies. TPI services include high-volume negotiations, marketing services and materials, information processing, training, and properietary travel packages for agency use.

Number of Franchisees: 23 in 8 states

In Business Since: 1983

Equity Capital Needed: $70,000

Financial Assistance Available: None

Training Provided: Managers quarterly, bookkeeping as needed—2 days, outside sales as needed—2 days, owners included in all of the above. Travel Professionals conducts a continuing education program for all franchise employees under the auspices of Dr. Bernard Strenecky, Ph.D.

Managerial Assistance Available: TPI develops all advertising materials, TV, radio, and print for franchisees. TPI provides on-site corporate sales, incentive, and group assistance. In the case of a new agency TPI provides hands on assistance in office development, hiring, bookkeeping, office layouts, and procedures.

Information Submitted: May 1987

TRAVEL TRAVEL FRANCHISE SYSTEM
P.O. Box 652
Encinitas, California 92024
James W. Hill, President

Description of Operation: An association of independently owned and operated travel agencies located throughout the entire U.S. receiving assistance and support through our centralized marketing, advertising, operations, accounting services, training, program, interior design package, and signage.

Number of Franchisees: 130 located throughout the United States.

In Business Since: 1979—merged with TravelMate Corporation in June 1983.

Equity Capital Needed: $67,000, fee included.

Financial Assistance Available: Assistance in securing outside financing.

Training Provided: 1 week of intensive training for owner and manager is provided. Ongoing training provided by field operations staff.

Managerial Assistance Available: Assistance is provided during start-up and on a continuous basis in the area of management, personnel, agency operations, tour packaging and business account development.

Information Submitted: May 1987

*UNIGLOBE TRAVEL (INTERNATIONAL), INC.
90-10551 Shellbridge Way
Richmond, British Columbia V6X 2W9
Canada
Michael Levy, Senior Vice President

Description of Operation: Uniglobe International is the master franchisor for the Uniglobe system, which is #1 in travel franchising and one of the Top Four travel organizations in North America. Uniglobe is designed to build the profitability of new and existing independent travel agencies. Uniglobe agencies benefit from a common image, professional training, business development assistance and ongoing support services. Uniglobe International has 19 of their 20 regions in operation in less than a 6 year period.

Being a Uniglobe franchisee entitles you to a vast array of services such as: national TV advertising, brand image, profitability software programs, ongoing business consultation, one-on-one agency visits for business development counseling, owners and managers meetings, preferred override programs, plus hundreds of hours of training. These services are coupled with the fact 200 staff members service the 520 plus independently owned and operated agencies. All resources of the regional offices are available to the franchisee.

Number of Franchisees: 520 as of April 1987, in USA and Canada.

In Business Since: 1980

Equity Capital Needed: Start up agency $125,000 includes franchise fee and working capital. Conversion agency $25,000 includes franchise fee, leasehold improvements and signage.

Financial Assistance Available: Depends on region.

Training Provided: Uniglobe provides ongoing training both at the international headquarters and in each region. This consists of approximately 100 days per month of continual training courses for its owners, managers and consultants. Certain courses are mandatory for the owners and managers.

Managerial Assistance Available: The Uniglobe Business Development Department works closely with agencies assisting, coaching and supporting new business development—much like an exclusive management consulting service. The Department is made up of seasoned travel professionals whose only goal is to help the franchisee become more successful.

Information Submitted: May 1987

RETAILING—ART SUPPLIES/FRAMES

ART MANAGEMENT SERVICES, INC.
Franchisor of the KOENIG ART EMPORIUMS
1777 Boston Post Road
Milford, Connecticut 06460

Description of Operation: Koenig Art Emporiums are retail artists, drafting supply picture frame stores selling to the creative person, amateur, professional, hobbyists, and the general public. Although primary sales stem from the artist, each Emporium's merchandise has a broad appeal to the general public through items such as fine writing instruments, framed posters and custom framing. Inventory is complemented by a full line catalogue. Average store size is 2,000 square feet.

Number of Franchisees: 70 in 19 States plus 15 company-owned stores.

In Business Since: 1933 (started franchising 1979)

Equity Capital Needed: Start-up franchises require a minimum cash investment of $50,000.

Financial Assistance Available: The total investment for a Koenig Art Emporium franchise is approximately $175,000-$225,000 included in the total investment is a franchise fee of $25,000. A.M.S. offers no financing arrangements directly to the franchisee, but will assist prospective franchisees with obtaining suitable financing from established lending institutions.

Training Provided: Training is of a minimum of 2 weeks' duration at A.M.S. headquarters, and will include familiarization with merchandise and its application, operating systems, do-it-yourself and custom picture framing techniques, computer reports, etc. In addition the franchisee will gain experience in store operations at an existing Koenig Art Emporium. Finally, A.M.S. will have a field representative on-site prior to and at the time of opening to instruct and assist the franchisee.

Managerial Assistance Available: A.M.S. provides a unique computerized inventory control system by interfacing its computer with the franchisee electric cash register. The computer will monitor inventory movement, generating orders automatically for timely stock replacement while providing meaningful reports to A.M.S. and the franchisee. A.M.S. also serves the franchisee as a continuing source of expertise in all facets of the store operation. The franchisee will also receive operations and employee manuals necessary for effective store procedures. A.M.S. will also offer advice with regard to the efficient and economical operation of the franchising Koenig Art Emporium.

Information Submitted: May 1987.

CREATIVE WORLD MANAGEMENT SERVICES, INC.
13450 Farmington
Livonia, Michigan 48150
Dennis R. Kapp, President

Description of Operation: Retail art/drafting materials and equipment, custom framing and teach painting classes.

Number of Franchisees: 5 in Michigan and Florida

In Business Since: 1946

Equity Capital Needed: $35,000

Financial Assistance Available: Inventory and fixture buy back agreements.

Training Provided: On location, and classroom—30 days or as required.

Managerial Assistance Available: Site location, construction management, store design, product acquisition, advertising and on-site training and technical advisor for 3 weeks minimum.

Information Submitted: August 1987

* DECK THE WALLS
A Division of WNS, INC.
P. O. Box 4586
Houston, Texas 77210
Houghton B. Hutcheson, Vice President, Franchise Development

Description of Operation: Deck The Walls is the nation's largest chain of retail stores specializing in popularly-priced prints, posters, frames and custom framing. Deck The Walls has tailored the art gallery concept to meet the tastes and needs of regional mall and shopping center shoppers. Many franchisees are involved in commercial art sales.

Number of Franchisees: 235 in 40 States

In Business Since: 1979

Equity Capital Needed: $50,000-$75,000

Financial Assistance Available: The total investment for a typical Deck The Walls franchise ranges from $150,000 to $200,000. WNS, Inc., assists qualified candidates in locating institutions which may provide SBA-guaranteed or other financing.

Training Provided: Extensive 10 day classroom training, including framing instruction, prepares franchisee for the daily operation of the store. Field staff continues training the franchisee and employees once the store is open, and ensures successful operation during the first critical weeks in business.

Managerial Assistance Available: Deck The Walls provides extensive assistance, including store construction specifications and plans; merchandise selection, pricing and visual presentation; national buying power; national and local marketing. Field staff make frequent store visits, supplemented by telecommunications, publications, regional meetings and an annual convention.

Information Submitted: May 1987

FRAME AND SAVE
1126 Dixie Highway
Erlanger, Kentucky 41018
Charles Karlosky, President

Description of Operation: Frame and Save offers to the public a "Do-It-Yourself and Custom FdPicture Framing Shop." Each store is approximately 1,600 square feet with a set up of 8 individual working booths. Frame and save has a line of quality moldings and mats.

Number of Franchisees: 40 in 7 States

In Business Since: 1973

Equity Capital Needed: $35,000

Financial Assistance Available: None

Training Provided: Intensive 2 weeks, mandatory training course is scheduled for all new franchisee's at one of our locations. This training, involves learning the techniques of cutting and assembling moulding, mats, glass, and conservation of valuable art work. Also, Frame and Save gives the franchisee one week of professional supervision at your location.

Managerial Assistance Available: Frame and Save provides continual contact with each individual franchisee with all update pricing and new techniques of the framing industry. District managers are available in all regions to work closely with the franchisees and visit the stores regularly to assist solving problems.

Information Submitted: May 1987

FRAME WORLD
P. O. Box 762
Decatur, Alabama 35602
Ronald Clark, President

Description of Operation: Frame World picture frame stores are unique retail stores. We specialize in all phases of retail picture framing indutry with emphasis on quality and volume.

Number of Franchisees: 5 in Alabama including 1 company-owned.

In Business Since: 1972

Equity Capital Needed: $22,500

Financial Assistance Available: None

Training Provided: 2 to 3 weeks in company-owned store, 2 to 3 weeks at franchisee store and assistance whenever needed.

Managerial Assistance Available: Managerial, technical and booking assistance provided in the above training period.

Information Submitted: May 1987

---

*THE GREAT FRAME UP SYSTEMS, INC.
9335 Belmont Avenue
Franklin Park, Illinois 60131
Arlene Kozemzak, Franchise Director

Description of Operation: Great Frame Up Centers are completely inventoried and equipped retail stores specializing in high volume sales of quality picture frames. All necessary materials and equipment are provided for the complete fulfillment of each customer's framing needs at absolute minimum prices.

Number of Franchisees: 95 in 23 States

In Business Since: 1975

Equity Capital Needed: Approximately $90,000

Financial Assistance Available: The licensor provides no direct financing of licensee locations. Licensor will assist licensee in preparing his/her own bank package. The licensor does indirectly offer financing through Allied Lending Corporation. With $22,000 in cash and $50,000 in equity a licensee may qualify for a $70,000 Small Business Administration Guaranteed Loan.

Training Provided: An intensive 6 week training period provides licensee with complete working knowledge of The Great Frame Up System of operation. Both "hands-on" and classroom situations and on-the-job training are part of the comprehensive program.

Managerial Assistance Available: The Great Frame Up Systems, Inc., is in constant touch with each of its licensees. It provides a flow of customer response to each store, field reports on each store operation, review of financial data, updating of operations and management manuals, a flow of advertising and public relations materials, and top level management review of stores in the system. Affiliates of the home company provide a complete line of inventory and equipment to all licensees at prices extremely competitive in the marketplace.

Information Submitted: May 1987

THE RINGGOLD CORPORATION
9605 Dalecrest
Houston, Texas 77080
Thomas J. Devine, President

Description of Operation: The "frame factory" and "framin place" shops are retail picture framing and art shops. Each shop is designed to allow the customer to select how their "picture" is to be framed, and then to do all of the work themselves in the shop. The shop personnel cuts and prepares all materials exactly as the customer chooses and then assist the customer in any way necessary to guarantee a professional job. All franchises offer custom framing.

Number of Franchisees: Approximately 100 in 28 States

In Business Since: 1971

Equity Capital Needed: Estimated maximum cost of $90,000. Equity of $30,000 required, balance financeable.

Financial Assistance Available: Assistance in arranging financing.

Training Provided: Not less than 3 weeks initially. Eight days immediately after the shop is opened. Regular seminars of shop owners are held for continuing education. Trade associations have regular local meetings and monthly periodicals.

Managerial Assistance Available: Managerial assistance is on a regular monthly basis. Technical assistance is provided on a group basis or when requested.

Information Submitted: May 1987

RETAILING—COMPUTER SALES/SERVICES

*COMPUTERLAND CORPORATION
2901 Peralta Oaks Court
Oakland, California 94605

Description of Operation: ComputerLand offers franchises for retail stores dealing in microcomputers, computer systems and related items, in a protected location, supported by marketing and purchasing services, under the name ComputerLand.

Number of Franchisees: 800 in 50 states and 24 foreign countries.

In Business Since: 1976

Equity Capital Needed: $200,000 to $600,000, depending on market size and location.

Financial Assistance Available: Financing of franchise fee available to qualified applicants. Franchisor will assist franchisee in preparing a loan proposal package to present to a bank or other loaning institution.

Training Provided: There is an initial training program for franchisees. Subjects covered are product knowledge, sales training and management, accounting, merchandising, and general franchise operation management. Updated and refresher courses are offered. Specific retail sales trainings are offered on an ongoing basis.

Managerial Assistance Available: Upon opening of the store, franchisor offers in-store aid and also supplies and keeps an updated operations manual which includes bookkeeping direction. Franchisor develops advertising aids for the franchisee, makes available inventory for purchase by franchisee at cost and protects the ComputerLand name.

Information Submitted: May 1987

COMPUTER RENAISSANCE, INC.
400 Penn Center Boulevard
Suite 900
Pittsburgh, Pennsylvania 15235
Stephen E. Gold, President

Description of Operation: Computer Renaissance franchises full service retail outlets offering used personal-computer systems, complimentary new and used peripherals, supplies, software, and related services.

Number of Franchisees: 7 in 5 States

In Business Since: 1984

Equity Capital Needed: $75,000-$115,000

Financial Assistance Available: Each franchisee is welcome to arrange their own financing. We will offer our advice and assistance in arranging financing on inventory requirements.

Training Provided: Franchisees and key management must attend and succsss-fully complete a 10 day training program provided at the parent company headquarters. Grand opening assistance is available. In addition, an operations specialist will work with you during your first week of operation. Seminars are offered on an ongoing basis.

Managerial Assistance Available: Computer Renaissance, Inc., provides ongoing support, service, training and assistance, and an updated operations manual which details policies and procedures. Additionally, they provide ongoing sourcing of inventory and purchasing assistance; quality pricing through the parent company; an integrated inventory system; strong financial control; continuous pricing guidelines; advertising assistance; and the benefit of an established trademark.

Information Submitted: May 1987

COMPUTERS UNLIMITED OF WISCONSIN
9055 D North 51st Street
Milwaukee, Wisconsin 53223
Kailas Rao, Director Franchise Development
Rick Kinder, Franchise Development Representative

Description of Operation: Computers Unlimited of Wisconsin offers franchises of specialty retail computer centers, under the name, ComputerBay. ComputerBay stores offer business clients tailored solutions to their computing needs, through inside and outside sales consultants. Each center adds value to the products it sells with service and training support. IBM Apple, Compaq.

Number of Franchisees: 12 centers in Miniesota, Pennsylvania, Illinois, Wisconsin, Florida and California.

In Business Since: 1981

Equity Capital Needed: $100,000 liquid assets total investment $200,000 to $500,000.

Financial Assistance Available: The franchisor does provide inventory financing programs. assistance.

Training Provided: The franchisor provides a 2 day training class for new franchisees at the corporate offices. All coordination of vendor training is provided. A 1 week training program is provided for the service personnel of each center. The franchisor also holds optional classes in sales, marketing and service.

Managerial Assistance Available: The franchisor provides continuing management and service support throughout the term of the agreement. This includes site visits by technical support and management personnel, assistance with store design, staff recruitment and inventory recommendations.

Information Submitted: May 1987

CONNECTING POINT OF AMERICA, INC.
7979 East Tufts Avenue Parkway
Suite 700
Denver, Colorado 80237
Peter Sherry

Description of Operation: The Connecting Point retail store is a single source for all computer hardware, software, training, and services.

Number of Franchisees: 78 in 26 States

In Business Since: 1982

Equity Capital Needed: At least $5,000 in liquid capital, plus $50,000 line of credit.

Financial Assistance Available: No direct financial assistance.

Training Provided: Customized sales and management training in all facets of store management, product knowledge, personnel management, inventory control, and sales techniques. All on site.

Managerial Assistance Available: Pre-opening assistance includes site selection, lease negotiation, store design, construction management, staff recruitment, recommended inventory planning, and extensive training. Ongoing support includes monthly advertising and promotional planning, inventory recommendations, and new product awareness.

Information Submitted: June 1987

* ENTRE COMPUTER CENTERS, INC.
1430 Spring Hill Road
McLean, Virginia 22102

Description of Operation: Entre Computer Centers, Inc., is America's largest publicly held franchisor of specialty retail computer centers. Each Entre Computer Center, utilizing a consultive sales process, provides business andprofessional clients with tailored solutions to their computing needs.

Number of Franchisees: 270 plus in 45 States, the District of Columbia, Canada, Europe, and Australia.

In Business Since: 1981

Equity Capital Needed: Minimum of $125,000 unencumbered liquid capital.

Financial Assistance Available: None

Training Provided: An extensive 5 plus week training program takes the franchisee and his/her personnel through the processes of operating a retail operation; developing a strategic plan; sales and marketing management; selling skills and technical training; entrepreneurism; advertising and promotion; public relations; hardware/software training; and more.

Managerial Assistance Available: A complete and ongoing support program is provided to franchisees through an organization of district support managers (DSM). Working with a specific group of stores, each DSM provides store support/assistance in such areas as: inventory planning; merchandising; promotional; tactical planning; and other critical areas of a franchisee's daily operations.

Information Submitted: August 1987

* INACOMP COMPUTER CENTERS
1800 West Maple Road
Troy, Michigan 48084
Richard Stopa, Vice President, National Franchising Department

Description of Operation: Inacomp Computer Centers are retailers of IBM, Apple and Compaq computers, and professional customer support services. Franchise stores are serviced by Regional Base/Distribution Centers which provide product and support programs to help franchisees maintain profitability and market control.

Number of Franchisees: 50 franchised outlets, 24 company-owned outlets, and 5 Regional Base/Distribution Centers.

In Business Since: 1976

Equity Capital Needed: Start-up investment required $215,000 to $300,000 plus approximately $100,000 in inventory (usually floorplanned).

Financial Assistance Available: No direct financial assistance. Floorplanning referrals only. We do provide leasing and credit programs for customer purchases.

Training Provided: Regional training centers provide; the initial 2-week and ongoing owner/management team training in advertising, merchandising, market forecasting, staff productivity, and customer support services, as well as the initial 2-week and ongoing staff training for sales/customer management skills, consultation analysis, product knowledge, and technical proficiency.

Managerial Assistance Available: Regional Base/Distribution Centers provide "localized" franchise support programs for marketing, advertising, merchandising, inventory forecasting, staff training; and customer support programs for consultation and education, leasing and credit cards, technical support and product repair.

Information Submitted: May 1987

* MICROAGE COMPUTER STORES, INC.
1475 West Alameda
Tempe, Arizona 85282
Thomas P. Krawczyk, Vice President of Franchising

Description of Operation: A professional sales organization operation from a computer store front. Commercial quality service, support, hardware and software are offered for voice and data forecasting needs.

Number of Franchisees: 178 in 38 States, Canada, Europe and Japan.

In Business Since: 1980

Equity Capital Needed: Cash—$120-$140,000. Total investment—$275,000-$500,000 (include above cash).

Financial Assistance Available: Franchisor does not make loans to franchisees. Extensive assistance is provided in the development by franchisee of a marketing and financial plan and bank presentation.

Training Provided: 2 weeks of training are provided prior to store opening. Ongoing training in the store as well as regional and home office located training is also provided.

Managerial Assistance Available: In store sales, store management, marketing, product mix and business services support are provided on an ongoing basis. Software and hardware technical support are continually provided.

Information Submitted: May 1987

RICHARD YOUNG, INC.
508 S. Military Trail
Deerfield Beach, Florida 33442
Jim Ziegler, Vice President, Franchise Sales

Description of Operation: The franchisor intends to offer franchises for the retail sale of computer accessories and supplies to businesses and individuals under the tradename "Richard Young Products." A four color catalog will be utilized to help promote sales. Direct contact, tele-marketing and customer mailings will be the main vehicles for selling product.

Number of Franchisees: 25 in Continental United States and its territories.

In Business Since: 1985

Equity Capital Needed: Approximately $150,000.

Financial Assistance Available: In special cases the franchisor will consider financing up to one half on the franchise fee.

Training Provided: There will be a 1 week start-up training program followed by a 1 week on-site training and support program.

Managerial Assistance Available: Richard Young provides continual management service for the duration of the franchise agreement in such areas as sales advertising, inventory control, purchasing and product research. A complete operations and procedural manual will be provided to all franchisees. District managers are available to work closely with franchises at their locations.

Information Submitted: July 1987

SAC DISTRIBUTORS INTERNATIONAL, INC.
3491 Pall Mall Drive 101
Jacksonville, Florida 32217
Sarai Cook, Executive Vice President

Description of Operation: SAC Distributors franchises are regional value-added resellers of computer systems, peripherals, software, supplies, and data communications equipment. Drawing on its experience in the retail sector, SAC Distributors has been highly innovative in implementing marketing strategies that are unparalleled in the industry. However, more important than any individual program is the company's efforts to keep available to it an unprecedented variety of products to market at consistently competitive prices. This policy clearly aligns SAC Distributors' best interests with those of its customers by remaining responsive to industry changes and customer needs. In addition, we have computerized many of the marketing, office, and accounting procedures involved in running a SAC Distributors franchise.

Number of Franchisees: 5 in Florida, Tennessee, Texas and Georgia

In Business Since: 1985

Equity Capital Needed: $31,000

Financial Assistance Available: An investment of $31,000 is required to open a SAC Distributors franchise. this includes training, computer, software, working capital, franchisee fee, and the rights to a protected territory consisting of a 300,000 (approximately) population area. We will provide financing for additional territory if desired by franchisee.

Training Provided: We require all new franchisees to attend an intensive 2 week training program at our corporate office. Training includes business operations, product training, principles of selling, interfacing, and time management.

Managerial Assistance Available: SAC Distributors International, Inc., regularly provides franchisees with incentive programs and information on new vendors, marketing strategies, and management techniques. An extensive database of product information is continually maintained and can be accessed via modem. Negotiations with new and existing vendors are ongoing to assure competitive pricing and service. An annual meeting is organized by SAC Distributors International, Inc., and on-site assistance at the franchisees' location is available.

Information Submitted: June 1987

SOFTWARE CENTRES INTERNATIONAL
1201 San Luis Obispo Avenue
Hayward, California 94544
Ted R. Torbuit, Director of Franchising

Description of Operation: Software Centre International specializes in providing a sophisticated mix of products and services geared exclusively to the personal computer after market; business and home entertainment software, peripheral products, supplies and accessories, high-tech publications, specialty furniture and more.

Number of Franchisees: 35 in 18 States

In Business Since: 1981

Equity Capital Needed: Approximately 4100,000. Total investment approximately $250,000

Financial Assistance Available: Franchisor assists in the preparation of a business plan/loan proposal and provides guidance in obtaining financing from outside sources.

Training Provided: Intensive 2 week training program is mandatory for all franchisees and managers. Special emphasis is placed on sales management, business planning, store operations, product knowledge, advertising, promotion and both retail and direct selling skills.

Managerial Assistance Available: Pre-opening assistance includes help with site selection, lease negotiation, professional store design, build out, initial inventory, personnel recruitment and other start-up issues. Continual management services are provided though numerous corporate-based programs and an organization of district field managers who regularly visit each store to assist with planning and operational issues. National franchisee conferences, regular regional training sessions and ongoing technical support are also provided.

Information Submitted: July 1987

STEP-SAVER DATA SYSTEMS
One Bala Plaza 417
Bala Cynwyd, Pennsylvania 19004
James S. Hammond, Director of Marketing

Description of Operation: Turnkey computer systems including IBM hardware to doctors.

Number of Franchisees: 23 in Florida, New Jersey, Pennsylvania, Maryland and New York.

In Business Since: 1981

Equity Capital Needed: $35,000

Financial Assistance Available: None

Training Provided: Initial 2 weeks classroom, thereafter, regular visits by field managers.

Managerial Assistance Available: 2 week in-house training on sales. Franchisor provides all technical help and computer installation. Franchisee only does sales.

Information Submitted: May 1987

*TODAYS COMPUTERS BUSINESS CENTERS
35 East Uwchlan Avenue
Suite 300
Exton, Pennsylvania 19341
Rex K. Reed, President

Description of Operation: For already successful businesses who have an existing customer base and solid reputation under their own name, the opportunity to set up a "company within their company." A commercial and retail franchise for computers and other intelligent electronic products.

Number of Franchisees: 66 in 31 States

In Business Since: 1982

Equity Capital Needed: Approximately $105,000.

Financial Assistance Available: Franchisor will assist franchisee in preparing a loan proposal package to present to a bank or other loaning institution, and obtaining inventory financing (floorplanning).

Training Provided: Initial 2 week training covering integration of computer sales and service into an existing operation with a focus on product knowledge. Additional courses to be provided as necessary.

Managerial Assistance Available: Pre-opening consultation on cost-efficient methods of developing the business, site improvement and fixturization guidance as necessary. Ongoing support through technical hot-line, manuals, dealer account manager, and corporate marketing support staff.

Information Submitted: August 1987

VALCOM
10810 Farnam
Omaha, Nebraska 68154
Mike Steffan, Director of Channel Development

Description of Operation: ValCom Computer Center is a complete one source, one stop, hands on store, concentrating on the business markets in selected locations throughout the United States. At the core of each ValCom Computer Center is a learning center. Not just some place to hold classes, but an intrical part of the total concept—the driving force behind the ValCom Computer Center.

Number of Franchisees: 170 stores in 40 States including company-owned.

In Business Since: 1982

Equity Capital Needed: $125,000-$300,000

Financial Assistance Available: No direct financing available; however, franchisor does assist franchisee in preparing a business plan that can be presented to a bank or other loan institutions.

Training Provided: 1 week for the store manager and 1 week for the learning center manager. Subjects covered are product knowledge, sales training and management, accounting and merchandising. Updating and refresher courses are offered as need arises both at corporate headquarters and/or the franchisees location. Currently no charge to franchisee.

Managerial Assistance Available: The franchisor provides continuing managerial and technical support services throughout the term of the franchise, through a field of regional managers that work with a group of 10 franchisees and live within their territories.

Information Submitted: August 1987

RETAILING—FLORIST

AFFORDABLE LOVE, INC.
7103 Crosswyck Court
Wexford, Pennsylvania 15090
Richard Finley, President

Description of Operation: Drive-thru flower and gift shops. Unique roadside flower and gift business that combines quality products, low prices and convenience.

Number of Franchisees: 2 in Pennsylvania

In Business Since: 1983

Equity Capital Needed: $25,000 to $29,000

Financial Assistance Available: None

Training Provided: 3 days of on-the-job training in Pittsburgh, Pennsylvania. A detailed operating manual and sales manual.

Managerial Assistance Available: Ongoing

Information Submitted: May 1987

* AMLINGS FRANCHISE INTERNATIONAL CORP.
540 West Ogden Avenue
Hinsdale, Illinois 60521
Scott D. Graunke, Vice President, Franchise Development
Kenneth J. Young, Director, Franchise Administration

Description of Operation: Amlings FLowers and Gifts franchise is a full service retail floral and gift store, selling fresh and artificial flowers, live and silk plants, cards, giftware, and related items. Stores range in size from 1,000 to 6,000 square feet.

Number of Franchisees: 4 plus 14 company-owned in Illinois

In Business Since: 1890, franchising since 1987

Equity Capital Needed: Minimum investment for a conversion floral store is $43,000. Minimum initial investment for new store is $120,000.

Financial Assistance Available: None

Training Provided: Intensive, 16 day mandatory training course is scheduled for all new franchises, including 4 days of classroom instruction and 12 days of field training in a company-owned Amlings Flowers and Gifts outlet.

Managerial Assistance Available: Continuous guidance and assistance in store operations, purchasing, advertising, merchandising, marketing, employee training, budgeting, record keeping and accounting. Complete Amlings Flowers and Gifts operating manual. Field representatives work with franchisees and visit stores on a regular basis.

Information Submitted: June 1987

BUNNING THE FLORIST, INC.
P. O. Box 14428
Ft. Lauderdale, Florida 33302
Edward P. Thal, President
Arthur O. Stone, Chairman of the Board

Description of Operation: Buning The Florist, Inc., offers unique retail florist shops throughout Florida and Western New York. Franchise package includes assistance in site selection and store layout, complete training program at headquarters in Ft. Lauderdale. Company operates 21 wholly owned units in addition to franchise locations.

Number of Franchisees: 11 in Florida, 1 in New York.

In Business Since: 1925 and began franchising in 1969.

Equity Capital Needed: $50,000

Financial Assistance Available: No financial assistance is provided by the franchisor.

Training Provided: 2 weeks provided at company headquarters in Ft. Lauderdale, Florida, plus continuing training in-store under company supervision.

Managerial Assistance Available: Franchisor assists franchisee in all aspects of shop operation, record keeping, advertising, promotion and selling techniques. Manuals of operation and counseling are provided. Home office personnel are available for periodic visits to stores.

Information Submitted: May 1987

* CONROY'S FLORISTS
11260 Playa Court
Culver City, California 90230
Carter S. Miller, President

Description of Operation: Conroy's, Inc., full service florists and mass merchandisors of floral product, licenses individuals to operate under the Conroy's Florists name and system of retail flowers and plant stores. The stores are generally free-standing (approximately 2,000 square feet) and located on high exposure signalized intersections. Conroy's performs real estate site acquisition, upon store opening provides a full-time field service representative to assist in day to day operations, coordinates initial set-up and grand opening, provides complete computerized accounting services consisting of profit and loss and balance sheets, and the processing of accounts receivable billings. Conroy's also coordinates and manages local and regional advertising programs utilizing television, radio, newspaper, direct mail and outdoor billboard advertising.

Number of Franchisees: 74 stores including company-owned.

In Business Since: 1960—Franchising since 1974.

Equity Capital Needed: Minimum $100,000 in cash.

Financial Assistance Available: None.

Training Provided: Training in a company-owned and operated training store will be provided. Training encompasses all phases of retail flower and plant operation including personnel recruitment and management, holiday programs, floral design, purchasing and all phases of retail operation.

Managerial Assistance Available: Conroy's provides opportunities for mass purchasing allowing licensees to obtain products at low prices (no obligation to purchase from Conroy's). Conroy's provides licensees with skilled and highly trained operational personnel to assist in opening licensee's store and provides support to licensees on an ongoing basis as required.

Information Submitted: May 1987

* FLOWERAMA OF AMERICA, INC.
3165 West Airline Highway
Waterloo, Iowa 50703
Chuck Nygren, Vice President

Description of Operation: Flowerama of America, Inc., franchise offers a unique and innovative approach to the retail floral business. Two types of stores (kiosk-450 square feet and in-line-1,000 square feet) located in prime locations in enclosed mall shopping centers only, offer fresh cut flowers, floral arrangements, potted plants, and other horticultural related products plus related floral accessories and gifts, to the consumer public at popular prices. Flowerama provides a service, from site selection to store design and construction under long-term leases to its franchisees.

Number of Franchisees: 86 in 23 States plus 12 company-owned shops.

In Business Since: 1966

Equity Capital Needed: $20,000 to $40,000 cash requirement.

Financial Assistance Available: Assists franchisee in obtaining financing from local bank. Supplies merchandise for resale on 30-day account basis.

Training Provided: 5 days at home office, 5 days on-the-job training and 10 days to 2 weeks at shop location.

Managerial Assistance Available: Flowerama provided continual management service for the life of the franchise in such areas as bookkeeping, advertising, store operations, inventory control. COmplete manuals of operations, forms, and directions are provided. Field representatives and staff personnel are continually available to provide franchise owners with assistance in the operation of their retail floral shop.

Information Submitted: May 1987

OMALLEY'S FLOWERS, INC.
15303 Ventura Boulevard 800
Sherman Oaks, California 91403
Daniel Martin, Director of Franchising

Description of Operation: OMalley's Flowers is an exciting flow, gift and antique retail operation. An average store is 1,500 square feet and is open either 6 or 7 days a week. No prior retail or floral background is required. The company provides extensive ongoing support to its franchisees.

Number of Franchisees: 26 in California, Oregon, Arizona and Nevada

In Business Since: 1977

227

Equity Capital Needed: Total investment between $105,000 and $130,000 plus.

Financial Assistance Available: The company will assist franchisee with financing from outside sources.

Training Provided: A very extensive training program is provided by the company. It is a 30 day program and includes all facets of the business. In addition our representative spends the first 10 days of the store opening in the franchisees store for additional training.

Managerial Assistance Available: A comprehensive training manual is provided, district and field managers are available in all regions to work closely with franchisees and visit stores regularly to assist in solving problems.

Information Submitted: July 1987

SHE'S FLOWERS, INC.
740 South Olive Street
Los Angeles, California 90014
Marty Shih

Description of Operation: Full service retail florist.

Number of Franchisees: 3 in California

In Business Since: 1979

Equity Capital Needed: $103,000-$156,000

Financial Assistance Available: The company may assist a franchisee with arrangements for financing through third parties.

Training Provided: 7 weeks of training. The initial training program will include instruction in flower handling, design, and floral arrangements; care for perishable floral commodities; inventory controls, purchasing methods, and procedures; administrative record keeping and accounting controls; local merchandising techniques and obligations; gross sales reporting; employee and customer relations; delivery procedures; and other features of the SHE'S Florists business system.

Managerial Assistance Available: Pre-opening assistance in site selection, design assistance, initial training program, operation manual and time to opening. Past opening assistance in inventory assistance, continuing supervision, accounting, promotion, updating of merchandising and supplier lists.

Information Submitted: May 1987

SILK PLANTS ETC. FRANCHISE SYSTEMS, INC.
1755 Butterfield Road
Libertyville, Illinois 60048
George W. Burns, Vice President, Franchising

Description of Operation: Silk plant and flower shops, size varies: 1,400-1,600 square feet. Silk plants anf lowers can be purchased direct from parent company which owns factories overseas—savings to purchasers of franchise about 30 percent. Retail prices 50 percent below department store prices.

Number of Franchisees: 151 including co-owned stores in most states.

In Business Since: 1985

Equity Capital Needed: $44,000 to $54,000.

Financial Assistance Available: None.

Training Provided: 7 days in corporate office—5 days in store.

Managerial Assistance Available: New product development advertising ma terials, national ads, new display and promotion ideas.

Information Submitted: May 1987.

WESLEY BERRY FLOWERS
15305 Schoolcraft
Detroit, Michigan 48227
Wesley L. Berry, III

Description of Operation: Wesely Berry Flowers offers full service flower shop franchises. Franchise outlets will participate in a $5.3 billion a year industry. Product line will include fresh cut flowers, blooming plants, green plants, floral arrangements, fine gifts, cards, and other such associated gift items. Complete advertising and public relations programs utilizing television, radio, newspapers and direct mail are available and in use in the Detroit metropolitan market.

Number of Franchisees: 9 in Michigan, and 10 in various stages of development.

In Business Since: 1946. Franchising began in late 1984.

Equity Capital Needed: $61,500.

Financial Assistance Available: From various financial institutions.

Training Provided: A 2 week intensified and personal training program covering floral design, shop operations and management skills. Further, a comprehensive training and policy manual is provided.

Managerial Assistance Available: Throughout the term of the agreement, the franchisor shall provide continuous sales, marketing and operational assistance by way of advice, consultations, periodical visits and telephone conferences.

Information Submitted: May 1987

RETAILING—NOT ELSEWHERE CLASSIFIED

ADELE'S ENTERPRISES, INC.
2832 Angelo Drive
Los Angeles, California 90077
Ted Margulis, President

Description of Operation: Adele's is a personalized gift boutique. The original store concept was established in Beverly Hills in 1945. The shops generally are 1,500-2,000 square feet and display between 2,000 to 3,500 sample items from which orders are taken from. Every item sold is personalized by either the store, or by one of 700 outside vendors. The items range from new born gifts to gifts for a new graduate and every gift giving event in between including weddings, anniversaries, etc.

Number of Franchisees: 5 in California

In Business Since: 1945 original store. Frachise operation since 1984.

Equity Capital Needed: $81,100-$161,000.

Financial Assistance Available: Yes through SBA.

Training Provided: A minimum of 10 days of intensive training in selling and management and product knowledge. Periodic consultation with the franchisee by a principal of the franchisor. A 300 plus page operations manual and all business operation forms including a vendor list of about 700 vendors and a purchase order system for initial ordering of samples. Complete computer/cash register system program.

Managerial Assistance Available: Operations manual visits by a principal and a monthly newsletter. At opening, up to 3 days of assistance by one of the training staff, if necessary.

Information Submitted: May 1987

* ADVENTURELAND VIDEO, INC.
4516 South 700 E
Suite 260
Salt Lake City, Utah 84107

Description of Operation: Video rental franchising.

Number of Franchisees: Over 600 units in 38 States.

In Business Since: 1981

Equity Capital Needed: $65,000 to $75,000

Financial Assistance Available: None

Training Provided: Initial training of owners and/or managers. Ongoing service.

Managerial Assistance Available: Regional service representatives, a monthly newsletter, a monthly consolidated store report and periodical training sessions. Training tapes and handbooks for employees and managers. Quarterly franchise meetings, store audits, store analysis, and store business plans.

Information Submitted: August 1987

AGWAY, INC.
P. O. Box 4933
Syracuse, New York 13221
Kenneth L. Gregg, Director of Representatives

Description of Operation: Agway Inc., operates company-owned stores that distribute principally farm-input supplies to its farmer-members and other patrons. The company also franchises stores to independent operators that sell agriculturally related products to small farm operators and homeowners. The franchised product line consists of primarily animal feeds, lawn and garden supplies, hardware and outdoor living supplies.

Number of Franchisees: 342 franchises, 265 company-owned stores and 103 local cooperatives in 12 States.

In Business Since: 1964

Equity Capital Needed: The total cost of an Agway outlet is not ascertainable due to variables such as land cost, construction cost, lease costs, delays and contingencies. It can be assumed, however, that the total initial cost will exceed $150,000.

Financial Assistance Available: Agway's wholly-owned subsidiary, Telmark, Inc., provides leasing services for equipment and buildings. Agway may provide for the purchase of inventory and supplies and may lease the premises. Terms and conditions vary with the need for credit and the credit worthiness of the franchisee.

Training Provided: The Agway training program covers all appropriate aspects of the operation of an Agway outlet. It is conducted in Syracuse, New York for 1 week. The course is mandatory and must be successfully completed. The franchisee will also participate in 40 hours of continuing education per year.

Managerial Assistance Available: Agway provides a continual business advisory service through a staff of zone managers. Accounting and tax preparation services are provided the first year and are available at cost thereafter. Operations and identification manuals are provided. Advertising materials are provided at cost. An extensive staff of technicians and researchers are available to answer questions on a continual basis.

Information Submitted: May 1987

AMERICAN FAST PHOTO AND CAMERA, INC.
157 S. Pine Street
Spartanburg, South Carolina 29302
Steve Bend, Vice President Development

Description of Operation: Full service 1 hour photofinishing outlet, portrait studio, cameras and retail accessories, black and white and enlargement services, slides, video transfer. All services done in house to insure maximum profitability.

Number of Franchisees: 20 in Michigan and South Carolina.

In Business Since: 1984

Equity Capital Needed: $35,000 to $60,000

Finacial Assistance Available: Equipment lease, full equipment price, SBA, up to 70 percent of package price.

Training Provided: Technical training, 2 weeks, management training, retail, and marketing, 1 week. Onsite training, 1 week.

Managerial Assistance Available: Site selection, lease negotiation, 4 week training program, technical staff, operations staff, building layouts.

Information Submitted: May 1987

ANIMATION STATION
10800 W. Pico Blvd.
Suite 387
Los Angeles, California 90064

Description of Operation: Animation Station is one of America's fun-packed retail franchise concepts which features a circus of cartoon merchandise. The cartoon merchandise mix run the gamut from comic strip and early animated characters including apparel, plush animal toys, greeting cards, candy, pins, posters, comic books and other traditional animated merchandise products.

Number of Franchisees: 6 in California

In Business Since: 1985

Equity Capital Needed: Total investment, including initial franchise fee, ranges from $65,000 to $150,000.

Financial Assistance Available: None

Training Provided: Management and operation, with a minimum of 2 weeks instruction.

Managerial Assistance Available: The franchisor will periodically inspect the franchise premises to provide on-site operations assistance. The franchisor may also periodically make available advertising plans and advice and in-shop merchandising materials for franchisees' local use and may assist in designing special advertising and promotional programs. Additional training courses or programs may become available to franchisee at the discretion of the franchisor to include sales techniques, training of personnel, performance standards, advertising programs and merchandising procedures.

Information Submitted: June 1987

ANNIE'S BOOK STOP, INC.
15 Lackey Street
Westbourough, Massachusetts 01581
Anne Adams

Description of Operation: Franchisor sells franchises to establish bookstore centers for the sale and exchange of pre-read paperback books, for the sale of new books, both paperback and hardcover editions, and for the sale of other book related or gift items.

Number of Franchisees: 84 in 14 states

In Business Since: 1981

Equity Capital Needed: $24,000 to $43,000

Financial Assistance Available: None

Training Provided: On hand training plus detailed manual duration, 2 weeks plus.

Managerial Assistance Available: Ongoing through phone and mail for life of franchise.

Information Submitted: May 1987

* APPLAUSE VIDEO
2622 South 156th Circle
Omaha, Nebraska 68130
Bruce Shackman, President

Description of Operation: Applause Video Corporation establishes a unique retail environment for the video industry. Each store is approximately 3,500 square feet with ample store front parking and is open 10 a.m. to 10 p.m. seven days a week. An extensive inventory providing the proper selection as well as depth tailored to the individual community is part of what makes Applause so successful.

Number of Franchisees: 18 franchised outlets plus 21 company-owned outlets in Nebraska and Iowa.

In Business Since: 1983

Equity Capital Needed: $75,000 minimum.

Financial Assistance Available: Provide no financial assistance.

Training Provided: We provide an intensive 2 week mandatory training course with in-store training at one of our company-owned locations in Omaha, Nebraska. In addition, we provide on premise management for the franchisee's store for the first week of operation.

Managerial Assistance Available: Applause Video provides continual management services for the life of the franchise in such areas as bookkeeping, advertising, promotion and inventory control. Field managers will work closely with franchisee and visit stores regularly to assist in solving problems.

Information Submitted: May 1987

ARMCHAIR SAILOR INTERNATIONAL, INC.
126 Thames Street
Newport, Rhode Island 02840
Perry Lewis, Vice President

Description of Operation: Armchair Sailor is a network of interactive marine book and navigation centers, emphasizing complete lines of marine and travel books and nautical charts. Franchisees are expected to provide professional level skills in navigation. custom software, design and inventory packages are provided.

Number of Franchisees: 9 in California, Florida, Rhode Island, Maryland, New York and Pennsylvania and South Carolina.

In Business Since: 1985

Equity Capital Needed: The franchise fee is $28,000. An additional $100,000 to $125,000 is required to open a center.

Financial Assistance Available: None

Training Provided: A 2 week training period in Newport for 2 employees. Assistance is provided at the opening and is available at all times by telephone, by modem and by periodic personal visits.

Managerial Assistance Available: Ongoing assistance is available by telephone, modem and personal visits. The 400 page manual is continuously scrutinized for revisions which are provided at all times.

Information Submitted: May 1987

BALLOON-AGE
P. O. Box 881
Chatham, New Jersey 07928
Roy R. Ruttenberg

Description of Operation: Gifts and decorations retail operation—specializes in balloon deliveries, sales promotions, party decorations and other gift items. Carries its own line of balloons, chocolates, mugs, T-shirts and other gifts.

Number of Franchisees: 8 in New York, New Jersey, Ohio and Georgia. Company-owned stores: 2 in New Jersey.

In Business Since: 1980

Equity Capital Needed: $40,000 to $60,000

Financial Assistance Available: May offer limited financial assistance to qualified prospects.

Training Provided: 2 weeks of training is provided.

Managerial Assistance Available: Balloon-Age provides continual management assistance for the duration of the franchise in areas such as: advertising, promotions, new product introduction, bookkeeping. Balloon-Age sponsors meeting of franchises to discuss all parts of their business.

Information Submitted: August 1987

*BATH & A-HALF FRANCHISE SYSTEMS, INC.
999 Elmhurst Road
Suite C-11
Mt. Prospect, Illinois 60056
Sandra K. Kreeger, President

Description of Operation: Retail stores specializing in bath accessories and bath related merchandise and gift lines, including towels, shower curtains, rugs, and coordinated bath accessories. Franchisor creates speciality merchandise and imports exclusive lines for Bath & A-Half stores only. Emphasis on coordinated ensembles and coordinates created for theme programs. Stores are located primarily in high traffic major enclosed mall shopping centers requiring approximately 1,200 square feet. Store are inventoried according to market and varied according to income levels.

Number of Franchisees: 13 stores in Illinois, Texas, Wisconsin and Minnesota, including 7 company-owned stores.

In Business Since: 1985

Equity Capital Needed: $80,000 to $100,000

Financial Assistance Available: None. Franchisee must obtain own financing. Generally, the franchisee must have 50 percent of the needed capital to obtain an additional 50 percent bank financing.

Training Provided: Intensive 1 week mandatory training course is scheduled for all franchisees or their store managers or operators. Training held in home office and actually includes working in company-owned Bath & A-Half stores. A second week of training and assistance is provided in franchisee's outlet. An annual Managers Mart is held for special training and merchandise selection.

Managerial Assistance Available: Bath & A-Half has complete operating manuals, vendor catalogs for purchasing aids, accounting systems, monthly newsletters, window and theme decor planning aids, annual buying program for holiday planning and advertising assistance. Field supervisors will work closely with the franchisees and visit stores regularly to assist with any problems. Bath & A-Half will provide regular newsletters and special bulletins to advise of new product opportunities, special allowances, seasonal items and merchandise specials.

Information Submitted: May 1987

*BATHTIQUE INTERNATIONAL, LTD
Carnegie Place—247 Goodman Street
Rochester, New York 14607
Don A. Selpel, President

Description of Operation: A retail bath, bed and gift specialty shop offering the latest products and accessories.

Number of Franchisees: 91 in 35 States, Puerto Rico and the Virgin Island including 23 company-owned shops.

In Business Since: 1969

Equity Capital Needed: $20-$35,000. No direct financing, but assistance in acquiring funding through local banks.

Financial Assistance Available: No direct financing but assistance in acquiring financing through local banks.

Training Provided: A concentrated 1 week training period is conducted for all new franchisees. Individuals for each franchise participate in a 1 week manager training program. This program includes a classroom and on-the-job training under experienced managers. An additional 2 weeks of on-site location assistance isprovided by the home office staff at the time the franchisees' shop opens. A follow-up briefing session is conducted on-site after opening.

Managerial Assistance Available: Bathtique International provides continuing review and feedback concening shop operations in areas such as sales, purchasing, advertising, and labor schedule. Merchandising is recommended to franchisees after testing in company shop. Merchandise is bought directly from recommended suppliers, quantity discounts available. A continuous personnel training program is strongly emphasized. Advertising materials and co-op funds are provided regularly including direct mail books. Annual and regional conferences are offered throughout the country.

Information Submitted: May 1987

BLIND DESIGNS, INC.
106 Bayview Boulevard
Oldsmar, Florida 33557

Description of Operation: Blind Designs is a specialty window treatment store offering a complete line of window coverings for both the commercial and residential customer. Our concept is unique: as we showcase them with lifesize displays. Our selling formula is to offer the consumer the best value, quality and service. As a franchise system of operation, Blind Designs stores are located in cities where there is immediate potential for further growth, and where the income and purchasing levels are in the middle to upper range. Our stores are conveniently located in strip centers of a modern type with a minimum suggested square feet of 600.

Number of Franchisees: 8 in Florida. Actively seeking franchises in Florida and New Jersey.

In Business Since: 1979, franchising since 1984

Equity Capital Needed: $15,000 franchise fee and up to $15,000 start up expenses.

Financial Assistance Available: None

Training Provided: Training covers insdie and outside sales, including soliciting and closing sales; management; hiring and firing of personnel, accounting and bookkeeping procedures, installing; product knowledge and pricing; advertising, and promotion, a 3 week training program and a representative for 1 seek for in store after opening.

Managerial Assistance Available: Our producrs are national brand products of the highest quality. Due to volume purchasing, the manufacturers we select will offer quick delivery, good service and competitive pricing. A representative will visit your location once every two montsh for a review and assist with any problems. Additional hlep will come in the way of a newsletter, pricing updates, sales techniques, new products and sales seminars.

Information Submitted: May 1987

BOOK RACK MANAGEMENT, INC.
2703 E. Commercial Boulevard
Ft. Lauderdale, Florida 33308
Fred M. Darnell

Description of Operation: Used paper back books, and new books.

Number of Franchisees: 248 in 34 states

In Business Since: 1963

Equity Capital Needed: $12,000

Financial Assistance Available: None

Training Provided: 1 or 2 weeks training and site location. Help supply inventory, yearly meeting and monthly newsletter.

Managerial Assistance Available: Ongoing assistance

Information Submitted: May 1987

BOWL AND BOARD
12 St. Marks Place
New York, New York 10003
Charles Fitzgerald, President

Description of Operation: Specialized retailing concept of all-wood items for home and kitchen. Parent company designs, develops, manufacturers unique and useful wood products; supplied to franchisee at competitive prices. Simple one source inventory control and management. Annual fee of $1,000 to $2,000 depending on size of location.

Number of Franchisees: 8

In Business Since: 1963

Equity Capital Needed: $15,000 to $45,000 for starting inventory plus annual fee of $1,000 to $2,000.

Financial Assistance Available: No financial assistance but a provision for return of goods for full credit.

Training Provided: Optional informal agreement where prospective franchisee will work in parent company outlet for at least 2 weeks providing all necessary training.

Managerial Assistance Available: Provide continually changing line of goods and system of management. Telephone advice on store location, decor, display and sales.

Information Submitted: May 1987

THE BOX SHOPPE, INC.
7165 East 87th Street
Indianapolis, Indiana 46256
Duke Smith

Description of Operation: We are a retail and wholesale business involved in the sale of gift boxes, moving boxes, storage boxes, bows, ribbons, gift wrap, etc.

Number of Franchisees: 27 in Indiana, Illinois, Kentucky, Ohio and Michigan.

In Business Since: 1984

Equity Capital Needed: $20,000

Financial Assistance Available: None at present.

Training Provided: Extensive 3 day training program at franchisor's headquarters, additional on-site assistance as necessary.

Managerial Assistance Available: None required.

Information Submitted: May 1987

BUDGET TAPES & RECORDS, INC.
10625 East 47th Avenue
Denver, Colorado 80239
Evan Lasky

Description of Operation: Retail tapes, records, and compact discs.

Number of Franchisees: 85 in 17 States

In Business Since: 1970

Equity Capital Needed: $55,000-$80,000

Financial Assistance Available: Assist in loan proposal preparation.

Training Provided: 2 to 3 weeks retail and warehouse training.

Managerial Assistance Available: Assistance in site selection and lease negotiation, preparation of store layout and design, selection of initial inventory and furniture and fixtures, development of advertising and promotional material and programs, assist in operation, financial planning and management of store, provide training in retail store and wholesale warehouse settings.

Information Submitted: May 1987

* BUTTERFIELDS DEVELOPMENT, INC.
600 Broadway
Suite 640
Kansas City, Missouri 64105
Larry K. Childers, President

Description of Operation: Gourmet kitchen store— featuring gadgets, accessories, decorator items, small appliances, and novelties. Locations are in regional shopping malls.

Number of Franchisees: 12 in Texas, Oklahoma and Louisiana

In Business Since: 1979

Equity Capital Needed: $110,000-$130,000

Financial Assistance Available: None

Training Provided: 2 weeks—1 week at headquarters and 1 week on-site of new store.

Managerial Assistance Available: Franchisor provides ongoing supervision and purchasing aids—keeping franchisee informed on new items and trends in the business.

Information Submitted: August 1987

* CAMERAAMERICA FRANCHISING, INC.
1404 Gornto Road
Valdosta, Georgia 31601
B. Daniel Bish, Vice President, Sales

Description of Operation: Sales of franchises to operate 1-hour photofinishing and retail camera/accessories store.

Number of Franchisees: 71 in 14 States

In Business Since: 1984

Equity Capital Needed: $50,000

Financial Assistance Available: Assistance in financing of lab and leasehold improvements.

Training Provided: 2 week initial training; periodic training annually.

Managerial Assistance Available: Buildout of store, merchandising, advertising, accounting, personnel as well as photo finishing, sales and camera assistance.

Information Submitted: May 1987

* CELLULAND
10717 Sorrento Valley Road
San Diego, California 92121
Teresa Beck, Franchise Sales Administrator

Description of Operation: Retail cellular car phone sales and service center offering a wide selection of cellular phones, products, installations, customer service, warranty work, cellular phone number activations and other communications products.

Number of Franchisees: 17 plus 1 company-owned in Arizona, California, Colorado, Minnesota and Nevada

In Business Since: 1985

Equity Capital Needed: $150,000 to $225,000

Financial Assistance Available: None

Training Provided: 6 weeks at franchisor's location plus ongoing support.

Managerial Assistance Available: Site selection assistance, store design, on-site support, cellular phone service contracts, central purchasing for products, computer software provided for lead tracking to customer cost of goods and profit reports.

Information Submitted: May 1987

CHAD'S RAINBOW, INC.
1778 North Plano Road
Suite 120
Richardson, Texas 75081
Dale Brandon

Description of Operation: Chad's Rainbow is a unique franchise of retail toy stores specializing in educational and developmental toys, books, and teaching aids. Store size is approximately 1,500 to 2,000 square feet located in major shopping malls or high traffic strip centers.

Number of Franchisees: 24 in 9 states.

In Business Since: 1981

Equity Capital Needed: $35,000

Financial Assistance Available: None at present time. Total investment needed for a Chad's Rainbow franchise is $127,000. Franchisee must arrange for outside financing.

Training Provided: Training includes 1 day of preliminary training to introduce franchisee to initial responsibilities as a new business owner. 10 days of training are conducted at franchisee's store location prior to grand opening. Ongoing training is provided as needed.

Managerial Assistance Available: Chad's Rainbow, Inc., provides continuing support and training for the life of the franchise in all areas of operation such as inventory selection and control, advertising, etc. Periodic owners meetings are held to share information on new inventory, advertising mediums, customer service, etc.

Information Submitted: May 1987

CLEANING IDEAS, INC.
4219 Center Gate
San Antonio, Texas 78217
Attention: Franchise Director

Description of Operation: Cleaning Ideas is a unique retail/wholesale store operation. Cleaning Ideas stores sell over 1,600 items and chemicals to be used for cleaning. All chemical items are manufactured by Cleaning Ideas, thus gross profits run as high as 60 percent. All products are sold with a money back guarantee. Each store is 1,000 square feet.

Number of Franchisees: 12 in Texas

In Business Since: 1931

Equity Capital Needed: $6,000 minimum

Financial Assistance Available: A total investment of $15,000 is necessary to open a Cleaning Ideas franchise. The down payment of $6,000 pays for sign, shelving, 1/2 inventory, training. Cleaning Ideas will finance the balance, with no interest (90 days).

Training Provided: Intensive 6 day mandatory training course is scheduled for all new franchisees. All training is performed in company-owned stores.

Managerial Assistance Available: Cleaning Ideas provides ongoing managerial and technical assistance, for the duration of the franchise agreement.

Information Submitted: May 1987

COLONEL VIDEO
2425 Bay Area Boulevard
Houston, Texas 77058
Vijay Gupta, President

Description of Operation: Video equipment, audio equipment computer equipment, telephone and other consumer electronics items. The franchise package also includes assistance in site selection, store layout and includes each store in a discount purchasing program. We also rent video movies.

Number of Franchisees: 3 in Texas and Oklahoma

In Business Since: 1982

Equity Capital Needed: Total cost is about $340,000. $60,000 plus outside financing.

Financial Assistance Available: None, we assist you in preparing the package for financial assistance from banks, and inventory finance companies.

Training Provided: Minimum 2 weeks: site selection, financial assistance,

Managerial Assistance Available: We provide you with continuous business assistance for the life of the franchise. We are in constant communication with our franchisees, both by telephone and by newsletters, to inform them of new products and new programs. We provide you with a manager for grand opening. Complete assistance for advertising on an ongoing basis.

Information Submitted: May 1987

COMPACT DISC WAREHOUSE, INC.
15601 Producer Lane, Building A
Huntington Beach, California 92649
William E. Cline, General Manager

Description of Operation: Retail sale of compact audio discs, video discs, and related accessories. Store size varies with maximum size of 2,000 square feet.

Number of Franchisees: 2 in California

In Business Since: 1986

Equity Capital Needed: Approximately $140,000. Minimum estimated start-up cost, including franchise fee of $10,000.

Financial Assistance Available: None

Training Provided: 1-2 weeks initially at company headquarters and on-site, ongoing management assistance and additional training as needed.

Managerial Assistance Available: Including advertising assistance as needed, inventory control as well as updated, complete policy and operations manual.

232

Information Submitted: May 1987

COOK'S CORNER
6404 Nancy Ridge Drive
San Diego, California 92121

Description of Operation: Cook's corner offers a unique retail store operation. Each store is approximately 1,500-2,000 square feet and is located in regional shopping centers only. An extensive inventory in the product categories of cookware, housewares and gourmet coffees is maintained. Cook's Corner is the lease holder, with the franchisee as the subtenant. The stores are designed to be attractive and increase customer acceptance.

Number of Franchisees: 12 in California

In Business Since: 1977

Equity Capital Needed: $75,000 to $100,000

Financial Assistance Available: A total investment of approximately $250,000 is necessary to open a Cook's Corner. Cook's Corner will assist franchisee with financing through various lenders.

Training Provided: Intensive 5 day classroom training in corporate offices in San Diego, California. On-site at company trainings take up to 3 days, and up to 7 days at franchisee's store under supervision of a Cook's Corner representative.

Managerial Assistance Available: Cook's Corner provides continual management service for life of the franchise in such areas as merchandising, marketing, promotion, purchasing, record keeping and inventory control. Complete manuals of operations are provided. Field support representatives are available to work closely with franchisees and visit stores regularly to assist solving problems. Cook's Corner sponsors meetings of franchisees and conducts marketing and product research to maintain high consumer acceptance.

Information Submitted: August 1987

COPY MAT
46 Shattuck Square
Berkeley, California 94704
Kathleen Roche, Director of Franchising

Description of Operation: Copy Mat is a full service photo-copy center specializing in high-quality volume production (same day and overnight) and customer service. Store offer a whole range of ancillarly services including stationary sales, self-service typing booths, postal boxes, spiral and velo-binding, cassette duplication, and full and self service desktop publishing services. Each distinctively designed Copy Mat is located in a highly visible, well lighted area and shops usually average approximately 1,500 square feet. Stores feature customer self-service on a walk-in basis on all equipment and can meet the needs of almost all types of businesses and personal use.

Number of Franchisees: 47 in California

In Business Since: 1984

Equity Capital Needed: $38,500 initial franchise fee; total investment from $96,250 to $254,000.

Financial Assistance Available: Franchisor will aid in securing outside financing in an advisory role.

Training Provided: Comprehensive training program for manager and assistant manager which includes up to 5 weeks at the franchisor's headquarters or store nearby their home. Program provides an operating manual, hands-on experience and covers all the training phases of business including pre-opening checklist, marketing, operations, customer relations, staffing and training, budgeting, accounting, and purchasing.

Managerial Assistance Available: Franchisor aids in the purchase of equipment and supplies. Franchisee has access to company purchasing contracts and their discounts. Upon store opening, franchisor provides full-time assistance by the district manager for up to 30 days. A regional manager assists at the store at least 1 day monthly. There is continual marketing assistance at both regional and local levels. Management provides aid with business management; inventory control; bookkeeping; and customer relations. The firm also aids in site selection and leasehold arrangements, store design, grand opening, and technical assistance involving any phase of operations.

Information Submitted: June 1987

CREATE-A-BOOK
6380 Euclid Road
Cincinnati, Ohio 45236
Robert Young

Description of Operation: Create-A-Book is a company that prints and sells personalized childrens books. Any child can have his/her name printed throughout colorful storybooks along with friends, relatives, pets, age, hometown, etc. It takes four minutes from start to finish to print, bind and place a book in a hard cover. Franchisees have the equipment to completely print and bind the books. There are many, many different ways to sell and market the books. Training provided. Excellent home business.

Number of Franchisees: 200

In Business Since: 1980

Equity Capital Needed: $2,995 plus approximately $1,200 for equipment.

Financial Assistance Available: We do not offer any financial assistance.

Training Provided: Training is provided in Cincinnati, Ohio. For those people unable to attend the training, we provide a manual and video tape. Additional training is provided through seminars and meetings.

Managerial Assistance Available: Seminars and meetings are provided to update franchisees. Newsletters are sent to all franchisees throughout the year.

Information Submitted: May 1987

C-3 MANAGEMENT CORPORATION
1582 Annapolis Road
Odenton, Maryland 2113
Cynthia A. Livingston

Description of Operation: C-3 Management Corporation offers franchises for the establishment, development and operation of retail facilities for the rental and sales of pre-recorded video tapes, related merchandise, accessories and products and is granted the right to use the mark "THE CHANNEL 3 CONNECTION."

Number of Franchisees: 5 in Maryland

In Business Since: 1975

Equity Capital Needed: $35,000 minimum

Financial Assistance Available: Assistance in preparing documents for outside financing.

Training Provided: Extensive 1 week training course in-store for all franchisees and 2 persons they may designate in all areas of operation and administration of The Channel 3 Connection video store concept.

Managerial Assistance Available: C-3 Management Corp. provides continual management service for the life of the franchise in such areas as bookkeeping, advertising, inventory control. Complete manuals of operations, forms and directions are provided. Managers are available to work closely with franchisees and visit stores regularly to assist solving problems. C-3 Management Corp. sponsors meetings of franchisees and conducts marketing and product research to maintain high consumer acceptance.

Information Submitted: May 1987

* CURTIS MATHES CORPORATION
P. O. Box 223607
Dallas, Texas 75225-0607
Larry Randolph, Director, Franchise Sales and Development

Description of Operation: Curtis Mathes Corporation authorizes franchisees to operate Curtis Mathes Home Entertainment Centers, which sell, rent and lease a broad line of high quality electronic home entertainment products carrying extended warranties. The stores also offer video movie rental clubs, satelite antenna systems and complete service capability.

Number of Franchisees: 600 in 46 States

In Business Since: 1920

Equity Capital Needed: $125,000

Financial Assistance Available: The total investment in a Curtis Mathes Home Entertainment Center is $125,000-$200,000, depending upon the type and size of the location. Neither the franchisor nor any affiliate directly offers financing to the franchisee. However, the franchisor indirectly offers inventory and consumer credit financing to the franchisee through third party lending institutions.

Training Provided: An intensive, 25 day, mandatory training program is scheduled for all new franchisees and their key personnel. 15 days are conducted at the home office training school in Dallas. 5 days are conducted at selected training stores around the country. 5 days are conducted at the franchisees outlet under the supervision of full-time Curtis Mathes employees.

Managerial Assistance Available: Continuing managerial and technical assistance are provided for the duration of the franchise in such areas as site selection, store design and layout, advertising and promotional materials, inventory and consumer credit financing, inventory control, etc. Complete manuals of operations, forms, and directions are provided. District and field managers are available to work closely with franchisees and visit stores regularly to assist in solving problems. Curtis Mathes sponsors meetings of franchisees and conducts extensive marketing and product research.

Information Submitted: April 1987

DELPHI STAINED GLASS CENTERS, INC.
2116 East Michigan
Lansing, Michigan 48912
Daniel L. Fattaleh, President, Franchise Sales Director

Description of Operation: Delphi Stained Glass Centers are retail stores which sell stained glass supplies—glass, tools, patterns, books and related merchandise used in the creation of stained glass windows, lampshades, mirrors and other items. Cneters also provide customers with the opportunities to develop techniques and upgrade skills in the art of stained glass, through an extensive program of stained glass classes, workshops and seminars. 1-800-248-2048 (Nat.) 1-800-292-5936 (in MI).

Number of Franchisees: 11 franchises in 5 States plus 2 company-owned.: In Business Since: 1982

Equity Capital Needed: Approximately $60,000-$65,000.

Financial Assistance Available: Franchisor helps in developing a business plan to obtain financing through local financial institutions.

Training Provided: New Delphi Stained Glass Center franchisees receive training in the areas of management, retail sales, promotion, advertising, finance and glass teaching skills.

Managerial Assistance Available: Delphi Stained Glass Centers, Inc., offers opening assisstance by reviewing with the franchisee the center location, lease, floor plan and fixture set up. An operations manual, stained glass instructors manual and an advertising kit are also provided. Continuing assistance is provided in the areas of advertising, marketing, operations and classes. Meetings between all the franchisees and the franchisor are held, on an semiannual basis.

Information Submitted: April 1986

DESCAMPS
A Division of THE DOLLFUS MIEG COMPANY, INC.
454 Columbia Avenue
New York, New York 10024

Description of Operation: Descamps franchise is in the business of linens, bath products and related items. The motor company is French and has at present 170 stores in 11 different countries. Each store has approximately 1,000 square feet, operates in using tradename, service marks, logos and designs summarized in a technical book provided bl franchisor.

Number of Franchisees: 3 in California and Texas. plus 6 company owned stores.

In Business Since: 1980

Equity Capital Needed: $130,000

Financial Assistance Available: Help in negotiating lease and most of time franchisor finds locations and in anycase has to give his approbation. Measurements and supply of plans are provided to franchisee in a technical book. An experienced Descamps merchandiser is sent during construction, to decorate prior to opening (during different trips to the site) helps for the opening, and afterwards twice a year at least for guidance and animation. A credit for opening in 30 days was given to franchisees in 1981.

Training Provided: 2 weeks of training in our Madison Avenue, New York store.

Managerial Assistance Available: Technical assistance is provided during all term of franchise contract through relation with our New York office to solve problems such as advertising, size of collection, financial analysis.

Information Submitted: September 1987

* DOLLAR DISCOUNT STORES
1362 Naamans Creek Road
Bothwyn, Pennsylvania 19061
Thomas Fleisher, Franchise Director

Description of Operation: Dollar Discount Stores has developed a successful retail concept for the discount shopper market. Its stores offer a wide variety of low priced, high demand close-out and general merchandise.

Number of Franchisees: 11

In Business Since: 1982

Equity Capital Needed: $77,000-$107,000 total investment.

Financial Assistance Available: None

Training Provided: Initial training consists of 10 days in the classroom and in actual stores and covers all aspects of the business such as: store management, merchandising, personnel management, policies and procedures, ordering, bookkeeping, hiring and training, theft prevention, etc. An experienced manager also will spend a minimum of 1 week on-site with each franchisee for the grand opening.

Managerial Assistance Available: Dollar Discount Stores assists its franchisees with site selection and development advice, lease negotiation, advertising and public relations, national and international product selection and purchasing, and ongoing operational support by a team of seasoned managers.

Information Submitted: July 1987

FAN FAIR DEVELOPMENT CORPORATION
12425 Knoll Rd.
Elm Grove, Wisconsin 53122

Description of Operation: Fan Fair offers a unique retail store operation. Merle Harmon's Fan Fair is billed as the "Sports Fans Gift Shop," featuring gifts and clothing bearing the team logos and colors from all professional teams and over 100 collegiate teams. Each store is about 1,000 square feet, located in a major regional shopping center, and merchandised according to local sports markets.

Number of Franchisees: 85 in 23 States

In Business Since: 1977

Equity Capital Needed: $80,000-$110,000

Financial Assistance Available: None. Franchisee must obtain own financing. Generally, the franchisee must have 50 percent of the needed capital to obtain an additional 50 percent bank financing.

Training Provided: Intensive 2-4 week mandatory training course is scheduled for all franchisees or their store operators. 10-14 days at the franchisees outlet under the supervision of our training supervisors ongoing.

Managerial Assistance Available: Fan Fair has complete operating manuals, vendor catalogs for purchasing aids, accounting systems, forms, reports, co-op buying sessions, and a distribution center for store support on many items. Field supervisors will work closely with the franchisees and visit stores regularly to assist with problems. Fan Fair constantly advises franchisees of new product opportunities, special allowances, and seasonal merchandising ideas.

Information Submitted: May 1987

FRIEDMAN FRANCHISORS
2301 Broadway
Oakland, California 94612
Arthur Friedman, General Partner

Description of Operation: Friedman's Microwave Ovens: Microwave specialty stores selling only microwave ovens and accessories enhanced by microwave cooking schools. A unique business with a focus on complete customer satisfaction by offering 60 day free exchange, competitive prices, free schools for life and discounts on accessories.

Number of Franchisees: 95 in 23 States

In Business Since: 1976, franchising since 1979

Equity Capital Needed: $25,000-$35,000

Financial Assistance Available: None

Training Provided: Week long training session held at Oakland, California headquarters, on-site training prior, during and after opening, telephone assistance always available.

Managerial Assistance Available: Included in the above.

Information Submitted: May 1987

GALLERY 1 AFFORDABLE ART
6601 NW 14th Street
Suite 2
Plantation, Florida 33313
Fred Goldstein, Vice President

Description of Operation: Gallery 1 Affordable Art manufactures and markets ready to hang fine art and graphic art in retail stores situated in high traffic areas of enclosed malls, value oriented malls and strip centers. We sell a wide selection of moderately priced fine art prints, graphic reproductions, and some original lithographs. Custom framing services are also provided.

Number of Franchisees: 6 in Florida and 1 in North Carolina

In Business Since: 1986

Equity Capital Needed: $69,200

Financial Assistance Available: None

Training Provided: 4-7 days of complete training in all phases of operation.

Managerial Assistance Available: Ongoing managerial, technical and marketing assistance is provided by franchisor to franchisee.

Information Submitted: May 1987

GOODWILL CANDLE & INCENSE FRANCHISE CORP.
300 East Milwaukee
Detroit, Michigan 48202
Chester Flam

Description of Operation: Wholesale and retail sales of proprietary and non proprietary religious goods including candles, incense, oils, status, books, etc. Primarily to the Black and Spanish areas of cities.

Number of Franchisees: 2 in Michigan and Georgia

In Business Since: 1975

Equity Capital Needed: $13,500 to $20,000

Financial Assistance Available: None

Training Provided: 1 week in Detroit and on location.

Managerial Assistance Available: Unlimited and ongoing.

Information Submitted: September 1987

HAMMETT'S LEARNING WORLD
Division of the J. L. HAMMETT COMPANY
P. O. Box 515 Hammett Place
Braintree, Massachusetts 02184
Richard A. Krause, Vice President, Retail/Franchising

Description of Operation: As a part of the $60 million Hammett business, the Learning World retail stores supply public and private school systems, businesses, hobbyists and "whiz kids" with educational supplies, office and art materials, games, toys and books. The complete line includes 7,000 items of retail stock supported by a catalog offering 14,000 additional items. Hammett's volume buying power provides a competitive pricing edge.

Number of Franchisees: 20, including company-owned, in 11 States

In Business Since: 1863 Hammett's, the oldest school supply company in America, began when its founder invented the chalk-board eraser and manufactured the first kindergarten materials in the United States.

Equity Capital Needed: Franchise fee $25,000; leasehold improvements $10,000-$70,000; supplies and inventory $50,000-$75,000; working capital $5,000-$7,000.

Financial Assistance Available: No financial assistance is available from the franchisor, however, all necessary information for loan proposals are provided.

Training Provided: Intensive 2 week in-house, hands-on training stresses the areas crucial to the retail operation, including administrative systems, marketing, merchandising, site selection and opening assistance.

Managerial Assistance Available: Continuous operational and merchandising assistance provided by the corporate staff, plus on-site support by district managers. Also, direct mailings, seasonal advertising and special promotions for continued success.

Information Submitted: August 1987

HAPPI-BATHER
c/o HAPPI-STORES, INC.
1225 Park Place Mall
Memphis, Tennessee 38119
J. Richard Holley, President

Description of Operation: A bath boutique featuring bath accessories and fragrances.

Number of Franchisees: 1 in 1 State

In Business Since: 1982

Equity Capital Needed: $50,000-$90,000

Financial Assistance Available: None

Training Provided: Total training program before and during installation—then ongoing as needed over entire period of franchise.

Managerial Assistance Available: Inventory control system, cash flow management and sales training.

Information Submitted: August 1987

HAPPI-COOK
c/o HAPPI-STORES, INC.
1225 Park Place Mall
Memphis, Tennessee 38119
J. Richard Holley, President

Description of Operation: Gourmet cook retail store featuring cookware, cook gadgets, books and accessories as well as homemade fudge, gourmet candies and other basket goods.

Number of Franchisees: 3 in 2 States

In Business Since: 1982

Equity Capital Needed: $50,000-$90,000

Financial Assistance Available: None

Training Provided: Total training program before and during installation—then ongoing as needed over entire period of franchise.

Managerial Assistance Available: Inventory control system, cash flow management and sales training.

Information Submitted: August 1987

HAPPI-NAMES
c/o HAPPI-STORES, INC.
1225 Park Place Mall
Memphis, Tennessee 38119
J. Richard Holley, President

Description of Operation: Presonalized gift stores with demonstrating artist on premises at all times.

Number of Franchisees: 24 in 10 States

In Business Since: 1982

Equity Capital Needed: $50,000-$90,000

Financial Assistance Available: None

Training Provided: Total training program during installation—then ongoing as needed over entire period of franchise.

Managerial Assistance Available: Inventory control systems, cash flow management and sales training.

Information Submitted: August 1987

HERITAGE CLOCK AND BRASSMITHS
P. O. Drawer 1577
Lexington, North Carolina 27293-1577
J. Curtis Williams, President

Description of Operation: Heritage Clock and Brassmiths offers a unique factory outlet store operation. Each store is approximately 2,500 square feet with ample store-front parking and is open 10 hours a day, Monday through Saturday and 5 hours on sunday. An extensive inventory of clocks, genuine solid brass beds and other brass gift items manufactured by Heritage as well as selected brand names is maintained.

Number of Franchisees: 5 company-owned in North Carolina, Virginia, Wash ington, D.C. and South Carolina.

In Business Since: 1971

Equity Capital Needed: $19,000 to $75,000

Financial Assistance Available: None

Training Provided: Both classroom and on-the-job training required at company headquarters; plus on-the-job training in the franchisee's store.

Managerial Assistance Available: Continuous consultation services plus catalogs, price lists and other sales materials.

Information Submitted: May 1987

HEROES WORLD CENTERS, INC.
66 Morris Street
P. O. Box 2244R
Morristown, New Jersey 07460
Ivan Snyder

Description of Operation: Retail store located in regional malls catering to items relating to fictional and real to life super heroes, super stars, and cartoon characters. Featuring toys, books, novelties, plush items, T-shirts and wearing apparel, new and collector comics and books featuring Smurfs, Strawberry Shortcake, Snoopy, Spiderman, Bateman, Star Wars, etc.

Number of Franchisees: 2 in 2 States plus 8 company-owned stores in 4 States

In Business Since: 1976

Equity Capital Needed: Minimum of $55,000 plus additional credit of $25,000-$40,000.

Financial Assistance Available: No financial assistance is provided.

Training Provided: Both classroom and on-the-job training required at company headquarters; plus on-the-job training in the franchisee's store.

Managerial Assistance Available: Operations manual and continuous managerial assistance from field personnel. Membership in Heroes World buying co-op erative. Site evaluation, and selection, lease negotiations.

Information Submitted: September 1987

THE HOUSE OF WATCH BANDS FRANCHISE CORPORATION
29223 Southfield Road
Southfield, Michigan 48076
Michael A. Max, Vice President

Description of Operation: The House of Watch Bands Franchise Corporation offers a unique retail store operation. Each store is approximately 1,000 square feet with ample store-front parking and open 9 hours daily, 6 days a week, with one late night (9-9). An extensive inventory of House of Watch Bands products as well as brand name watch banks and accessories is maintained.

Number of Franchisees: 3 in Michigan

In Business Since: 1927

Equity Capital Needed: $67,200

Financial Assistance Available: A total investment of $67,500 is necessary to open a House of Watch Bands franchise. Franchisee has option to arrange own outside financing.

Training Provided: Intensive, 14 day, mandatory training course is scheduled for all new franchisees and their personnel. In addition to the 2 week training at headquarters, franchisees receive on-site training at franchisee's own store during the first few weeks of operation under the supervision of the franchise corporation's training staff.

Managerial Assistance Available: The House of Watch Bands Franchise Corporation provides continual management service for the life of the franchise in such areas as bookkeeping, advertising, personnel management, and inventory control. Complete manuals of operations, forms, and directions are provided. District and field managers are available in all regions to work closely with franchisees and visit stores regularly to assist solving problems. The House of Watch Bands Franchise Corporation sponsors meetings of franchisees and conducts marketing and product research to maintain high House of Watch Bands consumer acceptance.

Information Submitted: August 1987

*THE INCREDIBLE MACHINE, INC.
17922 Sky Park circle
Suite H
Irvine, California 92714

Description of Operation: The Incredible Machine, Inc., offers investment opportunities for both single and multi-unit franchisees. A personalizing gift and award store that has virtually no competition. Images are engraved upon acrylic gift items by The Incredible Machine engraver—the only engraver to do so in the world. Locations are in regional shopping centers. High mark-ups of 300-700 percent.

Number of Franchisees: 35 locations

In Business Since: 1980

Equity Capital Needed: $89,900 to $98,700—does not include leasehold improvements, deposits and miscellaneous expenses.

Financial Assistance Available: Franchisor will assist franchisees in obtaining equipment financing.

Training Provided: 1 to 2 weeks training in operations, retail sales and merchandising.

Managerial Assistance Available: Ongoing managerial assistance is available along with merchandise discounts, site selection assistance and additional training.

Information Submitted: August 1987

INTILE DESIGNS FRANCHISE SYSTEMS, INC.
9716 Old Katy Road
Suite 110
Houston, Texas 77055
C. William Cox, Chairman of the Board

Description of Operation: The sale of imported ceramic tiles and marble and the supplies necessary for its installation and cleaning, in addition to offering decorating suggestions for the use of tile. Intile Designs imports and warehouses the tile and marble and distributes for wholesale and retail sales to each franchisee.

Number of Franchisees: 6 franchisees plus 4 company-owned stores in 4 States; Texas, New Mexico, Arizona, and Florida.

In Business Since: 1976

Equity Capital Needed: $131,000-$168,000.

Financial Assistance Available: No financing offered by Intile Designs. We will assist franchisees in obtaining credit and equipment financing if necessary.

Training Provided: 1 week mandatory training at the corporate headquarters. One additional week optional at franchisee's location. Constant communication and assistance available from franchisor to franchisee. Routine visits to franchisee by franchisor.

Managerial Assistance Available: Because our franchisees do not maintain their own inventory, we assist in inventory purchasing and control. Each franchisee and the managers and sales staff are required to attend and complete our training courses.

Information Submitted: May 1987

ISLAND WATER SPORTS
1985A NE 2nd Street
Deerfield Beach, Florida 33441
Kirk G. Cottrell, President

Description of Operation: Action Aports (surfing, skateboarding, sailboating, etc.) is one of the nations fastest growing industries and Island Water Sports is here to meet the nations demand, not just in the equipment itself but also the unlimited area of apparel and accessories that related to the image.

Number of Franchisees: 21 in Florida, Virginia, Missouri, Washington, DC, and South Carolina.

In Business Since: 1978

Equity Capital Needed: $70,000

Financial Assistance Available: Franchisee must provide his own financing.

Training Provided: 4 weeks of training: 1 week in the office, 2 weeks in the corporate store and 1 week in the franchisee's store.

Managerial Assistance Available: Island Water Sports provides ongoing experienced staff and support in the area of financial planning, central purchasing and/or buying assistance, operations assistance, central computerization, local advertising assistance and national advertising. Complete manuals are provided. Corporate personnel visit the store regularly. Semi-annual franchise meetings are held.

Information Submitted: August 1987

JET PHOTO INTERNATIONAL, INC.
123 South Main Street
P.O. Box 1609
Minot, South Dakota 58702

Description of Operation: 1 hour photo processing.

Number of Franchisees: 11 in 5 states.

In Business Since: 1982

Equity Capital Needed: $95,000 to $112,000

Financial Assistance Available: None.

Training Provided: Technical, management, retailing, counter activities, plus comprehensive study and the processing of film through on-the-job training. Expert training in the fields of quality control, color analysis, primary and secondary systems, machine maintenance and operation of the processor and the printer.

Managerial Assistance Available: Regular contact with regards to manage ment and technical assistance is available.

Information Submitted: May 1987.

JUST BASKETS INTERNATIONAL
1239 East Newport Center Drive
Suite 115
Deerfield Beach, Florida 33442
D'Arcy J. Williams

Description of Operation: Decorative Basket Centers including decorative gift baskets, center pieces, as well as certain other reltaed products and services at the retail and wholesale level.

Number of Franchisees: 5 in Florida

In Business Since: 1983

Equity Capital Needed: $25,000

Financial Assistance Available: None

Training Provided: 2 week training program covering sales, production, accounting and operational management.

Managerial Assistance Available: Continuing operational assistance, provide with creative workshops, product buying assistance and advertising.

Information Submitted: July 1987

JUST CHAIRS, INC.
1029 C Street
San Rafael, California 94901
Donald E. Sutton, President

Description of Operation: Business to business retail selling commercial seating to all sizes of end-users.

Number of Franchisees: 2 in California

In Business Since: 1984

Equity Capital Needed: $75,000-$125,000

Financial Assistance Available: None

Training Provided: 2 weeks, then ongoing assistance.

Managerial Assistance Available: Group purchasing, product evaluation, financial analysis, advertising materials, and advice hotline.

Information Submitted: May 1987

JUST CLOSETS FRANCHISE INC.
25 Pelican Way
San Rafael, California 94901
Michael Brachman, Vice President

Description of Operation: Closet organization. Complete retail store featuring an exclusive, computerized closet design service, ready-to-assemble closet systems plus over 500 accessories.

Number of Franchisees: 5 in California and Nevada

In Business Since: 1980

Equity Capital Needed: $89,000 per store

Financial Assistance Available: Yes

Training Provided: 2 weeks plus ongoing support

Managerial Assistance Available: Life of agreement. Just Closets provides support in site selection and lease negotiation, store management and sales training, inventory selection and control, advertising and promotional programs. Complete operations manuals, forms and collateral materials are supplied.

Information Submitted: May 1987

KITS CAMERAS, INC.
6051 South 194th
Kent, Washington 98032
Corporate Development Manager

Description of Operation: A Kits Camera franchise system offers a unique opportunity in the opration of a specialty photographic equpment and supplies tore. Most stores are located in enclosed shopping centers. The store carries an extensive line of brand name and private label merchandise.

Number of Franchisees: 40 on the West Coast

In Business Since: 1975

Equity Capital Needed: Total investment of approximately $100,000 to which $50,000 has to be cash.

Financial Assistance Available: Franchisor will assist franchisee in arranging the balance from a commercial bank.

Training Provided: 4-6 weeks course at the head office and company stores. Successful completion of training course a pre-requisite to obtaining a franchise.

Managerial Assistance Available: Kits Cameras provide continuous management service for the life of the franchise in areas of bookkeeping, advertising, merchandising and store operations. Coordinators visit stores regularly to provide assistance. Semi-annual conventions are sponsored by Kits Cameras.

Information Submitted: May 1987

JABIROTOPE, INC.
dba L'DREAM
3007 Longhorn Boulevard
Suite 100
Austin, Texas 78759
Billie M. Dixon, President

Description of Operation: L'Dream offers a unique franchise arrangement for part-time and full-time involvement, marketing imported French fragrance items. Available is an excellent retail profit plus a wholesaling profit for supplying other retailers involved in the networking system within the franchisee's area.

Number of Franchisees: 4 in Texas and California

In Business Since: 1973

Equity Capital Needed: $6,500 minimum

Financial Assistance Available: None

Training Provided: Intensive 2 day training school with ongoing on location support is scheduled for franchisees.

Managerial Assistance Available: An annual franchise training meeting is held with advance notice on location. Regular communication concerning new and supportive product, networking, sales, and training information from france and U.S. office for duration of franchisor-franchisee relationship.

Information Submitted: May 1987

LEMSTONE BOOK BRANCH
1123 Wheaton Oaks Ct.
Wheaton, Illinois 60187
Philip O. Darr, Vice President Development

Description of Operation: Christian bookstores located in large regional shopping malls which stock a unique variety of books, Bibles, Bible study material, gifts, music, greeting cards designed to meet the needs of the family as well as the institutional church market. Telelphone (312) 682-1400.

Number of Franchisees: 25 stores in 10 States

In Business Since: 1981

Equity Capital Needed: Approximately $30,000.

Financial Assistance Available: Lemstone Book Branch will assist franchisee in obtaining outside local financing if needed.

Training Provided: One week managers training class prior to opening at franchise headquarters. 400 page manual of operation detailing every aspect of store operations and procedure. On-site training during 5 days of new store

set-up. Ongoing regular field visits throughout the year by member of franchise team. Regional advanced management seminars annually. Annual franchise convention in Chicago area.

Managerial Assistance Available: Will assist franchisee hire sales staff. Regular field visits by franchise operations staff as well as regular franchise seminars. Comprehensive marketing and promotion program plus computerized inventory control and accounting systems provided. All aspects of financial accounting reviewed including monthly open to buy, cash flow projections, and actual to budget performance tracked monthly.

Information Submitted: July 1987

*LITTLE PROFESSOR BOOK CENTERS, INC.
110 North Fourth Street
Suite 400
Ann Arbor, Michigan 48104
Carla Garbin, Senior Vice President

Description of Operation: Little Professor Book Centers are full-line, full-service retail book stores. Each store (most are approximately 2,000 square feet) carries a complete selection of hardcover and papercover titles; magazines and newspapers. Franchisor provides complete assistance and counsel needed to open and operate a book store, from site selection to store opening and throughout the life of the franchise agreement.

Number of Franchisees: 115 stores in 35 States

In Business Since: 1969

Equity Capital Needed: $30,000 to $45,000—total $95,000.

Financial Assistance Available: Little Professor Book Centers, Inc., will assist in the loan application process, but provides no direct financial assistance.

Training Provided: Little Professor Book Center franchise owners participate in an established training program to learn the important aspects of retailing including: inventory control, general operations, financial management, advertising and other forms of sales promotion. The training program is conducted for 9 days; 5 days at company headquarters in Ann Arbor, Michigan, 4 days on-site in the new store.

Managerial Assistance Available: Little Professor Book Centers, Inc., provides continuous assistance and counsel in bookstore operation throughout the length of the franchise. Periodic visits are made by representatives of Little Professor Book Centers, Inc. Performance and results are evaluated and recommendations are offered on improving sales and profits. Experienced personnel are always available to assist in the solution of any problems. Comprehensive marketing and inventory management programs are provided.

Information Submitted: May 1987

LOESCHHORN'S FOR RUNNERS
10810 Warner Avenue
Fountain Valley, California 92708
John Loeschhorn, President

Description of Operation: Loeschhorn's For Runners franchises are retail stores that specialize in serving the needs of the running and aerobic sport oriented public. The stores are between 800 and 2,000 square feet and stock shoes, clothing and accessory items of interest to joggers, runners and aerobic dancers. Each store is deeply involved in running, sponsoring clinics, races and clubs.

Number of Franchisees: 3 in California

In Business Since: 1975

Equity Capital Needed: $65,000 to $100,000

Financial Assistance Available: None

Training Provided: Each franchisee receives a comprehensive training manual and intensive training in every aspect of our business at our Fountain Valley facility. The training normally lasts 5 working days, but can be repreated or extended according to individual needs.

Managerial Assistance Available: The franchisor makes regular visits to all franchises and is available to render assistance at reasonable times whenever necessary. The franchisor sponsor regular management meetings on a monthly basis. These meetings are held at various places in Southern California. These meetings are for the general benefit of all franchisees and are offered at no charge. Attendance is optional, but highly recommended as advertising programs, special buys, promotions and other important business related topics are normally discussed.

Information Submitted: August 1987

237

MEHTA HOLDINGS, INC.
30 Concourse Gate
Suite 205
Nepean, Ontario
K2E 7V7 Canada

Description of Operation: Mehta Holdings Inc., has acquired the rights from Athena International of Britain to open Athena Galleries under a franchising program in Canada and the State of Alaska in the U.S. Athena International is one of Britains largest publishers of fine art and contemporary art and a major exporter of a variety of art and stationery products. The outstanding array of merchandise, together with a most efficiently organized retailing concept, makes for an unusually profitable unit.

Number of Franchisees: 18 plus 1 company-owned stores in Canada with 5 more committed for 1987/88.

In Business Since: 1983

Equity Capital Needed: $45,000-$55,000 minimum

Financial Assistance Available: The franchisor will assist in preparation of information and presentation to the bank for financing.

Training Provided: Up to 1 week of intensive training at head office.

Managerial Assistance Available: Ongoing assistance provided in merchandising and in improving profitability.

Information Submitted: July 1987

MISS BOJANGLES, INC.
P. O. Box 14589
Baton Rouge, Louisiana 70898
Mike Stokes

Description of Operation: Retail jewelry stores.

Number of Franchisees: 47 in 14 States

In Business Since: 1974

Equity Capital Needed: $20,000

Financial Assistance Available: Negotiable

Training Provided: Complete training in all aspects of running a retail business—from ordering, personnel, advertising techniques, etc. One week on-site training.

Managerial Assistance Available: Merchandising memo's, feedback forum and convention.

Information Submitted: May 1987

MOBILITY CENTER, INC.
6693 Dixie
Bridgeport, Michigan 48722
Allan Thiene, President

Description of Operation: Mobility Center retail stores sell a variety of contemporary mobility aids for those with walking disabilities, including the Amigo, the original 3 wheel, battery-powered wheelchair. Mobility Center, Inc., is a wholly-owned subsidiary of Amigo Mobility International.

Number of Franchisees: 19 in 10 States

In Business Since: 1984

Equity Capital Needed: $60,000-$110,000

Financial Assistance Available: No financing provided by franchisor.

Training Provided: 2 weeks intensive training course provided by franchisor, covering marketing, sales, administration and service.

Managerial Assistance Available: Continual support service provided for all areas of business operations.

Information Submitted: May 1987

* **MOTO PHOTO**
4444 Lake Center Drive
Dayton, Ohio 45426
Michael Adler, President

Description of Operation: One Hour Moto-Photo is the world's largest franchisor of photo processing service. Each store develops and prints on-site color negative film and offers enlargements, portraits and video transfer.

Number of Franchisees: 215 stores in 26 States

In Business Since: 1981

Equity Capital Needed: $160,000 to $190,000.

Financial Assistance Available: Equipment leasing available. SBA financing available to qualified franchisees.

Training Provided: Company provides up to 3 weeks of training. The training program includes up to 2 weeks training at franchisor's facility in operation and management of the store and marketing of the processing services, and 1 week in the store.

Managerial Assistance Available: The company's personnel are available on a continuing basis for management and technical consultation. As a part of the company's quality control program, franchisee may participate in periodic training programs offered by the company. Additionally, the company develops all advertising materials.

Information Submitted: May 1987

MOVIES AND MORE FRANCHISE CORPORATION
2517 Warwick Avenue
Warwick, Rhode Island 02889
Arnold I. Kornstein, President

Description of Operation: We operate video specialty stores for the rental of pre-recorded movies, usually under a movie club plan; and the sale of video cassette recorders, color television sets, camcorders, blank tapes, movies and video accessories; and the rental of video cassette recorders and television sets on a short-term or rental-to-own program. Franchises are being solicited in the Continental United States.

Number of Franchisees: 45 in Rhode Island, Massachusetts, Connecticut, New Jersey, and Delaware.

In Business Since: 1981

Equity Capital Needed: $75,000

Financial Assistance Available: Franchisor extends credit to franchisee to secure as many VCR's as needed to operate short-term VCR rental program; generally ranges from $2,500-$10,000. Franchisor also assists in securing balance of financing needed.

Training Provided: Franchisor provides training in sales, movie club operation and in the operation of the VCR rental programs; usually 1 week but longer if needed. Updated training provided on an ongoing basis at changes or new developments occur within the franchise system or in the video industry.

Managerial Assistance Available: Franchisor provides the systems for bookkeeping, inventory control, the movie club program and for the VCR-TV rental programs, both short-term and rent-to-own. Franchisor also assists in personnel training, pricing of inventory and services, in th buying and merchandising and in the advertising and planning of promotions. This assistance is provided as needed both before the store opens for business and after the opening. Franchisor also arranges for franchisee to have his own direct accounts with suppliers and secures lines of credit for him. Franchisor provides store design and interior layout and assists in securing necessary fixtures and computer systems.

Information Submitted: May 1987

MR. LOCKSMITHY CONVENIENCE CENTERS
1828 Tribute Road
Suite M
Sacramento, California 95815
Don L. Rumbaugh, President & C.E.O.

Description of Operation: Mr. Locksmithy Convenience Centers offer a unique opportunity to be in business for one's self, and provide numerous services and sales of "hard to find" items such as; all types of engraving, making rubber stamps, scissor and knife sharpening, laminating, badge making, cassette duplication, key duplication, lock service, copying documents and other "hard to find", high profit items and services. Emphasis is on Quality Personal Service with a 100 percent satisfaction guarantee.

Number of Franchisees: 19 in California

In Business Since: 1975

Equity Capital Needed: $37,500

Financial Assistance Available: Various

Training Provided: Classroom training is provided in all facets of operations. additionally, individual hands-on instruction is made available throughout the duration of the franchise.

Managerial Assistance Available: Regular in person contacts, meetings, and a toll free hot line. We "back you all the way."

Information Submitted: May 1987

NAMESAKES PERSONALIZED GIFTS
2423 Post Oak Boulevard
Houston, Texas 77056
Nancy Holliman, President

Description of Operation: Gift shops that offer a wide variety of personalized gifts—hand painted, imprinted, monogrammed, engraved—most priced under $20. Can be opened in strip centers or malls with 800-1,000 square feet store front.

Number of Franchisees: 3 in Texas and Kansas

In Business Since: 1978

Equity Capital Needed: $44,000-$63,000 total investment.

Financial Assistance Available: None

Training Provided: 3 days at home office for manager and artists, 3 days at site when opening, ongoing traning and updating of services and products.

Managerial Assistance Available: The most unique part of the Namesake franchise package is handpainting of merchandise done while you wait. Constant retraining and quality control of the artist's work is an integral part of the assistance that is given. Training and supervision of the managerial staff and help with the financial aspects of the retail operations are major concerns of Namesakes and will be a part of annual seminars that cover new ideas and the artist retraining.

Information Submitted: August 1987

*NATIONAL VIDEO, INC.
7325 Northeast 55th Avenue
P. O. Box 18220
Portland, Oregon 97218
Ron Berger, President

Description of Operation: The company offers a unique opportunity to persons interested in operating a video-cassette retail store which deals primarily in rental and sales. The franchise offers professional advertising support, group purchasing benefits in many areas, and the benefits of a national identity.

Number of Franchisees: 1,350 in all 50 States, and Canada.

In Business Since: 1977—selling franchises since 1981.

Equity Capital Needed: $90,000 to $250,000 with liquid assets of at least 15 percent of the total investment. This can be individual or multiple investors.

Financial Assistance Available: None

Training Provided: The initial franchise fee entitles the franchisee to a training visit by a field staff member for several days prior to the store opening, and training at the national training center for 5 days. These visits are entirely at the franchisor's expense.

Managerial Assistance Available: A complete, tested operations manual covering basic bookkeeping, store operations procedures, video problems, video related law, sales concepts, and forms handling is provided upon signing. Advertising and marketing support and advice are provided throughout the length of the agreement. Additional management advice is offered upon request at no charge. The company conducts meetings from time to time in which additional training (at no charge) is provided, as well as new programs discussed.

Information Submitted: May 1987

NEIGHORHOOD VIDEO & 1-HOUR PHOTO CENTER, INC.
1801 Avenue of the Stars
Los Angeles, California 90067
Harmon Cogert, C.E.O., President

Description of Operation: Neighborhood Video and 1-Hour Photo Center, Inc., has combined two businesses (video/photo) under one roof that works with the same personnel saving rental and labor overheads.

Number of Franchisees: 13 in California and New Jersey

In Business Since: 1984

Equity Capital Needed: $109,000

Financial Assistance Available: 50 percent financed.

Training Provided: 1 week of intensive classroom training with the 1-hour photo processing equipment in addition to a 3 day in-store training period focusing on all facets of the movie rental business and the photo business (purchasing, marketing, display, etc.)

Managerial Assistance Available: Ongoing support from the franchisor to the franchisee.

Information Submitted: May 1987

NEVADA BOB'S PRO SHOPS, INC.
3333 East Flamingo Road
Las Vegas, Nevada 89121
Mel Mead, President

Description of Operation: Selling discount golf equipment in an attractive atmosphere, specializing in top of the line golf clubs, golf bags and accessories from MacGregor, Spalding, Prima, Mizuno, Dunlop, etc. Also, professional advice on all golf equipment given by our professional staff.

Number of Franchisees: 100 located throughout the United States and Canada

In Business Since: 1974

Equity Capital Needed: $225,000 investment—$200,000 start-up cost and $125,000 credit line.

Financial Assistance Available: No financial assistance available at this time.

Training Provided: 1 week extensive training at the headquarters in Las Vegas. Training includes all aspects of the golf industry. Also on-site assistance upon opening of franchise.

Managerial Assistance Available: Continuing assistance with all phases of operations. Annual convention sales seminars, weekly updating of product trends by phone and written correspondence.

Information Submitted: May 1987

*PAK MAIL CENTERS OF AMERICA, INC.
10555 East Dartmouth
Suite 360
Aurora, Colorado 80014
Director of Franchise Sales

Description of Operation: Franchisor of retail convenience centers offering residential and business consumers a wide variety of packaging, shipping, mail, communications, and related services.

Number of Franchisees: 70 in 19 States

In Business Since: 1984

Equity Capital Needed: $33,000-$50,000

Financial Assistance Available: None

Training Provided: Complete training program (1-1/2-2-1/2 weeks) including technical, managerial, advertising and promotion accounting and bookkeeping. Both classroom and on-location (on-the-job) training.

Managerial Assistance Available: Market survey, site selection, lease negotiation assistance, building construction program, decor/signage/graphics, start-up equipment, supplies and inventory, training, grand opening program, and toll free "owners" hotline. Advertising and promotional materials, technical support, management visits and consultation. Purchasing discounts, research and development, monthly newsletter, annual convention and seminars.

Information Submitted: April 1987

*PALMER VIDEO CORPORATION
1767 Morris Avenue
Union, New Jersey 07083
Richard Finch, Sales Manager

Description of Operation: Palmer Video stores are in the business of rental and sales of video cassettes, video recorders, and related video recorders and related video products, video recorder servicing, and film-to video transfers.

Number of Franchisees: 98 in New Jersey, New York, Pennsylvania, Ohio, Illinois, Florida, Michigan, Alabama, and Massachusetts.

In Business Since: 1981, franchising since 1982.

Equity Capital Needed: $70,525-$144,125

Financial Assistance Available: No financial assistance available; however, franchisor will refer to appropriate lending agencies whenever possible, as well as be available for consultation with lenders.

Training Provided: Complete hands-on training in one of the franchisor's company-owned stores with additional training at franchisee's location immediately prior to and at the time of opening.

Managerial Assistance Available: Ongoing operational, promotional and advertising assistance, operations manual, monthly newsletters, recommended purchases, and constant helpful communications to franchisees.

Information Submitted: May 1987

THE PERFUMERY, INC.
6721 Portwest Drive, #160
Houston, Texas 77024
Beth Marshall, President

Description of Operation: Stores which average 300 square feet, are generally located in shopping malls but may be placed in strip shopping centers. Stores carry The Perfumery's line of approximately 110 reproduction and original fragrances. Stores also provide fragrance compatability testing and custom blending of men's and women's fragrances.

Number of Franchisees: 14 in Texas, Louisana, Tennessee and New Jersey.

In Business Since: 1983

Equity Capital Needed: Total investment required $30,000-$100,000. No minimum equity required.

Financial Assistance Available: The franchise fee ranges from $5,000 to $20,000 and averages $10,000. A total investment of $30,000 to $100,000 is required, of which $15,000 is inventory. No financing is currently provided by franchisor.

Training Provided: 6 days of training at company headquarters and company stores in Houston, Texas. Three days of training in franchisees store at opening.

Managerial Assistance Available: Franchisor provides ongoing support in marketing, product development and training. Support includes periodic inspections of premises and evaluation of controls. A complete manual covering accounting controls, custom blending, fragrances and marketing is provided and video training on product knowledge.

Information Submitted: May 1987

PINCH A PENNY, INC.
14480 62nd Street North
Clearwater, Florida 33520
Fred A. Thomas, President

Description of Operation: Retail pool and patio supplies.

Number of Franchisees: 70 in Florida and Arizona

In Business Since: 1976

Equity Capital Needed: $90,000-$250,000

Financial Assistance Available: None

Training Provided: 4-6 weeks field training in retail stores and in the field doing service and repair. Regular calls on store by company representative. For advice/guidance on ordering, merchandising account and data processing, technical. Access to full service ad agency included in fees. Access to specialty promotion programs.

Managerial Assistance Available: Franchisor offers franchise owners an initial training program of up to 6 weeks duration at franchisor's headquarters or at such other sites as may be designated by franchisor. Offers ongoing management support, including current product information, marketing data, bookkeeping services, inventory control and advertising ideas ot its franchises.

Information Submitted: May 1987

P.O.P. AMERICA CORPORATION
6426 Coldwater Canyon
North Hollywood, California 91606
Bryan Anderson

Description of Operation: Nation's first service merchandising franchise. Manufacturers representative product distribution service based on heavy product promotion targeted to impulse sales at the retail level. Provides a rare opportunity for those seeking a way of establishing their own business by initially commiting just a few hours each week. Franchisor supplies a general merchandise product line, in-store audio-visual aid program; heavy point of purchase promotions' pre-established retail outlets, comprehensive training, ongoing guidance and support.

Number of Franchisees: 500 plus throughout the U.S.

In Business Since: 1980

Equity Capital Needed: $16,000-$18,000

Financial Assistance Available: Total cost of franchise is just under $30,000. Interest-free financing is available to qualified applicants.

Training Provided: Intensive field training program provides franchisee with step-by-step instruction in bookkeeping, inventory procedures, site locations, and assembly/set-up techniques associated with franchisor's, audio visual systems and merchandising aids.

Managerial Assistance Available: As long as franchisee is working under the franchise program, continued assistance is provided to franchisee. This includes introduction of new products, merchandising concepts, and an up-dated product catalog.

Information Submitted: August 1987

PRO GOLF OF AMERICA, INC.
Tall Oaks Office Center
31884 Northwestern Highway
Farmington Hills, Michigan 48018
Bob Sage, President

Description of Operation: Golf equipment discount stores.

Number of Franchisees: 80 in 24 States

In Business Since: 1964

Equity Capital Needed: $150,000-$200,000

Financial Assistance Available: Franchisor assists in opening credit with all major suppliers.

Training Provided: Initial 2 week training in Michigan. Assistance with grand opening on-site. Ongoing communications and training as long as franchise is owned.

Managerial Assistance Available: Continuous outgoing communications with regional co-ordinators and corporate advertising department. Monthly newsletter and news bulletins. Ordering, pricing and inventory assistance. Stores are visited regularly by field supervisors.

Information Submitted: May 1987

*THE PRO IMAGE
380 North 200 West
Suite 203
Bountiful, Utah 84010
Mark Gilleland, National Marketing Director

Description of Operation: The Pro Image carries "Everything for the Sports Fan." These unique retail stores feature gifts and clothing that is licensed and approved by the professional and collegiate teams. The stores are generally 1,000 square feet and are located in regional shopping malls.

Number of Franchisees: 100 in 25 States

In Business Since: 1985

Equity Capital Needed: $60,000 to $90,000

Financial Assistance Available: None. The Pro Image assists in arranging third party financing.

Training Provided: The franchisee is trained in all phases of operations, merchandising, advertising, inventory control, management, bookkeeping, customer relations, and purchasing. Five to 10 days home office and field training.

Managerial Assistance Available: The Pro Image assists the franchisee in site selection and leasehold arrangements. The company provides complete operating manuals and accounting system. The Pro Image also allows the franchisee access to company purchasing system and its discounts. The company assists with grand opening and provides ongoing assistance for new products, promotions, and merchandising ideas.

Information Submitted: May 1987

PROJECT MULTIPLICATION INTERNATIONAL, INC.
12239 SW 132nd Court
Miami, Florida 33186
Bruce F. Bales

Description of Operation: Retail concept featuring inter coordinated fashion accessories...jewelry, belts, hats, handbags, scarves. One of a kind FMI design group merchandise—accentuate and SKB originals and other name brand merchandise featured—emphasis on service and custom design plus wardrobe accessorizing.

Number of Franchisees: 4 in Florida and Georgia

In Business Since: 1981, retail stores and consulting, franchising 1986.

Equity Capital Needed: $65,000 to $85,000 includes inventory, fixtures, fee, sign, carpet and painting.

Financial Assistance Available: None, will assist in developing loan package.

Training Provided: 1 week at Miami training facility. 2 days (2 people) store set-up. 1 day (1 person) in store and ongoing helpline service.

Managerial Assistance Available: Full training and operations manual and systems linked to computer cash register, monthly report sales, cost/retail, percentage of gross profit, O.T.B. by classifications, helpline, all operations forms, personnel package, monthly newsletter featuring merchandise, store promotions, and merchandise plans, marketing program for advertising and initial layout and real estate assistance.

Information Submitted: May 1987

*RADIO SHACK DIVISION
TANDY CORPORATION
1600 One Tandy Center
Fort Worth, Texas 76102
Robert Owens, Vice President

Description of Operation: Radio Shack presently offers a licensing program to established retailers in towns of 8,500 or less in population. The dealerships are called Authorized Sales Centers. Applicants must be already established in a retail business.

Number of Franchisees: 2,200 in all States, West Indies, Central America, South America, Guam, American Samoa, and Saudi Arabia.

In Business Since: 1971

Equity Capital Needed: $15,000 to $40,000

Financial Assistance Available: Assist with bank presentation. No direct financial aid provided by franchisors.

Training Provided: Since dealerships are granted only to existing retailers, no formal training is provided. Procedures manual, display guide and miscellaneous instructional materials supplied upon approval of applicant.

Managerial Assistance Available: Weekly scheduled phone consultation, periodic visits (usually twice a year) for review of performance. Free ad mat service to introduce new lines and explain advertising and promotional plans. Provide technical manuals covering operational and servicing of consumer electronics merchandise.

Information Submitted: May 1987

RECEPTIONS PLUS, INC.
1970 Jerome Avenue
Bronx, New York 10453
David J. Lesser, President

Description of Operation: Receptions Plus offers a unique retail operation; a complete wedding service under one roof. Receptions plus provides high quality products and services, for low prices, and offers the convenience of shop at home service. Products and services include: catering, photography, video, cakes, flowers, limousines, tuxedos, invitations, souveniors, travel, music, and jewelry.

Number of Franchisees: 4 in Connecticut and Pennsylvania

In Business Since: 1969, franchising since September 1985.

Equity Capital Needed: Initial investments are available ranging from $61,000-$225,000.

Financial Assistance Available: The franchisor at the present time offers no financing assistance to franchisees.

Training Provided: Receptions plus provides a comprehensive 3 week training program at its corporate headquarters. The training schedule accounts for every 15 minutes of each training day, and includes a 1,750 page operations manual and a complete set of 9 video training tapes covering every aspect of the operation. Training is also provided to operate and implement the receptions plus custom developed computer software programs. Additional training also includes 1 week on-site with an operations specialist from headquarters and extensive operations and follow up support.

Managerial Assistance Available: Receptions Plus provides continual management service for the life of the franchise in such areas as bookkeeping, advertising, inventory, purchasing, and business relations. Complete manuals of operations, forms, and instructions are provided. Headquarters representatives are always available to work closely with franchisees and visit stores regularly. At headquarters there are always operations specialists to assist franchisees with problems. Headquarters is a perfect prototype of the operation and is always involved with the business and its day to day dealings with respect to research and development.

Information Submitted: May 1987

RE-SELL-IT SHOPS, INC.
2667 Camino del Rio South
Suite 215
San Diego, California 92108
Florence Kalanquin, President

Description of Operation: Sophisticated consignment stores: shops handle home furnishings and the boutique shops handle clothing.

Number of Franchisees: 3 in California plus 1 company-owned.

In Business Since: 1979, in California since 1981.

Equity Capital Needed: $20,000

Financial Assistance Available: 50 percent of franchise fee for 2 years. 50 percent of franchise fee over 2 years, amortized. Total amount financed $4,750. Interest 12 percent, payment 4570 per month.

Training Provided: Complete in-house training previous to opening at corporate office and store. Assistance at store opening by corporation representative, then ongoing assistance whenever requested plus bi-monthly newsletter and advertising, including ad copy monthly. Periodic visits by corporation representative.

Managerial Assistance Available: Managerial skills will be presented in origination training and on-site assistance at store opening. Periodic meetings to present new ideas and systems on an ongoing basis. Corporate help is available any time upon request.

Information Submitted: June 1987

*RUSLAN DISCOUNT PETMART
(Lanrus, Inc.)
7390 Trade Street
San Diego, California 92121-9899
Dennis J. Kelly, Vice President

Description of Operation: Ruslan Discount Petmart is a one of a kind franchise opportunity offering turnkey retail pet supply stores. The stores offer only the highest quality foods and supplies for dogs, cats, birds, and fish without livestock. Stores are approximately 1,500 square feet and located in shopping centers with a supermarket anchor tenant.

Number of Franchisees: 23 in California

In Business Since: 1973

Equity Capital Needed: $61,000 to $77,000

Financial Assistance Available: Franchisor will assist in preparation of loan package for presentation to financial institution or SBA.

Training Provided: 1 week of classroom studies focused on pet care and product knowledge and 1 week in store business management training. Training is conducted in San Diego, California.

Managerial Assistance Available: Complete ongoing managerial assistance is provided by field support staff and informational toll-free hot line. In-store signage, advertising campaigns, purchasing guidance, and business analysis are provided.

Information Submitted: May 1987

THE SCIENCE SHOP, INC.
140-B Archer Street
San Jose, California 95112
Rudy Yannitte, President

Description of Operation: Retail and wholesale store selling scientific equipment. A complete line of chemicals and laboratory equipment is presented in our company catalog. We also carry many scientific educational kits for schools and colleges.

Number of Franchisees: 2 in California including company-owned.

In Business Since: 1978

Equity Capital Needed: Approximately $100,000. Financing is available.

Financial Assistance Available: All financial assistance depends upon the individual franchisee and his/her current financial position. The maximum amount financed would be approximately 50 percent of the cost of the franchise.

Training Provided: Training is extensive. Our company will provide up to 3 months of on-site training to the new franchisee. All training will be provided by a professional competent manager from one of our company-owned stores.

Managerial Assistance Available: Support and assistance will be provided as long as necessary so that the franchisee will feel confident is the operation.

Information Submitted: May 1987

SILVER SCREEN VIDEO, INC.
1412B Baytree Road
P. O. Box 3724
Valdosta, Georgia 31604
L. L. Baggett, Jr., Franchise Marketing Manager

Description of Operation: Silver Screen Video grants franchises the right to operate retail video stores using its name, logo, decor, and operating procedures. Stores offer for sale and rental, video tape cassettes, recorders and players, accessories, services and other video related products. Silver Screen Video offers its own computer and software packages using a bar code scanner at pont-of-sale.

Number of Franchisees: 15 in Colorado, Kansas, Nebraska, New Mexico, Georgia, and Florida

In Business Since: 1984

Equity Capital Needed:

Financial Assistance Available: An initial investment of $25,000 to $40,000 is required, which applies to the purchase of tapes, store fixtures, franchise fee and operating capital. Qualified franchisees may elect to lease machines and the computer package.

Training Provided: All franchisees and certain key employees are required to successfully complete a 2 day training course covering advertising, merchandising, product knowledge, store set-up, customer relations, selling, daily operations, management and employee relations, and computer training.

Managerial Assistance Available: Silver Screen Video offers ongoing management support, including current product information, marketing data, bookkeeping services, inventory control, and advertising ideas to its franchisees.

Information Submitted: May 1987

SOFTWARE CITY
1415 Queen Ann Road
Teaneck, New Jersey 07666
Shep Altshuler, President

Description of Operation: Leading chain of franchised software specialty stores. Discounted programs for recreation, education and business. Stores also carry a wide selection of books, magazines, peripherals, accessories, disks, etc.

Number of Franchisees: Over 100 stores throughout U.S. and Overseas.

In Business Since: 1980

Equity Capital Needed: Approximately $65,000.

Financial Assistance Available: None

Training Provided: 1 week training in various phases of store operations is conducted at the home office and retail location in Teaneck, New Jersey.

Managerial Assistance Available: Continual management assistance, group buying power, national advertising, in-store assistance, meetings and information bulletins.

Information Submitted: May 1987

SPACE OPTIONS FRANCHISING CORP.
1411 Opus Place
Suite 670
Downers Grove, Illinois 60515
W. Michael McMayon, Director of Franchise Operations

Description of Operation: Space Options is a unique retail store that serves the needs of their customers by providing free space organization consulting in their homes or offices. We custom design and manufacture a system that best utilizes the space they need organized. The retail store carries storage products.

Number of Franchisees: 3 in Ohio, Illinois and United Kingdom

In Business Since: 1984

Equity Capital Needed: $50,000 minimum

Financial Assistance Available: We can help arrange financial package to take to a lending institution.

Training Provided: 2 weeks of extensive training at our corporate headquarters. We also provide 3-5 weeks of on-site assistance.

Managerial Assistance Available: We provide the franchisee with a comprehensive 700 plus page operations manual. During build out and grand opening members of our staff are on hand to assist. Regular seminar and training sessions are planned throughout the year along with visits from the corporate staff. We have a franchisee council to develop new products and methods.

Information Submitted: May 1987

*SPORT-ABOUT, INC.
1557 Coon Rapids Boulevard
Coon Rapids, Minnesota 55433
Adrian Antoniu, President

Description of Operation: Sport-About, Inc., a network of sporting goods businesses operating under the name Sport-About. Sporting goods equipment, athletic footwear, active sportswear and team uniforms are the type of products carried by Sport-About dealers. Franchisor provides access to suppliers through a centralized buying and billing system and a central warehouse program. Franchisor negotiates discounts and special buying programs with suppliers on behalf of dealers. Toll free consultation, advertising and promotion programs, monthly newsletter, operations manual, supplier catalogs, store design and layout assistance and much more. Sport-About also assists dealers in developing a direct marketing program for their Sport-About store. Advertising and promotion assistance also available. Site selection and lease negotiations available to licensee.

Number of Franchisees: 60 retail stores in 30 States

In Business Since: 1978

Equity Capital Needed: Minimum $35,000—total investment $150,000

Financial Assistance Available: Company will counsel licensee, will assist in determining financial needs and will assist licensee in preparing a financial package which may be necessary in securing funds.

Training Provided: Yes, a comprehensive 2 weeks training program covers basic operations skills, sales and marketing and other topics selected by franchisor. Part of the training is a "hands on" training at the corporate retail store facility. A part of the training is devoted to learning the exclusive, to Sport-About franchisees, point of sale computer system. Also Sport-About personnel will work directly with the franchisee on-site to properll prepare for the retail store opening.

Managerial Assistance Available: Ongoing WATS line consultation is provided by corporate staff on a continual basis. Newsletters are sent out monthly. Management, industry and product knowledge seminars are held during annual corporate trade shows. Area managers are available for on-site consultation.

Information Submitted: July 1987

*SPORTING LIFE, INC.
(LAS VEGAS DISCOUNT GOLF & TENNIS)
5325 South Valley View Boulevard
Suite 10Las Vegas, Nevada 89118

Description of Operation: Sporting Life, Inc., the exclusive franchisors of Las Vegas Discount Golf & Tennis, offers you a complete retail golf and tennis facility. Stores range in size from 3,500 square feet to 6,000 square feet. You will benefit from our enormous buying power in the industry as well as carry the exclusive St. Andrews brand of golf equipment. Sporting Life, Inc., provides you with all necessary training and operational assistance needed to operate a golf and tennis operation.

Number of Franchisees: 24 in 11 States—2 in Canada

In Business Since: 1984

Equity Capital Needed: Minimum of $150,000 cash—total investment of $300,000.

Financial Assistance Available: None provided by franchisor. However all necessary information for loan applications is available.

Training Provided: Intensive classroom on-site training in the original Las Vegas store provided for all franchisees and their managerial staff. The course runs 14 days and covers every aspect of the golf and tennis retail industry. Refresher and new technique or product knowledge courses provided as needed.

Managerial Assistance Available: Sporting Life, Inc., provides complete site-selection and lease negotiating for all franchisees. Complete manuals of operations, forms and directions provided. New product and special purchase announcements provided on a continual basis. Field representatives to work closely with the franchisees and visit stores regularly to assist in any problem solving needed. Continual ongoing support and assistance for all franchisees.

Information Submitted: May 1987

THE SPORTING LIFE, LTD.
5302 Eisenhower Avenue
Alexandria, Virginia 22304
Andrea M. Weiss, Vice President, Retail Stores

Description of Operation: A national mail order catalog, with a division of franchise stores.

Number of Franchisees: 9 in 8 States and Washington, D.C.

In Business Since: 1973

Equity Capital Needed: $35,000 franchise fee, $185,000 start-up cost including inventory.

Financial Assistance Available: None

Training Provided: 10 days training and assistance (for new store openings), 2 days per year consultation trip to stores.

Managerial Assistance Available: Constant communication by telephone. Assist in buying trips 4 times a year and weekly and monthly correspondence regarding market trends.

Information Submitted: August 1987

SPORTS ARENA, LTD.
414 N. Orleans St.
Chicago, Illinois 60610
Michael Conwisher, President

Description of Operation: We sell only the official licensed merchandise from all of the teams in Major League Baseball, the National Foodball League, the N.B.A., the N.H.L. and various colleges. The majority of sales come from the official jackets, jerseys and caps that the players wear as well as all other souvenir items.

Number of Franchisees: 5 in Illinois, including 4 company-owned.

In Business Since: 1981

Equity Capital Needed: $60,000-$90,000

Financial Assistance Available: None

Training Provided: A 2 week course in our O&O stores to learn the complete procedures and then we stay with them in their store until they have complete understanding of everything. From there the communication continues weekly as needed.

Managerial Assistance Available: We are always visiting the stores and assisting in any buying, advertising, inventory control, or any other situations which may arise. the advertising and promotions we arrange are always very significant.

Information Submitted: May 1987

*SPORT SHACKS, INC.
Birch Lake Professional Building
1310 East Highway 96
White Bear Lake, Minnesota 55110

Description of Operation: Retail sporting goods stores operating within the Sport Shack franchise system comprise the largest chain of its type in the U.S. These stores sell a combination of athletic equipment, footwear and apparel. The Sport Shack program provides the franchisee with these benefits: (a) store location and lease negotiation; (b) loan application preparation; (c) national buying programs and merchandise item selection; (d) national non-merchandise programs such as store layout, fixtures, interior and exterior signs, computer system package, etc.; (e) 5-day training program and (f) advertising preparation and/or production for print or radio.

Number of Franchisees: 200 in the United states, of which 70 are retail stores.

In Business Since: 1974

Equity Capital Neede: Minimum of $35,000 cash—total investment of $130,000 and up (dependant on state size).

Financial Assistance Available: None. However, necessary projections and other loan application assistance are provided to franchisees.

Training Provided: 5 day home office orientation program covering product knowledge, merchandising, inventory, display, store operations, accounting, advertising.

Managerial Assistance Available: Management assistance is provided via training, a 230-page operations manual, bulletins and newsletters, wats lines to HQ and periodic store visits or regional meetings by HQ personnel.

Information Submitted: May 1987

STANDARD TILE SUPPLY CO., INC.
1700 Pomona Avenue
San Jose, California 95110
Derol Briscoe

Description of Operation: Retail and wholesale ceramic tile and accessories.

Number of Franchisees: 3 in California plus 3 company-owned stores.

In Business Since: 1979

Equity Capital Needed: $20,000

Financial Assistance Available: None

Training Provided: 60 days—30 days at our location and 30 days at their new location.

Managerial Assistance Available: Imported ceramic tile is made available to franchisee at very low prices. We are available anytime for advertising advice or sales assistance.

Information Submitted: August 1987

THE TINDER BOX INTERNATIONAL, LTD.
Franchise Development Office
16945 North Chase Drive, Suite 1590
Houston, Texas 77060
Benjamin J. Scordello, Vice President, Franchising

Description of Operation: Specialty retail mall chain with product mix consisting of unique gifts as well as pipes, cigars, and tobaccos.

Number of Franchisees: 150 stores in 37 States plus 44 company-owned stores.

In Business Since: 1928

Equity Capital Needed: Minimum $50,000—total investment $135,000-$200,000 including inventory.

Financial Assistance Available: Financing assistance or direct financing available through company.

Training Provided: 8 day intensive training for franchisee and/or manager at franchisor's headquarters plus in-store set up and training.

Managerial Assistance Available: Franchisor provides ongoing merchandising, advertising, marketing and accounting assistance. Also available are site selection, store design and lease assistance, operation manuals, training videos and various fliers and publications. Annual convention including a private gift and tobacco show.

Information Submitted: May 1987

USA DORACO CORP.
20 East Herman Street
Philadelphia, Pennsylvania 19144
Dan Puleio, President

Description of Operation: Retail sales of residential custom doors and windows direct to the homeowner. Sales are made through retail showrooms. All products are custom made therefore there is virtually no inventory other than showroom displays. No inventory combined with the retail orientation means no cash tied up in slow moving products and no accounts receivable.

Number of Franchisees: None, 6 company-owned units in 3 States

In Business Since: 1987

Equity Capital Needed: $35,000 to $85,000

Financial Assistance Available: None, however help is available for prospective franchises to prepara a loan proposal for their bank.

Training Provided: Intensive 1 week training program provided at company headquarters in Philadelphia, Pennsylvania followed by 6 days of on-site assistance.

Managerial Assistance Available: At the franchisers request, assistance in management, sales and accounting is available on a per diem basis.

Information Submitted: July 1987

VARNET CORPORATION
1601 Belvedere Road
Suite 110
West Palm Beach, Florida 33406
Howard Reisman

Description of Operation: The Varnet franchise program provides the value-added reseller with all key elements of success including name identification, advertising, a complete business format, training, ongoing support and access to brand name hardware at discount prices. A standardized library of fourth-generation vertical market solutions and ongoing market research and development.

Number of Franchisees: 2 in Canada

In Business Since: 1985

Equity Capital Needed:

Financial Assistance Available: None

Training Provided: Business orientation, 2 weeks and product orientation 2 weeks.

Managerial Assistance Available: 1 week on-site for business, 1 week on-site for product plus daily ongoing support.

Information Submitted: May 1987

VIDEO BIZ, INC.
2981 West S/R 434
Suite 100
Longwood FL 32779
Edward Fainelli

Description of Operation: Video movies and video equipment sales and rentals. Also film to tape transfer and accessories sale, special club member enrollments.

Number of Franchisees: 225 plus 75 affiliates in over 200 cities.

In Business Since: 1981

Equity Capital Needed: $55,000

Financial Assistance Available: Yes

Training Provided: Total training at franchisee's location 3 to 5 days and site selection assistance and national and regional advertising.

Managerial Assistance Available: Complete operations manual including all printing forms required for operation, inventory control systems, company constantly available for consultation, technical assistance and opening manager provided. Computer store program provided.

Information Submitted: May 1987

VIDEO DATA SERVICES
24 Grove Street
Pittsford, New York 14534
Stuart J. Dizak

Description of Operation: Video taping services, legal, real estate, social, inventories and retail sales of video equipment.

Number of Franchisees: 142 in 34 States

In Business Since: 1980

Equity Capital Needed: $16,000

Financial Assistance Available: Assistance in local bank financing.

Training Provided: 3 day school and continuous correspondence training.

Managerial Assistance Available: Marketing, technical consulting and co-op advertising.

Information Submitted: July 1987

THE VIDEO EXCHANGE, INC.
198 Union Boulevard
Suite 100
Lakewood, Colorado 80228
Allen F. Kenfield, President

Description of Operation: One of the fastest growing and aggressive video rental and sales operations in the country. Franchisees rent and sell video tapes and video recorders from attractive, functional decorated stores.

Number of Franchisees: 116 in Colorado, Wyoming, Iowa, Kansas, Missouri and Texas

In Business Since: 1981

Equity Capital Needed: $25,000 to $35,000

Financial Assistance Available: There is no direct or indirect financing provided at this time. However, assistance is available in putting together loan packages.

Training Provided: Classroom training, in-store training, operations and procedures manual. Classroom training, 1 week. In-store training usually dependent on an individual basis, usually 2 to 3 days.

Managerial Assistance Available: Initial training, quarterly regional owner's meetings, annual convention, field visits, national advisory council, group advertising and buying power, ongoing service and support and marketing programs.

Information Submitted: May 1987

*VIDEO UPDATE, INC.
World Headquarters
261 East 5th Street
Suite 322
St. Paul, Minnesota 55101-1945

Description of Operation: A Video Update franchise enables franchisees to run a state-of-the-art video store while maximizing their independence and self reward.

Number of Franchisees: 90 plus in 17 States and New Zealand

In Business Since: 1982

Equity Capital Needed: $75,000 to $225,000

Financial Assistance Available: Will help franchisee in obtaining financing. In some instances, through the Small Business Administration.

Training Provided: Video Update provides ongoing educational services and support through the life of the franchise agreement including an intensive 5 day training program; 3 days at Video Update World Headquarters and 2 days at the franchise location; monthly regional meetings and an annual international meeting.

Managerial Assistance Available: Video Update provides continual management assistance through its toll-free phone lines and maintains a highly trained staff to answer all questions and concerns that may arise. In addition, franchisees are provided with Video Update's own computer software and hardware support programs, national distribution center carrying over 200 Video Update specialty items, a pre-store opening manual, advertising manual and operations manual.

Information Submitted: May 1987

VIDEO USA
P. O. Box 198
West Bountiful, Utah 84087
Garth Hansen, President

Description of Operation: Video sales and rentals.

Number of Franchisees: 35 in 13 States

In Business Since: 1981

Equity Capital Needed: $50,000-$100,000

Financial Assistance Available: Assist in obtaining financing.

Training Provided: Mandatory training for all new franchisees. 2 days conducted at the on-site company store—2-4 days at the franchisee's outlet.

Managerial Assistance Available: Complete manuals of operations, forms, and directions. District managers available. Video USA sponsors franchise meetings, for duration of franchise.

Information Submitted: August 1987

VIDEO VILLAGE
1746 Melmar Drive
Huntingdon Valley, Pennsylvania 19006
Alvaro Munoz, C.E.O.

Description of Operation: Video Village are community oriented video stores involved in the sale and rental of pre-recorded movies, and the sale of all related accessories.

Number of Franchisees: 12 in Pennsylvania, New Jersey and Delaware

In Business Since: 1980

Equity Capital Needed: $100,000 total

Financial Assistance Available: None

Training Provided: An initial program of training is followed by a continuing support program.

Managerial Assistance Available: Assistance is provided in all aspects of the video business by company professionals. Stores are visited on a regular basis and company people are available at all times for consultation. Full-time advertising, public relations and promotional assistance is available at any time.

Information Submitted: July 1987

WEDDING BELL BRIDAL BOUTIQUES (WEBB)
27 West Judson Avenue
Youngstown, Ohio 44507
Theodore E. Khoury, President

Description of Operation: A unique merchandising approach to the bridal customer. Features a complete merchandise plan for selling gowns, tuxedos, accessories and stationery. There are options for smaller operations. Suitable for malls, shopping centers or in a house if space is adequate. Training during set-up and opening. Protected territory, cooperative advertising, group purchases and exclusive designs. Conversions possible, also can be adapted to other existing businesses.

Number of Franchisees: 2 in Ohio

In Business Since: 1960, franchising since 1982

Equity Capital Needed: $30,000 to $35,000 depending on size of store.

Financial Assistance Available: None

Training Provided: A mandatory cooperative training program for owners and managers of franchise at franchisor's headquarters or at a selected WBBB site, also on-site training.

Managerial Assistance Available: Operational assistance is provided at regular intervals. A complete operations manual (work standards, methods and procedures). A 24-hour answering service direct to WBBB headquarters management.

Information Submitted: May 1987

WEE WIN TOYS AND ACCESSORIES, INC.
15340 Vantage Parkway E.
Suite 250
Houston, Texas 77032
James D. Flanagan

Description of Operation: Wholesale 2 lines of toys, Christian toys and wholesome toys.

Number of Franchisees: 181 in entire U.S.A.

In Business Since: 1984

Equity Capital Needed: $9,500 initial investment.

Financial Assistance Available: None.

Training Provided: 3 day training meeting held once each month. We encourage distributors to come as often as possible.

Managerial Assistance Available: Continued, ongoing training by "Wee Win" managers.

Information Submitted: August 1987.

*WEST COAST VIDEO
9990 Global Road
Philadelphia, Pennsylvania 19115
John L. Barry, Vice President, Franchise Sales

Description of Operation: Retail video stores.

Number of Franchisees: 150 plus 45 company-owned in 15 States and the United Kingdom.

In Business Since: 1983

Equity Capital Needed: $120,000 minimum

Financial Assistance Available: None

Training Provided: 1 week training for 2 people.

Managerial Assistance Available: Ongoing support and consultation thru computer, seminars, regional training, field support, etc.

Information Submitted: May 1987

*WICKS 'N' STICKS DIVISION
WNNS, INC.
P. O. Box 4586
Houston, Texas 77210-4586
Houghton B. Hutcheson, Vice President, Franchise Development

Description of Operation: Wicks 'N' Sticks is the nation's largest specialty retailer of candles, room fragrancing products and related home decorating accessories. Merchandise, including private-label and exclusive products, comes from vendors worldwide. Stores are located in major regional malls, today's most desirable retail setting.

Number of Franchisees: 283 in 43 States

In Business Since: 1968

Equity Capital Needed: $50,000-$65,000

Financial Assistance Available: The total investment for a typical Wicks 'N' Sticks franchise ranges from $150,000 to $200,000. WNS, Inc., assists qualified candidates in locating institutions which may provide SBA-guaranteed or other financing.

Training Provided: Extensive 1-week classroom training prepares franchisee for the daily operation of the store. Field staff continues training the franchisee and employees once the store is open, and ensures successful operation during the first critical weeks in business.

Managerial Assistance Available: Wicks 'N' Sticks provides extensive assistance, including site selection guidelines, construction specifications and plans; merchandise selection, pricing guidelines and visual presentation recommendations; national buying power; marketing support materials. Field staff make frequent store visits, supplemented by telecommunications, publications, regional meetings and an annual convention.

Information Submitted: May 1987

WIDE WORLD OF MAPS FRANCHISE CORPORATION
2626 West Glenrosa Avenue
Phoenix, Arizona 85017
James L. Willinger, Vice President

Description of Operation: A complete retail map store marketing a wide selection of over 10,000 different maps, globes, atlases, map related accessories, special interest books and travel guides; stores include a shop that performs decorative services such as mounting, laminating, and custom framing.

Number of Franchisees: Three company-owned in Arizona.

In Business Since: 1974

Equity Capital Needed: Approximately initial investment $17,500—total investment $125,000 to $165,000.

Financial Assistance Available: Assistance in preparing a business plan and in how to prepare a financial package for lenders.

Training Provided: Minimum of 6 business days training at company headquarters. Minimum of 80 hours additional training conducted at franchisees premises.

Managerial Assistance Available: An operating manual is provided detailing all aspects of the systems and procedures for running this specialized retail store. Additional training, managerial and technical assistance provided on a continuing basis at franchisee's premises, through newsletters, and at annual workshops.

Information Submitted: May 1987

WILD BIRDS UNLIMITED, INC.
1430 Broad Ripple Avenue
Indianapolis, Indiana 46220
James R. Carpenter, President

Description of Operation: Wild Birds Unlimited, Inc., offers unique retail shops that specialize in supplying birdseed, feeders, and gift items for the popular hobby of backyard bird feeding. The franchise package includes assistance in site selection and store layout, and includes each store in a discount purchasing program for both feeders and birdseed. Franchises are currently available in the Midwest and New England States.

245

Number of Franchisees: 15 in Indiana, Ohio, and Michigan plus 2 company-owned stores.

In Business Since: 1981

Equity Capital Needed: $20,000 to $25,000

Financial Assistance Available: No financial assistance is provided by the franchisor.

Training Provided: The franchisor provides up to 1 week of training at one of the company-owned stores and provides 2 training manuals, 1 for store operations, 1 for knowledge about bird feeding and sales techniques. Additional visits to the franchisee's store once opened will concentrate on displays, inventory and advertising techniques.

Managerial Assistance Available: Wild Birds Unlimited, Inc., provides continuing management assistance in areas such as group purchasing, advertising, new product information and help with any problems in the operation of the store.

Information Submitted: May 1987

WILLIAM ERNEST BROWN, LTD.
P. O. Box 153 (Sur House)
Big Sur, California 93920
James M. Josoff, Vice President

Description of Operation: Retail stationery shops, featuring very high quality custom designing of stationery and invitations.

Number of Franchisees: 21 in 11 States

In Business Since: 1970

Equity Capital Needed: Approximately $100,000.

Financial Assistance Available: None

Training Provided: Initial training and buying—3 to 4 weeks, continuing basis. Seminars, in-shop training, newsletters are provided on a continuing basis to all franchisees.

Managerial Assistance Available: As above.

Information Submitted: August 1987

WORLD BAZAAR
Division of MUNFORD, INC.
P. O. Box 7701, Station C
Atlanta, Georgia 30357
William A. Richardson

Description of Operation: A proven new complete method of efficiently acquiring and selling at retail various imported and domestic home decorative and gift items, including stylized store, premises, signs, display and merchandise.

Number of Franchisees: 40 within 146 units plus 165 company-owned stores in 32 States

In Business Since: In 1965 the company opened its first World Bazaar and began franchising in 1968.

Equity Capital Needed: Approximately 220,000 to 275,000, less than $95,000 fianced by Munford Inc.

Fiancial Assistance Available: $50,000 franchise fee, $5,000 down, $45,000 financed over 5 years, interest free. $50,000 note on merchandise and equipment purchased from World bazaar for 5 years at prime interest rate plus 1 percent.

Training Provided: 2 to 3 days in East Point, Georgia office, plus further training in a open and operating store is suggested. Training is an expense of the franchisee.

Managerial Assistance Available: Ongoing periodic visits by franchise representative to observe and advise, to provide merchandise and oerational guidance, and to recommend best selling merchandise. A real estate department to handle site selection, lease negotiation, and store construction. A market ing/merchandising department to handle store opening, including selecting and placing of fixtures, merchandise, and promotions. Advertising department that produces ad art and draws ad layouts. Staff that travels overseas buying in foreign countries and distribution center that delivers merchandise to stores.

Information Submitted: May 1987

YERUSHALMI, INC.
2400 Western Avenue
Las Vegas, Nevada 89102
Mordechai Yerushalmi, President

Description of Operation: Jewelry sales.

Number of Franchisees: 3 in Florida, New Jersey and Tennessee

In Business Since: 1985

Equity Capital Needed: $200,000 to $250,000

Financial Assistance Available: None

Training Provided: 1 week at location and 1 week at prospective store.

Managerial Assistance Available: Ongoing assistance when needed.

Information Submitted: May 1987

SECURITY SYSTEMS

CHAMBERS FRANCHISED SECURITY SYSTEMS, INC.
1103 Fredericksburg Road
San Antonio, Texas 78201
David Morris, President

Description of Operation: A signaling service primarily to protect businesses, industry and homeowners against the threats of burglary, fire, holdup, employee dishonesty. A full service organization providing equipment, installation, monitoring and maintenance thru a system lease program. Reoccuring monthly lease revenue assures company stability after startup. franchisor buy-back available.

Number of Franchisees: 2 plus 5 company units

In Business Since: 1978

Equity Capital Needed: $50,000-$200,000 operating till break-even.

Financial Assistance Available: Loan packaging assistance. Our sources or yours.

Training Provided: Orientation at national headquarters in San Antonio (2 days). Field training in startup city with company field trainer (2 weeks). Video cassette based ongoing training and follow-up.

Managerial Assistance Available: We train for "turnkey" operations. We provide assistance in employee selection, site selection, employee training, specific market potential and competitor analysis.

Information Submitted: May 1987

DICTOGRAPH SECURITY SYSTEMS
26 Columbia Turnpike
Florham Park, New Jersey 07932
Myles C. Goldberg, Senior Vice President

Description of Operation: The first company in industry to franchise; with a 40-year history of assisting entrepreneurial businessmen and industry-experienced individuals alike in the sale, installation, maintenance and monitoring of security systems for the residential, commercial, industrial and institutional markets. Extensive line of proprietary and private labeled products, including automatic burglar, fire and smoke alarm systems, access control devices, electronic article surveillance equipment, and auto alarms. Also a vast line of leading-edge closed circuit television systems for loss control and building management, including a unique transaction verification system particularly well-suited for the high large and small scale retail market of convenience stores, gas stations, liquor stores and the like. Fully computerized central monitoring station enables dealers to produce continuing monthly income.

Number of Franchisees: Over 90 in most every State; several overseas.

In Business Since: Founding company since 1902; became affilate of Sargent & Greenleaf Lock Company and Safemasters service network under umbrella Security Group, Inc., in 1985.

Equity Capital Needed: Territorial variations. Inventory refundable on 1 year money back guarantee.

Financial Assistance Available: Expansion promoted by unique dealer equipment assistance loan program. Dealers can participate in share of lease income generated by active national accounts development program. Company offers dealers opportunity to provide residential customers with purchase financing.

Training Provided: Dealer receives 2 weeks of intensive training in all facets of business at company's national headquarters training academy. Company provides dealer with opportunity to send sales, technical, installation and administrative personnel to headquarters training academy for specific classes held throughout the year. Periodic regional meetings hend each year for attendance by dealer and key personnel. Yearly national convention features 3-5 days of important seminars, training courses and new product introductions.

Managerial Assistance Available: The company is constantly developing new material and programs including manuals, sales presentations, technical memorandums and marketing communications materials. Each dealer assigned a dealer advisor who remains a source of information and assistance regarding every facet of the business. Technical and field assistance available to help dealer with equipment applications and troubleshooting, sales development, recruiting and training. Monthly communications packets keep dealers apprised of business developments as they occur. Company coducts national sales contest as incentive for dealers sales personnel. National and local advertising and public relations handled by in-house staff who will assist as needed in developing dealer's local marketing efforts through use of various media.

Information Submitted: July 1987

*DYNAMARK SECURITY CENTERS, INC.
P. O. Box 2068
Hagerstown, Maryland 21742-2068
Wayne E. Alter, Jr., President and Chief Executive Officer

Description of Operation: Dynamark Security Centers, over the past ten years, has developed a unique program and method of marketing residential and light commercial security and fire protection devices, Utilizing standardized trade names, service marks and trademarks, advertising plus training and instructions in operating an exclusive DSC business, franchisees purchase from DSC at bonafide wholesale prices, then sell, install and service devices at retail prices in their marketing territories. Central station monitoring services are available through a DSC subsidiary, DynaWatch, Inc.

Number of Franchisees: Approximately 150 in 33 States.

In Business Since: 1977 as Amtronics, Inc., and in 1984 changed name to Dynamark Security Centers, Inc.

Equity Capital Needed: $39,355. This includes franchise fees, initial classroom and on-the-job training, opening inventory, working capital and miscellaneous costs.

Financial Assistance Available: DSC does not guarantee to obtain nor provide financing for franchisee.

Training Provided: 6 day mandatory initial training course scheduled at national training center for all new franchisees and/or their operations managers. Ongoing advanced training conducted at national training center and at regional locations.

Managerial Assistance Available: DSC provides management services in such areas as marketing and sales, advertising and public relations, and bookkeeping. A complete manual of operations, forms, guidelines and directions is provided. corporate staff as well as technical advisors work via phone in the field with franchise organizations for training and problem solving purposes. DSC sponsors national and regional meetings of franchisees in addition to conducting ongoing marketing research and development to maintain leadership position with the consumer public.

Information Submitted: May 1987

THE SECURITY ALLIANCE CORPORATION
1865 Miner Street
Des Plaines, Illinois 60016
Ron Davis, President

Description of Operation: Security Alliance Corporation is a franchisor of companies who wish to be in the residential and mini-commercial security systems business. Utilizing state-of-the-art, supervised wireless systems, Security Alliance members are provided with a broad range of training, advertising and promotional support.

Number of Franchisees: 110 in 25 States

In Business Since: 1974

Equity Capital Needed: $15,000

Financial Assistance Available: Financing is available on a limited basis, although support is provided to obtain SBA assistance to qualified franchisees.

Training Provided: 1 week initial training, followed by one week of sales training plus quarterly regional training seminars plus monthly visitations.

Managerial Assistance Available: Franchisor provides ongoing telephone, in person support and managerial assistance through seminars. Three separate types of seminars are offered every 45 days, ranging from technical and sales support to sales management and management seminars. In addition, five field marketing people are available for in field visitations, usually on a monthly basis.

Information Submitted: May 1987

SONITROL CORPORATION
424 North Washington Street
Alexandria, Virginia 22314
Zaccheus M. Quincey, Market Development Manager

Description of Operation: Sonitrol Corporation is a manufacturer of audio intrusion detection alarm systems. A franchised Sonitrol dealer is granted a geographic area of primary responsibility where they are responsible for maintaining a sales effort of Sonitrol security alarm systems to businesses or residential end-users and monitoring those systems at a central monitoring station.

Number of Franchisees: 170 in 32 States

In Business Since: 1964

Equity Capital Needed: One-third of $100,000-$400,000 total capital required; which varies according to size of market and franchisees business plan.

Financial Assistance Available: A subsidiary, Sonitrol Financial Corporation, can provide lease financing for central monitoring station equipment.

Training Provided: Each new franchisee is assigned a mentor to supervise the critical path events to organizing and opening the dealership. Classroom or on-site training is provided as appropriate for dealer/general manager, sales manager, sales persons, alarm installers, equipment technicians, and monitoring console operators.

Managerial Assistance Available: Assistance to the franchise network is provided in the areas of national sales and marketing programs; consultation from field sales representatives to address local dealerships needs; formal training programs for management, sales, installation and service, operators; and hot-line service engineering response for installers to monitoring equipment technicians. Operating standards are published and periodic formal inspections are conducted to maintain a consistent level of service quality. Corporate product R&D is ongoing to maintain a differentiated technology edge in Sonitrol's audio listen-in security system.

Information Submitted: May 1987

SWIMMING POOLS

CALIFORNIA POOLS, INC.
4600 Santa Anita Avenue
El Monte, California 91731
David G. Morrill, Vice President

Description of Operation: Swimming pool contracting, selling and installation.

Number of Franchisees: 30 in California

In Business Since: 1952

Equity Capital Needed: $25,000

Financial Assistance Available: None

Training Provided: 1 week extensive. One day each month thereafter. Previous experience is normally required.

Managerial Assistance Available: Franchisor is in constant contact with franchisee. All bookkeeping and accounting is done by centralized computer.

Information Submitted: August 1987

CARIBBEAN CLEAR, INC.
939 Brodie Road
Leesville, South Carolina 29070
Patricia B. Minchey, President

Description of Operation: Caribbean Clear offers a revolutionary new method of purifying swimming pools without chlorine using technology developed by NASA. Franchisee sells units directly to pool owners in his exclusive area.

Number of Franchisees: 3 in South Carolina plus 50 distributors to be converted to franchisees.

In Business Since: 1977

Equity Capital Needed: $22,500 for initial inventory.

Financial Assistance Available: No financing provided at this time.

Training Provided: Intensive 2 day, mandatory training course for all new franchisees.

Managerial Assistance Available: Caribbean Clear provides continual management and technical consulting. A staff of engineers, chemist and managers are available to work directly with the franchisee as needed.

Information Submitted: May 1987.

TOOLS, HARDWARE

AD A BOY TOOL RENTAL, INC.
6655 S. Sweetwater Road
Lithia Springs, Georgia 30057
Jimmy Sorrells, President

Description of Operation: Ad A Boy Tool Rental offers a small equipment and tool rental business with a broad range of items to serve the homeowner, contractor, medical, party, and industrial customer. Store owners select their markets based on our feasibility study and their own personal preferences. Building required—1,800 to 3,200 square feet with outside storage and good traffic flow.

Number of Franchisees: 6 in Georgia and Florida

In Business Since: 1986

Equity Capital Needed: $24,000 plus $6,000 to $10,000 working capital. No franchise fee or royalty payments.

Financial Assistance Available: Your down payment of $24,000 is applied to the purchase of $85,000 of equipment, tools, and opening supplies. Balance can be financed with local banks. Guidance is provided in securing financing to qualified applicants.

Training Provided: Complete on-site training at the new store on a one to one basis for 2 full days. Training is very personalized to the individual store owners requirements. Complete information on the equipment and how to run the rental business.

Managerial Assistance Available: Initial consultation covers market survey and feasibility study, site evaluation, lease negotiation, financing, insurance, advertising, bookkeeping, rental contracts, and rental rates. After the store is in operation consultation is provided in-store on an ongoing basis. topics include operation and development of the rental business.

Information Submitted: May 1987

IMPERIAL HAMMER, INC.
9226 North Second Street
Rockford, Illinois 01111
John R. Sassaman, President

Description of Operation: Manufacturer of industrial hammers and vise jaws. Light non-ferrous metal foundry, selling and servicing industry and maintenance plants of all types.

Number of Franchisees: 3 in 3 States

In Business Since: 1957

Equity Capital Needed: $55,000 depending on size of territory.

Financial Assistance Available: Financial assistance is available to qualified individuals.

Training Provided: 2 weeks in franchisor's plant and office to learn complete operation.

Managerial Assistance Available: Assistance always available to help find location, assist, advise and counsel at all times.

Information Submitted: August 1987

MAC TOOLS, INC.
P. O. Box 370
South Fayette Street
Washington Court House, Ohio 43160
Bill Robertson and/or James Aylward

Description of Operation: Distributors carrying complete inventory of over 9,000 tools, calling directly on mechanics and light industry. These tools consist of a complete assortment of all small hand tools, sockets, wrenches, punches, chisels, screwdrivers, tool boxes, pneumatic tools, as well as special tools designed for the automotive after market.

Number of Franchisees: Over 1,800 throughout the United States and Canada.

In Business Since: 1938

Equity Capital Needed: $52,000

Financial Assistance Available: The $52,000 starting amount includes a basic starting inventory, initial deposit on a new tool truck, business supplies, and backup capital. There are no franchise fee and the original investment is protected by a buy-back agreement. Financing for the starter inventory is available for qualified applicants.

Training Provided: After new distributor training in Ohio, each distributor is assigned to a district manager who lives in the local area and does all necessary follow-up training, will aid in displaying the trucks, establishing bookkeeping systems, and technical knowledge. they spend approximately 3 weeks with any new distributor and then maintain a monthly contact. Also will continue to work with the distributor as he deems necessary.

Managerial Assistance Available: Same as above.

Information Submitted: May 1987

TOOL SHACK
TOOL STORES, INC.
5236 Colodny Drive
Suite 201
Agoura Hills, California 91301

Description of Operation: Tool stores selling name brand tools at discount prices with full guarantees to professional tradesmen.

Number of Franchisees: 42 in California, Arizona, Texas, Oklahoma, and Mississippi.

In Business Since: 1978, franchising since 1980.

Equity Capital Needed: Minimum $30,000 cash investment. Total package $95,000 franchise fee $30,000; balance of $65,000 used for inventory, deposits, working capital, etc.

Financial Assistance Available: SBA loans from 55,000 are available. Inventory of approximately $60,000 is provided at cost and financing available on balance.

Training Provided: Training in all phases of business conducted in actual operating store. One week to 10 days minimum duration, more if necessary. Additional days of training are provided during the grand opening of franchisee's store.

Managerial Assistance Available: The company provides a heavy concentration of radio, television and newspaper advertising on a consistent basis. Mass buying power is available to franchisees through warehouse affiliate and other tool distributors and factories. Site selection, lease negotiation and store set up are also provided to franchisee.

Information Submitted: May 1987

VULCAN TOOLS
1359 Louis Avenue
Elk Grove Village, Illinois 60007
Tom Zur, President

Description of Operation: Independent dealers and warehouse owners purchase mechanics' hand tools, shop supplies and equipment from the company at a very favorable discount. They in turn market these items from a van type truck directly to the user at a suggested mechanic net price. territories are assigned based on the number of potential customers rather than by geographic size. Customers include garages, truck and bus fleets, new and used car dealers, service stations, contractors, marinas, airports, appliance shops and all mechanics therein employed.

Number of Franchisees: 100 plus throughout the U.S., Puerto Rico and Canada.

In Business Since: 1960

Equity Capital Needed: Dealers: $15,000 minimum. Warehouse: $50,000 minimum.

Financial Assistance Available: Dealer financing: dealer must own suitable vehicle and have cash investment of not less than $15,000 for inventory. Thirty day financing for sales made to established commercial accounts. Warehouse financing: none available. Dealer, customer L.T. financing also available.

Training Provided: Training on use of catalog, sales book, reporting forms, truck and demonstration assistance offered. Sales and business procedure meetings and ongoing field service and training. Instruction booklets furnished on all equipment items. Also supported by numerous sales promotions and ongoing product addition.

Managerial Assistance Available: Training in all forms necessary for conduct of business. Counseling on inventory and accounts receivable turnover. No handling charge on dealer return of saleable inventory plus discontinued product protection. Assistance in taking physical inventory and computation at no charge.

Information Submitted: June 1987

VENDING

FORD GUM & MACHINE COMPANY, INC.
Division of LEAF, INC.
New and Hoag Streets
Akron, New York 14001
George H. Stege, Vice President

Description of Operation: Manufacturer and distributor of chewing gum, candy, and candy coated confections for sale through self-service vending machines, also manufactured and distrubuted to franchisees by the company.

Number of Franchisees: 183 in all States, canada and Puerto Rico.

In Business Since: 1934 with manufacturing plant in Akron, New York.

Equity Capital Needed: $5,000-$30,000 depending on area.

Financial Assistance Available: Extended credit to new franchisees for: a. expansion of franchised territory; b. purchase of existing franchise from retiring franchisee, and c. purchase of equipment and supplies.

Training Provided: On-the-job training in machine and service operation in franchisee's area.

Managerial Assistance Available: See above.

Information Submitted: May 1987

MECHANICAL SERVANTS, INC.
4615 North Clifton Avenue
Chicago, Illinois 60640
David A. Baum, President

Description of Operation: Mechanical Servants, Inc., manufactures and distrubutes general merchandise and amusement vending machines and a full line of general merchandise for use in these and other venders. Franchisees are offered a complete service including an exclusive territory, vending machines, special merchandise for sale through these machines, displays and other sales aids and a complete program for servicing, operating and maintaining them. The franchise can be operated from a residence on a full- or part-time basis depending upon the number of machines.

Number of Franchisees: 25 plus 26 company-owned in 24 States

In Business Since: 1953

Equity Capital Needed: $5,000 minimum

Financial Assistance Available: Total investment ranges from $10,000 depending upon the number of machines and market potential. Mechanical Servants, Inc., will finance franchisee with good credit background (10 years-120 payment basis).

Training Provided: Intensive on location training by company staff with optional home office training.

Managerial Assistance Available: Mechanical Servants, Inc., provides continual management service for the life of the franchise in such areas as record keeping, new product development, location acquisition and machine maintenance. Complete manual of operation, forms, and direction are provided. Field supervisors are available in all regions to work closely with franchisee and aid in solving problems. M.S.I. continually tests new products and its sales staff continually seeks new locations. Vending machines and parts (with a few exceptions) are guaranteed against defects in material and workmanship for the life of the franchise.

Information Submitted: May 1987

SERVAPURE COMPANY
1101 Columbus Avenue
Bay City, Michigan 48708
Howard or Richard Herzberger

Description of Operation: Coin operated pure water vending machines. Bottling of purified water.

Number of Franchisees: in Michigan

In Business Since: 1954

Equity Capital Needed: Minimum $25,000

Financial Assistance Available: Possible lease purchase to qualified party.

Training Provided: Initial training as necessary and ongoing technical support.

Managerial Assistance Available: As needed (see above).

Information Submitted: May 1987

UNITED SNACKS OF AMERICA, INC.
dba SNACKPACKER
P. O. Box 33488
Raleigh, North Carolina 27808
David A. Kachuck

Description of Operation: Snackpacker is an industrial snack food vending system. It provides a snack food service to small offices and shops.

Number of Franchisees: 5 in North Carolina, New Jersey and Georgia.

In Business Since: 1980

Equity Capital Needed: $75,000

Financial Assistance Available: None

Training Provided: Field training, classroom and on-site assistance as necessary, duration of training not guaranteed.

Managerial Assistance Available: Operating manual plus on-site assistance duration is not guaranteed. Periodic on-site and telephone consultation assistance for the life of the franchise.

Information Submitted: August 1987

WESTROCK VENDING VEHICLES CORP.
1565D 5th Industrial Court
Bayshore, New York 11706
Stephen L. Kronrad, President

Description of Operation: Westrock Vending Vehicles Corp., is offering a proven highly respected franchise opportunity. Mobile trailers and step vans for the selling of submarine sandwiches, hot food, soda and ice cream in industrial and high traffic areas. Operator works on high profit with very low overhead.

Number of Franchisees: 26 in New York

In Business Since: 1970

Equity Capital Needed: Trailers start at $12,000 and trucks $30,000. As little as 10 percent down to qualified buyers of trucks or trailers with the balance financed.

Financial Assistance Available: A total investment of $116,000 is necessary to open a "Master Distribution Center" franchise, the down payment of $41,000 pays for 25 vehicles, freezer, tools, inventory and fees. Westrock can arrange to finance the balance for qualified individuals. Franchisee may arrange their own outside financing.

Training Provided: Westrock will assist in your training and any questions you might have.

Managerial Assistance Available: Westrock provides the most comprehensive managerial and technical assistance programs available in the industry. The franchisee is advised in the areas: managerial science and business administration, bookkeeping, advertising, inventory control, vehicles and equipment maintenance, and specific information related to the industry. Manuals of operation, forms, and directions are provided. Westrock executives are always available to assist in solving problems. Consulting expertise is available.

Information Submitted: April 1987

WATER CONDITIONING

CULLIGAN INTERNATIONAL COMPANY
One Culligan Parkway
Northbrook, Illinois 60062

Description of Operation: Parent company is supplier to franchisee for water treatment equipment. Franchisee sells, leases, maintains and repairs water treatment equipment for domestic, commercial, and industrial consumers.

Number of Franchisees: 845 in the U.S. and Canada

In Business Since: 1936

Equity Capital Needed: $42,500 and up

Financial Assistance Available: Franchisor has various credit arrangements available for qualified franchisees with reference to the purchase of equipment from franchisor.

Training Provided: Franchisor provides training at Northbrook, Illinois headquarters. Franchisor also provides management training and technical training through frequent visits to franchisee's dealership by company personnnel.

Managerial Assistance Available: Franchisor has continuing managerial and technical assistance to franchisee through traveling, district service training engineers, district managers, and industrial sales managers. This assistance is available to all franchisees as needed.

Information Submitted: March 1987

*RAINSOFT WATER CONDITIONING CO.
2080 Lunt Street
Elk Grove Village, Illinois 60007
John R. Grayson, President

Description of Operation: Sell, lease, and rent water treatment equipment to homes, businesses, and industry.

Number of Franchisees: Over 200 in most States

In Business Since: 1953

Equity Capital Needed: Varies from $15,000 minimum.

Financial Assistance Available: Assist in establishing retail financing. Financing of rental equipment to qualified dealers on selected basis.

Training Provided: On-plant and field training in sales, service, and operation.

Managerial Assistance Available: Continuing contact for training and assistance through national and regional seminars, plus regular person-to-person contact from regional field representatives.

Information Submitted: May 1987

WATERCARE CORPORATION
1520 North 24th Street
Manitowoc, Wisconsin 54220
William K. Granger, President

Description of Operation: Water conditioning sales and service, domestic, industrial; institutional and commercial. Method of service and sales is portable exchange water conditioners; permanently installed water conditioners on a rental basis and outright sales.

Number of Franchisees: 130 dealers in 35 States

In Business Since: 1946

Equity Capital Needed: $15,000

Financial Assistance Available: After initial financing WaterCare provides dealer growth money on plant equipment and rental water conditioners.

Training Provided: Includes techniques of water conditioning, water analysis, sales and service of equipment, office procedures, management, all of which is done at our home office and plant in Manitowoc, Wisconsin and our "Dealer-Lab" company-owned retail operation at Green Bay, Wisconsin. Time is approximately 1 week in Wisconsin and 1 week by dealer counselor at the franchisee's place of operation. In addition, monthly call on franchisee by dealer counselor and semi-annual area work seminars.

Managerial Assistance Available: Same as above.

Information Submitted: August 1987

MISCELLANEOUS WHOLESALE AND SERVICE BUSINESSES

ADDHAIR TECHNOLOGIES, INC.
1525 Francisco Blvd.
Suite 5 East
San Rafael, California 94901
Gui R. Everitt

Description of Operation: Addhair Technologies is the formost leader in the hair replacement industry, using a technology which literally duplicates actual growing hair. The franchisor is Addhair Technologies, Inc., and the franchisees are Addhair Technologies Centers.

Number of Franchisees: 14 in California, Texas, Florida, and Illinois.

In Business Since: 10 years experience began franchising 3 years ago.

Equity Capital Needed: Minimum of $100,000

Financial Assistance Available: None

Training Provided: 2 weeks for management in San Francisco franchise outlet, 1 week for stylist in San Francisco franchise outlet.

Managerial Assistance Available: Same as above.

Information Submitted: May 1987

ADS & TYPE EXPRESS
ADS & TYPE GRAPHICS, INC.
P. O. Box 133
Fairview, New Jersey 07022
Louis C. Fernandez, President

Description of Operation: State-of-the-art wholesale typesetting and graphics/art service without investing a cent on expensive typesetting equipment. No typesetting or art skills required whatsoever. We do all the production work for you. You wholesale to quick- and commercial-printers. You could operate this business at home with minimum overhead. Protected territory.

Number of Franchisees: 4 in 3 States

In Business Since: 1985

Equity Capital Needed: Distributorship fee $1,500.

Financial Assistance Available: Credit-qualified individuals.

Training Provided: Complete training and continuous support. No typing, typesetting or art/graphics skills required.

Managerial Assistance Available: Continuous assistance via telephone "hot line" and periodic bulletins.

Information Submitted: July 1987

ALL-STATE WELDING AND INDUSTRIAL PRODUCTS
5112 Allendale Lane
Taneytown, Maryland 21787
John W. Jurasic, General Manager

Description of Operation: Mobile sales and service operation for welding products and services and other industrial products for maintenance and repair.

Number of Franchisees: 6 in Florida, Illinois, California, Washington, Louisiana and New York.

In Business Since: 1946

Equity Capital Needed: $75,000

Financial Assistance Available: Franchisee may sublease van from franchisor. Opening inventory of approximately $7,500 on 90 day payment terms.

Training Provided: 1 week product traning, 1 week sales training, 1 week business training and 1 week field training.

Managerial Assistance Available: Ongoing managerial and technical assistance available via 800 toll free number. Visitations to franchisee by managerial and technical staff as required. Literature and technical bulletins provided routinely to aid marketing effort. National trade magazine advertising.

Information Submitted: May 1987

ALMOST HEAVEN HOT TUBS, LTD.
Route 1-F
Renick, West Virginia 24966
Barry Glick, Franchise Director

Description of Operation: Manufacture of hot tubs, spas, jacuzzi whirlpool baths, sauna rooms, steam rooms and other leisure equipment.

Number of Franchisees: 1,097 in 50 States, Puerto Rico, Virgin Islands, and throughout the world.

In Business Since: 1968

Financial Assistance Available: Help in arranging financing through local banks.

Training Provided: Extensive training at manufacturing facility.

Managerial Assistance Available: Continual seminars, monthly bulletins, etc. 24-hour assistance, sales leads provided at no charge. Cooperative advertising program. Dealer territory protection.

Information Submitted: May 1987

THE ARMOLOY CORPORATION
1325 Sycamore Road
DeKalb, Illinois 60115
Jerome F. Bejbl, President

Description of Operation: Metal coating, that is electrodeposited chromium, for wear and corrosion precision parts.

Number of Franchisees: 7 in 6 States, 1 in the United Kingdom, and 1 in West Germany.

In Business Since: 1955

Equity Capital Needed: $300,000/$400,000

Financial Assistance Available: None

Training Provided: Complete training period at corporate headquarters for key personnel. Continuing assistance in any phase of the business.

Managerial Assistance Available: Technical assistance is run by our quality control laboratory, and corporate provides any managerial help that is needed. We have advertising, administrative and sales help available.

Information Submitted: May 1987

ARMOR SHIELD, INC.
4090 Rosehill Avenue
Cincinnati, Ohio 45229
Douglas J. Meester, Marketing Director

Description of Operation: Interior inspection, repair and coating of underground storage vessels containing petroleum products. Primary customers: major oil companies.

Number of Franchisees: 18 in 16 States

In Business Since: 1972

Equity Capital Needed: $80,000-$120,000

Financial Assistance Available: Very limited.

Training Provided: 3 weeks in field plus continual guidance.

Managerial Assistance Available: Annual seminar for managers and exchange of information. Technical assistance available.

Information Submitted: April 1987

BALLOON BOUQUETS, INC.
69 Kilburn Road
Belmont, Massachusetts 02178

Description of Operation: Balloon delivery and decorating service.

Number of Franchisees: 20 in 13 States and Washington, D.C.

In Business Since: 1976

Equity Capital Needed: None

Financial Assistance Available: None

Training Provided: 2 days: business management, office operations, balloon delivery and balloon decorating.

Managerial Assistance Available: Continuing technical assistance. Advertising, purchasing, nationwide customer referrals to franchisees through toll-free "800" lines: 1-800-424-2323.

Information Submitted: May 1987

BAVARIAN WAX ART
6380 Euclid Road
Cincinnati, Ohio 45236
Robert Young

Description of Operation: Bavarian Wax Art is a special art form of statues, wall plaques and Christmas ornaments, utilizing special casting wax from Germany to create beautiful and lasting decorative sculpture for home and office. These hand crafted works of wax art have a significant tradition, legend or historical link to the original piece of art. Their hard to believe details goes down to 1/64th of an inch. They are hand finished with great care. When finished these pieces have a natural wood finish. The franchisee will take the figures, buff them with a cloth, dip them in a special liquid solution and then give them a final buffing. The figures will then be ready for sale. There are many ways to market and sell the figures. Training provided. Excellent home based business.

Number of Franchisees: 5

In Business Since: 1984

Equity Capital Needed: $1,995

Financial Assistance Available: None

Training Provided: Training is provided in Cincinnati, Ohio. For those people unable to attend the training, we provide a manual. Additional training will be provided through seminars.

Managerial Assistance Available: Seminars and meetings are provided.

Information Submitted: May 1987

CHEMSTATION INTERNATIONAL, INC.
3201 Encrete Lane
Dayton, Ohio 45439
George F. Homan, President

Description of Operation: Chemical (cleaners) sales and distribution to institutions and industry in unique "bulk" ranks tailored to the individual users needs.

Number of Franchisees: 6 in Ohio, Michigan and Indiana

In Business Since: 1980

Equity Capital Needed: $50,000-$100,000

Financial Assistance Available: Help with third-party equipment leases, up to $30,000.

Training Provided: "In field" and equipment use, training 5-10 days or as required up to 30 days.

Managerial Assistance Available: Ongoing managerial assistance through duration of 10 year agreement. Forecasting, sales analysis, product development, national account development, government supply development.

Information Submitted: August 1987

COMPOSIL NORTH AMERICA, INC.
6944 Sunbelt Drive South
San Antonio, Texas 78218
C. T. Amundsen, Director of Franchising

Description of Operation: Texile protection service for both commercial and residential accounts using an internationally proven product. Involves the marketing and application of the products for use on carpeting, wall fabric, upholstered fabric, and draperies.

Number of Franchisees: 9 in Texas, Kansas, Colorado, Arizona and Florida.

In Business Since: 1985

Equity Capital Needed: $21,000 to $27,000 depending on initial inventory desired.

Financial Assistance Available: None

Training Provided: Franchisee will take a mandatory 3-day training course that is scheduled for all new franchisees and key personnel. This 3-day process will be conducted at the corporate headquarters free of charge.

Managerial Assistance Available: Composil provides continual management service for the life of the franchise. A complete manual covering all aspects of operations, forms, and advertising will be provided. Composil sponsors seminars for franchisees and conducts marketing and product research to maintain Composil consumer acceptance.

Information Submitted: August 1987

CROWN TROPHY, INC.
1034 Yonkers Avenue
Yonkers, New York 10704
Chuck Wersenfeld, President

Description of Operation: Manufacturer—all types of awards, signs, trophies, plaques, medals, ribbons, desk accessories and advertising specialties.

Number of Franchisees: 6 in New York

In Business Since: 1978

Equity Capital Needed: $48,000-$60,000

Financial Assistance Available: 100 percent financing for qualified buyers.

Training Provided: 2 weeks training, 1 week at home office and 1 week on-site.

Managerial Assistance Available: We will assist the buyer until he has enough knowledge on all the aspects of running his business.

Information Submitted: May 1987

*DATAGAS, INC.
P. O. Box 360
Ankeny, Iowa 50021
Russell H. Buchanan, President, CEO

Description of Operation: Marketing gasoline with ATM type computer terminals.

Number of Franchisees: 5 in Iowa

In Business Since: 1985

Equity Capital Needed: $100,000

Financial Assistance Available: None

Training Provided: 3 basic types of training: classroom 1 week, on-the-job 1 week and operations manual, ongoing.

Managerial Assistance Available: The kinds of assistance provided with depends somewhat on the skills and needs of the specific franchisee. However, we will have available: market research—customer base—site selection, prints and drawings—bills of material—approved supplier lists, advertising and promotion— marketing, selling techniques, administration and accounting, credit and collections, and facilities operations—maintenance. All of the foregoing will be available as long as the franchisee has a need.

Information Submitted: May 1987

FIRE DEFENSE CENTERS
3919 Morton Street
Jacksonville, Florida 32217

Description of Operation: Sale and service of fire extinguishers sales and service of automatic fire extinguishing dry chemical restaurant systems and sales plus service of first aid kits.

Number of Franchisees: 2 in Florida

In Business Since: 1973, franchising since 1985

Equity Capital Needed: $25,000-$29,500

Financial Assistance Available: None

Training Provided: Sale, marketing, bookkeeping, legal, service—complete turnkey operation, duration—7 days; followed by assistance at franchisee location— as needed.

Managerial Assistance Available: All managerial training in training, sales, marketing, bookkeeping, hiring, servicing, at regular intervals at home office and at franchisee's location.

Information Submitted: May 1987

FIRE PROTECTION USA/INC.
1787 East Fort Union Boulevard #201
P. O. Box 06357
Salt Lake City, Utah 84121
F. Darrell Lindsey

Description of Operation: Fire protection dealer/installer of fire retardant (interior and exterior), fire extinguishers, smoke alarms, escape ladders, emergency road kits, dead bolt locks and peep holes, fire proof blankets and clothing for homes and small businesses.

Number of Franchisees: 35 in 16 states.

In Business Since: 1986

Equity Capital Needed: No financial assistance.

Financial Assistance Available: $12,500 includes all equipment and supplies for turnkey business.

Training Provided: 3 days home office with all expenses paid and 2 weeks in field followup.

Managerial Assistance Available: Complete manuals, video tapes for telemarketing training of employees, all operating forms, customer letters, advertising, etc. franchisor holds annual conventions, visits franchisees several times each year, has 800 wats line for full support, has west coast and east coast corporate offices. Also affiliates with nationwide carpet cleaning franchise for cleaning.

Information Submitted: August 1987

FOLIAGE DESIGN SYSTEMS FRANCHISE CO.
1553 S.E. Fort King Avenue
Ocala, Florida 32671
John S. Hagood, C.E.O.

Description of Operation: The franchisor plans to authorize others to operate live foliage businesses, which sell foliage leasing and maintenance contracts to other businesses. The franchisee retains a contract from a business to provide and maintain live foliage plants on a lease basis or on a sale and maintenance basis. The plants are supplied to a business and are maintained by the franchisee, including replacing plants that need care in the greenhouse. The franchisee will also provide consultation with the businesses as to the number of live foliage plants, the types of plants and the location within the business that plants are to be placed and can sell plants to the business, maintain them, or provide a guaranteed maintenance agreement, so that the business contracting with the franchisee would always maintain high grade foliage plants without having to be concerned with maintenance, replacement, greenhouse activities, and the like. The franchisee will maintain a local greenhouse, a van, and other facilities to properly maintain plants and to store an inventory of live foliage plants. The franchise businesses will be located mostly in urban or heavily populated suburban areas, where various types of businesses that might desire live foliage plants as part of the office decor can be found. The Foliage Design Systems Franchise Company makes no representation as to the amount of income the franchisee might expect from such franchise.

Number of Franchisees: 30 in 12 States

In Business Since: 1971, franchising since 1980.

Equity Capital Needed: $20,000-$50,000

Financial Assistance Available: None

Training Provided: At least 1 week at franchise headquarters at Ocala, Florida, then 2 visits each of which are 3-5 days each to help with set up of greenhouse and marketing help.

Managerial Assistance Available: Foliage design Systems Franchise Company provides continual supervision of the life of the franchise. Manuals of operations, directories, and continued education are provided. The company makes available promotional advertising material plus the company runs regional and national advertising for the benefit of the franchisees. In addition, the company publishes an inch office mews letter quarterly that the franchisees can use.

Information Submitted: May 1987

FRIGFIX REFRIGERATION SERVICE
255 Park Avenue
Nutley, New Jersey 07110
Joseph J. Delmaestro, President

Description of Operation: This is a business of major household applicance repair and services, more particularly, household and light commercial refrigerators and freezers.

Number of Franchisees: 3.

In Business Since: 1974

Equity Capital Needed: $17,500.

Financial Assistance Available: Yes.

Training Provided: 3 weeks on the job training.

Information Submitted: June 1987.

*GREAT EXPECTATIONS CREATIVE MANAGEMENT
dba GREAT EXPECTATIONS
11040 Santa Monica Boulevard
Suite 300
Los Angeles, California 90025
Jeffrey Ullman, President

Description of Operation: Great Expectations is the oldest and largest singles introduction service in America. In 1976 it created "video dating" so that singles could meet each offer for a committed romantic relationship. Currently, video dating is only one of several unique services offered to its singles membership.

Number of Franchisees: 17 in 14 States and Washington, DC

In Business Since: 1976

Equity Capital Needed: $175,000-$255,000

Financial Assistance Available: Negotiable

Training Provided: Intensive and comprehensive 1 week training at Los Angeles headquarters followed up by a 1 month training visit to franchisee's centre. Additional training visits at franchisee's centre as well as at main headquarters are available. Training includes a 225 page operations manual.

Managerial Assistance Available: Besides training at franchisee's home centre and franchisor's headquarters, frequent communication is maintained through telephone and letter correspondance. Franchisee is encouraged to "pick up the phone and call franchisor or fellow franchisees." Each franchisee is able to participate in co-operative advertising.

Information Submitted: June 1987

GREEN KEEPERS INTERNATIONAL, INC.
5300 150 Avenue North
Clearwater, FLorida 33546
Robert Abrahams, President

Description of Operation: The franchisor plans to authorize the use of its registered tradename and associated mark to the franchisee for the design, sales, leasing and maintenance of live interior foliage plants. The franchisee sells or leases plants to commercial establishments and then maintains the plants under contract for a monthly service fee. Franchisee will maintain a local greenhouse to properly store inventory. Franchisor will supply any and all plants, containers and other ongoing inventories at lower costs than their competitors may purchase these items at, due to franchisors mass volume purchasing power.

Number of Franchisees: 2 in Florida

In Business Since: 1973, franchising since 1984.

Equity Capital Needed: $15,000-$32,000

Financial Assistance Available: The franchisor does not offer any direct financing, but will assist franchisee, through a third-party in securing funds.

Training Provided: Franchisor provides an in-depth 2 week training course at its headquarters in Clearwater, Florida. Training includes all aspects of horticultural practices, design, sales and an extensive course in business operations. Franchisor will also assist franchisee for 1 week at franchisees headquarters.

Managerial Assistance Available: Franchisor offers ongoing managerial and technical assistance to franchisee throughout the term of the franchise agreement. Operations manuals, sales brochures and presentation packages, national account reference lists, internal business forms and our exclusive custom graphics design kits are all offered to the franchises on a continual basis. Franchisor will also visit franchisees location on regular intervals throughout the year as well as holding semi-annual regional seminars.

Information Submitted: August 1987

* **HAIR ASSOCIATES, INC.**
dba HAIR REPLACEMENT SYSTEMS
Route 100, Old High School Building
P. O. Box 939
Waitsfield, Vermont 05673

Description of Operation: Retail sales on non-surgical, custom hair replacement.

Number of Franchisees: 44 studios in 20 States.

In Business Since: 1980

Equity Capital Needed: $11,380 to $37,450

Financial Assistance Available: Assistance in obtaining.

Training Provided: Complete initial training in business operations, sales and technical skills plus free ongoing training provided by franchisor.

Managerial Assistance Available: Toll-free line into HRS administrative offices, support of administrative staff, professional consultants, plus other franchisees, annual national business meeting.

Information Submitted: June 1987

* **HEEL QUIK**
1720 Cumberland Point Drive
Suite 15
Marietta, Georgia 30067

Description of Operation: Instant while you wait shoe repair operations. Either as an add on business or full independent store located in a mall or any high traffic area.

Number of Franchisees: 36 in 12 states.

In Business Since: 1984

Equity Capital Needed: $15,000-$25,000

Financial Assistance Available: None

Training Provided: Prior to the opening of licensee's Heel Quik, licensor trains staff designated by the licensee during a 1 to 2 week period. All training is performed at company training facilities and 1 week on site.

Managerial Assistance Available: In addition to training described above, licensor provides: established total concept system of while you wait shoe repair methodology, sales, marketing techniques, trademarks and ongoing supervision and support, advertising package, training manuals and video tapes.

Information Submitted: May 1987

* **MACHINERY WHOLESALERS CORP.**
3510 Biscayne Boulevard
Miami, Florida 33137
Mark Fields, President

Description of Operation: Machinery Wholesalers is a totally unique industrial machinery brokerage network providing a computerized seller-to-buyer service thru our computer center—with a data bank of more than 60,000 buyers, with offices coast to coast.

Number of Franchisees: Over 35 multiple territories in 32 States.

In Business Since: 1974

Equity Capital Needed: Territories $7,500 to $15,000.

Financial Assistance Available: Up to 50 percent, depending on amount of territories purchased by franchisee.

Training Provided: 3 working days of training from 8 am to 7 pm.

Managerial Assistance Available: Continuous supply of information, we are part of every sale.

Information Submitted: August 1987

MEISTERGRAM
3517 West Wendover Avenue
Greensboro, NC 27407
Stephen R. Gluskin, Vice President/
General Manager

Description of Operation: Meistergram is the originator and largest source of monogram embroidery equipment and supplies and has been in business since 1931. Much of our equipment is sold to department stores and manufacturers. several thousand of our accounts are individuals who acquire equipment to set up their own monogram service in their homes or shops. New products—also include the Etchmaster 2000 and Etchmaster 3000 equipment used to personalize glass and other hard line products.

Number of Franchisees: 6,000 in 50 States and overseas.

In Business Since: 1931

Equity Capital Needed: $5,000-$15,000

Financial Assistance Available: Leasing and financing plan available to qualified applicants.

Training Provided: Training available on premises.

Managerial Assistance Available: Factory trained instructor installs machine on premises and teaches franchisee how to operate and maintain equipment, work with different materials and garments. Complete supplies and service available.

Information Submitted: May 1987

MID CONTINENT SYSTEMS, INC.
310 Mid Continent Plaza
P. O. Box 1370
West Memphis, Arkansas 72301
Joe E. Gurley, Executive Vice President

Description of Operation: Mid Continent systems, Inc., offers a complete line of products and services for motor carriers throughout the country. The company also operates a regional chain of motels and sells property and casualty insurance tailored to the needs of truck stop operators and petroleum distributors.

Number of Franchisees: 208 in all States except, Deleware, Maine, Vermont and New Hampshire.

In Business Since: 1968

Equity Capital Needed: Varies, based upon situation.

Financial Assistance Available: None

Training Provided: Manuals and personal assistance as needed. Varies with time desired and involvement of franchisee in related service areas.

Managerial Assistance Available: Above, plus telephone (800 number) advise and counseling.

Information Submitted: May 1987

OXYGEN THERAPY INSTITUTE, INC.
21369 Hatcher Avenue
Ferndale, Michigan 48220

Description of Operation: Manufacturer of portable emergency oxygen inhalators.

253

Number of Franchisees: 47 in 30 states and Canada

In Business Since: 1967

Financial Assistance Available:

Training Provided: A training program is provided.

Managerial Assistance Available: Ongoing in all aspects of the operation.

Information Submitted: August 1987

* QUAL KROM FRANCHISING, INC.
301 Florida Avenue
Fort Pierce, Florida 33450
George W. Fluegel, President

Description of Operation: Restoration of chrome on antique automobiles, chrome plating marine, street rod parts, precious metal restoration, industrial plating and rechroming.

Number of Franchisees: 2 company-owned units in Florida and New York.

In Business Since: 1985

Equity Capital Needed: $50,000-$100,000

Financial Assistance Available: None

Training Provided: 6 weeks of initial training.

Managerial Assistance Available: Ongoing for term of agreement.

Information Submitted: May 1987

REDI NATIONAL PEST ELIMINATORS, INC.
2001 6th Avenue
Suite 1612
Seattle, Washington 98121
Dean Wilcox, Director of Franchise Sales

Description of Operation: Redi National Pest Eliminator, Inc., offers a highly successful system for operating a Pest Control Business including marketing programs and materials, technical methods and assistance and management systems.

Number of Franchisees: 11 in Alaska, Washington, Oregon and Arizona

In Business Since: 1980

Equity Capital Needed: $20,000

Financial Assistance Available: None

Training Provided: 15 day training program at the home office is mandatory. Follow-up training at franchisee's location as necessary to meet minimum requirements.

Managerial Assistance Available: Ongoing support is provided to franchisee's including advertising, sales development programs, and field consultants to assist in all phases of operations. In addition, operations manuals, forms and materials are provided and continually updated.

Information Submitted: May 1987

THE SPORTS SECTION PHOTOGRAPHY, INC.
4958 Hammermill Road
Atlanta, Georgia 30084
R. Daniel Burger, President

Description of Operation: TSS, a custom-color production facility, specializes in youth and youth sports photography. Franchisees with strengths in sales and marketing are trained in photography and become a part of our network of professionals offering unique photographic products and highly organized services to youth groups as a part- or full-time venture. Franchisees are encouraged to work from their homes. There is no merchandise to maintain, a protected territory of 100,000 to 800,000 population is worked year-round.

Number of Franchisees: 35 in 18 States

In Business Since: 1983

Equity Capital Needed: $7,900 for minimum 100,000 population; additional territory will be financed; or 420,000 for 500,000 including all training in territory.

Financial Assistance Available: None, except above mentioned.

Training Provided: Sales and marketing training in territory for 1-2 days and complete photography training in territory. Additional training available according to size of territory and needed assistance.

Managerial Assistance Available: Turnkey operation provided including all materials necessary for success. Sales and photography training provided in $20,000 franchise. Sales seminar in Atlanta headquarters for $7,900 franchise. Sales and photographic experts on call throughout U.S.

Information Submitted: May 1987

* STAINED GLASS OVERLAY, INC.
151 Kalmus Drive J-4
Costa Mesa, California 92626
Barry L. Rupp, President

Description of Operation: Franchisees are exclusive distributors of the unique "Overlay" process, which they apply to windows (without removing them from their mountings), mirrors, skylights, ceiling panels, etc. Just as beautiful as cut stained glass, Overlay has many benefits: it's seamless—no air or water leakage; it strengthens the glass; intricate designs are completed easily and quickly; over 200 colors coordinates with any decor; it can be used in residential and commercial markets anywhere—even where safety glass is specified. The corporation is continuously involved in market research and testing of new products and services. Complementary products available to franchisees now: oak doors and beveled glass, carved glass and designer rugs.

Number of Franchisees: 350 plus (United States, Australia, Canada, England, France, Germany, and Switzerland Japan and Israel).

In Business Since: 1974; franchising since 1981.

Equity Capital Needed: Franchise fee $34,000; start-up materials and supplies $11,000.

Financial Assistance Available: Initial cash investment required $45,000.

Training Provided: Minimum 40 hours training at corporate headquarters, including (but not limited to) Overlay application, marketing, and business administration. Ongoing updates and training through regional seminars and company newsletter.

Managerial Assistance Available: Corporate office provides continuous assistance in all phases of business operations and management, finances and record keeping, marketing and personnel. Upon request, a corporate representative will provide assistance at franchisee's location.

Information Submitted: June 1987

STARVING STUDENTS FRANCHISE CORPORATION
P. O. Box 351206
Los Angeles, California 90035
Ethan H. Margalith, President

Description of Operation: Moving and storage—local, intrastate and interstate.

Number of Franchisees: 12 "partnership" offices, 8 company-owned offices, and 2 licensee.

In Business Since: 1973

Equity Capital Needed: $16,950 to $40,000 ($10,000 to $25,000 franchise fee, $6,950 to $15,000 capital to begin business).

Financial Assistance Available: In some cases, for uniquely qualified individuals, franchisor will finance 100 percent under a partnership type arrangement! In some cases franchisor will accept a promissory note for $5,000 of the franchise fee.

Training Provided: Initial training lasts up to 8 weeks, depending upon prior experience. Additionally, ongoing training is provided as necessary, during the duration of the franchise relationship.

Managerial Assistance Available: All phases of operations, moving company accounting, advertising and promotion, etc. Duration of assistance will vary with individual's experience and background.

Information Submitted: May 1987

STELLARVISION, INC.
7028 NE 79th Court 1
Portland, Oregon 97218
James G. Stotler, President

Description of Operation: In a natural blend of science, high technology, art and cosmic wonder our franchisees create an extremely realistic illusion that lets you lay back relaxed with thousands of stars overhead, all in their astronomicly correct positions. A StellarVision installation produces a relaxing and intrigueing interior design feature which adds value and beauty with the unique quality of only being seen in the dark. You must see a StellarVision installation to really appreciate just how wonderful it is.

Number of Franchisees: 25 in 10 States and Qatar

In Business Since: 1985

Equity Capital Needed: $15,000 up

Financial Assistance Available: Franchisee is to arrange own outside financing if needed. Franchisor may help with these arrangements upon request.

Training Provided: A 1 week intensive training school is required and provided in the franchise fee for 2 individuals. The training is completed at the Portland, Oregon Corp. facilities with additional pre-training study and additional hands-on experience required before official certification is given.

Managerial Assistance Available: Franchisor will provide information on new products and engage in the development of new products and methods for the StellarVision franchise system.

Information Submitted: May 1987

SUNBANQUE ISLAND TANNING
2533 A Yonge Street
Toronto, M4P 2N9
Canada
Joel Giusto

Description of Operation: SunBanque has full service tanning salons with indoor and outdoor related products. State-of-the-art equipment. Full computerization with total inventory and sales control.

Number of Franchisees: 12 in Massachusetts and Canada

In Business Since: 1983

Equity Capital Needed: $40,000 (depending on lease hold improvements).

Financial Assistance Available: Full financing.

Training Provided: Provided in advertising, public relations and merchandising techniques.

Managerial Assistance Available: Site selection, lease negotiations, training/operations manuals, supplies, advertising materials and ongoing support.

Information Submitted: June 1987

* SUDDENLLY SUN & FIRM
33900 Station Street
Solon, Ohio 44139
Terri Mrklas

Description of Operation: Service industry look and feeling good (health and fitness) tanning and passive resistance exercising tables, nutritional and body products (weight control).

Number of Franchisees: 7 in Ohio

In Business Since: 1981 as distributor, 1984 as franchisor.

Equity Capital Needed: $30,000-$50,000

Financial Assistance Available: Will help direct to financial institutes.

Training Provided: Complete training a company headquarters, 1 week. Seminars throughout year.

Managerial Assistance Available: Constant ongoing.

Information Submitted: June 1987

TEMPACO, INC.
1701 Alden Road
P. O. Box 7667
Orlando, Florida 32854
Charles T. Clark, President

Description of Operation: Wholesale parts and controls for heating, air conditioning and refrigeration.

Number of Franchisees: 8—6 in Florida, and 1 in Mississippi.

In Business Since: 1946

Equity Capital Needed: Approximately $60,000 to $75,000

Financial Assistance Available: None

Training Provided: 2 weeks—introductory training, supplemental and retraining on a non-scheduled basis. Ongoing.

Managerial Assistance Available: Continuous management counsel in areas of bookkeeping, inventory control, accounts receivable, operational procedures, training, advertising and publicity, purchasing control, sales in accordance with the need of the franchisee.

Information Submitted: May 1987

TOGETHER DATING SERVICE
763 Farmington Avenue
Farmington, Connecticut 06032
Brian J. Pappas, Jeff M. Pappas

Description of Operation: Personal dating service.

Number of Franchisees: 62 offices nationwide; 17 company-owned offices.

In Business Since: 1974

Equity Capital Needed: Minimum $50,000.

Financial Assistance Available: Franchisor will finance up to 66-2/3 percent of initial franchise fee.

Training Provided: In our training offices and in the franchisee's office.

Managerial Assistance Available: Ongoing assistance in managerial and marketing especially—in the supply of new advertising materials, which include TV commercials, radio commercials, etc.

Information Submitted: August 1987

NEW BUSINESS INVESTMENT CORPORATION
Franchisor of THE ULTIMATE TAN
408 Warren Avenue
Suite AA
Normal, Illinois 61761
Lawrence Pritts, President

Description of Operation: We plan 8 bed tanning salons. We are qualified in lease negotiations, sight selection, decorating, floor plans, general contracting and all facets of the tanning business.

Number of Franchisees: 4 units including company-owned in Illinois

In Business Since: 1984

Equity Capital Needed: Minimum cost: $100,000 and maximum cost: $150,000.

Financial Assistance Available: Yes

Training Provided: 2 weeks on-the-job training in one of franchisors tanning salons plus ongoing assistance. This training will be received by the person who will manage franchisee store.

Managerial Assistance Available: Periodic inspections and ongoing managerial and technical assistance by telephone and mail will be provided for the duration of the agreement.

Information Submitted: May 1987

UNITED AIR SPECIALISTS, INC.
4440 Creek Road
Cincinnati, Ohio 45242

Description of Operation: Sales and service of Smokeeter electronic air cleaners.

Number of Franchisees: 65 in all 50 States

In Business Since: 1966

Equity Capital Needed: $10,000 initial inventory with additional $25,000 working capital available.

Financial Assistance Available: On an individual basis.

Training Provided: Comprehensive 4 day factory seminar, field training, regional and national meetings.

Managerial Assistance Available: Factory and field training, support and managerial consultation. Comprehensive national marketing and advertising support program.

Information Submitted: June 1987

UNITED DIGNITY, INC.
Sweetbriar Building
2500 Hillsboro Road
Nashville, Tennessee 37212
Ralph E. Staus, Executive Vice President

Description of Operation: United Dignity is structured as a national franchise network offering the public simple inexpensive and dignified funeral services. Family has option to choose embalming or refrigeration; and burial or cremation. Each facility is approximately 1,700 square feet and designed to be efficiently operated with minimal manpower and limited product inventory. Conversion of existing funeral establishment possible. Only vehicle required is a customized station wagon utilized as a herse.

Number of Franchisees: 5 in Arizona, Florida, New Mexico, Ohio and Texas.

In Business Since: 1981

Equity Capital Needed: $70,000 to $175,000 depending upon geographical location and whether facility is leased or purchased.

Financial Assistance Available: Financing package assistance.

Training Provided: An informal 4 day training seminar is available, but optional at corporate office. There is no fee, but all expenses are borne by franchisee. This training session is directed toward business technique, marketing and overall concepts. Mortuary science education is left to institutions specializing in that field with the corresponding licensing requirements in the hands of individual State Boards.

Managerial Assistance Available: A procedures manual which stresses operational methods and guidelines is furnished to each franchisee. United Dignity provides expertise in all segments of start up operation and thereafter; allowing franchisee to concentrate efforts on professional aspects of the business. UDI sponsors ongoing regional seminars and maintains briefings via newsletters. Manual is updated regularly. If franchisee subscribes to bookkeeping services, statement analysis is submitted for review with suggested operational adjustments.

Information Submitted: July 1987

UNITED WORTH HYDROCHEM CORPORATION
P. O. Box 366
Fort Worth, Texas 76101
Roy Coleman, President

Description of Operation: Chemical water treating and chemical cleaning service for cooling towers, boilers, closed systems and heat exchangers. Program built around personal service. Start as one person operation and grow from there. Territory is fully protected.

Number of Franchisees: 20 in 8 States

In Business Since: 1959

Equity Capital Needed: $1,500

Financial Assistance Available: Franchisee must have personal capital or income to support his family needs during first year.

Training Provided: Training school of 2 weeks at home office for theory. Close training in the field during first few months. Close technical support from there on.

Managerial Assistance Available: Worth provides continuous management, sales and technical service to all franchisers. Laboratory support is available on a no charge basis. Technical seminars are held on a semi-annual basis. Worth conducts continuous product research.

Information Submitted: May 1987

VIDEO SHUTTLE
445 8th Avenue, NW
St. Paul, Minnesota 55112
Nancy Evert

Description of Operation: Video Shuttle is a network of franchisees who provide wholesale distribution service to video outlets; both specialty and non-specialty stores. Our van showrooms are stocked with new and used video tapes. Our franchisees exchange tapes, trade tapes, buy in bulk and lease tapes or video movies. We offer a pre-buy program. We use FAX Machines to communicate.

Number of Franchisees: 6 in Minnesota

In Business Since: 1984

Equity Capital Needed: $28,000

Financial Assistance Available: None

Training Provided: The franchisor will at its expense, provide a training program at corporate headquarters to educate and familiarize the franchisee or manager with the business practices of operating a Video Shuttle business. The 4 day training program (will include 2 days classroom, and 2 days with a Video Shuttle trainer in an established territory conducting actual business) will be scheduled at

the discretion of franchisor. The franchisee is responsible for all personal expenses, including travel costs and living expenses incurred in connection with attendance at the training program.

Managerial Assistance Available: Upon request of the franchisee, the franchisor will provide, at the franchisee's expense, additional training to train the franchisee and/or their employees in customer relations, business management and use of the operations manual. This training will take place in the franchisee's territory. The trainer's travel, food, lodging, and related expenses for this assistance shall be borne by the franchisee.

Information Submitted: May 1987

WATSCO, INC.
1943 Oakley
Topeka, Kansas 66604
Larry G. Waters, President

Description of Operation: Wat-A-Egg—Watsco, Inc., provides processing and marketing assistance to egg companies to enter the market of hard-cooked peeled egg processors. Wat-A-Heater—Wat-A-Heater is a waste heat water heater for residential use. Watsco, Inc., trains licensees to market and install these low cost units that reduce utility bills and increase volume of hot water. Licensees are in water softeners or plumbing.

Number of Franchisees: 31 in 12 States, Canada, United Kingdom, South Africa, Australia, The Netherlands, Belgium, Switzerland and Puerto Rico.

In Business Since: 1970

Equity Capital Needed: $5,000

Financial Assistance Available: None

Training Provided: 1 week at Watsco, Inc., home office.

Managerial Assistance Available: Initial training in installation and marketing at home office and continuous support in the field.

Information Submitted: June 1987

YOUR ATTIC, INC.
1659 West Big Beaver Road
Troy, Michigan 48084
George F. Field, Jr., President

Description of Operation: Your Attic, Inc., is the only franchisor of self-storage real estate propreties (mini-warehouses). operated under the Federally-registered tradename, Your Attic, storage spaces, rented on a month-to-month basis, are used by both individuals and a variety of businesses. Particular emphasis is placed on business tenants. Your Attic facilities also provide a wide range of services and products for tenant convenience and project revenue.

Number of Franchisees: 10 in Michigan

In Business Since: 1982

Equity Capital Needed: The amount of equity required depends both on the financial capabilities of the franchisee as well as the size of the project. the typical project will provide 60,000 to 70,000 rentable square feet at a total project cost of $1.4 to $4 million. Cash equity required typically approximates 25 percent of total project cost and may be generated through real estate syndication.

Financial Assistance Available: No direct assistance is provided, although the franchisor shares mortgage funding sources and assists in syndication.

Training Provided: Training materials are provided in the form of audio-visual tapes and prepared manuals addressing all facets of facility operation for both the on-site managers and the principal. certain services are optional in the development, construction and management process.

Managerial Assistance Available: Your Attic provides continual updates and management consultation for the life of the franchise in such areas as bookkeeping, marketing and promotional strategies and programs, product development and facility enhancements, and operational review. Complete manuals of operations, forms and directions are provided, as well as complete information for development and construction of the facility.

Information Submitted: July 1987

RECEIVED TOO LATE TO CLASSIFY

A-PERM-O-GREEN LAWNS, INC.
P. O. Box 562687
Dallas, Texas 75356-1687
Tommy Isbell, Owner

Description of Operation: A-Perm-O-Green Lawns franchisees provide professional lawn care services (fertilizing, weed control, insect and disease control) and tree/shrub care services (fertilizing, insect and disease control) to residential customers.

Number of Franchisees: 5 in Texas and Louisiana

In Business Since: 1976

Equity Capital Needed: $20,000 minimum

Financial Assistance Available: Financial assistance available to qualified persons.

Training Provided: Technical, sales and managerial training. Bookkeeping service available.

Managerial Assistance Available: Ongoing

Information Submitted: September 1987

THE DIET WORKSHOP, INC.
111 Washington Street
Brookline, Massachusetts 02146
William E. Seltz

Description of Operation: The Diet Workshop offers weight control support to members attending one of its three divisions: Flexi-Groups, Quick Loss Clinics, and Workplace. In its group weight control classes it offers diet, nutrition, behavior modification and mild toning exercises and related weight control products such as vitamins, low-calorie dried food, diet salad dressing and other nutritious items as well as diet related literature.

Number of Franchisees: 34 in 20 States

In Business Since: 1965

Equity Capital Needed: A minimum of $40,000

Financial Assistance Available: None

Training Provided: New franchises receive training at the national offices and regular follow-up and advice during the initial start-up period.

Managerial Assistance Available: A franchise receives ongoing support through regular mailings and seminars concerning promotions, weight related products, motivation and administration.

Information Submitted: October 1987

INFORMATION DEPOT OPEN UNIVERSITY
Division of AM ED RELEVANT EDUCATION, INC.
4970 Reseda Boulevard
Tarzana, California 91356
Robert I. Goldstein, President

Description of Operation: Information Depot Open University provides short, relevant classes and seminars in broad range of topics to specifically fit needs and interests of it's local community. Information Depot serves it's community by training its students in computers and other relevant job skills as well as self improvement topics; also leisure and physical fitness areas. Students appreciate the ability to take exactly the courses they want. Easy registration and low prices, qualified and interesting and inspiring teachers.

Number of Franchisees: 2 in California

In Business Since: 1985

Equity Capital Needed: $78,000-$100,000

Financial Assistance Available: None

Training Provided: 3 weeks extensive training program at operating Open University plus 3 days at grand opening.

Managerial Assistance Available: 3 day assistance provided at time of grand opening. Representatives of home office will assist franchisee in all aspects of businss prior to, during and after start-up, including securing location, planning, and visits to franchisee's site. Franchisees receive extensive training in screening, hiring and supervising teachers for classes and seminars in professional computing, job advancement, physical fitness, real estate investment, aerobics, dancing, how to start your own business, and many others.

Information Submitted: September 1987

INTROMARKETING OF AMERICA
30161 Southfield
Suite 315
Southfield, Michigan 48076
James A. Mirro, President

Description of Opreation: IntroMarketing of America provides product demonstration and other point-of-purchase or marketing services. Call (313) 540-5000.

Number of Franchisees: 2

In Business Since: 1987

Equity Capital Needed: $25,000 minimum (includes $9,500 franchise fee).

Financial Assistance Available: None

Training Provided: 2 week training program at corporate headquarters, plus 3 day on-site assistance.

Managerial Assistance Available: Aid in setting up payroll/billing system, advertising program, accounting system, demonstrator training, operations manual/forms, computer software system, promotional merchandise, product information, insurance needs and ongoing advice/consultation.

Information Submitted: October 1987

PREVENT-A-CRACK
c/o National Finance Services, Inc.
500 East Thomas Road, Suite 306
Phoenix, Arizona 85012
Kenneth M. Hollowell, President

Description of Operation: Prevent-A-Crack operates as a mobile repair service that repairs damaged windshields of cars, trucks and vans at fraction of the cost of replacement.

Number of Franchisees: 3 in Arizona

In Business Since: 1985

Equity Capital Needed: $7,500

Financial Assistance Available: None

Training Provided: Franchisor offers a 2 day training program in Phoenix, Arizona in all phases of running the Prevent-A-Crack business, then within 30 days after the business is operating the franchisor spends 3 days working with the franchisee in his territory.

Managerial Assistance Available: Franchisor offers seminars, workshops from time to time to provide up-to-date sales methods and introduced the latest technology improvements in repairs of glass and windshields.

Information Submitted: September 1987

QUIZNO'S INTERNATIONAL, INC.
714 Lincoln Street
Denver, Colorado 80203
Boyd R. Bartlett, General Manager

Description of Operation: Fast food franchise shops offering "Classic Subs" made of the finest, freshest ingredients. Quizno's compliments the "Classic Subs" with a unique salad and dessert menu.

Number of Franchisees: 31 in 2 States

In Business Since: 1981

Equity Capital Needed: Minimum of $40,000 (depending upon location).

Financial Assistance Available: Financial assistance provided to qualified franchisees.

Training Provided: Franchisees complete a comprehensive training program in company store prior to franchise opening.

Managerial Assistance Available: Management representatives spend first 2 weeks assisting new franchisees in shops. Comprehensive operations manual provided with appropriate adjustments made to keep manuals updated. Operation hours response service available to franchisees to call for advice and problem solving.

Information Submitted: October 1987

Using the Franchise Index/Profile

Before You Start

One of the biggest mistakes you can make is to be in too much of a hurry to get into the franchise business. If you shortcut the information-gathering profile outlined in this section, you might neglect to examine other franchises that are perhaps better and more suitable than your initial selection, or you might be pressured into a franchise that is not right for you.

Although most franchises are managed by reputable businessmen, you should be aware that some may be poorly managed, financially weak, or have questionable practices. This profile is intended to guide your franchise investigation in such a way that you can avoid involvement with disreputable businesses.

Before getting into a thorough evaluation of any franchise, here is a quick test that can save you much time, money, and aggravation.

1. Were you promised high profits in exchange for minimum effort?
2. Did the representative pressure you to sign a contract immediately?
3. Were you told that this was your last chance to sign and that if you did not, the opportunity would no longer be available?
4. Did the representative refuse to answer questions or give specific answers?
5. Were you told of services such as training, management assistance, etc., without specific examples of each?
6. Was the representative reluctant to give you a list of references?
7. Did you feel that the representative was more interested in selling you a franchise than in your being successful in business?
8. Did the representative try to discourage you from having your attorney review the contract before you signed it?

In addition, it might be wise for you to call or visit one of the operating franchises and talk to the owner about his business and find out:

1. Does the franchisor deliver what he promises?
2. Does the franchisee consider the franchisor competent in his business?

If the answers to questions 1–8 are *NO*, and if you are satisfied with your discussion with the franchisee, then proceed with the following Franchise Index/Profile. After it is completed, you will have a fairly accurate picture of the franchise, know whether it is the right business for you, and have weeded out the bad risks from the field of prospects.

Franchise Index/Profile
A Franchise Evaluation Process

A. Franchise—General   Yes No

1. Is the Product or Service:
   a. Considered reputable? (Talk to people familiar with the product or service, check it out yourself, and write to the Better Business Bureau in your city and the city of the franchise headquarters.) ___ ___
   b. Part of a growing market? (The market may be slow, as long as it is "taking off." Be sure that it isn't a declining market. Request marketing data from the franchisor, write to applicable trade magazines, and check with your local business library or regional Small Business Administration office.) ___ ___
   c. Needed in your area? (Make sure that products or services have year-round appeal in your area.) ___ ___
   d. Of interest to you? (Only invest in a franchise that is in a field of interest to you.) ___ ___
   e. Safe? (If a product rather than a service is involved, be sure that it meets quality standards with no restrictions.) ___ ___
      Protected? (Is the product protected by patent or liability insurance, and is the same protection afforded to the franchisor?) ___ ___
      Covered by guarantee? (Obtain a copy and be sure of your responsibilities and obligations as a franchisee.) ___ ___
   f. Linked to the name of a well-known personality? ___ ___
      A sound franchise without a well-known personality? (Assuming that the personality maintains a good reputation, it is important that he or she has an actual investment in the franchise. Don't be fooled by a glamour name.)

2. What is the Area of the Franchise? **Yes No**
   a. Local _____ _____
      Regional _____ _____
      International _____ _____
      (A franchise that is only local or regional may be in the beginning or test stage. A national or international franchise is probably better established and known—of particular importance if the product is a consumer one.)

   b. Full time _____ _____
      Part time _____ _____
      Full time possible in future _____ _____
      (There are very few part-time franchises that are as good as they profess to be. If you do get involved in a part-time franchise, make sure that it could later be expanded into a profitable full-time venture.)

3. Existing Franchises:
   a. How long was the company in business before the first franchise was awarded? _____ years. (Favor the company that started *before* it entered the franchise business.)

   b. What date was the company founded and what date was the first franchise awarded? Company founded _____. First franchise awarded _____. (Keep in mind that the dates you want are related to the franchise and not the parent company. Many franchises are actually owned by major corporations.)

   c. How many franchises of a particular company are currently in operation or under construction? _____. (This will indicate the popularity of the franchise. Also find out if there are many existing franchises in one specific area. If a franchise claims to be national and in business for over three years, the spread should be fairly even. The franchisor should provide names and addresses of several franchises in operation in markets like yours. Call or visit these locations.) Franchises to contact:
   Franchise #1
   Owner: _____
   Address: _____
   Telephone: _____
   Date Started: _____
   Franchise #2
   Owner: _____
   Address: _____
   Telephone: _____
   Date Started: _____
   Franchise #3
   Owner: _____
   Address: _____
   Telephone: _____
   Date Started: _____
   d. How many franchises are planned for the next 12 months (not including those awarded and not yet in operation)? _____. (Keep in mind that part of what you pay for in the franchise fee is service, advice, and training. If the home office is not planning properly, they will not be able to give what they promise.)

4. Why Have Franchises Failed?
   a. How many franchises have failed? _____. How many of these have been in the last two years? _____. (The number of failures is not as crucial as the reasons for them—unless the figure is high in relation to the number in operation. If the failure rate is clustered prior to the past two years, perhaps the causes have been remedied.)

   b. Why have franchises failed? (This is one of the most important questions—and the most difficult to answer accurately. First ask the franchisor, then ask the franchisees who have failed. Finally, check with the local Better Business Bureau. Remember that the franchisor and franchisee may be biased against each other. Use your judgment and draw your own conclusions.)
   Franchisor's Reasons: _____

   Franchisee's Reasons: _____

   Better Business Bureau's Reasons: _____
   _____

5. Franchise in Local Market Area
   a. Has a franchise ever been awarded in this area? _____. (The franchise you are investigating might already be in operation in your market. This is not a drawback, since in the cases of fast food and personal service franchises each benefits from the visibility of the other.)
   Franchise in Operation
   Owner: _____
   Address: _____
   Telephone: _____ Date Started: _____
   Franchise that Failed
   Owner: _____
   Address: _____
   Date Started: _____ Date Ended: _____
   Reasons for Failure: _____

6. What Product or Service Will Be Added to the Franchise Package?
   a. Within 12 months (as an indication of short-term future growth): _____
   _____

   b. Within two years (to keep up with the market and changing conditions): _____
   _____

   c. Within two to five years (regarding the long-range corporate goals of the franchisor): _____

7. Competition:
   a. What is your competition? (Look through the Yellow Pages of the telephone directo-

ries in your area for potential competition. Visit several of the major franchises and speak with the owners. Determine whether or not the market is saturated with the product or service.) _____
_____

8. Are All Franchises Independently Owned?
   a. Of the total outlets, _____ are franchised, and _____ are company owned. (Some major franchise companies buy back franchises from their owners so that stronger corporate control can be maintained.)
   b. If some outlets are company owned, did they start out that way, or were they repurchased from a franchisee? Date of most recent company acquisition _____. (If it is a recent date, most likely a repurchase program is under way. Find out the terms of the repurchase agreement.)

9. Franchise Distribution Pattern:
   a. Is the franchise exclusive or nonexclusive? _____
      (Many franchises are not exclusive as far as territory is concerned. The obvious disadvantage of the nonexclusive arrangement is a smaller sales potential. This should be understood before you sign a contract.)
   b. Is the franchise a distributorship or a dealership? _____
      (A franchisor "packages" the product and sells it to distributors, who sell it to dealers, who in turn sell it to customers. The distributor covers a fairly large area; the dealer covers a local one. If you do not have a strong business background and substantial cash reserves, start with a dealership. Develop a good working relationship with your distributor.)
      Distributor's or Dealer's Name: _____
      _____
      Address: _____
      How long has he been a distributor or dealer? _____

10. Franchise Operations:
    a. What facilities are required and must you build or lease? (Some franchises can be operated from your home; others require office space, manufacturing facilities, or a separate building. The franchisor should offer guidance and assistance for the arrangements.)

	Build	Lease
Office	_____	_____
Building	_____	_____
Manufacturing facility	_____	_____
Warehouse	_____	_____
Other	_____	_____

    b. To begin a franchise, who is responsible for what? (If your franchise requires that customers come to your place of business, the franchisor should provide you with a feasibility study, including the following information: traffic count of possible locations, average income of the people in the area, potential customers, etc. Make sure that any money "put down" on the basis of a feasibility study would be refunded if the results are negative. If you must have anything designed or constructed, the franchisor should guide you every step of the way.)

	Franchisor	Franchisee
Feasibility Study	_____	_____
Design	_____	_____
Construction	_____	_____
Furnishings	_____	_____

B. **Franchise Company**
   (The purpose of this section is to get as much information about the company's reputation, financial stability, and management leadership.)
   1. The Company:
      a. What is the name of the parent company if it is different from the franchise company? (Remember that being part of a larger company can be an important asset in terms of financial stability and visibility.)
         Name of Parent Company: _____
         _____
         Address: _____
      b. Is the parent company public or private?
         _____
      c. If the company is public, where is its stock traded? (Check publications at your local public library or stock broker to get a report about the company.)
         New York Stock Exchange _____
         American Stock Exchange _____
         Over the Counter _____
         Other _____
      d. If the company is private, who is the president? _____
         (It is more difficult to check on private companies. Ask a franchisor for references; write to the Better Business Bureau for a report.)
         Bank Reference: _____
         Address: _____

C. **Legal and Financial**
   (In this section, you should determine exactly what is included in your franchise package, and what you can expect to get in terms of return.)
   1. Where to Get Advice:
      a. Lawyer (Before you sign anything, have a lawyer advise you about the terms of any contract. Make sure that your liabilities are covered by insurance.
         Lawyer: _____
         Address: _____
         Telephone: _____
      b. Accountant (In dealing with financial matters, consult with an accountant who is knowledgeable in advising small businessmen.)
         Accountant: _____
         Address: _____

Telephone: _____

  c. Management (Contact the Small Business Administration Regional Office for advice about business management. You can also receive assistance from the Service Corps of Retired Executives (SCORE) via the Small Business Administration.

    Manager: _____
    Address: _____
    Telephone: _____

2. Total Franchise Cost:

  a. How much must you pay the franchisor to get started? $_____
    (This consists primarily of the following expenses: (1) *Franchise fee*—You must buy the right to use and promote a franchise name and identification program. (2) *Services*—These should include complete operating manuals on all phases of the franchise business and personal assistance from home office experts. (3) *Product*—The initial cost of the franchise may or may not include an opening inventory of the products for sale. (4) *Real Estate*—You may be required to purchase or lease the land for the construction of your place of business. (5) *Equipment*—If the cost of equipment and fixtures is not included in your initial fees, you must add this to your personal expenses.

    Franchise Fee: $_____
    Services: $_____
    Products: $_____
    Real Estate: $_____
    Equipment: $_____
    Other: $_____
    Is any of the initial franchise cost refundable? _____
    If so, on what basis? _____

  b. How much money does it take to start a franchise? (Make out your own forecast of required finances, which includes initial franchise cost, first-year operating and personal expenses.)

    Franchise Cost (Total of 2a) $_____
    Operating Costs (First year) $_____
    Personal Costs (First year) $_____
    TOTAL $_____

3. Financing:

  a. Is part of the initial cost to the franchise financed by the franchise company? ____ If so, how much $_____. This represents what percentage of the total initial cost? _____%

  b. What is the interest rate? _____% When does the loan have to be paid back? _____ (Many franchise companies have subsidiaries whose business it is to lend money to the franchisee. Make sure the interest rates are competitive. Check with the Small Business Administration to see if you can qualify for an SBA loan.)

4. Forecast of Income and Expenses:

  a. Is a forecast of income and expenses provided? _____
    Is it based on actual franchise operations, a franchisor's outlet, or is it a theoretical estimation? _____
    (The forecast should be based on the experience of successful franchises and a conservative forecast of sales. Have your accountant review it with you.)

  b. If a forecast is provided by the franchisor, does it:

	Yes	No
Relate to your market area?	___	___
Meet your personal goals?	___	___
Provide adequate return on your investment?	___	___
Provide for adequate personnel and promotions?	___	___

5. Legal Structure:

  a. What is the best legal structure for a franchise? According to the Small Business Administration's Management Aid No. 80, there are three main choices for a legal structure:

    (1) *Proprietorship*—The easiest and most flexible structure, which requires no governmental approval. Business profits are taxed as personal income and the owner is personally liable for debts and taxes.

    (2) *Partnership*—An arrangement whereby two or more business partners are taxed separately and are personally liable for all debts and taxes.

    (3) *Corporation*—The most formal structure, which operates under state laws, with its scope of activity restricted by a charter. Business profits are taxed separately from earnings of executives and owners. Only the company (not the owners and managers) is liable for its debts and taxes.

6. The Franchise Contract:

  a. Are all details of the agreement covered in a written contract? _____
    (Do not accept a verbal agreement. Review all the major points listed below with your lawyer and accountant before signing the contract.)

	Yes	No
Advertising and promotion	___	___
Commissions and royalties	___	___
Exclusive vs. nonexclusive business	___	___
Financing	___	___
Franchise fee	___	___
Home-office services	___	___
Patent and liability protection	___	___
Selling and renewal	___	___
Termination clause	___	___
Territory	___	___
Training	___	___

D. **Training**

1. Initial Training:

  a. Does the franchisor provide formal initial

training? _____ If so, how long does it last? _____ (Depending on how complicated the business is, training can range from one day to two months. Equally important is what happens after you begin your business. If the franchisor does not provide on-the-job assistance, consider this a drawback.)

b. Are training costs:

	Yes	No
Included in the franchise fee?	___	___
Inclusive of all materials?	___	___
Inclusive of transportation?	___	___
Inclusive of room and board?	___	___

If not included in the franchise fee, what is the total cost of training expenses? $_____

c. What does the training course include?

	Yes	No
Finance	___	___
Franchise operations	___	___
Management	___	___
Manufacturing and maintenance	___	___
Personnel	___	___
Promotion	___	___
Sales	___	___
Training	___	___
Other	___	___
_____		

d. How do you train your initial staff? _____ Is a training program provided for them? _____

Does the franchisor provide an instructor from the home office to teach? _____
What materials are included in the staff training program? _____

2. Additional Training:
a. Are there any advanced training programs or seminars? _____
If so, how much are they? $_____
Are special materials required? _____
What is the cost? $_____

E. **Marketing**
1. How Is the Product or Service Sold?

	Yes	No
Customer's home		
by appointment	___	___
door to door	___	___
Customer's business address		
by appointment	___	___
door to door	___	___
Mail	___	___
Store (or place of business)	___	___
Telephone	___	___
Other	___	___

2. Sales Leads:
(In some cases the franchisor generates sales through national advertising, public relations, and direct mail, which he then turns over to the franchisee for follow-up. On the other extreme, the franchisee must secure all sales leads without cooperative advertising or support from the franchisor. Remember a satisfied customer is your best advertisement.)

	Franchisor		Franchisee	
	Yes	No	Yes	No
Direct Mail	___	___	___	___
Print Advertising	___	___	___	___
Telephone	___	___	___	___
Trade Shows	___	___	___	___
Other	___	___	___	___

3. Potential Customers for Products or Services:
(It is imperative that you know who your prospects are. In most businesses, 20 percent of your customers account for 80 percent of your business. For consumer products, the profile will be described by type of business, annual sales volume, number of employees, and purchaser's title.)
Outline a brief customer profile for your franchise: _____
_____

4. What Is the Franchisor's National Advertising Program? _____
_____

a. What is the national advertising budget? $_____
b. What are the primary advertising media? (Samples of the advertising should be available to the prospective franchisees.)
Direct mail _____
Magazine _____
Newspaper _____
Outdoor print _____
Radio _____
Television _____

5. Local Advertising and Promotion:
(This should be an extension of the national marketing program. The franchisor should provide packaged programs for your use including: ad mats, radio scripts, TV commercials, sample media and direct-mail programs, publicity releases, photographs, etc. Ask to see sample kits.)

	Yes	No
Is a packaged advertising program available?	___	___
Is there a co-op advertising program?	___	___
Is there a grand-opening package?	___	___

6. Advertising Agencies:
a. Should you have an advertising agency?
_____
(This shouldn't be necessary because the franchise package should include a tested advertising program along with complete instructions on how to use it. You should also get some assistance from the franchisor's field man, if one exists.)

F. **Home Office Support**
1. Principals and Directors:
a. Who are the key people in the day-to-day operation of the business? (Look for sound business and financial experience and a depth of expertise in the particular franchise.)

Name	Title	Background
___	___	_____
___	___	_____
___	___	_____

b. Who are the members of the board of directors? (Again, these people should have backgrounds related to the business of the franchise.)

Name	Business Association
___	_____

2. Consultants:
   a. Who are the consultants for the company? (These are specialists in their fields who sell their services on a retainer basis to companies that hire them.)

Name	Business Specialty
___	_____
___	_____

3. Service Departments:
   a. What service departments are available to you? (These exist to serve the franchise; learn what is available and make use of it. Remember, research and development is of vital importance to the future of any product or service line.)

	Yes	No
Advertising and promotion	___	___
Construction	___	___
Finance and accounting	___	___
Manufacturing and operations	___	___
Personnel and training	___	___
Purchasing	___	___
Real estate	___	___
Research and development	___	___
Sales and marketing	___	___

4. Field Support:
   a. Do you have a field man assigned to your franchise? If so, what is his name? _____ How many other franchises is he assigned to? _____ Can you get in touch with him? _____

GOVERNMENT ASSISTANCE PROGRAMS

Minority Business Development Agency

Expansion of minority-owned businesses contributed to the creation of jobs and the introduction of innovative goods and services in the U.S. economy. Recognizing this, the Federal Government has established policies and programs to ensure continued growth of minority enterprise.

The major agency that implements federal policies benefiting minority entrepreneurship is the Minority Business Development Agency (MBDA), established within the Department of Commerce by Executive Order 11625. Among the functions MBDA performs are the following:

• Funds 100 **Minority Business Development Centers (MBDc)** in areas across the country with the largest minority populations. MBDCs provide management, marketing, and technical assistance at the local level aimed at increasing sales opportunities in both U.S. and foreign markets for minority firms.

• Awards **grants and cooperative agreements** to other organizations, such as State and local government agencies and trade associations, to assist minority entrepreneurs.

• Maintains an **Information Clearinghouse** to answer inquiries concerning minority business development, make referrals, provide information kits, and disseminate reports, statistics, and research on minority business.

• Operates the **Minority Vendor PROFILE System** a computerized database listing some 30,000 minority firms. PROFILE is designed to match minority entrepreneurs with marketing opportunities.

• Conducts, funds, and promotes **research** on various aspects of minority buinsess in the U.S.

• Works with **other federal agencies and departments** that have programs of value to minority firms.

MBDA has six Regional and six District Offices. If you operate a minority business enterprise or plan to start one, and need information or assistance, contact one of the MBDA Regional or District Offices listed below. Its staff can refer you to the MBDC nearest you.

ATLANTA REGIONAL OFFICE

Carlton Eccles
Atlanta Region
MBDA Regional Director
1371 Peachtree St., N.W. Suite 505
Atlanta, Georgia 30309
Tel: (404) 881-4091

ATLANTA REGIONAL OFFICE—Continued

Rudy Swarez
MBDA District Officer
930 Federal Building
Miami, Florida 33130
Tel: (305) 350-5054

CHICAGO REGIONAL OFFICE

David Vega
Chicago Region
MBDA Regional Director
55 E. Monroe St, Room 1440
Chicago, Illinois 60603
Tel: (312) 353-0182

DALLAS REGIONAL OFFICE

Melda Cabrera
Dallas Region
MBDA Acting Regional Director
1100 Commerce, Room 7B19
Dallas, Texas 75242
Tel: (214) 767-8001

NEW YORK REGIONAL OFFICE

Georgina Sanchez
MBDA Regional Director
26 Federal Plaza, Suite 37-20
New York, New York 10278
Tel: (212) 264-3262

R. K. Schwartz
MBDA District Officer
441 Stuart Street, 9th Floor
Boston, Massachusetts 02116
Tel: (617) 223-3726

SAN FRANCISCO REGIONAL OFFICE

Xavier Mena
San Francisco Region
MBDA Regional Director
221 Main Street, Room 1280
San Francisco, California 94102
Tel: (415) 974-9597

Rudy Guerra
MBDA District Officer
2500 Wilshire Boulevard, Room 908
Los Angeles, California 90057
Tel: (213) 688-7157

U.S. Department of Commerce International Trade Administration

DISTRICT OFFICE DIRECTORY
October 1987

ALABAMA

Birmingham—Gayle C. Shelton, Jr., Director, Suite 2015, 2nd Avenue N. 3rd Floor, Berry Building 35203, Tel: (205) 264-1331

ALASKA

Anchorage—Richard Lenahan, Director, 701 C Street, P.O. Box 32, 99513, Tel: (907) 271-5041

ARIZONA

Phoenix—Donald W. Fry, Director, Federal Building & U.S. Courthouse, 230 North 1st Avenue, Room 3412, 85025, Tel: (602) 261-3285

ARKANSAS

Little Rock—Lon J. Hardin, Director, Suite 811, Savers Federal Building, 320 W. Capitol Avenue, 72201, Tel: (501) 378-5794

CALIFORNIA

Los Angeles—Daniel J. Young, Director, Room 800, 11777 San Vicente Boulevard, 90049, Tel: (213) 209-6705

San Francisco—Betty D. Neuhart, Director, Federal Building, Box 36013, 450 Golden Gate Avenue, 94102, Tel: (415) 556-5860

COLORADO

Denver—Paul G. Bergman, Acting Director, Room 119, U.S. Customhouse, 721-19th Street, 80202, Tel: (303) 844-3246

CONNECTICUT

Hartford—Eric B. Outwater, Director, Room 610-B, Federal Office Building, 450 Main Street, 06103, Tel: (203) 240-3530

FLORIDA

Miami—Ivan A. Cosimi, Director, Suite 224, Federal Building, 51 S.W. First Avenue, 33130, Tel: (305) 536-5267

GEORGIA

Atlanta—George T. Norton, Jr., Director, Suite 504, 1365 Peachtree Street, N.E., 30309, Tel: (404) 881-7000

Savannah—James W. McIntire, Director, 120 Barnard Street, A-107, 31402, Tel: (912) 944-4204

HAWAII

Honolulu—George Dolan, Director, 4106 Federal Building, P.O. Box 50026, 300 Ala Moana Boulevard, 96850, Tel: (808) 541-1782

ILLINOIS

Chicago—Michael V. Simon, Director, 1406 Mid Continental Plaza Building, 55 East Monroe Street, 60603, Tel: (312) 353-4450

INDIANA

Indianapolis—Mel R. Sherar, Director, 357 U.S. Courthouse & Federal Office Building, 46 East Ohio Street, 46204, Tel: (317) 269-6214

IOWA

Des Moines—Jesse N. Durden, Director, 817 Federal Building, 210 Walnut Street, 50309, Tel: (515) 284-4222

KENTUCKY

Louisville—Donald R. Henderson, Director, Room 636B, U.S. Post Office and Courthouse Building, 40202, Tel: (502) 582-5066

LOUISIANA

New Orleans—Paul L. Guidry, Director, 432 International Trade Mart, No. 2 Canal Street, 70130, Tel: (504) 589-6546

MARYLAND

Baltimore—LoRee P. Silloway, Director, 415 U.S. Customhouse, Gay and Lombard Streets, 21202, Tel: (301) 962-3560

MASSACHUSETTS

Boston—Francis J. O'Connor, Director, World Trade Center, S-307, Commonwealth Pier Area, Tel: (617) 565-8563

MICHIGAN

Detroit—Bill Dahlin, Director, 1140 McNamara Building, 477 Michigan Avenue, 48226, Tel: (313) 226-3650

MINNESOTA

Minneapolis—Ronald E. Kramer, Director, 108 Federal Building, 110 South Fourth Street, 55401, Tel: (612) 348-1638

MISSISSIPPI

Jackson—Mark E. Spinney, Director, Jackson Mall Office Center, Suite 328, 300 Woodrow Wilson Boulevard, 39213, Tel: (601) 965-4388

MISSOURI

St. Louis—Donald R. Loso, Director, 7911 Forsyth Boulevard, Suite 610, 63106, Tel: (314) 425-3302-4

Kansas City—James D. Cook, Director, Room 635, 601 East 12th Street, 64106, Tel: (816) 374-3141

NEBRASKA

Omaha—George H. Payne, Director, Empire State Building, 11133 "O" Street, 68137, Tel: (402) 221-3664

NEVADA

Reno—Joseph J. Jeremy, Director, 1755 E. Plumb Lane, #152, 89502, Tel: (702) 784-5203

NEW JERSEY

Trenton—Thomas J. Murray, Director, 3131 Princeton Pike Building, Suite 211, 08648, Tel: (609) 989-2100

NEW MEXICO

Albuquerque—(Vacant), Director, 517 Gold, S.W., Room S-4303, 87102, Tel: (505) 766-2386

NEW YORK

Buffalo—Robert F. Magee, Director, 1312 Federal Building, 111 West Huron Street, 14202, Tel: (716) 846-4191

New York—Milton A. Eaton, Director, Room 3718, Federal Office Building, 26 Federal Plaza, Foley Square, 10278, Tel: (212) 264-0634

NORTH CAROLINA

Greensboro—Samuel Troy, Director, 203 Federal Building, West Market Street, P.O. Box 1950, 27402, Tel: (919) 333-5345

OHIO

Cincinnati—Gordon B. Thomas, Director, 9504 Federal Office Building, 550 Main Street, 45202, Tel: (513) 684-2944

Cleveland—Toby Zettler, Director, Room 600, 666 Euclid Avenue, 44114, Tel: (216) 522-4750

OKLAHOMA

Oklahoma City—Ronald L. Wilson, Director, 5 Broadway Executive Park, S-200, 6601 Broadway Extension, 73116, Tel: (405) 231-5302

OREGON

Portland—Lloyd R. Porter, Director, Room 618, 1220 S.W. 3rd Avenue, 97204, Tel: (503) 221-3001

PENNSYLVANIA

Philadelphia—Robert E. Kistler, Director, 9448 Federal Building, 600 Arch Street, 19106, Tel: (215) 597-2866

Pittsburgh—John A. McCartney, Director, 2002 Federal Building, 1000 Liberty Avenue, 15222, Tel: (412) 644-2850

PUERTO RICO

San Juan (Hato Rey)—J. Enrique Vilella, Director, Room 659, Federal Building, 00918, Tel: (809) 753-4555, Ext. 555

SOUTH CAROLINA

Columbia—Edgar L. Rojas, Director, Strom Thurmond Federal Building, Suite 172, 1835 Assembly Street, 29201, Tel: (803) 765-5345

TENNESSEE

Nashville—James Charlet, Director, Suite 1114, 404 James Robinson Parkway, 37219, Tel: (615) 736-5161

TEXAS

Dallas—C. Carmon Stiles, Director, Room 7A5, 1100 Commerce Street, 75242, Tel: (214) 767-0542

Houston—James D. Cook, Director, 2625 Federal Building Courthouse, 515 Rusk Street, 77002, Tel: (713) 229-2578

UTAH

Salt Lake City—Stephen P. Smoot, Director, U.S. Courthouse, 350 S. Main Street, 84101, Tel: (801) 524-5116

VIRGINIA

Richmond—Philip A. Ouzts, Director, 8010 Federal Building, 400 North 8th Street, 23240, Tel: (804) 771-2246

WASHINGTON

Seattle—C. Franklin Foster, Director, 3131 Elliot Avenue, Suite 290, 98121, Tel: (206) 442-5616

WEST VIRGINIA

Charleston—Roger L. Fortner, Director, 3402 New Federal Building, 500 Quarrier Street, 25301, Tel: (304) 347-5123

WISCONSIN

Milwaukee—Patrick A. Willis, Director, Federal Building, U.S. Courthouse, 517 East Wisconsin Avenue, 53202, Tel: (414) 291-3473

Small Business Administration

The Small Business Administration aids those planning to enter business, as well as to those already in business. This assistance includes counseling and possible financial aid.

Counseling may be by SBA specialists or retired executives under the Service Corps of Retired Executives (SCORE) program, and could include various seminars or courses, or a combination of services including reference publications.

Financial assistance may take the form of loans or the participation in, or guaranty of, loans made by financial institutions. Such assistance can be given only to those eligible applicants who are unable to provide the money from their own resources and cannot obtain it on reasonable terms from banks, franchisors, or other usual business sources.

The Small Business Administration financial support under its own legislation can provide up to $350,000 with the usual maximum maturity of 6 years for working capital and up to 10 years for fixtures and equipment. Under some circumstances, portions of a loan involving construction can qualify for longer terms up to 20 years. For those who qualify, loans made under Title IV of the Economic Opportunity Act can be up to $100,000 and the maturity can be up to 10 for working capital and 15 years for fixed assets.

A list follows of Small Business Administration field offices as of September 1, 1986, where more detailed information regarding the various services available can be obtained.

REGIONAL OFFICES

Region 1
(Connecticut, Maine,Massachusetts, New Hampshire, Rhode Island, Vermont)
   60 Batterymarch Street, Boston, MA 02110, Tel: (617) 223-3204

Region 2
(New Jersey, New York, Puerto Rico, Virgin Islands)
   26 Federal Plaza, Room29-118, New York, NY 10278, Tel: (212) 264-7772

Region 3
(Delaware, District of Columbia, Maryland, Pennsylvania, Virginia West Virginia)
   231 St. Asaphs Road, Suite 640-W, Bala Cynwyd, PA 19004, Tel: (215) 596-5889

Region 4
(Alabama, Florida, Georgia, Kentucky, Mississippi, North Carolina, South Carolina, Tennessee)
   1375 Peachtree Street, N.E., Atlanta, GA 30367 Tel: (404) 347-2797

Region 5
(Illinois, Indiana, Michigan, Minnesota, Ohio, Wisconsin)
   230 South Dearborn Street, Room 510, Chicago, IL 60604, Tel: (312) 353-0359

REGIONAL OFFICES—Continued

Region 6
(Arkansas, Louisiana, New Mexico, Oklahoma, Texas)
   8625 King George Drive, Dallas, TX 75235, Tel: (214) 767-7643

Region 7
(Iowa, Kansas, Missouri, Nebraska)
   911 Walnut Street, 13rd Floor, Kansas City, MO 64106, Tel: (816) 374-5288

Region 8
(Colorado, Montana, North Dakota, South Dakota, Utah, Wyoming)
   1405 Curtis Street, 22nd Floor, Denver, CO 80202, Tel: (303) 844-5441

Region 9
(Arizona, California, Hawaii, Nevada, Pacific Islands)
   Federal Building, 450 Golden Gate Avenue, Room 15307, San Francisco, CA 94102, Tel: (415) 556-7487

Region 10
(Alaska, Idaho, Oregon, Washington)
   2615 4th Avenue, Room 440, Seattle, WA 98104 Tel: (206) 442-5676

DISTRICT OFFICES

Region 1
   10 Causeway Street, Boston, MA 02222, Tel: (617) 565-5590

   Federal Building, 40 Western Avenue, Room 512, Augusta, ME 04330, Tel: (207) 622-8378

   55 Pleasant Street, Room 209, Concord, NH 03301, Tel: (603) 225-1400

   330 Main Street, Hartford, CT 06106, Tel: (203) 722-3600

   Federal Building, 87 State Street, Room 205, Montpelier, VT 05602, Tel: (802) 828-4474

   380 Westminister Mall, Providence, RI 02903, Tel: (401) 528-4586

Region 2
   Carlos Chardon Avenue, Hato Rey, PR 00918, Tel: (809) 753-4002

   60 Park Place, Newark, NJ 07102, Tel: (201) 645-2434

   100 State Street, Room 601, Rochester, NY 14614, Tel: (716) 263-6700

   Federal Building, Room 1071, 100 South Clinton Street, Syracuse, NY 13202, Tel: (315) 423-5383

   111 West Huron Street, Room 1311, Federal Building, Buffalo, NY 14202, Tel: (716) 846-4301

   333 E. Water Street, Elmira, NY 14901, Tel: (607) 734-8130

   445 Broadway, Albany, NY 12207, Tel: (518) 472-6300

DISTRICT OFFICES—Continued

Region 3

168 W. Main Street, Clarksburg, WV 26301, Tel: (304) 623-5361

960 Penn Avenue, Pittsburgh, PA 15222, Tel: (412) 644-2780

Federal Building, 400 North 8th Street, Room 3015, Richmond, VA 23240, Tel: (804) 771-2617

1111 18th Street, N.W., Washington, DC 20417, Tel: (202) 634-4950

100 Chestnut Street, Harrisburg, PA 17101, Tel: (717) 782-3840

20 N. Pennsylvania Avenue, Wilkes-Barre, PA 18702, Tel: (717) 826-6497

844 King Street, Federal Building, Room 5207, Wilmington, DE 19801, Tel: (302) 573-6294

600 Federal Place, Louisville, KY 40202, Tel: (503) 582-5976

Region 4

2121 8th Avenue, N., Suite 200, Birmingham, AL 35203, Tel: (205) 731-1344

222 S. Church Street, Room 300, Charlotte, NC 29202, Tel: (704) 371-6563

1835 Assembly Street, Columbia, SC 29202, Tel: (803) 765-5376

100 West Capitol Street, Jackson, MS 39269, Tel: (601) 965-4378

Federal Building, 400 West Bay Street, Room 261, Jacksonville, FL 32202, Tel: (904) 791-3782

2222 Ponce de Leon Bovlevard, 5th Floor, Miami, FL 33184, Tel: (305) 536-5521

404 James Robertson Parkway, Nashville, TN 37219, Tel: (615) 736-5881

700 Twiggs Street, Suite 607, Tampa, FL 33602, Tel: (813) 228-2594

1720 Peachtree Road, NW, 6th Floor, Atlanta, GA 30309, Tel: (404) 347-4749

Region 5

Four North Old State Capital Plaza, Springfield, IL 62701, Tel: (217) 492-4416

1240 East 9th Street, Room 317, Cleveland, OH 44199, Tel: (216) 522-4180

85 Marconi Boulevard, Columbus, OH 43215, Tel: (614) 469-6860

Federal Building, 550 Main Street, Cincinnati, OH 45202, Tel: (513) 684-2814

477 Michigan Avenue, McNamara Building, Detroit, MI 48226, Tel: (313) 226-6075

DISTRICT OFFICES—Continued

575 N. Pennsylvania Avenue, Century Building, Indianapolis, IN 46204, Tel: (317) 269-7272

212 East Washington Avenue, Room 213, Madison, WI 53703, Tel: (608) 264-5261

100 North 6th Street, Minneapolis, MN 55403, Tel: (612) 349-3550

220 W. Washington Street, Marquette, MI 49855, Tel: (906) 225-1108

Federal Building, 517 East Wisconsin Avenue, Room 246, Milwaukee, WI 53202, Tel: (414) 291-3941

500 South Barstow Street, Room 16, Federal Office Building, & U.S. Courthouse, Eau Claire, WI 54701, Tel: (715) 834-9012

Region 6

5000 Marble Avenue, N.E., Patio Plaza Building, Albuquerque, NM 87100, Tel: (505) 262-6171

2525 Murworth, Houston, TX 77054, Tel: (713) 660-4401

320 West Capitol Avenue, Little Rock, AR 72201, Tel: (501) 378-5871

1611 Tenth Street, Lubbock, TX 79401, Tel: (806) 762-7466

222 East Van Buren Street, Harlingen, TX 78550, Tel: (512) 423-8934

100 South Washigton Street, Marshall, TX 75670, Tel: (214) 935-5257

1661 Canal Street, New Orleans, LA 70113, Tel: (504) 589-6685

200 N.W. 5th Street, Suite 670, Oklahoma City, OK 73102, Tel: (405) 231-4301

727 E. Durango, Room A-513, San Antonio, TX 78206, Tel: (512) 229-6250

1100 Commerce Street, Dallas, TX 75242, Tel: (214) 767-0605

10737 Gateway W., Suite 320, El Paso, TX 79902, Tel: (915) 541-7586

400 Main Street, Corpus Christi, TX 78401, Tel: (512) 888-3331

Region 7

New Federal Building, 210 Walnut Street, Room 749, Des Moines, IA 50309, Tel: (515) 284-4422

11145 Mill Valley Road, Omaha, NE 68154, Tel: (402) 221-4691

815 Olive Street, St. Louis, MO 63101, Tel: (314) 425-6600

110 East Waterman, Wichita, KA 67202, Tel: (316) 269-6571

DISTRICT OFFICES—Continued

Region 8

Room 4001, Federal Building, 100 East B Street, Casper, WY 82601, Tel: (307) 261-5761

301 S. Park, Room 528, Helena, MT 59626, Tel: (406) 449-5381

Federal Building, 657 2nd Avenue, North, Room 218, Fargo, ND 58102, Tel: (701) 237-5771

Federal Building, 125 South State Street, Room 2237, Salt Lake City, UT 84138, Tel: (801) 524-5800

101 South Main Avenue, Sioux Falls, SD 57102, Tel: (605) 336-2980

Region 9

300 Ala Moana Boulevard, Honolulu, HI 96850, Tel: (808) 546-8950

350 S. Figueroa Street, Los Angeles, CA 90071, Tel: (213) 688-2956

211 Main Street, San Francisco, CA 94105, Tel: (415) 974-0642)

2005 N. Central Avenue, Phoenix, AZ 85004, Tel: (602) 261-3732

880 Front Street, San Diego, CA 92101, Tel: (619) 293-5440

301 E. Stewart, Las Vegas, NV 89121, Tel: (702) 388-6611

2202 Monterey Street, Fresno, CA 93721, Tel: (209) 487-5189

Region 10

1020 Main Street, Boise, ID 83702, Tel: (208) 334-1696

1220 S.W. Third Avenue, Portland, OR 97205, Tel: (503) 423-5221

W 920 Riverside Avenue, Spokane, WA 99201, Tel: (509) 456-3783

8th & C Streets, Anchorage, AK 99501, Tel: (907) 271-4022

Internal Revenue Service, Department of the Treasury

The Internal Revenue Service offers a number of services to assist new business executives in understanding and meeting their Federal tax obligations. For example, a *Mr. Businessman's Kit* (Publication 454) which contains informational publications, forms, instructions, and samples of notices which the IRS issues to business concerns is available free.

The kit is a convenient place for storing retained copies of tax returns and employee information. It also contains a checklist of tax returns and a tax calendar of due dates for filing returns and paying taxes identified on the folder. Copies of the kit may be obtained from local offices of the Internal Revenue Service. Employees of the IRS are available to explain items in the kit and answer questions about the tax forms, how to complete them, requirements for withholding, depositing, reporting Federal income and social security taxes, and the Federal unemployment tax. Copies of the kit may also be obtained by writing to the District Director who will have it delivered and explained at a mutually convenient time.

The Tax Guide for Small Business (Publication 334) may also be obtained at local office of the IRS, the District Director, or the Superintendent of Documents, U.S. Government Printing Office, Washington, D.C. 20402. Free.

NON-GOVERNMENTAL ASSISTANCE AND INFORMATION

Better Business Bureaus

Files on many firms that distribute through the franchise method are maintained by Better Business Bureaus. A summary report for a specific company on which a Bureau has a record can be obtained free of charge from the BBB in the area where the franchising company is headquartered.

If the address of the local Bureau is not known, send a postage paid, self-addressed envelope with the complete name and address of the company on which information is desired, to the Council of Better Business Bureaus, Inc., 1515 Wilson Blvd., Arlington, Va., 22209. The Council will either refer your request to, or provide the address of, the appropriate Bureau.

International Franchise Association

The International Franchise Association (IFA) is a nonprofit trade association representing more than 550 franchising companies in the U.S. and around the world. It is recognized as the spokesman for responsible franchising.

The IFA was founded in 1960 by a group of franchising executives who saw the need for an organization that would speak on behalf of franchising, provide services to member companies and those interested in franchising, set standards of business practice, serve as a medium for the exchange of experience and expertise, and offer educational programs for top executives and managers.

The IFA is highly selective in its membership. The Association's Executive Committee approves all memberships. Not all companies applying for membership are accepted.

A full member must have a satisfactory financial condition; have been in business for at least two years; have at least 10 franchisees, one of which must have been in business at least two years; have complied with all applicable state and federal full disclosure requirements; and have satisfactory business and personal references. Full members are granted the use of the IFA seal in their advertising.

The Associate membership category is reserved for those companies who are new in franchising, considering franchising, or who cannot meet all of the requirements of full membership. Associate members may not use the IFA seal. They are admitted so that they can be guided by more experienced franchising companies. Like full members, their membership is contingent upon continuing adherence to the IFA Code of Ethics.

IFA also offers international memberships on an information exchange basis to franchising organizations in other countries. Educational memberships are offered at low cost to business and law departments of colleges and universities.

IFA historically has supported the principal of full disclosure of all pertinent information to potential franchisees. It annually distributes thousands of copies of its booklet, "Investigate Before Investing," which provides guidance for potential franchisees, and its Code of Ethics and Ethical Advertising Code are widely respected. The Small Business Administration, in its booklet, "Franchise Index/Profile," reprints the Codes and the IFA's membership requirements and suggests: "It is worth a letter to the IFA requesting a copy of the International Franchise Association Membership Directory to determine whether or not the franchise you are interested in is a member. The codes themselves are reassuring."

A Directory of Membership, which incorporates the "Investigate Before Investing," is available for free on a walk-in basis or for $1.95 (postage and handling) or $3.95 (first class mail).

The Association traditionally has been an advocate of reasonable legislation and has actively supported legislation which would assure greater protection to potential investors. It has many thousands of communications yearly with persons and organizations seeking franchise information and cooperated with the Midwest Securities Administrators Association (now the North American Securities Administrators Association) to develop a Uniform Franchise Offering Circular to further uniformity in legislation and regulation throughout the states. IFA believes such uniformity benefits the states, franchising companies and potential franchisees.

One of IFA's main functions is to keep members alert to changes in franchising law and regulation. The association holds an annual legal symposium which covers franchise issues in-depth, and a series of regional legal roundtable discussions covering specific legal aspects of franchising. The IFA closely monitors legislation affecting franchising and and works with legislators and agencies to develop laws and regulations that benefit franchising.

IFA carries out an extensive educational program dealing with all phases of franchise management and operations. Educational meetings are held regularly throughout the year, both on a regional and national basis. One of IFA's new ventures is the establishment of an educational foundation to promote franchising courses in the nation's universities and business schools. The foundation will also provide research on franchising and act as a resource center.

The International Franchise Association is unique in its status as the foremost medium for information about franchising. A quarterly newsletter, "Franchising World," is distributed to members and contains the most recent information about developing trends in franchising. Also circulated to IFA members is the "Current Legal Digest," which contains updated information on the status of franchise legislation as well as summaries and analyses of the most recent decisions from the courts and administrative agencies relating to franchising.

Of great importance to the Association and its members is its effort to make IFA membership connotative of the highest standards of business ethics and conduct.

Further information on its services and membership requirements may be obtained from Association's executive offices at 1350 New York Avenue, N.W., Suite 900, Washington, D.C. 20005. IFA's telephone number is (202) 628-8000.